AMERICAN HISTORY

A SURVEY
VOLUME I: TO 1877

TWELFTH EDITION

AMERICAN HISTORY

A SURVEY
VOLUME I: TO 1877

Alan Brinkley
Columbia University

Boston   Burr Ridge, IL   Dubuque, IA   Madison, WI   New York   San Francisco   St. Louis
Bangkok   Bogotá   Caracas   Kuala Lumpur   Lisbon   London   Madrid   Mexico City
Milan   Montreal   New Delhi   Santiago   Seoul   Singapore   Sydney   Taipei   Toronto

The **McGraw·Hill** Companies

Mc Graw Hill Higher Education

AMERICAN HISTORY: A SURVEY, VOLUME I: TO 1877
Published by McGraw-Hill, a business unit of The McGraw-Hill Companies, Inc., 1221 Avenue of the Americas, New York, NY, 10020.

ISBN-13: 978-0-07-312501-5
ISBN-10: 0-07-312501-6

Editor in Chief:: *Emily Barrosse*
Publisher: *Lyn Uhl*
Director of Development: *Lisa Pinto*
Developmental Editor: *Kristen Mellitt*
Marketing Manager: *Katherine Bates*
Managing Editor: *Jean Dal Porto*
Lead Project Manager: *Susan Trentacosti*
Art Director: *Jeanne Schreiber*
Lead Designer: *Gino Cieslik*
Text Designer: *Maureen McCutcheon*
Cover Designer: *Gino Cieslik*
Art Editor: *Katherine McNab*
Photo Research Coordinator: *Nora Agbayani*
Photo Researcher: *PhotoSearch, Inc.*
Senior Supplement Producer: *Louis Swaim*
Senior Production Supervisor: *Carol A. Bielski*
Lead Media Producer: *Sean Crowley*
Media Project Manager: *Kate Boylan*
Composition: *10/12 Garamond Book by Techbooks/GTS – Los Angeles, CA Campus*
Printing: *45# Pub Matte Plus, R.R. Donnelley & Sons*
Cover Credits: Top: Courthouse, Philadelphia *(oil on canvas) by Russell William Thompson Smith (1812–98). (detail). © Atwater Kent Museum*
of Philadelphia, Courtesy of Historical Society of Pennsylvania Collection, Philadelphia, PA/Bridgeman Art Library
Bottom: Lake George, *1870 by John Frederick Kensett (1816–72). (detail). © Brooklyn Museum of Art, Brooklyn,*
NY/Bridgeman Art Library

Library of Congress Control Number: 2005936582

www.mhhe.com

About the Author

ALAN BRINKLEY is the Allan Nevins Professor of History and Provost at Columbia University. He is the author of *Voices of Protest: Huey Long, Father Coughlin, and the Great Depression,* which won the 1983 National Book award; *The Unfinished Nation: A Concise History of the American People; The End of Reform: New Deal Liberalism in Recession and War;* and *Liberalism and Its Discontents.* He was educated at Princeton and Harvard, and he has taught at Harvard, Princeton, the City University of New York Graduate School, and Oxford University, where he was the Harmsworth Professor of American History. He won the Joseph R. Levenson Memorial Teaching Award at Harvard in 1987 and the Great Teacher Award at Columbia in 2003. He is a member of the American Academy of Arts and Sciences, a member of the board of trustees of the National Humanities Center, and chairman of the board of trustees of the Century Foundation.

Brief Contents

Preface xvii

The Twelfth Edition xix

A Guided Tour of *American History: A Survey* xxiii

List of Illustrations, Maps, and Charts xxix

1 The Meeting of Cultures 2

2 Transplantations and Borderlands 32

3 Society and Culture in Provincial America 64

4 The Empire in Transition 100

5 The American Revolution 126

6 The Constitution and the New Republic 158

7 The Jeffersonian Era 180

8 Varieties of American Nationalism 214

9 Jacksonian America 232

10 America's Economic Revolution 258

11 Cotton, Slavery, and the Old South 292

12 Antebellum Culture and Reform 314

13 The Impending Crisis 338

14 The Civil War 366

15 Reconstruction and the New South 400

Appendixes A-1

Index I-1

Contents

PREFACE   xvii

THE TWELFTH EDITION   xix

A GUIDED TOUR OF *AMERICAN HISTORY: A SURVEY*   xxiii

LIST OF ILLUSTRATIONS, MAPS, AND CHARTS   xxix

CHAPTER 1
THE MEETING OF CULTURES 2

SIGNIFICANT EVENTS   2

AMERICA BEFORE COLUMBUS   4
   The Civilizations of the South   4
   The Civilizations of the North   5
   Tribal Cultures   8

EUROPE LOOKS WESTWARD   9
   Commerce and Nationalism   9
   Christopher Columbus   11
   The Conquistadores   12
   Spanish America   14
   Northern Outposts   16
   The Empire at High Tide   17
   Biological and Cultural Exchanges   18
   Africa and America   20

THE ARRIVAL OF THE ENGLISH   23
   The Commercial Incentive   23
   The Religious Incentive   24
   The English in Ireland   27
   The French and the Dutch in America   27
   The First English Settlements   29
   Roanoke   29

WHERE HISTORIANS DISAGREE
Why Do Historians So Often Differ?   6

WHERE HISTORIANS DISAGREE
The American Population Before Columbus   8

AMERICA IN THE WORLD
The Atlantic Context of Early American History   22

CONCLUSION   30

INTERACTIVE LEARNING   31

FOR FURTHER REFERENCE   31

CHAPTER 2
TRANSPLANTATIONS AND BORDERLANDS 32

SIGNIFICANT EVENTS   32

THE EARLY CHESAPEAKE   34
   The Founding of Jamestown   34
   Reorganization   34
   Tobacco   35
   Expansion   36
   Exchanges of Agricultural Technology   37
   Maryland and the Calverts   38
   Turbulent Virginia   39
   Bacon's Rebellion   39

THE GROWTH OF NEW ENGLAND   40
   Plymouth Plantation   40
   The Massachusetts Bay Experiment   42
   The Expansion of New England   43
   Settlers and Natives   45
   The Pequot War, King Philip's War, and the Technology of
     Battle   46

THE RESTORATION COLONIES 48
    The English Civil War 48
    The Carolinas 48
    New Netherland, New York, and New Jersey 50
    The Quaker Colonies 51

BORDERLANDS AND MIDDLE GROUNDS 52
    The Caribbean Islands 53
    Masters and Slaves in the Caribbean 53
    The Southwestern Borderlands 55
    The Southeast Borderlands 56
    The Founding of Georgia 57
    Middle Grounds 58

THE EVOLUTION OF THE BRITISH EMPIRE 59
    The Drive for Reorganization 59
    The Dominion of New England 61
    The "Glorious Revolution" 61

WHERE HISTORIANS DISAGREE
Native Americans and "The Middle Ground" 58

CONCLUSION 62

INTERACTIVE LEARNING 62

FOR FURTHER REFERENCE 63

CHAPTER 3
SOCIETY AND CULTURE IN PROVINCIAL AMERICA 64

SIGNIFICANT EVENTS 64

THE COLONIAL POPULATION 66
    Indentured Servitude 66
    Birth and Death 67
    Medicine in the Colonies 68
    Women and Families in the Chesapeake 69
    Women and Families in New England 70
    The Beginnings of Slavery in British America 71
    Changing Sources of European Immigration 75

THE COLONIAL ECONOMIES 78
    The Southern Economy 78
    Northern Economic and Technological Life 78
    The Extent and Limits of Technology 80
    The Rise of Colonial Commerce 81
    The Rise of Consumerism 82

PATTERNS OF SOCIETY 83
    The Plantation 83
    Plantation Slavery 85
    The Puritan Community 86
    The Witchcraft Phenomenon 87
    Cities 88

AWAKENINGS AND ENLIGHTENMENT 90
    The Pattern of Religions 90
    The Great Awakening 91
    The Enlightenment 92
    Education 93
    The Spread of Science 93
    Concepts of Law and Politics 96

WHERE HISTORIANS DISAGREE
The Origins of Slavery 72

WHERE HISTORIANS DISAGREE
The Witchcraft Trials 89

PATTERNS OF POPULAR CULTURE
Colonial Almanacs 94

CONCLUSION 97

INTERACTIVE LEARNING 98

FOR FURTHER REFERENCE 98

CHAPTER 4
THE EMPIRE IN TRANSITION 100

SIGNIFICANT EVENTS   100

LOOSENING TIES   102
   A Tradition of Neglect   102
   The Colonies Divided   102

THE STRUGGLE FOR THE CONTINENT   103
   New France and the Iroquois Nation   103
   Anglo-French Conflicts   104
   The Great War for the Empire   105

THE NEW IMPERIALISM   107
   Burdens of Empire   108
   The British and the Tribes   109
   The Colonial Response   110

STIRRINGS OF REVOLT   113
   The Stamp Act Crisis   113
   The Townshend Program   115
   The Boston Massacre   116
   The Philosophy of Revolt   117
   The Tea Excitement   118

COOPERATION AND WAR   121
   New Sources of Authority   121
   Lexington and Concord   122

PATTERNS OF POPULAR CULTURE
Taverns In Revolutionary Massachusetts   120

CONCLUSION   124

INTERACTIVE LEARNING   125

FOR FURTHER REFERENCE   125

CHAPTER 5
THE AMERICAN REVOLUTION 126

SIGNIFICANT EVENTS   126

THE STATES UNITED   128
   Defining American War Aims   128
   The Decision for Independence   129
   Responses to Independence   129
   Mobilizing for War   131

THE WAR FOR INDEPENDENCE   133
   The First Phase: New England   134
   The Second Phase: The Mid-Atlantic Region   135
   The Iroquois and the British   138
   Securing Aid from Abroad   138
   The Final Phase: The South   139
   Winning the Peace   142

WAR AND SOCIETY   143
   Loyalists and Minorities   144
   The War and Slavery   144
   Native Americans and the Revolution   145
   Women's Rights and Women's Roles   146
   The War Economy   148

THE CREATION OF STATE GOVERNMENTS   149
   The Assumptions of Republicanism   149
   The First State Constitutions   149
   Revising State Governments   150
   Toleration and Slavery   150

THE SEARCH FOR A NATIONAL GOVERNMENT   151
   The Confederation   151
   Diplomatic Failures   151
   The Confederation and the Northwest   151

Indians and the Western Lands 153
Debts, Taxes, and Daniel Shays 154

WHERE HISTORIANS DISAGREE
The American Revolution 130

AMERICA IN THE WORLD
The Age of Revolutions 142

CONCLUSION 156

INTERACTIVE LEARNING 156

FOR FURTHER REFERENCE 156

CHAPTER 6
THE CONSTITUTION AND THE NEW REPUBLIC 158

SIGNIFICANT EVENTS 158

FRAMING A NEW GOVERNMENT 160
Advocates of Centralization 160
A Divided Convention 162
Compromise 162
The Constitution of 1787 163
Federalists and Antifederalists 166
Completing the Structure 168

FEDERALISTS AND REPUBLICANS 168
Hamilton and the Federalists 168
Enacting the Federalist Program 170
The Republic Opposition 170

ESTABLISHING NATIONAL SOVEREIGNTY 172
Securing the Frontier 172
Native Americans and the New Nation 172
Maintaining Neutrality 173
Jay's Treaty and Pinckney's Treaty 173

THE DOWNFALL OF THE FEDERALISTS 174
The Election of 1796 175
The Quasi War with France 175
Repression and Protest 176
The "Revolution" of 1800 177

WHERE HISTORIANS DISAGREE
The Background of the Constitution 164

CONCLUSION 178

INTERACTIVE LEARNING 179

FOR FURTHER REFERENCE 179

CHAPTER 7
THE JEFFERSONIAN ERA 180

SIGNIFICANT EVENTS 180

THE RISE OF CULTURAL NATIONALISM 182
Patterns of Education 182
Medicine and Science 183
Cultural Aspirations in the New Nation 184
Religious Skepticism 185
The Second Great Awakening 186

STIRRINGS OF INDUSTRIALISM 188
Technology in America 188
Transportation Innovations 190
The Rising Cities 192

JEFFERSON THE PRESIDENT 193
The Federal City and the "People's President" 194
Dollars and Ships 198
Conflict with the Courts 198

DOUBLING THE NATIONAL DOMAIN 200
    Jefferson and Napoleon 200
    The Louisiana Purchase 201
    Lewis and Clark Explore the West 202
    The Burr Conspiracy 202

EXPANSION AND WAR 204
    Conflict on the Seas 204
    Impressment 204
    "Peaceable Coercion" 205
    The "Indian Problem" and the British 206
    Tecumseh and the Prophet 207
    Florida and War Fever 208

THE WAR OF 1812 209
    Battles with the Tribes 209
    Battles with the British 209
    The Revolt of New England 211
    The Peace Settlement 212

AMERICA IN THE WORLD
The Global Industrial Revolution 190

PATTERNS OF POPULAR CULTURE
Horse Racing 194

CONCLUSION 213

INTERACTIVE LEARNING 213

FOR FURTHER REFERENCE 213

CHAPTER 8
VARIETIES OF AMERICAN NATIONALISM 214

SIGNIFICANT EVENTS 214
A GROWING ECONOMY 216
    Banking, Currency, and Protection 216
    Transportation 217
EXPANDING WESTWARD 219
    The Great Migrations 219
    The Plantation System in the Southwest 220
    Trade and Trapping in the Far West 220
    Eastern Images of the West 221
THE "ERA OF GOOD FEELINGS" 222
    The End of the First Party System 222
    John Quincy Adams and Florida 223
    The Panic of 1819 224
SECTIONALISM AND NATIONALISM 224
    The Missouri Compromise 225
    Marshall and the Court 225
    The Court and the Tribes 226
    The Latin American Revolution and the Monroe Doctrine 227
THE REVIVAL OF OPPOSITION 228
    The "Corrupt Bargain" 228
    The Second President Adams 229
    Jackson Triumphant 229

CONCLUSION 230

INTERACTIVE LEARNING 231

FOR FURTHER REFERENCE 231

CHAPTER 9
JACKSONIAN AMERICA 232

SIGNIFICANT EVENTS 232

THE RISE OF MASS POLITICS 234
The Expanding Electorate 234
The Legitimization of Party 236
"President of the Common Man" 237

"OUR FEDERAL UNION" 238
Calhoun and Nullification 239
The Rise of Van Buren 239
The Webster-Hayne Debate 240
The Nullification Crisis 241

THE REMOVAL OF THE INDIANS 242
White Attitudes Toward the Tribes 242
The Black Hawk War 242
The "Five Civilized Tribes" 243
Trails of Tears 243
The Meaning of Removal 245

JACKSON AND THE BANK WAR 246
Biddle's Institution 246
The "Monster" Destroyed 247
The Taney Court 247

THE CHANGING FACE OF AMERICAN POLITICS 249
Democrats and Whigs 249
Van Buren and the Panic of 1837 250
The Log Cabin Campaign 252
The Frustration of the Whigs 252
Whig Diplomacy 253

WHERE HISTORIANS DISAGREE
The "Age of Jackson" 236

PATTERNS OF POPULAR CULTURE
The Penny Press 254

CONCLUSION 256

INTERACTIVE LEARNING 256

FOR FURTHER REFERENCE 257

CHAPTER 10
AMERICA'S ECONOMIC REVOLUTION 258

SIGNIFICANT EVENTS 258

THE CHANGING AMERICAN POPULATION 260
The American Population, 1820–1840 260
Immigration and Urban Growth, 1840–1860 261
The Rise of Nativism 263

TRANSPORTATION, COMMUNICATIONS, AND TECHNOLOGY 265
The Canal Age 265
The Early Railroads 268
The Triumph of the Rails 269
Innovations in Communications and Journalism 270

COMMERCE AND INDUSTRY 271
The Expansion of Business, 1820–1840 271
The Emergence of the Factory 272
Advances in Technology 273
Innovations in Corporate Organization 274

MEN AND WOMEN AT WORK 274
Recruiting a Native Work Force 274
The Immigrant Work Force 277
The Factory System and the Artisan Tradition 277
Fighting for Control 278

PATTERNS OF INDUSTRIAL SOCIETY 279
    The Rich and the Poor 279
    Social Mobility 280
    Middle-Class Life 281
    The Changing Family 282
    Women and the "Cult of Domesticity" 283
    Leisure Activities 285

THE AGRICULTURAL NORTH 288
    Northeastern Agriculture 288
    The Old Northwest 288
    Rural Life 290

PATTERNS OF POPULAR CULTURE
Shakespeare in America 286

CONCLUSION 290

INTERACTIVE LEARNING 291

FOR FURTHER REFERENCE 291

CHAPTER 11
COTTON, SLAVERY, AND THE OLD SOUTH 292

SIGNIFICANT EVENTS 292

THE COTTON ECONOMY 294
    The Rise of King Cotton 294
    Southern Trade and Industry 295
    Sources of Southern Difference 298

WHITE SOCIETY IN THE SOUTH 298
    The Planter Class 298
    "Honor" 300
    The "Southern Lady" 301
    The Plain Folk 301

SLAVERY: THE "PECULIAR INSTITUTION" 303
    Varieties of Slavery 303
    Life Under Slavery 304
    Slavery in the Cities 307
    Free African Americans 307
    The Slave Trade 308
    Slave Resistance 308

THE CULTURE OF SLAVERY 310
    Language and Music 310
    African-American Religion 310
    The Slave Family 312

WHERE HISTORIANS DISAGREE
The Character of Slavery 306

PATTERNS OF POPULAR CULTURE
The Slaves' Music 311

CONCLUSION 313

INTERACTIVE LEARNING 313

FOR FURTHER REFERENCE 313

CHAPTER 12
ANTEBELLUM CULTURE AND REFORM 314

SIGNIFICANT EVENTS 314

THE ROMANTIC IMPULSE 316
Nationalism and Romanticism in American Painting 316
Literature and the Quest for Liberation 316
Literature in the Antebellum South 318
The Transcendentalists 318
The Defense of Nature 319
Visions of Utopia 319
Redefining Gender Roles 320
The Mormons 321

REMAKING SOCIETY 322
Revivalism, Morality, and Order 323
The Temperance Crusade 323
Health Fads and Phrenology 324
Medical Science 326
Reforming Education 326
Rehabilitation 327
The Indian Reservation 328
The Rise of Feminism 329

THE CRUSADE AGAINST SLAVERY 330
Early Opposition to Slavery 330
Garrison and Abolitionism 330
Black Abolitionists 331
Anti-Abolitionism 332
Abolitionism Divided 334

AMERICA IN THE WORLD
The Abolition of Slavery 333

PATTERNS OF POPULAR CULTURE
Sentimental Novels 334

CONCLUSION 337

INTERACTIVE LEARNING 337

FOR FURTHER REFERENCE 337

CHAPTER 13
THE IMPENDING CRISIS 338

SIGNIFICANT EVENTS 338

LOOKING WESTWARD 340
Manifest Destiny 340
Americans in Texas 341
Tensions Between the United States and Mexico 341
Oregon 343
The Westward Migration 343
Life on the Trail 344

EXPANSION AND WAR 346
The Democrats and Expansion 346
The Southwest and California 346
The Mexican War 347

THE SECTIONAL DEBATE 351
Slavery and the Territories 351
The California Gold Rush 351
Rising Sectional Tensions 353
The Compromise of 1850 353

THE CRISES OF THE 1850s 355
The Uneasy Truce 355
"Young America" 355
Slavery, Railroads, and the West 355
The Kansas-Nebraska Controversy 356
"Bleeding Kansas" 356

The Free-Soil Ideology   357
The Pro-Slavery Argument   359
Buchanan and Depression   359
The Dred Scott Decision   360
Deadlock over Kansas   361
The Emergence of Lincoln   362
John Brown's Raid   362
The Election of Lincoln   363

PATTERNS OF POPULAR CULTURE
Lyceums   360

CONCLUSION   364

INTERACTIVE LEARNING   364

FOR FURTHER REFERENCE   365

C H A P T E R 1 4
THE CIVIL WAR   366

SIGNIFICANT EVENTS   366

THE SECESSION CRISIS   368
The Withdrawal of the South   368
The Failure of Compromise   368
Fort Sumter   368
The Opposing Sides   370

THE MOBILIZATION OF THE NORTH   371
Economic Measures   371
Raising the Union Armies   374
Wartime Politics   375
The Politics of Emancipation   376
African Americans and the Union Cause   377
The War and Economic Development   377
Women, Nursing, and the War   378

THE MOBILIZATION OF THE SOUTH   379
The Confederate Government   379
Money and Manpower   379
States' Rights versus Centralization   382
Economic and Social Effects of the War   382

STRATEGY AND DIPLOMACY   383
The Commanders   384
The Role of Sea Power   386
Europe and the Disunited States   387
The American West and the War   388

THE COURSE OF BATTLE   388
The Technology of Battle   388
The Opening Clashes, 1861   389
The Western Theater   390
The Virginia Front, 1862   390
1863, Year of Decision   393
The Last Stage, 1864–1865   395

WHERE HISTORIANS DISAGREE
The Causes of Civil War   372

AMERICA IN THE WORLD
The Consolidation of Nations   380

PATTERNS OF POPULAR CULTURE
Baseball and the Civil War   384

CONCLUSION   398

INTERACTIVE LEARNING   399

FOR FURTHER REFERENCE   399

CHAPTER 15
RECONSTRUCTION AND THE NEW SOUTH 400

SIGNIFICANT EVENTS   400

THE PROBLEMS OF PEACEMAKING   402
  The Aftermath of War and Emancipation   402
  Competing Notions of Freedom   403
  Issues of Reconstruction   404
  Plans for Reconstruction   404
  The Death of Lincoln   405
  Johnson and "Restoration"   405

RADICAL RECONSTRUCTION   406
  The Black Codes   406
  The Fourteenth Amendment   406
  The Congressional Plan   407
  The Impeachment of the President   409

THE SOUTH IN RECONSTRUCTION   409
  The Reconstruction Governments   409
  Education   411
  Landownership and Tenancy   411
  The Crop-Lien System   412
  The African-American Family in Freedom   413

THE GRANT ADMINISTRATION   414
  The Soldier President   414
  The Grant Scandals   415
  The Greenback Question   415
  Republican Diplomacy   415

THE ABANDONMENT OF RECONSTRUCTION   416
  The Southern States "Redeemed"   416
  The Ku Klux Klan Acts   416
  Waning Northern Commitment   417
  The Compromise of 1877   417
  The Legacies of Reconstruction   420

THE NEW SOUTH   421
  The "Redeemers"   421
  Industrialization and the "New South"   421
  Tenants and Sharecroppers   424
  African Americans and the New South   425
  The Birth of Jim Crow   427

WHERE HISTORIANS DISAGREE
Reconstruction   418

PATTERNS OF POPULAR CULTURE
The Minstrel Show   422

WHERE HISTORIANS DISAGREE
The Origins of Segregation   428

CONCLUSION   430

INTERACTIVE LEARNING   431

FOR FURTHER REFERENCE   431

APPENDIXES   A-1
INDEX   I-1

Preface

This book strives to tell the remarkable story of the history of the American people and the nation they created. Like any history, it is a product of its time and reflects the views of our past that historians have developed over recent generations. A comparable book published a generation from now will likely seem as different from this one as this seems different from textbooks published generations ago. The writing of history changes constantly—not, of course, because the past changes, but because of changes in the way historians, and the publics they serve, ask questions about the past. There are now, as there have always been, critics of changes in historical understanding; people who believe that history is simply a collection of facts and should not be subject to reinterpretation. But historians understand that facts alone are only the beginning of historical understanding, and that it is up to both the writers and readers of history to bring to the past their own questions, concerns, and knowledge.

Among the changes in this twelfth edition of *American History: A Survey* is a continuing effort to link our understanding of our nation's past to an understanding of the world. The United States has from its beginning been part of a global process of change, and it has become far more so in our own time. It is important, therefore, to consider some of the ways we might draw new perspectives on our own past by looking at the histories of other societies.

Our age has also been profoundly affected by an explosive growth in scientific and technological knowledge. But it is important to recall that such knowledge has played a major role in all periods of history and that understanding that role is a critical part of understanding our past. This edition continues the effort of previous editions to deepen its engagement with the history of science and technology.

The power of the environmental movement, which has developed rapidly over the last several decades, has encouraged historians to take a new interest in environmental history. That history includes, but is not restricted to, the history of the modern environmental movement itself. It also draws our attention to the ways in which human interaction with the environment has shaped American life from its earliest beginnings. This edition incorporates substantial new material on environmental history into the text. I remain very grateful to the distinguished historian William Cronon, whose excellent essays on the American environment were part of this book for several editions. Because environmental history is now more integrated into the text itself, these essays no longer appear in this book.

Despite these and other changes, which are described in detail in the section immediately following this preface, I have tried to retain in this edition what I believe has long been the principal strength of this book: a picture of the American past that connects the newer histories of society and culture of the last several decades to the more traditional histories of politics, diplomacy, and great public events. The United States is a nation of extraordinary diversity, and understanding its history requires us to examine the experiences of the many different groups and cultures that have shaped it. But the United States is also a nation, whose people share a common political system, a connection to an integrated national economy, and a familiarity with a shared and, in our time, enormously powerful popular culture. To understand the American past, therefore, it is necessary to study both the nation's enormous diversity and the powerful forces that have drawn it together and have allowed it to survive and flourish as a nation.

As always, I am grateful to many people for their help in producing this new edition. I was particularly fortunate to have the help of Kevin Murphy, Moshik Temkin, and Timothy White as I worked on this most recent revision. I also appreciate the very helpful reviews I received from a group of talented scholars and teachers:

Steven R. Boyd, *The University of Texas, San Antonio;* Joan Cashin, *Ohio State University;* Charles Orson Cook, *University of Houston/St. John's School;* Edward R. Crowther, *Adams State College;* Lane Fenrich, *Northwestern University;* Lorri Glover, *University of Tennessee;* Mathew M. Hanson, *St Joseph's University;* Debra Meyers, *Northern Kentucky University;* Marla Miller, *University of Massachusetts, Amherst;* Robyn Muncy, *University of Maryland, College Park;* Kevin Roberts, *New Mexico State University;* David Stebenne, *Ohio State University;* Jack W. Traylor, *Bryan College;* and Austin White, *City College of San Francisco.*

I am grateful as well to the many people at McGraw-Hill who have helped bring this new edition to completion: Lyn Uhl, Steve Drummond, Kristen Mellitt, Susan Trentacosti, Gino Cieslik, and Deborah Bull. My wife, Evangeline Morphos, as always, brought her own impressive critical skills to bear on this book.

Finally, I am grateful to the students, teachers, and other readers of this book who have sent me comments, criticism, and corrections. I hope they will continue to do so by writing me at 205 Low Library, Columbia University, New York, NY 10027; or by e-mail to ab65@ columbia.edu.

Alan Brinkley
Columbia University
New York, NY

The Twelfth Edition

Although this book tells the large and complex story of the history of the United States, it has a simple purpose. It aspires to be a thorough, balanced, and versatile account of America's past that instructors and students will find accessible and appropriate no matter what approach to the past a course chooses. It includes, as it has from its first edition, a careful, scrupulous examination of American political and diplomatic history. But it is, today, at least as committed to exploring the many other areas of the American past that are of interest to scholars and students alike.

Many of today's American history textbooks emerged out of the particular interests of their authors and their commitment to bringing new kinds of history to the attention of students—social history, regional histories, cultural history, women's history. This book, by contrast, exists to provide students and instructors with a broad account of a diverse American past, one in which no single approach or theme predominates. The twelfth edition is committed to representing the many newer forms of history that have emerged over a generation and more of scholarly innovation.

ORGANIZATION AND COVERAGE

American History: A Survey is organized in a way that reflects the typical United States history course. The thirty-four chapters follow the history of the United States chronologically, and the subheadings allow instructors to select portions of chapters to suit their syllabi. The text is divided into two volumes with an overlapping Chapter Fifteen that covers the "Reconstruction and the New South," providing flexibility for two-semester courses. While this organization makes it easy for instructors to use the text, it also allows for coverage of traditional topics in fresh ways.

NARRATIVE

The book is most notable for the balance among the many elements of the past it presents and for the connections it draws among them to weave a coherent narrative. In each new edition it has expanded its scope while maintaining the clear prose and the straightforward structure that have always made it so accessible and versatile for students and instructors. Today, the traditional political narrative is woven together with newer, equally important narratives: the history of women and gender, of race and ethnicity, of economic growth and the changing character of labor, of region and religion, of popular culture and intellectual life, and of the environment and the economy. *American History: A Survey* is at the cutting edge of the effort to put politics into social history and to put society and culture into political history.

ONE VOICE

One distinctive feature of this book is that it represents the work of one author. Multiauthored books, of course, tend to bring together many scholars with different forms of expertise in different areas of the past. But a single author has the advantage of bringing a unified organizing conception to the book, of writing in a consistent style, and of providing greater coherence to the narrative.

GLOBALIZATION

Recently, a great deal of attention has been given to the subject of thinking about and teaching the American experience in a way that places it in a larger international and global context. To study the history of our country in isolation from the many varied international influences and other national histories is to neglect an important part of the story. This edition continues to present American history in a more international context, while preserving the distinctiveness of the nation's past. This coverage can be found within both the narrative of the text and in a new set of "America in the World" essays placing events in American history in a global context. Two new essays have been added to this edition: one on social democracy in Chapter 21, and one on the cinema in Chapter 24.

THE NATURE OF HISTORICAL SCHOLARSHIP

The book is written in clear and accessible prose, but it does not condescend to students and does not shy away from complex issues and complicated debates. The "Where Historians Disagree" essays, which have always been a popular feature of this book, suggest its commitment to helping students understand the contested quality of much of the American past. This feature encourages them to think for themselves about what different aspects of our history actually mean. Three new "Where Historians Disagree" essays have been added to this edition: "Native Americans and 'the Middle Ground'" in Chapter 2, "The Witchcraft Trials" in Chapter 3, and "The Civil Rights Movement" in Chapter 31.

CONTENT

American History: A Survey continues to win praise from both instructors and students for its balanced presentation of political, cultural, and social history, its clear and accessible prose, its reliable scholarship, its versatility of use, and its excellent map and illustration program. The "Patterns of Popular Culture," "Where Historians Disagree," and "America in the World" features continue to provide exciting and informative presentations of cutting-edge scholarship. All of these strengths have been preserved and enhanced in the new twelfth edition.

Integrated throughout the twelfth edition is additional information about women in American history. Highlights include:

- Expanded material about women entering the workforce and its social effects (Chapter 17)

- Expanded sections about the growing popularity of literature and formation of book clubs by women (Chaper 18)

- More on lynching, particularly the role played by southern women in opposing lynching (Chapter 21)

- New material on the "Women's Bureau," an agency dedicated to protecting the interests of women in the workforce (Chapter 23)

- New material on legislation passed in response to woman suffrage, including the Shepard Towner Maternity and Infancy Act and the 1922 Cable Act (Chapter 23)

- Material from "The American Environment" essays has been integrated into the main text narrative

- New "Patterns of Popular Culture" essay on Louisa May Alcott (Chapter 17)

- Judicious edits throughout to tighten the narrative

Other revisions to the twelfth edition include the integration of "The American Environment" essays into the main text narrative, to present environmental history in context, expanded material on the effect of European colonists on America in Chapter 2, additional information about the growth of cities in Chapter 18, and new material on the role of the same-sex marriage issue in the 2004 elections in Chapter 32. As always, the book gives particular attention to the very recent past, including new material on President George W. Bush's efforts to restructure the social security system; the state of the U.S. economy through 2005; the "digital divide"; the ongoing war on terror, including the War in Iraq and the debate over the treatment of terrorism suspects; and a new conclusion focusing on America in the first years of the twenty-first century.

PEDAGOGICAL FEATURES

The telling of a good story is only part of the task facing those who teach American history. Instructors also have to engage students in the enterprise of learning and the more actively engaged they are, the more they learn. Pedagogical tools within a textbook have become an important complement to the narrative, aiding students in participating actively in the learning process.

American History: A Survey has always provided students with clear, accessible, and useful pedagogical support. The twelfth edition continues this tradition by retaining the strong features of past editions, refining and updating these features, and adding several new ones.

Chapter Introductions and Conclusions

Each chapter opens with an introduction that sets the stage for understanding the material to follow. For the twelfth edition, introductions have been expanded to present a more comprehensive overview of the chapter. Chapters then end with conclusions that highlight key themes. These features preserve the engaging narrative style, while helping students focus on the main points in the chapter.

Timelines

One of the most commonly voiced frustrations for instructors is that students lack a sense of chronology. Each chapter of this book contains a timeline focusing on significant events covered within the chapter narrative. These timelines have been placed at the beginning of each chapter and include events that correspond to many of the chapter subtitles, as well as other events mentioned throughout the narrative.

Clear Headings and Marginal Notes

Clear thematic titles and precise headings guide students through the chapter. Marginal notes also highlight key terms and concepts contained within the narrative.

For Further Reference Sections

The bibliographies that conclude each chapter have been updated to provide students and instructors with assistance in accessing additional resources, including books, films, and materials on the book's companion Online Learning Center.

Integrated Map Program

Because a sense of geography is essential to the study of history, the text includes a wealth of full-color maps. New to the twelfth edition are a map of West Africa (Chapter 1), a map of the Caribbean islands in the seventeenth century (Chapter 2), and a map of the Election of 2004 (Chapter 34). Every map features a caption that discusses the map content in detail and poses thought questions In addition, many maps in the book have a Web icon that links them to interactive versions on the Online Learning Center.

SUPPLEMENTS

For the Instructor

Instructor's Resource CD-ROM

This CD-ROM organizes a diverse range of instructor's tools in one place. It features an electronic Instructor's Manual, featuring chapter summaries, themes and objectives for the instructor's use, suggestions for classroom discussion, and more. A computerized test bank is also included, offering questions of varying types and levels of difficulty. McGraw-Hill's EZ Test is a flexible and easy-to-use electronic testing program. The program allows instructors to create tests from book-specific items. It accommodates a wide range of question types and instructors may add their own questions. Multiple versions of the test can be created and any test can be exported for use with course management systems such as WebCT, BlackBoard or PageOut. EZ Test Online is a new service and gives you a place to easily administer your EZ Test created exams and quizzes online. The program is available for Windows and Macintosh environments. Instructors can also use the Instructor's Resource CD-ROM to illustrate classroom lectures and discussions with text-specific PowerPoint presentations, or integrate images from a gallery of maps and photographs into their own presentations.

The Primary Source Investigator American History iPod Instructor's Presentation Tool

The PSiPod contains over 250 speeches and musical selections organized chronologically and into topical play lists. These can be imported into any compatible music management program, organized into new play lists, and amplified on any standard speaker. In addition to the Audio Collection, the American History iPod also contains an Historical Image Collection of over 350 images organized chronologically and into topical albums. These can be imported into any compatible photo management program, organized into new slide shows, and displayed on any projector or television. Music can be played along with slide shows for a complete multi-media experience. Please contact your local McGraw-Hill Sales representative for more information. Adoption requirements apply.

Instructor's Manual for Advanced Placement Teachers

This specially focused manual for AP teachers includes free response questions; key terms, concepts, and names; document-based questions, creative extensions, and other resources for every chapter of the book.

Overhead Transparency Acetates

This comprehensive package of 150 transparencies, most of them full-color, is designed to support the text's unique integrated art program.

U.S. History Video and CD-ROM Library

Contact your local sales representative for a complete listing of the many videos and CD-ROMs available from the Films for the Humanities American History catalog. Adoption requirements apply.

Instructor's Online Learning Center

www.mhhe.com/brinkley12

At the homepage to the text-specific website, instructors will find a series of online tools to meet a wide range of classroom needs. The Instructor's Manual and most PowerPoint presentations can be downloaded by instructors, but are password-protected to prevent tampering. Instructors can also create Web-based homework assignments or classroom activities by linking to the Student Online Learning Center, and can create an interactive course syllabus using McGraw-Hill's PageOut (www. mhhe.com/pageout).

PageOut

On the PageOut Web site, instructors can create their own course websites. PageOut requires no prior knowledge of HTML, no long hours of coding, and no design skills on the instructor's part. Simply plug the course information into a template and click on one of sixteen designs. The process takes no time at all and leaves instructors with a professionally designed Web site. Powerful features include an interactive course syllabus that lets instructors post content and links, an online gradebook, lecture notes, bookmarks, and even a discussion board where instructors and students can discuss course-related topics.

Readers

McGraw-Hill publishes a number of readers that complement *American History*. These can be sold with our texts with a price break for students. Please visit www.mhhe.com or contact your local McGraw-Hill representative for more information on these titles.

After the Fact: The Art of Historical Detection, 5/e, Davidson and Lytle
The American Record, 5/e, Graebner and Richards
Life, Liberty, and the Pursuit of Happiness, Corbett and Naugle
American Portraits: Biographies in United States History, 2/e, Weisner and Hartford
Annual Editions: American History, 18/e, Maddox
Taking Sides: American History, 11/e, Madaras and SoRelle

For the Student

Primary Source Investigator CD-ROM

Packaged free with every copy of the book, the **Primary Source Investigator CD-ROM** includes hundreds of sources to explore, including images, short documentary movies, interactive maps, photographs, and much more. Each source has tools accompanying it that teach students to examine a source the way a historian would. PSI also tutors student on how to write a paper based on their work with the sources. Find more information about the CD-ROM where it is packaged in your book.

McGraw-Hill American History EduBlog

Our new American history blog serves as a personal teaching assistant for both instructors and students. Find out what historians and other students are saying about American history. For further information, please contact your local McGraw-Hill Sales representative or visit www.mhhe.com/brinkley12.

Student Study Guide with Map Exercises

Available in two volumes, the Study Guide helps students to process and master important concepts covered in the text. For each chapter, it offers valuable pedagogical tools such as chapter summaries and reviews, chapter outlines, learning objectives, short answer and essay questions, and mapping exercises.

U.S. History Map Atlas

This is a valuable collection of more than fifty clear and colorful historical maps covering all major periods in American history. It is available for packaging with the textbook. Please contact your local sales representative for more information.

After the Fact Interactive CD-ROM—The Visible and Invisible Worlds of Salem
After the Fact Interactive CD-ROM—Who Freed the Slaves?

After the Fact Interactive CD-ROM—USDA Government Inspected
After the Fact Interactive CD-ROM—From Rosie to Lucy

After the Fact Interactive helps students practice the art of historical detection on real historical controversies. Rich, visually appealing modules on the Salem witch trials, the freeing of the slaves, the passage of the Meat Inspection Act of 1906, and the changing roles of women after World War II introduce them to three basic steps taken by practicing historians: Ask, Research, and Argue; provide them with numerous rich original sources to examine, including video, audio, and images; and guide them in constructing an argument based on their research.

Student Online Learning Center

www.mhhe.com/brinkley12
At the homepage to the text-specific Web site, students can work with an interactive study guide, including online essay questions, timelines, mapping exercises, and a variety of objective questions to guide them through the text material. Links to related Web sites and Internet exercises make the student Online Learning Center a great place to begin Web-based research.

PowerWeb: American History

This online supplement, accessed through the Online Learning Center, is a collection of readings delivered electronically, along with other tools for conducting research in history. Student study tools, Web research tips and exercises, and free access to the Northern Lights search engine are included. A card with a password for accessing PowerWeb has been packaged with the textbook.

Advanced Placement Online Learning Center

At the homepage to the text-specific site students can work with the Advanced Placement Online Learning Center. The Center, developed for use with *American History*, 12th Edition, was created specifically for advanced placement courses and provides students with exercises, activities, projects, sample free response questions, and sample multiple choice questions similar to those on the AP Exam.

As a full-service publisher of quality education products, McGraw-Hill does much more than just sell textbooks to students. We create and publish an extensive array of print, video, and digital supplements to support instruction on your campus. Orders of new (versus used) textbooks help us to defray the cost of developing such supplements, which is substantial. Please consult your McGraw-Hill sales representative to learn more about the availability of the supplements that accompany *American History: A Survey*, 12th Edition.

The author of *American History: A Survey* has made every effort to provide the most accurate, complete, and accessible textbook possible. With this goal in mind, he has included a number of helpful study aids that augment the narrative and heighten the drama and excitement of America's past. The following "Guided Tour" gives examples of many of these special features and suggests how to make the best use of them.

Chapter Introduction

Every chapter opens with an expanded introduction that focuses on the chapter's main themes and direction. In addition, timelines that correspond to many of the chapter heads, as well as other events contained throughout the narrative, are placed at the beginning of the chapters. These introductions, in addition to serving as a guide to the chapter, are also valuable for review in preparation for tests.

IMMIGRANT GROUPS IN COLONIAL AMERICA, 1760 Even though the entire Atlantic seaboard of what is now the United States had become a series of British colonies by 1760, the population consisted of people from many nations. As this map reveals, English settlers dominated most of the regions of North America. But note the large areas of German settlement in the western Chesapeake and Pennsylvania; the swath of Dutch settlement in New York and New Jersey; the Scots-Irish regions in the western regions of the South; and the large areas in which Africans were becoming the majority of the population, even if subjugated by the white minority. ◆ *What aspects of the history of these colonies help explain their ethnic composition?*

For an interactive version of this map go to www.mhhe.com/brinkley12ch3maps

them Roman Catholics who had been defeated in rebellions in 1715 and 1745, immigrated into several colonies, North Carolina above all. Presbyterian Lowlanders, faced in Scotland with high rents in the country and unemployment in the towns, left for America in large numbers shortly before the American Revolution, joining earlier groups of Scots, who had arrived in the late seventeenth century. They became a significant influence in New Jersey and Pennsylvania and helped established Presbyterianism as an important religion in those colonies. The Catholic Irish migrated steadily over a long period, and by the time of the Revolution they were almost as numerous as the Scots, although less conspicuous. Many of them had by then abandoned their Roman Catholic religion and with it much of their ethnic identity.

Continuing immigration and natural increase contributed to a rapid population growth in the colonies in the eighteenth century. In 1700, the non-Indian population of the colonies totaled less than 250,000; by 1775, it was over 2 million—a nearly tenfold increase. Throughout the colonial period, the non-Indian population nearly doubled every twenty-five years.

Maps

This textbook includes a wealth of full-color maps that enhance the study of American history. Captions make specific reference to map content and include thought questions for every map. In addition, many maps in the book feature a Web icon that links them to an interactive version on the text's Online Learning Center.

Interactive Maps

Interactive maps, related to those maps within the text distinguished by a Web icon, offer a variety of learning functions. On one level you can use the interactive maps to view topography, territories, borders, urban development, developing trends, and other such topics. On a second level, the interactive maps provide you with a multiple-choice quiz that tests your understanding of the information provided on the map, questions for deeper analysis, suggestions for projects, and an audio component that provides an overview of the map. Visit the site at www.mhhe.com/brinkley12.

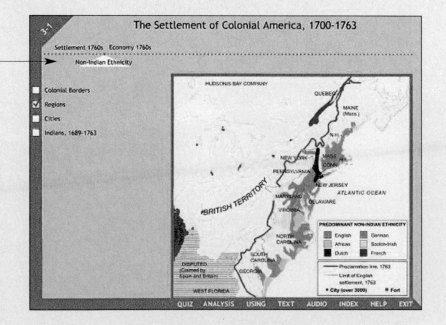

Where Historians Disagree

This well-received feature clearly demonstrates that history is not simply a collection of facts; rather, it consists of many stories that are often complex and open to interpretation. The "Where Historians Disagree" essays illustrate the contested quality of much of the American past. This feature encourages thinking about what different aspects of American history mean and provide a taste of the thrill of historical investigation.

WHERE HISTORIANS DISAGREE

The Character of Slavery

No issue in American history has produced a richer literature or a more spirited debate than the nature of American slavery. The debate began even before the Civil War, when abolitionists strove to expose slavery to the world as a brutal, dehumanizing institution, while southern defenders of slavery tried to depict it as a benevolent, paternalistic system. That same debate continued for a time after the Civil War; but by the late nineteenth century, with white Americans eager for sectional conciliation, both northern and southern chroniclers of slavery began to accept a romanticized and unthreatening picture of the Old South and its "peculiar institution."

The first major scholarly examination of slavery was fully within this romantic tradition. Ulrich B. Phillips's *American Negro Slavery* (1918) portrayed slavery as an essentially benign institution in which kindly masters looked after submissive, childlike, and generally contented African Americans. Phillips's apologia for slavery remained the authoritative work on the subject for nearly thirty years.

In the 1940s, as concern about racial injustice increasingly engaged the attention of white Americans, challenges to Phillips began to emerge. In 1941, Melville J. Herskovits challenged Phillips's contention that black Americans retained little of their African cultural inheritance. In 1943, Herbert

(Historic New Orleans Collection, 1975.93.2 (detail))

(General Research Division, New York Public Library, Astor, Lenox and Tilden Foundations)

Aptheker published a chronicle of slave revolts as a way of challenging Phillips's claim that blacks were submissive and content.

A somewhat different challenge to Phillips emerged in the 1950s from historians who emphasized the brutality of the institution. Kenneth Stampp's *The Peculiar Institution* (1956) and, even more damningly, Stanley Elkins's *Slavery* (1959) described a labor system that did serious physical and psychological damage to its victims. Stampp and Elkins portrayed slavery as something like a prison, in which men and women had virtually no space in which to develop their own social and cultural lives. Elkins compared the system to Nazi concentration camps during World War II and likened the childlike "Sambo" personality of slavery to the distortions of character that many scholars believed the Holocaust had produced.

In the early 1970s, an explosion of new scholarship on slavery shifted the emphasis away from the damage the system inflicted on African Americans and toward the striking success of the slaves in building a culture of their own despite their enslavement. John Blassingame in 1973, echoing Herskovits's claims of thirty years earlier, argued that "the most remarkable aspect of the whole process of enslavement is the extent to which the American-born slaves were able to retain their ancestors' culture." Herbert Gutman, in *The Black Family in Slavery and Freedom* (1976) challenged the prevailing belief that slavery had weakened and even destroyed the African-American family. On the contrary, he argued, the black family survived slavery with

impressive strength, although with some significant differences from the prevailing form of the white family. Eugene Genovese's *Roll, Jordan, Roll* (1974) and other works revealed how African Americans manipulated the paternalist assumptions at the heart of slavery to build a large cultural space of their own within the system where they could develop their own family life, social traditions, and religious patterns. That same year, Robert Fogel and Stanley Engerman published their controversial *Time on the Cross*, a highly quantitative study that supported some of the claims of Gutman and Genovese about black achievement, but that went much further in portraying slavery as a successful and reasonably humane (if ultimately immoral) system. Slave workers, they argued, were better treated and lived in greater comfort than most northern industrial workers of the same era. Their conclusions produced a storm of criticism.

Some of the most important recent scholarship on slavery has focused on the role of women within it. Elizabeth Fox-Genovese's *Within the Plantation Household* (1988) examined the lives of both white and black women on the plantation. Rejecting the claims of some feminist historians that black and white women shared a common female identity born of their shared subordination to men, she portrayed slave women as defined by their dual roles as members of the plantation work force and anchors of the black family. Slave women, she argued, professed loyalty to their mistresses when forced to serve them as domestics; but their real loyalty remained to their own communities and families.

306

AMERICA IN THE WORLD

The Cinema

There is probably no cultural or commercial product more closely identified with the United States than motion pictures — or, as movies are known in much of the world, the cinema. Although the technology of film emerged from the work of inventors in England and France as well as the United States, the production and distribution of films has been dominated by Americans almost from the start. The United States was the first nation to create a film "industry," and it did so at a scale vaster than that of any other country. The 700 feature films a year that Hollywood produced in the 1920s was more than ten times the number created by any other nation, and even then its films were dominating not only the vast American market, but much of the world's market as well. Seventy percent of the films seen in Latin America, and 95 percent of the movies viewed in Canada and Great Britain were produced in the United States in the 1920s. As early as the 1930s, the penetration of other nations by American movies was already troubling many governments. The Soviet Union responded to the popularity of Walt Disney's Micky Mouse cartoons by inventing a cartoon hero of its own — a porcupine, designed to entertain in a way consistent with socialist values and not the capitalist ones that they believed Hollywood conveyed. During World War II, American films were banned in occupied France (prompting some anti-fascist dissidents to screen such American films as Frank Capra's *Mr. Smith Goes to Washington* in protest).

American dominance was a result in part of World War I and its aftermath, which debilitated European film-making just as movies were vigorously growing in the United States. By 1915, the United States had gained complete control of its own vast market and had so saturated it with movie theaters that by the end of World War I, half the theaters of the world were in America. Two decades later, after an extraordinary expansion of theaters in other nations, the United States continued to have over 40 percent of the world's cinemas. And while the spread of theaters through

other areas of the world helped launch film industries in many other countries, it also increased the market (and the appetite) for American films and strengthened American supremacy in their production. "The sun, it now appears," the *Saturday Evening Post* commented in the mid-1920s, "never sets on the British empire and the American motion picture." Movies were then, and perhaps remain still, America's most influential cultural export. Even American popular music, which has enormous global reach, faces more significant local competition than American movies do in most parts of the world.

Despite this American dominance, however, film-making has flourished and continues to flourish in many countries around the world. India's fabled "Bollywood," for example, produces an enormous number of movies for its domestic market — almost as many as the American industry creates, even though few of them are widely exported. This global dominance has had a significant impact on American film-making, just as American films have influenced film-makers abroad. The small British film industry had a strong early influence on American movies partly because of the quality and originality of British films, and partly because of the emigration of talented actors, directors, and screenwriters to the United States. The great Alfred Hitchcock, for example, made his first films in London before moving to Hollywood, where he spent the rest of his long career. After World War II, French "new wave" cinema helped spawn a new generation of highly individualistic directors in the United States. Asian cinema — especially the thriving film industry in Hong Kong with its gritty realism — helped lead to some of the powerfully violent American films of the 1980s and beyond, as well as the genre of martial-arts films that has become popular around the world. German, Italian, Swedish, Dutch, Japanese, Australian, and Indian film-makers also had enormous influence on Hollywood — and over time perhaps even greater influence on the large and growing "independent film" movement in the United States.

VALENTINO The popularity of the film star Rudolph Valentino among American women was one of the most striking cultural phenomena of the 1920s. Valentino was slight and of more than average height — the conventional image of manliness. But he became — in enormous ways — among women, in part as this poster is obviously intended to suggest — by baring his body on screen. Valentino was Italian, which made him seem somehow strange and foreign to many older-stock Americans, and he was almost always cast in exotic roles, never as an American. His sudden death in 1926 (at the age of 31) created enormous outpourings of grief among American women. *(George Kleiman/Bettmann/Corbis)*

In recent decades, as new technologies and new styles have transformed films around the world, the American movie industry has continued to dominate global cinema. But national boundaries no longer adequately describe movie-making in the twenty-first century. It is becoming a truly globalized enterprise in the same way that so many other commercial ventures are becoming "American" films today are often produced abroad, often have non-American directors and actors, and are often paid for with international financing. Hollywood still dominates worldwide film-making, but Hollywood itself is now an increasingly global community.

649

America in the World

The "America in the World" features place America in a more global context. America has never existed in isolation from the rest of the world, and these essays demonstrate the importance of the many international influences on the American story.

Patterns of Popular Culture

"Patterns of Popular Culture" essays spotlight the ways popular culture has affected the lives of Americans at different times and places that culture in a larger historical context. The author has selected a wide variety of high-interest topics ranging from *Horse Racing, Baseball and the Civil War, Louisa May Alcott, The Slaves' Music, Rock Music in the Sixties, Lucy and Desi, The Age of Swing, Coney Island, The Wild West Show, Yellow Journalism,* and *The Golden Age of Comic Books.* (See the Contents for a complete listing.)

The Novels of Horatio Alger

A young boy, perhaps an orphan, makes his perilous way through life on the rough streets of the city by selling newspapers or peddling matches. One day, his energy and determination catches the eye of a wealthy man, who gives him a chance to improve himself. Through honesty, charm, hard work, and aggressiveness, the boy rises in the world to become a successful man.

That, in a nutshell, is the story that Horatio Alger presented to his vast public in novel after novel—over 100 of them in all—for over forty years. During his lifetime, Americans bought over 100 million copies of his novels. After his death in 1899, his books (and others written in his name) continued to sell at an astonishing rate. Even today, when the books themselves are largely forgotten, the name Horatio Alger has come to represent the idea of individual advancement through (in a phrase Alger coined) "pluck and luck."

Alger was born in 1832 into a middle-class New England family, attended Harvard, and spent a short time as a Unitarian minister. He himself never experienced the hardships he later chronicled. In the mid-1850s, he turned to writing stories and books, and continued to do so for the rest of his life. His most famous novel, *Ragged Dick*, was published in 1868; but there were many others that were almost identical to it: *Tom, the Bootblack; Sink or Swim; Jed, the Poorhouse Boy; Phil, the Fiddler; Andy Grant's Pluck.* Most of his books were aimed at young people, and almost all of them were fables of a young man's rise "from rags to riches." The purpose of his writing, he claimed, was twofold. He wanted to "exert a salutary influence upon the class of whom [I] was writing, by setting before them inspiring examples of what energy, ambi-

A NEWSBOY'S STORY Alger's novels were even more popular after his death in 1899 than they had been in his lifetime. This reprint of one of his many "rags-to-riches" stories—about the rise of a New York newsboy to wealth and success—includes in the background a rendering of the "Met Life Building," an early skyscraper built in 1909.

tion, and an honest purpose may achieve." He also wanted to show his largely middle-class readers "the life and experiences of the friendless and vagrant children to be found in all our cities."

But Alger's intentions probably had little to do with the success of his books. Most Americans of the late nineteenth and early twentieth centuries were attracted to Alger because his stories helped them to believe in one of the most cherished of all their national myths: that it is possible for individuals to rise in the world with willpower and hard work, that anyone can become a "self-made man." That belief was all the more important in the late nineteenth

century when the rise of large-scale corporate industrialization was making it increasingly difficult for individuals to control their own fates.

Alger placed great emphasis on the moral qualities of his heroes; their success was a reward for their virtue. But many of his readers ignored the moral message and clung simply to the image of sudden and dramatic success. After the author's death, his publishers responded to that yearning by abridging many of Alger's works to eliminate the parts of his stories where the heroes do good deeds. Instead, they emphasized the success of Alger's heroes in rising in the world.

Alger himself had very mixed feelings about the new industrial order he described. His books were meant to reveal not just the opportunities for advancement it sometimes created, but also its cruelty. That was one reason that in almost all his books, his heroes triumphed not just because of their own virtues or efforts, but because of some amazing stroke of luck. To Alger, at least, the modern age did not guarantee success through hard work alone; there had to be some providential assistance as well. Over time, however, Alger's admirers came to ignore his own misgivings about industrialism and to portray his books purely as celebrations of (and justifications for) laissez-faire capitalism and the accumulation of wealth.

An example of the transformation of Alger into a symbol of individual achievement is the Horatio Alger Award, established in 1947 by the American Schools and Colleges Association to honor "living individuals who by their own efforts had pulled themselves up by their bootstraps in the American tradition." Among its recipients have been Presidents Dwight D. Eisenhower and Ronald Reagan, Evangelist Billy Graham, and Supreme Court Justice Clarence Thomas.

and schools, institutions he believed would help the poor to help themselves.

The notion of private wealth as a public blessing existed alongside another popular concept: the notion of great wealth as something available to all. Russell H. Conwell,

a Baptist minister, became the most prominent spokesman for the idea by delivering one lecture, "Acres of Diamonds," more than 6,000 times between 1880 and 1900. Conwell told a series of stories, which he claimed were true, of

Russell Conwell

474

The Novels of Louisa May Alcott

If Horatio Alger's rags-to-riches tales captured the aspirations of many men of the late nineteenth century, Louisa May Alcott's enormously popular novels helped give voice to the often unstated ambitions of many young women.

Alcott was born in 1832, the daughter of a prominent if generally impoverished reformer and educator, Bronson Alcott—a New England transcendentalist committed to abolishing slavery and advancing women's rights. Louisa May Alcott grew up wanting to write, one of the few serious vocations available to women. As a young adult, she wrote a series of popular adventure novels under the pen-name A. M. Barnard, populated by conventional male heroes. But after serving as a nurse in the Civil War (during which she contracted typhoid, from which she recovered, and mercury poisoning through her treatment, from which she suffered until her death in 1888), she chose a different path—writing more realistic fiction, and basing it on the lives and experiences of women. The publication of *Little Women* (1868, 1869) established Alcott as a major literary figure and as an enduring, if sometimes puzzling, inspiration for girls and, indeed, women of all ages.

Little Women—and its successors *Little Men* (1871) and *Jo's Boys* (1886)—were in many ways wholly unlike the formulaic Horatio Alger stories, in which young men inevitably rose from humble circumstances to great success. And yet they both echoed and altered the message of those books. The fictional March family in the novels was in fact modeled on Alcott's own impoverished if intellectually lively childhood, and much of *Little Women* is a chroni-

(Bettmann/Corbis)

cle of poverty, suffering, and even death. But it is also the story of a young girl—Jo March, modeled to some degree on Alcott herself—who struggles to build a life for herself that is not defined by conventional women's roles and ambitions. Jo March, like Louisa May Alcott herself, becomes a writer. She spurns a conventional marriage (to her attractive and wealthy neighbor Laurie). Unlike Alcott, who never married, Jo does find a husband—an older man, a German professor who does not support Jo's literary ambitions.

Many readers have found this marriage troubling—and false to the message of the book. It seems to contradict Alcott's belief that women can have intellectual independence and achievement. But to Alcott, this unconventional marriage was a symbol of her own repudiation of an ordinary domestic life. "Girls write to ask who the little

women marry, as if that was the only end and aim of a woman's life," Alcott wrote a friend after the publication of the first volume of the novel. "I won't marry Jo to Laurie to please any one." Jo's marriage to Professor Bhaer is in many ways a concession. "Jo should have remained a literary spinster [like Alcott herself]," she once wrote, "but so many enthusiastic ladies wrote to me clamorously demanding that she should marry Laurie, and out of perversity I didn't dare to refuse and out of perversity went and made a funny match for her."

It is tempting to see Louisa May Alcott's life—as an independent woman, a writer, and an active suffragist—as a better model to her readers than the characters in her fiction. But it was through *Little Women* and her other novels that Alcott mostly affected her time; and, whatever their limitations, they present a group of young women who do challenge, even if indirectly, the expectations of their era. Jo March is willful, rebellious, stubborn, ambitious, and often selfish, not the poised, romantic, submissive woman of most sentimental novels of her time. She hates housekeeping and drudgery. She yearns at times to be a boy. She resists society's expectations—through her literary aspirations, her sharp temper, and ultimately her unconventional marriage. Through those qualities, she captured the imaginations of late nineteenth-century female readers and continues to capture the imaginations of readers today. *Little Women* has survived far longer than the Horatio Alger stories did precisely because it presents a story of growing up that, unlike Alger's, is not predictable but complicated, conflicted, and surprising.

individuals who had found opportunities for extraordinary wealth in their own backyards. (One such story involved a modest farmer who discovered a vast diamond mine in his own fields in the course of working his land.) "I say to you," he told his rapt audiences, "that you have 'acres of diamonds' beneath you right here . . . that the men and women sitting here have within their reach opportunities to get largely wealthy. . . . I say that you ought to get rich, and that it is your duty to get rich." Most of the millionaires in the country, Conwell claimed (inac-

curately), had begun on the lowest rung of the economic ladder and had worked their way to success. Every industrious individual had the chance to do likewise.

Horatio Alger was the most famous promoter of the success story. (See "Patterns of Popular Culture," p. 474.) Alger was originally a minister in a small town in Massachusetts but was driven from his pulpit as a result of a sexual scandal. He moved to New York, where he wrote his celebrated novels—more than 100 in all, which together sold more than

Horatio Alger

475

New Interactive Learning Paragraphs

New Interactive Learning paragraphs at the end of every chapter list relevant material on the Primary Source Investigator CD-ROM packaged with every book.

INTERACTIVE LEARNING

The *Primary Source Investigator CD-ROM* offers the following materials related to this chapter:

- A short documentary movie, **Documenting the Depression**, examining the 1930s documentary film *The River* (D17).
- Interactive maps: **U.S. Elections** (M7) and **Unemployment Relief** (M26).
- Documents, images, and maps related to the onset of the Great Depression, the suffering of the people, and the ordeal of President Herbert Hoover. Highlights include "Migrant Mother" and other striking images by

Farm Security Administration photographer Dorothea Lange; an image of the Depression-era shantytowns dubbed "Hoovervilles"; photographs of a dust storm and other images of Dust Bowl life; and an image of the Bonus Army shacks in Washington D.C.

Online Learning Center
(www.mhhe.com/brinkley12)

For quizzes, Internet resources, references to additional books and films, and more, consult this book's Online Learning Center.

FOR FURTHER REFERENCE

Donald Worster scathingly indicts agricultural capitalism for its destruction of the plains environment in *Dust Bowl: The Southern Plains in the 1930s* (1979). In *The Great Depression: Delayed Recovery and Economic Change in America, 1929–1939* (1987), Michael Bernstein argues that we should ask not so much why the economy crashed in 1929 but rather why the expected recovery from the crash was so slow. Richard Pells, *Radical Visions and American Dreams: Culture and Social Thought in the Depression Years* (1973) is an important survey of the cultural and intellectual history of the 1930s. Studs Terkel, *Hard Times* (1970) is an excellent oral history of the Depression. Susan Ware analyzes the effect of the Great Depression on women in *Holding Their Own: American Women in the 1930s* (1987). The Communist Party's most popular period in

the United States is the subject of Harvey Klehr's *The Heyday of American Communism: The Depression Decade* (1984) and, from quite different viewpoints, Robin D. G. Kelley, *Hammer and Hoe: Alabama Communists During the Great Depression* (1990) and Michael Denning, *The Cultural Front: The Laboring of American Culture in the Twentieth Century* (1997). Joan Hoff Wilson, *Herbert Hoover: Forgotten Progressive* (1975) argues that President Hoover was in many ways a surprisingly progressive thinker about the American social order. *The Great Depression* (1993), a multipart film by Blackside Productions, is an eloquent picture of many aspects of the depression decade. *Union Maids* (1997) is a vivid film history of women organizing in the 1930s. *The Lemon Grove Incident* (1985) is a film providing a rare glimpse of Mexican-American civil rights activism over school integration in the early 1930s.

Depression Families

The economic hardships of the Depression years placed great strains on American families, many of whom had become accustomed in the 1920s to a steadily rising standard of living but now found themselves plunged suddenly into uncertainty.

Retreat from Consumerism   Such circumstances forced many families to retreat from the consumer patterns they had developed in the 1920s. Women often returned to sewing clothes for themselves and their families and to preserving their own food rather than buying such products in stores. Others engaged in home businesses—taking in laundry, selling baked goods, accepting boarders. Many households expanded to include more distant relatives. Parents often moved in with their children and grandparents with their grandchildren, or vice versa.

But the Depression also eroded the strength of many family units. There was a decline in the divorce rate, but largely because divorce was now too expensive for some. More common was the informal breakup of families, particularly the desertion of families by unemployed men bent on escaping the humiliation of being unable to earn a living. The marriage and birth rates declined simultaneously for the first time since the early nineteenth century.

THE DEPRESSION AND AMERICAN CULTURE

The Great Depression was a traumatic experience for millions of Americans, and it shook the confidence of many people in themselves or in their nation or both. Out of the crisis emerged some of the most probing criticisms of American society and the American economic system of the industrial age. At the same time, the Depression produced powerful confirmations of more traditional values and reinforced many traditional goals. There was not one Depression culture, but many.

Depression Values

Prosperity and industrial growth had done much to shape American values in the 1920s. Mainstream culture, at least, had celebrated affluence and consumerism and had stressed the importance of personal gratification through both. Many Americans assumed, therefore, that the experience of hard times would have profound effects on the nation's social values. In general, however, American social values seemed to change relatively little in response to the Depression. Rather, many people responded to hard times by redoubling their commitment to familiar ideas and goals. The sociologists Robert and Helen Merrell Lynd, who had published a celebrated

study of Muncie, Indiana, *Middletown*, in 1929, returned there in the mid-1930s to see how the city had changed. They concluded in their 1937 book, *Middletown in Transition*, that in most respects "the texture of Middletown's culture has not changed. . . . Middletown is overwhelmingly living by the values by which it lived in 1925." Above all, the men and women of "Middletown"—and by implication many other Americans—remained committed to the traditional American emphasis on the individual.

Persistence of the "Success Ethic"   No assumption would seem to have been more vulnerable to erosion during the Depression than the belief that the individual was in control of his or her own fate, that anyone displaying sufficient talent and industry could become a success. And in some respects, the economic crisis did work to undermine the traditional "success ethic" in America. Many people began to look to government for assistance; many blamed corporate moguls, international bankers, "economic royalists," and others for their distress. Yet the Depression did not, in the end, seriously erode the success ethic.

Self Blame   The survival of the ideals of work and individual advancement was evident in many ways, not least in the reactions of those most traumatized by the Depression: ordinary working people who suddenly found themselves without employment. Some expressed anger and struck out at the economic system. Many, however, seemed to blame themselves. Nothing so surprised foreign observers of America in the 1930s as the apparent passivity of the unemployed, many of whom were so ashamed of their joblessness that they refused to leave their homes. Perhaps that was why people who continued in the 1930s to work and to live more or less as they always had sometimes found it easy to forget that there was an economic crisis. The Depression was sometimes hard to see, because the unemployed tended to hide themselves, unwilling to display to the world what many of them considered their own personal failure.

At the same time, millions responded eagerly to reassurances that they could, through their own efforts, restore themselves to prosperity and success. Dale Carnegie's self-help manual *How to Win Friends and Influence People* (1936), was one of the best-selling books of the decade. Carnegie's message was not only that personal initiative was the route to success; it was also that the best way for people to get ahead was to fit in and make other people feel important. Similarly, Harry Emerson Fosdick, a Protestant theologian who preached the virtues of positive thinking and individual initiative, attracted large audiences with his radio addresses.

Marginal Icons

Marginal icons refer to related mini-documentaries on the corresponding Primary Source Investigator CD-ROM.

did prove highly divisive and that gradually became entwined with each other: railroads and slavery.

Transcontinental Railroad and Slavery
As the nation expanded westward, the problem of communication between the older states and the areas west of the Mississippi River became more and more critical. As a result, broad support began to emerge for building a transcontinental railroad. The problem was where to place it—and in particular, where to locate the railroad's eastern terminus, where the line could connect with the existing rail network east of the Mississippi. Northerners favored Chicago, the rapidly growing capital of the free states of the Northwest. Southerners supported St. Louis, Memphis, or New Orleans—all in slave states. The transcontinental railroad, in other words, had become part of the struggle between the North and the South.

Gadsden Purchase
Pierce's secretary of war, Jefferson Davis of Mississippi, removed one obstacle to a southern route. Surveys indicated that a railroad with a southern terminus would have to pass through an area in Mexican territory. But in 1853 Davis sent James Gadsden, a southern railroad builder, to Mexico, where he persuaded the Mexican government to accept $10 million in exchange for a strip of land that today comprises part of Arizona and New Mexico. The so-called Gadsden Purchase only accentuated the sectional rivalry.

The Kansas-Nebraska Controversy

As a senator from Illinois, a resident of Chicago, and the acknowledged leader of northwestern Democrats, Stephen A. Douglas naturally wanted the transcontinental railroad for his own city and section. He also realized the strength of the principal argument against the northern route west of the Mississippi: that it would run mostly through country with a substantial Indian population. As a result, he introduced a bill in January 1854 to organize (and thus open to white settlement) a huge new territory, known as Nebraska, west of Iowa and Missouri.

Douglas knew the South would oppose his bill because it would prepare the way for a new free state; the proposed territory was in the area of the Louisiana Purchase north of the Missouri Compromise line (36°30′) and hence closed to slavery. In an effort to make the measure acceptable to southerners, Douglas inserted a provision that the status of slavery in the territory would be determined by the territorial legislature—that is,

Kansas-Nebraska Act
according to "popular sovereignty." In theory, the region could choose to open itself to slavery (although few believed it actually would). When southern Democrats demanded more, Douglas agreed to an additional clause

explicitly repealing the Missouri Compromise. He also agreed to divide the area into two territories—Nebraska and Kansas—instead of one. The new, second territory (Kansas) was more likely to become a slave state. In its final form the measure was known as the Kansas-Nebraska Act. President Pierce supported the bill, and after a strenuous debate, it became law in May 1854 with the unanimous support of the South and the partial support of northern Democrats.

No piece of legislation in American history produced so many immediate, sweeping, and ominous consequences. It divided and destroyed the Whig Party, which disappeared almost entirely by 1856. It divided the northern Democrats (many of whom were appalled at the repeal of the Missouri Compromise, which they considered an almost sacred part of the fabric of the Union) and drove many of them from the party. Most important of all, it spurred the creation of

Birth of the Republican Party
a new party that was frankly sectional in composition and creed. People in both major parties who opposed Douglas's bill began to call themselves Anti-Nebraska Democrats and Anti-Nebraska Whigs. In 1854, they formed a new organization and named it the Republican Party. It instantly became a major force in American politics. In the elections of that year, the Republicans won enough seats in Congress to permit them, in combination with allies among the Know-Nothings, to organize the House of Representatives.

"Bleeding Kansas"

Events in Kansas itself in the next two years increased the political turmoil in the North. White settlers from both the North and the South began moving into the territory almost immediately after the passage of the Kansas-Nebraska Act. In the spring of 1855, elections were held for a territorial legislature. There were only about 1,500 legal voters in Kansas by then, but thousands of Missourians, some traveling in armed bands into Kansas, swelled the vote to over 6,000. The result was that pro-slavery forces elected a majority to the legislature, which immediately legalized slavery. Outraged free-staters elected their own delegates to a constitutional convention, which met at Topeka and adopted a constitution excluding slavery. They then chose their own governor and legislature and petitioned Congress for statehood. President Pierce denounced them as traitors and threw the full support of the federal government behind the pro-slavery territorial legislature. A few months later a pro-slavery federal marshal assembled a large posse, consisting mostly of Missourians, to arrest the free-state leaders, who had set up their headquarters in Lawrence. The posse sacked the town, burned the "governor's" house,

Marginal Notes

Marginal notes highlight key, terms, events, and concepts as they appear within the narrative. These notes are useful both in reading through the text and in reviewing to prepare for tests.

For Further Reference

For Further Reference lists at the end of every chapter highlight the most significant books available about topics covered in the chapter, allowing readers to do further research or follow up on a topic of particular interest.

FOR FURTHER REFERENCE

William E. Leuchtenburg, *Franklin D. Roosevelt and the New Deal* (1963) is a classic short history of the New Deal. Anthony Badger, *The New Deal: The Depression Years* (1989) is another fine overview. David Kennedy, *Freedom from Fear: The American People in Depression and War, 1929–1945* (1999) is an important narrative history, a volume in the Oxford History of the United States. Geoffrey Ward, *Before the Trumpet: Young Franklin Roosevelt, 1882–1905* (1985) and *A First-Class Temperament: The Emergence of Franklin Roosevelt* (1989) are superb biographical accounts of the pre-presidential FDR. Frank Freidel, *Franklin D. Roosevelt: A Rendezvous with Destiny* (1990) is a one-volume biography by one of FDR's most important biographers. Ellis Hawley, *The New Deal and the Problem of Monopoly* (1967) is a classic examination of the economic policies of the Roosevelt administration in its first five years. Colin Gordon, *New Deals: Business, Labor, and Politics in America, 1920–1935* (1994) is a challenging reinterpretation of the early New Deal years. The transformation of liberalism after 1937 is the subject of Alan Brinkley, *The End of Reform: New Deal Liberalism in Recession and War* (1995). Jennifer Klein, *For All These Rights: Business, Labor, and the Shaping of America's Public-Private Welfare State* (2003) sees the origin of the modern welfare state as a product in part of struggles between labor and capital. Linda Gordon, *Pitied But Not Entitled: Single Mothers and the History of Welfare* (1994) is a pioneering work on women as the recipients and also the authors of government welfare policies. Alice Kessler-Harris, *In Pursuit of Equity: Women, Men, and the Quest for Economic Citizenship in Twentieth-Century America* (2001) is an important study of the intersection of gender and economic rights. The efforts of Chicago workers to protest and organize is the subject of Lizabeth Cohen, *Making a New Deal: Industrial Workers in Chicago, 1919–1939* (1990). Nelson Lichtenstein, *The Most Dangerous Man in Detroit: Walter Reuther and the Fate of American Labor* (1995) is a valuable study of one of the early leaders of the CIO. Richard Lowitt, *The New Deal and the West* (1984) pays particular attention to water policy and agriculture in the New Deal years. Jordan Schwarz, *The New Dealers: Power Politics in the Age of Roosevelt* (1993) examines the proponents of state-funded economic development of the South and West. Alan Brinkley, *Voices of Protest: Huey Long, Father Coughlin, and the Great Depression* (1982) examines some of the most powerful challenges to the New Deal. Bruce Shulman, *From Cotton Belt to Sunbelt* (1991) explores the New Deal's effort to transform the region Roosevelt and others considered the nation's number one economic problem, the American South. Harvard Sitkoff, *A New Deal for Blacks* (1978) and Nancy J. Weiss, *Farewell to the Party of Lincoln: Black Politics in the Age of FDR* (1983) take contrasting positions on what the New Deal did for African Americans.

FDR (1994), a documentary by David Grubin, gives viewers a fine view of the private and public life of Franklin D. Roosevelt. One of the president's most vocal and powerful critics is featured in another film, by Ken Burns, *Huey Long* (1986). *The World of Tomorrow* (1984) is a provocative documentary on the 1939 World's Fair.

List of Illustrations

Frobisher and the Eskimos 2
Indians of New France 5
Cahokia Indian Mounds 6
Iroquois Women 10
The Indian Village of Secoton (c. 1585),
    by John White 10
Christopher Columbus 11
Balboa Discovering the Pacific 12
The Mexicans Strike Back 14
Pizarro in Peru 14
De Soto in North America 15
Smallpox Among the Indians 19
Sculpture of Djenne 20
The Docks of Bristol, England 25
John Calvin 26
Elizabeth I 27
The "Restitution" of New Amsterdam 28
Roanoke 30
Advice to Migrants 32
Tobacco Plant 36
The Maryland Proprietor, c. 1670 38
Colonial Currency 42
Portrait of a Boston Woman 43
Anne Hutchinson Preaching in Her
    House in Boston 45
A Pequot Village Destroyed 47
Charleston, South Carolina 49
New Amsterdam 50
A Quaker Meeting 51
Making Molasses in Barbados 54
Savannah in 1734 60
Dr. William Gleason 64
Servants for Sale 68
Guide to the Seasons 70
Africans Bound for America 74
The Slave Ship *Brookes* 75
The Pennsylvania Dutch 76
Preparing Tobacco 79
Commerce in New England 80
Tea Party in the Time of George I 83
Mulberry Plantation, 1770 85
A Study of Witchcraft 88
Sinners in Hell, 1744 91
George Whitefield 92
A "Dame School" Primer 94
Poor Richard's Almanac 94
Town and Country-Man's Almanac 95
Benjamin Franklin on Electricity 96
Punishment in New England 97
The Boston Massacre (1770),
    by Paul Revere 100
An Appeal for Colonial Unity 103
The Siege of Louisbourg, 1758 106
George III 110
Preparing to Meet the Paxton Boys 112
The Alternatives of William Burg 114
"The Tory's Day of Judgment" 115
The Boston Massacre (1770),
    by Paul Revere 117

"The Cruel Fate of the Loyalists" 117
The Boston Tea Party 119
The Scales of Justice 120
Tavern Billiards 120
Paying the Exciseman 121
Recruiting Patriots 122
The British Retreat from
    Concord, 1775 124
The British Surrender 126
Common Sense 128
Voting for Independence 132
Revolutionary Soldiers 133
Battle of Germantown 134
The Battle of Bunker Hill, 1775 136
The British on the Hudson, 1776 141
Storming the Bastille 142
The British Infantry 147
Banner of the Society of Pewterers 148
A Free Black Man 150
The Grid, Illinois 153
Little Turtle 155
Daniel Shays and Job Shattuck 155
The American Star 158
George Washington at Mount Vernon 160
A Broadside Against "Nobility" 161
The Grand Convention 163
Federalist #1 166
Bank Note 169
The Jeffersonian Idyll 171
A Comment on the Whiskey Rebellion 173
Mount Vernon 174
John Adams 175
The XYZ Affair 176
Congressional Brawlers 177
The Burning of Washington 180
Moravian Boys' School ca. 1800 182
The Pennsylvania Hospital 184
Methodist Camp Meeting, 1837 187
The Cotton Gin 188
Pawtucket Bridge and Falls 189
The English Canal Age 191
A Scene of the Road 192
Oakland House and Race Course 194
The Eclipse-Henry Match Race 195
Washington City, 1821 197
Thomas Jefferson 197
Jefferson the Architect 197
West Point 199
The Journal of Lewis and Clark 202
New Orleans in 1803 203
Protection from Impressment 205
The Treaty of Greenville 206
Tecumseh 207
James and Dolly Madison 208
The Bombardment of Fort McHenry 211
Attacking the Federalists 212
Fourth of July Picnic at Weymouth Landing (c. 1845), by
    Susan Merrett 214
An Early Mill in New England 216

List of Maps

How the Early North Americans Lived 4
European Exploration and Conquest, 1492-1583 13
Spanish America 16
Europe and West Africa in the Fifteenth Century 21
The Growth of the Chesapeake, 1607-1750 35
The Growth of New England, 1620-1750 44
The Non-Indian Population of New England, 1620-1700 44
The Seventeenth-Century Caribbean 55
America in 1700 66
Immigrant Groups in Colonial America, 1760 77
The "Triangular Trade" 81
African Population as a Proportion of Total Population,
    c. 1775 84
The New England Town: Sudbury, Massachusetts,
    17th Century 87

The Thirteen Colonies in 1763 108
North America in 1763 111
The Battles of Lexington and Concord, 1775 123
The Revolution in the North, 1775-1776 135
The Revolution in the Middle Colonies, 1776-1778 137
The Revolution in the South, 1778-1781 140
The Conflict over Western Lands 152
Land Survey: Ordinance of 1785 154
America in 1800 193
Washington, D.C. in the Early Nineteenth Century 196
Exploring the Louisiana Purchase, 1804-1807 201
The War of 1812 210
The Missouri Compromise, 1820 224
The Election of 1828 230

List of Charts

The Non-Indian Population of the Chesapeake, 1607–1700 37

The Non-Indian Population of New England, 1620–1700 44

The Non-Indian Population of North America, 1700–1780 67

The African Population of the British Colonies, 1620–1780 76

Wealth Distribution in Colonial Cities, 1687–1771 90

American Imports and Exports, 1790–1820 217

Participation in Presidential Elections, 1824–1860 234

Population Growth, 1620–1860 260

Immigration, 1820–1840 260

Sources of Immigration, 1820–1840 261

Immigration, 1840–1860 264

Sources of Immigration, 1840–1860 264

Union and Confederate Resources 370

AMERICAN HISTORY

A SURVEY

FROBISHER AND THE ESKIMOS In 1577, the English explorer Martin Frobisher embarked on an elusive search that enchanted a generation of Europeans—the search for the "Northwest Passage," a waterway through North America to the Pacific. He sailed into the Arctic regions of eastern Canada, deep into Baffin Bay, before finding his route blocked by impassable ice. Along the way, he encountered groups of Baffinland Eskimos, who—as this John White drawing (repainted by his contemporary Hans Sloan) shows—attacked his party. Even outnumbered, the Frobisher party had the advantage of firearms and escaped serious harm. *(British Museum, London/The Bridgeman Art Library)*

SIGNIFICANT EVENTS

14,000– ▶ Asians begin migrating to North America across
12,000 B.C.   the Bering Strait

1347 ▶ Black Death begins in Europe

1480s ▶ Portuguese explorers travel down west coast of
        Africa in search of sea route to Asia

1492 ▶ Columbus sails west from Spain in search of Asia,
       reaches Bahama Islands in the Caribbean

1494 ▶ Papal decree divides New World between Spain and
       Portugal

1497 ▶ John Cabot establishes first English claim in North
       America

1502 ▶ First African slaves arrive in Spanish America

CHAPTER 1

The Meeting of Cultures

*T*he discovery of America did not begin with Christopher Columbus. It began many thousands of years earlier when human beings first crossed an ancient land bridge over the Bering Strait into what is now Alaska and—almost certainly without realizing it—began to people a new continent. No one is certain when these migrations began; recent estimates suggest between 12,000 and 14,000 years ago, but some scholars believe the first crossings were much earlier. They were probably a result of the development of new stone tools—spears and other hunting implements—with which it became possible to pursue the large animals that regularly crossed between Asia and North America. Year after year, a few at a time, these nomadic peoples—all of them apparently from a Mongolian stock similar to that of modern-day eastern Siberia—entered the new continent and moved ever deeper into its heart. Ultimately, perhaps as early as 9,000 B.C., the migrations reached the southern tip of South America. By the end of the fifteenth century A.D., when the first important contact with Europeans occurred, America was the home of many millions of men and women. Scholars estimate that more than 50 million people— and perhaps as many as 75 million, more than lived in Europe— lived in the Americas by 1500 and that as many as 10 million lived in the territory that now constitutes the United States.

These ancient civilizations had experienced many changes and many catastrophes during their long history. But it is likely that none of these experiences was as tragically transforming as the arrival of Europeans beginning in the late fifteenth century. In the long term, European settlers came to dominate entirely most areas of the Americas. But even in the short term—in the first violent years of Spanish and Portuguese exploration and conquest—the impact of the new arrivals was profound. Europeans brought with them diseases (most notably smallpox) to which natives, unlike the invaders, had no immunity. The result was a great demographic catastrophe that killed millions of people, weakened existing societies, and greatly aided the Spanish and Portuguese in their rapid and devastating conquest of the existing American empires.

But neither in the southern regions of the Americas, nor in the northern areas where the English and French eventually created settlements, were the European immigrants ever able to eliminate the influence of the existing peoples (which they came to call "Indians"). Battles between natives and Europeans continued into the late nineteenth century. But there were also more peaceful interactions through which these very different civilizations affected one another, learned from one another, and changed each other permanently and profoundly.

1517 ▶ Martin Luther challenges Catholic Church, sparking Protestant Reformation in Europe

1518–1530 ▶ Smallpox epidemic ravages Indian societies of Central and South America

1519–1522 ▶ Magellan expedition circumnavigates globe

1521 ▶ Cortes captures Tenochtitlán and conquers Aztec Empire in Mexico

1532–1538 ▶ Pizarro conquers Incas in Peru

1558 ▶ Elizabeth I ascends English throne

1565 ▶ St. Augustine founded in Florida

1566 ▶ English conquest of Ireland begins

1587 ▶ "Lost Colony" established on Roanoke Island

1598 ▶ Don Juan de Oñate establishes Spanish colony in present-day New Mexico

1603 ▶ James I succeeds Elizabeth I in England

1608 ▶ French establish Quebec, their first permanent settlement in America

1609 ▶ Spanish colonists found Santa Fe

1624 ▶ Dutch establish permanent settlements in what is now New York

1680 ▶ Pueblos revolt and drive Spanish colonists from present-day New Mexico

1692 ▶ Spanish return to New Mexico

1696 ▶ Spanish crush last Pueblo revolt in New Mexico

AMERICA BEFORE COLUMBUS

As settlement spread, early peoples began to adapt themselves to their surroundings. For many centuries, they lived primarily in small nomadic bands, subsisting through hunting, fishing, and occasionally primitive agriculture, depending on the resources in their various regions. Gradually, however, they developed substantial civilizations—some of them of vast size and power. There was as much variety among the civilizations of the Americas as among the civilizations of Europe, Asia, and Africa.

The Civilizations of the South

The most elaborate of these societies emerged in South and Central America and in Mexico. In Peru, the Incas created a powerful empire of perhaps 6 million people. They developed a complex political system and a large network of paved roads that welded together the populations of many tribes under a single rule. In Central America and on the Yucatán peninsula of Mexico, the Mayas built a sophisticated culture with a written language, a numerical system similar to the Arabic (and superior to the Roman), an accurate calendar, and an advanced agricultural system. They were succeeded by the Aztecs, a once-nomadic warrior tribe from the north. In the late thirteenth century, the Aztecs established a precarious rule over much of central and southern Mexico and built elaborate administrative, educational, and medical systems comparable to the most advanced in Europe at the time. The Aztecs also developed a harsh religion that required human sacrifice. Their Spanish conquerors discovered the skulls of 100,000 victims in one location when they arrived in 1519. Finds such as these help explain why many Europeans came to consider the Aztecs "savages" despite their impressive accomplishments (and despite holy wars and witch burnings throughout Christian Europe).

The economies of these societies were based primarily on agriculture, but there were also substantial cities. In them lived, among others, many of the warriors and priests who ruled the empires and formed their hereditary elites. Some of these cities were as large as the

> Incas, Mayans, and Aztecs

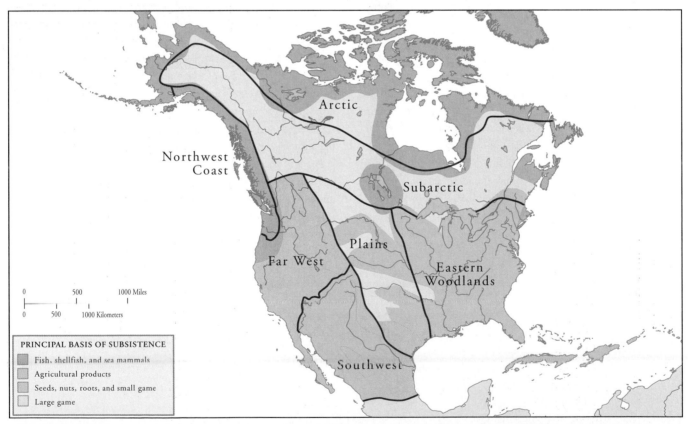

HOW THE EARLY NORTH AMERICANS LIVED This map shows the various ways in which the native tribes of North America supported themselves before the arrival of European civilization. Like most precommercial peoples, the native Americans survived largely on the resources available in their immediate surroundings. Note, for example, the reliance on the products of the sea of the tribes along the northern coastlines of the continent, and the way in which tribes in relatively inhospitable climates in the North—where agriculture was difficult—relied on hunting large game. Most native Americans were farmers. ◆ *What different kinds of farming would have emerged in the very different climates of the agricultural regions shown on this map?*

 For an interactive version of this map go to www.mhhe.com/brinkley12ch1maps

greatest capitals of Europe. Tenochtitlán, the Aztec capital built on the site of present-day Mexico City, had a population of over 100,000 in 1500 (larger than any European city of that time) and an impressive complex of majestic public buildings—including temples equal in size to the great pyramids of Egypt. The Mayas (at Mayapán and elsewhere) and the Incas (in such cities as Cuzco and Machu Picchu) produced similarly elaborate settlements with striking religious and ceremonial structures of their own. These achievements are all the more remarkable for their having been attained without some of the important technologies that Asian and European civilizations possessed. The Incas, for example, never had any system of writing or any equivalent for paper. And as late as the sixteenth century, no American society had yet developed wheeled vehicles.

The Civilizations of the North

The peoples north of Mexico—in the lands that became the United States and Canada—did not develop empires as large or political systems as elaborate as those of the Incas, Mayas, and Aztecs. They did, however, build complex civilizations of great variety. Societies that subsisted on hunting, gathering, fishing, or some combination of the three emerged in the northern regions of the continent. The Eskimos of the Arctic Circle fished and hunted seals; their civilization spanned thousands of miles of largely frozen land, which they traversed by dogsled. The big-game hunters of the northern forests led nomadic lives based on pursuit of moose and caribou. The tribes of the Pacific Northwest, whose principal occupation was salmon fishing, created substantial permanent settlements along the coast and engaged in constant and often violent competition with one another for access to natural resources.

Complex and Varied Civilizations

Another group of tribes spread through relatively arid regions of the Far West and developed successful communities—many of them quite wealthy and densely populated—based on fishing, hunting small game, and gathering. Other societies in North America were primarily agricultural. Among the most elaborate were those in the Southwest. The people of that region built large irrigation systems to allow farming on their relatively dry land, and they constructed substantial towns that became centers of trade, crafts, and religious and civic ritual. Their densely populated settlements at Chaco Canyon and elsewhere consisted of stone and adobe terraced structures, known today as pueblos, many of which resembled the large apartment buildings of later eras in size and design. In the Great Plains region, too, most tribes were engaged in sedentary farming (corn and other grains) and lived in substantial permanent settlements, although there were some small nomadic tribes that subsisted by hunting buffalo. (Only in the eighteenth century, after Europeans had introduced the horse to North America, did buffalo hunting begin to support a large population in the region; at that point, many once-sedentary farmers left the land to pursue the great migratory buffalo herds.)

The eastern third of what is now the United States—much of it covered with forests and inhabited by people who have thus become known as the Woodland Indians—had the greatest food resources of any region of the continent. Many tribes lived there, and most of them engaged simultaneously in farming, hunting, gathering, and fishing. In the South there were for a time substantial permanent settlements and large trading networks based on corn and other grains grown in the rich lands of the Mississippi River valley. Among the major cities that emerged as a result of trade was Cahokia (near present-day St. Louis), which at its peak in 1200 A.D. had a population of 40,000 and contained a great complex of large earthen mounds.

INDIANS OF NEW FRANCE The drawing is by the cartographer Charles Bécard de Granville, who was employed by the French government to make maps of its territories in North America. Granville also produced drawings of the flora and fauna of the region and of the natives he encountered. This depiction of Indian hunters traveling by river dates from approximately 1701. *(From the Collection of Gilcrease Museum, Tulsa)*

Why Do Historians So Often Differ?

There was a time, early in the twentieth century, while the professional study of history was still relatively new, when many historians believed that questions about the past could be answered with the same certainty and precision that questions in other, more scientific fields could be answered. By using precise methods of research and analysis, and by deploying armies of scholars to sift through available records and produce careful, closely argued accounts of the past, it would be possible to create something close to definitive histories that would survive without controversy for many generations. Scholars who believed this were known as "positivists," and they shared the views of such European thinkers as Auguste Comte and Thomas Henry Huxley that real knowledge can only be derived from direct, scientific observation of clear "facts." Historians, therefore, set out to answer questions for which extensive archival or statistical evidence was available.

Although a vigorous debate continues to this day over whether historical research can or should be truly objective, almost no historian any longer accepts the "positivist" claim that history could ever be anything like an exact science. Disagreement about the past is, in fact, at the very heart of the effort to understand history—just as disagreement about the present is at the heart of efforts to understand our own time. Critics of contemporary historical scholarship often denounce the way historians are constantly revising earlier interpretations; some denounce the act of interpretation itself. History, they claim, is "what happened." Historians should "stick to the facts." That scholars almost always find it impossible to do so helps account for the many controversies surrounding the historical profession today.

Historians differ with one another both because the "facts" are seldom as straightforward as their critics claim, and because facts by themselves mean almost nothing without an effort to assign meaning to them. There are, of course, some historical "facts" that are not in dispute. Everyone agrees, for example, that the Japanese bombed Pearl Harbor on December 7, 1941, or that Abraham Lincoln was elected president in 1860. But many other "facts" are much harder to determine—among them, for example, the question of how large the American population was before the arrival of

(Library of Congress)

Columbus, which is discussed later in this chapter. How many slaves resisted slavery? This sounds like a reasonably straightforward question, but it is almost impossible to answer with any certainty—in part because the records of slave resistance are spotty, and in part because the definition of "resistance" is a matter of considerable dispute.

CAHOKIA INDIAN MOUNDS The great earthen mounds constructed by the Cahokia Indians near present-day St. Louis have endured into modern times as part of the Missouri landscape. One of them is pictured here, rising above a farm field. *(Missouri Historical Society, St. Louis)*

Even when a set of facts is reasonably clear and straightforward, historians disagree—sometimes quite radically—over what they mean. Those disagreements can be the result of political and ideological disagreements. Some of the most vigorous debates in recent decades have been between scholars who believe that economic interests and class divisions are the key to understanding the past, and those who believe that ideas and culture are at least as important as material interests. The disagreements can be a result of the particular perspectives that people of different backgrounds bring to the study of the past. Whites and people of color, men and women, people from the American South and people from the North, young people and older people: these and many other points of difference find their way into scholarly disagreements. And debates can be a result as well of differences over methodology – differences, for example, between those who believe that quantitative studies can answer important historical questions and those who believe that other methods come closer to the truth.

Most of all, perhaps, historical interpretation changes in response to the time in which it is written. Historians may strive to be "objective" in their

(Historic New Orleans Collection, 1975.93.2)

work, but no one can be entirely free from the assumptions and concerns of the present. In the 1950s, the omnipresent shadow of the Cold War had a profound effect on the way most historians viewed the past and produced much work that seemed to validate the American democratic experience in contrast to the new and dangerous alternatives that seemed to be challenging it at the time. In the 1960s, concerns about racial justice and disillusionment with the Vietnam War altered the way many historians viewed the past. Those events introduced a much more critical tone to scholarship and turned the attention of scholars away from politics and government and toward the study of society and culture.

Many areas of scholarship in the late twentieth century are embroiled in a profound debate over whether there is such a thing as "truth." The world, some scholars argue, is simply a series of "narratives" constructed by people who view life in very different and often highly personal ways. "Truth" does not really exist. Everything is a product of interpretation. Not many historians embrace such radical ideas; most would agree that interpretations, to be of any value, must rest on a solid foundation of observable facts. But historians do recognize that even the most compelling facts are subject to many different interpretations and that the process of understanding the past is a forever continuing—and forever contested—process.

The agricultural societies of the Northeast were more mobile than those in other regions. Farming techniques there were designed to exploit the land quickly rather than to develop permanent settlements. Natives often cleared the land by setting forest fires or cutting into trees to kill them. They then planted crops—corn, beans, squash, pumpkins, and others—among the dead or blackened trunks. After a few years, when the land became exhausted or the filth from a settlement began to accumulate, they moved on and established themselves elsewhere. In some parts of eastern North America, villages dispersed every winter and families foraged for themselves in the wilderness until warm weather returned; those who survived then reassembled to begin farming again.

Many of the tribes living east of the Mississippi River were linked together loosely by common linguistic roots. The largest of the language groups was the Algonquin

tribes, which lived along the Atlantic seaboard from Canada to Virginia. More elaborately organized was the Iroquois Confederation, which emerged in the mid-fifteenth century, centered in what is now upstate New York. The Iroquois included at least five distinct northern "nations"—the Seneca, Cayuga, Onondaga, Oneida, and Mohawk—and had links as well with the Cherokees and the Tuscaroras farther south, in the Carolinas and Georgia. The third largest language group—the Muskogean—included the tribes in the southernmost region of the eastern seaboard: the Chickasaws, Choctaws, Creeks, and Seminoles. Alliances among the various Indian societies (even among those with common languages) were fragile, since the peoples of the Americas did not think of themselves as members of a single civilization. When Europeans arrived and began to threaten their way of

Mobile Societies

7

The American Population Before Columbus

No one knows how many people lived in the Americas in the centuries before Columbus. But scholars and others have spent more than a century and have written many thousands of pages debating the question nevertheless. Interest in this question survives, despite the near impossibility of answering it, because the debate over the pre-Columbian population is closely connected to the much larger debate over the consequences of European settlement of the Western Hemisphere.

Throughout the nineteenth century, Native Americans—in the midst of their many losing battles against the spread of white civilization—spoke often of the great days before Columbus when there were many more people in their tribes. They drew from their own rich tradition of oral history handed down through storytelling from one generation to another. The painter and ethnographer George Catlin, who spent much time among the tribes in the 1830s painting portraits of a race that he feared was "fast passing to extinction," listened to these oral legends and estimated that there had been 16 million Indians in North

America before the Europeans came. Most other white Americans who thought about this issue dismissed such claims as preposterous and insisted that the native population could not have been even as large as a million. Indian civilization was far too primitive, they claimed, to have been able to sustain so large a population.

In the early twentieth century, an ethnologist at the Smithsonian Institution, James Mooney, set out to find a method of estimating the early North American population that would be more scientific than the methods of the previous century, which were essentially guesses. He drew from early accounts of soldiers and missionaries in the sixteenth century and in 1928 came up with the implausibly precise figure of 1.15 million natives who lived north of Mexico in the early sixteenth century. That was a larger figure than nineteenth-century writers had suggested, but still much smaller than the Indians themselves claimed. A few years later, the anthropologist Alfred Kroeber used many of Mooney's methods to come up with an estimate of the population of the entire Western

(Biblioteca Mediceo Laurenziana, Firenze/IKONA, Rome)

Hemisphere—considerably larger than Mooney's, but much lower than Catlin's. He concluded in 1934 that there were 8.4 million people in the Americas in 1492, half in North America and half in the Caribbean and South America. His conclusions remained largely uncontested until the 1960s.

These low early estimates reflected, more than anything else, an assumption

life, Indians generally viewed the threat in terms of how it affected their own community and tribe, not in terms of how it affected any larger "Indian nation." Only rarely did tribes unite in opposition to challenges from whites.

Tribal Cultures

The enormous diversity of economic, social, and political structures among the North American Indians makes large generalizations about their cultures difficult. In the last centuries before the arrival of Europeans, however, Native Americans—like peoples in other areas of the world—were experiencing an agricultural revolution. In all regions of the United States (if in varying degrees from place to place), tribes were becoming more sedentary and were developing new sources of food, clothing, and shelter. Most regions were experiencing significant population growth. Virtually all were developing the sorts of elaborate social customs and rituals that only relatively stationary societies can produce. Religion was as important to Indian society as it was to most other cultures

Agricultural Revolution

and was usually closely bound up with the natural world on which the tribes depended. Native Americans worshipped many gods, whom they associated variously with crops, game, forests, rivers, and other elements of nature. Some tribes created elaborate, brightly colored totems as part of their religious ritual; most staged large festivals on such important occasions as harvests or major hunts.

As in other parts of the world, the societies of North America tended to divide tasks according to gender. All tribes assigned women the jobs of caring for children, preparing meals, and gathering certain foods. But the allocation of other tasks varied from one society to another. Some tribal groups (notably the Pueblos of the Southwest) reserved farming tasks almost entirely for men. Among others (including the Algonquins, the Iroquois, and the Muskogees), women tended the fields, while men engaged in hunting, warfare, or clearing land. Iroquois women and children were often left alone for extended periods while men were away hunting or fighting battles. As a result, women tended to control the social and economic organization of the settlements and that the arrival of the Europeans did not much reduce the native population. Given that assumption, it seemed reasonable to assume that the relatively low numbers of Indians that Europeans encountered in the late sixteenth and seventeenth centuries reflected the numbers of natives living in the Americas in earlier centuries as well. A dramatic change in the scholarly approach to the early population came as a result of the discovery by a number of scholars in the 1960s and 1970s that the early tribes had been catastrophically decimated by European plagues not long after the arrival of Columbus—meaning that the numbers Europeans observed even in the late 1500s were already dramatically smaller than the numbers in 1492. Drawing on early work by anthropologists and others who discovered evidence of widespread deaths by disease, historians such as William McNeill in 1976 and Alfred Crosby a decade later produced powerful accounts of the near extinction of some tribes and the dramatic depopulation of others in a pestilential catastrophe with few parallels in history. Almost all scholars now accept that much, perhaps most, of the native population was wiped out by disease—smallpox,

measles, tuberculosis, and other plagues imported from Europe—before white settlers began serious efforts to count.

The belief that the native population was much bigger in 1492 than it would be a few decades later has helped spur much larger estimates of how many people were in America before Columbus. Henry Dobyns, an anthropologist who was one of the earliest scholars to challenge the early, low estimates, claimed in 1966 that there were between 10 and 12 million people north of Mexico in 1492, and between 90 and 112 million in all of the Americas. He reached those figures by concluding that epidemics had destroyed 95 percent of the pre-Columbian population. He then took the best information on the population after Columbus and multiplied it by 20. No subsequent scholar has made so high a claim, and most historians have concluded that the 95 percent figure of deaths by disease is too high except for a few, relatively isolated areas such as the island of Hispaniola. But most subsequent estimates have been much closer to Dobyns's than to Kroeber's. The geographer William M. Denevan, for example, argued in 1976 that the American population in 1492

was around 55 million and that the population north of Mexico was under 4 million. Those are among the lowest of modern estimates, but still dramatically higher than the nineteenth-century numbers.

The vehemence with which scholars, and at times the larger public, have debated these figures is not just because it is very difficult to determine population size. It is also because the debate over the population is part of the debate over whether the arrival of Columbus—and the millions of Europeans who followed him—was a great advance in the history of civilization (as most Americans believed in 1892 when they joyously celebrated the 400th anniversary of Columbus's voyage) or an unparalleled catastrophe that virtually exterminated a large and flourishing native population (as some Americans and Europeans argued during the far more somber commemoration of the 500th anniversary in 1992). How to balance the many achievements of European civilization in the New World after 1492 against the terrible destruction of native peoples that accompanied it is, in the end, less a historical question, perhaps, than a moral one.

played powerful roles within families (which in many tribes were traced back "matrilineally," or through the mother's line).

EUROPE LOOKS WESTWARD

Europeans were almost entirely unaware of the existence of the Americas before the fifteenth century. A few early wanderers—Leif Eriksson, an eleventh-century Norse seaman, and perhaps others—had glimpsed parts of the New World and had demonstrated that Europeans were capable of crossing the ocean to reach it. But even if their discoveries had become common knowledge (and they did not), there would have been little incentive for others to follow. Europe in the Middle Ages (roughly 500–1500 A.D.) was not an adventurous civilization. Divided into innumerable small duchies and kingdoms, its outlook was overwhelmingly provincial. Subsistence agriculture predominated, and commerce was limited; few merchants looked beyond the boundaries of their own regions. The Roman Catholic Church

exercised a measure of spiritual authority over most of the continent, and the Holy Roman Empire provided at least a nominal political center. Even so, real power was for the most part widely dispersed; only rarely could a single leader launch a great venture. Gradually, however, conditions in Europe changed so that by the late fifteenth century interest in overseas exploration had grown.

Commerce and Nationalism

Two important and related changes provided the first incentive for Europeans to look toward new lands. One was a result of the significant population growth in fifteenth-century Europe. The Black Death, a catastrophic epidemic of the bubonic plague that began in Constantinople in 1347, had decimated Europe, killing (according to some estimates) more than a third of the people of the continent and debilitating its already limited economy. But a century and a half later, the population had rebounded. With that growth came a rise in land values, a reawakening of commerce, and a general increase in

IROQUOIS WOMEN This 1734 French engraving shows Iroquois women at work in a settlement somewhere in what is now upstate New York. In the foreground, women are cooking. Others are working in the fields. Men spent much of their time hunting and soldiering, leaving the women to govern and dominate the internal lives of the villages. Property in Iroquois society was inherited through the mother, and women occupied positions of great honor and authority within the tribes. *(Library of Congress)*

THE INDIAN VILLAGE OF SECOTON (C. 1585), BY JOHN WHITE
John White created this illustration of life among the Eastern Woodland Indians in coastal North Carolina. It shows the diversified agriculture practiced by the natives: squash, tobacco, and three varieties of corn. The hunters shown in nearby woods suggest another element of the native economy. At bottom right, Indians perform a religious ritual, which White described as "strange gestures and songs." *(British Museum)*

prosperity. Affluent landlords became eager to purchase goods from distant regions, and a new merchant class emerged to meet their demand. As trade increased, and as advances in navigation and shipbuilding made long-distance sea travel more feasible, interest in developing new markets, finding new products, and opening new trade routes rapidly increased.

| A Reawakening of Commerce |

Paralleling the rise of commerce in Europe, and in part responsible for it, was the rise of new governments that were more united and powerful than the feeble political entities of the feudal past. In the western areas of Europe, the authority of the distant pope and the even more distant Holy Roman Emperor was necessarily weak. As a result, strong new monarchs emerged there and created centralized nation-states, with national courts, national armies, and—perhaps most important—national tax systems. As these ambitious kings and queens consolidated their power and increased their wealth, they became eager to enhance the commercial growth of their nations.

| Centralized Nation-States |

Ever since the early fourteenth century, when Marco Polo and other adventurers had returned from Asia bearing exotic goods (spices, fabrics, dyes) and even more exotic tales, Europeans who hoped for commercial glory had dreamed above all of trade with the East. For two centuries, that trade had been limited by the difficulties of the long, arduous overland journey to the Asian courts. But in the fourteenth century, as the maritime capabilities of several western European societies increased and as Muslim societies seized control of the eastern routes to Asia, there began to be serious talk of finding a faster, safer sea route to Asia. Such dreams gradually found a receptive audience in the courts of the new monarchs. By the late fifteenth century, some of them were ready to finance daring voyages of exploration.

The first to do so were the Portuguese. They were the preeminent maritime power in the fifteenth century, in large part because of the work of one man, Prince Henry the Navigator. Henry's own principal interest was not in

Prince Henry the Navigator

finding a sea route to Asia, but in exploring the western coast of Africa. He dreamed of establishing a Christian empire there to aid in his country's wars against the Moors of northern Africa; and he hoped to find new stores of gold. The explorations he began did not fulfill his own hopes, but they ultimately led farther than he had dreamed. Some of Henry's mariners went as far south as Cape Verde, on Africa's west coast. In 1486 (six years after Henry's death), Bartholomeu Dias rounded the southern tip of Africa (the Cape of Good Hope); and in 1497–1498 Vasco da Gama proceeded all the way around the cape to India. In 1500, the next fleet bound for India, under the command of Pedro Cabral, was blown westward off its southerly course and happened upon the coast of Brazil. But by then another man, in the service of another country, had already encountered the New World.

Christopher Columbus

Christopher Columbus, who was born and reared in Genoa, Italy, obtained most of his early seafaring experience in the service of the Portuguese. As a young man, he became intrigued with the possibility, already under discussion in many seafaring circles, of reaching Asia by going not east but west. Columbus's hopes rested on several basic misconceptions. He believed that the world was far smaller than it actually is. He also believed that the Asian continent extended farther eastward than it actually does. He assumed, therefore, that the Atlantic was narrow enough to be crossed on a relatively brief voyage. It did not occur to him that anything lay to the west between Europe and Asia.

Columbus failed to win support for his plan in Portugal, so he turned to Spain. The Spaniards were not yet as advanced a maritime people as the Portuguese, but they were at least as energetic and ambitious. And in the fifteenth century, the marriage of Spain's two most powerful regional rulers, Ferdinand of Aragon and Isabella of Castile, had produced the strongest monarchy in Europe. Like other young monarchies, it soon grew eager to demonstrate its strength by sponsoring new commercial ventures.

Columbus appealed to Queen Isabella for support for his proposed westward voyage. In 1492, having consolidated the monarchy's position within Spain itself, Isabella agreed to Columbus's request. Commanding

Columbus's First Voyage

ninety men and three ships—the *Niña,* the *Pinta,* and the *Santa María*—Columbus left Spain in August 1492 and sailed west into the Atlantic on what he thought was a straight

CHRISTOPHER COLUMBUS In this somewhat idealized drawing, created several years after Christopher Columbus's historic voyage to the New World, Columbus stands in the bow of his ship, a suit of armor ready at his feet, approaching a shore in the New World that he believed was in fact part of Asia. *(Library of Congress)*

course for Japan. Ten weeks later, he sighted land and assumed he had reached his target. In fact, he had landed on an island in the Bahamas. When he pushed on and encountered Cuba, he assumed he had reached China. He returned to Spain in triumph, bringing with him several captured natives as evidence of his achievement. (He called the natives "Indians" because he believed they were from the East Indies in the Pacific.)

But Columbus had not, of course, encountered the court of the great khan in China or the fabled wealth of the Indies. A year later, therefore, he tried again, this time with a much larger expedition. As before, he headed into the Caribbean, discovering several other islands and leaving a small and short-lived colony on Hispaniola. On a third voyage, in 1498, he finally reached the mainland and cruised along the northern coast of South America. When he passed the mouth of the Orinoco River (in present-day Venezuela), he concluded for the first time that what he had discovered was not in fact an island off the coast of China, as he had assumed, but a separate continent; such a large freshwater stream, he realized, could emerge only from a large body of land. Still, he remained convinced that Asia was only a short distance away. And although he failed in his efforts to sail around the northeastern coast of South America to the Indies (he was blocked by the Isthmus of Panama), he returned to Spain believing that he had explored at least the fringes of the Far East. He continued to believe that until he died.

Columbus's celebrated accomplishments made him a popular hero for a time, but he ended his life in obscurity. When Europeans at last gave a name to the New World, they ignored him. The distinction went instead to a Florentine merchant, Amerigo Vespucci, a member of a later Portuguese expedition to the New World who wrote a series of vivid descriptions of the lands he visited and who recognized the Americas as new continents.

Columbus has been celebrated for centuries as the "Admiral of the Ocean Sea" (a title he struggled to have officially bestowed on him during his lifetime) and as a representative of the new, secular, scientific impulses of Renaissance Europe. But Columbus was also a deeply religious man, even something of a mystic. His voyages were inspired as much by his conviction that he was fulfilling a divine mission as by his interest in geography and trade. A strong believer in biblical prophecies, he came to see himself as a man destined to advance the coming of the millennium. "God made me the messenger of the new heaven and the new earth," he wrote near the end of his life, "and he showed me the spot where to find it." A similar combination of worldly and religious passions lay behind many subsequent efforts at exploration and settlement of the New World.

Religious Motives for Exploration

Partly as a result of Columbus's initiative, Spain began to devote greater resources and energy to maritime exploration and gradually replaced Portugal as the leading seafaring nation. The Spaniard Vasco de Balboa fought his way across the Isthmus of Panama in 1513 and became the first known European to gaze westward upon the great ocean that separated America from China and the Indies. Seeking access to that ocean, Ferdinand Magellan, a Portuguese in the employ of the Spanish, found the strait that now bears his name at the southern end of South America, struggled through the stormy narrows and into the ocean (so calm by contrast that he christened it the "Pacific"), then proceeded to the Philippines. There Magellan died in a conflict with the natives, but his expedition went on to complete the first known circumnavigation of the globe (1519–1522). By 1550, Spaniards had explored the coasts of North America as far north as Oregon in the west and Labrador in the east, as well as some of the interior regions of the continent.

Ferdinand Magellan

BALBOA DISCOVERING THE PACIFIC The Spanish historian Herrera created this engraving to commemorate Vasco de Balboa's discovery of the Pacific Ocean, which he encountered after fighting his way across the Isthmus of Panama. Balboa's contemporaries called the Pacific *"El Mar del Sur,"* the "South Sea." *(Bettmann/Corbis)*

The Conquistadores

In time, Spanish explorers in the New World stopped thinking of America simply as an obstacle to their search for a route to the East. They began instead to consider it a possible source of wealth rivaling and even surpassing the original Indies. On the basis of Columbus's discoveries, the Spanish claimed for themselves the whole of the New World, except for a piece of it (today's Brazil) that was reserved by a papal decree for the Portuguese. By the mid-sixteenth century, the Spanish were well on their way to establishing a substantial American empire.

The early Spanish colonists, beginning with those Columbus brought on his second voyage, settled on the islands of the Caribbean, where they tried to enslave the Indians and find gold. They had little luck in either effort. But then, in 1518, Hernando Cortés led a small military expedition of about 600 men into Mexico. Cortés had been a Spanish government official in Cuba for fourteen years and to that point had achieved little success. But when he heard stories of great treasures in Mexico, he decided to go in search of them. He met strong and resourceful resistance from the Aztecs and their powerful emperor, Montezuma. The first Spanish assault on Tenochtitlán, the Aztec capital, failed. But Cortés and his army had, unknowingly, unleashed an assault on the Aztecs far more devastating than military attack: they had exposed the natives to smallpox. A smallpox epidemic decimated the population and made it possible for the Spanish to triumph in their second attempt at conquest. The Spanish saw the epidemic as vindication of their efforts. When the Christians were exhausted from war, one follower of Cortés said at the time, "God saw fit to send the Indians smallpox."

Cortés Conquers the Aztecs

EUROPEAN EXPLORATION AND CONQUEST, 1492–1583 This map shows the many voyages of exploration to and conquest of North America launched by Europeans in the late fifteenth and sixteenth centuries. Note how Columbus and the Spanish explorers who followed him tended to move quickly into the lands of Mexico, the Caribbean, and Central and South America, while the English and French explored the northern territories of North America. ♦ *What factors might have led these various nations to explore and colonize these different areas of the New World?*

For an interactive version of this map go to www.mhhe.com/brinkley12ch1maps

Through his ruthless suppression of the surviving natives, Cortés established a lasting reputation as the most brutal of the Spanish *conquistadores* (conquerors).

The news that silver was to be found in Mexico attracted the attention of other Spaniards. From the island colonies and from Spain itself, a wave of conquistadores descended on the mainland in search of fortune—a movement comparable in some ways to the nineteenth-century gold rushes elsewhere in the world, but far more vicious. Francisco Pizarro, who conquered Peru (1532–1538) and revealed to Europeans the wealth of the Incas, opened the way for other advances into South America. His one-time deputy Hernando de Soto, in a futile search for gold, silver, and jewels, led several expeditions (1539–1541) through Florida west into the continent and became the first white man known to have

THE MEXICANS STRIKE BACK In this vivid scene from the Duran Codex, Mexican artists illustrate a rare moment in which Mexican warriors gained the upper hand over the Spanish invaders. Driven back by native fighters, the Spanish have taken refuge in a room in the royal palace in Tenochtitlán while brightly attired Mexican warriors besiege them. Although the Mexicans gained a temporary advantage in this battle, the drawing illustrates one of the reasons for their inability to withstand the Spanish in the longer term. The Spanish soldiers are armed with rifles and crossbows, while the Indians carry only spears and shields. *(Oronoz Archivo)*

crossed the Mississippi River. Francisco Coronado traveled north from Mexico (1540–1542) into what is now New Mexico in a similarly fruitless search for gold and jewels; in the process, he helped open the Southwest of what is now the United States to Spanish settlement.

PIZARRO IN PERU A European artist depicted Pizarro's arrival on the coast of Peru in the early 1530s, where he was greeted by crowds of hostile Indians. By 1538, Pizarro had conquered the empire of the Incas. *(British Museum)*

The story of the Spanish warriors is one of great military daring and achievement. It is also a story of remarkable brutality and greed. The conquistadores subjugated and, Brutality and Greed in some areas (through a combination of warfare and disease), almost exterminated the native populations. In this horrible way, they made possible the creation of a vast Spanish empire in the New World.

Spanish America

Lured by dreams of treasure, Spanish explorers, conquistadores, and colonists established a vast empire for Spain in the New World. New European diseases and Spanish military power forced the previously powerful Aztec Ordinances of Discovery and Incan empires into submission. The history of the Spanish empire spanned three distinct periods. The first was the age of discovery and exploration—beginning with Columbus and continuing through the first two decades of the sixteenth century. The second was the age of the conquistadores, in which Spanish military forces (aided by the diseases they unleashed) established their dominion over the lands once ruled by natives. The third phase began in the 1570s, when new Spanish laws—the Ordinances of Discovery—banned the most brutal military conquests. From that

DE SOTO IN NORTH AMERICA This gruesome drawing portrays Spanish troops under Hernando de Soto massacring a group of Mobile Indians in what is now Alabama, in the winter of 1540–1541. De Soto had been governor of Cuba, but in 1539 he sailed to Florida with 600 troops and for the next several years traveled through large areas of what would later become the southern United States until dying of fever in 1542. Here, as elsewhere, his troops dealt with the Indian tribes they encountered along the way with unrestrained brutality. *(Rare Books and Special Collections/ Library of Congress)*

point on, the Spanish expanded their presence in America through colonization.

The first Spaniards to arrive in the New World, the conquistadores, had been interested in only one thing: getting rich. And in that they were fabulously successful. For 300 years, beginning in the sixteenth century, the mines in Spanish America yielded more than ten times as much gold and silver as the rest of the world's mines put together. These riches made Spain the wealthiest and most powerful nation on earth.

After the first wave of conquest, however, most Spanish settlers in America traveled to the New World for other reasons. Many went in hopes of creating a profitable agricultural economy. Unlike the conquistadores, who left little but destruction behind them, these settlers helped establish elements of European civilization in America that permanently altered both the landscape and the social structure.

At least as important as a force for colonization was the Catholic Church. Ferdinand and Isabella, in establishing Spain's claim to most of the Americas from Mexico south, bowed to the wishes of the Church and established the requirement that Catholicism must be the only religion of the new territories. Spain abided by that condition. As a result, the characteristic Spanish settlements in the new world were highly religious in character. Although the Spanish founded several commercial and military centers in the sixteenth century, the most common settlement by the early seventeenth century was the mission. Missions had commercial lives, to be sure. But their primary purpose, at least at first, was converting natives to Catholicism. There were usually military garrisons connected to the missions, to protect them from hostile natives. *Presidios* (military bases) often grew up nearby to provide additional protection. Other Spaniards went to America to spread the Christian religion. Indeed, after the era of the conquistadores came to a close in the 1540s, the missionary impulse became one of the principal motives for European emigration to America. Priests or friars accompanied all colonizing ventures. Through the work of zealous missionaries, the gospel of the Catholic Church ultimately extended throughout South and Central

Catholic Missions

OUTPOSTS ON THE NORTHERN FRONTIER OF NEW SPAIN
(Not simultaneous; through the 18th century)

- • Missions
- • Forts (Sometimes with missions)
- • Settlements

World divided into Spanish and Portuguese hemispheres: Treaty of Tordesillas (1494)

Aztec Empire at the time of Spanish Conquest

Inca Empire at the time of Spanish Conquest

Colonial boundaries and provincial names are for the late 18th century

SPANISH AMERICA From the time of Columbus's initial voyage in 1492 until the mid-nineteenth century, Spain was the dominant colonial power in the New World. From the southern regions of South America to the northern regions of the Pacific northwest, Spain controlled one of the world's vastest empires. Note how much of the Spanish empire was simply grafted upon the earlier empires of native peoples—the Incas in what is today Chile and Peru, and the Aztecs across much of the rest of South America, Mexico, and the Southwest of what is now the United States. ◆ *What characteristics of Spanish colonization would account for their preference for already settled regions?*

 For an interactive version of this map go to www.mhhe.com/brinkley12ch1maps

America, Mexico, and into the South and Southwest of the present United States.

Northern Outposts

The Spanish fort established in 1565 at St. Augustine, Florida, became the first permanent European settlement in the present-day United States. It served as a military outpost, an administrative center for Franciscan missionaries, and a headquarters for unsuccessful campaigns among North American natives that were ultimately abandoned. But it did not mark the beginning of a substantial effort at colonization in the region.

St. Augustine

A more substantial colonizing venture began thirty years later in the Southwest. In 1598, Don Juan de Oñate traveled north from Mexico with a party of 500 men and claimed for Spain some of the lands of the Pueblo Indians that Coronado had passed through over fifty years before. The Spanish migrants began to establish a colony, modeled roughly on those the Spanish had created farther south, in what is now New Mexico. Oñate distributed *encomiendas,* which were licenses to exact labor and tribute from the natives in specific areas (a system first used in dealing with the Moors in Spain). The Spanish began demanding tribute from the local Indians (and at times commandeering them as laborers). Spanish colonists founded Santa Fe in 1609.

Oñate's harsh treatment of the natives (who greatly outnumbered the small Spanish population) threatened the stability of the new colony and led to his removal as governor in 1606. Over time, relations between the Spanish and the Pueblos improved. Substantial numbers of Pueblos converted to Christianity under the influence of Spanish missionaries. Others entered into important trading relationships with the Spanish. The colony remained precarious nevertheless because of the danger from Apache and Navajo raiders, who threatened the Spanish and Pueblos alike. Even so, the New Mexico settlement continued to grow. By 1680, there were over 2,000 Spanish colonists living among about 30,000 Pueblos. The economic heart of the colony was not the gold and precious metals the early Spanish explorers had tried in vain to find. It was cattle and sheep, raised on the *ranchos* that stretched out around the small towns Spanish settlers established.

In 1680, the colony was nearly destroyed when the Pueblos rose in revolt. Despite the widespread conversions to Catholicism, most natives (including the converts) continued to practice their own religious rituals—

Pueblo Revolt of 1680

rituals that sustained their sense of tribal identity. In 1680, Spanish priests and the colonial government, which was closely tied to the missionaries, launched one of their periodic efforts to suppress these rituals. In response, an Indian religious leader named Pope led an uprising that killed hundreds of European settlers (including twenty-one priests), captured Santa Fe, and drove the Spanish temporarily from the region. But twelve years later the Spanish returned, resumed seizing Pueblo lands, and crushed a last revolt in 1696.

Spanish exploitation of the Pueblos did not end. But after the revolts, many Spanish colonists realized that they could not prosper in New Mexico if they remained constantly in conflict with a native population that greatly outnumbered them. They tried to solve the problem in two ways. On the one hand, the Spanish intensified their efforts to assimilate the Indians—baptizing Indian children at birth and enforcing observance of Catholic rituals. On the other hand, they now permitted the Pueblos to own land; they stopped commandeering Indian labor; they replaced the encomienda system with a less demanding and oppressive one; and they tacitly tolerated the practice of tribal religious rituals.

These efforts were at least partially successful. After a while, there was significant intermarriage between Europeans and Indians. Increasingly, the Pueblos came to consider the Spanish their allies in the continuing battles with the Apaches and Navajos. By 1750, the Spanish population had grown modestly to about 4,000. The Pueblo population had declined (through disease, war, and migration) to about 13,000, less than half what it had been in 1680. New Mexico had by then become a reasonably stable but still weak and isolated outpost of the Spanish empire.

The Empire at High Tide

By the end of the sixteenth century, the Spanish empire had become one of the largest in the history of the world. It included the islands of the Caribbean and the coastal areas of South America that had been the first targets of the Spanish expeditions. It extended to Mexico and southern North America, where a second wave of colonizers had established out-

Spain's Vast Empire

posts. Most of all, the empire spread southward and westward into the vast landmass of South America—the areas that are now Chile, Argentina, and Peru. In 1580, when the Spanish and Portuguese monarchies temporarily united, Brazil came under Spanish jurisdiction as well.

It was, however, a colonial empire very different from the one the English would establish in North America beginning in the early seventeenth century. Although the earliest Spanish ventures in the New World had been largely independent of the throne, by the end of the sixteenth century the monarchy had extended its authority directly into the governance of local communities. Colonists had few opportunities to establish political institutions independent of the crown. There was also a significant economic difference between the Spanish empire and the later British one. The Spanish were far more successful than the British would be in extracting great surface wealth—gold and silver—from their American colonies. But for the same reason, they concentrated relatively less energy on making agriculture and commerce profitable in their colonies. The strict and inflexible commercial policies of

Rigid Royal Control

the Spanish government made things worse. To enforce the collection of duties and to provide protection against pirates, the government established rigid and restrictive regulations. They required all trade with the colonies to go through a single Spanish port and only a few colonial ports, in fleets making but two voyages a year. The system stifled the economic development of the Spanish areas of the New World.

There was also an important difference between the character of the population in the Spanish empire and that of the colonies to the north. Almost from the beginning, the English, Dutch, and French colonies in North America concentrated on establishing permanent settlement and family life in the New World. The Europeans in North America reproduced rapidly after their first difficult years and in time came to outnumber the natives. The Spanish, by contrast, ruled their empire but did not people it. In the first century of settlement, fewer than 250,000 settlers in the Spanish colonies were from Spain itself or from any other European country. Only about 200,000 more arrived in the first half of the seventeenth century. Some additional settlers came from various outposts of Spanish civilization in the Atlantic—the Azores, the Cape Verde Islands, and elsewhere; but even with these other sources, the number of European settlers in Spanish America remained very small relative to the native population. Despite the ravages of disease and war, the vast majority of the population of the Spanish Empire continued to consist of natives. The Spanish, in other words, imposed a small ruling class upon a much larger existing population;

A Collision of Cultures

they did not create a self-contained European society in the New World as the English would attempt to do in the north.

Biological and Cultural Exchanges

The lines separating the races in the Spanish Empire gradually grew less distinct than they would be in the English colonies to the north, but European and native cultures never entirely merged. Indeed, significant differences remain today between European and Indian cultures throughout South and Central America. Nevertheless, the arrival of whites launched a process of interaction between different peoples that left no one unchanged.

Europeans would not have been exploring the Americas at all without their early contacts with the natives. From them, they first learned of the rich deposits of gold and silver. After that, the history of the Americas became one of increasing levels of exchanges—some beneficial, some catastrophic—among different peoples and cultures.

Increasing Levels of Exchange

The first and most profound result of this exchange was the importation of European diseases to the New World. It would be difficult to exaggerate the consequences of the exposure of Native Americans to such illnesses as influenza, measles, chicken pox, mumps, typhus, and above all smallpox—diseases to which Europeans had over time developed at least a partial immunity but to which Native Americans were tragically vulnerable. Millions died. (See "Where Historians Disagree," pp. 8–9.)

Native groups inhabiting some of the large Caribbean islands and some areas of Mexico were virtually extinct within fifty years of their first contact with whites. On Hispaniola—where the Dominican Republic and Haiti are today and where Columbus landed and established a small, short-lived colony in the 1490s—the native population quickly declined from approximately 1 million to about 500. In the Mayan areas of Mexico, as much as 95 percent of the population perished

Demographic Catastrophe

within a few years of their first contact with the Spanish. Some groups fared better than others; some (although far from all) of the tribes north of Mexico, whose contact with European settlers came later and was often less intimate, were spared the worst of the epidemics. But most areas of the New World experienced a demographic catastrophe at least as grave as, and in many places far worse than, the Black Death that had killed at least a third of the population of Europe two centuries before.

The decimation of native populations in the southern regions of the Americas was not, however, purely a result of this inadvertent exposure to infection. It was also a result of the conquistadores' quite deliberate policy of subjugation and extermination. Their brutality was in part a reflection of the ruthlessness with which Europeans waged war in all parts of the world. It was also a result of their conviction that the natives

Deliberate Subjugation and Extermination

were "savages"—uncivilized peoples whom they considered somehow not fully human. Paradoxically, the brutality was also a consequence of the high level of development of some native societies. Had the natives truly been as primitive as Europeans wanted to believe, there would have been little need to destroy them. But organized into substantial empires, they posed a threat to the conquistadores' ambitions.

That, more than anything else, accounts for the thoroughness with which the Spanish set about obliterating native cultures. They razed cities and dismantled temples and monuments. They destroyed records and documents (one reason why modern scholars have been able to learn so little about the histories of these native societies). They systematically killed Indian warriors, leaders, and priests. They tried, in short, to eliminate the underpinnings of existing native civilizations so as to bring the Indian population fully under Spanish control and to remove all obstacles to the spread of Christianity. By the 1540s, the combined effects of European diseases and European military brutality had all but destroyed the empires of Mexico and South America and had largely eliminated native resistance to the Spanish.

Not all aspects of the exchange were so disastrous to the natives. The Europeans introduced important new crops to America (among them sugar and bananas), domestic livestock (cattle, pigs, and sheep), and perhaps most significantly the horse, which had disappeared from the Western Hemisphere in the Ice Age and now returned aboard Spanish ships in the sixteenth century. The Europeans imported these things for their own use. But Indian tribes soon learned to cultivate the new crops, and European livestock proliferated rapidly and spread widely among natives. In the past, most tribes had possessed no domesticated animals at all other than dogs. The horse, in particular, became central to the lives of many natives and transformed their societies.

The exchange was at least as important (and more beneficial) to the Europeans. In both North and South

New Crops and Agricultural Techniques

America, the arriving white peoples learned new agricultural techniques from the natives, techniques often better adapted to the character of the new land than those they had brought with them from Europe. They discovered new crops, above all maize (corn), which became an important staple among the settlers. Columbus took it back to Europe from his first trip to America, and it soon spread through much of Europe as well. Such American foods as squash, pumpkins, beans, sweet potatoes, tomatoes, peppers, and potatoes also found their way back to Europe and in the process revolutionized European agriculture. Agricultural discoveries ultimately proved more important to the future of Europe than the gold and silver the conquistadores valued so highly.

In South America, Central America, and Mexico, a society emerged in which Europeans and natives lived in intimate, if unequal, contact with one another. As a result, Indians adopted many features of European civilization, although those features seldom survived the transfer to America unchanged. Many natives gradually

came to learn Spanish or Portuguese, but in the process they created a range of dialects, combining the European languages with their own. European missionaries—through both persuasion and coercion—spread Catholicism through most areas of the Spanish Empire. But native Christians tended to connect the new creed with features of their old religions, creating a hybrid of faiths that were, while essentially Christian, nevertheless distinctively American.

Colonial officials were expected to take their wives with them to America, but among the ordinary settlers —the majority—European men outnumbered European women by at least ten to one. Not surprisingly, therefore, the Spanish immigrants had substantial sexual contact with native women. Intermarriage became frequent, and before long the population of the colonies came to be dominated (numerically, at

A Complex Racial Hierarchy

least) by people of mixed race, or *mestizos*. Through much of the Spanish Empire, as a result, an elaborate racial hierarchy developed, with Spanish at the top, natives at the bottom, and people of mixed races distributed in between. Racial categories, however, were much more fluid than the Spanish wanted to believe and could not long remain fixed. Over time, the wealth and influence of a family often came to define its place in the "racial" hierarchy more decisively than race itself. A successful or powerful person could become "Spanish" regardless of his or her actual racial ancestry.

The frequency of intermarriage suggests a great deal about how the society of the Spanish Empire was taking shape. It reveals, of course, that men living alone in a strange land craved female companionship and the satisfactions of family life and that they sought those things in the only places they could—among the native population. It shows the desperate need for labor among the white settlers, including the domestic labor that native wives could provide; in some cases, intermarriage was a form of labor recruitment. Finally, it suggests why the lines separating the races in the areas of Spanish settlement did not remain as distinct as they did in the later English colonies, which were peopled largely by families and in which intermarriage with natives was consequently rare.

Intermarriage was not, however, just a result of the needs and desires of white men. Some Indian women entered marriages to white men only under coercion, but the extent of intermarriage suggests that not all women resisted. Native women might have seen some advantage in marrying Spanish men because the male populations of their tribes were so depleted by warfare or enslavement by the Spaniards. There were also long-established customs of intermarriage among some Indian tribes as a way of forming or cementing alliances. Since many Indians considered the white settlers little more foreign than some rival native groups, that custom probably contributed to the frequency of intermarriage as well.

Reasons for Intermarriage

Natives were the principal labor source for the Europeans. Virtually all the commercial, agricultural, and mining enterprises of the Spanish and Portuguese colonists depended on an Indian work force. Different labor systems emerged in different areas of the empire. In some places, Indians were sold into slavery. More often, colonists used a wage system closely related, but not identical, to slavery, by which Indians were forced to work in the mines and on the plantations for fixed periods, unable to leave without the consent of their employers. Such work forces survived in some areas of the South American mainland for many centuries. So great was the need for native labor that European settlers were less interested in acquiring land than they were in gaining control over Indian villages, which could become a source of labor and tribute to landlords.

Varied Labor Systems

Even so, the native population could not meet all the labor needs of the colonists—particularly since the native population had declined (and in some places virtually vanished) because of disease and war. As early as 1502, therefore, European settlers began importing slaves from Africa.

Africa and America

Most of the black men and women who were forcibly taken to America came from a large region in west Africa below the Sahara Desert, known as Guinea. It was the home of a wide variety of peoples and cultures. Since over half of all the new arrivals in the New World between 1500 and 1800 were Africans, those cultures,

too, greatly affected the character of American civilization. Europeans and white Americans came to portray African society as primitive and uncivilized (in part to justify the enslavement of Africa's people). But most Africans were, in fact, civilized peoples with well-developed economies and political systems.

Humans began settling in west Africa at least 10,000 years ago. By the fifteenth century A.D., they had developed extensive civilizations and complex political systems. The residents of upper Guinea had substantial commercial contact with the Mediterranean world—trading ivory, gold, and slaves for finished goods. Largely as a result, they became early converts to Islam. After the collapse of the ancient kingdom of Ghana around 1100 A.D., the even larger empire of Mali emerged and survived well into the fifteenth century. Its great city, Timbuktu, became fabled as a trading center and a seat of education.

Ghana and Mali

Africans further south were more isolated from Europe and the Mediterranean. They were also more politically fragmented. The central social unit in much of the south was the village, which usually consisted of members of an extended family group. Some groups of villages united in small kingdoms—among them Benin, Congo, and Songhay. But no large empires emerged in the south comparable to the Ghana and Mali kingdoms farther north. Nevertheless, these southern societies developed extensive trade—in woven fabrics, ceramics, and wooden and iron goods, as well as crops and livestock—both among themselves and, to a lesser degree, with the outside world.

Benin, Congo, and Songhay

The African civilizations naturally developed economies that reflected the climates and resources of their lands. In upper Guinea, fishing and rice cultivation, supplemented by the extensive trade with Mediterranean lands, were the

SCULPTURE OF DJENNE Many of the Africans forcibly exported from their homes to America in the seventeenth and eighteenth centuries were natives of Mali, the seat of an ancient east African civilization. This terra cotta sculpture, discovered in the 1940s, dates from between 600 and 900 years ago. It may be an image of an ancestor created for use in a family shrine. *("Seated Prisoner", 11th/16th Century, Djenne, Founders Society Purchase, Robert H. Tannahill Foundation Fund. Photograph ©1995 The Detroit Institute of the Arts)*

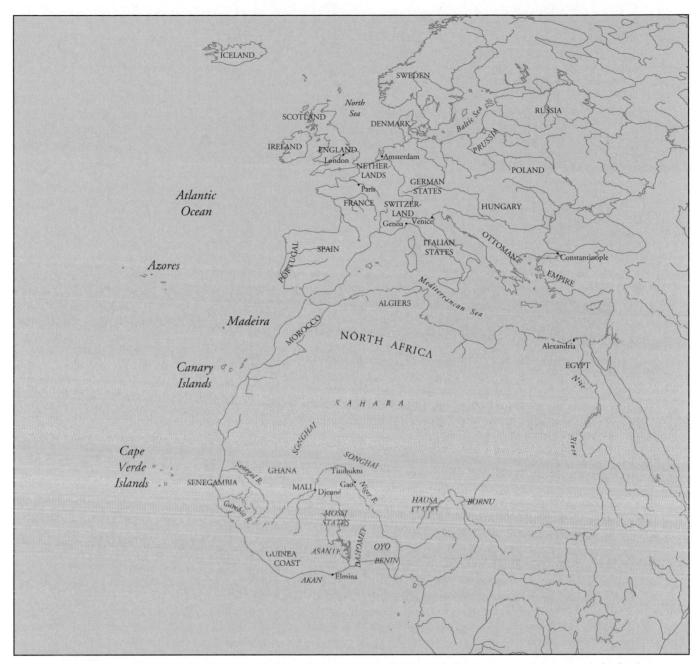

EUROPE AND WEST AFRICA IN THE FIFTEENTH CENTURY Exploration of North and South America was in part an outgrowth of earlier European trade in the Eastern Hemisphere. Europeans delivered cloth and other manufactures to northern Africa; then camels carried the cargoes across the Sahara to cities such as Timbuktu, Gao, and Djenné. There they loaded gold, ivory, and kola nuts for return to the Mediterranean. Africans also traded with Asia to obtain cloth, porcelain, and spices. ◆ *What areas of trade were most important to the early interaction between Africa and America?*

foundation of the economy. Farther south, Africans grew wheat and other food crops, raised livestock, and fished. There were some more nomadic tribes in the interior, which subsisted largely on hunting and gathering and developed less elaborate social systems. But most Africans were sedentary people, linked together by elaborate political, economic, and familial relationships.

Like many Native American societies, but unlike those in Europe, African societies tended to be matrilineal— which means that people traced their heredity through, and inherited property from, their mothers rather than their fathers. When a couple married, the husband left his own family to join the family of his wife. Like most other peoples, Africans divided work by gender, but the nature of that division varied greatly from place to place. Women played a major role, often the dominant role, in trade; in many areas they were the principal farmers (while the men hunted, fished, and raised livestock); everywhere, they managed child care and food preparation. Most

Matrilineal Societies

The Atlantic Context of Early American History

Most Americans understand that our nation has become intimately bound up with the rest of the world—that we live in a time that is sometimes called the "age of globalization." In recent years, scholars have also begun to re-examine the way we explain the American past and have revealed a host of connections between what happened in the Americas and what was happening in the rest of the world. They have, in short, taken our modern notion of globalization and used it to explain some aspects of our more distant past. This re-examination has included the earliest period of European settlement of the Americas. Many scholars of early American history now examine what happened in the "New World" in the context of what has become known as the "Atlantic World."

The idea of an "Atlantic World" rests in part on the obvious connections between western Europe and the Spanish, British, French, and Dutch colonies in North and South America. All the early European civilizations of the Americas were part of a great imperial project launched by the major powers of Europe. The massive European immigration to the Americas beginning in the sixteenth century, the defeat and devastation of native populations, the creation of European agricultural and urban settlements, and the imposition of imperial regulations on trade, commerce, landowning, and political life—all of these forces reveal the influence of Old World imperialism on the history of the New World.

But the creation of empires is only one part of the creation of the Atlantic World. At least equally important—and closely related—is the expansion of commerce from Europe to the Americas. Although some Europeans traveled to the New World to escape oppression or to search for adventure, the great majority of European immigrants were in search of economic opportunity. Not surprisingly, therefore, the European settlements in the Americas were almost from the start intimately connected to Europe through the growth of commerce between them—commerce that grew more extensive and more complex with every passing year. The commercial relationship between America and Europe was responsible not just for the growth of trade, but also for the increases in migration over time—as the demand for labor in the New World drew more and more settlers from the Old World. Commerce was also the principal reason for the rise of slavery in the Americas, and for the growth of the slave trade between European America and Africa. The Atlantic World, in other words, included not just Europe and the Americas, but Africa as well.

Religion was another force binding together the Atlantic World. The vast majority of people of European descent were Christians and most of them maintained important religious ties to Europe. Catholics, of course, were part of a hierarchical church based in Rome and maintained close ties with the Vatican. But the Protestant faiths that predominated in North America were intimately linked to their European counterparts as well. New religious ideas and movements spread back and forth across the Atlantic with astonishing speed. Great revivals that began in Europe moved quickly to America. The "Great Awakening" of the mid-eighteenth century, for example, began in Britain and traveled to America in large part through the efforts of the English evangelist George Whitefield. American evangelists later carried religious ideas from the New World back to the Old.

The early history of European America was also closely bound up with the intellectual life of Europe. The Enlightenment—the cluster of ideas that emerged in Europe in the seventeenth and eighteenth centuries emphasizing the power of human reason—moved quickly to the Americas, producing considerable intellectual ferment throughout the New World, but particularly in the British colonies in North America and the Caribbean. The ideas of the British philosopher John Locke, for example, helped shape the founding of Georgia. The English Constitution, and the idea of the "rights of Englishmen," shaped the way North Americans shaped their own concepts of politics. Many of the ideas that lay behind the American Revolution were products of British and continental philosophy that had traveled across the Atlantic. The reinterpretation of those ideas by Americans to help justify their drive to independence—by, among others, Thomas Paine—moved back across the Atlantic to Europe and helped, among other things, to inspire the French Revolution. Scientific and technological knowledge—another product of the Enlightenment—moved rapidly back and forth across the Atlantic. Americans borrowed industrial technology from Britain. Europe acquired much of its early knowledge of electricity from experiments done in America. But the Enlightenment was only one part of the continuing intellectual connections within the Atlantic World, connections that spread artistic, scholarly, and political ideas widely through the lands bordering the ocean.

Instead of thinking of the early history of what became the United States simply as the story of the growth of thirteen small colonies along the Atlantic seaboard of North America, the idea of the "Atlantic World" encourages us to think of early American history as a vast pattern of exchanges and interactions—trade, migration, religious and intellectual exchange, and many other relationships—among all the societies bordering the Atlantic: western Europe, western Africa, the Caribbean, and North and South America.

(The I.N. Phelps Stokes Collection of American Historical Prints, Prints Division, The New York Public Library, Astor, Lenox and Tilden Foundations.)

tribes also divided political power by gender, with men choosing leaders and systems for managing what they defined as male affairs and women choosing parallel leaders to handle female matters. Tribal chiefs generally were men (although in some places there was a female counterpart), but the position customarily passed down not to the chief's son but to the son of the chief's eldest sister. African societies, in short, were characterized by a greater degree of sexual equality than those of most other parts of the world.

In those areas of west Africa where indigenous religions had survived the spread of Islam (which included most of the lands south of the empire of Mali), people worshipped many gods, whom they associated with various aspects of the natural world and whose spirits they believed lived in trees, rocks, forests, and streams. Most Africans also developed forms of ancestor worship and took great care in tracing family lineage; the most revered priests (who were often also important social and political leaders as well) were generally the oldest people.

African societies had elaborate systems of social ranks (or hierarchies). Small elites of priests and nobles stood at the top. Most people belonged to a large middle group of farmers, traders, crafts workers, and others. At the bottom of society were slaves—men and women who were put into bondage after being captured in wars or because of criminal behavior or unpaid debts. Slavery in Africa was not usually permanent; people were generally placed in bondage for a fixed period and in the meantime retained certain legal protections (including the right to marry). Their children, moreover, did not inherit their parents' condition of bondage. The slavery that Africans would experience at the hands of the Europeans was to be very different.

The African slave trade began long before the European migration to the New World. As early as the eighth century A.D., west Africans began selling slaves to traders from the Mediterranean. They were responding to a demand from affluent families who wanted black men and women as domestic servants. They were also responding to more general labor shortages in some areas of Europe and North Africa. When Portuguese sailors began exploring the coast of Africa in the fifteenth century, they too bought slaves—usually criminals and people captured in war—and took them back to Portugal, where there was a small but steady demand.

In the sixteenth century, however, the market for slaves grew dramatically as a result of the rising European demand for sugar cane. The small areas of sugar cultivation in the Mediterranean were proving inadequate, and production soon moved to the island of Madeira off the African coast, which became a Portuguese colony. Not long after that, it moved to the Caribbean islands and Brazil. Sugar was a labor-intensive crop, and the demand for workers in

Growth of the African Slave Trade

these new areas increased rapidly. European slave traders responded to that demand by increasing the recruitment of workers from along the coast of west Africa (and from some areas of east Africa as well). As the demand increased, African kingdoms warred with one another in an effort to capture potential slaves to exchange for European goods. At first the slave traders were overwhelmingly Portuguese and, to a lesser extent, Spanish. By the seventeenth century, the Dutch had won control of most of the slave market. In the eighteenth century, the English dominated it. (Despite some recent claims, Jews were never significantly involved in the slave trade.) By 1700 slavery had begun to spread well beyond its original locations in the Caribbean and South America and into the English colonies to the north.

THE ARRIVAL OF THE ENGLISH

England's first documented contact with the New World came only five years after Spain's. In 1497, John Cabot (like Columbus a native of Genoa) sailed to the northeastern coast of North America on an expedition sponsored by King Henry VII. Other English navigators continued Cabot's unsuccessful search for a northwest passage through the New World to the Orient. They explored other areas of North America during the sixteenth century. But even though England claimed dominion over the lands its explorers surveyed, nearly a century passed before the English made any serious efforts to establish colonies there. Like other European nations, England had to experience an internal transformation before it could begin settling new lands. That transformation occurred in the sixteenth century.

John Cabot

The Commercial Incentive

Part of the attraction of the New World to the English was its newness, its contrast to their own troubled land. America seemed a place where human settlement could start anew, where a perfect society could be created without the flaws and inequities of the Old World. Such dreams began to emerge in England only a few years after Columbus's voyages. They found classic expression in Sir Thomas More's *Utopia* (published in Latin in 1516, translated into English thirty-five years later), which described a mythical and nearly perfect society on an imaginary island supposedly discovered by a companion of Amerigo Vespucci in the waters of the New World.

More's picture of an ideal community was, among other things, a comment on the social and economic ills of the England of his own time. The people of Tudor England suffered from frequent and costly European wars, from almost constant religious strife, and above all from a harsh economic transformation of the

The Enclosure Movement

countryside. Because the worldwide demand for wool was growing rapidly, many landowners were finding it profitable to convert their land from fields for crops to pastures for sheep. The result was a significant growth in the wool trade. But that meant land worked at one time by serfs and later by rent-paying tenants was steadily enclosed for sheep runs and taken away from the farmers. Thousands of evicted tenants roamed the countryside in gangs, begging from (and at times robbing) the more fortunate householders through whose communities they passed.

The government passed various laws designed to halt enclosures, relieve the worthy poor, and compel the able-bodied or "sturdy beggars" to work. Such laws had little effect. The enclosure movement continued unabated, and relatively few of the dislocated farmers could find reemployment in raising sheep or manufacturing wool. By removing land from cultivation, the enclosure movement also limited England's ability to feed its population, which grew from 3 million in 1485 to 4 million in 1603. Both because of the dislocation of farmers and the restriction of the food supply, therefore, the nation had a serious problem of surplus population.

Amid this growing distress, a rising class of merchant capitalists was prospering from the expansion of foreign trade. At first, England had exported little except raw wool; but new merchant capitalists helped create a domestic cloth industry that allowed them to begin marketing finished goods at home and abroad. At first, most exporters did business almost entirely as individuals. In time, however, some merchants joined forces and formed chartered companies.

Chartered Companies

Each such enterprise operated on the basis of a charter acquired from the monarch, which gave the company a monopoly for trading in a particular region. Among the first of these were the Muscovy Company (1555), the Levant Company (1581), the Barbary Company (1585), the Guinea Company (1588), and the East India Company (1600). Investors in these companies often made fantastic profits from the exchange of English manufactures, especially woolens, for exotic goods; and they felt a powerful urge to continue the expansion of their profitable trade.

Central to this drive was the emergence of a new concept of economic life known as mercantilism, which was gaining favor throughout Europe. Mercantilism rested on the assumption that the nation as a whole was the principal actor in the economy, not the individuals within it. The goal of economic activity should be to increase the nation's total wealth. Mercantilists believed that the world's wealth was finite. One person or nation could grow rich only at the expense of another. A nation's economic health depended, therefore, on extracting as much wealth as possible from foreign lands and exporting as little wealth as possible from home.

The principles of mercantilism guided the economic policies of virtually all the European nation-states in the sixteenth and seventeenth centuries. Mercantilism greatly enhanced the position of the new merchant capitalists,

Mercantilism

whose overseas ventures were thought to benefit the entire nation and to be worthy of government assistance. It also increased competition among nations. Every European state was trying to find markets for its exports while trying to limit its imports. One result was the increased attractiveness of acquiring colonies, which could become the source of goods that a country might otherwise have to buy from other nations.

In England, the mercantilistic program thrived at first on the basis of the flourishing wool trade with the European continent, and particularly with the great cloth market in Antwerp. Beginning in the 1550s, however, that glutted market collapsed, and English merchants found themselves obliged to look elsewhere for overseas trade. The establishment of colonies seemed to be a ready answer to that and other problems. Richard Hakluyt, an Oxford clergyman and the out-

Richard Hakluyt's Argument for Colonies

standing English propagandist for colonization, argued that colonies would not only create new markets for English goods, they would also help alleviate poverty and unemployment by siphoning off the surplus population. For the poor who remained in England "idly to the annoy of the whole state," there would be new work as a result of the prosperity the colonies would create. Perhaps most important, colonial commerce would allow England to acquire products from its own new territories for which the nation had previously been dependent on foreign rivals—products such as lumber, naval stores, and, above all, silver and gold.

The Religious Incentive

In addition to these economic motives for colonization, there were also religious ones, rooted in the events of the European and English Reformations. The Protestant Reformation began in Germany in 1517, when Martin Luther openly challenged some of the basic practices and beliefs of the Roman Catholic Church—until then, the supreme religious authority and also one of the strongest political authorities throughout western Europe. Luther, an Augustinian monk and ordained priest, challenged the Catholic belief that salvation could be achieved through good works or through loyalty (or payments) to the church itself. He denied the church's claim that God communicated to the world through the pope and the clergy. The Bible, not the church, was the authentic voice of God, Luther claimed, and salvation was to be found not through "works" or through the formal practice of religion, but through faith alone. Luther's challenge quickly won him a wide following among ordinary men and

THE DOCKS OF BRISTOL, ENGLAND By the eighteenth century, when this scene was painted, Bristol had become one of the principal English ports serving the so-called triangular trade among the American colonies, the West Indies, and Africa. The lucrativeness of that trade is evident in the bustle and obvious prosperity of the town. Even earlier, however, Bristol was an important port of embarkation for the thousands of English settlers migrating to the New World. (Docks and Quay. *English School (18th Century). City of Bristol Museum and Art Gallery/The Bridgeman Art Library, London*)

women in northern Europe. He himself insisted that he was not revolting against the church, that his purpose was to reform it from within. But when the pope excommunicated him in 1520, Luther defied him and began to lead his followers out of the Catholic Church entirely. A schism within European Christianity had begun that was never to be healed.

As the spirit of the Reformation spread rapidly throughout Europe, creating intellectual ferment and (in some places) war, other dissidents began offering alternatives to orthodox Catholicism.

Doctrine of Predestination

The Swiss theologian John Calvin was, after Luther, the most influential reformer and went even further than Luther had in rejecting the Catholic belief that human institutions could affect an individual's prospects for salvation. Calvin introduced the doctrine of predestination. God "elected" some people to be saved and condemned others to damnation; each person's destiny was deter-

mined before birth, and no one could change that predetermined fate. But while individuals could not alter their destinies, they could strive to know them. Calvinists believed that the way people led their lives might reveal to them their chances of salvation. A wicked or useless existence would be a sign of damnation; saintliness, diligence, and success could be signs of grace. Calvinism created anxieties among its followers, to be sure; but it also produced a strong incentive to lead virtuous, productive lives. The new creed spread rapidly throughout northern Europe and produced (among other groups) the Huguenots in France and the Puritans in England.

The English Reformation began, however, more because of a political dispute between the king and the pope than as a result of these doctrinal revolts. In 1529 King **The English Reformation** Henry VIII became angered by the pope's refusal to grant him a divorce from his Spanish wife (who had failed to

JOHN CALVIN Next to Martin Luther, John Calvin was the most important figure of the European Reformation. His belief in predestination was central to the Puritan faith of early New England. *(Bettman/Corbis)*

bear him the son he desperately wanted). In response, he broke England's ties with the Catholic Church and established himself as the head of the Christian faith in his country. He made relatively few other changes in English Christianity, however, and after his death the survival of Protestantism remained in doubt for a time. When Henry's Catholic daughter Mary ascended the throne, she quickly restored England's allegiance to Rome and harshly persecuted those who refused to return to the Catholic fold. Many Protestants were executed (the origin of the queen's enduring nickname, "Bloody Mary"); others fled to the European continent, where they came into contact with the most radical ideas of the Reformation. Mary died in 1558, and her half-sister, Elizabeth, became England's sovereign. Elizabeth once again severed the nation's connection with the Catholic Church (and, along with it, an alliance with Spain that Mary had forged).

The Church of England, as the official religion was now known, satisfied the political objectives of the queen, but it failed to satisfy the religious desires of many English Christians. Large groups of Catholics continued to claim allegiance to the pope. Others, affected by the teachings of the European Reformation, believed the new Church of England had abandoned Rome without abandoning Rome's offensive beliefs and practices. Under Elizabeth, the church began to incorporate some of the tenets of Calvinism, but never enough to satisfy its critics—particularly the many exiles who had fled the country under Mary and who now returned, bringing their new, more radical religious ideas with them. They continued to clamor for reforms that would "purify" the church; as a result, they became known as "Puritans."

A few Puritans took what were, by the standards of the time, genuinely radical positions. They were known as Separatists, and they were determined to worship as they **Puritan Separatists** pleased in their own independent congregations. That determination flew in the face of English law—which outlawed unauthorized religious meetings, required all subjects to attend regular Anglican services, and levied taxes to support the established church. The radicalism of the Separatists was visible in other ways as well, including their rejection of prevailing assumptions about the proper religious roles of women. Many Separatist sects, perhaps most prominently the Quakers, permitted women to serve as preachers and to assume a prominence in other religious matters that would have been impossible in the established church.

Most Puritans resisted separatism. Still, their demands were by no means modest. They wanted to simplify Anglican forms of worship. They wanted to reduce the power of the bishops, who were appointed by the crown and who were, in many cases, openly corrupt and highly extravagant. Perhaps above all they wanted to reform the local clergy, a group composed in large part of greedy, uneducated men with little interest in (or knowledge of) theology. The more moderate Puritans wished, in short, to see the church give more attention to its spiritual role and less to its worldly ambitions. No less than the Separatists, they grew increasingly frustrated by the refusal of either the political or ecclesiastical leaders of the nation to respond to their demands.

Puritan discontent, already festering, grew rapidly after the death of Elizabeth, the last of the Tudors, and the accession to the throne of James I, a **Puritan Discontent** Scotsman and the first of the Stuarts, in 1603. James believed kings ruled by divine right, and he felt no obligation to compromise with his opponents. He quickly antagonized the Puritans, a group that included most of the rising businessmen, by resorting to arbitrary taxation, by favoring English Catholics in the granting of charters and other favors, and by supporting "high church" forms of ceremony. By the early seventeenth century, some religious nonconformists were beginning to look for places of refuge outside the kingdom. Along with the other economic and social incentives for colonization, such religious discontent helped turn England's gaze to distant lands.

ELIZABETH I The flemish artist Marcus Gheeraerts the younger moved to England in 1568 (along with his father, also a painter) as a Protestant refugee from his homeland. In approximately 1593 he painted this portrait of the English queen, portraying her as she was seen by many of her contemporaries: a strong, confident ruler presiding over an ambitious, expansionist nation. She stands here on a map of England. *(National Portrait Gallery, London)*

The English in Ireland

England's first experience with colonization came not in the New World, but in a land separated from Britain only by a narrow stretch of sea: Ireland. The English had long laid claim to the island and had for many years maintained small settlements in the area around Dublin. Only in the second half of the sixteenth century, however, did serious efforts at large-scale colonization begin. Through the 1560s and 1570s, would-be colonists moved through Ireland, capturing territory and attempting to subdue the native population. In the process they developed many of the assumptions that would guide later English colonists in America.

The most important of these assumptions was that the native population of Ireland—approximately 1 million people, loyal to the Catholic
Subjugation of Ireland Church, with their own language (Gaelic) and their own culture—was a collection of wild, vicious, and ignorant "savages." The Irish lived in ways the English considered crude and wasteful ("like

beasts"), and they fought back against the intruders with a ferocity that the English considered barbaric. Such people could not be tamed, the English concluded. They certainly could not be assimilated into English society. They must, therefore, be suppressed, isolated, and if necessary destroyed. Eventually, they might be "civilized," but only after they were thoroughly subordinated.

Whatever barbarities the Irish may have inflicted on the colonizers, the English more than matched in return. Sir Humphrey Gilbert, who was later to establish the first British colony in the New World (an unsuccessful venture in Newfoundland), served for a time as governor of one Irish district and suppressed native rebellions with extraordinary viciousness. Gilbert was an educated and supposedly civilized man. But he considered the natives somehow less than human, and therefore not entitled to whatever decencies civilized people reserved for their treatment of one another. As a result, he managed to justify, both to himself and to others, such atrocities as beheading Irish soldiers after they were killed in battle. Gilbert himself, Sir Walter Raleigh, Sir Richard Grenville, and others active in Ireland in the mid-sixteenth century derived from their experiences there an outlook they would take to America, where they made similarly vicious efforts to subdue and subjugate the natives.

The Irish experience led the English to another important (and related) assumption about colonization: that English settlements in distant lands must retain a rigid separation from the native populations. In Ireland, English colo- The Plantation Model
nizers established what they called "plantations," transplantations of English society in a foreign land. Unlike the Spanish in America, the English in Ireland did not try simply to rule a subdued native population; they tried to build a complete society of their own, peopled with emigrants from England itself. The new society would exist within a "pale of settlement," an area physically separated from the natives. That concept, too, they would take with them to the New World, even though in Ireland, as later in America, the separation of peoples and the preservation of "pure" English culture proved impossible.

The French and the Dutch in America

English settlers in North America, unlike those in Ireland, were to encounter not only natives but also other Europeans who were, like them, driven by mercantilist ideas to establish economic outposts abroad. To the south and southwest was the Spanish Empire. Spanish ships continued to threaten English settlements along the coast for years. But except for Mexico and scattered outposts such as those in Florida and New Mexico, the Spanish made little serious effort to colonize North America.

England's more formidable North American rivals in the early sixteenth century were the French. France founded its first permanent settlement in America at Quebec in 1608, less than a year after the English started their first colony at Jamestown. The French colony's population grew very slowly. Few French Catholics felt any inclination to leave their homeland, and French Protestants who might have wished to emigrate were excluded from the colony. The French, however, exercised an influence in the New World disproportionate to their numbers, largely because of their relationships with Native Americans. Unlike the English, who for many years hugged the coastline and traded with the Indians of the interior through intermediaries, the French forged close, direct ties with natives deep inside the continent. French Jesuit missionaries were among the first to penetrate Indian societies, and they established some of the first contacts between the two peoples. More important still were the *coureurs de bois*—adventurous fur traders

Coureurs de Bois

and trappers—who also penetrated far into the wilderness and developed an extensive trade that became one of the underpinnings of the French colonial economy.

The fur trade was, in fact, more an Indian than a French enterprise. The *coureurs de bois* were, in many ways, little more than agents for the Algonquins and the Hurons, who were the principal fur traders among the Indians of the region and from whom the French purchased their pelts. The French traders were able to function only to the degree that they could form partnerships with the Indians. Successful partnerships often resulted from their ability to become virtually a part of native society, living among the Indians and at times marrying Indian women. The fur trade helped open the way for the other elements of the French presence in North America—the agricultural estates (or *seigneuries*) along the St. Lawrence River,

the development of trade and military centers at Quebec and Montreal, and the creation of an alliance with the Algonquins and others—that enabled the French to compete with the more numerous British in the contest for control of North America. That alliance also brought the French into conflict with the Iroquois, the Algonquins' ancient enemies, who assumed the central role in the English fur trade. An early result of these tensions was a 1609 attack led by Samuel de Champlain, the founder of Quebec, on a band of Mohawks, apparently at the instigation of his Algonquin trading partners.

The Dutch, too, were establishing a presence in North America. Holland had won its independence from Spain in the early seventeenth century and was one of the leading trading nations of the world. Its merchant fleet was larger than England's, and its

Henry Hudson

traders were active not only in Europe but also in Africa, Asia, and—increasingly—America. In 1609 an English explorer in the employ of the Dutch, Henry Hudson, sailed up the river that was to be named for him in what is now New York State. Because the river was so wide, he believed for a time that he had found the long-sought water route through the continent to the Pacific. He was wrong, of course, but his explorations led to a Dutch claim on territory in America and to the establishment of a permanent Dutch presence in the New World.

For more than a decade after Hudson's voyage, the Dutch maintained an active trade in furs in and around New York. In 1624, the Dutch West India Company established

New Amsterdam

a series of permanent trading posts on the Hudson, Delaware, and Connecticut Rivers. The company actively encouraged settlement of the region—not just from

THE "RESTITUTION" OF NEW AMSTERDAM This is a detail from an elaborate engraving created to celebrate the "Restitutio" (or return) of New Amsterdam to the Dutch in 1673. England had captured New Amsterdam in 1664 and made claim to the entire province of New Netherland. But in 1672, war broke out between England and the Netherlands, and the Dutch recaptured their lost province. In celebration of that event, this heroic picture of the Dutch fleet in New York was created for sale in the Netherlands. Early in 1674, at the conclusion of the war, the Dutch returned the colony to England. *(Museum of the City of New York)*

Holland itself, but from such other parts of northern Europe as Germany, Sweden, and Finland. It transported whole families to the New World and granted vast feudal estates to landlords (known as "patroons") on condition that they bring still more immigrants to America. The result was the colony of New Netherland and its principal town, New Amsterdam, on Manhattan Island. Its population, diverse as it was, remained relatively small; the colony was only loosely united, with chronically weak leadership.

The First English Settlements

The first enduring English settlement in the New World was established at Jamestown, in Virginia, in 1607. But for nearly thirty years before that, English merchants and adventurers had been engaged in a series of failed efforts to create colonies in America. Through much of the sixteenth century, the English had mixed feelings about the New World. They knew of its existence and were intrigued by its possibilities. Under the strong leadership of Elizabeth I, they were developing a powerful sense of nationalism that encouraged dreams of expansion. At the same time, however, England was leery of Spain, which remained the dominant force in America and, it seemed, the dominant naval power in Europe.

But much changed in the 1570s and 1580s. English "sea dogs" such as Sir Francis Drake staged successful raids on Spanish merchant ships and built confidence in England's ability to challenge Spanish sea power. More

The Spanish Armada

important was the attempted invasion of England by the Spanish Armada in 1588. Philip II, the powerful Spanish king, had recently united his nation with Portugal. He was now determined to end England's challenges to Spanish commercial supremacy and to bring the English back into the Catholic Church. He assembled one of the largest military fleets in the history of warfare—known to history as the "Spanish Armada"—to carry his troops across the English Channel and into England itself. Philip's bold venture turned into a fiasco when the smaller English fleet dispersed the Armada and, in a single stroke, ended Spain's domination of the Atlantic. The English now felt much freer to establish themselves in the New World.

The pioneers of English colonization were Sir Humphrey Gilbert and his half brother Sir Walter Raleigh—both friends of Queen Elizabeth, and both veterans of the earlier colonial efforts in Ireland. In 1578 Gilbert obtained from Elizabeth a patent granting him the exclusive right for six years "to inhabit and possess at his choice all remote and heathen lands not in the actual possession of any Christian prince."

After numerous setbacks, Gilbert led an expedition to Newfoundland in 1583 and took possession of it in the

Gilbert's Expedition to Newfoundland

queen's name. He proceeded southward along the coast, looking for a good place to build a military outpost that might eventually grow into a profitable colony. But a storm sank his ship, and he was lost at sea.

Roanoke

Raleigh was undeterred by Gilbert's misfortune. The next year, he secured from Elizabeth a six-year grant similar to Gilbert's and sent a small group of men on an expedition to explore the North American coast. They returned with two captive Indians and glowing reports of what they had seen. They were particularly enthusiastic about an island the natives called Roanoke and about the area of the mainland just beyond it (in what is now North Carolina). Raleigh asked the queen for permission to name the entire region "Virginia" in honor of Elizabeth, "the Virgin Queen." But while Elizabeth granted the permission, she did not offer the financial assistance Raleigh had hoped his flattery would produce. So he turned to private investors to finance another expedition.

In 1585 Raleigh recruited his cousin, Sir Richard Grenville, to lead a group of men (most of them from the English plantations in Ireland) to Roanoke to establish a colony. Grenville deposited the settlers on the island, remained long enough to antagonize the

The First Roanoke Colony

natives by razing an Indian village as retaliation for a minor theft, and returned to England. The following spring, Sir Francis Drake unexpectedly arrived in Roanoke. With supplies and reinforcements from England long overdue, the beleaguered colonists boarded Drake's ships and left.

Raleigh tried again in 1587, sending an expedition carrying ninety-one men, seventeen women (two of them pregnant), and nine children—the nucleus, he hoped, of a viable "plantation." The settlers landed on Roanoke and attempted to take up where the first group of colonists had left off. (Shortly after arriving, one of the women—the daughter of the commander of the expedition, John White—gave birth to a daughter, Virginia Dare, the first American-born child of English parents.) White returned to England after several weeks (leaving his daughter and granddaughter behind) in search of supplies and additional settlers; he hoped to return in a few months. But the hostilities with Spain intervened, and White did not return to the island for three years. When he did, in 1590, he found the island utterly deserted, with no clue to the settlers' fate other than the cryptic inscription "Croatoan" carved on a post. Some have argued that the colonists were slaughtered by the Indians in retaliation for Grenville's (and perhaps their own) hostilities. Others have contended that they left their settlement and joined native society, ultimately becoming entirely assimilated. But no conclusive solution to the mystery of the "Lost Colony" has ever been found.

The Roanoke disaster marked the end of Sir Walter Raleigh's involvement in English colonization of the New World. In 1603, when James I succeeded Elizabeth to the

ROANOKE A drawing by one of the English colonists in the ill-fated Roanoke expedition of 1585 became the basis for this engraving by Theodore DeBry, published in England in 1590. A small European ship carrying settlers approaches the island of Roanoke, at left. The wreckage of several larger vessels farther out to sea and the presence of Indian settlements on the mainland and on Roanoke itself suggest some of the perils the settlers encountered. *(New York Public Library Astor, Lenox and Tilden Foundations)*

throne, Raleigh was accused of plotting against the king, stripped of his monopoly, and imprisoned for more than a decade. Finally (after being released for one last ill-fated maritime expedition), he was executed by the king in 1618. No later colonizer would receive grants of land in the New World as vast or undefined as those Raleigh and Gilbert had acquired. But despite the discouraging example of these early experiences, the colonizing impulse remained alive.

In the first years of the seventeenth century, a group of London merchants to whom Raleigh had assigned his charter rights decided to renew the attempt at colonization in Virginia. A rival group of merchants, from Plymouth and other West Country towns, were also interested in American ventures and were sponsoring voyages of exploration farther north, up to Newfoundland, where West Country fishermen had been going for many years. In 1606 James I issued a new charter, which divided America **New Colonial Charters** between the two groups. The London group got the exclusive right to colonize in the south, and the Plymouth merchants received the same right in the north. Through their efforts, the first enduring English colonies were planted in America.

CONCLUSION

The lands that Europeans eventually named the Americas were the home of many millions of people before the arrival of Columbus. Having migrated from Asia thousands of years earlier, the pre-Columbian Americans spread throughout the Western Hemisphere and eventually created great civilizations. Among the most notable of them were the Incas in Peru, and the Mayas and Aztecs in Mexico. In the regions north of what was later named the Rio Grande, the human population was smaller and the civilizations less advanced than they were further south. Even so, North American natives created a cluster of civilizations that thrived and expanded. There were probably 10 million people living north of Mexico by the time Columbus arrived.

In the century after European contact, these native populations suffered a series of catastrophes that all but destroyed the civilizations they had built: brutal invasions by Spanish and Portuguese conquistadores and, even more devastating, a series of plagues inadvertently imported by Europeans that decimated native populations. By the middle of the sixteenth century, the Spanish and Portuguese—no longer faced with effective resistance from the native populations—had established

colonial control over all of South America and much of North America, creating one of the largest empires in the world.

In the parts of North America that would eventually become the United States, the European presence was for a time much less powerful. The Spanish established an important northern outpost in what is now New Mexico, a society in which Europeans and Indians lived together intimately, if unequally. They created a fort at St. Augustine, Florida. On the whole, however, the North American Indians remained largely undisturbed by Europeans until the English, French, and Dutch migrations began in the early seventeenth century.

INTERACTIVE LEARNING

The *Primary Source Investigator CD-ROM* offers the following materials related to this chapter:

- Interactive maps: **Early Native Peoples** (M1) and **The Atlantic World** (M68).

- Documents, images, and maps related to the Native Americans, early European explorations and settlements in North America, and the meeting of cultures. Some highlights include early paintings of Native

American farming techniques made by European explorers and European maps of the area.

Online Learning Center (www.mhhe.com/brinkley12)

For quizzes, Internet resources, references to additional books and films, and more, consult this book's Online Learning Center.

FOR FURTHER REFERENCE

Alvin M. Josephy, ed., *America in 1492: The World of the Indian Peoples Before the Arrival of Columbus* (1993) and Brian M. Fagan, *The Great Journey: The Peopling of Ancient America* (1987) provide introductions to pre-Columbian history. William M. Denevan, ed., *The Native Population of the Americas in 1492* (1976) and Russell Thornton, *American Indian Holocaust and Survival: A Population History since 1492* (1987) are important contributions to the debate over the size and character of the American population before Columbus. Alfred Crosby, *The Columbian Exchange: Biological and Cultural Consequences of 1492* (1972) explores the results of European-Indian contact in both the Americas and Europe. Hugh Thomas, *Rivers of Gold: The Rise of the Spanish Empire from Columbus to Magellan* (2004) is a good popular history of the Spanish Empire. D. W. Meinig, *The Shaping of America, Vol. I: Atlantic*

America, 1492–1800 (1986) is an account of the early contacts between Europeans and the New World. Gary Nash, *Red, White and Black: The Peoples of Early America* (1982) provides a brief, multiracial survey of colonial America. Philip Curtin, *The Atlantic Slave Trade: A Census* (1969) has become the indispensable starting point for understanding African forced migration to the Americas. John Thornton, *Africa and Africans in the Making of the Atlantic World* (1998) examines the impact of slavery and the slave trade on the entire Atlantic world from the fifteenth through the eighteenth centuries. One outstanding collection of essays that summarizes modern scholarship on colonial America is Jack P. Greene and J.R. Pole, eds, *Colonial British America: Essays in the New History of the Early Modern Era* (1984). *Columbus and the Age of Discovery* (1991) is a seven-part documentary film series on Christopher Columbus, his era, and his legacy.

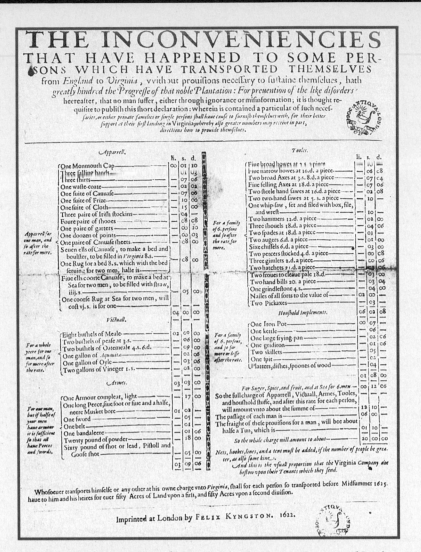

ADVICE TO MIGRANTS This 1622 handbill by the Virginia Company of London provides a detailed list of items that people contemplating a voyage to America should plan to take with them. The list reflects the company's awareness of how few finished goods were yet available in America (and also their realization that they themselves could profit from selling such goods to their passengers). *(Rare Books Division, New York Public Library, Astor, Lenox and Tilden Foundations)*

SIGNIFICANT EVENTS

1607 ▶ Jamestown founded

1608 ▶ Pilgrims flee to Holland from England

1612 ▶ Tobacco production established in Virginia

1619 ▶ First African workers arrive in Virginia

▶ Virginia House of Burgesses meets for first time

1620 ▶ Pilgrims found Plymouth colony

1620s ▶ English colonization accelerates in the Caribbean

1622 ▶ Powhatan Indians attack English colony in Virginia

1624 ▶ Dutch establish settlement on Manhattan Island

1629 ▶ New Hampshire and Maine established

1630 ▶ Puritans establish Massachusetts Bay colony at Boston

1634 ▶ First English settlements founded in Maryland

1635 ▶ Hartford settled in Connecticut

1636 ▶ Roger Williams founds settlement in Rhode Island

1637 ▶ Anne Hutchinson expelled from Massachusetts Bay colony

▶ Pequot War fought

1638 ▶ Swedes and Finns establish New Sweden on the Delaware River

1642–1649 ▶ English Civil War

1644 ▶ Last major Powhatan uprisings against English settlers in Virginia

1649 ▶ Charles I executed

CHAPTER 2

Transplantations and Borderlands

The Roanoke fiasco dampened the colonizing enthusiasm in England—for a time. But the lures of the New World were too strong to be suppressed for very long. Propagandizers such as Richard Hakluyt kept the image of America alive in English society. By the early seventeenth century, the effort to establish permanent colonies in the New World resumed.

Lure of the New World

The first of these new efforts were much like the earlier, failed ones. They were largely private ventures, with little planning or direction from the English government. They were small, fragile settlements, and generally unprepared for the hardships they were to face. They met with terrible disasters.

These first permanent English settlements were business enterprises. They were financed by private companies, and, in most cases, they were expected to produce a profit. As in Ireland, there were few efforts to blend English society with the society of the natives. The Europeans attempted, as best they could, to isolate themselves from the Indians and create enclosed societies that would be entirely their own—"transplantations" of the English world they had left behind. And almost nothing worked out as they had planned--largely because the English could not effectively isolate themselves from the world around them, a world populated by Native American tribes, but also by colonists, explorers, and traders from Spain, France, and the Netherlands, and immigrants from other parts of Europe. However much the settlers tried to re-create English society in the New World, American society very quickly began to develop its own habits and institutions. The English colonies were also different from one another. Although all areas of British North America were primarily agricultural, there was also a growing merchant class clustered in a few cities—most notably Boston, New York, and Philadelphia. In the South, where there were opportunities to cultivate marketable crops for export such as tobacco, cotton, and rice, a plantation system—reliant on indentured and later slave labor—dominated the region. Politically, too, the colonies were very different from one another. Some were governed by representatives of the king, others by locally chosen leaders, and others still by private companies. In virtually all of the colonies, however, there were at least some institutions of self-government, and most institutions provided representation only to white males, and in some cases only to particular religious or social groups.

Characteristics of English Settlements

1655 ▸ Civil war in Maryland temporarily unseats Catholic proprietor

1660 ▸ English Restoration: Charles II becomes king

▸ First Navigation Act passed

1663 ▸ Carolina colony chartered

▸ Second Navigation Act passed

1664 ▸ English capture New Netherland

▸ New Jersey chartered

1673 ▸ Third Navigation Act passed

1675–1676 ▸ King Philip's War in New England

1676 ▸ Bacon's Rebellion in Virginia

1681 ▸ William Penn receives charter for Pennsylvania

1685 ▸ James II becomes king

1686 ▸ Dominion of New England established

1688 ▸ Glorious Revolution in England: William and Mary ascend throne

1689 ▸ Glorious Revolution in America: rebellion breaks out against Andros in New England

▸ Leisler leads rebellion in New York

1732 ▸ Georgia chartered

THE EARLY CHESAPEAKE

After James I issued his 1606 charters to the London and Plymouth Companies, the principal obstacle to founding new American colonies was, as usual, money. The Plymouth group made an early, unsuccessful attempt to establish a colony at Sagadahoc, on the coast of Maine; but in the aftermath of that failure, it largely abandoned its colonizing efforts. The London Company, by contrast, moved quickly and decisively. Only a few months after receiving its charter, it launched a colonizing expedition headed for Virginia—a party of 144 men aboard three ships: the *Godspeed,* the *Discovery,* and the *Susan Constant.*

The Founding of Jamestown

Only 104 men survived the journey. They reached the American coast in the spring of 1607, sailed into the Chesapeake Bay and up a river they named the James, and established their colony on a peninsula extending from the river's northern bank. They called it Jamestown. The colonists had chosen their site poorly. In an effort to avoid the mistakes of Roanoke (whose residents were assumed to have been killed by Indians), they selected what they believed to be an easily defended location—an inland setting that they believed would offer them security. But the site was low and swampy, hot and humid in the summer, and prey to outbreaks of malaria. It was surrounded by thick woods, which were difficult to clear for cultivation. And it lay within the territories of powerful local Indians, a confederation led by the imperial chief Powhatan. The result could hardly have been more disastrous.

The initial colonists, too many of whom were adventurous gentlemen and too few of whom were willing laborers, ran into serious difficulties from the moment they landed. Much like the Indians to the south who had succumbed quickly to European diseases when first exposed to them, these English settlers had had no prior exposure, and thus no immunity, to the infections of the new land. Malaria, in particular, debilitated the colony, killing some and weakening others so they could do virtually no work. Because the promoters in London demanded a quick return on their investment, the colonists spent much of their limited and dwindling energy on futile searches for gold. They made only slightly more successful efforts to pile up lumber, tar, pitch, and iron for export. Growing food was a low priority.

Early Problems

The London Company promoters had little interest in creating a family-centered community, and at first they sent no women to Jamestown. The absence of English women made it difficult for the settlers to establish any semblance of a "society." The colonists were seldom able (and also seldom willing) to intermarry with native women, and hence Jamestown was at first an entirely male settlement. Without women, settlers could not establish real households, could not order their domestic lives, and had difficulty feeling any sense of a permanent stake in the community.

Greed and rootlessness contributed to the failure to grow sufficient food; inadequate diets contributed to the colonists' vulnerability to disease, the ravages of disease made it difficult for the settlers to recover from their early mistakes. The result was a community without the means to sustain itself. By January 1608, when ships appeared with additional men and supplies, all but 38 of the first 104 colonists were dead. Jamestown, now facing extinction, survived the crisis largely because of the efforts of twenty-seven-year-old Captain John Smith. He was already a famous world traveler, the hero of implausible travel narratives he had written and published. But he was also a capable organizer. Leadership in the colony had been divided among the several members of a council who quarreled continually. In the fall of 1608, however, Smith became council president and asserted his will. He imposed work and order on the community. He also organized raids on neighboring Indian villages to steal food and kidnap natives. During the colony's second winter, fewer than a dozen (in a population of about 200) died. By the summer of 1609, when Smith was deposed from the council and returned to England to receive treatment for a serious powder burn, the colony was showing promise of survival.

John Smith

Reorganization

The London Company (now calling itself the Virginia Company) was, in the meantime, dreaming of bigger things. In 1609 it obtained a new charter from the king, which increased its power over the colony and enlarged the area of land to which it had title. The company raised additional capital by selling stock to "adventurers" who would remain in England but share in future profits. It attracted new settlers by offering additional stock to "planters" who were willing to migrate at their own expense. And it provided free passage to Virginia for poorer people who would agree to serve the company for seven years. In the spring of 1609, confident that it was now poised to transform Jamestown into a vibrant, successful venture, the company launched a "great fleet" of nine vessels with about 600 people (including some women and children) aboard—headed for Virginia.

More disaster followed. One of the Virginia-bound ships was lost at sea in a hurricane. Another ran aground on one of the Bermuda islands and was unable to free itself for months. Many of those who reached Jamestown, still weak from their long and stormy voyage, succumbed to fevers before the cold weather came. The winter of 1609–1610 became known as the "starving time," a period worse than anything before. The local Indians,

The Starving Time

antagonized by John Smith's raids and other hostile actions by the early English settlers, killed off the livestock in the woods and kept the colonists barricaded within their palisade. The Europeans lived on what they could find: "dogs, cats, rats, snakes, toadstools, horsehides," and even the "corpses of dead men," as one survivor recalled. The following May, the migrants who had run aground and been stranded on Bermuda finally arrived in Jamestown. They found only about 60 people (out of 500 residents the previous summer) still alive—and those so weakened by the ordeal that they seemed scarcely human. There seemed no point in staying on. The new arrivals took the survivors onto their ship, abandoned the settlement, and sailed downriver for home.

That might have been the end of Jamestown had it not been for an extraordinary twist of fate. As the refugees proceeded down the James toward the Chesapeake Bay, they met an English ship coming up the river—part of a fleet bringing supplies and the colony's first governor, Lord De La Warr. The departing settlers agreed to turn around and return to Jamestown. New relief expeditions with hundreds of colonists soon began to arrive, and the effort to turn a profit in Jamestown resumed.

De La Warr and his successors (Sir Thomas Dale and Sir Thomas Gates) imposed a harsh and rigid discipline on the colony. They organized settlers into work gangs. They sentenced offenders to be flogged, hanged, or broken on the wheel. But this communal system of labor did not function effectively for long. Settlers often evaded work, "presuming that howsoever the harvest prospered, the general store must maintain them." Governor Dale soon concluded that the colony would fare better if the colonists had personal incentives to work. He began to permit the private ownership and cultivation of land. Landowners would repay the company with part-time work and contributions of grain to its storehouses.

Under the leadership of these first, harsh governors, Virginia was not always a happy place. But it survived and even expanded. New settlements began lining the river above and below Jamestown. The expansion was partly a result of the order and discipline the governors at times managed to impose. It was partly a product of increased military assaults on the local Indian tribes, which provided protection for the new settlements. But it also occurred because the colonists had at last discovered a marketable crop: tobacco.

De La Warr's Harsh Discipline

Tobacco

Europeans had become aware of tobacco soon after Columbus's first return from the West Indies, where he had seen the Cuban natives smoking small cigars (*tabacos*), which they inserted in the nostril. By the early seventeenth century, tobacco from the Spanish colonies was already in wide use in Europe. Some critics denounced it as a poisonous weed, the cause of many diseases. King James I himself led the attack with *A Counterblaste to Tobacco* (1604), in which he urged his people not to imitate "the barbarous and beastly manners of the wild, godless, and slavish Indians, especially in so vile and stinking a custom." Other critics were concerned because England's tobacco purchases from the

THE GROWTH OF THE CHESAPEAKE, 1607–1750 This map shows the political forms of European settlement in the region of the Chesapeake Bay in the seventeenth and early eighteenth centuries. Note the several different kinds of colonial enterprises: the royal colony of Virginia, controlled directly by the English crown after the failure of the early commercial enterprises there; and the proprietary regions of Maryland, northern Virginia, and North Carolina, which were under the control of powerful English aristocrats. ◆ *Did these political differences have any significant effect on the economic activities of the various Chesapeake colonies?*

TOBACCO PLANT This 1622 woodcut, later hand-colored, represents the tobacco plant cultivated by English settlers in Virginia in the early seventeenth century after John Rolfe introduced it to the colonists. On the right is an image of a man smoking the plant through a very large pipe. *(Getty Images)*

Spanish colonies meant a drain of English gold to the Spanish importers. Still, the demand for tobacco soared.

Then in 1612, the Jamestown planter John Rolfe began to experiment in Virginia with a harsh strain of tobacco that local Indians had been growing for years. He produced crops of high quality, and he found ready buyers in England. Tobacco cultivation quickly spread up and down the James. The char-

Emergence of the Tobacco Economy

acter of this tobacco economy— its profitability, its uncertainty, its land and labor demands—transformed Chesapeake society in fundamental ways.

Of most immediate importance, perhaps, was the pressure tobacco cultivation created for territorial expansion. Tobacco growers needed large areas of farmland to grow their crops; and because tobacco exhausted the soil after only a few years, the demand for land increased even more. English farmers began establishing plantations deeper and deeper in the interior, isolating themselves from the center of European settlement at Jamestown and encroaching on territory the natives considered their own.

Expansion

Even the discovery of tobacco cultivation was not enough to help the Virginia Company. By 1616, there were still no profits, only land and debts. Nevertheless, the promoters continued to hope that the tobacco trade would allow them finally to turn the corner. In 1618, they launched a last great campaign to attract settlers and make the colony profitable.

Part of that campaign was an effort to recruit new settlers and workers to the colony. The company established what they called the "headright" system. Headrights were fifty-acre grants of land, which new settlers could

The Headright System

acquire in a variety of ways. Those who already lived in the colony received 100 acres apiece. Each new settler received a single headright for himself or herself. This system encouraged family groups to migrate together, since the more family members traveled to America, the larger the landholding the family would receive. In addition, anyone (new settler or old) who paid for the passage of other immigrants to Virginia would receive an additional headright for each new arrival—thus, it was hoped, inducing the prosperous to import new laborers to America. Some colonists were able to assemble sizable plantations with the combined headrights they received for their families and their servants. In return, they contributed a small quitrent (one shilling a year for each headright) to the company.

The company added other incentives as well. To diversify the colonial economy, it transported ironworkers and other skilled craftsmen to Virginia. In 1619, it sent 100 Englishwomen to the colony (which was still overwhelmingly male) to become the wives of male colonists. (The women could be purchased for 120 pounds of tobacco and enjoyed a status somewhere between indentured servants and free people, depending on the good will—or lack of it—of their husbands.) It promised the colonists the full rights of Englishmen (as provided in the original charter of 1606), an end to the strict and arbitrary rule of the communal years, and even a share in self-government. On July 30, 1619, in the Jamestown church, delegates from the various communities met as the House of Burgesses. It was the first meeting of an elected legislature, a representative assembly, within what was to become the United States.

A month later, another event in Virginia established a very different but no less momentous precedent. As John Rolfe recorded, "about the latter end of August" a Dutch ship brought in "20 and odd Negroes." The status and fate of these first Africans in the English colonies remains obscure. There is some reason to believe that the colonists did not consider them slaves, that they thought of them as servants to be held for a term of years and then freed, like the white servants with whom the planters were already familiar. For a time, moreover, the use of black labor remained limited. Although Africans continued to trickle steadily into the colony, planters continued to prefer European indentured servants until at least the 1670s, when such servants began to become scarce and expensive. But whether or not anyone realized it at the time, the small group of black people who arrived in 1619 marked a first step toward the enslavement of Africans within what was to be the American republic.

The expansion of the colony was able to proceed only because of effective suppression of the local Indians,

Suppression of the Powhatan Indians

who resisted the expanding English presence. For two years, Sir Thomas Dale led unrelenting assaults against the Powhatan Indians and in the process kidnapped the great chief Powhatan's daughter Pocahontas. When Powhatan refused to ransom her, she converted to Christianity and in 1614 married John Rolfe. He agreed to the marriage in part to contribute to what he considered the uplifting of her people and, by doing so, to bring greater glory to England. (Pocahontas accompanied her husband back to England, where, as a Christian convert and a gracious woman, she stirred interest in projects to "civilize" the Indians. She died while abroad.) At that point, Powhatan ceased his attacks on the English in the face of overwhelming odds. But after his death several years later, his brother, Opechancanough, became head of the native confederacy and resumed the effort to defend tribal lands from European encroachments. On a March morning in 1622, tribesmen called on the white settlements as if to offer goods for sale, then suddenly attacked. Not until 347 whites of both sexes and all ages (including John Rolfe) lay dead or dying were the Indian warriors finally forced to retreat. The surviving English struck back mercilessly at the Indians and turned back the threat for a time. Only after Opechancanough led another unsuccessful uprising in 1644 did the Powhatans finally cease to challenge the eastern regions of the colony.

By then the Virginia Company in London was defunct.

Demise of the Virginia Company

The company had poured virtually all its funds into its profitless Jamestown venture and in the aftermath of the 1622 Indian uprising faced imminent bankruptcy. In 1624, James I revoked the company's charter, and the colony came under the control of the crown. It would remain so until 1776.

Exchanges of Agricultural Technology

The hostility the early English settlers expressed toward their Indian neighbors was in part a result of their conviction that their own civilization was greatly superior to that of the natives—and perhaps above all that they were more technologically advanced. The English, after all, had great ocean-going vessels, muskets and other advanced implements of weaponry, and many other tools that the Indians had not developed. Indeed, when John Smith and other early Jamestown residents grew frustrated at their inability to find gold and other precious commodities, they often blamed the backwardness

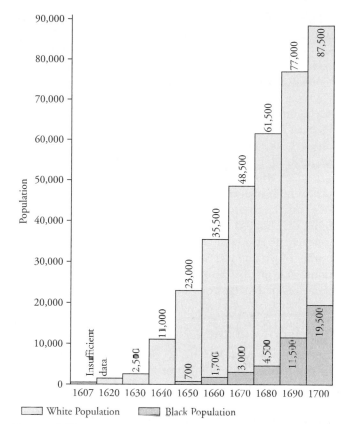

THE NON-INDIAN POPULATION OF THE CHESAPEAKE, 1607–1700 This graph shows the very rapid growth of the population of the Chesapeake during its first century of European settlement. Note the very dramatic increases in the first half of the century, and the somewhat slower increase in the later decades. If the forcibly imported slave population were not counted in the last two decades of the century, the non-Indian population would have grown virtually not at all. ◆ *What impact would the growth of African slavery have had on the rate of immigration by Europeans?*

of the natives. The Spanish in South America, Smith once wrote, had grown rich because the natives there had built advanced civilizations and mined much gold and silver. If Mexico and Peru had been as "ill peopled, as little planted, laboured and manured as Virginia," he added, the Spanish would have found no more wealth than the English did.

Yet the survival of Jamestown was, in the end, largely a result of agricultural technologies developed by Indians and borrowed by the English. Native

Indian Agricultural Techniques

agriculture was far better adapted to the soil and climate of Virginia than the agricultural traditions the English settlers brought with them. The Indians of Virginia were not nomadic hunters, but settled farmers whose villages were surrounded by neatly ordered fields in which grew a variety of crops—beans, pumpkins, vegetables, and above all maize (known to us as corn), which had been previously unknown to the English. Some of the Indian farmlands stretched over hundreds of acres and supported substantial populations.

The English settlers did not adopt all the Indian agricultural techniques. Natives cleared fields not, as the English did, by cutting down and uprooting all the trees. Instead they killed trees in place by "girdling" them (that is, making deep incisions around the base) in the areas in which they planted or setting fire to their roots; and they planted crops not in long, straight rows, but in curving patterns around the dead tree trunks. But in other respects, the English learned a great deal from the Indians about how to grow food in the New World. In particular, they quickly recognized the great value of corn, which proved to be easier to cultivate and to produce much greater yields than any of the European grains the English had known at home. Corn was also attractive to the settlers because its stalks could be a source of sugar and it spoiled less easily than other grains. The English also learned the advantages of growing beans alongside corn to enrich the soil.

Maryland and the Calverts

Maryland was founded under circumstances very different from those of Virginia, but it nonetheless developed in ways markedly similar to its neighbor to the south. The new colony was the dream of George Calvert, the first Lord Baltimore, a recent convert to Catholicism and a shrewd businessman. Calvert envisioned establishing a colony both as a great speculative venture in real estate and as a retreat for English Catholics, many of whom felt oppressed by the Anglican establishment at home. He died before he could receive a charter from the king. But in 1632, his son Cecilius, the second Lord Baltimore, received a charter remarkable not only for the extent of the territory it granted him—an area that encompassed parts of what are now Pennsylvania, Delaware, and Virginia, in addition to present-day Maryland—but also for the powers it bestowed on him. He and his heirs were to hold their province as "true and absolute lords and proprietaries," and were to acknowledge the ultimate sovereignty of the king only by paying an annual fee to the crown.

Proprietary Rule

Lord Baltimore named his brother, Leonard Calvert, governor and sent him with another brother to oversee the settlement of the province. In March 1634, two ships—the *Ark* and the *Dove*—bearing 200 to 300 passengers entered the Potomac River and turned into one of its eastern tributaries. On a high and dry bluff, these first arrivals laid out the village of St. Mary's (named, diplomatically, for the queen). The neighboring Indians, who were more worried about rival tribes in the region than they were about the new arrivals, befriended the settlers, provided them with temporary shelter, sold them land, and supplied them with corn. Unlike the Virginians, the early Marylanders experienced no Indian assaults, no plagues, no starving time.

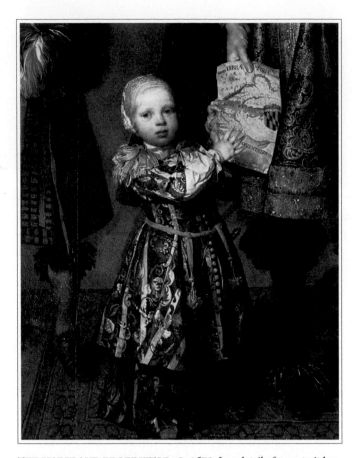

THE MARYLAND PROPRIETOR, C. 1670 In a detail of a portrait by the court painter to King Charles II, the young Cecilius Calvert reaches for a map of Maryland. His grandfather and namesake, the second Lord Baltimore (1606–1675), holds it out to him. George Calvert, the father of the elder Cecilius, began negotiations to win a royal charter for Maryland; his son completed them in 1632 and became the first proprietor of the colony. He published the map shown here in 1635 as part of an effort to attract settlers to the colony. By the time this portrait was painted, Lord Baltimore's son, Charles, was governor of Maryland. The boy Cecilius, the heir apparent, died in 1681 before he could assume his title. *(Enoch Pratt Free Library, Baltimore)*

The Calverts had invested heavily in their American possessions, and they needed to attract many settlers to make the effort profitable. As a result, they had to encourage the immigration of Protestants as well as their fellow English Catholics, who were both relatively few in number (about 2 percent of the population of England) and generally reluctant to emigrate. The Protestant settlers (mostly Anglicans) outnumbered the Catholics from the start, and the Calverts quickly realized that Catholics would always be a minority in the colony. They prudently adopted a policy of religious toleration. To appease the non-Catholic majority, Calvert appointed a Protestant as governor in 1648. A year later, he sent from England the draft of an "Act Concerning Religion," which assured freedom of worship to all Christians.

Religious Toleration

Nevertheless, politics in Maryland remained plagued for years by tensions between the Catholic minority (which included the proprietor) and the Protestant majority. Zealous Jesuits and crusading Puritans frightened and antagonized their opponents with their efforts to establish the dominance of their own religion. At one point, the Protestant majority barred Catholics from voting and repealed the Toleration Act. There was frequent violence, and in 1655 a civil war temporarily unseated the proprietary government and replaced it with one dominated by Protestants.

By 1640, a severe labor shortage in the colony had forced a change in the land grant procedure; and Maryland, like Virginia, adopted a "headright" system—a grant of 100 acres to each male settler, another 100 for his wife and each servant, and 50 for each of his children. Like Virginia, Maryland became a center of tobacco cultivation; and like Virginia, planters worked their land with the aid, first, of indentured servants imported from England and then, beginning late in the seventeenth century, with slaves imported from Africa.

Turbulent Virginia

By the mid-seventeenth century, the Virginia colony had survived its early disasters, and both its population and the complexity and profitability of its economy were increasing. It was also growing more politically contentious, as emerging factions within the province began to compete for the favor of the government. Perhaps the most important dispute involved policy toward the natives. As settlement moved west, further into Indian lands, border conflicts grew increasingly frequent. Much of the tension within English Virginia in the late seventeenth century revolved around how to respond to those conflicts.

Virginia's Westward Expansion

Sir William Berkeley arrived in Virginia in 1642 at the age of thirty-six, appointed governor by King Charles I. With but one interruption he remained in control of the government until the 1670s. Berkeley was popular at first as he sent explorers across the Blue Ridge Mountains to open up the western interior of Virginia. He organized the force that put down the 1644 Indian uprising. The defeated Indians ceded a large area of land to the English, but Berkeley agreed to prohibit white settlement west of a line he negotiated with the tribes.

This attempt to protect Indian territory—like many such attempts later in American history—was a failure from the start, largely because of the rapid growth of the Virginia population. Oliver Cromwell's victory in 1649 in the English Civil War (see p. 48) and the flight of many of his defeated opponents to the colony contributed to what was already a substantial population increase. Between 1640 and 1650, Virginia's population doubled from 8,000 to 16,000. By 1660, it had more than doubled again, to 40,000. As the choice lands along the tidewater became scarce, new arrivals and indentured servants completing their terms or escaping from their masters pressed westward into the piedmont. By 1652, English settlers had established three counties in the territory promised to the Indians. Unsurprisingly, there were frequent clashes between natives and whites.

By the 1660s, Berkeley had become a virtual autocrat in the colony. When the first burgesses were elected in 1619, all men aged seventeen or older were entitled to vote. By 1670, the vote was restricted to landowners, and elections were rare. The same burgesses, loyal and subservient to the governor, remained in office year after year. Each county continued to have only two representatives, even though some of the new counties of the interior contained many more people than the older ones of the tidewater area. Thus the more recent settlers in the "backcountry" were underrepresented or (if living in areas not yet formally organized as counties) not represented at all.

Berkeley's Autocratic Rule

Bacon's Rebellion

In 1676, backcountry unrest and political rivalries combined to create a major conflict. Nathaniel Bacon, a wealthy young graduate of Cambridge University, arrived in Virginia in 1673. He purchased a substantial farm in the west and won a seat on the governor's council. He established himself, in other words, as a member of the backcountry gentry.

But the new and influential western landowners were soon squabbling with the leaders of the tidewater region in the east. They disagreed on many issues, but above all on policies toward the natives. The backcountry settlements were in constant danger of attack from Indians, because many of these settlements were being established on lands reserved for the tribes by treaty. White settlers in western Virginia had long resented the governor's attempts to hold the line of settlement steady so as to avoid antagonizing the natives. That policy was, they believed, an effort by the eastern aristocracy to protect its dominance by holding down the white population in the west. (In reality, the policy was at least as much an effort by Berkeley to protect his own lucrative fur trade with the Indians.)

Backcountry Grievances

Bacon, an aristocratic man with great political ambitions, had additional reasons for unhappiness with Berkeley. He resented his exclusion from the inner circle of the governor's council (the so-called Green Spring group, whose members enjoyed special access to patronage). Bacon also fumed about Berkeley's refusal to allow him a piece of the Indian fur trade. He was developing grievances that made him a natural leader of an opposing faction.

Bloody events thrust him into that role. In 1675, some Doeg Indians—angry about the European intrusions into their lands—raided a western plantation and killed a white servant. Bands of local whites struck back angrily and haphazardly, attacking not only the small Doeg tribe but the powerful Susquehannock as well. The Indians responded with more raids on plantations and killed many more white settlers. As the fighting escalated, Bacon and other concerned landholders—unhappy with the governor's cautious response to their demand for help—defied Berkeley and struck out on their own against the Indians. Berkeley dismissed Bacon from the governor's council and proclaimed him and his men rebels. At that point what had started as an unauthorized assault on the Indians became a military challenge to the colonial government, a conflict known as Bacon's Rebellion. It was the largest and most powerful insurrection against established authority in the history of the colonies, one that would not be surpassed until the Revolution.

Twice, Bacon led his army east to Jamestown. The first time he won a temporary pardon from the governor; the second time, after the governor reneged on the agreement, he burned the city and drove the governor into exile. In the midst of widespread social turmoil throughout the colony, Bacon stood on the verge of taking command of Virginia. Instead, he died suddenly of dysentery; and Berkeley, his position bolstered by the arrival of British troops, soon managed to regain control. In 1677, the Indians (aware of their inability to defeat the white forces militarily) reluctantly signed a new treaty that opened additional lands to white settlement.

Bacon's Rebellion was significant for several reasons. It was part of the continuing struggle to define the boundary between Indian and white lands in Virginia; it showed how unwilling the English settlers were to abide by earlier agreements with the natives, and how unwilling the Indians were to tolerate further white movement into their territory. It revealed the bitterness of the competition between eastern and western landowners. But it also revealed something that Bacon himself had never intended to unleash: the potential for instability in the colony's large population of free, landless men. These men—most of them former indentured servants, propertyless, unemployed, with no real prospects—had formed the bulk of Bacon's constituency during the rebellion. They had become a large, unstable, floating population eager above all for access to land. Bacon had for a time maintained his popularity among them by exploiting their hatred of Indians. Gradually, however, he found himself unintentionally leading a movement that reflected the animosity of these landless men toward the landed gentry of which Bacon himself was a part.

Significance of Bacon's Rebellion

One result was that landed people in both eastern and western Virginia began to recognize a common interest in preventing social unrest from below. That was one of several reasons that they turned increasingly to the African slave trade to fulfill their need for labor. Enslaved blacks might pose dangers too, but the events of 1676 suggested that the perils of importing a large white subordinate class were even greater.

THE GROWTH OF NEW ENGLAND

The first enduring settlement in New England—the second in English America—resulted from the discontent of a congregation of Puritan Separatists in England. For years, Separatists had been periodically imprisoned and even executed for defying the government and the Church of England; some of them, as a result, began to contemplate leaving England altogether in search of freedom to worship as they wished—even though Puritans did not believe in religious freedom for all others.

Religious Repression

Plymouth Plantation

It was illegal to leave England without the consent of the king. In 1608, however, a congregation of Separatists from the hamlet of Scrooby began emigrating quietly, a few at a time, to Leyden, Holland, where they could worship without interference. They were, however, barred from the Dutch craft guilds and had to work at unskilled and poorly paid jobs. They were also troubled by the effects of the tolerant atmosphere of Dutch society, which threatened their dream of a close-knit Christian community as had the repression in England. As a result, some of the Separatists decided to move again, this time across the Atlantic, where they hoped to create the kind of community they wanted and where they could spread "the gospel of the Kingdom of Christ in those remote parts of the world."

Leaders of the Scrooby group obtained permission from the Virginia Company to settle in Virginia. From the king, they received informal assurances that he would "not molest them, provided they carried themselves peaceably." (This was a historic concession by the crown, for it opened English America to settlement not only by the Scrooby group but by other dissenting Protestants.) Several English merchants agreed to advance the necessary funds in exchange for a share in the profits of the settlement at the end of seven years.

The migrating Puritans "knew they were pilgrims" even before they left Holland, their leader and historian, William Bradford, later wrote. In September 1620 they left the port of Plymouth, on the English coast, in the *Mayflower* with thirty-five "saints" (Puritan Separatists) and sixty-seven "strangers" (people who were not full members of the leaders' church) aboard. By the time they sighted land in November, it was too late in the year to go on. Their original destination was probably the mouth of the Hudson River, in what is now New York.

But they found themselves instead on Cape Cod. After exploring the region for a while, they chose a site for their settlement in the area just north of the cape, an area Captain John Smith had named "Plymouth" (after the English port from which the Puritans had sailed) during an exploratory journey some years before. Plymouth lay outside the London Company's territory, and the settlers realized they had no legal basis for settling there.

The Mayflower Compact

As a result, forty-one of the "saints" signed a document, the Mayflower Compact, which established a civil government and proclaimed their allegiance to the king. Then, on December 21, 1620, the Pilgrims stepped ashore at Plymouth Rock.

They settled on cleared land that had once been an Indian village until, three years earlier, a mysterious epidemic—known as "the plague" and probably brought to the region by earlier European explorers—had swept through the region and substantially depopulated it. The Pilgrims' first winter was a difficult one; half the colonists perished from malnutrition, disease, and exposure. But the colony survived.

Like the Spanish and Spanish Portuguese colonists in the southern regions of the Americas, the Pilgrims (and other future English colonists) brought more to the New World than people and ideas. They also created profound changes in the natural landscape of New England. A smallpox epidemic created by English carriers almost eliminated the Indian population in the areas around Plymouth in early 1630s, which transformed the social landscape of the region. The English demand for furs, animal skins, and meat greatly depleted the number of wild animals in the areas around Plymouth, one reason colonists worked so hard to develop stocks of domestic animals—many of them (such as horses, cattle, sheep, and hogs) imported from Europe and never before seen in America. The Pilgrims and later English settlers also introduced new crops (wheat, barley, oats, and others), while incorporating many native foods (among them corn, potatoes, and peas) into their own diets—and eventually exporting them back to England and the rest of Europe. Gradually, colonial society imposed a European pattern onto the American landscape, as the settlers fenced in pastures, meadows, orchards, and fields for cultivation.

The Pilgrims' experience with the Indians was, for a time at least, very different from the experiences of the early English settlers farther south. That was in part because the remaining natives in the region—their numbers thinned by disease—were significantly weaker than their southern neighbors and realized they had to get along with the Europeans. It was also probably because the Pilgrims were less actively hostile to the natives than the colonists in Virginia were. In the end, the survival and growth of the colony depended crucially on the assistance they received from natives. Important Indian

friends—Squanto and Samoset, among others—showed them how to gather seafood, cultivate corn, and hunt local animals. Squanto, a Pawtuxet who

Relations with the Indians

had earlier been captured by an English explorer and taken to Europe, spoke English and was of particular help to the settlers in forming an alliance with the local Wampanoags, under Chief Massasoit. After the first harvest, in 1621, the settlers marked the alliance by inviting the Indians to join them in an October festival, the first Thanksgiving.

But the relationship between the settlers and the local Indians was not happy for long. Thirteen years after the Pilgrims' arrival, a devastating smallpox epidemic—a result of contact with English settlers—wiped out much of the Indian population around Plymouth.

The Pilgrims could not hope to create rich farms on the sandy, marshy soil, and their early fishing efforts produced no profits. In 1622, the military officer Miles Standish, one of the leaders of the colony, established a semimilitary regime to impose discipline on the settlers. Eventually the Pilgrims began to grow enough corn and other crops to provide them with a modest trading surplus. They also developed a small fur trade with the Abenaki Indians of Maine. From time to time new colonists arrived from England, and in a decade the population reached 300.

The people of "Plymouth Plantation," as they called their settlement, chose William Bradford again and again to be their governor. As early as 1621, he persuaded the Council

William Bradford

for New England (the successor to the old Plymouth Company, which had charter rights to the territory) to give them legal permission to live there. He ended the communal labor plan Standish had helped create, distributed land among the families, and thus, as he explained it, made "all hands very industrious." He and a group of fellow "undertakers" took over the colony's debt to its original financiers in England and, with earnings from the fur trade, finally paid it off—even though the financiers had repeatedly cheated them and had failed to send them promised supplies.

The Pilgrims were always a poor community. As late as the 1640s, they had only one plow among them. But they clung to the belief that God had put them in the New World to live as a truly Christian community; and they were, on the whole, content to live their lives in what they considered godly ways.

At times, they spoke of serving as a model for other Christians. Governor Bradford wrote in retrospect: "As one small candle may light a thousand, so the light here kindled hath shone to many, yea in some sort to our whole nation." But the Pilgrims were less committed to grand designs, less concerned about how they were viewed by others, than the Puritans who settled the larger and more ambitious English colonies to their north.

The Massachusetts Bay Experiment

Turbulent events in England in the 1620s (combined with the example of the Plymouth colony) created strong interest in colonization among other groups of Puritans. James I had been creating serious tensions for years between himself and Parliament through his effort to claim the divine right of kings and by his harsh, repressive policies toward the Puritans. The situation worsened after his death in 1625, when he was succeeded by his son, Charles I. By trying to restore Roman Catholicism to England and destroy religious nonconformity, he started the nation down the road that in the 1640s would lead to civil war. The Puritans were particular targets of Charles's policies. Some were imprisoned for their beliefs, and many began to consider the climate of England intolerable. The king's disbanding of Parliament in 1629 (it was not to be recalled until 1640) ensured that there would be no political solution to the Puritans' problems.

In the midst of this political and social turmoil, a group of Puritan merchants began organizing a new enterprise

Massachusetts Bay Company

designed to take advantage of opportunities in America. At first their interest was largely an economic one. They obtained a grant of land in New England for most of the area now comprising Massachusetts and New Hampshire; they acquired a charter from the king (who was evidently unaware that they were Puritans) allowing them to create the Massachusetts Bay Company and to establish a colony in the New World; and they bought equipment and supplies from a defunct fishing and trading company that had attempted (and failed) to establish a profitable enterprise in North America. In 1629, they were ready to dispatch a substantial group of settlers to New England.

Among the members of the Massachusetts Bay Company, however, were a number of Puritans who saw the enterprise as something more than a business venture. They began to consider emigrating themselves and creating a haven for Puritans in New England. Members of this faction met secretly in Cambridge in the summer of 1629 and agreed to buy out the other investors and move en masse to America.

As governor, the new owners of the company chose

John Winthrop

John Winthrop, an affluent, university-educated gentleman with a deep piety and a forceful character. Winthrop had been instrumental in organizing the migration, and he commanded the expedition that sailed for New England in 1630: seventeen ships and 1,000 people (who were, unlike the earlier migrants to Virginia, mostly family groups). It was the largest single migration of its kind in the seventeenth century. Winthrop carried with him the charter of the Massachusetts Bay Company, which meant that the colonists would be responsible to no company officials in England, only to themselves.

COLONIAL CURRENCY This seal was created in 1690 by the Massachusetts Bay Company to validate the paper "bills of credit" with which colonists conducted many financial transactions. Paper money met considerable resistance at first. Many people doubted its value and would not accept it, preferring instead the Spanish silver coins that were in wide circulation at the time. Gradually, however, a shortage of silver required increasing reliance on this and other paper devices. The seal shows an Indian saying "Come over and help us," which represents an English belief in the superiority of white European society. *(Courtesy of the Massachusetts Historical Society)*

The Massachusetts migration quickly produced several different new settlements. The port of Boston, at the mouth of the Charles River, became the company's headquarters and the colony's capital. But in the course of the next decade colonists moved into a number of other new towns in eastern Massachusetts: Charlestown, Newtown (later renamed Cambridge), Roxbury, Dorchester, Watertown, Ipswich, Concord, Sudbury, and others.

The Massachusetts Bay Company soon transformed itself into a colonial government. According to the original company charter, the eight stockholders (or "freemen") were to meet as a general court to choose officers and adopt rules for the corporation. But eventually the definition of "freemen" changed to include all male citizens, not just the stockholders. John Winthrop dominated colonial politics just as he had dominated the original corporation, but after 1634 he and most other officers of the colony had to face election each year.

Unlike the Separatist founders of Plymouth, the founders of Massachusetts had no intention of breaking from the Church of England. Yet if they continued to feel any real attachment to the Anglican establishment, they gave little sign of it. In every town, the community

PORTRAIT OF A BOSTON WOMAN Anne Pollard, a member of the original Winthrop expedition to Boston, was 100 years old when this portrait was painted in 1721. In 1643, thirteen years after her arrival in Massachusetts, she married a Boston innkeeper with whom she had 13 children. After her husband's death in 1679, she continued to manage the tavern on her own. When she died in 1725, at the age of 104, she left 130 direct descendants. The artist who painted this early portrait is unknown, but is assumed to be an American working in the relatively primitive style common in New England before the arrival in 1729 of the first academically trained portraitists from England. *(Courtesy of the Massachusetts Historical Society)*

The Congregational Church church had (in the words of the prominent minister John Cotton) "complete liberty to stand alone," unlike churches in the highly centralized Anglican structure in England. Each congregation chose its own minister and regulated its own affairs. In both Plymouth and Massachusetts, this form of parish organization eventually became known as the Congregational Church.

The Massachusetts Puritans were not grim or joyless, as many observers would later portray them. They were, however, serious and pious people. They strove to lead useful, conscientious lives of thrift and hard work, and they honored material success as evidence of God's favor. "We here enjoy God and Jesus Christ," Winthrop wrote to his wife soon after his arrival; "is this not enough?" He and the other Massachusetts founders believed they were founding a holy commonwealth—a "city upon a hill"—that could serve as a model for the rest of the world.

If Massachusetts was to become a beacon to others, it had first to maintain its own "holiness." Ministers had no formal political power, but they exerted great influence on **A Theocratic Society** church members, who were the only people who could vote or hold office. The government in turn protected the ministers, taxed the people (members and non-members alike) to support the church, and enforced the law requiring attendance at services. Dissidents had no more freedom of worship in America than the Puritans themselves had had in England. Colonial Massachusetts was, in effect, a "theocracy," a society in which the line between the church and the state was hard to see.

Like other new settlements, the Massachusetts Bay colony had early difficulties. During their first winter, an unusually severe one, nearly a third of the colonists died; others left in the spring. But more rapidly than Jamestown or Plymouth, the colony grew and prospered. The Pilgrims and neighboring Indians helped with food and advice. Affluent incoming settlers brought needed tools and other goods, which they exchanged for the cattle, corn, and other produce of the established colonists and the natives. The large number of family groups in the colony (a sharp contrast to the early years at Jamestown) helped ensure a feeling of commitment to the community and a sense of order among the settlers. It also allowed the population to reproduce itself more rapidly. The strong religious and political hierarchy ensured a measure of social stability.

The Expansion of New England

As the population grew, more and more people arrived in Massachusetts who did not accept all the religious tenets of the colony's leaders or who were not Puritan "saints" and hence could not vote. New- **Growing Religious Dissent** comers had a choice of conforming to the religious practices of the colony or leaving. Many left, helping to begin a process that would spread settlement throughout present-day New England and beyond.

The Connecticut Valley, about 100 miles west of the edge of European settlement around Boston, began attracting English families as early as the 1630s. The valley appealed in particular to Thomas Hooker, a minister of Newtown (Cambridge), who defied the Massachusetts government in 1635 and led his congregation through the wilds to establish the town of Hartford. Four years later, the people of Hartford and of two other towns established a colonial government of their own and adopted a constitution known as the Fundamental Orders of Connecticut.

Another Connecticut colony, the project of a Puritan minister and a wealthy merchant from England, grew up

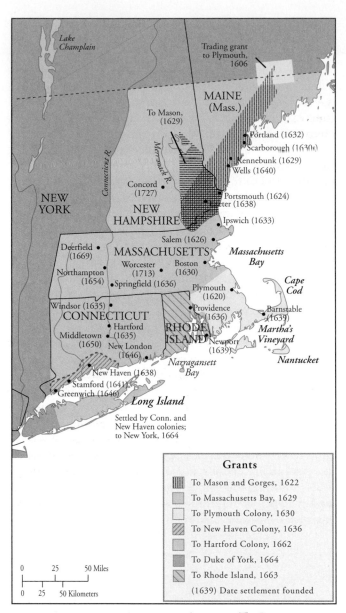

THE GROWTH OF NEW ENGLAND, 1620–1750 The European settlement of New England, as this map reveals, traces its origins primarily to two small settlements on the Atlantic coast. The first was the Pilgrim settlement at Plymouth, which began in 1620 and spread out through Cape Cod, southern Massachusetts, and the islands of Martha's Vineyard and Nantucket. The second, much larger settlement began in Boston in 1630 and spread rapidly through western Massachusetts, north into New Hampshire and Maine, and south into Connecticut. ◆ *Why would the settlers of Massachusetts Bay have expanded so much more rapidly and expansively than those of Plymouth?*

For an interactive version of this map go to www.mhhe.com/brinkley12ch2maps

around New Haven on the Connecticut coast. It reflected impatience with what its founders considered increasing religious laxity in Massachusetts. The Fundamental Articles of New Haven (1639) established a religious government even stricter than that in Boston. New Haven remained independent until 1662, when a royal charter combined it with Hartford to create the colony of Connecticut.

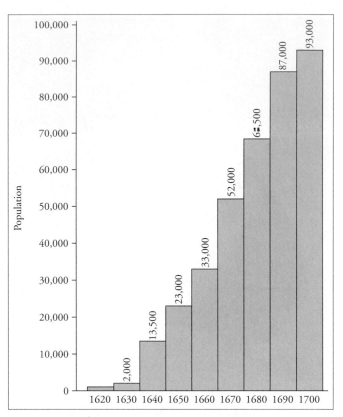

THE NON-INDIAN POPULATION OF NEW ENGLAND, 1620–1700 As in the Chesapeake colonies, the European population of New England grew very rapidly after settlement began in 1620. The most rapid rate of growth, unsurprisingly, came in the first thirty years, when even a modest wave of immigraton could double or triple the small existing population. But the largest numbers of new immigrants arrived between 1650 and 1680. ◆ *What events in England in those years might have led to increased emigration to America in that period?*

Rhode Island had its origins in the religious and political dissent of Roger Williams, an engaging but controversial young minister who lived for a time in Salem, Massachusetts. Even John Winthrop, who considered Williams a heretic, called him a "sweet and amiable" man, and William Bradford described him as "a man godly and zealous." But he was, Bradford added, "very unsettled in judgment." Williams, a confirmed Separatist, argued that the Massachusetts church should abandon all allegiance to the Church of England. More disturbing to the clergy, he called for a complete separation of church and state— to protect the church from the corruption of the secular world. The colonial government, alarmed at this challenge to its spiritual authority, banished him. During the bitter winter of 1635–1636, he took refuge with Narragansett tribesmen; the following spring he bought a tract of land from them and, with a few followers, created the town of Providence on it. Other communities of dissidents followed him to what became Rhode Island, and in 1644 Williams obtained a charter from Parliament permitting him to establish a government.

Roger Williams

ANNE HUTCHINSON PREACHING IN HER HOUSE IN BOSTON
Anne Hutchinson was alarming to many of Boston's religious leaders
not only because she openly challenged the authority of the clergy, but
also because she implicitly challenged norms of female behavior in
Puritan society. *(Bettmann/Corbis)*

Rhode Island's government gave no support to the church
and allowed "liberty in religious concernments." For a
time, it was the only colony in which members of all faiths
(including Jews) could worship without interference.

An even greater challenge to the established order in
Massachusetts Bay emerged in the person of Anne
Hutchinson, an intelligent and charismatic woman from
a substantial Boston family. Hutchinson had come to
Massachusetts with her husband in 1634. She antagonized the leaders of the colony by arguing vehemently
that the members of the Massachusetts clergy who were
not among the "elect"—that is, had not undergone a conversion experience—had no right to spiritual office. Over
time, she claimed that many clergy—among them her
own uninspiring minister—were among the nonelect and
had no right to exercise authority over their congregations. She eventually charged that all the ministers in
Massachusetts—save community leader John Cotton and

| Anne Hutchinson | her own bother-in-law—were |
| | not among the elect. Alongside |

such teachings (which her critics called 'Antinomianism,'
from the Greek meaning 'hostile to the law'), Hutchinson
also created alarm by affronting prevailing assumptions
about the proper role of women in Puritan society. She

was not a retiring, deferential wife and mother, but a
powerful religious figure in her own right.

Hutchinson developed a large following among
women, to whom she offered an active role in religious
affairs. She also attracted support from others (merchants, young men, and dissidents of many sorts) who
resented the oppressive character of the colonial government. As her influence grew the Massachusetts leadership mobilized to stop her. Hutchinson's followers
were numerous and influential enough to prevent
Winthrop's reelection as governor in 1636, but the next
year he returned to office and put her on trial for heresy.
Hutchinson embarrassed her accusers by displaying a
remarkable knowledge of theology; but because she continued to defy clerical authority (and because she
claimed she had herself communicated directly with the
Holy Spirit—a violation of the Puritan belief that the age
of such revelations had passed), she was convicted of
sedition and banished as "a woman not fit for our society." Her unorthodox views had challenged both religious
belief and social order in Puritan Massachusetts. With her
family and some of her followers, she moved to Rhode
Island, and then into New Netherland (later New York),
where in 1643 she died during an Indian uprising.

Alarmed by Hutchinson's heresy, male clergy began to
restrict further the already limited public activities
of women within congregations. As a result, many of
Hutchinson's followers began to migrate out of Massachusetts Bay, especially to New Hampshire and Maine.

Colonies had been established there in 1629 when
two English proprietors, Captain John Mason and Sir
Ferdinando Gorges, had received

	New Hampshire and
a grant from the Council for	Maine
New England and divided it	

along the Piscataqua River to create two separate
provinces. But despite their lavish promotional efforts,
few settlers had moved into these northern regions until
the religious disruptions in Massachusetts Bay. In 1639,
John Wheelwright, a disciple of Anne Hutchinson, led
some of his fellow dissenters to Exeter, New Hampshire.
Other groups—of both dissenting and orthodox
Puritans—soon followed. New Hampshire became a separate colony in 1679. Maine remained a part of Massachusetts until 1820.

Settlers and Natives

Indians were less powerful rivals to the early New
England immigrants than natives were to the English settlers further south. By the mid-1630s, the native population, small to begin with, had been almost extinguished
by the epidemics. The surviving Indians sold much of
their land to the English (a great boost to settlement,
since much of it had already been cleared). Some
natives—known as "praying Indians"—even converted to
Christianity and joined Puritan communities.

Indians provided crucial assistance to the early settlers as they tried to adapt to the new land. Whites learned from the natives about vital local food crops: corn, beans, pumpkins, and potatoes.

Importance of Indian Assistance

They also learned such crucial agricultural techniques as annual burning for fertilization and planting beans to replenish exhausted soil. Natives also served as important trading partners to European immigrants, particularly in the creation of the thriving North American fur trade. They were an important market for such manufactured goods as iron pots, blankets, metal-tipped arrows, eventually guns and rifles, and (often tragically) alcohol. Indeed, commerce with the Indians was responsible for the creation of some of the first great fortunes in British North America and for the emergence of wealthy families who would exercise influence in the colonies (and later the nation) for many generations.

But as in other areas of white settlement, there were also conflicts; and the early peaceful relations between whites and Indians did not last. Tensions soon developed as a result of the white colonists' insatiable appetite for land. The expanding white demand for land was also a result of a change in the colonists' agrarian economy. As wild animals began to disappear from overhunting, colonists began to concentrate more and more on raising domesticated animals: cattle, sheep, hogs, horses, and others. As the herds expanded, so did the colonists' need for new land. As a result, they moved steadily into territories such as the Connecticut Valley where they came into conflict with natives that were more numerous and more powerful than those along the Massachusetts coast.

The character of those conflicts—and the brutality with which whites assaulted their Indian foes—emerged in part out of changing Puritan attitudes toward the natives. At

Shifting Attitudes

first, many white New Englanders had looked at the Indians with a slightly condescending admiration. Before long, however, they came to view them primarily as "heathens" and "savages," and hence as a constant threat to the existence of a godly community in the New World. Some Puritans believed the solution to the Indian "problem" was to "civilize" the natives by converting them to Christianity and European ways, and some English missionaries had modest success in producing converts. One such missionary, John Eliot, even translated the Bible into an Algonquian language. Other Puritans, however, envisioned a harsher "solution": displacing or, if that failed, exterminating the natives.

To the natives, the threat from the English was very direct. European settlers were penetrating deeper and deeper into the interior, seizing land, clearing forests, driving away much of the wild game on which the tribes depended for food. English farmers often let their livestock run wild, and the animals often destroyed natives' crops. Now land and food shortages exacerbated the drastic Indian population decline that had begun as a result of epidemic diseases. There had been more than 100,000 Indians in New England at the beginning of the seventeenth century; by 1675, only 10,000 remained. This decline created despair among New England natives. It drove some Indians to alcoholism and others to conversion to Christianity. But it drove others to war.

The Pequot War, King Philip's War, and the Technology of Battle

The first major conflict came in 1637, when hostilities broke out between English settlers in the Connecticut Valley

The Pequot War

and the Pequot Indians of the region as a result of competition over trade with the Dutch in New Netherland and friction over land. In what became known as the Pequot War, English settlers allied with the Mohegan and Narragansett Indians, (rivals of the Pequots). The greatest savagery in the conflict was the work of the English. In the bloodiest act of the war, white raiders under Captain John Mason marched against a palisaded Pequot stronghold and set it afire. Hundreds of Indians either burned to death in the flaming stockade or were killed as they attempted to escape. Those who survived were hunted down, captured, and sold as slaves. The Pequot tribe was almost wiped out.

The most prolonged and deadly encounter between whites and Indians in the seventeenth century began in 1675, a conflict that the English would remember for generations as King Philip's War. As in the earlier Pequot War in Connecticut, an Indian tribe—in this case the Wampanoags, under the leadership of a chieftain known to the white settlers as King Philip and among his own people as Metacomet—rose up to resist the English. The Wampanoags had not always been hostile to the settlers; indeed, Metacomet's grandfather had once forged an alliance with the English. But by the 1670s, they had become convinced that only armed resistance could protect them from English incursions into their lands and, more immediately, from the efforts by the colonial governments to impose English law on the natives. (A court in Plymouth had recently tried and hanged several Wampanoags for murdering a member of their own tribe.)

For three years, the natives—well organized and armed with guns—terrorized a string of Massachusetts towns, destroying

King Philip's War

twenty of them and causing the deaths of as many as a thousand people (including at least one-sixteenth of the white males in the colony). The war greatly weakened both the society and economy of Massachusetts. But, in 1676, the white settlers fought back and gradually prevailed. They received critical aid from the Mohawks, long-time rivals of the Wampanoags, and guides, spies, and soldiers recruited from among the so-called praying Indians of the region. While white militiamen attacked

A PEQUOT VILLAGE DESTROYED An English artist drew this view of a fortified Pequot village in Connecticut surrounded by English soldiers and their allies from other tribes during the Pequot War in 1637. The invaders massacred more than 600 residents of the settlement. *(Rare Book Division, New York Public Library Astor, Lenox and Tilden Foundations)*

Indian villages and destroyed native food supplies, a group of Mohawks ambushed, shot, and killed Metacomet, then bore his severed head to Boston to present to the colonial leaders. After that, the fragile alliance that Metacomet had managed to forge among local tribes collapsed. Europeans were soon able to crush the uprising. Some Wampanoag leaders were executed; others were sold into slavery in the West Indies. The Wampanoags and their allies, their populations depleted and their natural resources reduced, were now powerless to resist the English.

Yet these victories by the white colonists did not end the danger to their settlements. Other Indians in other tribes survived, and were still capable of attacking English settlements. The New England settlers also faced competition not only from the natives but also from the Dutch and the French, who claimed the territory on which some of the outlying settlements were established. The French, in particular, would pose a constant threat to the English through their alliance with the Algonquins. In later years, they would join forces with Indians in their attacks on the New England frontier.

The character of the Pequot War, King Philip's War, and many other conflicts between natives and settlers in the years that followed was crucially affected by earlier exchanges of technology between the English and the tribes. In particular, the Indians made effective use of a relatively new weapon introduced to New England by Myles Standish and others: the flintlock rifle. It replaced the earlier staple of colonial musketry, the matchlock rifle, which proved too heavy, cumbersome, and inaccurate to

Flintlock Musket

be useful in the kind of combat characteristic of Anglo-Indian struggles. The matchlock had to be steadied on a fixed object and ignited with a match before firing; the flintlock could be held up without support and fired without a match. (Indians using bows and arrows often outmatched settlers using the clumsy matchlocks.)

Many English settlers were slow to give up their cumbersome matchlocks for the lighter flintlocks. But the Indians recognized the advantages of the newer rifles right away and began purchasing them in large quantities as part of their regular trade with the colonists. Despite rules forbidding colonists to instruct natives on how to use and repair the weapons, the natives learned to handle the rifles, and even to repair them, very effectively on their own. They even built a substantial forge for shaping and repairing rifle parts. In King Philip's War, the very high casualties on both sides were a result of the use of these more advanced rifles.

Indians also used more traditional military technologies in their conflicts with the English—especially the construction of forts. The Narragansetts, allies of the Wampanoags in King Philip's War, built an enormous fort in the Great Swamp of Rhode Island in 1675, which became the site of one of the bloodiest battles of the war before English attackers burned it down. After that, a band of Narragansetts set out to build a large stone fort, with the help of a member of the tribe who had learned masonry while working with the English. When English soldiers discovered the stone fort in 1676, after the end of King Philip's War, they killed most of its occupants and destroyed it. In the end, the technological skills of the Indians (both those they borrowed from the

English and those they drew from their own traditions) proved no match for the overwhelming advantages of the English settlers in both numbers and firepower.

THE RESTORATION COLONIES

By the end of the 1630s, English settlers had established six significant colonies in the New World: Virginia, Massachusetts, Maryland, Connecticut, Rhode Island, and New Hampshire. (Maine remained officially part of Massachusetts until after the American Revolution.) But for nearly thirty years after Lord Baltimore received the charter for Maryland in 1632, the English government launched no additional colonial ventures. It was preoccupied with troubles of its own at home.

The English Civil War

England's problems had begun during the rule of James I, who attracted widespread opposition before he died in 1625 but never openly challenged Parliament. His son, Charles I, was not so prudent. After he dissolved Parliament in 1629 and began ruling as an absolute monarch, he steadily alienated a growing number of his subjects—and the members of the powerful Puritan community above all. Finally, desperately in need of money, Charles called Parliament back into session and asked it to levy new taxes. But he antagonized the members by dismissing them twice in two years. In 1642, some of them organized a military challenge to the king, thus launching the English Civil War.

Origins

The conflict between the Cavaliers (the supporters of the king) and the Roundheads (the forces of Parliament, who were mostly Puritans) lasted seven years. Finally, in 1649, the Roundheads defeated the king's forces, captured Charles himself, and—in an action that horrified not only much of continental Europe at the time but also future generations of English men and women—beheaded the monarch. To replace him, they elevated the stern Roundhead leader Oliver Cromwell to the position of "protector," from which he ruled for the next nine years. When Cromwell died in 1658, his son and heir proved unable to maintain his authority. Two years later, King Charles II, son of the beheaded monarch, returned from exile and claimed the throne.

Among the many results of the Stuart Restoration was the resumption of colonization in America. Charles II quickly began to reward faithful courtiers with grants of land in the New World; and in the twenty-five years of his reign, he issued charters for four additional colonies: Carolina, New York, New Jersey, and Pennsylvania. The new colonies were all proprietary ventures (modeled on Maryland rather than on Virginia and Massachusetts), thus exposing an important change in

New Proprietary Colonies

the nature of American settlement. No longer were private companies interested in launching colonies, realizing at last that there were no quick profits to be had in the New World. The goal of the new colonies was not so much quick commercial success as permanent settlements that would provide proprietors with land and power.

The Carolinas

Carolina (a name derived from the Latinate form of "Charles") was, like Maryland, carved in part from the original Virginia grant. Charles II awarded the territory to a group of eight court favorites, all prominent politicians already active in colonial affairs. In successive charters issued in 1663 and 1665, the eight proprietors received joint title to a vast territory stretching south to the Florida peninsula and west to the Pacific Ocean. Like Lord Baltimore, they received almost kingly powers over their grant.

Also like Lord Baltimore, they expected to profit as landlords and land speculators. They reserved large estates for themselves, and they proposed to sell or give away the rest in smaller tracts (using a headright system similar to those in Virginia and Maryland) and to collect annual payments ("quitrents") from the settlers. Although committed Anglicans themselves, they welcomed any settlers they could get. The charter of the colony guaranteed religious freedom to everyone who would worship as a Christian. The proprietors also promised a measure of political freedom; laws were to be made by a representative assembly. With these incentives, they hoped to attract settlers from the existing American colonies and thus to avoid the expense of financing expeditions from England.

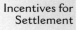

Incentives for Settlement

Their initial efforts failed dismally, and some of the original proprietors gave up. But one man—Anthony Ashley Cooper, soon to become the earl of Shaftesbury—persisted. Cooper convinced his partners to finance migrations to Carolina from England. In the spring of 1670, the first of these expeditions—a party of 300—set out from England. Only 100 people survived the difficult voyage; those who did established a settlement in the Port Royal area of the Carolina coast. Ten years later they founded a city at the junction of the Ashley and Cooper Rivers, which in 1690 became the colonial capital. They called it Charles Town. (It was later renamed Charleston.)

The earl of Shaftesbury, troubled by the instability in England, wanted a planned and well-ordered community. With the aid of the English philosopher John Locke, he drew up the Fundamental Constitution for Carolina in 1669, which created an elaborate system of land distribution and an elaborately designed social order. In fact, however, Carolina developed along lines quite different from the almost utopian vision of Shaftesbury and Locke. For one thing, the

Fundamental Constitution for Carolina

CHARLESTON, SOUTH CAROLINA This unusual map, drawn on deerskin by an Indian chief around 1730, illustrates the close juxtaposition of the ordered English settlement in Charleston, South Carolina, seen on the left, and the more fluid Indian settlements near the town, on the right. *(Getty Images)*

colony was never really united in anything more than name. The northern and southern regions remained both widely separated and socially and economically distinct from one another. The northern settlers were mainly backwoods farmers, isolated from the outside world, scratching out a meager existence through subsistence agriculture. They developed no important aristocracy and for many years imported virtually no African slaves. In the south, fertile lands and the good harbor at Charles Town promoted a more prosperous economy and a more aristocratic society. Settlements grew up rapidly along the Ashley and Cooper Rivers, and colonists established a flourishing trade in corn, lumber, cattle, pork, and (beginning in the 1690s) rice—which was to become the colony's principal commercial crop. Traders from the interior used Charles Town to market furs and hides they had acquired from Indian trading partners; some also marketed Indian slaves, generally natives captured by rival tribes and sold to the white traders.

Southern Carolina very early developed close ties to the large (and now overpopulated) English colony on the island of Barbados. For many years, Barbados was Carolina's most important trading partner. During the first ten years of settlement, most of the new settlers in Carolina were Barbadians, some of whom arrived with large groups of African workers and established themselves quickly as substantial landlords. African slavery had taken root on Barbados earlier than in any of the mainland colonies (see pp. 53–54); and the white Caribbean migrants—tough, uncompromising profit seekers—established a similar slave-based plantation society in Carolina. (The proprietors, four of whom had a financial interest in the African slave trade, also encouraged the importation of Africans.)

For several decades, Carolina remained one of the most unstable English colonies in America. There were tensions between the small farmers of the Albemarle region in the north and the wealthy planters in the south. There were conflicts between the rich Barbadians in southern Carolina and the smaller landowners around them. After Lord Shaftesbury's death, the

North and South Carolina

NEW AMSTERDAM The small Dutch settlement on Manhattan Island, known before 1664 as New Amsterdam, fell to the English in 1664. This painting shows buildings clustered at the southern tip of the island, which remained the center of what became New York City until the nineteenth century. *(Bettmann/Corbis)*

proprietors proved unable to establish order, and in 1719 the colonists seized control of the colony from them. Ten years later, the king divided the region into two royal colonies, North and South Carolina.

New Netherland, New York, and New Jersey

In 1664, one year after he issued the Carolina charter, Charles II granted to his brother James, the duke of York, all the territory lying between the Connecticut and Delaware Rivers. But much of the territory included in the grant was already claimed by the Dutch, who had established substantial settlements at New Amsterdam and other strategic points beginning in 1624.

The emerging conflict between the English and Dutch in America was part of a larger commercial rivalry between the two nations throughout the world. But the English particularly resented the Dutch presence in America, because it served as a wedge between the northern and southern English colonies and because it provided bases for Dutch smugglers evading English customs laws. And so in 1664, an English fleet under the command of Richard Nicolls sailed into

Capture of New Amsterdam

the lightly defended port of New Amsterdam and extracted a surrender from its unpopular Dutch governor, Peter Stuyvesant, who had failed to mobilize resistance to the invasion. Under the Articles of Capitulation, the Dutch colony surrendered to the British in return for assurances that the Dutch settlers would not be displaced. In 1673, the Dutch briefly reconquered New Amsterdam. But they lost it for good in 1674.

James, the duke of York, his title to New Netherland now clear, renamed the colony New York and prepared to govern a colony of extraordinary diversity. New York contained not only Dutch and English, but Scandinavians, Germans, French, Africans (imported as slaves by the Dutch West India Company), and members of several different Indian tribes. There were, of course, many different religious faiths among these groups. James made no effort to impose his own Roman Catholicism on the colony. Like other proprietors before him, he remained in England and delegated powers to a governor and a council. But he provided for no representative assembly, perhaps because a parliament had executed his own father, Charles I. The laws did, however, establish local governments and guarantee religious toleration. Nevertheless, there were immediate tensions over the distribution of power in the colony. The great Dutch "patroons" (large landowners) survived with their economic and political power largely intact. James granted large estates as well to some of his own political supporters in an effort to create a class of influential landowners loyal to him. Power in the colony thus remained widely and unequally dispersed—among wealthy English landlords, Dutch patroons, fur traders (who forged important alliances with the Iroquois), and the duke's political appointees. Like Carolina, New York would for many years be a highly factious society.

It was also a growing and generally prosperous colony. By 1685, when the duke of York ascended the English throne as James II, New York contained approximately 30,000 people, about four times as many as when James had received his grant twenty years before. Most of them still lived within the Hudson Valley, close to the river itself, with the largest settlement at its mouth, in the town of New York (formerly New Amsterdam).

Originally, James's claims in America extended south of the Hudson to the Delaware Valley and beyond. But shortly after receiving his charter, he gave a large portion of that land to a pair of political allies, Sir John Berkeley and Sir George Carteret, both of whom were also Carolina proprietors. Carteret named the territory New Jersey, after the island in the English channel on which he had been born. In 1702, after nearly a decade of political squabbling and economic profitlessness, the proprietors ceded control of the territory back to the crown and New Jersey became a royal colony.

Establishment of New Jersey

Like New York (from which much of the population had come), New Jersey was a place of enormous ethnic and religious diversity. But unlike New York, New Jersey developed no important class of large landowners; most of its residents remained small farmers. Nor did New Jersey (which, unlike New York, had no natural harbor) produce any single important city.

The Quaker Colonies

Pennsylvania, like Massachusetts, was born out of the efforts of dissenting English Protestants to find a home for their own religion and their own distinctive social order. The Society of Friends originated in mid-seventeenth-century England and grew into an important force as a result of the preachings of George Fox, a Nottingham shoemaker, and Margaret Fell. Their followers came to be known as Quakers because Fox urged them to "tremble at the name of the Lord." Unlike the Puritans, Quakers rejected the concepts of predestination and original sin. All people had divinity within themselves (an "Inner Light," which could guide them along the path of righteousness), and all who cultivated that divinity could attain salvation. Also unlike the Puritans, Quakers granted women a position within the church generally equal to that of men. Women and men alike could become preachers and define church doctrine, an equality symbolized by the longtime partnership between Fox and Fell.

The Society of Friends

Of all the Protestant sectarians of the time, the Quakers were the most anarchistic and democratic. They had no church government, only periodic meetings of representatives from congregations. They had no paid clergy, and in their worship they spoke up one by one as the spirit moved them. Disregarding distinctions of

A QUAKER MEETING An anonymous artist painted this view of a Quaker meeting in approximately 1790. Because the Society of Friends (or Quakers) believed that all people were equal in the eyes of God, they appointed no ministers and imposed no formal structure on their religious services. Members of the congregation stood up to speak at will. *(Museum of Fine Arts, Boston, Bequest of Maxim Karolik)*

gender and class, they addressed one another with the terms "thee" and "thou," words then commonly used in other parts of English society only in speaking to servants and social inferiors. And as confirmed pacifists, they refused to fight in wars. The Quakers were unpopular enough in England as a result of these beliefs and practices. They increased their unpopularity by occasionally breaking up other religious groups at worship. Many were jailed.

As a result, like the Puritans before them, the Quakers looked to America for asylum. A few went to New England. But except in Rhode Island, they were greeted there with fines, whippings, and banishment; three men and a woman who refused to leave were actually put to death. Others migrated to northern Carolina, and there became the fastest-growing religious community in the region. They were soon influential in colonial politics. But many Quakers wanted a colony of their own. As a despised sect, they had little chance of getting the necessary royal grant without the aid of someone influential at court. But fortunately for Fox and his followers, a

William Penn

number of wealthy and prominent men had become attracted to the faith. One of them was William Penn—the son of an admiral in the Royal Navy who was a landlord of valuable Irish estates. He had received the gentleman's education expected of a person of his standing, but he resisted his father in being attracted to untraditional religions. Converted to the doctrine of the Inner Light, the younger Penn became an evangelist for Quakerism. With George Fox, he visited the European continent and found Quakers there who, like Quakers in England, longed to emigrate to the New World. He set out to find a place for them to go.

Penn turned his attention first to New Jersey and soon became an owner and proprietor of part of the colony. But in 1681, after the death of his father, Penn inherited his father's Irish lands and also his father's claim to a large debt from the king. Charles II, short of cash, paid the debt with a grant of territory between New York and Maryland—an area larger than England and Wales combined and which (unknown to him) contained more valuable soil and minerals than any other province of

Pennsylvania Founded

English America. Penn would have virtually total authority within the province. At the king's insistence, the territory was named Pennsylvania, after Penn's late father.

Like most proprietors, Penn wanted Pennsylvania to be profitable for him and his family. And so he set out to attract settlers from throughout Europe through informative and honest advertising in several languages. Pennsylvania soon became the best known of all the colonies among ordinary people in England and on the European continent, and also the most cosmopolitan. Settlers flocked to the province from throughout Europe, joining several hundred Swedes and Finns who

had been living in a small trading colony—New Sweden—established in 1638 at the mouth of the Delaware River. But the colony was never profitable for Penn and his descendants. Indeed, Penn himself, near the end of his life, was imprisoned in England for debt and died in poverty in 1718.

Penn was more than a mere real estate promoter, however, and he sought to create in Pennsylvania what he called a holy experiment. In 1682, he sailed to America and personally supervised the laying out of a city between the Delaware and the Schuylkill Rivers, which he named Philadelphia ("Brotherly Love"). With its rectangular streets, like those of Charles Town, Philadelphia helped set the pattern for most later cities in America. Penn believed, as had Roger Williams, that the land belonged to the Indians, and he was careful to see that they were reimbursed for it, as well as to see that they were not debauched by the fur traders' alcohol. Indians respected Penn as an honest white man, and during his lifetime the colony had no major conflicts with the natives. More than any other English colony, Pennsylvania prospered from the outset (even if its proprietor did not), because of Penn's successful recruitment of emigrants, his thoughtful planning, and the region's mild climate and fertile soil.

But the colony was not without conflict. By the late 1690s, some residents of Pennsylvania were beginning to resist the nearly absolute power of the proprietor. Southern residents in particular complained that the government in Philadelphia was unresponsive to their needs. As a result, a substantial opposition emerged to challenge Penn.

Charter of Liberties

Pressure from these groups grew to the point that in 1701, shortly before he departed for England for the last time, Penn agreed to a Charter of Liberties for the colony. The charter established a representative assembly (consisting, alone among the English colonies, of only one house), which greatly limited the authority of the proprietor. The charter also permitted "the lower counties" of the colony to establish their own representative assembly. The three counties did so in 1703 and as a result became, in effect, a separate colony: Delaware—although until the American Revolution, it had the same governor as Pennsylvania.

BORDERLANDS AND MIDDLE GROUNDS

The English colonies clustered along the Atlantic seaboard of North America eventually united, expanded, and became a great nation. But in the seventeenth and early eighteenth centuries, their future was not all clear. In those years, they were small, frail settlements surrounded by other, competing societies and settlements. The British Empire in North America was, in fact, a much smaller and weaker one than the great Spanish Empire to the South, and not, on the surface at least, clearly stronger than the enormous French empire to the North.

The continuing contest for control of North America, and the complex interactions among the diverse peoples populating the continent, were most clearly visible in areas around the borders of English settlement—the Caribbean and along the northern, southern, and western borders of the coastal colonies.

The Caribbean Islands

Throughout the first half of the seventeenth century, the most important destination for English immigrants was not the mainland, but rather the islands of the Caribbean and the northern way station of Bermuda. More than half the English migrants to the New World in those years settled on these islands. The island societies had close ties to English North America from the beginning and influenced the development of the mainland colonies in several ways. But they were also surrounded by, and sometimes imperiled by, outposts of the Spanish Empire.

The English Caribbean

Before the arrival of Europeans, most of the Caribbean islands had substantial native populations—the Arawaks, the Caribs, and the Ciboney. But beginning with Christopher Columbus's first visit in 1492, and accelerating after the Spanish established their first colony on Hispaniola in 1496, the native population was all but wiped out by European epidemics. Indians were never a significant factor in European settlement of the Caribbean. Indeed, by the time significant European settlement of the islands began, many were almost entirely deserted.

Imperial Conflict

The Spanish Empire claimed title to all the islands in the Caribbean, but there was substantial Spanish settlement only on the largest of them: Cuba, Hispaniola, and Puerto Rico. English, French, and Dutch traders began settling on some of the smaller islands early in the sixteenth century, although these weak colonies were always vulnerable to Spanish attack. After Spain and the Netherlands went to war in 1621 (distracting the Spanish navy and leaving the English in the Caribbean relatively unmolested), the pace of English colonization increased. By mid-century, there were several substantial English settlements on the islands, the most important of them on Antigua, St. Kitts, Jamaica, and Barbados. Even so, through the seventeenth century, the English settlements in the Caribbean were the targets of almost constant attacks and invasions by the Spanish, the Portuguese, the French, the Dutch, and the remaining Indians of the region. The world of the Caribbean was a violent and turbulent place.

The Caribbean colonies built their economies on raising crops for export. In the early years, English settlers experimented unsuccessfully with tobacco and cotton. But they soon discovered that the most lucrative crop was sugar, for which there was a substantial and growing market in Europe. Sugar cane could also be distilled into rum, for which there was also a booming market abroad. Within a decade of the introduction of sugar cultivation to the West Indies, planters were devoting almost all of their land to sugar cane. In their appetite for more land for sugar cane, they cut down forests and destroyed the natural habitats of many animals, and greatly reduced the amount of land available for growing food.

Because sugar was a labor-intensive crop, and because the remnant of the native population was too small to provide a work force, English planters quickly found it necessary to import laborers. As in the Chesapeake, they began by bringing indentured servants from England. But the arduous work discouraged white laborers; many found it impossible to adapt to the harsh tropical climate so different from that of England. By mid-century, therefore, the English planters in the Caribbean (like the Spanish colonists who preceded them) were relying more and more

Sugar and Slavery

heavily on an enslaved African work force, which soon substantially outnumbered them.

On Barbados and other islands where a flourishing sugar economy developed, the English planters were a tough, aggressive, and ambitious breed. Some of them grew enormously wealthy; and since their livelihoods depended on their work forces, they expanded and solidified the system of African slavery there remarkably quickly. By the late seventeenth century, there were four times as many African slaves as there were white settlers. By then the West Indies had ceased to be an attractive destination for ordinary English immigrants; most now went to the colonies on the North American mainland instead.

Masters and Slaves in the Caribbean

A small, mostly wealthy white population, and a large African population held in bondage made for a potentially explosive combination. As in other English colonies in the New World in which Africans came to outnumber Europeans, whites in the Caribbean grew fearful of slave revolts. They had good reason, for there were at least seven

Slave Revolts

major slave revolts in the islands, more than the English colonies of North America experienced in their entire history as slave societies. As a result, white planters monitored their labor forces closely and often harshly. Beginning in the 1660s, all the islands enacted legal codes to regulate relations between masters and slaves and to give white people virtually absolute authority over Africans. A master could even murder a slave with virtual impunity.

There was little in either the law or in the character of the economy to compel planters to pay much

MAKING MOLASSES IN BARBADOS African slaves, who constituted the vast majority of the population of the flourishing sugar-producing island of Barbados, work here in a sugar mill grinding sugar cane and then boiling it to produce refined sugar, molasses, and—after a later distillation process not pictured here—rum. *(Arents Collections, Rare Books Division, New York Public Library. Astor, Lenox and Tilden Foundations)*

attention to the welfare of their workers. Many white slaveowners concluded that it was cheaper to buy new slaves periodically than to protect the well-being of those they already owned, and it was not uncommon for masters literally to work their slaves to death. Few African workers survived more than a decade in the brutal Caribbean working environment—they were either sold to planters in North America or died. Even whites, who worked far less hard than did the slaves, often succumbed to the harsh climate; most died before the age of forty—often from tropical diseases to which they had no immunity.

Establishing a stable society and culture was extremely difficult for people living in such harsh and even deadly conditions. Many of the whites were principally interested in getting rich and had no long-term commitment to the islands.

Unstable Societies

Those who could returned to England with their fortunes and left their estates in the hands of overseers. A large proportion of the European settlers were single men, and many of them either died or left at a young age. Those who remained, many of them common white farmers and laborers living in desperate poverty, were too poor to contribute much to the development of the society. With few white women on the islands and little intermarriage between blacks and whites, Europeans in the Caribbean lacked many of the institutions that gave stability to the North American settlements: church, family, community.

Africans in the Caribbean faced even greater difficulties, of course, but they managed to create a world of their own despite the hardships. They started families (although many of them were broken up by death or the slave trade); they sustained African religious and social traditions (and showed little interest in Christianity); and within the rigidly controlled world of the sugar plantations, they established patterns of resistance.

The Caribbean settlements were connected to the North American colonies in many ways. They were an important part of the Atlantic trading world in which many Americans became involved—a

Connection to British North America

source of sugar and rum and a market for goods made in the mainland colonies and in England. They were the principal source of African slaves for the mainland colonies; well over half the slaves in North America came from the islands, not directly from Africa. And because Caribbean planters established an elaborate plantation system earlier than planters in North America, they provided models that many mainland people consciously or

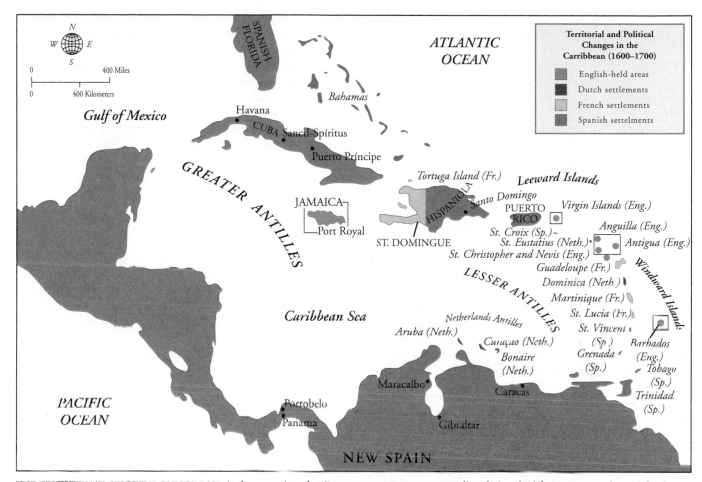

THE SEVENTEENTH-CENTURY CARIBBEAN At the same time that European powers were expanding their colonial presence on the mainland of the American continents, they were also establishing colonies in the islands of the Caribbean. In some cases, these islands were even more important to the Atlantic economy than many of the mainland possessions, particular the large, heavily populated sugar growing islands (among them Jamaica and Barbados), in which the majority of the population consisted of African slaves ◆ *What role did the Caribbean islands play in the spread of slavery in North America?*

unconsciously copied. In the American South, too, planters grew wealthy at the expense of poor whites and, above all, of African slaves.

The Southwestern Borderlands

By the end of the seventeenth century, the Spanish empire had established only a small presence in the regions that became the United States. In Mexico and regions further south, the Spanish had established a sophisticated and impressive empire. Their capital, Mexico City, was the most dazzling metropolis in the Americas. The Spanish residents, well over a million of them, enjoyed much greater prosperity than all but a few English settlers in North America.

But the principal Spanish colonies north of Mexico— Florida, Texas, New Mexico, Arizona, and California— although attracting religious minorities, Catholic missionaries, independent ranchers fleeing the heavy hand of imperial authority, and Spanish troops defending the

northern flank of the empire, remained weak and peripheral parts of the great empire to their south.

Spain's Northern Colonies

New Mexico was the most prosperous and populous of these Spanish outposts. Once the Spanish quelled the Pueblo revolt there in 1680 (see p. 17), they worked effectively with the natives of the region to develop a flourishing agriculture. By the early nineteenth century, New Mexico had a non-Indian population of over 10,000—the largest European settlement west of the Mississippi and north of Mexico—and it was steadily expanding through the region. But New Mexico was prosperous only when compared to other borderlands. Its residents were far less successful than the Spanish in Mexico and other more densely settled regions.

The Spanish began to colonize California once they realized that other Europeans—among them English merchants and French and Russian trappers—were beginning to establish a presence in the region. Formal

Spanish settlement of California began in the 1760s,

California

when the governor of Baja California was ordered to create outposts of the empire further north. Soon a string of missions, forts (or *presidios*), and trading communities were springing up along the Pacific coast, beginning with San Diego and Monterey in 1769 and eventually San Francisco (1776), Los Angeles (1781), and Santa Barbara (1786). As in other areas of European settlement, the arrival of the Spanish in California (and the diseases they imported) had a devastating effect on the native population. Approximately 65,000 at the time of the first Spanish settlements, by 1820 it had declined by two-thirds. As the new settlements spread, however, the Spanish insisted that the remaining natives convert to Catholicism. That explains the centrality of missions in almost all the major Spanish outposts in California. But the Spanish colonists were also intent on creating a prosperous agricultural economy, and they enlisted Indian laborers to help them do so. California's Indians had no choice but to accede to the demands of the Spanish, although there were frequent revolts by natives against the harsh conditions imposed upon them. Already decimated by disease, the tribes now declined further as a result of malnutrition and overwork at the hands of the Spanish missions.

In the late seventeenth and early eighteenth centuries, the Spanish considered the greatest threat to the northern borders of their empire to be the growing ambitions of the French. In the 1680s, French explorers traveled down the Mississippi Valley to the mouth of the river and claimed the lands they had traversed for their king, Louis XIV. They called the territory Louisiana. Fearful of French incursions further west, and unsettled by the nomadic Indians driven into the territory by the French, the Spanish began to fortify their claim to Texas by establishing new forts, missions, and settlements there, including San Fernando (later San Antonio) in 1731. The region that is now Arizona was also becoming increasingly tied to the Spanish empire. Northern Arizona was a part of the New Mexico colony and was governed from Santa Fe. The rest of Arizona (from Phoenix south) was controlled by the Mexican region of Sonora. As in California, much of the impetus for these settlements came from Catholic missionaries (in this case Jesuits), eager to convert the natives. But the missionary project met with little success. Unlike the sedentary Pueblos around Santa Fe, the Arizona natives were nomadic peoples, unlikely to settle down or to Christianize, frequently at war with rival tribes, and—like natives elsewhere—tragically vulnerable to smallpox, measles, and other imported diseases. As in California, epidemics reduced the native population of Arizona by two-thirds in the early eighteenth century.

Although peripheral to the great Spanish Empire to the south, the Spanish colonies in the Southwest nevertheless helped create enduring societies very unlike those being established by the English along the Atlantic seaboard. The Spanish colonies were not committed to displacing the native populations, but rather to enlisting them. They sought to convert them to Catholicism, to recruit them (sometimes forcibly) as agricultural workers, and to cultivate them as trading

Importance of the Spanish Borderlands

partners. The Spanish did not generally consider the natives to be their equals, certainly, and they did not often treat them very well. But neither did they consider them merely as obstacles to their own designs, as many English settlers in the East did.

The Southeast Borderlands

A more direct challenge to English ambitions in North America was the Spanish presence in the southeastern areas of what is now the United States. After the establishment of the Spanish claim to Florida in the 1560s (see p. 16), missionaries and traders began moving northward into Georgia and westward into what is now known as the panhandle, and some ambitious Spaniards began to dream of expanding their empire still further north, into what became the Carolinas, and perhaps beyond. The founding of Jamestown in 1607 replaced those dreams with fears. The English colonies, they believed, could threaten their existing settlements in Florida and Georgia. As a result, the Spanish built forts in both regions to defend themselves against the slowly increasing English presence there. Throughout the eighteenth century, the area between the Carolinas and Florida was the site of continuing tension, and frequent conflict, between the Spanish and the English—and, to a lesser degree, between the Spanish and the French, who were threatening their northwestern borders with settlements in Louisiana and in what is now Alabama.

There was no formal war between England and Spain in these years, but that did not dampen the hostilities in the Southeast. English pirates continually harassed the Spanish settlements and, in 1668, actually sacked St. Augustine. Both sides in this conflict

Hostilities in the Southeast

sought to make use of the native tribes. The English encouraged Indians in Florida to rise up against the Spanish missions. The Spanish, for their part, offered freedom to African slaves owned by Carolina settlers if they agreed to convert to Catholicism. About 100 Africans accepted the offer, and the Spanish later organized some of them into a military regiment to defend the northern border of New Spain. The English correctly viewed the Spanish recruitment of their slaves as an effort to undermine their economy. By the early eighteenth century, the constant fighting in the region had driven almost all the Spanish settlers out of Florida. The Spanish presence was almost entirely confined to St. Augustine on the Atlantic coast and Pensacola on the Gulf Coast, and to the modest colonies that surrounded the forts there. Because they were so few and so weak, they came to rely—far more than most British did—on natives and Africans and intermarried frequently with them.

Eventually, after more than a century of conflict in the southeastern borderlands, the English prevailed—acquiring Florida in the aftermath of the Seven Years' War (known in America as the French and Indian war; see pp. 105–107) and rapidly populating it with settlers from their colonies to the North. Before that point, however, protecting the southern boundary of the British empire in North America was a continual concern to the English and contributed in crucial ways to the founding of the colony of Georgia.

The Founding of Georgia

Georgia was unique in its origins. Its founders were a group of unpaid trustees led by General James Oglethorpe, a member of Parliament and military hero. They were interested in economic success, but they were

James Oglethorpe's Vision

driven primarily by military and philanthropic motives. They wanted to erect a military barrier against the Spanish lands on the southern border of English America, and they wanted to provide a refuge for the impoverished, a place where English men and women without prospects at home could begin anew.

The need for a military buffer between South Carolina and the Spanish settlements in Florida was particularly urgent in the first years of the eighteenth century. In a 1676 treaty, Spain had recognized England's title to lands already occupied by English settlers. But conflict between the two colonizing powers had continued. In 1686, a force of Indians and Creoles from Florida, directed by Spanish agents, attacked and destroyed an outlying South Carolina settlement south of the treaty line. And when hostilities broke out again between Spain and England in 1701 (known in England as Queen Anne's War and on the continent as the War of the Spanish Succession), the fighting renewed in America as well.

Oglethorpe, himself a veteran of Queen Anne's war, was keenly aware of the military advantages of an English colony south of the Carolinas. Yet his interest in settlement rested even more on his philanthropic commitments. As head of a parliamentary committee investigating English prisons, he had grown appalled by the plight of honest debtors rotting in confinement. Such prisoners, and other poor people in danger of succumbing to a similar fate, could, he believed, become the farmer-soldiers of the new colony in America.

In 1732, King George II granted Oglethorpe and his fellow trustees control of the land between the Savannah and Altamaha Rivers. Their colonization policies reflected the vital military purposes of the colony. They limited the size of landholdings to make the settlement compact and easier to defend against Spanish and Indian attacks. They excluded Africans, free or slave; Oglethorpe feared slave labor would produce internal revolts, and that disaffected slaves might turn to the Spanish

Georgia's Military Rationale

as allies. The trustees prohibited rum (both because Oglethorpe disapproved of it on moral grounds and because the trustees feared its effects on the natives). They strictly regulated trade with the Indians, again to limit the possibility of wartime insurrection. They also excluded Catholics for fear they might collude with their coreligionists in the Spanish colonies to the south.

Oglethorpe himself led the first colonial expedition to Georgia, which built a fortified town at the mouth of the Savannah River in 1733 and later constructed additional forts south of the Altamaha. In the end, only a few debtors were released from jail and sent to Georgia. Instead, the trustees brought hundreds of impoverished tradesmen and artisans from England and Scotland and many religious refugees from Switzerland and Germany. Among the immigrants was a small group of Jews. English settlers made up a lower proportion of the European population of Georgia than of any other English colony.

The strict rules governing life in the new colony stifled its early development and ensured the failure of Oglethorpe's vision. Settlers in Georgia—many of whom were engaged in labor-intensive agriculture—needed a work force as much as those in other southern colonies. Almost from the start they began demanding the right to buy slaves. Some opposed the restrictions on the size of individual property holdings. Many resented the nearly absolute political power of Oglethorpe and the trustees. As a result, newcomers to the region generally preferred to settle in South Carolina, where there were fewer restrictive laws.

Oglethorpe (whom some residents of Georgia began calling "our perpetual dictator") at first bitterly resisted the demands of the settlers for social and political reform. Over time, however, he wearied of the conflict in the colony and grew frustrated at its failure to grow. He also suffered military disappointments, such as a 1740 assault on the Spanish outpost at St. Augustine, Florida, which ended in failure. Oglethorpe, now disillusioned with his American venture, began to loosen his grip.

Transformation of Georgia

Even before the 1740 defeat, the trustees had removed the limitation on individual landholdings. In 1750, they removed the ban on slavery. A year later they ended the prohibition of rum and returned control of the colony to the king, who immediately permitted the summoning of a representative assembly. Georgia continued to grow more slowly than the other southern colonies, but in other ways it now developed along lines roughly similar to those of South Carolina. By 1770, there were over 20,000 non-Indian residents of the colony, nearly half of them African slaves.

Native Americans and "The Middle Ground"

For many generations, historians chronicling the westward movement of European settlement in North America incorporated Native Americans into the story largely as weak and inconvenient obstacles swept aside by the inevitable progress of "civilization." Indians were presented either as murderous savages or as relatively docile allies of white people, but rarely as important actors of their own. Francis Parkman, the great nineteenth-century American historian, described Indians as a civilization "crushed" and "scorned" by the march of European powers in the New World. Many subsequent historians departed little from his assessment.

In more recent years, historians have challenged this traditional view by examining how white civilization victimized the tribes. Gary Nash's *Red, White, and Black* (1974) was one of the first important presentations of

this approach, and Ramon Guttierez's *When Jesus Came, the Corn Mothers Went* (1991) was a more recent contribution. They, and other scholars, rejected the optimistic, progressive view of white triumph over adversity and presented, instead, a picture of white brutality and futile Indian resistance, ending in defeat.

More recently, however, a new view of the relationship between the peoples of the Old and New Worlds has emerged. It sees Native Americans and Euro-Americans as uneasy partners in the shaping of a new society in which, for a time at least, both were a vital part. Richard White's influential 1991 book, *The Middle Ground,* was among the first important statements of this view. White examined the culture of the Great Lakes Region in the eighteenth century, in which Algonquin Indians created a series of complex trading and political relationships with

French, English, and American settlers and travelers in the region. In this "borderland" between the growing European settlements in the East and the still largely intact Indian civilizations further west, a new kind of hybrid society emerged in which many cultures intermingled. James Merrell's *Into the American Woods* (1999) contributed further to this new view of collaboration by examining the world of negotiators and go-betweens along the western Pennsylvania frontier in the seventeenth and eighteenth centuries. Like White, he emphasized the complicated blend of European and Native American diplomatic rituals that allowed both groups to conduct business, make treaties, and keep the peace.

Daniel Richter extended the idea of a "middle ground" further in two important books: *The Ordeal of the Longhouse* (1992) and *Facing East from*

Middle Grounds

The struggle for the North American continent was, of course, not just one among competing European empires. It was also a contest between the new European immigrants and the native populations.

In some parts of the British empire—Virginia and New England, for example—English settlers fairly quickly established their dominance, subjugating and displacing most natives until they had established societies that were dominated almost entirely by Europeans. But elsewhere the balance of power remained far more precarious. Along the western borders of English settlement, in particular, Europeans and Indians lived together in regions in which neither side was able to establish clear dominance. In these "middle grounds," as they have been called, the two populations—despite frequent conflicts—carved out ways of living together, with each side making concessions to the other. Here the Europeans found themselves obliged to adapt to tribal expectations at least as much as the Indians had to adapt to European ones.

To the Indians, the European migrants were both menacing and appealing. They feared the power of these strange people: their guns, their rifles, their forts. But they also wanted the French and British settlers to behave like "fathers"—to help them mediate their own internal disputes, to offer them gifts, to help them moderate their conflicts. Europeans came from a world in

Conflict and Accommodation

which the formal institutional and military power of a nation or empire governed relationships between societies. But the natives had no understanding of the modern notion of a "nation" and thought much more in terms of ceremony and kinship. But gradually, Europeans learned to fulfill at least some of their expectations.

In the seventeenth century, before many English settlers had entered the interior, the French were particularly adept at creating mutually beneficial relationships with the tribes. They welcomed the chance to form close relationships with—even to marry within—the tribes. They also recognized the importance of treating tribal chiefs with respect and channeling gifts and tributes through them. But by the mid-eighteenth century, French influence in the interior was in decline, and British settlers gradually became the dominant European group in the "middle grounds." It took the British a considerable time to learn the lessons that the French had long ago absorbed—that simple commands and raw force were much less effective in creating a workable relationship with the tribes than were gifts and ceremonies and mediation. Eventually they did so, and in large western regions—especially those around the Great Lakes—they established a precarious peace with the tribes that lasted for several decades.

Mutually Beneficial Relations

But as the British (and after 1776) American presence in the region grew, the balance of power between

(Rare Book Division, New York Public Library, Astor, Lenox and Tilden Foundations)

Indian Country (2001). Richter demonstrates that the Iroquois Confederacy was an active participant in the power relationships in the Hudson River basin, and in his later book, he tells the story of European colonization from the Native American perspective, revealing how western myths of "first contact" such as the story of John Smith and Pocahantas look entirely different when seen through the eyes of Native Americans, who remained in many ways the more powerful of the two societies in the seventeenth century.

How did these important collaborations collapse? What happened to the "middle ground"? Over time, the delicate partnerships along the frontiers of white settlement gave way to the sheer numbers of Europeans (and in some places Africans) who moved westward. Joyce Chaplin's *Subject Matter* (2001) argues as well that Old World Americans at first admired the natives as a kind of natural nobility until European diseases ravaged the tribes, helping to strengthen the sense of superiority among Europeans that had been a part of their view of Indians from the beginning. Jill Lepore's *The Name of War* (1998) describes how the violence of King Philip's War in seventeenth-century New England helped transform English views of the tribes both because of the white victory over the Indians, and because of their success in turning this victory into a rationale for the moral superiority of Europeans (who, in reality, had used as much "savagery" against the natives as the natives had used against them) by portraying the Indians as brutal, uncivilized people. As the pressures of white settlement grew, as the Indian populations weakened as a result of disease and war, and as the relationship between the tribes and the European settlers grew more and more unequal, the cultural "middle ground" that for many decades characterized much of the contact between the Old and New Worlds gradually disappeared. By the time historians began seriously chronicling this story in the late nineteenth century, the Indian tribes had indeed become the defeated, helpless "obstacles" that they portrayed. But for generations before, the relationship between white Americans and Native Americans was a much less unequal one than it later became.

Europeans and natives shifted. Newer settlers had difficulty adapting to the complex rituals of gift-giving and mediation that the earlier migrants had developed. The stability of the relationship between the Indians and whites deteriorated. By the early nineteenth century, the "middle ground" had collapsed, replaced by a European world in which Indians were ruthlessly subjugated and eventually removed. Nevertheless, it is important to recognize that for a considerable period of early American history, the story of the relationship between whites and Indians was not simply a story of conquest and subjugation, but also—in some regions—a story of a difficult but stable accommodation and mutual adaptation. The Indians were not simply victims in the story of the growth of European settlement in North America. They were also important actors, sometimes obstructing and sometimes facilitating the development of the new societies.

The Shifting Balance

THE EVOLUTION OF THE BRITISH EMPIRE

The English colonies in America had originated as quite separate projects, and for the most part they grew up independent of one another. But by the mid-seventeenth century, the growing commercial success of the colonial ventures was producing pressure in England for a more rational, uniform structure to the empire.

The Drive for Reorganization

Imperial reorganization, many people in England claimed, would increase the profitability of the colonies and the power of the English government to supervise them. Above all, it would contribute to the success of the mercantile system, the foundation of the English economy. Colonies would provide a market for England's manufactured goods and a source for raw materials it could not produce at home, thus increasing the total wealth of the nation. But for the new possessions truly to promote mercantilist goals, England would have to exclude foreigners (as Spain had done) from its colonial trade. According to mercantilist theory, any wealth flowing to another nation could come only at the expense of England itself. Hence the British government sought to monopolize trade relations with its colonies.

Mercantilism

In theory, the mercantile system offered benefits to the colonies as well by providing them with a ready market for the raw materials they produced and a source for the manufactured goods they did not. But some colonial goods were not suitable for export to England, which itself produced wheat, flour, and fish and had no interest in obtaining them from America. Colonists also found it more profitable at times to trade with the Spanish, French, or Dutch even in goods that England did import. Thus, a considerable trade soon developed between the English colonies and non-English markets.

SAVANNAH IN 1734 This early view of the English settlement at Savannah by an English artist shows the intensely orderly character of Georgia in the early moments of European settlement there. As the colony grew, its residents gradually abandoned the rigid plan created by Georgia's founders. *(I.N. Phelps Stokes Collection of American Historical Prints, New York Public Library, Astor, Lenox and Tilden Foundations)*

For a time, the English government made no serious efforts to restrict this challenge to the principles of mercantilism, but gradually it began passing laws to regulate colonial trade. During Oliver Cromwell's "Protectorate," in 1650 and 1651, Parliament passed laws to keep Dutch ships out of the English colonies. After the Restoration, the government of Charles II adopted three Navigation Acts designed to regulate colonial commerce even more strictly. The first of them, in 1660, closed the colonies to all trade except that carried in English ships. This law also required the colonists to export certain items, among them tobacco, only to England or English possessions. The second act, in 1663, provided that all goods being shipped from Europe to the colonies had to pass through England on the way; that would make it possible for England to tax them. The third act, in 1673, was a response to the widespread evasion of the first two laws by the colonial shippers, who frequently left port claiming to be heading for another English colony but then sailed to a foreign port. It imposed duties on the coastal trade among the English colonies,

The Navigation Acts

and it provided for the appointment of customs officials to enforce the Navigation Acts. These acts formed the legal basis of England's mercantile system in America for a century.

The system created by the Navigation Acts had obvious advantages for England. But it had some advantages for the colonists as well. By restricting all trade to British ships, the laws encouraged the colonists (who were themselves legally British subjects) to create an important shipbuilding industry of their own. And because the English wanted to import as many goods as possible from their own colonies (as opposed to importing them from other, rival nations), they encouraged—and at times subsidized—the development of American production of goods they needed, among them iron, silk, and lumber. Despite the bitter complaints the laws provoked in America in the late seventeenth century, and the even more bitter conflicts they would help to provoke decades later, the system of the Navigation Acts served the interests of the British and the Americans alike reasonably well through most of the eighteenth century.

The Dominion of New England

Enforcement of the Navigation Acts required not only the stationing of customs officials in America, but the establishment of an agency in England to oversee colonial affairs. In 1679, Charles II attempted to increase his control over Massachusetts (which behaved at times as if its leaders considered it an independent nation) by stripping the colony of its authority over New Hampshire and chartering a separate, royal colony there whose governor he would himself appoint. Five years later, after the Massachusetts General Court defied instructions from Parliament to enforce the Navigation Acts, Charles revoked the Massachusetts corporate charter and made it a royal colony.

Charles II's brother and successor, James II, who came to the throne in 1685, went much further. In 1686, he created a single Dominion of New England, which combined the government of Massachusetts with the governments of the rest of the New England colonies and, in 1688, with those of New York and New Jersey as well. He eliminated the existing assemblies within the new Dominion and appointed a single governor, Sir Edmund Andros, to supervise the entire region from Boston. Andros was an able administrator but a stern and tactless man; his rigid enforcement of the Navigation Acts, his brusque dismissal of the colonists' claims to the "rights of Englishmen," and his crude and arbitrary tactics made him quickly and thoroughly unpopular. He was particularly despised in Massachusetts, where he tried to strengthen the Anglican Church.

Sir Edmund Andros

The "Glorious Revolution"

James II was not only losing friends in America; he was making powerful enemies in England by attempting to exercise autocratic control over Parliament and the courts. He was also appointing his fellow Catholics to high office, inspiring fears that he would try to reestablish Catholicism as England's official religion. By 1688, his popular support had all but vanished.

Until 1688, James's heirs were two daughters—Mary and Anne—both of whom were Protestant. But in that year the king had a son and made clear that the boy would be raised a Catholic. Some members of Parliament were so alarmed that they invited the king's daughter Mary and her husband, William of Orange, ruler of the Netherlands and Protestant champion of Europe, to assume the throne together. When William and Mary arrived in England with a small army, James II (perhaps remembering what had happened to his father, Charles I) offered no resistance and fled to France. As a result of this bloodless coup, which the English called "the Glorious Revolution," William and Mary became joint sovereigns.

When Bostonians heard of the overthrow of James II, they moved quickly to unseat his unpopular viceroy in New England. Andros managed to escape an angry mob, but he was arrested and imprisoned as he sought to flee the city dressed as a woman. The new sovereigns in England chose not to contest the toppling of Andros and quickly acquiesced in what the colonists had, in effect, already done: abolishing the Dominion of New England and restoring separate colonial governments. They did not, however, accede to all the colonists' desires. In 1691, they combined Massachusetts with Plymouth and made it a royal colony. The new charter restored the General Court, but it gave the crown the right to appoint the governor. It also replaced church membership with property ownership as the basis for voting and officeholding and required the Puritan leaders of the colony to tolerate Anglican worship.

End of the Dominion

Andros had been governing New York through a lieutenant governor, Captain Francis Nicholson, who enjoyed the support of the wealthy merchants and fur traders of the province—the same groups who had dominated the colony for years. Other, less favored colonists—farmers, mechanics, small traders, and shopkeepers—had a long accumulation of grievances against both Nicholson and his allies. The leader of the New York dissidents was Jacob Leisler, a German immigrant and a prosperous merchant who had married into a prominent Dutch family but had never won acceptance as one of the colony's ruling class. Much like Nathaniel Bacon in Virginia, the ambitious Leisler resented his exclusion and eagerly grasped the opportunity to challenge the colonial elite. In May 1689, when news of the Glorious Revolution in England and the fall of Andros in Boston reached New York, Leisler raised a militia, captured the city fort, drove Nicholson into exile, and proclaimed himself the new head of government in New York. For two years, he tried in vain to stabilize his power in the colony amid fierce factional rivalry. In 1691, when William and Mary appointed a new governor, Leisler briefly resisted this challenge to his authority. Although he soon yielded, his hesitation allowed his many political enemies to charge him with treason. He and one of his sons-in-law were hanged, drawn, and quartered. Fierce rivalry between what became known as the "Leislerians" and the "anti-Leislerians" dominated the politics of New York for many years thereafter.

In Maryland, many people erroneously assumed when they heard news of the Glorious Revolution that their proprietor, the Catholic Lord Baltimore, who was living in England, had sided with the Catholic James II and opposed William and Mary. So in 1689, an old opponent of the proprietor's government, John Coode, started a new revolt which drove out Lord Baltimore's officials in the name of Protestantism. Through an elected convention, his supporters chose a committee to run the government and petitioned the crown for

John Coode's Rebellion

a charter as a royal colony. In 1691, William and Mary complied, stripping the proprietor of his authority. The colonial assembly established the Church of England as the colony's official religion and forbade Catholics to hold public office, to vote, or even to practice their religion in public. Maryland became a proprietary colony again in 1715, but only after the fifth Lord Baltimore joined the Anglican Church.

As a result of the Glorious Revolution, the colonies revived their representative assemblies and successfully thwarted the plan for colonial unification. In the process, they legitimized the idea that the colonists had some rights within the empire, that the English government needed to consider their views in making policies that affected them. But the Glorious Revolution in America was not, as many Americans later came to believe, a clear demonstration of American resolve to govern itself or a clear victory for colonial self-rule. In New York and Maryland, in particular, the uprisings had more to do with local factional and religious divisions than with any larger vision of the nature of the empire. And while the insurgencies did succeed in eliminating the short-lived Dominion of New England, their ultimate results were governments that increased the crown's potential authority in many ways. As the first century of English settlement in America came to its end and as colonists celebrated their victories over arbitrary British rule, they were in fact becoming more a part of the imperial system than ever before.

CONCLUSION

The English colonization of North America was part of a larger effort by several European nations to expand the reach of their increasingly commercial societies. Indeed, for many years, the British empire in America was among the smallest and weakest of the imperial ventures there, overshadowed by the French to the North and the Spanish to the South.

In the British colonies along the Atlantic seaboard, new agricultural and commercial societies gradually emerged—in the South centered on the cultivation of tobacco and cotton, and reliant on slave labor; and in the northern colonies centered on more traditional food crops and based mostly on free labor. Substantial trading centers emerged in such cities as Boston, New York, Philadelphia, and Charleston, and a growing proportion of the population became prosperous and settled in these increasingly complex communities. By the early eighteenth century, English settlement had spread from northern New England (in what is now Maine) south into Georgia.

But this growing British empire coexisted with, and often found itself in conflict with, the presence of other Europeans—most notably the Spanish and the French—in other areas of North America. In these borderlands, societies did not assume the settled, prosperous form they were taking in the Tidewater and New England. They were raw, sparsely populated settlements in which Europeans, including over time increasing numbers of English, had to learn to accomodate not only one another but also the still-substantial Indian tribes with whom they shared these interior lands. By the middle of the eighteenth century, there was a significant European presence across a broad swath of North America—from Florida to Maine, and from Texas to Mexico to California—only a relatively small part of it controlled by the British. But changes were underway within the British empire that would soon lead to its dominance through a much larger area of North America.

INTERACTIVE LEARNING

The *Primary Source Investigator CD-ROM* offers the following materials related to this chapter:

- Interactive maps: **The Atlantic World** (M68) and **Growth of Colonies** (M3).

- Documents, images, and maps related to the English colonization of North America, the borderlands, and the meeting of cultures. Highlights include letters and documents relating to the peace resulting from the marriage of Pocahontas to John Rolfe, and the eventual breakdown of that peace; early materials related to the origins of slavery in America, including a document that presents one of the earliest restrictive slave codes in the British colonies; and images of an early slave trading fort on the coast of West Africa.

 Online Learning Center (www.mhhe.com/brinkley12)

For quizzes, Internet resources, references to additional books and films, and more, consult this book's Online Learning Center.

FOR FURTHER REFERENCE

William Cronon, *Changes in the Land: Indians, Colonists, and the Ecology of New England* (1983) examines the social and environmental effects of English settlement in colonial America. Richard White, *The Middle Ground: Indians, Empires, and Republics in the Great Lakes Region, 1650–1815* (1991) is an important study of the accommodations that Indians and early European settlers made in the continental interior. James H. Merrell, *The Indians' New World* (1991) and *Into the American Woods: Negotiators on the Pennsylvania Frontier* (1999) are among the best examinations of the impact of European settlement on eastern tribes. Perry Miller, *The New England Mind: From Colony to Province* (1953) is a classic exposition of the Puritan intellectual milieu. David Hall, *Worlds of Wonder, Days of Judgment* (1990) is a good, recent counterpoint to Miller. George Marsden, *Jonathan Edwards: A Life* is an important biography of one of the most influential religious leaders of the colonial era. Michael Kammen, *Colonial New York* (1975) illuminates the diversity and pluralism of New York under the Dutch and the English. Russell Shorto, *The Island at the Center of the World* (2003) is a portrait of Dutch Manhattan. Edmund Morgan, *American Slavery, American Freedom* (1975) is a compelling narrative of political and social development in early Virginia. Peter Wood, *Black Majority* (1974) describes the early importance of slavery in the founding of South Carolina. Richard S. Dunn, *Sugar and Slaves: The Rise of the Planter Class in the English West Indies, 1624–1713* (1972) is important for understanding the origins of British colonial slavery. David J. Weber, *The Spanish Frontier in North America* (1992) and James C. Brooks, *Captains and Cousins: Slavery, Kinship, and Community in the Southwest Borderlands* (2002) examine the northern peripheries of the Spanish empire.

DR. WILLIAM GLEASON The American artist Winthrop Chandler painted this image of a doctor examining a female patient in 1780. The doctor obviously considers it inappropriate to view a woman lying in bed, so he takes her pulse as she slips her hand through the curtain obscuring her. *(Ohio State Historical Society)*

SIGNIFICANT EVENTS

1636 ▶ Harvard College founded in Massachusetts

1640 ▶ Instability in tobacco markets begins

1647 ▶ Massachusetts law requires a public school in every town

1650 ▶ Population of New England begins to grow by natural increase

1662 ▶ Halfway Covenant established in New England

1670s ▶ Flow of indentured servants declines

▶ Slave traders begin importing slaves directly from Africa to North America

1685 ▶ Edict of Nantes revoked in France; Huguenots begin migrating to North America

1690s ▶ Rice production becomes central to South Carolina economy

▶ Slave trade expands as prices decline

CHAPTER 3

Society and Culture in Provincial America

The British colonies were, most people in both England and America believed, outposts of the British world. And it is true that as the colonies grew and became more prosperous, they also became more English. The colonists adopted the tastes, styles, and customs of England, bought goods made in England, read books and pamphlets published in England, and modeled most of their political, cultural, and educational institutions on their English equivalents. Some of the early settlers had come to America to escape what they considered English tyranny. But by the early eighteenth century, many, perhaps most, colonists considered themselves Englishmen just as much as the men and women in England itself did.

At the same time, however, life in the colonies was diverging in many ways from that in England simply by the nature of the New World. The physical environment was very different—vaster

Diverging Societies

and less tamed. The population was more diverse as well. Beginning with the Dutch settlements in New York, the area that would become the United States was a magnet for immigrants from many lands other than England: Scotland, Ireland, the European continent, as well as migrants from the Spanish and French empires already established in America. And beginning with the first importation of slaves into Virginia, English North America became the destination for thousands of forcibly transplanted Africans. At least equally important, Europeans and Africans were interacting constantly with a native population that for many years outnumbered them. Despite the efforts of the colonists to isolate themselves from Indian society and create a culture all their own, the European and Native American worlds could not remain entirely separate.

To the degree that the colonists emulated English society, they were becoming more and more like one another. To the degree that they were shaped by the character of their own regions, they were becoming more and more diverse. Indeed, the pattern of society in some areas of North America resembled that of other areas scarcely at all. Although Americans would ultimately discover that they had enough in common to join together to form a single nation, these regional differences continued to affect their society well beyond the colonial period.

1691 ▶ Official toleration of Catholics ends in Maryland

1692 ▶ Witchcraft trials begin in Salem

1693 ▶ College of William and Mary founded in Virginia

1697 ▶ Royal African Company monopoly of slave trade broken; slave importations begin to increase

1701 ▶ Yale College founded in Connecticut

1708–1709 ▶ First major migration of Palatinate Germans to North America begins

1710 ▶ Major Scotch-Irish migrations to North America begin

▶ German-Swiss establish settlements in North Carolina

1720 ▶ Cotton Mather initiates smallpox inoculations in Massachusetts

1734 ▶ Great Awakening begins in Massachusetts

▶ Peter Zenger tried in New York

1739 ▶ George Whitefield arrives in North America

▶ Great Awakening intensifies

▶ Stono slave rebellion in South Carolina

1740s ▶ Indigo production begins in South Carolina

1746 ▶ College of New Jersey founded at Princeton

1754 ▶ King's College (later Columbia University) founded in New York

1755 ▶ Academy and College of Philadelphia (later University of Pennsylvania) founded

1764 ▶ Major ironworks established in New Jersey

THE COLONIAL POPULATION

Not until long after the beginning of European colonization did Europeans and Africans in North America outnumber the native population. But after uncertain

Immigration and Natural Increase

beginnings at Jamestown and Plymouth, the nonnative population grew rapidly and substantially, through continued immigration and through natural increase, until by the late seventeenth century Europeans and Africans became the dominant population groups along the Atlantic coast.

A few of the early English settlers were members of the upper classes—usually the younger sons of the lesser gentry, men who stood to inherit no land at home and aspired to establish estates for themselves in America. For the most part, however, the early English population was very unaristocratic. It included some members of the emerging middle class, businessmen who migrated to America for religious or commercial reasons, or (like John Winthrop) both. But the dominant element was English laborers. Some came to the New World independently. The religious dissenters who formed the bulk of the population of early New England, for example, were men and women of modest means who arranged their own passage, brought their families with them, and established themselves immediately on their own land. But in the Chesapeake, at least three-fourths of the immigrants in the seventeenth century arrived as indentured servants.

Indentured Servitude

The system of temporary servitude in the New World developed out of existing practices in England. Young men and women bound themselves to masters for a fixed term of servitude (usually four to five years). In return they received passage to America, food, and shelter.

Origins

Upon completion of their terms of service, male indentures were supposed to receive such benefits as clothing, tools, and occasionally land; in reality, however,

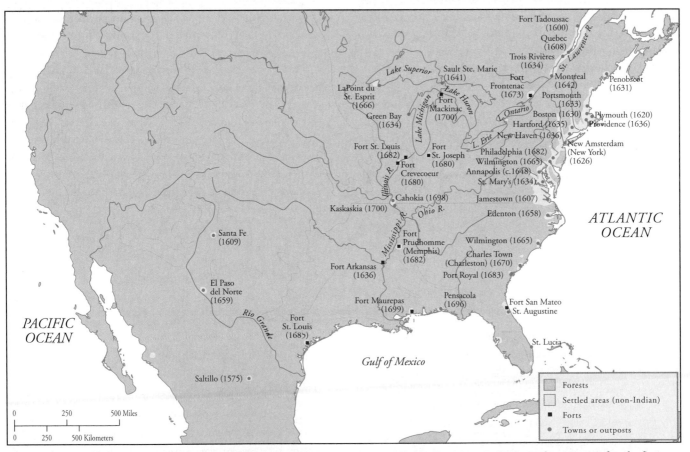

AMERICA IN 1700 This map reveals how tiny a proportion of North America was settled by Europeans in 1700, nearly a century after the first English settlements there. The largest area of settlement was the thin fringe of colonies along the northern Atlantic seaboard. There were additional scattered settlements, almost all of them tiny, in eastern Canada, along the southern Atlantic coast, in the Mississippi valley, and in the Southwest.

◆ *What would account for the isolated colonies in noncoastal areas of North America?*

 For an interactive version of this map go to www.mhhe.com/brinkley12ch3maps

many left service without anything at all, unprepared and unequipped to begin earning livings on their own. Roughly one-fourth of the indentures in the Chesapeake were women, most of whom worked as domestic servants. Because men greatly outnumbered women in the region in the seventeenth century, they could reasonably expect to marry when their terms of servitude expired. Male domestic servants, however, usually had no such options.

Most indentured servants came to the colonies voluntarily, but not all. Beginning as early as 1617, the English government occasionally dumped shiploads of convicts in America to be sold into servitude, although some criminals, according to Captain John Smith, "did chuse to be hanged ere they would go thither, and were." The government also sent prisoners taken in battles with the Scots and the Irish in the 1650s, as well as other groups deemed undesirable: orphans, vagrants, paupers, and those who were "lewd and dangerous." Other involuntary immigrants were neither dangerous nor indigent but simply victims of kidnapping, or "impressment," by aggressive and unscrupulous investors and promoters.

It was not difficult to understand why the system of indentured servitude proved so appealing to colonial employers—particularly once it became clear, as it quickly did, that the Indian population could not easily be transformed into a servile work force. The indenture system provided a means of coping with the severe labor shortage in the New World. In the Chesapeake, the headright system (by which masters received additional land grants for every servant they imported) offered another incentive. For the servants themselves, the attractions were not always so clear. Those who came voluntarily often did so to escape troubles in England; others came in the hope of establishing themselves on land or in trades of their own when their terms of service expired. Yet the reality often differed sharply from the hope.

Some former indentures managed to establish themselves successfully as farmers, tradespeople, or artisans.

Realities of Indentured Servitude

Others (mostly males) found themselves without land, without employment, without families, and without prospects. A large floating population of young single men traveled restlessly from place to place in search of work or land and were a potential (and at times actual) source of social unrest, particularly in the Chesapeake. Even free laborers who found employment or land and settled down with families often did not stay put for very long. The phenomenon of families simply pulling up stakes and moving to another, more promising location every several years was one of the most prominent characteristics of the colonial population.

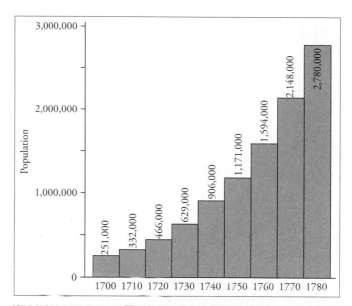

THE NON-INDIAN POPULATION OF NORTH AMERICA, 1700–1780 The European population of North America grew much more dramatically in the eighteenth century than it had in the seventeenth, exceeding 2 million by 1770. But unlike the seventeenth century, the most important reason for this expansion was natural increase (children born in America), replacing immigration from Europe. ◆ *Why would the natural increase have been so much larger than in the past?*

Indentured servitude remained an important source of population growth well into the eighteenth century, but beginning in the 1670s the flow began to decline substantially. A decrease in the English birth rate and an increase in English prosperity reduced the pressures on many men and women who might otherwise have considered emigrating. After 1700, those who did travel to America as indentured servants generally avoided the southern colonies, where working conditions were arduous and prospects for advancement were slim, and took advantage of the better opportunities in the mid-Atlantic colonies, especially Pennsylvania and New York. In the Chesapeake, landowners themselves began to find the indenture system less attractive, in part because they were troubled by the instability that former servants created or threatened to create. That was one reason for the increasing centrality of African slavery in the southern agricultural economy.

Birth and Death

At first, new arrivals in most colonies, whatever their background or status, could anticipate great hardship: inadequate food, frequent epidemics, and in an appalling number of cases, early death. Gradually, however, conditions improved enough to allow the non-Indian population to begin to expand. By the end of the seventeenth century, the non-Indian population in the English colonies of North America had grown to over a quarter of a million, of whom about 25 percent were Africans.

SERVANTS FOR SALE The *South Carolina Gazette* of Charles Town ran this advertisement in November 1749 to announce the arrival of a group of English "indentures"—men and women who had accepted passage to America in exchange for their agreement to sell themselves as servants for a fixed period of years once they arrived. Indentures were the most common form of labor in most of the colonies during much of the seventeenth century, but by 1749 the system was already beginning to die out—replaced in the South by the enslavement of Africans. The appeal at the end of this advertisement for help in capturing two German indentures who had run away was similar to many such advertisements in many southern papers over the next century appealing for help in finding runaway slaves. *(Charleston Library Society, Charleston, South Carolina)*

Although immigration remained for a time the greatest source of population increase, marked improvement in the reproduction rate began in New England and the mid-Atlantic colonies in the second half of the seventeenth century, and after the 1650s natural increase became the most important source of population. The New England population more than quadrupled through reproduction alone in the second half of the seventeenth century. This was less a result of unusual fertility (families in New England and in other regions were probably equally fertile) than of exceptional longevity. Indeed, the life spans of residents of some areas of New England were nearly equal to those of people in the twentieth century. In the first generation of American-born colonists, according to one study, men who survived infancy lived to an average age of seventy-one, women to seventy. The next generation's life expectancy declined somewhat—to sixty-five for men who survived infancy—but remained at least ten years higher than the English equivalent and

Exceptional Longevity in New England

approximately twenty years higher than life expectancy in the South. Scholars disagree on the reasons for these remarkable life spans, but contributing factors probably include the cool climate and the relatively disease-free environment it produced, clean water (a stark contrast to England in these years), and the absence of large population centers that might breed epidemics.

Conditions improved much more slowly in the South. The mortality rates for whites in the Chesapeake region remained markedly higher than those elsewhere until the mid-eighteenth century (and the mortality rates for Africans higher still). Throughout the seventeenth century, the average life expectancy for white men in the region was just over forty years, and for white women slightly less. One in four children died in infancy, and fully half died before the age of twenty. The high death rate among adults meant that only about a third of all marriages lasted more than ten years; thus those children who survived infancy often lost one or both of their parents before reaching maturity. Widows, widowers, and orphans formed a substantial proportion of the white population of the Chesapeake. The continuing ravages of disease (particularly malaria) and the prevalence of salt-contaminated water kept the death rate high in the South; only after the settlers developed immunity to the local diseases (a slow process known as "seasoning") did life expectancy increase significantly. Population growth was substantial in the region, but largely as a result of immigration.

Natural increases in the population, wherever they occurred, were in large part a result of a steady improvement in the sex ratio through the seventeenth century. In the early years of settlement, more than three-quarters of the white population of the Chesapeake consisted of men. And even in New England, which from the beginning had attracted more families (and thus more women) than the southern colonies, 60 percent of the white inhabitants in 1650 were male. Gradually, however, more women began to arrive in the colonies; and increasing birth rates, which of course produced roughly equal numbers of males and females, contributed to shifting the sex ratio as well. Not until well into the eighteenth century did the ratio begin to match that in England (where women were a slight majority), but by the late seventeenth century, the proportion of males to females in all the colonies was becoming more balanced.

More Balanced Sex Ratio

Medicine in the Colonies

The very high death rates of women who bore children illustrate the primitive nature of medical knowledge and practice in the colonies. Seventeenth- and eighteenth-century physicians had little or no understanding of infection and sterilization. As a result, many people died from infections contracted during childbirth or surgery from dirty instruments or dirty hands. Because communities were unaware of bacteria, many were plagued with infectious diseases transmitted by garbage or unclean water.

One result of the limited extent of medical knowledge was that it was relatively easy for people to enter the field, even without any professional training. The biggest beneficiaries of this ease of access were women, who established themselves in considerable numbers as midwives. Midwives assisted women in childbirth, but they

Midwives

also dispensed other medical advice—usually urging their patients to use herbs or other natural remedies. Midwives were popular because they were usually friends and neighbors of the people they treated, unlike physicians, who were few and therefore not often well known to their patients. Male doctors felt threatened by the midwives and struggled continually to drive them from the field, although they did not make substantial progress in doing so until the nineteenth century.

Midwives and doctors alike practiced medicine on the basis of the prevailing assumptions of their time, most of them derived from the theory of "humoralism" popularized by the second century Roman physician Galen. Galen argued that the human body was governed by four "humors" that were lodged in four bodily fluids: yellow bile (or "choler"), black bile ("melancholy"), blood, and phlegm. In a healthy body, the four humors existed in balance. Illness represented an imbalance and suggested the need for removing from the body the excesses of whatever fluid was causing the imbalance. That was the rationale that lay behind the principal medical techniques of the seventeenth century: purging, expulsion, and bleeding. Bleeding was the most extreme of the treatments (and the most destructive), and it was practiced mostly by male physicians. Midwives preferred more homeopathic treatments and favored "pukes" and laxatives. The great majority of early Americans, however, had little contact with physicians, or even midwives, and sought instead to deal with illness on their own, confident that their abilities were equal to those of educated physicians— which, given the state of medical knowledge, was often true.

That seventeenth-century medicine rested so much on ideas produced 1,400 years before is evidence of how little support there was for the scientific method—which rests on experimentation and observation rather than on inherited faiths—in England and America at the time. Bleeding, for example, had been in use for hundreds of years, during which time there had been no evidence at all that it helped people recover from illness; indeed, if anyone had chosen to look for it, there was considerable evidence that bleeding could do great harm. But what would seem in later eras to be the simple process of testing scientific assumptions was not yet a common part of Western thought. Only with the birth of the Enlightenment in the late seventeenth century—with its faith in human reason and its belief in the capacity of individuals and societies to create better lives—would the scientific method find acceptance.

Women and Families in the Chesapeake

The importance of reproduction in the labor-scarce society of seventeenth-century America had particularly significant effects on women. The high sex ratio meant that few women remained unmarried for long. The average European woman in America married for the first time at twenty or twenty-one years of age, considerably earlier than in England; in some areas of the Chesapeake, the average bride was three to four years younger. In the Chesapeake, the most important factor affecting women and families remained, until at least the mid-eighteenth century, the extraor-

Male Authority Undermined

dinarily high mortality rate. Under those circumstances, the traditional male-centered family structure of England—by which husbands and fathers exercised firm, even dictatorial control over the lives of their wives and children—was difficult to maintain. Because so few families remained intact for long, rigid patterns of male authority were constantly undermined. Standards of sexual behavior were also more flexible in the South than they were in England or other parts of America. Because of the large numbers of indentured servants who were forbidden to marry until their terms of service expired, premarital sexual relationships were frequent. Female servants who became pregnant before the expiration of their terms could expect harsh treatment: heavy fines, whippings if no one could pay the fines, an extra year or two of service added to their contract, and the loss of their children after weaning. Bastard children were themselves bound out as indentures at a very early age. On the other hand, a pregnant woman whose term of service expired before the birth of her child or whose partner was able to buy her remaining time from her master might expect to marry quickly. Over a third of Chesapeake marriages occurred with the bride already pregnant.

Women in the Chesapeake could anticipate a life consumed with childbearing. The average wife became pregnant every two years. Those who lived long enough bore an average of eight children apiece (up to five of whom typically died in infancy or early childhood). Since childbirth was one of the most frequent causes of female death, relatively few women survived to see all their children grow to maturity.

For all the hardships women encountered in the seventeenth-century South, they also enjoyed more power and a greater level of freedom than women in other areas (or than southern women in later years). Because men were plentiful and women scarce, females had considerable latitude in choosing husbands. (They also often had no fathers or other male relatives nearby trying to control their choices.) Because women generally married at a much younger age than men, they also tended to outlive their husbands (even though female life expectancy was somewhat shorter than male). Widows were often left with several children and with responsibility for managing a farm or plantation, a circumstance of enormous hardship but one that also gave them significant economic power.

Greater Independence in the South

Widows seldom remained unmarried for long, however. Those who had no grown sons to work the tobacco farms and plantations had particular need for male assistance, and marriage was the surest way to secure it. Since many widows married men who were themselves widowers, complex combinations of households were frequent. With numerous stepchildren, half brothers, and half sisters living together in a single household, women often had to play the role of peacemaker—a role that may have further enhanced their authority within the family.

By the early eighteenth century, the character of the Chesapeake population was beginning to change, and with it the nature of the typical family. Life expectancy was increasing; indentured servitude was in decline; and natural reproduction was becoming the principal source of white population increase. The sex ratio was becoming more equal. One result of these changes was that life for white people in the region became less perilous and less arduous. Another result was that women lost some of the power that their small numbers had once given them. As families grew more stable, traditional patterns of male authority revived. By the mid-eighteenth century, southern families were becoming highly "patriarchal," that is, dominated by the male head of the family.

Revival of Patriarchy

Women and Families in New England

In New England, where many more immigrants arrived with family members and where death rates declined quickly, family structure was much more stable than it was in the Chesapeake and hence much more traditional. Because the sex ratio was reasonably balanced, most men could expect to marry.

GUIDE TO THE SEASONS Among their many purposes, almanacs sought to help farmers predict weather and plan for the demands of changing seasons. This illustration, part of a "calendar" of farming images, shows a man and woman tending fields in July, in preparation for the coming harvest. *(American Antiquarian Society)*

Women, however, remained in the minority; and as in the Chesapeake, they married young, began producing children early, and continued to do so well into their thirties. In contrast to the South, however, northern children were more likely to survive (the average family raised six to eight children to maturity), and families were more

Male-Dominated New England

likely to remain intact. Fewer New England women became widows, and those who did generally lost their husbands later in life. Hence women were less often cast in roles independent of their husbands. Young women, moreover, had less control over the conditions of marriage, both because there were fewer unmarried men vying for them and because their fathers were more often alive and able to exercise control over their choice of husbands.

Among other things, increased longevity meant that, unlike in the Chesapeake (where three-fourths of all children lost at least one parent before the age of twenty-one), white parents in New England usually lived to see their children and even their grandchildren grow to maturity. Still, the lives of most New England women were nearly as consumed by childbearing and child rearing as those of women in the Chesapeake. Even women who lived into their sixties spent the vast majority of their mature years with young children in the home. The longer lives in New England also meant that parents continued to control their children far longer than did parents in the South. Although they were less likely than parents in England actually to "arrange" marriages for their children, few sons and daughters could choose spouses entirely independent of their parents' wishes. Men usually depended on their fathers for land—generally a prerequisite for beginning families of their own. Women needed dowries from their parents if they were to attract desirable husbands. Stricter parental supervision of children meant, too, that fewer women became pregnant before marriage than in the South (although even in Puritan New England the premarital pregnancy rate was not insubstantial—as high as 20 percent in some communities).

For New Englanders more than for residents of the Chesapeake, family relationships and the status of women were defined in part by religious belief. In the South, established churches were relatively weak. But in New England the Puritan church was a powerful institutional and social presence. In theory, the Puritan belief that men and women were equal before God and hence equally capable of interpreting the Bible created possibilities for women to emerge as spiritual leaders. But in reality, religious authority remained securely in the hands of men, who used it in part to reinforce a highly patriarchal view of society. The case of Anne Hutchinson (see p. 45) is an example of both the possibilities and the limits of female spiritual power.

Puritanism placed a high value on the family, which was the principal economic and religious unit within every community. At the same time, however, Puritanism reinforced the idea of nearly

The Patriarchal Puritan Family

absolute male authority and the assumption of female weakness and inferiority. Women were expected to be modest and submissive. (Such popular girls' names as Prudence, Patience, Chastity, and Comfort suggest something about Puritan expectations of female behavior.) A wife was expected to devote herself almost entirely to serving the needs of her husband and household.

Women were of crucial importance to the New England agricultural economy. Not only did they bear and raise children who at relatively young ages became part of the work force, but they themselves were continuously engaged in tasks vital to the functioning of the farm—gardening, tending livestock, spinning, and weaving, as well as cooking, cleaning, and washing.

The Beginnings of Slavery in British America

Almost from the beginning of European settlement in America, there was a demand for black servants to supplement the always scarce southern labor supply. The demand grew rapidly once tobacco cultivation became a staple of the Chesapeake economy. But the supply of African laborers was limited during much of the seventeenth century, because the Atlantic slave trade did not at first serve the English colonies in America. Portuguese slavers, who had dominated the trade since the sixteenth century, shipped captive men and women from the west coast of Africa to the new European colonies in South America and the Caribbean. Gradually, however, Dutch and French navigators joined the slave trade. A substantial commerce in slaves grew up within the Americas, particularly between the Caribbean islands and the southern colonies of English America. By the late seventeenth century, the supply of black workers in North America was becoming plentiful.

As the commerce in slaves grew more extensive and sophisticated, it also grew more horrible. Before it ended in the nineteenth century, it was responsible for the forced immigration of as many as 11 million Africans to the New World. (Until

The Middle Passage

the late eighteenth century, the number of African immigrants to the Americas was higher than that of Europeans.) Native African chieftains captured members of enemy tribes in battle, tied them together in long lines, or "coffles," and sold them in the flourishing slave marts on the African coast. Then, after some haggling on the docks between the

The Origins of Slavery

The debate among historians over how and why white Americans created a system of slave labor in the seventeenth century—and how and why they determined that people of African descent and no others should populate that system—has been a long and unusually heated one. At its center is the question of whether slavery was a result of white racism or helped to create it.

In 1950, Oscar and Mary Handlin published an influential article, "Origins of the Southern Labor System," which noted that many residents of the American colonies (and of England) lived in varying degrees of "unfreedom" in the seventeenth century, although none resembling slavery as it came to be known in America. The first Africans who came to America lived for a time in conditions not very different from those of white indentured servants. But slavery came ultimately to differ substantially from other conditions of servitude. It was permanent bondage, and it passed from one generation to the next. That it emerged in America, the Handlins argued, resulted from efforts by colonial legislatures to increase the available labor force. That it included African Americans and no others was because black people had few defenses and few defenders. Racism emerged to justify slavery; it did not cause slavery.

In 1959, Carl Degler became the first of a number of important historians to challenge the Handlins. In his essay "Slavery and the Genesis of American Race Prejudice," he argued that Africans had never been like other servants in the Chesapeake; that "the Negro was actually never treated as an equal of the white man, servant or free." Racism was strong "long before slavery had come upon the scene." It did not result from slavery, but helped cause it. Nine years later, Winthrop D. Jordan argued similarly that white racism, not economic or legal conditions, produced slavery. In *White Over Black* (1968) and other, earlier writings, Jordan argued that Europeans had long viewed people of color—and black Africans in particular—as inferior beings appropriate for serving whites. Those attitudes migrated with white Europeans to the New World, and white racism shaped the treatment of Africans in America—and the nature of the slave labor system—from the beginning.

George Fredrickson has echoed Jordan's emphasis on the importance of racism as an independent factor reinforcing slavery; but unlike Jordan, he has argued that racism did not precede slavery. "The treatment of blacks," he wrote, "engendered a cultural and psycho-social racism that after a certain point took on a life of its own. . . . Racism, although the child of slavery, not only outlived its parent but grew stronger and more independent after slavery's demise."

(*View of Mulberry (House and Street)*) *by Thomas Coram. Gibbes Museum of Art/Carolina Art Association*)

European traders and the African suppliers, the terrified victims were packed into the dark, filthy holds of ships for the horrors of the "middle passage"—the journey to America. For weeks, sometimes even months, the black prisoners remained chained in the bowels of the slave ships. Conditions varied from one ship to another. Some captains took care to see that their potentially valuable cargo remained reasonably healthy. Others accepted the deaths of numerous Africans as inevitable and tried to cram as many as possible into their ships to ensure that enough would survive to yield a profit at journey's end. On such ships, the African prisoners were sometimes packed together in such close quarters that they were unable to stand, hardly able to breathe. Some ships supplied them with only minimal food and water. Women were often victims of rape and other sexual abuse. Those who died en route were simply thrown overboard. Upon arrival in the New World, slaves were auctioned off to white landowners and transported, frightened and bewildered, to their new homes.

The first black laborers arrived in English North America before 1620, and as English seamen began to establish themselves in the slave trade, the flow of Africans to the colonies gradually increased. But North America was always a much less important market for Africans than were other parts of the New World, especially the Caribbean islands and Brazil, whose labor-intensive sugar economies created an especially large demand for slaves. Fewer than 5 percent of the Africans imported to the Americas went directly to the English colonies on the mainland. Most blacks

Peter Wood's *Black Majority* (1974), a study of seventeenth-century South Carolina, moved the debate back away from racism and toward social and economic conditions. Wood demonstrated that blacks and whites often worked together on relatively equal terms in the early years of settlement. But as rice cultivation expanded, finding white laborers willing to do the arduous work became more difficult. The forcible importation of African workers, and the creation of a system of permanent bondage, was a response to a growing demand for labor and to fears among whites that without slavery a black labor force would be difficult to control. Similarly, Edmund Morgan's *American Slavery, American Freedom* (1975) argued that the southern labor system was at first relatively flexible and later grew more rigid. In colonial Virginia, he claimed, white settlers did not at first intend to create a system of permanent bondage. But as the tobacco economy grew and created a high demand for cheap labor, white landowners began to feel uneasy about their dependence on a large group of dependent white workers, since such workers were difficult to recruit and control. Thus slavery was less a result of racism than of the desire for white landowners to find a reliable and stable labor force. Racism, Morgan contended, was a result of slavery, an ideology created to justify a system that

had been developed to serve other needs. And David Brion Davis, in *The Problem of Slavery in the Age of Revolution* (1975), argued that while prejudice against blacks had a long history, racism as a systematic ideology was crystallized during the American Revolution—as Americans such as Thomas Jefferson struggled to explain the paradox of slavery existing in a republic committed to individual freedom.

Robin Blackburn's *The Making of New World Slavery* (1996) is perhaps the most emphatic statement of the economic underpinnings of slavery. Why, he asks, did the American colonies create a thriving slave labor system at a time when slavery had almost entirely died out in Europe? He concedes that race was a factor; Africans were "different" in appearance, culture, and religion from European colonists, and it was easier to justify enslaving them than it was to justify enslaving English, French, or Spanish workers. But the real reasons for slavery were hardheaded economic decisions by ambitious entrepreneurs, who realized very early that a slave-labor system in the labor-intensive agricultural world of the American South and the Caribbean was more profitable than a free-labor system. Slaveowning planters, he argues, not only enriched themselves; they created wealth that benefited all of colonial society and provided significant capital for the rapidly devel-

(National Maritime Museum, London)

oping economy of England. Thus, slavery served the interests of a powerful combination of groups: planters, merchants, governments, industrialists, and consumers. Race may have been a rationale for slavery, allowing planters and traders to justify to themselves the terrible human costs of the system. But the most important reason for the system was not racism, but the pursuit of profit—and the success of the system in producing it. Slavery was not, according to Blackburn, an antiquated remnant of an older world. It was, he uncomfortably concludes, a recognizably modern labor system that, however horrible, served the needs of an emerging market economy.

who ended up in what became the United States spent time first in the West Indies. Not until the 1670s did traders start importing blacks directly from Africa to North America. Even then, however, the flow remained small for a time, mainly because a single group, the Royal African Company of England, maintained a monopoly on trade in the mainland colonies and managed as a result to keep prices high and supplies low.

A turning point in the history of the African population in North America came in the mid-1690s, when the Royal African Company's monopoly was finally broken. With the trade now opened to English and colonial merchants on a competitive basis, prices fell and the number of Africans arriving in North America rapidly increased. By the end of the century, only about

one in ten of the residents of the colonies was African (about 25,000 in all). But because Africans were so heavily concentrated in a few southern colonies, they were already beginning to outnumber Europeans in some areas. The high ratio of men to women among African immigrants (there were perhaps two males to one female in most areas) retarded the natural increase of the black population. But in the Chesapeake at least, more new slaves were being born by 1700 than were being imported from Africa. In South Carolina, by contrast, the difficult conditions of rice cultivation—and the high death rates of those who worked in the rice fields—ensured that the black population would barely be able to sustain itself through natural increase until much later.

Growing Slave Population

AFRICANS BOUND FOR AMERICA Shown here are the below-deck slave quarters of a Spanish vessel en route to the West Indies. A British warship captured the slaver, and a young English naval officer (Lt. Francis Meynell) made this watercolor sketch on the spot. The Africans seen in this picture appear somewhat more comfortable than prisoners on some other slave ships, who were often chained and packed together so tightly that they had no room to stand or even sit. *(National Maritime Museum, London)*

Between 1700 and 1760, the number of Africans in the colonies increased tenfold to about a quarter of a million. A relatively small number (16,000 in 1763) lived in New England; there were slightly more (29,000) in the middle colonies. The vast majority, however, continued to live in the South. By then the flow of free white laborers to that region had all but stopped, and Africans had become securely established as the basis of the southern work force.

It was not entirely clear at first that the status of black laborers in America would be fundamentally different from that of white indentured servants. In the rugged conditions of the seventeenth-century South, it was often difficult for Europeans and Africans to maintain strictly separate roles. In some areas—South Carolina, for example, where the number of African arrivals swelled more quickly than anywhere else—whites and blacks lived and worked together for a time on terms of relative equality. Some blacks were treated much like white hired servants, and some were freed after a fixed term of servitude. A few Africans themselves became landowners, and some apparently owned slaves of their own.

Uncertain Status

By the early eighteenth century, however, a rigid distinction had become established between black and white. (See "Where Historians Disagree," pp. 72–73.) Masters were contractually obliged to free white servants after a fixed term of servitude. There was no such necessity to free black workers, and the assumption slowly spread that blacks would remain in service permanently. Another incentive for making the status of Africans rigid was that the children of slaves provided white landowners with a self-perpetuating labor force.

White assumptions about the inferiority of people of color contributed to the growing rigidity of the system. Such assumptions came naturally to the English settlers. They had already defined themselves as a superior race in their relations with the native Indian population (and earlier in their relations with the Irish). The idea of subordinating a supposedly inferior race was, therefore, already established in the English imagination by the time substantial numbers of Africans appeared in America.

In the early eighteenth century, colonial assemblies began to pass "slave codes," limiting the rights of blacks

THE SLAVE SHIP *BROOKES* The British slave ship *Brookes* provided this plan of its "stowage" of slaves to conform to 1798 legislation from Parliament. It illustrates vividly the terrible conditions under which slaves were shipped from Africa to the Americas—human beings squeezed into every available space like cargo for the long, dangerous passage during which many Africans died. *(Library of Congress)*

in law and ensuring almost absolute authority to white masters. One factor, and one factor only, determined whether a person was subject to the slave codes: color. In contrast to the colonial societies of Spanish America, where people of mixed race had a different (and higher) status than pure Africans, English America recognized no such distinctions. Any African ancestry was enough to classify a person as black.

Slave Codes

Changing Sources of European Immigration

By the early eighteenth century, the flow of immigrants from England itself began to decline substantially—a result of better economic conditions there and of new government restrictions on emigration in the face of massive depopulation in some regions of the country. But as English immigration declined, French, German, Swiss, Irish, Welsh, Scottish, and Scandinavian immigration continued and increased.

The earliest, although not the most numerous, of these non-English European immigrants were the French Calvinists, or Huguenots. A royal proclamation, the Edict of Nantes of 1598, had allowed them to become practically a state within the state in Roman Catholic France. In 1685, however, the French government revoked the edict. Soon after that, Huguenots began leaving the country. A total of about 300,000 left France in the following decades, and a small proportion of them traveled to the English colonies in North America. Many German Protestants suffered similarly from the arbitrary religious policies of their rulers; and all Germans, Catholics as well as Protestants, suffered from the devastating wars with King Louis XIV of France (the "Sun King"). The Rhineland of southwestern Germany, the area known as the Palatinate, experienced particular hardships. Because it was close to France, its people were particularly exposed to slaughter and ruin at the hands of invaders. The unusually cold winter of 1708–1709

Huguenots and Pennsylvania Dutch

THE AFRICAN POPULATION OF THE BRITISH COLONIES, 1620-1780 From tiny beginnings in the seventeenth century, the African population of the British colonies grew rapidly in the eighteenth century. The growth of slavery was a result of both supply (a readily available population of African workers in the Caribbean islands) and demand (the growth of tobacco, rice, and cotton cultivation in larger areas of the South). The slave population in the colonies also increased naturally in this period at a far greater rate than in the past, largely because living conditions for African workers improved. ◆ *Why would slaveowners have invested in better conditions for their slaves?*

THE PENNSYLVANIA DUTCH This painting of a gentleman in traditional dress was a familiar subject of Pennsylvania Dutch folk art in the eighteenth century. The Pennsylvania Dutch were, in fact, German immigrants. They were known to their neighbors in Pennsylvania as "Dutch" because that was how their native word for their nationality ("Deutsch") sounded to most English-speakers. *(Free Library of Philadelphia)*

dealt a final blow to the precarious economy of the region. More than 12,000 Palatinate Germans sought refuge in England, and approximately 3,000 of them soon found their way to America. They arrived in New York and tried at first to make homes in the Mohawk Valley, only to be ousted by the powerful landlords of the region. Some of the Palatines moved farther up the Mohawk, out of reach of the patroons; but most made their way to Pennsylvania, where they received a warm welcome (and where they ultimately became known to English settlers as the "Pennsylvania Dutch," a corruption of their own word for "German": "Deutsch"). The Quaker colony became the most common destination for Germans, who came to America in growing numbers. (Among them were Moravians and Mennonites, with religious views similar in many ways to those of the Quakers.) Many German Protestants went to North Carolina as well, especially after the founding of New Bern in 1710 by a company of 600 German-speaking Swiss.

The most numerous of the newcomers were the Scots-Irish—Scottish Presbyterians who had settled in northern Ireland (in the province of Ulster) in the early seventeenth century. The Ulster colonists had prospered for a time despite the barren soil and the constant, never wholly successful, struggle to suppress the Catholic natives. But in the first years of the eighteenth century,

Parliament prohibited Ulster from exporting to England the woolens and other products that had become the basis of the northern Irish economy; at the same time, the English government virtually outlawed the practice of the Presbyterian religion in Ulster and insisted on conformity with the Anglican church. After 1710, moreover, the long-term leases of many Scots-Irish expired; English landlords doubled and even tripled the rents. Thousands of tenants embarked for America.

Often coldly received at the colonial ports, many of the Scots-Irish pushed out to the edges of European settlement. There they occupied land without much regard for who actually claimed to own it, whether absentee whites, Indians, or the colonial governments. They were as ruthless in their displacement and suppression of the Indians as they had been with the native Irish Catholics.

Scots-Irish

Immigrants from Scotland itself and from southern Ireland added other elements to the colonial population in the eighteenth century. Scottish Highlanders, some of

IMMIGRANT GROUPS IN COLONIAL AMERICA, 1760 Even though the entire Atlantic seaboard of what is now the United States had become a series of British colonies by 1760, the population consisted of people from many nations. As this map reveals, English settlers dominated most of the regions of North America. But note the large areas of German settlement in the western Chesapeake and Pennsylvania; the swath of Dutch settlement in New York and New Jersey; the Scots-Irish regions in the western regions of the South; and the large areas in which Africans were becoming the majority of the population, even if subjugated by the white minority. ◆ *What aspects of the history of these colonies help explain their ethnic composition?*

For an interactive version of this map go to www.mhhe.com/brinkley12ch3maps

them Roman Catholics who had been defeated in rebellions in 1715 and 1745, immigrated into several colonies, North Carolina above all. Presbyterian Lowlanders, faced in Scotland with high rents in the country and unemployment in the towns, left for America in large numbers shortly before the American Revolution, joining earlier groups of Scots, who had arrived in the late seventeenth century. They became a significant influence in New Jersey and Pennsylvania and helped established Presbyterianism as an important religion in those colonies. The Catholic Irish migrated steadily over a long period, and

by the time of the Revolution they were almost as numerous as the Scots, although less conspicuous. Many of them had by then abandoned their Roman Catholic religion and with it much of their ethnic identity.

Continuing immigration and natural increase contributed to a rapid population growth in the colonies in the eighteenth century. In 1700, the non-Indian population of the colonies totaled less than 250,000; by 1775, it was over 2 million—a nearly tenfold increase. Throughout the colonial period, the non-Indian population nearly doubled every twenty-five years.

THE COLONIAL ECONOMIES

To those who remained in Europe, and even to some who settled in North America, the English colonies often appeared so small and isolated as to seem virtually at the end of the world. But from the beginning, almost all the English colonies were commercial ventures and were tied in crucial ways to other economies. They developed substantial trade with the native population of North America, with the French settlers to the north, and, to a lesser extent, with Spanish colonists to the south and west. And over time they developed an even more substantial trade within the growing Atlantic economy of the sixteenth and seventeenth centuries, of which they became a critical part.

Rapid Population Growth

American colonists engaged in a wide range of economic pursuits. But except for a few areas in the West where the small white populations subsisted largely on the fur and skin trade with the Indians, farming dominated all areas of European and African settlement throughout the seventeenth and eighteenth centuries. Some farmers engaged in simple subsistence agriculture; but whenever possible American farmers attempted to grow crops for the local, intercolonial, and export markets.

The Southern Economy

In the Chesapeake region, tobacco early established itself as the basis of the economy. A strong European demand for the crop enabled some planters to grow enormously wealthy and at times allowed the region as a whole to prosper. But production frequently exceeded demand, and as a result the price of tobacco periodically suffered severe declines. The first major bust in the tobacco economy occurred in 1640, and the boom-and-bust pattern continued throughout the colonial period and beyond. Growing more tobacco only made the problem of overproduction worse, but Chesapeake farmers never understood that. Those planters who could afford to do so expanded their landholdings, enlarged their fields, and acquired additional laborers. After 1700, tobacco plantations employing several dozen slaves or more were common.

Tobacco

The staple of the economies of South Carolina and Georgia was rice. By building dams and dikes along the many tidal rivers, farmers managed to create rice paddies that could be flooded and then drained. Rice cultivation was arduous work, performed standing knee-deep in the mud of malarial swamps under a blazing sun, surrounded by insects. It was a task so difficult and unhealthful that white laborers generally refused to perform it. As a result, planters in South Carolina and Georgia were even more dependent than those elsewhere on African slaves. It was not only because Africans could be compelled to perform difficult work that whites found them so valuable. It was also because they were much better at it. They showed from the beginning a greater resistance to malaria and other local diseases (although the impact of disease on African workers was by no means inconsiderable). And they proved more adept at the basic agricultural tasks required, in part because some of them had come from rice-producing regions of west Africa (a fact that has led some historians to argue that Africans were responsible for introducing rice cultivation to America). It was also because most Africans were more accustomed to hot and humid climates such as those of the rice-growing regions than were the Europeans.

In the early 1740s, another staple crop contributed to the South Carolina economy: indigo. Eliza Lucas, a young Antiguan woman who managed her family's North American plantations, experimented with cultivating the West Indian plant (which was the source of a blue dye in great demand in Europe) on the mainland. She discovered that it could grow on the high ground of South Carolina, which was unsuitable for rice planting, and that its harvest came while the rice was still growing. Indigo became an important complement to rice and a popular import in England.

Indigo

Because of the South's early dependence on large-scale cash crops, the southern colonies developed less of a commercial or industrial economy than the colonies of the North. The trading in tobacco and rice was handled largely by merchants based in London and, later, in the northern colonies. Few cities of more than modest size developed in the South. No substantial local merchant communities emerged. A pattern was established that would characterize the southern economy, and differentiate it from that of other regions, for more than two centuries.

Northern Economic and Technological Life

In the North, agriculture also continued to dominate, but it was agriculture of a more diverse kind. Agriculture, however, did not remain the only major economic activity in the North because conditions for farming were less favorable there. In northern New England, in particular, colder weather and hard, rocky soil made it difficult for colonists to develop the kind of large-scale commercial farming system that southerners were creating. Conditions for agriculture were better in southern New England and the middle colonies, where the soil was fertile and the weather more temperate. New York, Pennsylvania, and the Connecticut River valley were the chief suppliers of wheat to much of New England and to parts of the South. Even there, however, a substantial commercial economy emerged alongside the agricultural one.

More Diverse Agriculture in the North

PREPARING TOBACCO This 1790 engraving is designed to illustrate the African origins of the enslaved workers who processed tobacco in Virginia. Their "primitive" costumes seemed to the artist, a French visitor to America, to be in keeping with the crude processes they had created for drying, rolling, and sorting tobacco. *(The Stapleton Collection/Bridgeman Art Library)*

Almost every colonist engaged in a certain amount of industry at home. Occasionally these home industries provided families with surplus goods they could trade or sell. Beyond these domestic efforts, craftsmen and artisans established themselves in colonial towns as cobblers, blacksmiths, riflemakers, cabinetmakers, silversmiths, and printers. In some areas, entrepreneurs harnessed water power to run small mills for grinding grain, processing cloth, or milling lumber. And in several places, large-scale shipbuilding operations began to flourish.

The first effort to establish a significant metals industry in the colonies was an ironworks established in Saugus, Massachusetts, in the 1640s after iron ore deposits had been discovered in the region. Iron

Saugus Ironworks

technology was already advancing rapidly in England, and the colonists attempted to transfer those skills to America. The Saugus works used water power to drive a bellows, which controlled the heat in a charcoal furnace. As the ore melted, it trickled down into molds or was taken in the form of simple "sow bars" to a forge to be shaped into marketable objects. The Saugus works was a tech-

nological success; indeed, it could boast technological capabilities equal to any ironworks in Europe at the time. But it was a financial failure. It began operations in 1646; in 1668, its financial problems forced it to close its doors.

Metal works, however, gradually became an important part of the colonial economy. The largest industrial enterprise anywhere in English North America was the ironworks of the German ironmaster Peter Hasenclever in northern New Jersey. Founded in 1764 with British capital, it employed several hundred laborers, many of them imported from ironworks in Germany. There were other, smaller ironmaking enterprises in every northern colony (with particular concentrations in Massachusetts, New Jersey, and Pennsylvania), and there were ironworks as well in several of the southern colonies. Even so, these and other growing industries did not become the basis for the kind of explosive industrial growth that Great Britain experienced in the late eighteenth century—in part because English parliamentary regulations such as the Iron Act of 1750 restricted metal processing in the colonies. Similar prohibitions limited the manufacture of woolens, hats, and other goods. But the biggest obstacles

COMMERCE IN NEW ENGLAND This late-eighteenth-century painting of the home, wharves, countinghouse, and fleet of a prosperous New England fisherman gives some indication of how commerce was expanding even in such relatively small places as Duxbury, Massachusetts. The owner, Joshua Winsor, was active in the mackerel and cod fishing industry. The painting—evidently an effort to celebrate Winsor's great material success and record it for posterity—was by his son-in-law, Dr. Rufus Hathaway. *(A View of Mr. Joshua Winsor's House, 1793–95. By Rufus Hathaway. Museum of American Folk Art, New York. Promised anonymous gift.)*

to industrialization in America were an inadequate labor supply, a small domestic market, and inadequate transportation facilities and energy supplies.

More important than manufacturing were industries that exploited the natural resources of the continent. By the mid-seventeenth century, the flourishing fur trade of earlier years was in decline. Taking its place were lumbering, mining, and fishing, particularly in the waters off the New England coast. These industries provided commodities that could be exported to England in exchange for manufactured goods. And they helped produce the most distinctive feature of the northern economy: a thriving commercial class.

Extractive Industries

The Extent and Limits of Technology

Despite the technological progress that was occurring in some parts of America in the seventeenth and eighteenth centuries, much of colonial society was conspicuously lacking in even very basic technological capacities. Up to

half the farmers in the colonies were so primitively equipped that they did not even own a plow. Substantial numbers of households owned no pots or kettles for cooking. And only about half the households in the colonies owned guns or rifles—with rural people almost as unlikely to have firearms as urban people. The relatively low levels of ownership of these and other elementary tools was not because such things were difficult to make, but because most Americans remained too poor or too isolated to be able to afford them. Many households had few if any candles, because they were unable to afford candle molds or tallow (wax), or because they had no access to commercially produced candles. In the early eighteenth century, very few farmers owned wagons. Most made do with two-wheeled carts, which could be hauled by hand (or by horse) around the farm but which were not very efficient for transporting crops to market. The most commonly owned tool on American farms was the axe, which suggests how much time most farmers had to spend clearing land. But throughout the colonies, the ability of people to acquire manufactured implements lagged far behind the economy's capacity to produce them.

Even so, few colonists were self-sufficient in the late seventeenth and early eighteenth centuries. The popular image of early American households is of people who

Myth of Self-Sufficiency

had little connection to the market, who grew their own food, made their own clothes, and bought little from anyone else. In fact, relatively few colonial families owned spinning wheels or looms, which suggests that most people purchased whatever yarn and cloth they needed, or could afford, from merchants. Most farmers who grew grain took it to centralized facilities for processing.

The Rise of Colonial Commerce

Perhaps the most remarkable feature of colonial commerce in the seventeenth century was that it was able to survive at all. American merchants faced such bewildering and intimidating obstacles, and lacked so many of the basic institutions of trade, that they managed to stay afloat only with great difficulty. There was, first, no commonly accepted medium of exchange. The colonies

Shortage of Currency

had almost no specie (gold or silver coins). They experimented at times with different forms of paper currency—tobacco certificates, for example, which were secured by tobacco stored in warehouses; or land certificates, secured by

property. Such paper was not, however, acceptable as payment for any goods from abroad and it was in any case ultimately outlawed by Parliament. For many years, colonial merchants had to rely on a haphazard barter system or on crude money substitutes such as beaver skins.

A second obstacle was the near impossibility of imposing order on their trade. In the fragmented, jerrybuilt commercial world of colonial America, no merchants could be certain that the goods on which their commerce relied would be produced in sufficient quantity; nor could they be certain of finding adequate markets for them. Few channels of information existed to inform traders of what they could expect in foreign ports; vessels sometimes stayed at sea for several years, journeying from one market to another, trading one commodity for another, attempting to find some way to turn a profit. Engaged in this chaotic commerce, moreover, were an enormous number of small, fiercely competitive companies, which made the problem of stabilizing the system even more acute.

Despite these and other problems, commerce in the colonies not only survived but grew. There was an elaborate coastal trade, through which the colonies did business with one another and with the West Indies, largely in such goods as rum, agricultural products, meat, and fish. The mainland colonies received sugar, molasses, and

Triangular Trade

slaves from the Caribbean markets in return. There was as well an expanding transatlantic trade, which linked the

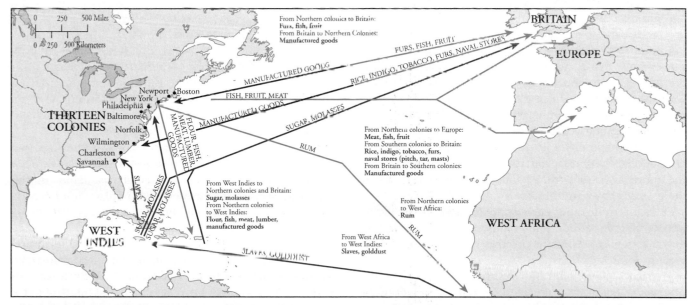

THE "TRIANGULAR TRADE" This map illustrates the complex pattern of trade that fueled the colonial American economy in the seventeenth and eighteenth centuries. A simple explanation of this trade is that the American colonies exported raw materials (agricultural products, furs, and others) to Britain and Europe and imported manufactured goods in return. But while that explanation is accurate, it is not complete, largely because the Atlantic trade was not a simple exchange between America and Europe, but a complex network of exchanges involving the Caribbean, Africa, and the Mediterranean. Note the important exchanges between the North American mainland and the Caribbean islands; the important trade between the American colonies and Africa; and the wide range of European and Mediterranean markets in which Americans were active. Not shown on this map, but also very important to colonial commerce, was a large coastal trade among the various regions of British North America.
◆ *Why did the major ports of trade emerge almost entirely in the northern colonies?*

 For an interactive version of this map go to www.mhhe.com/brinkley12ch3maps

North American colonies in an intricate network of commerce with England, continental Europe, and the west coast of Africa. This commerce has often been described, somewhat inaccurately, as the "triangular trade," suggesting a neat process: merchants carried rum and other goods from New England to Africa; exchanged their merchandise for slaves, whom they then transported to the West Indies (hence the term "middle passage" for the dreaded journey—it was the second of the three legs of the voyage); and then exchanged the slaves for sugar and molasses, which they shipped back to New England to be distilled into rum. In fact, the system was almost never so simple. The "triangular" trade in rum, slaves, and sugar was in fact part of a maze of highly diverse trade routes: between the northern and southern colonies, America and England, America and Africa, the West Indies and Europe, and other combinations.

Out of this complex and highly risky trade emerged a group of adventurous entrepreneurs who by the mid-eighteenth century were beginning to constitute a distinct merchant class. Concentrated in the port cities of the North (above all, Boston, New York, and Philadelphia), they enjoyed protection from foreign competition within the English colonies—the British Navigation Acts had excluded all non-British ships from the colonial carrying trade. They had access to a market in England for such American products as furs, timber, and ships. That did not, however, satisfy all their commercial needs. Many colonial products—fish, flour, wheat, and meat, all of which England could produce for itself—required markets altogether outside the British empire. Ignoring laws restricting colonial trade to England and its possessions, many merchants developed markets in the French, Spanish, and Dutch West Indies, where prices were often higher than in the British colonies. The profits from this commerce enabled the colonies to import the manufactured goods they needed from Europe.

Emerging Merchant Class

In the course of the eighteenth century, the colonial commercial system began to stabilize. In some cities, the more successful merchants expanded their operations so greatly that they were able to dominate some sectors of trade and curb some of the destabilizing effects of competition. Merchants managed, as well, to make extensive contacts in the English commercial world, securing their positions in certain areas of transatlantic trade. But the commercial sector of the American economy remained open to newcomers, largely because it—and the society on which it was based—was expanding so rapidly.

The Rise of Consumerism

Among relatively affluent residents of the colonies, the growing prosperity and commercialism of British America created both new appetites and new opportunities to satisfy them. The result was a growing preoccupation with the consumption of material goods—and of the association of possessions with social status.

One thing that spurred the growth of eighteenth-century consumerism was the increasing division of American societies by class. As the difference between the upper and lower classes became more glaring, people of means became more intent on demonstrating their own membership in the upper ranks of society. The ability to purchase and display consumer goods was an important way of doing so, particularly for affluent people in cities and towns, who did not have large estates with which they could demonstrate their success. But the growth of consumerism was also a product of the early stages of the industrial revolution. Although there was relatively little industry in America in the eighteenth century, England and Europe were making rapid advances and producing more and more affordable goods for affluent Americans to buy. The new manufacturing was dependent, of course, on customers for its products. In an increasingly commercial society, therefore, there were many people committed to creating a climate in which purchasing consumer goods could be considered a positive social good. Consumption also grew because of an increasing tendency among colonists to take on debt to finance purchases, and the willingness of some merchants to offer credit.

Growing Consumerism

To facilitate the new consumer appetites, merchants and traders began advertising their goods in journals and newspapers. Agents of urban merchants—the ancestors of the traveling salesman—fanned out through the countryside, attempting to interest wealthy landowners and planters in the luxury goods now available to them. George and Martha Washington, for example, spent considerable time and money ordering elegant furnishings for their home at Mount Vernon, goods that were shipped to them mostly from England and Europe.

One feature of a consumer society is that things that once were considered luxuries quickly come to be seen as necessities once they are readily available. In the colonies, items that became commonplace after having once been expensive luxuries included tea, household linens, glassware, manufactured cutlery, crockery, and furniture, and many other things. Another result of consumerism is the association of material goods—of the quality of a person's home and possessions and clothing, for example—with virtue and "refinement." The ideal of the cultivated "gentleman" and the gracious "lady" became increasingly powerful throughout the colonies in the eighteenth century, and many colonists strove to emulate that ideal. In part that meant striving to become educated and "refined"—"gentlemanly" or "ladylike" in speech and behavior. Americans read books on manners and fashion. They bought magazines about London society.

Social Consequences

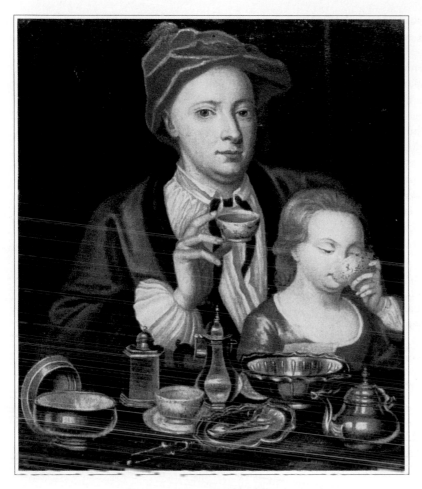

TEA PARTY IN THE TIME OF GEORGE I This painting by an unknown artist dates from the 1720s and shows a prosperous Virginian posing with a fashionable and expensive tea service, some of it from China. His eagerness to display his possessions in this way is a sign of the growing interest in the badges of refinement among colonial Americans of means in the eighteenth century. *(Colonial Williamsburg Foundation)*

And they strove to develop themselves as witty and educated conversationalists. They also commissioned portraits of themselves and their families, devoted large portions of their homes to entertainment, built shelves and cases in which they could display fashionable possessions, constructed formal gardens, and lavished attention on their wardrobes and hairstyles.

The growing importance of consumption and refinement was visible in the public spaces as well. Eighteenth-century cities—in America as in England and Europe—began to plan their growth to ensure that there would be elegant and gracious public squares, parks, and boulevards. In the past, social interaction in American communities had largely been between neighbors and relatives, or at most among members of church congregations. Now that a wider "society" was emerging within cities, it became important to create not just private but also public stages for social display.

PATTERNS OF SOCIETY

Although there were sharp social distinctions in the colonies, the well-defined and deeply entrenched class system of England failed to reproduce itself in America.

In England, where land was scarce and the population large, the relatively small number of people who owned property had enormous power over the great majority who did not; the imbalance between land and population became a foundation of the English economy and the cornerstone of its class system. In America, the opposite was true. Land was abundant, and people were scarce. Aristocracies emerged in America, to be sure. But they tended to rely less on landownership than on control of a substantial work force, and they were generally less secure and less powerful than their English counterparts. Far more than in England, there were opportunities in America for social mobility—both up and down.

There emerged, too, new forms of community whose structure reflected less the British model than the realities of the American environment. These forms varied greatly from one region to another, but several basic—and distinctly American—types emerged.

Social Mobility

The Plantation

The plantation defined a distinctive way of life for many white and black southerners that would survive, in varying forms, until the Civil War. The first plantations emerged in the early settlements of Virginia and Maryland, once tobacco became the economic basis of the Chesapeake.

In a few cases, plantations were of enormous size—much like some of the great estates of England. The Maryland plantation of Charles Carroll of Carrollton, reputedly the wealthiest man in the colonies, covered 40,000 acres and contained 285 slaves. On the whole, however, seventeenth-century colonial plantations were rough and relatively small estates. In the early days in Virginia, they were little more than crude clearings where landowners and indentured servants worked side by side in conditions so horrible that death was an everyday occurrence. Even in later years, when the death rate declined and the landholdings became more established, plantation work forces seldom exceeded thirty people.

The economy of the plantation, like all agricultural economies, was a precarious one. In good years, suc-

Vagaries of the Plantation Economy

cessful growers could earn great profits and expand their operations. But since they could not control their markets, even the largest planters were constantly at risk. When prices for their crops fell—as tobacco prices did, for example, in the 1660s—they faced ruin.

Because plantations were sometimes far from cities and towns—which were, in any case, relatively few in the South—they tended to become self-contained communities. Residents lived in close proximity to one another in a cluster of buildings that included the "great house" of the planter himself (a house that was usually, although not always, far from great), the service buildings, the barns, and the cabins of the slaves. Wealthier planters often created something approaching a full town on their plantations, with a school (for white children only), a chapel, and a large population. Smaller planters lived more modestly, but still in a relatively self-sufficient world. In some parts of the South, for example, the region around Charleston, South Carolina, planters often divided their time between the city and their relatively nearby plantations.

On the larger plantations, the presence of a substantial slave work force altered not only the economic, but the family lives of the planter class. Plantation mistresses, unlike the wives of small farmers, could rely on servants to perform ordinary household chores and could thus devote more time to their husbands and children than their counterparts in other parts of colonial society. But there were also frequent sexual liaisons between their husbands or sons and black women of the slave community. Southern women generally learned to pretend not to notice these relationships, but they were almost certainly a source of anxiety and resentment. Black women, naturally, had even greater cause to resent such liaisons.

Southern society was highly stratified. Within given areas, great landowners controlled not only the lives of

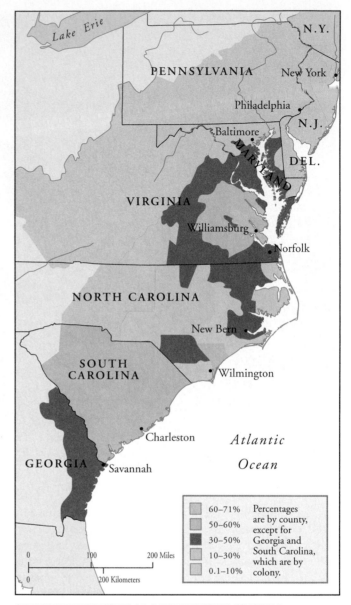

AFRICAN POPULATION AS A PROPORTION OF TOTAL POPULATION, c. 1775 This map illustrates the parts of the colonies in which the slave population was a large proportion of the whole—in some areas actually a majority. The densest African population was in Tidewater Virginia, but there were black majorities as well in South Carolina and parts of North Carolina. The slave population was smallest in the western regions of the southern colonies and in the area north of the Chesapeake, although there remained a significant African population in parts of New Jersey and New York (some slave, some free). ◆ *What explains the dense concentrations of slaves in these areas of the South?*

those who worked on their own plantations but also the liveli-

Stratified Southern Society

hoods of small farmers who could not effectively compete with the wealthy planters and thus depended on them to market crops and receive credit. Small farmers, working modest plots of land with few or no slaves to help them, formed the majority of the southern agrarian population, but it was the planters who dominated the southern agrarian economy. Most landowners lived in rough cabins or houses, with their servants or slaves nearby. Relatively few lived in anything resembling aristocratic splendor.

Plantation Slavery

African slaves, of course, lived very differently. On the smaller farms with only a handful of slaves, there was not always a rigid social separation between whites and blacks. But by the mid-eighteenth century, over three-fourths of all blacks lived on plantations of at least ten slaves; nearly half lived in communities of fifty slaves or more. In these larger establishments, Africans developed a society and culture of their own—influenced by their white masters, to be sure, but also partly independent of them.

Although whites seldom encouraged formal marriages among slaves, Africans themselves developed a strong and elaborate family structure. This became possible beginning in the eighteenth century as a result of the increased life expectancy of slaves, the gradual equalization of the sex ratio, and the growth of the population through natural increase. Slaves attempted to construct nuclear families, and they managed at times to build stable households, even to work together growing their own food in gardens provided by their masters. But such efforts were in constant jeopardy. Any family member could be sold at any time to another planter, even to one in another colony. As a result, the black family evolved along lines in many ways different from its white counterpart. Africans placed special emphasis on extended kinship networks. They even created surrogate "relatives" for those who were separated entirely from their own families. They adapted themselves, in short, to difficult conditions over which they had limited control.

African workers also developed languages of their own. In South Carolina, for example, the early slaves communicated with one another in Gullah, a hybrid of English and African tongues, that not only reinforced a sense of connection with their African ancestry but enabled **Slave Culture** them to engage in conversations their white masters could not understand. There emerged, too, a distinctive slave religion, which blended Christianity with African folklore and which became a central element in the emergence of an independent black culture.

Nevertheless, slave society was subject to constant intrusions from and interaction with white society. African house servants, for example, at times lived in what was, by the standards of slavery, great luxury; but they were also isolated from their own community and under constant surveillance from whites. Black women

MULBERRY PLANTATION, 1770 This painting of a rice plantation in South Carolina is unusual in placing the slave quarters in the forefront of the picture. The steep roofs of the slave cabins, which were built by the slaves themselves, reflected African architectural styles. The high roofs helped keep the cabins cool by allowing the heat to rise into the rafters. The master's house and adjacent chapel, built in more conventionally European style, is in the background. *(View of Mulberry (House and Street)* by Thomas Coram, *Gibbes Museum of Art/Carolina Art Association)*

were subject to usually unwanted sexual advances from owners and overseers and hence to bearing mulatto children, who were rarely recognized by their white fathers but who were generally accepted as members of the slave community. On some plantations, African workers received kindness and even affection from their masters and mistresses and at times displayed genuine devotion in return. On others, they encountered physical brutality and occasionally even sadism, against which they were virtually powerless.

There were occasional acts of individual resistance by slaves against masters, and at least twice during the colonial period there were actual slave rebellions. In the most important such revolt, the so-called Stono Rebellion in South Carolina in 1739, about 100 Africans rose up, seized weapons, killed several whites, and attempted to escape south to Florida. Whites quickly crushed the uprising and executed most participants. The most frequent form of resistance was simply running away, but for most slaves that provided no real solution either. There was nowhere to go.

Most slaves, male and female, worked as field hands (with women shouldering the additional burdens of cooking and child rearing). But on the larger plantations that aspired to genuine self-sufficiency, some slaves learned trades and crafts: blacksmithing, carpentry, shoemaking, spinning, weaving, sewing, midwifery, and others. These skilled craftsmen and craftswomen were at times hired out to other planters. Some set up their own establishments in towns or cities and shared their profits with their owners. On occasion, they were able to buy their freedom. There was a small free black population living in southern cities by the time of the Revolution.

The Puritan Community

A very different form of community emerged in Puritan New England, but one that was also distinctively American. The characteristic social unit in New England was not the isolated farm, but the town. Each new settlement drew up a "covenant" among its members, binding all residents together in a religious and social commitment to unity and harmony. Some such settlements consisted of people who had immigrated to America together (occasionally entire Puritan congregations who had traveled to the New World as a group).

The structure of the towns reflected the spirit of the covenant. Colonists laid out a village, with houses and a meetinghouse arranged around a central pasture, or "common." They also divided up the outlying fields and woodlands of the town among the residents; the size and location of a family's field depended on the family's numbers, wealth, and social station. But wherever their lands might lie, families generally lived in the village with their neighbors close by, reinforcing the strong sense of community.

Once established, a town was generally able to run its own affairs, with little interference from the colonial government. Residents held a yearly "town meeting" to decide important questions and to choose a group of "selectmen," who governed until the next meeting. Only adult males were permitted to participate in the meeting. But even among them, important social distinctions remained, the most crucial of which was membership in the church. Only those residents who could give evidence of grace, of being among the elect (the "visible saints") confident of salvation as a result of a conversion experience, were admitted to full membership, although other residents of the town were still required to attend church services.

The English system of primogeniture—the passing of all inherited property to the firstborn son—did not take root in New England. Instead, a father divided up his lands among all his sons. His control of this inheritance was one of the most effective means of exercising power over the male members of his family. Often a son would reach his late twenties before his father would allow him to move into his own household and work his own land. Even then, sons would usually continue to live in close proximity to their fathers. Young women were generally more mobile than their brothers, since they did not stand to inherit land; their dowries and their inheritances consisted instead of movable objects (furniture, household goods, occasionally money or precious objects) and thus did not tie them to a particular place.

As the years passed and the communities grew, the tight-knit social structure of the Puritans experienced strains. This was partly because of the increasing commercialization of New England society. But it was also a result of other pressures that developed even within purely agricultural communities, pressures that were a result primarily of population growth.

As towns grew larger, residents tended to cultivate lands farther and farther from the community center. Some moved out of the town center to be nearer their lands and thus began to find themselves far away from the church. Some groups of outlying residents would eventually apply for permission to build a church of their own, which was usually the first step toward creation of a wholly new town. Such applications were frequently the occasion for bitter quarrels between the original townspeople and those who proposed to break away.

The practice of distributing land through the patriarchal family structure also helped create tensions in the Puritan community. In the first generations, fathers generally controlled enough land to satisfy the needs of all their sons. After several generations, however, when

Stono Rebellion

Patterns of Settlement

Puritan Democracy

Population Pressure

THE NEW ENGLAND TOWN: SUDBURY, MASSACHUSETTS, 17TH CENTURY Just as the plantation was a characteristic social form in the southern colonies, the town was the most common social unit in New England. This map shows the organization of Sudbury, Massachusetts, a town just west of Boston, in its early years in the seventeenth century. Note the location of the houses, which are grouped mostly together around a shared pasture (or "commons") and near the church. Note, too, the outlying fields, which were divided up among residents of the town, even though they were often not connected to the land on which they lived. The map illustrates the holdings of a single resident of Sudbury, John Goodnow, whose house was on the Common, but whose lands were scattered over a number of areas of Sudbury. • *What aspects of New England life might help explain the clustering of residences at the center of the town? (From Sumner Chilton Powell,* Puritan Village: The Formation of a New England Town. *Copyright © 1963 by Wesleyan University. Reprinted by permission from Wesleyan University Press)*

such lands were being subdivided for the third or fourth time, there was often too little to go around, particularly in communities surrounded by other towns, with no room to expand outward. The result was that in many communities, groups of younger residents began breaking off and moving elsewhere—at times far away—to form towns of their own where land was more plentiful.

Even within the family, economic necessity often undermined the patriarchal model to which most Puritans, in theory at least, subscribed. It was not only the Generational Conflict sons who needed their fathers (as a source of land and wealth); fathers needed their sons, as well as their wives and daughters, as a source of labor to keep the farm and the household functioning. Thus, while in theory men had nearly dictatorial control over their wives and children, in reality relationships were more contractual, with the authority of husbands and fathers limited by economic necessity (and, of course, bonds of affection).

The Witchcraft Phenomenon

The gap between the expectation of a cohesive, united community and the reality of an increasingly diverse and fluid one was difficult for early New Englanders to accept. At times, such tensions could produce bizarre and disastrous events. One example was the widespread hysteria in the 1680s and 1690s over supposed witchcraft in New England.

The most famous outbreak (although by no means the only one) was in Salem, Massachusetts, where adolescent girls began to exhibit strange behavior and leveled accusations of witchcraft against several West Indian servants steeped in voodoo lore. The hysteria they produced spread throughout the town, and before it was over, hundreds of Salem Witch Trials people (most of them women) were accused of witchcraft. As the crisis in Salem grew, accusations shifted from marginal women like the West Indians to more prominent and substantial people. Nineteen residents of Salem were put to death before the trials finally ended in 1692; the girls who had been the original accusers later recanted and admitted that they had made up the story.

But the Salem experience was only one of many. Accusations of witchcraft spread through many New England towns in the early 1690s (and indeed had emerged regularly in Puritan society for many years before). Research into the background of accused witches reveals that most were middle-aged women, often widowed, with few or no children. Many accused witches were of low social position, were often involved in domestic conflicts, had frequently been accused of other crimes, and were considered abrasive by their neighbors. Others were women who, through inheritance or enterprise, had come into possession of substantial land and property on their own and hence also challenged the gender norms of the community. Puritan society had little tolerance for "independent" women. That so many "witches" were women who were not securely lodged within a male-dominated family structure (and that many seemed openly to defy the passive,

A STUDY OF WITCHCRAFT This pamphlet, originally published in 1697 near the height of the witchcraft phenomenon in New England, was one of many contemporary studies to take the idea of witchcraft seriously. Belief in witches as agents of Satan was widespread in early New England society (and in many other parts of the Christian world as well), and many of the charges that seem preposterous in our time appeared entirely plausible, even among educated people, in theirs. *(Courtesy Peabody Essex Museum, Salem, MA)*

submissive norms society had created for them) suggests that tensions over gender roles played a substantial role in generating the crisis.

Above all, however, the witchcraft controversies were a reflection of the highly religious character of these societies. New Englanders believed in the power of Satan and his ability to assert his power in the world. Belief in witchcraft was not a marginal superstition, rejected by the mainstream. It was a common feature of Puritan religious conviction.

Cities

To call the commercial centers that emerged along the Atlantic coast in the eighteenth century

Growth of Colonial Cities

"cities" would be to strain the modern definition of that word. Even the largest colonial community was scarcely bigger than a modern small town. Yet by the standards of the eighteenth century, cities did indeed exist in America. In the 1770s the two largest ports—Philadelphia and New York—had populations of 28,000 and 25,000, respectively, which made them larger than most English urban centers. Boston (16,000), Charles Town (later Charleston), South Carolina (12,000), and Newport, Rhode Island (11,000), were also substantial communities by the standards of the day.

Colonial cities served as trading centers for the farmers of their regions and as marts for international trade. Their leaders were generally merchants who had acquired substantial estates. Disparities of wealth were features of almost all communities in America, but in cities they seemed particularly glaring. Moving beside them were the numerous minor tradesmen, workers, and indigents, who lived in crowded and often filthy conditions. More than in any other area of colonial life (except, of course, in the relationship between masters and slaves), social distinctions were real and visible in urban areas.

Cities were also the centers of much of what industry there was in the colonies, such as ironworks and distilleries for turning imported molasses into exportable rum. And they were the locations of the most advanced schools and the most sophisticated cultural activities, and of shops where imported goods could be bought. In addition, they were communities with peculiarly urban social prob-

Commercial and Cultural Importance

lems: crime, vice, pollution, epidemics, traffic. Unlike smaller towns, cities were required to establish elaborate governments. They set up constables' offices and fire departments. They developed systems for supporting the urban poor, whose numbers grew steadily and became especially large in times of economic crisis.

Cities were also particularly vulnerable to fluctuations in trade. When a market for a particular product

The Witchcraft Trials

The witchcraft trials of the 1690s—which began in Salem, Massachusetts, and spread to other areas of New England—have been the stuff of popular legend for centuries. They have also engaged the interest of generations of historians, who have tried to explain why these seventeenth-century Americans became so committed to the belief that some of their own neighbors were agents of Satan. Although there have been many explanations of the witchcraft phenomenon, some of the most important in recent decades have focused on the central place of women in the story.

Through the first half of the twentieth century, most historians dismissed the witchcraft trials as "hysteria," prompted by the intolerance and rigidity of Puritan society. This interpretation informed perhaps the most prominent popular portrayal of witchcraft in the twentieth century: Arthur Miller's play, *The Crucible*, first produced in 1953, which was clearly an effort to use the Salem trials as a comment on the great anticommunist frenzy of his own time. But at almost the same time, the renowned scholar of Puritanism Perry Miller argued in a series of important studies that belief in witchcraft was not a product of hysteria or intolerance, but a widely shared part of the religious worldview of the seventeenth century. To the Puritans, witchcraft seemed not only plausible, but scientifically rational.

A new wave of interpretation of witchcraft began in the 1970s, with the publication of *Salem Possessed* (1976), by Paul Boyer and Stephen Nissenbaum. Their examination of the town records of Salem in the 1690s led them to conclude that the witchcraft controversy there was a product of class tensions between the poorer, more marginal residents of one part of Salem and their wealthier, more privileged residents of another. These social

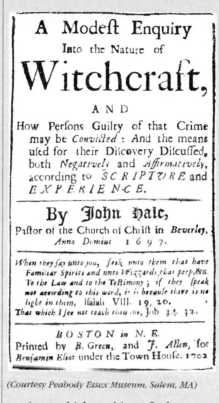

(Courtesy Peabody Essex Museum, Salem, MA)

tensions, which could not find easy expression on their own terms, led some poorer Salemites to lash out at their richer neighbors by charging them, or their servants, with witchcraft. A few years later, John Demos, in *Entertaining Satan* (1983), examined witchcraft accusations in a larger area of New England and similarly portrayed them as products of displaced anger about social and economic grievances that could not be expressed otherwise. Demos provided a far more complex picture of the nature of these grievances than had Boyer and Nissenbaum but like them saw witchcraft as a symptom of a persistent set of social and psychological tensions.

At about the same time, however, a number of scholars were beginning to look at witchcraft through the then relatively new scholarly lens of gender. Carol Karlsen's *The Devil in the Shape of a Woman* (1987) demonstrated through intensive scrutiny of records across New England that a disproportionate number of those accused of witchcraft were property-owning widows or unmarried women—in other words, women who did not fit comfortably into the normal pattern of male-dominated families. Karlsen concluded that such women were vulnerable to these accusations because they seemed threatening to people (including many women) who were accustomed to women as subordinate members of the community.

More recently, Mary Beth Norton's *In the Devil's Snare* (2002) placed the witchcraft trials in the context of other events of their time—and in particular the terrifying upheavals and dislocations that the Indian wars of the late seventeenth century created in Puritan communities. In the face of this crisis, in which refugees from King William's War were fleeing towns destroyed by the Indians and flooding Salem and other eastern towns, fear and social instability helped create a more-than-normal readiness to connect aberrant behavior (such as the actions of unusually independent or eccentric women) to supernatural causes. The result was a wave of witchcraft accusations that ultimately led to the execution of at least twenty people.

became glutted and prices fell, the effects on merchants and other residents could be severe. In the countryside, the impact was generally more muted. Finally, and of particular importance for the political future of the colonies, cities became places where new ideas could circulate and be discussed. Because there were printers, it was possible to have regular newspapers. Books and other publications from abroad introduced new intellectual influences. And the taverns and coffeehouses of cities provided forums in which people could gather and debate the issues of the day. It was not surprising that when the revolutionary crisis began to build in the 1760s and 1770s, it was first visible in the cities.

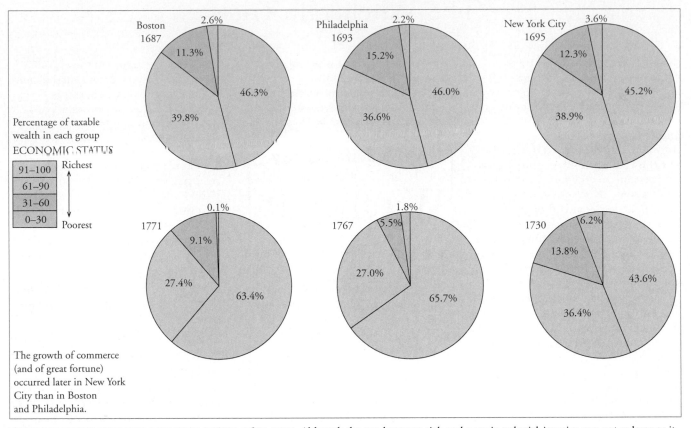

WEALTH DISTRIBUTION IN COLONIAL CITIES, 1687–1771 Although the gap between rich and poor in colonial America was not as large as it would become in the nineteenth and twentieth centuries, the rise of commerce in the early eighteenth century did produce increasing inequality. This chart shows the distribution of wealth in three important commercial cities—Boston, Philadelphia, and New York. The upper pie charts show the distribution of wealth in the late seventeenth century, and the lower charts show how that distribution had changed by the mid or late eighteenth centuries. Note the heavy concentration of wealth in the top 10 percent of the population in the seventeenth century, and the even heavier concentration of wealth in Boston and Philadelphia in the eighteenth century. In New York, by contrast, wealth distribution became slightly more equal between 1695 and 1730, because of the breaking up of the great Dutch estates once the colony came under the control of the British. In later years, New York would show the same pattern of growing inequality that Boston and Philadelphia experienced. ◆ *What aspects of colonial commerce helped concentrate so much wealth in the hands of a relatively small group?*

AWAKENINGS AND ENLIGHTENMENTS

Two powerful forces were competing in American intellectual life in the eighteenth century. One was the traditional outlook of the sixteenth and seventeenth centuries, with its emphasis on a personal God, intimately involved with the world, keeping watch over individual lives. The other was the new spirit of the Enlightenment, a movement sweeping both Europe and America, which stressed the importance of science and human reason. The old views supported such phenomena as the belief in witchcraft, and they placed great value on a stern moral code in which intellect was less important than faith. The Enlightenment, by contrast, suggested that people had substantial control over their own lives and the course of their societies, that the world could be explained and therefore could be structured along rational scientific lines. Much of the intellectual climate of colonial America was shaped by the tension between these two impulses.

The Pattern of Religions

Religious toleration flourished in many parts of America to a degree unmatched in any European nation, not because Americans deliberately sought to produce it but because conditions virtually required it. Settlers in America brought with them so many different religious practices that it proved difficult to impose a single religious code on any large area.

Roots of Religious Toleration

The Church of England was established as the official faith in Virginia, Maryland, New York, the Carolinas, and Georgia. Except in Virginia and Maryland, however, the laws establishing the Church of England as the official colonial religion were largely ignored. Even in New England, where the Puritans had originally believed that they were all part of a single faith, there was a growing tendency in the eighteenth century for different congregations to affiliate with different denominations, especially Congregationalism and Presbyterianism. In parts of

SINNERS IN HELL, 1744 This mid-eighteenth-century religious image illustrates both the fears and prejudices of many colonial Christians. The idyllic city of Sion, in the center of the drawing, is threatened on all sides by forces of evil, which include not just images of Satan and sin, but also of some of the perceived enemies of Protestants—the Catholic Church (symbolized by the image of the Pope) and Islam (symbolized by Turks). *(The Granger Collection, New York)*

New York and New Jersey, Dutch settlers had established their own Calvinist denomination, Dutch Reformed, which survived after the colonies became part of the British Empire. American Baptists (of whom Roger Williams is considered the first) developed a great variety of sects. All Baptists shared the belief that rebaptism, usually by total immersion, was necessary when believers reached maturity. But while some Baptists remained Calvinists (believers in predestination) others came to believe in salvation by free will.

Protestants extended toleration to one another more readily than they did to Roman Catholics. Many Protestants in America, like many in England, feared and hated the pope. New Englanders, in particular, viewed their Catholic neighbors in New France (Canada) not only as commercial and military rivals but also as dangerous agents of Rome. In most of the English colonies, however, Roman Catholics were too few to cause serious conflict. They were most numerous in Maryland, and even there they numbered no more than 3,000. Perhaps for that reason they suffered their worst persecution in that colony. After the overthrow of the original proprietors in 1691, Catholics in Maryland not only lost their political rights but also were forbidden to hold religious services except in private houses.

Anti-Catholicism

Jews in provincial America totaled no more than about 2,000 at any time. The largest community lived in New York City. Smaller groups settled in Newport and Charleston, and there were scattered Jewish families in all the colonies. Nowhere could they vote or hold office. Only in Rhode Island could they practice their religion openly.

By the beginning of the eighteenth century, some Americans were growing troubled by the apparent decline in religious piety in their society. The movement of the population westward and the wide scattering of settlements had caused many communities to lose touch with organized religion. The rise of commercial prosperity created a more secular outlook in urban areas. The progress of science and free thought in Europe—and the importation of Enlightenment ideas to America—caused at least some colonists to doubt traditional religious beliefs.

Concerns about weakening piety surfaced as early as the 1660s in New England, where the Puritan oligarchy warned of a decline in the power of the church. Sabbath after Sabbath, ministers preached sermons of despair (known as "jeremiads"), deploring the signs of waning piety. By the standards of other societies or other eras, the Puritan faith remained remarkably strong. But New Englanders measured their faith by their own standards, and to them the "declension" of religious piety seemed a serious problem.

Jeremiads

The Great Awakening

By the early eighteenth century, similar concerns about declining piety and growing secularism were emerging in other regions and among members of other faiths. The result was the first great American revival: the Great Awakening.

The Great Awakening began in earnest in the 1730s, reached its climax in the 1740s, and brought a new spirit of religious fervor to the colonies. The revival had particular appeal to women (who constituted the majority of converts) and to younger sons of the third or fourth generation of settlers—those who stood to inherit the least land and who faced the most uncertain futures. The rhetoric of the revival emphasized the potential for every person to break away from the constraints of the past and start anew in his or her relationship with God. Such beliefs may have reflected the desires of many people to break away from their families or communities and start a new life.

Powerful evangelists from England helped spread the revival. John and Charles Wesley, the founders of Methodism, visited Georgia and other colonies in the 1730s. George Whitefield, a powerful open-air preacher and for a time an associate of the Wesleys, made several evangelizing tours through the colonies and drew tremendous crowds. But the outstanding preacher of the Great Awakening was the New England Congregationalist Jonathan Edwards, a deeply orthodox Puritan but a highly original theologian. From his pulpit in Northampton, Massachusetts, Edwards attacked the new doctrines of easy salvation for all. He preached anew the traditional Puritan ideas of the absolute sovereignty of God, predestination, and salvation by God's grace alone. His vivid descriptions of hell could terrify his listeners.

The Great Awakening led to the division of existing congregations (between "New Light" revivalists and "Old Light" traditionalists) and to the founding of new ones. It also affected areas of society outside **Old Lights and New Lights** the churches. Some of the revivalists denounced book learning as a hindrance to salvation, and some communities repudiated secular education altogether. But other evangelists saw education as a means of furthering religion, and they founded or led schools for the training of New Light ministers.

The Enlightenment

The Great Awakening caused one great upheaval in the culture of the colonies. The Enlightenment, a very different—and in many ways competing—phenomenon, caused another.

The Enlightenment was to a large degree the product of some of the great scientific and intellectual discoveries in Europe in the seventeenth century. As scientists and other thinkers discovered natural laws that they believed regulated the workings of nature, they came to celebrate the power of human reason and scientific inquiry. Enlightenment thinkers argued that reason, not just faith, could create progress and advance knowledge. They argued that humans had a moral sense on which they could rely to tell the difference between right and wrong; that they did not need always to turn to God for guidance in making decisions. They insisted that men and women could, through the power of their own reason, move civilization to ever greater heights.

In celebrating reason, the Enlightenment slowly helped undermine the power of traditional authority—something the Great Awakening did as well. But unlike the Great Awakening, the Enlightenment encouraged men and women to look to themselves—not to God—for guidance as to how to live their lives and to shape society. **Traditional Authority Challenged** Enlightenment thought, with its emphasis on human rationality, encouraged a new emphasis on education, and a heightened interest in politics and government (for through governments, the believers in reason argued, society had its best chance of bettering itself). Most Enlightenment figures did not challenge religion and insisted that rational inquiry would support, not undermine, Christianity. But they challenged the notion of some religious groups that the answer to all questions about human society should, or could, come directly from God.

In the early seventeenth century, Enlightenment ideas in America were largely borrowed from abroad—from such earlier giants as Francis Bacon and John Locke, and from

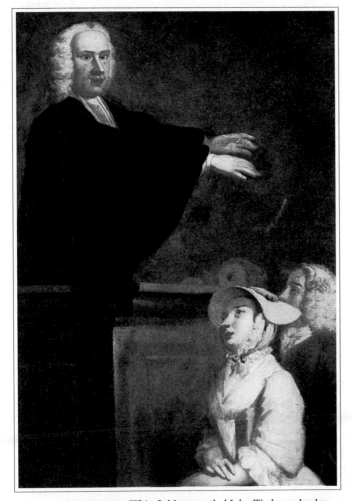

GEORGE WHITEFIELD Whitefield succeeded John Wesley as leader of the Calvinistic Methodists in Oxford, England. Like Wesley, he was a major force in promoting religious revivalism in both England and America. He made his first missionary journey to the New World in 1738 and returned in the mid-1740s for a celebrated journey through the colonies that helped spark the Great Awakening. *(National Portrait Gallery, London)*

contemporary Enlightenment thinkers in England and Scotland. Few Americans had yet made important contributions of their own to the new age of science and reason. Later, however, such Americans as Benjamin Franklin, Thomas Jefferson, Thomas Paine, and James Madison made their own vital contributions to the Enlightenment tradition.

Education

Even before Enlightenment ideas became common in America, colonists had placed a high value on education, despite the difficulties they confronted in gaining access to it. Some families tried to teach their children to read and write at home, although the heavy burden of work in most agricultural households limited the time available for schooling. In Massachusetts, a 1647 law required every town to support a public school, and while many communities failed to comply, a modest network of educational establishments emerged as a result. Elsewhere, the Quakers and other sects operated church schools. And in some communities, widows or unmarried women conducted "dame schools" by holding private classes in their homes. In cities, master craftsmen set up evening schools for their apprentices; at least a hundred such schools appeared between 1723 and 1770.

Only a relatively small number of children received education beyond the primary level; but white male

High White Literacy Rates

Americans, at least, achieved a high degree of literacy. By the time of the Revolution, well over half of all white men could read and write, a rate substantially higher than in most European countries. The large number of colonists who could read helped create a market for the first widely circulated publications in America other than the Bible: almanacs. (See pp. 94–95) The literacy rate for women lagged behind that of men until the nineteenth century; and while opportunities for further education were scarce for males, they were almost nonexistent for females. Nevertheless, in their early years colonial girls often received the same home-based education as boys, and their literacy rate too was substantially higher than that of their European counterparts. African slaves had virtually no access to education. Occasionally a master or mistress would teach slave children to read and write, but they had few real incentives to do so. Indeed, as the slave system became more firmly entrenched, strong social (and ultimately legal) sanctions developed to discourage any efforts to promote black literacy, lest it encourage slaves to question their station. Indians, too, remained largely outside the white educational system—to a large degree by choice; most tribes preferred to educate their children in their own way. But some white missionaries and philanthropists established schools for Native Americans and helped create a small but significant population of Indians literate in spoken and written English.

Nowhere was the intermingling of the influences of traditional religiosity and the new spirit of the Enlightenment clearer than in the colleges and universities that grew up in colonial America. Of the six colleges in operation by 1763, all but two were founded by religious groups primarily for the training of preachers. Yet in almost all, the influences of the new scientific, rational approach to knowledge could be felt. Harvard, the first American college, was established in 1636 by the General Court of Massachusetts at the behest of Puritan theologians, who wanted to create a training center for ministers. The college was named for a Charlestown minister, John Harvard, who had died and left his library and half his estate to the college. Decades later, in 1693, William and Mary College (named for the English king and queen) was established in Williamsburg, Virginia, by Anglicans; like Harvard, it was conceived as an academy to train clergymen. In 1701, conservative Congregationalists, dissatisfied with what they considered the growing religious liberalism of Harvard, founded Yale (named for one of its first benefactors, Elihu Yale) in New Haven, Connecticut. Out of the Great Awakening emerged the College of New Jersey, founded in 1746 and known later as Princeton (after the town in which it is located). One of its first presidents was Jonathan Edwards.

Despite the religious basis of these colleges, students at most of them could derive something of a liberal education from the curricula, which included not only theology, but logic, ethics, physics, geometry, astronomy, rhetoric, Latin, Hebrew, and Greek. From the beginning, Harvard attempted not only to provide an educated ministry but also to "advance learning and perpetuate it to posterity." Members of the Harvard faculty made strenuous

Liberal Curricula

efforts to desseminate new scientific ideas—particularly the ideas of Copernican astronomy—to a larger public, often publishing their ideas in popular almanacs. By doing so, they hoped to stamp out popular belief in astrology, which they considered pagan superstition.

King's College, founded in New York in 1754 and later renamed Columbia, was even more devoted to the spread of secular knowledge. It had no theological faculty and was interdenominational from the start. The Academy and College of Philadelphia, which became the University of Pennsylvania, was a completely secular institution, founded in 1755 by a group of laymen under the inspiration of Benjamin Franklin. It offered courses in utilitarian subjects—mechanics, chemistry, agriculture, government, commerce, and modern languages—as well as in the liberal arts. It also became the site of the first medical school in British America, founded in 1765.

The Spread of Science

The clearest indication of the spreading influence of the Enlightenment in America was an increasing interest in

Colonial Almanacs

Books were scarce and expensive in colonial America, and many families owned only one: the Bible. But starting very early in the life of the English colonies, men and women had another important source of information: almanacs, the most popular nonreligious literature in early America.

Almanacs had been popular in Europe since at least the mid-sixteenth century. They first appeared in America in 1638 or 1639 when printers in Cambridge, Massachusetts began publishing the *Philomath Almanac,* which combined an elaborate calendar of religious holidays with information about astronomy, astrology, and, as time went on, other popular interests. By the 1680s, the *Farmer's Almanac* began to rival the *Philomath.* It was a heavily illustrated publication that set a pattern for the future by adding medical advice, practical wisdom, navigational information, and humor. It also indulged in the European custom of prognostication; through a combination of superstition, popular folklore, and astronomical (and astrological) devices, it predicted weather patterns throughout the year, crop yields, and many other things. Almanac predictions were notoriously unreliable; but in the absence of any better alternatives, many people relied on them nevertheless.

By 1700, there were dozens, perhaps hundreds, of almanacs circulating

POOR RICHARD'S ALMANACK This page from a 1757 edition of *Poor Richard's Almanack* illustrates the wide range of material that almanacs presented to their readers—an uplifting poem, a calendar of holidays and weather predictions, and such scattered pieces of advice and wisdom as "A rich rogue is like a fat hog, who never does good till as dead as a log." *(New York Public Library Astor, Lenox and Tilden Foundations)*

throughout the colonies and even in the sparsely settled lands to the west and north. The most popular almanacs sold tens of thousands of copies every year. Most families had at least one, and many had several. "It is easy to prove," one almanac writer claimed in the mid-eighteenth century, "that no book we read (except the Bible) is so much valued and so serviceable to the community." America was a multilingual society, and although most almanacs were in English, some appeared in French, Dutch, Hebrew, Norwegian, Spanish, German, and various Indian languages. For five years just after the Revolution, Benjamin Banneker of Maryland was the only African-American almanac writer, publishing a book that occasionally included harsh commentary on slavery and the slave trade.

The best-known almanac in the colonies in the years before the American Revolution was published by Benjamin Franklin, a printer's son who ran away from an apprenticeship in his older brother's print shop in Rhode Island and eventually settled in Philadelphia. There, from 1732 to 1758, he published *Poor Richard's Almanack* under the pseudonym Richard Saunders. "I endeavor'd to make it both entertaining and useful," Franklin later wrote in his autobiography. "And observing that it was generally read, . . . I consider'd it as a proper vehicle for conveying instruction among the

A "DAME SCHOOL" PRIMER More than the residents of any other region of North America (and far more than those of most of Europe), the New England colonists strove to educate their children and achieved perhaps the highest level of literacy in the world. Throughout the region, young children attended institutions known as "dame schools" (because the teachers were almost always women) and learned from primers like this one. Puritan education emphasized both basic skills (the alphabet and reading) and moral and religious precepts, as this sample page suggests. *(American Antiquarian Society)*

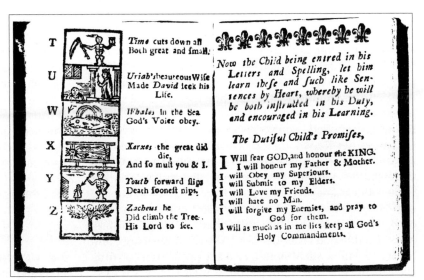

94

common people, who bought scarcely any other books." In issue after issue, Franklin accompanied his calendars, astronomical information, and other standard almanac fare with "proverbial sentences, chiefly such as inculcated industry and frugality." One of his favorite proverbs, which he said illustrated how difficult it was for a poor man always to act honestly, was "It is hard for an empty sack to stand upright." Poor Richard's many sayings became among the most familiar passages in America. Franklin was among many writers who used the almanac to promote the new scientific discoveries of his time and to try to discredit what he considered the backward superstitions that stood in the way of knowledge. He was particularly contemptuous of astrology.

Almanacs were virtually the only widely read publications in America that contained popular humor, and they are one of the best sources today for understanding what early Americans considered funny. Not unlike later generations, they delighted in humor that ridiculed the high and mighty (aristocrats, lawyers, clergymen, politicians), that made fun of relationships between men and women, and that expressed stereotypes about racial and ethnic groups. In the 1760s and 1770s, almanac humor was often used to disguise political ideas, in the way it ridiculed British officials and American

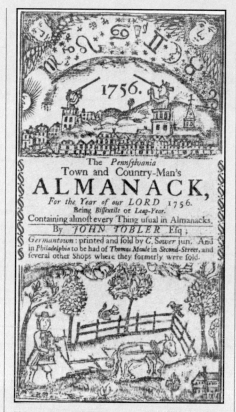

TOWN AND COUNTRY-MAN'S ALMANACK
As the population of colonial cities and towns grew, almanacs—originally targeted mainly at farmers—began to make explicit appeal to townspeople as well. *(Princeton University Library. Sinclair Hamilton Collection, Graphic Arts Division, Department of Rare Books and Special Collections)*

Tories. During the war itself, humorous anecdotes about military officers and political leaders reflected the uneasy views of Americans about the long and difficult struggle.

During and after the Revolution, much almanac humor consisted of admiring anecdotes about the man who was by then perhaps the most famous and beloved man in America—Poor Richard himself, Benjamin Franklin. Much less reverential, and probably funnier to readers, was the often ribald ethnic and racial humor in many almanacs. In *Beer's Almanac* of 1801, an Irishman boasted that he had owned a large estate in Ireland before leaving for America. Why, he was asked, had he left it to come to the United States? "Ah," he replied, "It was indeed under a small encumbrance; for another man's land lay right a top of it."

Almanacs remained enormously popular throughout the nineteenth century, and some are still published today. But they had their greatest influence in the early years of European settlement when, for thousands of Americans, they were virtually the only source of printed information people had. "A good Almanac," the printer Isaac Briggs wrote in 1798, in a preface to one of his own, "is, like iron, far more valuable (although much less valued) than gold, if we estimate its value by its absolute usefulness to the common purposes of life."

scientific knowledge. Most of the early colleges established chairs in the natural sciences and introduced some of the advanced scientific theories of Europe, including Copernican astronomy and Newtonian physics, to their students. But the most vigorous promotion of science in these years occurred outside the colleges, through the private efforts of amateurs and the activities of scientific societies. Leading merchants, planters, and even theologians became corresponding members of the Royal Society of London, the leading English scientific organization. Benjamin Franklin, the most celebrated amateur scientist in America, won international fame through his experimental proof of the nature of lightning and electricity and his invention of the lightning rod. His 1752 demonstration, using a kite,

of his theory that lightning and electricity were the same was widely celebrated in the colonies.

The high value that influential Americans were beginning to place on scientific knowledge was clearly demonstrated by the most daring and controversial scientific experiment of the eighteenth century: inoculation
Smallpox Inoculation
against smallpox. The Puritan theologian Cotton Mather heard, reportedly from his own slave, of the practice of deliberately infecting people with mild cases of smallpox in order to immunize them against the deadly disease. He learned, too, that experiments in inoculation were being conducted, with some success, in England. Mather was not, certainly, a wholly committed scientist. He continued to believe that disease was a punishment for sin.

BENJAMIN FRANKLIN ON ELECTRICITY The discovery of electricity was one of the great scientific events of the eighteenth century, even though large-scale practical use of electrical energy emerged much later. Benjamin Franklin was one of the first Americans, and certainly the most famous American, to experiment with electricity. This is the frontispiece for a book, originally published in 1750 in Philadelphia, that describes his "experiments and observations." The pages shown here are from the London edition, which appeared in 1774. *(Getty Images)*

Yet despite strong opposition from many of his neighbors, he urged inoculation on his fellow Bostonians during an epidemic in the 1720s. The results confirmed the effectiveness of the technique. Other theologians (including Jonathan Edwards) took up the cause, along with many physicians. By the mid-eighteenth century, inoculation had become a common medical procedure in America.

Concepts of Law and Politics

In seventeenth- and eighteenth-century law and politics, as in other parts of their lives, Americans of European descent believed that they were re-creating in the New World the practices and institutions of the Old. But as in other areas, they managed, without meaning to or even realizing it, to create something very different.

Changes in the law in America resulted in part from the scarcity of English-trained lawyers, who were almost unknown in the colonies until after 1700. Not until well into the eighteenth century did authorities in England try to impose the common law and the statutes of the realm upon the provinces. By then, it was already too late. Although the American legal system adopted most of the essential elements of the English system, including such ancient rights as trial by jury, significant differences had already become well established. Pleading and court procedures were simpler in America than in England, and punishments were different. Instead of the gallows or prison, colonists more commonly resorted to the whipping post, the branding iron, the stocks, and (for "gossipy" women) the ducking stool. In a labor-scarce society, it was not in the interests of communities to execute or incarcerate potential workers. Crimes were redefined. In England, a printed attack on a public official, whether true or false, was considered libelous. In the 1734–1735 trial of the New York publisher John Peter Zenger, who was powerfully defended by the Philadelphia lawyer Andrew Hamilton, the courts ruled that criticisms of the government were not libelous if factually true—a verdict that removed some restrictions on the freedom of the press. There was a subtle but decisive transformation in legal philosophy. Some colonists came to think of law as a reflection of the divine will; others saw it as a result of

PUNISHMENT IN NEW ENGLAND New England communities prescribed a wide range of punishments for misconduct and crime in the seventeenth and eighteenth centuries. Among the more common punishments were public humiliations—placing offenders in stocks, forcing them to wear badges of shame, or, as in this woodcut, publicly ducking them in a stream or pond to create both discomfort and embarrassment. *(The British Museum)*

the natural order. In neither case did they consider it an expression of the power of an earthly sovereign.

Even more significant for the future of the relationship between the colonies and England were important emerging differences between the American and British political systems. Because the royal government was so far away, Americans created a group

Colonial Governments

of institutions of their own that gave them—in reality, if not in theory—a large measure of self-government. In most colonies, local communities grew accustomed to running their own affairs with minimal interference from higher authorities. Communities also expected to maintain strict control over their delegates to the colonial assemblies, and those assemblies came to exercise many of the powers that Parliament exercised in England (even though in theory Parliament remained the ultimate authority in America). Provincial governors appointed by the crown had broad powers on paper, but in fact their influence was sharply limited. They lacked control over appointments and contracts; such influence resided largely in England or with local colonial leaders. They could never be certain of their tenure in office; because governorships were patronage appointments, a governor could be removed any time his patron in England lost favor. And in many cases, governors were not even familiar with the colonies they were meant to govern. Some governors were native-born Americans, but most were Englishmen who came to the colonies for the first time to assume their offices. The result of all this was that the focus of politics in the colonies became a local one. The provincial governments became accustomed to acting more or less independently of Parliament, and a set of assumptions and expectations about the rights of the colonists began to take hold in America that policymakers in England did not share. These differences caused few problems before the 1760s, because the British did little to exert the authority they believed they possessed. But when, beginning in 1763, the English government began attempting to tighten its control over the American colonies, a great imperial crisis developed.

CONCLUSION

What began as a few small, isolated, precarious settlements in the wilderness had evolved by the mid-eighteenth century into a large and complex society. The English colonies in America grew steadily between the 1650s and the 1750s: in population, in the size of their economies, and in the sophistication—and diversity—of their cultures. In many ways the colonies had become more like England by the mid-eighteenth century than they had been during their frail early years. In other ways, life in America and life in Britain had begun to diverge.

Many distinct societies developed in the colonies, but the greatest distinction was between the colonies of the North and those of the South. In the North, society was dominated by relatively small family farms and by towns

Regional Differences

and cities of growing size. A thriving commercial class was developing, and with it an increasingly elaborate urban culture. In the South, there were many family farms as well. But there were also large plantations cultivating tobacco, rice, indigo, and cotton for export. By the late seventeenth century, these plantations were relying heavily on African workers who had been brought to the colonies forcibly as slaves. There were few significant towns and cities in the South, and little commerce other than the marketing of crops.

The colonies did, however, also have much in common. Most white Americans accepted common assumptions about racial inequality. That enabled them to tolerate (and at times celebrate) the enslavement of African men and women and to justify a campaign of displacement and often violence against Native Americans that would continue for two centuries. Most white Americans (and, in different ways, most nonwhite Americans as well) were deeply religious. The Great Awakening, therefore, had a powerful impact throughout the colonies, North and South. And most white colonists shared a belief in certain basic principles of law and politics, which they considered embedded in the English constitution, and which in the years after the 1750s would lead to a great imperial crisis.

INTERACTIVE LEARNING

The *Primary Source Investigator CD-ROM* offers the following materials related to this chapter:

- A short documentary movie, **Witchcraft Crisis of 1692** (D1).
- Interactive maps; **The Atlantic World** (M68); **Salem Witchcraft** (M4); and **Settlement of Colonial America** (M5).
- Documents, images, and maps related to society and culture in provincial America, including a sermon from the famous itinerant preacher George White-

field, a poem by African-American poet Phyllis Wheatley, and various materials depicting life in the colonies and the rise of disputes between the colonial governments and the British authorities.

 Online Learning Center (www.mhhe.com/brinkley12)

For quizzes, Internet resources, references to additional books and films, and more, consult this book's Online Learning Center.

FOR FURTHER REFERENCE

Edward Countryman, *Americans: A Collision of Histories* (1996) includes a vivid picture of the many cultures that encountered one another in early America. Bernard Bailyn, *Voyagers to the West: A Passage in the Peopling of America on the Eve of the Reolution* (1986) reveals the complexity and scope of European emigration to North America. Bailyn's *The Origin of American Politics* (1968) remains an excellent introduction to colonial politics. David Hackett Fischer, *Albion's Seed* (1989) suggests four major folkways for English migrants to America. Jack P. Greene, *Pursuits of Happiness: The Social Development of Early Modern British Colonies and the Formation of American Culture* (1986) is a broad portrait of life in early American communities. Laurel Thatcher Ulrich, *Good Wives: Image and Reality in the Lives of Women in Northern New England, 1650–1750* (1982) examines women's roles in colonial New England, and Mary Beth Norton, *In the Devils Snare: The Salem Witchcraft Crisis of 1692* (2002) explores the role of gender in a sensa-

tional 17th century controversy. John Demos, *The Unredeemed Captive: A Family Story of Early America* (1994) is a vivid, unconventional account of the experiences of a New England girl captured by Indians. Ira Berlin, *Many Thousands Gone: The First Two Centuries of Slavery in North America* (1998) and Philip Morgan, *Slave Counterpoint: Black Culture in the Eighteenth-Century Chesapeake and Lowcountry* (1998) are two excellent studies of slavery in the colonial era. Robin Blackburn, *The Making of New World Slavery: From the Baroque to the Modern, 1492–1800* (1997) includes an important examination of the character of the institution in colonial America. Kathleen M. Brown, *Good Wives, Nasty Wenches, and Anxious Patriarchs: Gender, Race and Power in Colonial Virginia* (1996) places gender at the center of the development of slavery in the Chesapeake. Rhys Isaac, *The Transformation of Virginia, 1740–1790* (1982) uses the methods of cultural anthropology in an influential study of the world of the colonial Virginia gentry.

THE BOSTON MASSACRE (1770), BY PAUL REVERE This is one of many sensationalized engravings, by Revere and others, of the conflict between British troops and Boston laborers that became important propaganda documents for the Patriot cause in the 1770s. Among the victims of the massacre listed by Revere was Crispus Attucks, probably the first black man to die in the struggle for American independence. *(Burstein Collection/Corbis)*

SIGNIFICANT EVENTS

1713 ▶ Treaty of Utrecht concludes Queen Anne's War

1718 ▶ New Orleans founded to serve French plantation economy in Louisiana

1744–1748 ▶ King George's War

1749 ▶ French construct fortresses in Ohio Valley

1754 ▶ Albany Plan for intercolonial cooperation rejected

▶ Battle of Fort Duquesne begins French and Indian War

1756 ▶ Seven Years' War begins in Europe

1757 ▶ British policies provoke riots in New York

1758 ▶ Pitt returns authority to colonial assemblies

▶ British capture Louisbourg fortress and Fort Duquesne

1759 ▶ British forces under Wolfe capture Quebec

1760 ▶ George III becomes king

▶ French army surrenders to Amherst at Montreal

CHAPTER 4

The Empire in Transition

As late as the 1750s, few Americans saw any reason to object to their membership in the British Empire. The imperial system provided them with many benefits: opportunities for trade and commerce, military protection, political stability. And those benefits were accompanied by few costs; for the most part, the English government left the colonies alone. While Britain did attempt to regulate the colonists' external trade, those regulations were usually so laxly administered that they could be easily circumvented. Some Americans predicted that the colonies would ultimately develop to a point where greater autonomy would become inevitable. But few expected such a change to occur soon.

By the mid-1770s, however, the relationship between the American colonies and their British rulers had become so strained, so poisoned, so characterized by suspicion and resentment that the once seemingly unbreakable bonds of empire were ready to snap. And in the spring of 1775, the first shots were fired in a war that would ultimately win America its independence.

The revolutionary crisis emerged as a result of both long-standing differences between the colonies and England and particular events in the 1760s and 1770s. Ever since the first days of settlement in North America, the ideas and institutions of the colonies had been diverging from those in England in countless ways. Only because the relationship between America and Britain had been so casual had those differences failed to create serious tensions in the past. Beginning in 1763, however, the British government embarked on a series of new policies toward its colonies—policies dictated by changing international realities and new political circumstances within England itself—that brought the differences between the two societies into sharp focus. In the beginning, most Americans reacted to the changes with relative restraint. Gradually, however, as crisis followed crisis, a large group of Americans found themselves fundamentally disillusioned with the imperial relationship. By 1775, that relationship was, for all practical purposes, damaged beyond repair.

Sources of Crisis

1763 ▶ Peace of Paris ends Seven Years' (and French and Indian) War

▶ Grenville becomes prime minister

▶ Proclamation of 1763 restricts western settlement

▶ Paxton uprising in Pennsylvania

1764 ▶ Sugar Act passed

▶ Currency Act passed

1765 ▶ Stamp Act crisis

▶ Mutiny Act passed

1766 ▶ Stamp Act repealed

▶ Declaratory Act passed

1767 ▶ Townshend duties imposed

1768 ▶ Boston, New York, and Philadelphia merchants make nonimportation agreement

1770 ▶ Boston Massacre

▶ Most Townshend Duties repealed

1771 ▶ Regulator movement quelled in North Carolina

1772 ▶ Committees of correspondence established in Boston

▶ Gaspee incident in Rhode Island

1773 ▶ Tea Act passed

▶ Bostonians stage tea party

1774 ▶ Intolerable Acts passed

▶ First Continental Congress meets at Philadelphia

▶ North Carolina women sign Edenton Proclamation calling for boycott of British goods

1775 ▶ Clashes at Lexington and Concord begin American Revolution

LOOSENING TIES

After the Glorious Revolution of 1688 in England and the collapse of the Dominion of New England in America, the English government (which became the British government after 1707, when a union of England and Scotland created Great Britain) made no serious or sustained effort to tighten its control over the colonies for over seventy years. During those years, it is true, an increasing number of colonies were brought under the direct control of the king. New Jersey in 1702, North and South Carolina in 1729, Georgia in 1754—all became royal colonies, bringing the total to eight; in all of them, the king had the power to appoint the governors and other colonial officials. During those years, Parliament also passed new laws supplementing the original Navigation Acts and strengthening the mercantilist program—laws restricting colonial manufactures, prohibiting paper currency, and regulating trade. On the whole, however, the British government remained uncertain and divided about the extent to which it ought to interfere in colonial affairs. The colonies were left, within broad limits, to go their separate ways.

A Tradition of Neglect

In the fifty years after the Glorious Revolution, the British Parliament established a growing supremacy over the king. During the reigns of George I (1714–1727) and George II (1727–1760), both of whom were German born and unaccustomed to English ways, the prime minister and his fellow cabinet ministers began to become the nation's real executives. They held their positions not by the king's favor but by their ability to control a majority in Parliament.

Growing Power of Parliament

These parliamentary leaders were less inclined than the seventeenth-century monarchs had been to try to tighten imperial organization. They depended heavily on the support of the great merchants and landholders, most of whom feared that any such experiments would require large expenditures, would increase taxes, and would diminish the profits they were earning from the colonial trade. The first of the modern prime ministers, Robert Walpole, deliberately refrained from strict enforcement of the Navigation Acts, believing that relaxed trading restrictions would stimulate commerce.

Meanwhile, the day-to-day administration of colonial affairs remained decentralized and inefficient. There was no colonial office in London. The nearest equivalent was the Board of Trade and Plantations, established in 1696—a mere advisory body that had little role in any actual decisions. Real authority rested in the Privy Council (the central administrative agency for the government as a whole), the admiralty, and the treasury. But those agencies were responsible for administering

Decentralized Colonial Administration

laws at home as well as overseas; none could concentrate on colonial affairs alone. To complicate matters further, there was considerable overlapping and confusion of authority among the departments.

Few of the London officials, moreover, had ever visited America; few knew very much about conditions there. What information they did gather came in large part from agents sent to England by the colonial assemblies to lobby for American interests, and these agents, naturally, did nothing to encourage interference with colonial affairs. (The best known of them, Benjamin Franklin, represented not only his own colony, Pennsylvania, but also Georgia, New Jersey, and Massachusetts.)

It was not only the weakness of administrative authority in London and the policy of neglect that weakened England's hold on the colonies. It was also the character of the royal officials in America—among them the governors, the collectors of customs, and naval officers. Some of these officeholders were able and intelligent men; most were not. Appointments generally came as the result of bribery or favoritism, not as a reward for merit. Many appointees remained in England and, with part of their salaries, hired substitutes to take their places in America. Such deputies received paltry wages and thus faced great temptations to augment their incomes with bribes. Few resisted the temptation. Customs collectors, for example, routinely waived duties on goods when merchants paid them to do so. Even honest and well-paid officials usually found it expedient, if they wanted to get along with their neighbors, to yield to the colonists' resistance to trade restrictions.

Resistance to imperial authority centered in the colonial legislatures. By the 1750s the American assemblies had claimed the right to levy taxes, make appropriations, approve appointments, and pass laws for their respective colonies. Their legislation was subject to veto by the governor or the Privy Council. But the assemblies had leverage over the governor through their control of the colonial budget, and they could circumvent the Privy Council by repassing disallowed laws in slightly altered form. The assemblies came to look upon themselves as little parliaments, each practically as sovereign within its colony as Parliament itself was in England.

Powerful Colonial Legislatures

The Colonies Divided

Despite their frequent resistance to the authority of London, the colonists continued to think of themselves as loyal English subjects. In many respects, in fact, they felt stronger ties to England than they did to one another. "Fire and water," an English traveler wrote, "are not more heterogeneous than the different colonies in North America." New Englanders and Virginians viewed each other as something close to foreigners. A Connecticut man denounced the merchants of New York for their

AN APPEAL FOR COLONIAL UNITY This sketch, one of the first American editorial cartoons, appeared in Benjamin Franklin's Philadelphia newspaper, the *Pennsylvania Gazette*, on May 9, 1754. It was meant to illustrate the need for intercolonial unity and, in particular, for the adoption of Franklin's Albany Plan. *(Library Company of Philadelphia)*

"frauds and unfair practices," while a New Yorker condemned Connecticut because of the "low craft and cunning so incident to the people of that country." Only an accident of geography, it seemed, connected these disparate societies to each other.

Yet for all their differences, the colonies could scarcely avoid forging connections with one another. The growth of the colonial population produced an almost continuous line of settlement along the seacoast and led to the gradual construction of roads and the rise of intercolonial trade. The colonial postal service helped increase communication. In 1691, it had operated only from Massachusetts to New York and Pennsylvania. In 1711, it extended to New Hampshire in the North; in 1732, to Virginia in the South; and ultimately, all the way to Georgia.

Still, the colonists were loath to cooperate even when, in 1754, they faced a common threat from their old rivals, the French, and France's Indian allies. A conference of colonial leaders—with delegates from Pennsylvania, Maryland, New York, and New England—was meeting in Albany in that year to negotiate a treaty with the Iroquois, as the British government had advised the colonists to do. The delegates stayed on to talk about forming a colonial federation for defense against the Indians. Benjamin Franklin proposed, and the delegates tentatively approved, a plan by which Parliament would set up in America "one general government" for all the colonies (except Georgia and Nova Scotia). Each colony would "retain its present constitution," but would grant to the new general government such powers as the authority to govern all relations with the Indians. The central government would have a "president general"

| Albany Plan |

appointed and paid by the king (just as colonial governors were) and a legislature (a "grand council") elected by the colonial assemblies.

War with the French and Indians was already beginning when this Albany Plan was presented to the colonial assemblies. None approved it. "Everyone cries, a union is necessary," Franklin wrote to the Massachusetts governor, "but when they come to the manner and form of the union, their weak noodles are perfectly distracted."

THE STRUGGLE FOR THE CONTINENT

In the late 1750s and early 1760s, a great war raged through North America, changing forever the balance of power both on the continent and throughout the world. The war in America was part of a titanic struggle between England and France for dominance in world trade and naval power. The British victory in that struggle, known in Europe as the Seven Years' War, rearranged global power and cemented England's role as the world's great commercial and imperial nation. It also cemented its control of most of the settled regions of North America.

In America, however, the conflict was the final stage in a long battle among the three principal powers in northeastern North America: the English, the French, and the Iroquois. For more than a century prior to the conflict—which was known in America as the French and Indian War—these three groups had maintained an uneasy balance of power. The events of the 1750s upset that balance, produced a prolonged and open conflict, and established a precarious dominance for the English societies throughout the region.

| An Uneasy Balance of Power |

The French and Indian War was important to the English colonists in America for another reason as well. By bringing the Americans into closer contact with British authority than ever before, it raised to the surface some of the underlying tensions in the colonial relationship.

New France and the Iroquois Nation

The French and the English had coexisted relatively peacefully in North America for nearly a century. But by the 1750s, religious and commercial tensions began to produce new frictions and conflicts. The crisis began in part because of the expansion of the French presence in America in the late seventeenth century—a result of Louis XIV's search for national unity and increased world power. The lucrative fur trade drew immigrant French peasants deeper into the wilderness, while missionary zeal drew large numbers of French Jesuits into the interior in search of potential converts. The bottomlands of the Mississippi River valley attracted

| New Sources of Conflict |

French farmers discouraged by the short growing season in Canada.

By the mid-seventeenth century, the French Empire in America comprised a vast territory. Louis Joliet and Father Jacques Marquette, French explorers of the 1670s, journeyed together by canoe from Green Bay on Lake Michigan as far south as the junction of the Arkansas and Mississippi Rivers. A year later, René Robert Cavelier, Sieur de La Salle, began the explorations that in 1682 took him to the delta of the Mississippi, where he claimed the surrounding country for France and named it Louisiana in the king's honor. Subsequent traders and missionaries wandered to the southwest as far as the Rio Grande; and the explorer Pierre Gaultier de Varennes, Sieur de La Verendrye, pushed westward in 1743 from Lake Superior to a point within sight of the Rocky Mountains. The French had by then revealed the outlines of, and laid claim to, the whole continental interior.

To secure their hold on these enormous claims, they founded a string of widely separated communities, fortresses, missions, and trading posts. Fort Louisbourg, on Cape Breton Island, guarded the approach to the Gulf of St. Lawrence. Would-be feudal lords established large estates *(seigneuries)* along the banks of the St. Lawrence River; and on a high bluff above the river stood the fortified city of Quebec, the center of the French Empire in America. To the south was Montreal, and to the west Sault Sainte Marie and Detroit. On the lower Mississippi emerged plantations much like those in the southern colonies of English America, worked by black slaves and owned by "Creoles" (white immigrants of French descent). New Orleans, founded in 1718 to service the French plantation economy, soon was as big as some of the larger cities of the Atlantic seaboard; Biloxi and Mobile to the east completed the string of French settlement.

France's North American Empire

But the French were not, of course, alone in the continental interior. They shared their territories with a large and powerful Indian population—in regions now often labeled the "middle ground" (see pp. 58–59)—and their relations with the natives were crucial to the shaping of their empire. They also shared the interior with a growing number of English traders and settlers, who had been moving beyond the confines of the colonial boundaries in the East. Both the French and the English were aware that the battle for control of North America would be determined in part by which group could best win the allegiance of native tribes—as trading partners and, at times, as military allies. The Indians, for their part, were principally concerned with protecting their independence. Whatever alignments they formed with the European societies growing up around them were generally marriages of convenience, determined by which group offered the most attractive terms.

The English—with their more advanced commercial economy—could usually offer the Indians better and more plentiful goods. But the French offered something that was often more important: tolerance. Unlike the English settlers, most of whom tried to impose their own social norms on the Native Americans they encountered, the French settlers in the interior generally adjusted their own behavior to Indian patterns. French fur traders frequently married Indian women and adopted tribal ways. Jesuit missionaries interacted comfortably with the natives and converted them to Catholicism by the thousands without challenging most of their social customs. By the mid-eighteenth century, therefore, the French had better and closer relations with most of the tribes of the interior than did the English.

The most powerful native group, however, had a rather different relationship with the French. The Iroquois Confederacy—the five Indian nations (Mohawk, Seneca, Cayuga, Onondaga, and Oneida)

The Iroquois Confederacy

that had formed a defensive alliance in the fifteenth century—had been the most powerful tribal presence in the Northeast since the 1640s, when they had fought—and won—a bitter war against the Hurons. Once their major competitors were largely gone from the region, the Iroquois forged an important commercial relationship with the English and Dutch along the eastern seaboard—although they continued to trade with the French as well. Indeed, the key to the success of the Iroquois in maintaining their independence was that they avoided too close a relationship with either group and astutely played the French and the English off against each other. As a result, they managed to maintain an uneasy balance of power in the Great Lakes region.

The principal area of conflict among these many groups was the Ohio Valley. The French claimed it. Several competing Indian tribes (many of them refugees from lands farther east, driven into the valley by the English expansion) lived there. English settlement was expanding into it. And the Iroquois were trying to establish a presence there as traders. With so many competing groups jostling for influence, the Ohio Valley quickly became a potential battleground.

Anglo-French Conflicts

As long as England and France remained at peace in Europe, and as long as the precarious balance in the North American interior survived, the tensions among the English, French, and Iroquois remained relatively mild. But after the Glorious Revolution in England, the English throne passed to one of Louis XIV's principal enemies, William III, who was also the stadholder (chief magistrate) of the Netherlands and

European Seeds of Conflict

who had long opposed French expansionism. William's

successor, Queen Anne (the daughter of James II), ascended the throne in 1702 and carried on the struggle against France and its new ally, Spain. The result was a series of Anglo-French wars that continued intermittently in Europe for nearly eighty years.

The wars had important repercussions in America. King William's War (1689–1697) produced a few, indecisive clashes between the English and French in northern New England. Queen Anne's War, which began in 1701 and continued for nearly twelve years, generated more substantial conflicts: border fighting with the Spaniards in the South as well as with the French and their Indian allies in the North. The Treaty of Utrecht, which brought the conflict to a close in 1713, transferred substantial areas of French territory in North America to the English, including Acadia (Nova Scotia) and Newfoundland. Two decades later, European rivalries led to still more conflicts in America. Disputes over British trading rights in the Spanish colonies produced a war between England and Spain and led to clashes between the British in Georgia and the Spaniards in Florida. (It was in the context of this conflict that the last English colony in America, Georgia, was founded in 1733; see p. 57.) The Anglo-Spanish conflict soon merged with a much larger European war, in which England and France lined up on opposite sides of a territorial dispute between Frederick the Great of Prussia and Maria Theresa of Austria. The English colonists in America were soon drawn into the struggle, which they called King George's War; and between 1744 and 1748 they engaged in a series of conflicts with the French. New Englanders captured the French bastion at Louisbourg on Cape Breton Island; but the peace treaty that finally ended the conflict forced them (in bitter disappointment) to abandon it.

In the aftermath of King George's War, relations among the English, French, and Iroquois in North America quickly deteriorated. The Iroquois (in what in retrospect appears a major blunder) began for the first time to grant trading concessions in the interior to English merchants. In the context of the already tense Anglo-French relationship in America, that decision set in motion a chain of events disastrous for the Iroquois Confederacy. The French feared that the English were using the concessions as a first step toward expansion into French lands (which to some extent they were). They began in 1749 to construct new fortresses in the Ohio Valley. The English interpreted the French activity as a threat to their western settlements. They protested and began making military preparations and building fortresses of their own. The balance of power that the Iroquois had strove to maintain for so long rapidly disintegrated, and the five Indian nations allied themselves with the British and assumed an essentially passive role in the conflict that followed.

For the next five years, tensions between the English and the French increased. In the summer of 1754 the governor of Virginia sent a militia force (under the command of an inexperienced young colonel, George Washington) into the Ohio Valley to challenge French expansion. Washington built a crude stockade (Fort Necessity) not far from the larger French outpost, Fort Duquesne, on the site of what is now Pittsburgh. After the Virginians staged an unsuccessful attack on a French detachment, the French countered with an assault on Fort Necessity, trapping Washington and his soldiers inside. After a third of them died in the fighting, Washington surrendered.

Fort Necessity

That clash marked the beginning of the French and Indian War, the American part of the much larger Seven Years' War that spread through Europe at the same time. It was the climactic event in the long Anglo-French struggle for empire.

The Great War for the Empire

The French and Indian War lasted nearly nine years, and it proceeded in three distinct phases. The first of these phases lasted from the Fort Necessity debacle in 1754 until the expansion of the war to Europe in 1756. It was primarily a local, North American conflict, which the English colonists managed largely on their own.

The British provided modest assistance during this period, but they provided it so ineptly that it had little impact on the struggle. The British fleet failed to prevent the landing of large French reinforcements in Canada; and the newly appointed commander in chief of the British army in America, General Edward Braddock, failed miserably in a major effort in the summer of 1755 to retake the crucial site at the forks of the Ohio River where Washington had lost the battle at Fort Necessity. A French and Indian ambush a few miles from the fort left Braddock dead and what remained of his forces in disarray.

Braddock Defeated

The local colonial forces, meanwhile, were preoccupied with defending themselves against raids on their western settlements by the Indians of the Ohio Valley. Virtually all of them (except the Iroquois) were now allied with the French, having interpreted the defeat of the Virginians at Fort Duquesne as evidence of British weakness. Even the Iroquois, who were nominally allied with the British, remained fearful of antagonizing the French. They engaged in few hostilities and launched no offensive into Canada, even though they had, under heavy English pressure, declared war on the French. By late 1755, many English settlers along the frontier had withdrawn to the east of the Allegheny Mountains to escape the hostilities.

The second phase of the struggle began in 1756, when the governments of France and England formally opened hostilities and a truly international conflict (the Seven Years' War) began. In Europe, the war was marked by a realignment within the complex system of alliances.

THE SIEGE OF LOUISBOURG, 1758 The fortress of Louisbourg, on Cape Breton Island in Nova Scotia, was one of the principal French outposts in eastern Canada during the French and Indian War. It took a British fleet of 157 ships nearly two months to force the French garrison to surrender. "We had not had our Batteries against the Town above a Week," wrote a British soldier after the victory, "tho we were ashore Seven Weeks; the Badness of the Country prevented our Approaches. It was necessary to make Roads for the Cannon, which was a great Labour, and some Loss of Men; but the spirits the Army was in is capable of doing any Thing." *(The New Brunswick Museum, Saint John, NB)*

France allied itself with its former enemy, Austria; England joined France's former ally, Prussia. The fighting now spread to the West Indies, India, and Europe itself. But the principal struggle remained the one in North America, where so far England had suffered nothing but frustration and defeat.

Beginning in 1757, William Pitt, the English secretary of state (and future prime minister), began to transform the war effort in America by bringing it for the first time fully under British control. Pitt himself began planning military strategy for the North American conflict, appointing military commanders, and issuing orders to the colonists. Military recruitment had slowed dramatically in America after the defeat of Braddock. To replenish the army, British commanders began forcibly enlisting colonists (a practice known as "impressment"). Officers also began to seize supplies and equipment from local farmers and tradesmen and compelled colonists to offer shelter to British troops—all generally without compensation. The Americans had long ago become accustomed to running their own affairs and had been fighting for over two years without much

William Pitt Takes Charge

assistance or direction from the British. They resented these new impositions and firmly resisted them—at times, as in a 1757 riot in New York City, violently. By early 1758, the friction between the British authorities and the colonists was threatening to bring the war effort to a halt.

Beginning in 1758, therefore, Pitt initiated the third and final phase of the war by relaxing many of the policies that Americans found obnoxious. He agreed to reimburse the colonists for all supplies requisitioned by the army. He returned control over military recruitment to the colonial assemblies (which resulted in an immediate and dramatic increase in enlistments). And he dispatched large numbers of additional troops to America.

Finally, the tide of battle began to turn in England's favor. The French had always been outnumbered by the British colonists; after 1756, they suffered as well from a series of poor harvests. As a result, they were unable to sustain their early military successes. By mid-1758, the British regulars in America (who did the bulk of the actual fighting) and the colonial militias were seizing one French stronghold after another. Two brilliant English generals, Jeffrey Amherst and James Wolfe, captured the fortress at Louisbourg in July 1758; a few months later Fort Duquesne fell without a fight. The next year, at the

Siege of Quebec

end of a siege of Quebec, supposedly impregnable atop its towering cliff, the army of General James Wolfe struggled up a hidden ravine under cover of darkness, surprised the larger forces of the Marquis de Montcalm, and defeated them in a battle in which both commanders died. The dramatic fall of Quebec on September 13, 1759, marked the beginning of the end of the American phase of the war. A year later, in September 1760, the French army formally surrendered to Amherst in Montreal.

Not all aspects of the struggle were as romantic as Wolfe's dramatic assault on Quebec. The British resorted at times to such brutal military expedients as population dispersal. In Nova Scotia, for example, they uprooted several thousand French inhabitants, whom they suspected of disloyalty, and scattered them throughout the English colonies. (Some of these Acadians eventually made their way to Louisiana, where they became the ancestors of the present-day Cajuns.) Elsewhere, English and colonial troops inflicted even worse atrocities on the Indian allies of the French—for example, offering "scalp bounties" to those who could bring back evidence of having killed a native. The French and their Indian allies retaliated, and hundreds of families along the English frontier perished in brutal raids on their settlements.

Peace finally came after the accession of George III to the British throne and the resignation of Pitt, who, unlike the new king, wanted to continue hostilities. The

Peace of Paris

British achieved most of Pitt's aims nevertheless in the Peace of Paris, signed in 1763. Under its terms, the French ceded to Great Britain some of their West Indian islands and most of their colonies in India. They also transferred Canada and all other French territory east of the Mississippi, except New Orleans, to Great Britain. They ceded New Orleans and their claims west of the Mississippi to Spain, thus surrendering all title to the mainland of North America.

The French and Indian War had profound effects on the British Empire and the American colonies. It greatly expanded England's territorial claims in the New World. At the same time, it greatly enlarged Britain's debt; financing the vast war had been a major drain on the treasury. It also generated substantial resentment toward the Americans among British leaders who were contemptuous of the colonists for what they considered American military ineptitude during the war. They were angry that the colonists had made so few financial contributions to a struggle waged largely for American benefit; they were particularly bitter that some colonial merchants had been selling food and other goods to the French in the West Indies

throughout the conflict. All these factors combined to persuade many English leaders that a major reorganization of the empire, giving London increased authority over the colonies, would be necessary in the aftermath of the war.

The war had an equally profound but very different effect on the American colonists. It forced them, for the first time, to act in concert against a common foe. The friction of 1756–1757 over British requisition and impressment policies, and the 1758

Consequences of the Seven Years' War

return of authority to the colonial assemblies, established an important precedent in the minds of the colonists: it seemed to confirm the illegitimacy of English interference in local affairs. For thousands of Americans—the men who served in the colonial armed forces—the war was an important socializing experience. The colonial troops, unlike the British regiments, generally viewed themselves as part of a "people's army." The relationship of soldiers to their units was, the soldiers believed, in some measure voluntary; their army was a communal, not a coercive or hierarchical, organization. The contrast with the British regulars, whom the colonists widely resented for their arrogance and arbitrary use of power, was striking; and in later years, the memory of that contrast helped to shape the American response to British imperial policies.

For the Indians of the Ohio Valley, the third major party in the French and Indian War, the British victory was disastrous. Those tribes that had allied themselves with the French had earned the enmity of the victorious English. The Iroquois Confederacy, which had allied itself with Britain, fared only slightly better. English officials saw the passivity of the Iroquois during the war (a result of their effort to hedge their bets and avoid antagonizing the French) as evidence of duplicity. In the aftermath of the peace settlement, the Iroquois alliance with the British quickly unraveled, and the Iroquois Confederacy itself began to crumble from within. The Iroquois nations would continue to contest the English for control of the Ohio Valley for another fifty years; but increasingly divided and increasingly outnumbered, they would seldom again be in a position to deal with their white rivals on terms of military or political equality.

THE NEW IMPERIALISM

With the treaty of 1763, England found itself truly at peace for the first time in more than fifty years. But saddled with enormous debts and responsible for vast new lands in the New World, the imperial government could not long avoid expanding its involvement in its colonies.

THE THIRTEEN COLONIES IN 1763   This map is a close-up of the thirteen colonies at the end of the Seven Years' War. Like the previous map, it shows the line of settlement established by the Proclamation of 1763 (the red line), as well as the extent of actual settlement in that year (the green line). Note that in the middle colonies (North Carolina, Virginia, Maryland, and southern Pennsylvania), settlement had already reached the red line—and in one small area of western Pennsylvania moved beyond it—by the time of the Proclamation of 1763. Note also the string of forts established beyond the Proclamation line.   ◆ *How do the forts help to explain the efforts of the British to restrict settlement? And how does the extent of actual settlement help explain why it was so difficult for the British to enforce their restrictions?*

 For an interactive version of this map go to www.mhhe.com/brinkley12ch4maps

Burdens of Empire

The experience of the French and Indian War, however, suggested that such increased involvement would not be easy to achieve. Not only had the colonists proved so resistant to British control that Pitt had been forced to relax his policies in 1758, but the colonial assemblies had continued after that to respond to British needs slowly and grudgingly. Unwilling to be taxed by Parliament to support the war effort, the colonists were generally reluctant to tax themselves as well. Defiance of imperial trade regulations and other British demands continued, and even increased, through the last years of the war.

The problems of managing the empire became more difficult after 1763 because of a basic shift in Britain's imperial design. In the past, the English had viewed their colonial empire primarily in terms of trade; they had opposed acquisition of territory for its own sake. But by

Commercial versus Territorial Imperialists

the mid-eighteenth century, a growing number of English and American leaders (including both William Pitt and Benjamin Franklin) were beginning to argue that land itself was of value to the empire— because of the population it could support, the taxes it could produce, and the imperial splendor it would confer. The debate between the old commercial imperialists and the new territorial ones came to a head at the conclusion of the French and Indian War. The mercantilists wanted England to return Canada to France in exchange for Guadeloupe, the most commercially valuable of the French "sugar islands" in the West Indies. The territorialists, however, prevailed. The acquisition of the French territories in North America was a victory for, among others, Benjamin Franklin, who had long argued that the American people would need these vast spaces to accommodate their rapid and, he believed, limitless growth.

With the territorial annexations of 1763, the area of the British Empire was suddenly twice as great as it had been, and the problems of governing it were thus considerably more complex. Some argued that the empire should restrain rapid settlement in the western territories. To allow Europeans to move into the new lands too quickly, they warned, would run the risk of stirring up costly conflicts with the Indians. Restricting settlement would also keep the land available for hunting and trapping.

Other colonists wanted to see the new territories opened for immediate development, but they disagreed among themselves about who should control the western lands. Colonial governments made fervent, and often conflicting, claims of jurisdiction. Others argued that control should remain in England, and that the territories should be considered entirely new colonies, unlinked to the existing settlements. There were, in short, a host of problems and pressures that the British could not ignore.

At the same time, the government in London was running out of options in its effort to find a way to deal

Britain's Staggering War Debt

with its staggering war debt. Landlords and merchants in England itself were objecting strenuously to increases in what they already considered excessively high taxes. The necessity of stationing significant numbers of British troops on the Indian border after 1763 was adding even more to the cost of defending the American settlements. And the halfhearted response of the colonial assemblies to the war effort had suggested that in its search for revenue, England could

not rely on any cooperation from the colonial governments. Only a system of taxation administered by London, the leaders of the empire believed, could effectively meet England's needs.

At this crucial moment in Anglo-American relations, with the imperial system in desperate need of redefinition, the English government experienced a series of changes as a result of the accession to the throne of a new king. George III assumed power in 1760 on the death of his grandfather. And he brought two particularly unfortunate qualities to the office. First, he was determined, unlike his two predecessors, to be an active and responsible monarch. In part because of pressure from his ambitious mother, he removed from power the long-standing and relatively stable coalition of Whigs, who had (under Pitt and others) governed the empire for much of the century and whom the new king mistrusted. In their place, he created a new coalition of his own through patronage and bribes and gained an uneasy control of Parliament. The new ministries that emerged as a result of these changes were inherently unstable, each lasting in office an average of only about two years.

The king had serious intellectual and psychological limitations that compounded his political difficulties. He suffered, apparently, from a rare disease that produced intermittent bouts of insanity. (Indeed, in the last years of his long reign he was, according to most accounts, a virtual lunatic, confined to the palace and unable to perform

George III's Shortcomings

any official functions.) Yet even when George III was lucid and rational, which in the 1760s and 1770s was most of the time, he was painfully immature (he was only twenty-two when he ascended the throne) and insecure—striving constantly to prove his fitness for his position but time and again finding himself ill equipped to handle the challenges he seized for himself. The king's personality, therefore, contributed to both the instability and the intransigence of the British government during these critical years.

More immediately responsible for the problems that soon emerged with the colonies, however, was George Grenville, whom the king made prime minister in 1763. Grenville did not share his brother-in-law William Pitt's sympathy with the American point of view. He agreed instead with the prevailing opinion within Britain that the colonists had been too long indulged and that they should be compelled to obey the laws and to pay a part of the cost of defending and administering the empire. He promptly began trying to impose a new system of control upon what had been a loose collection of colonial possessions in America.

The British and the Tribes

The western problem was the most urgent. With the departure of the French, settlers and traders from the

GEORGE III George III was 22 years old when he ascended the throne in 1760, and for many years almost all portraits of him were highly formal, with the king dressed in elaborate ceremonial robes. This more informal painting dates from much later in his reign, after he had begun to suffer from the mental disorders that eventually consumed him. After 1810, he was blind and permanently deranged, barred from all official business by the Regency Act of 1811. His son (later King George IV) served as regent in those years. *(The Granger Collection, New York)*

English colonies had begun immediately to move over the mountains and into the upper Ohio Valley. The Indians of the region objected to this intrusion into their land and commerce; and an alliance of tribes, under the Ottawa chieftain Pontiac, struck back. To prevent an escalation of the fighting that might threaten western trade, the British government issued a ruling—the Proclamation of 1763—forbidding settlers to advance beyond a line drawn along the Appalachian Mountains.

The Proclamation of 1763 was appealing to the British for several reasons. It would allow London, rather than the provincial governments and their land-hungry constituents, to control the westward movement of the white population. Hence, westward expansion would proceed in an orderly manner, and conflicts with the tribes, which were both militarily costly and dangerous to trade, might be limited. Slower western settlement would also slow the population exodus from the coastal

Proclamation of 1763

colonies, where England's most important markets and investments were. And it would reserve opportunities for land speculation and fur trading for English rather than colonial entrepreneurs.

Although the tribes were not enthusiastic about the Proclamation, which required them to cede still more land to the white settlers, many tribal groups supported the agreement as the best bargain available to them. The Cherokee, in particular, worked actively to hasten the drawing of the boundary, hoping to put an end to white encroachments for good. Relations between the western tribes and the British improved in at least some areas after the Proclamation, partly as a result of the work of the Indian superintendents the British appointed. John Stuart was in charge of Indian affairs in the southern colonies and Sir William Johnson in the northern ones. Both were sympathetic to Native American needs and lived among the tribes; Johnson married a Mohawk woman, Mary Brant, who was later to play an important role in the American Revolution.

In the end, however, the Proclamation of 1763 failed to meet even the modest expectations of the Native Americans. It had some effect in limiting colonial land specula-

White Encroachment

tion in the West and in controlling the fur trade, but on the crucial point of the line of settlement it was almost completely ineffective. White settlers continued to swarm across the boundary and to claim lands farther and farther into the Ohio Valley. The British authorities tried repeatedly to establish limits to the expansion but continually failed to prevent the white colonists from pushing the line of settlement still farther west.

The Colonial Response

The Grenville ministry soon moved to increase its authority in the colonies in more direct ways. Regular British troops, London announced, would now be stationed permanently in America; and under the Mutiny Act of 1765 the colonists were required to assist in provisioning and maintaining the army. Ships of the British navy were assigned to patrol American waters and search for smugglers. The customs service was reorganized and enlarged. Royal officials were ordered to take up their colonial posts in person instead of sending substitutes. Colonial manufacturing was to be restricted, so that it would not compete with the rapidly expanding industry of Great Britain.

The Sugar Act of 1764, designed in part to eliminate the illegal sugar trade between the continental colonies and the French and Spanish West Indies, strengthened enforcement of the duty on sugar (while lowering the duty on molasses, further damaging the market for sugar grown in the colonies). It also established new vice-admiralty courts in America to try accused

Sugar, Currency, and Stamp Acts

NORTH AMERICA IN 1763 The victory of the English over the French in the Seven Years' War (or, as it was known in America, the French and Indian War) reshaped the map of colonial North America. Britain gained a vast new territory, formerly controlled by France—Canada, and a large area west of the Mississippi River, thus more than doubling the size of the British Empire in America. French possessions in the New World dwindled to a few islands in the Caribbean. Spain continued to control a substantial empire in the North American interior. The red line along the western borders of the English colonies represents the line of settlement established by Britain in 1763. White settlers were not permitted to move beyond that line. ◆ *Why did the British wish to restrict settlement of the western lands?*

OLC **For an interactive version of this map go to www.mhhe.com/brinkley12ch4maps**

smugglers—thus depriving them of the benefit of sympathetic local juries. The Currency Act of 1764 required the colonial assemblies to stop issuing paper money (a widespread practice during the war) and to retire on schedule all the paper money already in circulation. Most momentous of all, the Stamp Act of 1765 imposed a tax on most printed documents in the colonies: newspapers, almanacs, pamphlets, deeds, wills, licenses.

The new imperial program was an effort to reapply to the colonies the old principles of mercantilism. And in some ways, it proved highly effective. British officials were soon collecting more than ten times as much annual revenue from America as before 1763. But the new policies created many more problems than they solved.

The colonists may have resented the new imperial regulations, but at first they found it difficult to resist them effectively. For one thing, Americans continued to harbor as many grievances against one another as against the authorities in London. Often, the conflicts centered around tensions between the established societies of the Atlantic coast and the "backcountry" further west, whose

PREPARING TO MEET THE PAXTON BOYS The "Paxton Boys" were residents of western Pennsylvania who were declared outlaws by the assembly in Philadelphia after they launched an unauthorized attack on neighboring Conestoga Indians. Instead of surrendering, they armed themselves and marched on Philadelphia. This engraving satirizes the haphazard military preparations in the city for the expected invasion. An accompanying poem, expressing the contempt some colonists felt toward the urbanized, pacifist Quakers of Philadelphia, commented: "To kill the Paxtonians, they then did Advance, With Guns on their Shoulders, but how did they Prance." Benjamin Franklin finally persuaded the Paxton rebels not to attack in return for greater representation in the legislature. *(Library Company of Philadelphia)*

Paxton Boys residents often felt isolated from, and underrepresented in, the colonial governments. They sometimes felt beleaguered because they lived closer to the worlds of the Indian tribes than the societies of the East. In 1763, for example, a band of people from western Pennsylvania known as the Paxton Boys descended on Philadelphia with demands for relief from colonial (not British) taxes and for money to help them defend themselves against Indians; the colonial government averted bloodshed only by making concessions to them.

In 1771, a small-scale civil war broke out as a result of the so-called Regulator movement in North Carolina.

Regulator Movement The Regulators were farmers of the Carolina upcountry who organized in opposition to the high taxes that local sheriffs (appointed by the colonial governor) collected. The western counties were badly underrepresented in the colonial assembly, and the Regulators failed to win redress of their grievances there. Finally they armed themselves and began resisting tax collections by force. To suppress the revolt, Governor William Tryon raised an army of militiamen, mostly from the eastern counties, who defeated a band of 2,000 Regulators in the Battle of Alamance. Nine on each side were killed, and many others were wounded. Afterward, six Regulators were hanged for treason.

The bloodshed was exceptional, but bitter conflicts within the colonies were not. After 1763, however, the new policies of the British government began to create common grievances among virtually all colonists that to some degree counterbalanced these internal divisions.

Indeed, there was something in the Grenville program to antagonize virtually everyone. Northern merchants believed they would suffer from restraints on their commerce, from the closing of opportunities for manufacturing, and from the increased burden of taxation. Settlers in the northern backcountry resented the closing of the West to land speculation and fur trading. Southern planters, in debt to English merchants, feared having to pay additional taxes and losing their ability to ease their debts by speculating in western land. Professionals—ministers, lawyers, professors, and others—depended on merchants and planters for their livelihood and thus shared their concerns about the effects of English law. Small farmers, the largest group in the colonies, believed they would suffer from increased taxes and from the abolition of paper money, which had enabled them to pay their loans. Workers in towns opposed the restraints on manufacturing.

The new restrictions came, moreover, at the beginning of an economic depression. The British government, by pouring money into the colonies to finance the fighting, had stimulated a wartime boom; that flow of funds stopped after the peace in 1763, precipitating an

Postwar Depression

economic bust. Now the authorities in London proposed to aggravate the problem by taking money out of the colonies. The imperial policies would, many colonists feared, doom them to permanent economic stagnation and a declining standard of living.

In reality, most Americans soon found ways to live with (or circumvent) the new British policies. The American economy was not, in fact, being destroyed. But economic anxieties were rising in the colonies nevertheless, and they created a growing sense of unease, particularly in the cities—the places most resistant to British policies. Urban Americans were worried about the periodic economic slumps that were occurring with greater and greater frequency. They had been shocked by the frightening depression of the early 1760s and alarmed by the growth of a large and destabilizing group within the population who were unemployed or semi-employed. The result of all these anxieties was a feeling in some colonial cities—and particularly in Boston, the city suffering the worst economic problems—that something was deeply amiss.

Whatever the economic consequences of the British government's programs, the political consequences were—in the eyes of the colonists, at least—far worse. Perhaps nowhere else in the late-eighteenth-century world did so large a proportion of the people take an

Political Consequences of the Grenville Program

active interest in public affairs. That was partly because Anglo-Americans were accustomed (and deeply attached) to very broad powers of self-government; and the colonists were determined to protect those powers. The keys to self-government, they believed, were the provincial assemblies; and the key to the power of the provincial assemblies was their long-established right to give or withhold appropriations for the colonial governments which the British were now challenging. Home rule, therefore, was not something new and different that the colonists were striving to attain, but something old and familiar that they desired to keep. The movement to resist the new imperial policies, a movement for which many would ultimately fight and die, was thus at the same time democratic and conservative. It was a movement to conserve liberties Americans believed they already possessed.

STIRRINGS OF REVOLT

By the mid-1760s, therefore, a hardening of positions had begun in both England and America that would bring the colonies into increasing conflict with the mother country. The victorious war for empire had given the colonists a heightened sense of their own importance and a renewed commitment to protecting their political autonomy. It had given the British a strengthened belief in the need to tighten administration of the empire and a strong desire to use the colonies as a source of revenue. The result was a series of events that, more rapidly than anyone could imagine, shattered the English Empire in America.

The Stamp Act Crisis

Even if he had tried, Prime Minister Grenville could not have devised a better method for antagonizing and unifying the colonies than the Stamp Act of 1765. The Sugar

Effects of the Stamp Act

Act of a year earlier had affected few people other than the New England merchants whose trade it hampered. But the new tax fell on all Americans, and it evoked particular opposition from some of the most powerful members of the population. Merchants and lawyers were obliged to buy stamps for ships' papers and legal documents. Tavern owners, often the political leaders of their neighborhoods, were required to buy stamps for their licenses. Printers—the most influential group in distributing information and ideas in colonial society—had to buy stamps for their newspapers and other publications.

The actual economic burdens of the Stamp Act were, in the end, relatively light; the stamps were not very expensive. What made the law obnoxious to the colonists was not so much its immediate cost as the precedent it seemed to set. In the past, Americans had rationalized the taxes and duties on colonial trade as measures to regulate commerce, not raise money. Some Americans had even managed to persuade themselves that the Sugar Act, which was in fact designed primarily to raise money, was not fundamentally different from the traditional imperial duties. The Stamp Act, however, they could interpret in only one way. It was a direct attempt by England to raise revenue in the colonies without the consent of the colonial assemblies. If this new tax passed without resistance, the door would be open for more burdensome taxation in the future.

Few colonists believed that they could do anything more than grumble and buy the stamps—until the Virginia House of Burgesses sounded what one colonist called a "trumpet of sedition" that aroused Americans to action almost everywhere. The "trumpet" was the collective voice of a group of young Virginia aristocrats. They hoped, among other things, to challenge the power of tidewater planters who (in alliance with the royal governor) dominated Virginia politics. Foremost among the malcontents was Patrick Henry, who had already achieved fame for his fiery oratory and his occasional defiance of British authority. Henry made a dramatic speech to the House of Burgesses in May 1765, concluding

THE ALTERNATIVES OF WILLIAM BURG In the aftermath of the
Boston Tea Party, and in response to the Coercive Acts Great Britain
enacted to punish the colonists, the First Continental Congress called
on Americans to boycott British goods until the Acts were repealed. In
this drawing, a prosperous Virginia merchant is seen signing a pledge
to honor the nonimportation agreement—unsurprisingly given the
alternative, visible in the background of the picture: tar and feathers
hanging from a post labeled "A Cure for the Refractory." *(Colonial
Williamsburg Foundation)*

with a vague prediction that if present policies were not
revised, George III, like earlier tyrants, might lose his
head. There were shocked cries of "Treason!" and,
according to one witness, an immediate apology from
Henry (although many years later he was quoted as having made the defiant reply: "If this be treason, make the
most of it").

Henry introduced a set of resolutions declaring that
Americans possessed the same rights as the English, espe-

Virginia Resolves

cially the right to be taxed only
by their own representatives,
that Virginians should pay no taxes except those voted
by the Virginia assembly; and that anyone advocating the
right of Parliament to tax Virginians should be deemed
an enemy of the colony. The House of Burgesses defeated
the most extreme of Henry's resolutions, but all of them
were printed and circulated as the "Virginia Resolves"
(creating an impression in other colonies that the people
of Virginia were more militant than they actually were).

In Massachusetts at about the same time, James Otis
persuaded his fellow members of the colonial assembly
to call an intercolonial congress for action against the
new tax. In October 1765, the Stamp Act Congress met
in New York with delegates from nine colonies and
decided to petition the king and the two houses of
Parliament. Their petition conceded that Americans
owed to Parliament "all due subordination," but it denied
that the colonies could rightfully be taxed except
through their own provincial assemblies.

Meanwhile, in several colonial cities crowds began
taking the law into their own hands. During the summer
of 1765 serious riots broke out

Sons of Liberty

up and down the coast, the
largest of them in Boston. Men belonging to the newly
organized Sons of Liberty terrorized stamp agents and
burned the stamps. The agents, themselves Americans,
hastily resigned; and the sale of stamps in the continental
colonies virtually ceased. In Boston, a crowd also
attacked such pro-British "aristocrats" as the lieutenant
governor, Thomas Hutchinson (who had privately
opposed passage of the Stamp Act but who, as an officer
of the crown, felt obliged to support it once it became
law). The protestors pillaged Hutchinson's elegant house
and virtually destroyed it.

The Stamp Act crisis was a dangerous moment in the
relationship between the colonies and the British
government. But the crisis subsided, largely because
England backed down. The authorities in London did not
relent because of the resolutions by the colonial assemblies, the petitions from the Stamp Act Congress, or the
riots in American cities. They changed their attitude
because of economic pressure. Even before the Stamp
Act, many New Englanders had stopped buying English
goods to protest the Sugar Act of 1764. Now the colonial
boycott spread, and the Sons of Liberty intimidated those
colonists who were reluctant to participate in it. The
merchants of England, feeling the loss of much of their
colonial market, begged Parliament to repeal the Stamp
Act; and stories of unemployment, poverty, and discontent
arose from English seaports and manufacturing towns.

The Marquis of Rockingham, who succeeded
Grenville as prime minister in July 1765, tried to appease
both the English merchants and

Parliament Retreats

the American colonists, and he
finally convinced the king to kill the Stamp Act. On
March 18, 1766, Parliament repealed it. Rockingham's
opponents were strong and vociferous, and they insisted
that unless England compelled the colonists to obey the
Stamp Act, they would soon cease to obey any laws of
Parliament. So on the same day, to satisfy such critics,
Parliament passed the Declaratory Act, asserting Parliament's authority over the colonies "in all cases whatsoever." In their rejoicing over the repeal of the Stamp Act,
most Americans paid little attention to this sweeping
declaration of power.

"THE TORY'S DAY OF JUDGMENT" A mob of American Patriots hoists a Loyalist neighbor up a flagpole in this woodcut, which is obviously sympathetic to the victim. The crowd is shown as fat, rowdy, and drunken. Public humiliations of Tories were not infrequent during the war. More common, however, was seizure of their property. *(Library of Congress)*

The Townshend Program

The reaction in England to the Rockingham government's policy of appeasement was less enthusiastic than it was in America. English landlords, a powerful political force, angrily protested that the government had "sacrificed the landed gentlemen to the interests of traders and colonists." They feared that backing down from taxing the colonies would lead the government to increase taxes on them. The king finally bowed to their pressure and dismissed the Rockingham ministry. To replace it, he called upon the aging but still powerful William Pitt to form a government. Pitt had been a strong critic of the Stamp Act and, despite his acceptance of a peerage in 1766, had a reputation in America as a friend of the colonists. Once in office, however, Pitt (now Lord Chatham) was so hobbled by gout and at times so incapacitated by mental illness that the actual leadership of his administration fell to the chancellor of the exchequer, Charles Townshend—a brilliant, flamboyant, and at times reckless politician known to his contemporaries variously as "the Weathercock" and "Champagne Charlie."

Among Townshend's first challenges was dealing with the continuing American grievances against Parliament, now most notably the Mutiny (or Quartering) Act of 1765, which **Mutiny Act** required the colonists to provide quarters and supplies for the British troops in America. The British considered this a reasonable requirement. The troops were stationed in North America to protect the colonists from Indian or French attack and to defend the frontiers; lodging the troops in coastal cities was simply a way to reduce the costs to England of supplying them. To the colonists, however, the law was another assault on their liberties.

They did not so much object to quartering the troops or providing them with supplies; they had been doing that voluntarily ever since the last years of the French and Indian War. They resented that these contributions were now mandatory, and they considered it another form of taxation without consent. They responded with defiance. The Massachusetts Assembly refused to vote the mandated supplies to the troops. The New York Assembly soon did likewise, posing an even greater challenge to imperial authority, since the army headquarters were in New York City.

To enforce the law and to try again to raise revenues in the colonies, Townshend steered two measures through Parliament in 1767. The first disbanded the New York Assembly until the colonists **Internal and External Taxes** agreed to obey the Mutiny Act. (By singling out New York, Townshend thought he would avoid Grenville's mistake of arousing all the colonies at once.) The second levied new taxes (known as the Townshend Duties) on various goods imported to the colonies from England—lead, paint, paper, and tea. The colonists could not logically object to taxation of this kind, Townshend reasoned, because it met standards they themselves had accepted. Benjamin Franklin, as a colonial agent in London trying to prevent the passage of the Stamp Act, had long ago argued for the distinction between "internal" and "external" taxes and had denounced the stamp duties as internal taxation. Townshend himself had considered the distinction laughable; but he was nevertheless imposing duties on what he believed were clearly external transactions.

Yet Townshend's efforts to satisfy colonial grievances were to no avail. Townshend might call them external taxes, but they were no more acceptable to colonial merchants than the Stamp Act. Indirectly, colonial consumers would still have to pay them. Their purpose, Americans believed, was the same as that of the Stamp Act: to raise revenue from the colonists without their consent. And the suspension of the New York Assembly, far from isolating New York, aroused the resentment of all the colonies. They considered this assault on the rights of one provincial government a precedent for the annihilation of the rights of all of them.

The Massachusetts Assembly took the lead in opposing the new measures by circulating a letter to all the colonial governments urging them to stand up against every tax, external or internal, imposed by Parliament. At first, the circular evoked little response in some of the legislatures (and ran into strong opposition in Pennsylvania's). Then Lord Hillsborough, secretary of state for the colonies, issued a circular letter of his own from London in which he warned that assemblies endorsing the Massachusetts letter would be dissolved. Massachusetts defiantly reaffirmed its support for the circular. (The vote in the Assembly was 92 to 17, and for a time "ninety-two" became a patriotic rallying cry throughout British America.) The other colonies, including Pennsylvania, promptly rallied to the support of Massachusetts.

In addition to his other unpopular measures, Townshend tried to strengthen enforcement of commercial regulations in the colonies by, among other things, establishing a new board of customs commissioners in America. Townshend hoped the new board would stop the rampant corruption in the colonial customs houses, and to some extent his hopes were fulfilled. The new commissioners virtually ended smuggling in Boston, their headquarters, although smugglers continued to carry on a busy trade in other colonial seaports.

The Boston merchants—accustomed, like all colonial merchants, to loose enforcement of the Navigation Acts and doubly aggrieved now that the new commission was **Colonial Boycotts** diverting the lucrative smuggling trade elsewhere—were indignant, and they took the lead in organizing another boycott. In 1768, the merchants of Philadelphia and New York joined them in a nonimportation agreement, and later some southern merchants and planters also agreed to cooperate. Colonists boycotted British goods subject to the Townshend Duties; and throughout the colonies, American homespun and other domestic products became suddenly fashionable, while English luxuries fell from favor.

Late in 1767, Charles Townshend suddenly died—before the consequences of his ill-conceived program had become fully apparent. The question of dealing with colonial resistance to the Townshend Duties fell, therefore, to the new prime minister, Lord North. Hoping to break the nonimportation agreement and divide the colonists, Lord North secured the repeal of all the Townshend Duties except the tax on tea in March 1770.

The Boston Massacre

The withdrawal of the Townshend Duties never had a chance to pacify colonial opinion. Before news of the repeal reached America, an event in Massachusetts raised colonial resentment to a new level of intensity. The colonists' harassment of the new customs commissioners in Boston had grown so intense **Competition for Scarce Employment** that the British government had placed four regiments of regular troops inside the city. The presence of the "redcoats" was a constant affront to the colonists' sense of independence and a constant reminder of what they considered British oppression. In addition, British soldiers, poorly paid and poorly treated by the army, wanted jobs in their off-duty hours; and they competed with local workers in an already tight market. Clashes between them were frequent.

On the night of March 5, 1770, a few days after a particularly intense skirmish between workers at a ship-rigging factory and British soldiers who were trying to find work there, a crowd of dockworkers, "liberty boys," and others began pelting the sentries at the customs house with rocks and snowballs. Hastily, Captain Thomas Preston of the British regiment lined up several of his men in front of the building to protect it. There was some scuffling; one of the soldiers was knocked down; and in the midst of it all, apparently, several British soldiers fired into the crowd, killing five people (among them a mulatto sailor, Crispus Attucks).

This murky incident, almost certainly the result of panic and confusion, was quickly transformed by local resistance leaders into the "Boston Massacre"—a graphic symbol of British oppression and brutality. The victims became popular martyrs; the event became the subject of many lurid (and inaccurate) **Samuel Adams** accounts. A famous engraving by Paul Revere, widely reproduced and circulated, portrayed the massacre as a carefully organized, calculated assault on a peaceful crowd. A jury of Massachusetts colonists found the British soldiers guilty of manslaughter and sentenced them to a token punishment. Colonial pamphlets and newspapers, however, convinced many Americans that the soldiers were guilty of official murder. Year after year, resistance leaders marked the anniversary of the massacre with demonstrations and speeches. The leading figure in fomenting public outrage over the Boston Massacre was Samuel Adams, the most effective radical in the colonies. Adams (a distant cousin of John Adams, second president of the United States) was born in 1722 and was thus somewhat older than other leaders of colonial protest. As a member of an earlier generation with strong ties to New England's Puritan past, he was particularly inclined to view public events in stern moral terms. A failure in business, he became an unflagging voice expressing outrage at British oppression. England, he argued, had become a morass of sin and corruption; only in America did public virtue survive. He spoke frequently at Boston town meetings; and as one unpopular English policy followed another—the Townshend Duties, the placement of customs commissioners in Boston, the

THE BOSTON MASSACRE (1770), BY PAUL REVERE This is one of many sensationalized engravings, by Revere and others, of the conflict between British troops and Boston laborers that became important propaganda documents for the Patriot cause in the 1770s. Among the victims of the massacre listed by Revere was Crispus Attucks, probably the first black man to die in the struggle for American independence. *(Burstein Collection/Corbis)*

"THE CRUEL FATE OF THE LOYALISTS" This British cartoon, published near the end of the American Revolution, show three Indians, representing American revolutionaries, murdering six loyalists: four by hanging, one by scalping, and one—appealing to Fate—about to be killed by an axe-wielding native. By using Indians to represent Anglo-American soldiers, the British were trying to equate the presumed savagery of native Americans with the behavior of the revolutionaries. *(Library of Congress, LC-USZ62-15233)*

stationing of British troops in the city (with its violent results)—his message attracted increasing support. In 1772, he proposed the creation of a "committee of correspondence" in Boston to publicize the grievances against England throughout the colony. He became its first head. Other colonies followed Massachusetts's lead, and there grew up a loose network of political organizations that kept the spirit of dissent alive through the 1770s.

The Philosophy of Revolt

Although a superficial calm settled on the colonies for approximately three years after the Boston Massacre, the crises of the 1760s had helped arouse enduring ideological challenges to England and had produced powerful instruments for publicizing colonial grievances. Gradually a political outlook gained a following in America that would ultimately serve to justify revolt.

The ideas that would support the Revolution emerged from many sources. Some were drawn from religious (particularly Puritan) sources or from the political experiences of the colonies. Others came from abroad. Most important, perhaps, were the "radical" ideas of those in Great Britain who stood in opposition to their

government. Some were Scots, who considered the English state tyrannical. Others were embittered "country Whigs," who felt excluded from power and considered the existing system corrupt and oppressive. Drawing from some of the great philosophical minds of earlier generations—most notably John Locke—these English dissidents framed a powerful argument against their government.

Central to this emerging ideology was a new concept of what government should be. Because humans were inherently corrupt and selfish, government was necessary to protect individuals from the evil in one another. But because any government was run by corruptible people, the people needed safeguards against its possible abuses of power. Most people in both England and America considered the English constitution the best system ever devised to meet these necessities. By distributing power among the three elements of society—the monarchy, the aristocracy, and the common people—the English political system ensured that no individual or group could exercise authority unchecked by another. Yet by the mid-seventeenth century, dissidents in both England and America had become convinced that the constitution was in danger. A single center of power—the king and his ministers—was becoming so powerful that it could not be effectively checked, and the system was becoming a corrupt and dangerous tyranny.

Such arguments found little sympathy in most of England. The English constitution was not a written document or a fixed set of unchangeable rules. It was

> England's Balanced Constitution

a general sense of the "way things are done," and most people in England were willing to accept changes in it. Americans, by contrast, drew from their experience with colonial charters, in which the shape and powers of government were permanently inscribed on paper. They resisted the idea of a flexible, changing set of basic principles.

One basic principle, Americans believed, was the right of people to be taxed only with their own consent—a belief that gradually took shape in the widely repeated slogan, "No taxation without representation." This clamor about "representation" made little sense to the English. According to English constitutional theory, members of Parliament did not represent individuals or particular geographical areas. Instead, each member represented the interests of the whole nation and indeed the whole empire, no matter where the member happened to come from. The many boroughs of England that had no representative in Parliament, the whole of Ireland, and the colonies thousands of miles away—all were thus represented in the Parliament at London, even though they elected no representatives of their own. This was the theory of "virtual" representation. But Americans, drawing from their experiences with their town meetings and their colonial assemblies, believed in "actual" representation. Every community was entitled to its own representative, elected by the people of that community and directly responsible to them. Since the colonists had none of their own representatives in Parliament, it followed that they were not represented there. Americans believed that the colonial assemblies played the same role within the colonies that Parliament did within England. The empire, the Americans argued, was a sort of federation of commonwealths, each with its own legislative body, all tied together by common loyalty to the king.

Such ideas illustrated a fundamental difference of opinion between England and America over the nature of sovereignty—over the question of where ultimate power lay. By arguing that Parliament had the right to legislate for England and for the empire as a whole, but that only the provincial assemblies could legislate for the individual colonies, Americans were in effect arguing for a division of sovereignty. Parliament would be sovereign in some matters; the assemblies would be sovereign in others. To the British, such an argument was absurd. In any system of government there must be a single, ultimate authority. And since the empire was, in their view, a single, undivided unit, there could be only one authority within it: the English government of king and Parliament.

Virtual versus Actual Representation

The Tea Excitement

An apparent calm in America in the first years of the 1770s disguised a growing sense of resentment at the increasingly heavy-handed British enforcement of the Navigation Acts. The customs commissioners, who remained in the colonies despite the repeal of the Townshend Acts, were mostly clumsy, intrusive, and arrogant officials. They harassed colonial merchants and seamen constantly with petty restrictions, and they also enriched themselves through graft and through illegal seizures of merchandise.

Colonists also kept revolutionary sentiment alive through writing and talking. Dissenting leaflets, pamphlets, and books circulated widely through the colonies. In towns and cities, men gathered in churches, schools, town squares, and above all in taverns to discuss politics and express their growing disenchantment with English policy. The rise of revolutionary ideology was not simply a result of the ideas of intellectuals. It was also a product of a social process by which ordinary people heard, discussed, and absorbed new ideas.

Revolutionary Discourse

The popular anger lying just beneath the surface was also visible in occasional acts of rebellion. At one point, colonists seized a British revenue ship on the lower Delaware River. And in 1772, angry residents of Rhode Island boarded the British schooner *Gaspée,* set it afire, and sank it in Narragansett Bay. The British response to the *Gaspée* affair further inflamed American opinion. Instead of putting the accused attackers on trial in colonial courts, the British sent a special commission to America with power to send the defendants back to England for trial.

What finally revived the revolutionary fervor of the 1760s, however, was a new act of Parliament—one that the English government had expected to be relatively uncontroversial. It involved the business of selling tea. In 1773, Britain's East India Company (which had an official monopoly on trade with the Far East) was on the verge of bankruptcy and sitting on large stocks of tea that it could not sell in England. In an effort to save the company, the government passed the Tea Act of 1773, which gave the company the right to export its merchandise directly to the colonies without paying any of the navigation taxes that were imposed on the colonial merchants, who had traditionally served as the middlemen in such transactions. With these privileges, the East India Company could undersell American merchants and monopolize the colonial tea trade.

The act angered many colonists for several reasons. First, it enraged influential colonial merchants, who feared being replaced and bankrupted by a powerful monopoly. The East India Company's decision to grant franchises to certain American merchants for the sale of their tea created further resentments among those excluded from this lucrative trade. More important, however, the Tea Act revived American passions about the

Monday Morning, December 27, 1773.
THE Tea-Ship being arrived, every Inhabitant who will to preferve the Liberty of America, is defired to meet the STATE-HOUSE, This Morning, precifely at TEN o'Clock, advife what is beft to be done on this alarming Crifis.

To the PUBLIC.

THE Senfe of the City relative to the Landing the India Company's Tea, being fignified to Captain Lockyer, by the Committee, neverthelefs, it is the Defire of a Number of the Citizens, that at his Departure from hence, he fhould fee, with his own Eyes, their Deteftation of the Meafures purfued by the Miniftry and the India Company, to enflave this Country. This will be declared by the Convention of the People at his Departure from this City; which will be on next Saturday Morning, about nine o'Clock, when no Doubt, every Friend to this Country will attend. The Bells will give the Notice about an Hour before he embarks from Murray's Wharf.

By Order of the COMMITTEE.

NEW YORK, APRIL 21ß, 1774.

THE BOSTON TEA PARTY The artist Ramberg produced this wash drawing of the Boston Tea Party in 1773. A handbill in a Philadelphia newspaper ten days later and another distributed in New York the following April illustrate how quickly the spirit of resistance spread to other colonies (Left, *The Metropolitan Museum of Art, Bequest of Charles Allen Munn, 1924. (24.90.1865);* Upper Right, *Chicago Historical Society;* Bottom Right, *Bettmann/Corbis)*

The Tea Act

issue of taxation without representation. The law provided no new tax on tea. But the original Townshend duty on the commodity —the only one of the original duties that had not been repealed—survived. It was the East India Company's exemption from that duty that put the colonial merchants at such a grave competitive disadvantage. Lord North assumed that most colonists would welcome the new law because it would reduce the price of tea to consumers by removing the middlemen. But resistance leaders in America argued that it was another insidious example of the results of an unconstitutional tax. Many colonists responded by boycotting tea.

The boycott was an important event in the history of colonial resistance. Unlike earlier protests, most of which had involved relatively small numbers of people, the boycott mobilized large segments of the population. It also helped link the colonies together in a common experience of mass popular protest. Particularly important to the movement were the activities of colonial women, who were among the principal consumers of tea and now became leaders of the effort to boycott it.

Women had played a significant role in resistance activities from the beginning. Several women (most prominently Mercy Otis Warren) had been important in writing the dissident literature—in Warren's case satirical plays—that did much to fan colonial resentments in the 1760s. Women had participated actively in anti-British riots and crowd activities in the 1760s; they had formed an informal organization—the Daughters of Liberty— that occasionally mocked their male counterparts as insufficiently militant. Now, as the sentiment for a boycott grew, some women mobilized as never before, determined (as the Daughters of Liberty had written) "that rather than Freedom, we'll part with our Tea."

In the last weeks of 1773, with strong popular support, leaders in various colonies made plans to prevent the East India Company from landing its cargoes in colonial ports. In Philadelphia and New York, determined colonists kept the tea from leaving the company's ships. In Charleston, they stored it away in a public warehouse. In Boston, after failing to turn back the three ships in the harbor, local patriots staged a spectacular drama. On the

Boston Tea Party

evening of December 16, 1773, three companies of fifty men each, masquerading as Mohawks, passed through a tremendous crowd of spectators (which served to protect them from official interference), went aboard the three ships, broke open the tea chests, and heaved them into the harbor. As the electrifying news of the Boston "tea party" spread, other seaports followed the example and staged similar acts of resistance.

When the Bostonians refused to pay for the property they had destroyed, George III and Lord North decided on a policy of coercion, to be applied only against Massachusetts—the chief center of resistance. In four acts of 1774, Parliament closed the port of Boston, drastically reduced colonial self-government, permitted

Taverns in Revolutionary Massachusetts

In colonial Massachusetts, as in many other American colonies in the 1760s and 1770s, taverns (or "public houses," as they were often known) were crucial to the development of popular resistance to British rule. The Puritan culture of New England created some resistance to taverns, and there were continuing efforts by reformers to regulate or close them to reduce the problems caused by "public drunkenness," "lewd behavior," and anarchy. But as the commercial life of the colonies expanded, and as increasing numbers of people began living in towns and cities, taverns became a central institution in American social life—and eventually in its political life as well.

Taverns were appealing, of course, because they provided alcoholic drinks in a culture where the craving for alcohol—and the extent of drunkenness—was very high. But taverns had other attractions as well. There were few other places where people could meet and talk openly in public, and to many colonists the life of the tavern came to seem the only vaguely democratic experience available to them. Gradually, many came to see the attacks on the public houses as efforts to increase the power of existing elites and suppress the freedoms of ordinary people. The tavern was a mostly male institution, just as politics was considered a mostly male concern. And so the fusion of male camaraderie and political discourse emerged naturally out of the tavern culture.

As the revolutionary crisis deepened, taverns and pubs became the central meeting places for discussions of the ideas that fueled resistance to British polices. Educated and uneducated men alike joined in animated discussions of events. Those who could not read—and there were many—could learn about the contents of revolutionary pamphlets from listening to tavern discussions. They could join in the discussion of the new republican ideas emerging in the Americas by participating in tavern celebrations of, for example, the anniversaries of resistance to the Stamp Act. Those anniversaries inspired elaborate toasts in public houses throughout the colonies. Such toasts were the equivalents of political speeches, and illiterate men could learn much from them about the political concepts that were circulating through the colonies.

Taverns were important sources of information in an age before any wide distribution of newspapers. Tavernkeepers were often trusted informants and confidants to the Sons of Liberty and other activists, and they were fountains of information about the political and social turmoil of the time. Taverns were also the settings for political events. In 1770, for example, a report circulated through the taverns of Danvers, Massachusetts about a local man who was continuing to sell tea despite the colonial boycott. The Sons of Liberty brought the seller to the Bell Tavern and persuaded him to sign a confession and apology before a crowd of defiant men in the public room.

Almost all politicians found it necessary to visit taverns in colonial Massachusetts if they wanted any real contact with the public. Samuel Adams spent considerable time in the public houses of Boston, where he sought to encourage resistance to British rule while taking care to drink moderately so as not to erode his stature as a leader. His cousin John Adams was somewhat more skeptical of taverns, more sensitive to the vices they encouraged. But he, too, recognized their political value. In taverns, he once said, "bastards, and legislators are frequently begotten."

TAVERN BILLIARDS Gentlemen in Hanover Town, Virginia gather for a game of billiards in a local tavern in this 1797 drawing by Benjamin Henry Latrobe. *(Maryland Historical Society, Baltimore)*

THE SCALES OF JUSTICE This sign for a Hartford tavern promises hospitality (from "the charming Patroness") and "entertainment" as well as food and drink. *(The Connecticut Historical Society, Hartford)*

royal officers to be tried in other colonies or in England when accused of crimes, and provided for the quartering of troops in the colonists' barns and empty houses.

Parliament followed these Coercive Acts—or, as they were more widely known in America, Intolerable Acts—with the Quebec Act, which was separate from them in origin and quite different in purpose. Its object was to provide a civil government for the French-speaking Roman Catholic inhabitants of Canada and the Illinois country. The law extended the boundaries of Quebec to include

Coercive Acts

PAYING THE EXCISEMAN This eighteenth-century satirical drawing by a British artist depicts Bostonians forcing tea down the throat of a customs official, whom they have tarred and feathered. In the background, colonists are dumping tea into the harbor (presumably a representation of the 1773 Boston Tea Party); and on the tree at right is a symbol of the Stamp Act, which the colonists had defied eight years earlier. *(Art Resource, NY.)*

the French communities between the Ohio and Mississippi Rivers. It also granted political rights to Roman Catholics and recognized the legality of the Roman Catholic Church within the enlarged province. In many ways it was a tolerant and long overdue piece of legislation. But in the inflamed atmosphere of the time, many people in the thirteen English-speaking colonies considered it a threat. They were already alarmed by rumors that the Church of England was scheming to appoint a bishop for America who would impose Anglican authority on all the various sects. Since the line between the Church of England and the Church of Rome had always seemed to many Americans dangerously thin, the passage of the Quebec Act convinced some of them that a plot was afoot in London to subject Americans to the tyranny of the pope. Those interested in western lands, moreover, believed that the act would hinder westward expansion.

The Coercive Acts, far from isolating Massachusetts, made it a martyr to residents of other colonies and sparked new resistance up and down the coast. Colonial legisla- | Consequences

tures passed a series of resolves supporting Massachusetts. Women's groups throughout the colonies mobilized to extend the boycotts of British goods and to create substitutes for the tea, textiles, and other commodities they were shunning.

COOPERATION AND WAR

Revolutions do not simply happen. They need organizers and leaders. Beginning in 1765, colonial leaders developed a variety of organizations for converting popular discontent into direct action—organizations that in time formed the basis for an independent government.

New Sources of Authority

The passage of authority from the royal government to the colonists themselves began on the local level, where the tradition of autonomy was already strong. In colony after colony, local institutions responded to the resistance movement by simply seizing authority on their own. At times, entirely new, extralegal bodies emerged semi-spontaneously and began to perform some of the functions of government. In Massachusetts in 1768, for example, Samuel Adams called a convention of delegates from the towns of the colony to sit in place of the General Court, which the governor had dissolved. The Sons of Liberty, which Adams had helped organize in Massachusetts and which sprang up elsewhere as well, became another source of power. Its members at times formed disciplined bands of vigilantes who made certain that all colonists respected the boycotts and other forms of popular resistance. And in most colonies, committees of prominent citizens began meeting to perform additional political functions.

The most effective of these new groups were the committees of correspondence, which Adams had inaugurated in Massachusetts in 1772. Virginia later established the first intercolonial committees of correspondence, which made possible continuous cooperation among the colonies. Virginia also took | First Continental Congress

the greatest step of all toward united action in 1774 when, after the royal governor dissolved the assembly, a rump session met in the Raleigh Tavern at Williamsburg, declared that the Intolerable Acts menaced the liberties of every colony, and issued a call for a Continental Congress. Variously elected by the assemblies and by extralegal meetings, delegates from all the thirteen colonies except Georgia were present when, in September 1774, the First Continental Congress convened in Carpenter's Hall in Philadelphia. They made five major decisions. First, in a very close vote, they rejected a plan (proposed by Joseph Galloway of Pennsylvania) for a colonial union under British authority (much like the

RECRUITING PATRIOTS This Revolutionary War recruiting poster tries to attract recruits by appealing to their patriotism (asking them to defend "the liberties and independence of the United States"), their vanity (by showing the "handsome clothing" and impressive bearing of soldiers), and their greed (by offering them "a bounty of twelve dollars" and "sixty dollars a year"). *(Library of Congress)*

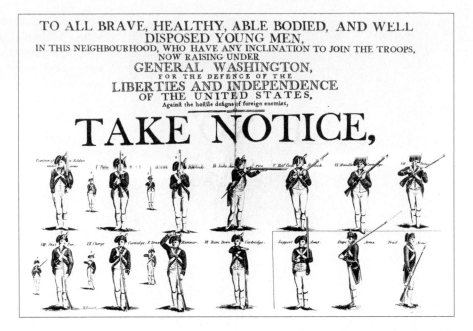

earlier Albany Plan). Second, they endorsed a statement of grievances, whose tortured language reflected the conflicts among the delegates between moderates and extremists. The statement seemed to concede Parliament's right to regulate colonial trade and addressed the king as "Most Gracious Sovereign"; but it also included a more extreme demand for the repeal of all the oppressive legislation passed since 1763. Third, they approved a series of resolutions, recommending, among other things, that the colonists make military preparations for defense against possible attack by the British troops in Boston. Fourth, they agreed to nonimportation, nonexportation, and nonconsumption as means of stopping all trade with Great Britain, and they formed a "Continental Association" to enforce the agreements. And fifth, when the delegates adjourned, they agreed to meet again the next spring, thus indicating that they considered the Continental Congress a continuing organization.

Through their representatives in Philadelphia the colonies had, in effect, reaffirmed their autonomous status within the empire and declared something close to economic war to maintain that position. The more optimistic of the Americans hoped that this economic warfare alone would win a quick and bloodless victory, but the more pessimistic had their doubts. "I expect no redress, but, on the contrary, increased resentment and double vengeance," John Adams wrote to Patrick Henry; "we must fight." And Henry replied, "By God, I am of your opinion."

During the winter, the Parliament in London debated proposals for conciliating the colonists. Lord Chatham (William Pitt), the former prime minister, urged the withdrawal of troops from America. Edmund Burke called for the repeal of the Coercive Acts. But their efforts were in vain. Lord North finally won approval early in 1775 for a series of measures known as the Conciliatory Propositions, but they were in fact far less conciliatory than the approaches Burke or Chatham had urged. Parliament now proposed that the colonies, instead of being taxed directly by Parliament, would tax themselves at Parliament's demand. With this offer, Lord North hoped to divide the American moderates, who he believed represented the views of the majority, from the extremist minority. But his offer was probably too little and, in any case, too late. It did not reach America until after the first shots of war had been fired.

> The Conciliatory Propositions

Lexington and Concord

For months, the farmers and townspeople of Massachusetts had been gathering arms and ammunition and training as "minutemen," preparing to fight on a minute's notice. The Continental Congress had approved preparations for a defensive war, and the citizen-soldiers awaited an aggressive move by the British regulars in Boston.

In Boston, General Thomas Gage, commanding the British garrison, knew of the military preparations in the countryside but considered his army too small to do anything until reinforcements arrived. He resisted the advice of less cautious officers, who assured him that the Americans would never dare actually to fight, that they would back down quickly before any show of British force. Major John Pitcairn, for example, insisted that a single "small action," such as the burning of a few towns, would "set everything to rights."

THE BATTLES OF LEXINGTON AND CONCORD, 1775 This map shows the fabled series of events that led to the first battle of the American Revolution. On the night of April 18, 1775, Paul Revere and William Dawes rode out from Boston to warn the outlying towns of the approach of British troops. Revere was captured just west of Lexington, but Dawes escaped and returned to Boston. The next morning, British forces moved out of Boston toward Lexington, where they met armed American minutemen on the Lexington common and exchanged fire. The British dispersed the Americans in Lexington. But they next moved on to Concord, where they encountered more armed minutemen, clashed again, and were driven back toward Boston. All along their line of march, they were harassed by riflemen. ◆ *What impact did the battles of Lexington and Concord (and the later battle of Bunker Hill, also shown on this map) have on colonial sentiment toward the British?*

When General Gage received orders from England to arrest the rebel leaders Sam Adams and John Hancock, known to be in the vicinity of Lexington, he still hesitated. But when he heard that the minutemen had stored a large supply of gunpowder in Concord (eighteen miles from Boston), he at last decided to act. On the night of April 18, 1775, he sent a detachment of about 1,000 soldiers out from Boston on the road to Lexington and Concord. He intended to surprise the colonials and seize the illegal supplies without bloodshed.

General Thomas Gage

But patriots in Boston were watching the British movements closely, and during the night two horsemen, William Dawes and Paul Revere, rode out to warn the villages and farms. When the British troops arrived in Lexington the next day, several dozen minutemen awaited them on the town common. Shots were fired and minutemen fell; eight of them were killed and ten more wounded. Advancing to Concord, the British discovered that the Americans had hastily removed most of the powder supply, but the British

burned what was left of it. All along the road from Concord back to Boston, farmers hiding behind trees, rocks, and stone fences harassed the British with continual gunfire. By the end of the day, the British had lost almost three times as many men as the Americans.

The first shots—the "shots heard round the world," as Americans later called them—had been fired. But who had fired them? According to one of the minutemen at Lexington, Major Pitcairn had shouted to the colonists on his arrival, "Disperse, ye rebels!" When the Americans ignored the command, he had given the order to fire. British officers and soldiers told a different story. They claimed that the minutemen had fired first, that only after seeing the flash of American guns had the British begun to shoot. Whatever the truth, the rebels succeeded in circulating their account well ahead of the British version, adorning it with lurid tales of British atrocities. The effect was to rally to the rebel cause thousands of colonists, north and south, who previously had had little enthusiasm for it.

The Retreat

From Concord to Lexington of the Army of Wild Irish Asses Defeated by the Brave American Militia
W. Deacon *M.* Loeings *M.* Mulikens *M.* Bonds Houses and Barn all Plunder'd and Burnt on April 19.*th*

THE BRITISH RETREAT FROM CONCORD, 1775 This American cartoon satirizes the retreat of British forces from Concord after the battle there on April 19, 1775. Patriot forces are lined up on the left, and the retreating British forces (portrayed with dog heads, perhaps because many of the soldiers were "wild" Irish) straggle off at right—some fleeing in panic, others gloating over the booty they have plundered from the burning homes above. In its crude and exaggerated way, the cartoon depicts the success of Patriot forces at the Old North Bridge in Concord in repulsing a British contingent under the command of Lord Percy. As the redcoats retreated to Lexington and then to Boston, they continued to encounter fire from colonial forces, not arrayed in battle lines as shown here, but hidden along the road. One British soldier described the nightmarish withdrawal: "We were fired on from Houses and behind Trees . . . the Country was . . . full of Hills, Woods, stone Walls . . . which the Rebels did not fail to take advantage of." *(Anne S.K. Brown Military Collection, Brown University Library)*

It was not immediately clear to the British, and even to many Americans, that the skirmishes at Lexington and Concord were the first battles of a war. Many saw them

The Revolution Begins

as simply another example of the tensions that had been afflicting Anglo-American relations for years. But whether they recognized it at the time or not, the British and the Americans had taken a decisive step. The War for Independence had begun.

CONCLUSION

When the French and Indian War ended in 1763, it might have seemed reasonable to expect that relations between the English colonists in America and Great Britain itself would have been cemented more firmly than ever. America and Britain had fought together in a great war against the French and their Indian allies. They had won impressive victories. They had vastly expanded the size of the British Empire.

But in fact the end of the French and Indian War altered the imperial relationship forever, in ways that ultimately drove Americans to rebel against English rule and begin a war for independence. To the British, the lesson of the war was that the colonies in America needed firmer control from London. The empire was now much bigger, and it needed better administration. The war had produced great debts, and the Americans—among the principal beneficiaries of the war—should help pay them. And so for more than a decade after the end of the fighting, the British tried one strategy after another to tighten control over and extract money from the colonies, all of them in the end failures.

To the colonists, this effort to tighten imperial rule was both a betrayal of the sacrifices they had made in the war and a challenge to their long-developing assumptions about the rights of English people to rule themselves. Gradually, white Americans came to see in the British policies evidence of a conspiracy to establish tyranny in the New World. And so throughout the 1760s and 1770s, the colonists developed ever more overt and effective forms of resistance. By the time the first shots were fired in the American Revolution in 1775, Britain and America—not long before bonded so closely to one another that most white Americans considered themselves as English as any resident of London—had come to view each other as two very different societies. Their differences, which came to seem irreconcilable, propelled them into a war that would change the course of history.

INTERACTIVE LEARNING

The *Primary Source Investigator CD-ROM* offers the following materials related to this chapter:

- Interactive maps: **The Atlantic World** (M68) and **Settlement of Colonial America** (M5).

- Documents, images, and maps related to the transition of the American colonies in the 1760s and 1770s, as one crisis after another led to a break with England. Highlights include texts of the British imperial acts that outraged the colonists and a gazette article describing the Boston Massacre.

Online Learning Center (www.mhhe.com/brinkley12)

For quizzes, Internet resources, references to additional books and films, and more, consult this book's Online Learning Center.

FOR FURTHER REFERENCE

Fred Anderson, *The Crucible of War: The Seven Years' War and the Fate of Empire in British North America, 1754–1766* (2000) is an excellent account of the critical years in which the British Empire transformed itself through its colonial wars in America. David Armitage, *The Ideological Origins of the British Empire* (2000) examines the ideas of those who promoted and sought to justify Britain's imperial ambitions. Francis Jennings, *The Ambiguous Iroquois Empire* (1984) examines the critical role of the Iroquois in the conflicts over empire in North America. Richard Bushman, *King and People in Colonial Massachusetts* (1987) traces the fracture between Massachusetts colonists and the imperial government. Gary Nash, *The Urban Crucible: The Northern Seaports and the Origins of the American Revolution* (1979) argues that increasing class stratification in northern cities contributed to the coming of the American Revolution. T.H. Breen, *The Marketplace of Revolution* (2004) argues that consumer politics played a major role in creating the Revolution. Jon Butler, *Becoming America: The Revolution Before 1776* (2000) argues for the emergence of a distinctive American culture in the eighteenth century. Robert R. Palmer, *The Age of Democratic Revolution: Vol. 1, The Challenge* (1959) and J. G. A. Pocock, *The Machiavellian Moment* (1975) both place the American Revolution in the context of a transatlantic political culture. Bernard Bailyn, *The Ideological Origins of the American Revolution* (1967) was one of the first works by an American historian to emphasize the importance of English republican political thought for the revolutionary ideology of the American colonists.

THE BRITISH SURRENDER This contemporary drawing depicts the formal surrender of British troops at Yorktown on October 19, 1781. Columns of American troops and a large French fleet flank the surrender ceremony, suggesting part of the reason for the British defeat. General Cornwallis, the commander of British forces in Virginia, did not himself attend the surrender. He sent a deputy in his place. *(Getty Images)*

SIGNIFICANT EVENTS

1774 ▶ Shawnee defeated by Virginia militia in Lord Dunmore's War

1775 ▶ Second Continental Congress meets

▶ George Washington appointed to command American forces

▶ Battle of Bunker Hill

▶ Montgomery assault on Quebec fails

1776 ▶ Thomas Paine's *Common Sense* published

▶ British troops leave Boston

▶ Declaration of Independence debated and signed (July 2–4)

▶ Howe routs Americans on Long Island

▶ Battle of Trenton

▶ First state constitutions written

1777 ▶ Articles of Confederation adopted

▶ Battles of Princeton, Brandywine, and Germantown

▶ Howe occupies Philadelphia

▶ Washington camps at Valley Forge for winter

▶ Burgoyne surrenders to Gates at Saratoga

1778 ▶ French-American alliance established

▶ Clinton replaces Howe

▶ British leave Philadelphia

▶ War shifts to the South

▶ British capture Savannah

CHAPTER 5

The American Revolution

*T*wo struggles occurred simultaneously during the seven years of war that began in April 1775. One was the military conflict with Great Britain. The second was a political struggle within America. The two struggles had profound effects on each other.

The military conflict was, by the standards of later wars, a relatively modest one. Battle deaths on the American side totaled fewer than 5,000. The technology of warfare was so crude that cannons and rifles were effective only at very close range, and fighting of any kind was virtually out of the question in bad weather. Yet the war in America was, by the standards of its own day, an unusually savage conflict, pitting not only army against army, but at times the population at large against a powerful external force. This shift of the war from a traditional, conventional struggle to a new kind of conflict—a revolutionary war for liberation—made it possible for the new American army finally to defeat the vastly more powerful British.

At the same time, Americans were wrestling with the great political questions the conflict necessarily produced: first, whether to demand independence from Britain; then, how to structure the new nation they had proclaimed. Only the first of these questions had been

Key Political Questions

resolved when the British surrendered at Yorktown in 1781. But by then the United States had already established itself—both in its own mind and in the mind of much of the rest of the world—as a new kind of nation, one with a special mission and dedicated to enlightened ideals. Thomas Paine, an important figure in shaping the Revolution, reflected the opinion of many when he claimed that the American War for Independence had "contributed more to enlighten the world, and diffuse a spirit of freedom and liberality among mankind, than any human event that ever preceded it."

Neither at the time nor later did the United States always follow those ideals. At the same time that revolutionaries were celebrating the "rights of man," they were consolidating the enslavement of African Americans, depriving loyalists (those who supported the British during the Revolution) of rights and property, barring women from participation in public life, and denying Indian tribes even some of the limited rights the British had accorded them. And yet despite these contradictions, the belief that the nation should try to live up to the ideals proclaimed in the Revolution exercised a continuing influence on the future history of the United States.

1780 ▶ British capture Charleston

▶ Cornwallis defeats Gates at Camden, South Carolina

▶ Patriots defeat Tories at King's Mountain, South Carolina

▶ Massachusetts state constitution ratified

▶ Slavery abolished in Pennsylvania

1781 ▶ Battles of Cowpens and Guilford Court House

▶ Cornwallis surrenders at Yorktown

▶ Articles of Confederation ratified

▶ Continental impost proposed

1782 ▶ American militiamen massacre Delaware Indians in Ohio

1781–1784 ▶ States cede western lands to Confederation

1783 ▶ Treaty of Paris with Great Britain recognizes American independence

▶ Slavery abolished in Massachusetts

1784 ▶ Postwar depression begins, aggravating currency problems

1784–1785 ▶ First ordinances establishing procedures for settling western lands enacted

1786 ▶ Virginia Statute of Religious Freedom passed

1786–1787 ▶ Shays's Rebellion in Massachusetts

1787 ▶ Northwest Ordinance enacted

1789 ▶ John Carroll named first bishop of Catholic Church of United States

1792 ▶ Mary Wollstonecraft's *Vindication of the Rights of Women* published in the United States

1794 ▶ Anthony Wayne defeats Indians in Ohio

THE STATES UNITED

Although many Americans had been expecting a military conflict with Britain for months, even years, the actual beginning of hostilities in 1775 found the colonies generally unprepared for the enormous challenges awaiting them. America was an unformed nation, with a population less than a third as large as the 9 million of Great Britain, and with vastly inferior economic and military resources. It faced the task of mobilizing for war against the world's greatest armed power. Americans faced that task, moreover, deeply divided about what they were fighting for.

Defining American War Aims

Three weeks after the battles of Lexington and Concord, the Second Continental Congress met in the State House in Philadelphia, with delegates from every colony except Georgia, which sent no representative until the following autumn. The members agreed to support the war. But they disagreed, at times profoundly, about its purpose.

At one pole was a group led by the Adams cousins (John and Samuel), Richard Henry Lee of Virginia, and others, who favored complete independence from Great Britain. At the other pole was a group led by such moderates as John Dickinson of Pennsylvania, who hoped for modest reforms in the imperial relationship that would permit an early reconciliation with Great Britain. Most of the delegates tried to find some middle ground between these positions. They demonstrated their uncertainty in two very different declarations, which they adopted in quick

Olive Branch Petition

succession. They approved one last, conciliatory appeal to the king, the "Olive Branch Petition." Then, on July 6, 1775, they adopted a more antagonistic "Declaration of the Causes and Necessity of Taking Up Arms." It proclaimed that the British government had left the American people with only two alternatives, "unconditional submission to the tyranny of irritated ministers or resistance by force."

The attitude of much of the public mirrored that of the Congress. At first, most Americans believed they were fighting not for independence but for a redress of grievances within the British Empire. During the first year of fighting, however, many of them began to change their minds, for several reasons. First, the costs of the war—human and financial—were so high that the original war aims began to seem too modest to justify them. Second, what lingering affection American Patriots retained for England greatly diminished when the British began trying to recruit Indians, African slaves, and foreign mercenaries (the hated Hessians) against them. Third, and most important, colonists came to believe that the British government was forcing them toward independence by rejecting the Olive Branch Petition and instead enacting a "Prohibitory Act," which closed the colonies to all overseas trade and made no concessions to American demands except an offer to pardon repentant rebels. The British enforced the Prohibitory Act with a naval blockade of colonial ports.

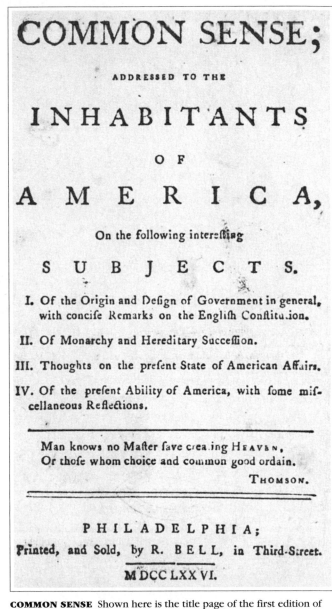

COMMON SENSE Shown here is the title page of the first edition of Thomas Paine's influential pamphlet, published anonymously in Philadelphia on January 10, 1776. Paine served in Washington's army during the campaigns in New Jersey and at the same time wrote a series of essays designed to arouse support for the Patriot cause. They were collectively titled *The Crisis* (the first of them contains the famous phrase "These are the times that try men's souls"). In later years Paine took an active part in the French Revolution, on behalf of which he published *The Rights of Man* (1791–1792). He also wrote *The Age of Reason* (1794–1796), which attacked conventional Christian beliefs and promoted his own "deist" philosophy. He returned to America in 1802 and spent the last years before his death in 1809 in poverty and obscurity. *(Library of Congress)*

But the growing support for independence remained to a large degree unspoken until January 1776, when an impassioned pamphlet appeared that galvanized many Americans. It was called, simply, *Common Sense.* Its author, unmentioned on the title page, was Thomas Paine, who had emigrated from England to America fifteen months before. Long a failure in various trades, Paine

Common Sense

now proved a brilliant success as a revolutionary propagandist. His pamphlet helped change the American outlook toward the war. Paine wanted to turn the anger of Americans away from the specific parliamentary measures they were resisting and toward what he considered the root of the problem—the English constitution itself. It was not enough, he argued, for Americans to continue blaming their problems on particular ministers, or even on Parliament. It was the king, and the system that permitted him to rule, that was to blame. It was, he argued, simple common sense for Americans to break completely with a government that could produce so corrupt a monarch as George III, a government that could inflict such brutality on its own people, a government that could drag Americans into wars in which America had no interest. The island kingdom of England was no more fit to rule the American continent, he claimed, than a satellite was fit to rule the sun.

The Decision for Independence

Common Sense sold more than 100,000 copies in its first few months. To many of its readers it was a revelation. Although sentiment for independence remained far from unanimous, support for the idea grew rapidly in the first months of 1776.

In the midst of all this, the Continental Congress was moving slowly and tentatively toward a final break with England. It declared American ports open to the ships of all nations except Great Britain. It entered into communication with foreign powers. It recommended to the

The Declaration of Independence

various colonies that they establish new governments independent of the British Empire, as in fact most already were doing. Congress also appointed a committee to draft a formal declaration of independence. On July 2, 1776, it adopted a resolution: "That these United Colonies are, and, of right, ought to be, free and independent states; that they are absolved from all allegiance to the British crown, and that all political connexion between them and the state of Great Britain is, and ought to be, totally dissolved." Two days later, on July 4, Congress approved the Declaration of Independence itself, which provided the formal justifications for the actions the delegates had in fact taken two days earlier.

Thomas Jefferson, a thirty-three-year-old delegate from Virginia, wrote most of the Declaration, with help from Benjamin Franklin and John Adams. As Adams later observed, Jefferson said little in the document that was new. Its virtue lay in the eloquence with which it expressed beliefs already widespread in America. In particular, it expressed ideas that had been voiced throughout the colonies in the preceding months in the form of at least ninety other, local "declarations of independence"—declarations drafted up and down the coast by town meetings, artisan and militia organizations, county officials, grand juries, Sons of Liberty, and colonial assemblies. Jefferson borrowed heavily from these texts, both for the ideas he expressed and, to some extent, for the precise language he used.

The document was in two parts. In the first, the Declaration restated the familiar contract theory of John Locke: that governments were formed to protect the rights of life, liberty, and property; Jefferson gave the theory a more idealistic tone by replacing "property" with "the pursuit of happiness." In the second part, the Declaration listed the alleged crimes of the king, who, with the backing of Parliament, had violated his "contract" with the colonists and thus had forfeited all claim to their loyalty.

The Declaration's ringing endorsement of the idea that "all men are created equal"—a phrase borrowed from an earlier document by Jefferson's fellow Virginian George Mason—later helped movements of liberation and reform of many kinds in the United States and abroad. It helped inspire, among other things, the French Revolution's own Declaration of the Rights of Man. More immediately, the Declaration—and its bold claim that the American colonies were now a sovereign nation, "The United States of America"—led to increased foreign aid for the struggling rebels and prepared the way for France's intervention on their side. The Declaration also encouraged American Patriots, as those opposing the British called themselves, to fight on and to reject the idea of a peace that stopped short of winning independence. At the same time it created deep divisions within American society.

Responses to Independence

At the news of the Declaration of Independence, crowds in Philadelphia, Boston, and other places gathered to cheer, fire guns and cannons, and ring church bells. But there were many in America who did not rejoice. Some had disapproved of the war from the beginning. Others had been willing to support it only so long as its aims did not conflict with their basic loyalty to the king. Such people were a minority, but a substantial one. They called themselves Loyalists; supporters of independence called them Tories.

In the aftermath of the Declaration of Independence, the colonies began to call themselves states—a reflection of their belief that each province was now in

Divided Americans

The American Revolution

Through most of its long life, the debate over the origins of the American Revolution has tended to reflect two broad schools of interpretation. One sees the Revolution largely as a political and intellectual event and argues that the revolt against Britain was part of a defense of ideals and principles. The other views the Revolution as a social and economic phenomenon and contends that material interests were at its heart.

The Revolutionary generation itself portrayed the conflict as a struggle over ideals, and their interpretation prevailed through most of the nineteenth century. For example, George Bancroft wrote in 1876 that the Revolution "was most radical in its character, yet achieved with such benign tranquillity that even conservatism hesitated to censure." Its aim, he argued, was to "preserve liberty" against British tyranny.

But in the early twentieth century, historians influenced by the reform currents of the progressive era began to identify social and economic forces that they believed had contributed to the rebellion. In a 1909 study of New York, Carl Becker wrote that two questions had shaped the Revolution: "The first was the question of home rule; the second was the question . . . of

(Anne S.K. Brown Military Collection, Brown University Library)

who should rule at home." The colonists were not only fighting the British; they were also engaged in a kind of civil war, a contest for power between radicals and conservatives that led to the "democratization of American politics and society."

Other "progressive" historians elaborated on Becker's thesis. In *The*

American Revolution Considered as a Social Movement (1926), J. Franklin Jameson argued that "the stream of revolution, once started, could not be confined within narrow banks, but spread abroad upon the land. . . . Many economic desires, many social aspirations, were set free by the political struggle, many aspects of society profoundly altered by the forces thus let loose." In a 1917 book, Arthur M. Schlesinger maintained that colonial merchants, motivated by their own interest in escaping the restrictive policies of British mercantilism, aroused American resistance in the 1760s and 1770s.

Beginning in the 1950s, a new generation of scholars began to re-emphasize the role of ideology and to de-emphasize the role of economic interests. Robert E. Brown (in 1955) and Edmund S. Morgan (in 1956) both argued that most eighteenth-century white Americans, regardless of station, shared basic political principles and that the social and economic conflicts the progressives had identified were not severe. The rhetoric of the Revolution, they suggested, was not propaganda, but a real reflection of the colonists' ideas. Bernard Bailyn, in *The Ideological Origins of the American Revolution*

some respects a separate and sovereign entity. Even before the Declaration, colonies were beginning to operate independently of royal authority, largely because the Parliament in London had suspended representative government in America. That suspension did not, as intended, end colonial self-government. It increased it, since the colonial assemblies continued to meet, now independent of imperial law. For the most part, the same men served in these assemblies as had served in the assemblies approved by London. After the Declaration of 1776, the former colonies marked their independence by writing formal constitutions for themselves. By 1781 most of the new states had produced such constitutions, which established republican governments. Some of these constitutions survived for many decades without significant change.

At the national level, however, the process of forming a government was more halting and less successful. For

a time, Americans were uncertain whether they even wanted a real national government; the Continental Congress had not been much more than a coordinating mechanism, and virtually everyone considered the individual colonies (now states) the real centers of authority. Yet fighting a war required a certain amount of central direction. Americans began almost immediately to do something they would continue to do for more than two centuries: balance the commitment to state and local autonomy against the need for some centralized authority.

In November 1777, Congress adopted the Articles of Confederation (which were not finally ratified until 1781). They did little more than confirm the

Articles of Confederation

weak, decentralized system already in operation. The Continental Congress would survive as the chief coordinating agency of the war effort. Its powers over the individual states would be very limited. Indeed, the Articles

(1967), demonstrated the complex roots of the ideas behind the Revolution and argued that this carefully constructed political stance was not a disguise for economic interests but a genuine ideology that itself motivated the colonists to act. The Revolution, he claimed, "was above all else an ideological, constitutional, political struggle and not primarily a controversy between social groups undertaken to force changes in the organization of the society or the economy."

By the late 1960s, however, a group of younger historians—many of them influenced by the New Left—were challenging the ideological interpretation again by illuminating social and economic tensions within colonial society that they claimed helped shape the Revolutionary struggle. Jesse Lemisch and Dirk Hoerder pointed to the actions of mobs in colonial cities as evidence of popular resentment of both American and British elites. Joseph Ernst re-emphasized the significance of economic pressures on colonial merchants and tradesmen. Gary Nash, in *The Urban Crucible* (1979), emphasized the role of growing economic distress in colonial cities in creating a climate in which Revolutionary sentiment could

(Gift of Edgar William and Bernice Chrysler Garbisch, © 1998 Board of Trustees, National Gallery of Art, Washington)

flourish. Edward Countryman and Rhys Isaac both pointed to changes in the nature of colonial society and culture, and in the relationship between classes in eighteenth-century America, as a crucial prerequisite for the growth of the Revolutionary movement.

Some newer social interpretations of the Revolution attempt to break free of the old debate pitting ideas against interests. The two things are not in competition with, but rather reinforce one another, more recent scholars argue. "Everyone has economic interests," Gary Nash has written, "and everyone . . . has an ideology." Only by exploring the relationships between the two can historians hope fully to understand either. Also, as Linda Kerber has written, newer interpretations have "reinvigorated the Progressive focus on social conflict between classes and extended it to include the experience not only of rich and poor but of a wide variety of interest groups, marginal communities, and social outsiders." That extension of focus to previously little-studied groups includes work by Mary Beth Norton on women, Silvia Frey on slaves, and Colin Calloway on Native Americans.

In 1992, Gordon Wood, in *The Radicalism of the American Revolution*, helped revive an interpretation of the Revolution that few historians have embraced in recent decades: that it was a genuinely radical event, which led to the breakdown of such long-standing patterns of society as deference, patriarchy, and traditional gender relations. Class conflict and radical goals may not have caused the Revolution; but the Revolution had a profound, even radical, ideological impact on society nevertheless.

---

did not make it entirely clear that the Congress was to be a real government at all. As a result, the new nation had to fight a war for its own survival with a weak and uncertain central government, never sure of its own legitimacy.

Mobilizing for War

The new governments of the states and the nation faced a series of overwhelming challenges: raising and organizing armies, providing them with the supplies and equipment they needed, and finding a way to pay for it all. Without access to the British markets on which the colonies had come to depend, finding necessary supplies was exceptionally difficult. Shortages persisted to the end.

America had many gunsmiths, but they could not come close to meeting the wartime demand for guns and ammunition, let alone the demand for heavy arms.

Although Congress created a government arsenal at Springfield, Massachusetts, in 1777, the Americans managed to manufacture only a small fraction of the equipment they used. They relied heavily on weapons and materiel they were able to capture from the British. But they got most of their war supplies from European nations, mainly from France.

Financing the war proved in many ways the most nettlesome problem. Congress had no authority to levy taxes directly on the people; it had to requisition funds from the state governments. But hard money was scarce in America, and the states were little better equipped to raise it than Congress was. None of them contributed more than a small part of their expected share. Congress tried to raise money by selling long-term bonds, but few Americans could afford them and those who could generally preferred to invest in more profitable ventures, such as privateering. In the end, the government had no choice but

VOTING FOR INDEPENDENCE The Continental Congress actually voted in favor of independence from Great Britain on July 2, 1776. July 4, the date Americans now celebrate as Independence Day, is when the Congress formally approved the Declaration of Independence. This painting by Edgar Pine-Savage re-creates the scene in Philadelphia as delegates from the various colonies made their momentous decision. *(Courtesy of The Historical Society of Pennsylvania Collection, Atwater Kent Museum of Philadelphia)*

to issue paper money. Continental currency came from the printing presses in large and repeated batches. The states printed sizable amounts of paper currency of their own.

The result, predictably, was inflation. Prices rose to fantastic heights, and the value of paper money plummeted. Many American farmers and merchants began to prefer doing business with the British, who could pay for goods in gold or silver coin. (That was one reason why George Washington's troops suffered from severe food shortages at Valley Forge in the winter of 1777–1778; many Philadelphia merchants would not sell to them.) Congress tried and failed repeatedly to stem the inflationary spiral. In the end, the new American government was able to finance the war effort only by borrowing heavily from other nations.

Financing the War

After the first great surge of patriotism faded in 1775, few Americans volunteered for military service. As a result, the states had to resort to persuasion and force: to paying bounties to attract new recruits and to drafting them. Even when it was possible to recruit substantial numbers of militiamen, they remained under the control of their respective states. Congress quickly recognized the disadvantages of this decentralized system and tried, with some success, to correct it. In the spring of 1775, it created a Continental army with a single commander in chief. George Washington, the forty-three-year-old Virginia planter-aristocrat who had commanded colonial forces during the French and Indian War, possessed more experience than any other American-born officer available. He had also been an early advocate of independence. Above all, he was admired, respected, and trusted by nearly all Patriots. He was the unanimous choice of the delegates, and he took command in June 1775.

Congress had chosen well. Throughout the war, Washington kept faithfully at his task, despite difficulties and discouragements that would have daunted a lesser man. He had to deal with serious problems of morale among soldiers who consistently received short rations and low pay; open mutinies broke out in 1781 among the Pennsylvania and New Jersey troops. The Continental Congress, Washington's "employers," always seemed too little interested in supplying him with manpower and equipment and too much interested in interfering with his conduct of military operations.

General George Washington

REVOLUTIONARY SOLDIERS Jean Baptiste de Verger, a French officer serving in America during the Revolution, kept a journal of his experiences illustrated with watercolors. Here he portrays four American soldiers carrying different kinds of arms: a black infantryman with a light rifle, a musketman, a rifleman, and an artilleryman. *(Anne S.K. Brown Military Collection, Brown University Library)*

Washington was not without shortcomings as a military commander. But he was, in the end, a great war leader. With the aid of foreign military experts such as the Marquis de Lafayette from France and Baron von Steuben from Prussia, he succeeded in building and holding together an army of fewer than 10,000 men that, along with state militias, ultimately prevailed against the greatest

Foreign Assistance

military power in the world. Even more important, perhaps, in a new nation still unsure of either its purposes or its structure, with a central government both weak and divided, Washington provided the army—and the people—with a symbol of stability around which they could rally. He may not have been the most brilliant of the country's early leaders, but in the crucial years of the war, at least, he was the most successful in holding the new nation together

THE WAR FOR INDEPENDENCE

On the surface, at least, all the advantages in the military struggle between America and Great Britain appeared to lie with the British. They possessed the greatest navy and the best-equipped army in the world.

They had access to the resources of an empire. They had a coherent structure of command. The Americans, by contrast, were struggling to create a new army and a new government at the same time that they were trying to fight a war.

Yet the United States had advantages that were not at first apparent. Americans were fighting on their own ground, while the English were far from their own land (and their own resources). The American Patriots were, on the whole, deeply committed to the conflict; the British people only halfheartedly supported the war. As Thomas Paine said at the time, "They cannot defeat an idea with an army." Beginning in 1777, moreover, the Americans

American Advantages

had the benefit of substantial aid from abroad, when the American war became part of a larger world contest in which Great Britain faced the strongest powers of Europe—most notably France—in a struggle for imperial supremacy.

The American victory was not, however, simply the result of these advantages. It was not simply a result, either, of the remarkable spirit and resourcefulness of the people and the army. It was a result, too, of a series of egregious blunders and miscalculations by the British

BATTLE OF GERMANTOWN On October 4, 1777, Washington launched an attack on General Howe's camp at Germantown, near Philadelphia. Although the Patriots were successful in the first hours of the battle, a heavy fog confused them and allowed the British finally to force them to retreat. This 1782 painting re-creates a part of the battle: an attack by American forces led by "Mad Anthony" Wayne. *(National Center for the American Revolution/Valley Forge Historical Society)*

in the early stages of the fighting, when England could (and probably should) have won. And it was, finally, a result of the transformation of the war—which proceeded in three different phases—into a new kind of conflict that the British military, for all its strength, could not win.

The First Phase: New England

For the first year of the fighting, the British remained uncertain about whether or not they were actually engaged in a war. Many English authorities continued to believe that British forces were simply attempting to quell pockets of rebellion in the contentious area around Boston. Gradually, however, colonial forces took the offensive and made almost the entire territory of the American colonies a battleground.

After the British withdrawal from Concord and Lexington in April 1775, American forces besieged the army of General Thomas Gage in Boston. The Patriots suffered severe casualties in the Battle of Bunker Hill (actually fought on Breed's Hill) on June 17, 1775, and were ultimately driven from their position there. But they inflicted much greater losses on the enemy than the enemy inflicted on them. Indeed, the British suffered their heaviest casualties of the entire war at Bunker Hill. After the battle, the Patriots continued to tighten the siege.

By the first months of 1776, the British had concluded that Boston was not the best place from which to wage war. Not only was it in the center of the most fervently anti-British region of the colonies, it was also tactically indefensible—a narrow neck of land, easily isolated and besieged. By late winter, in fact, Patriot forces had surrounded the city and occupied strategic positions on the heights. On March 17, 1776 (a date still celebrated in Boston as Evacuation Day), the British departed Boston for Halifax in Nova Scotia with hundreds of Loyalist refugees. Less than a year after the firing of the first shots, the Massachusetts colonists had driven the British—temporarily—from American soil.

Elsewhere, the war proceeded fitfully and inconclusively. To the south, at Moore's Creek Bridge in North Carolina, a band of Patriots crushed an uprising of Loyalists on February 27, 1776, and in the process discouraged a British plan to invade the southern states. The British had expected substantial aid from local Tories in the South; they realized now that such aid might not be as effective as they had hoped. To the north, Americans launched an invasion of Canada—hoping to remove the

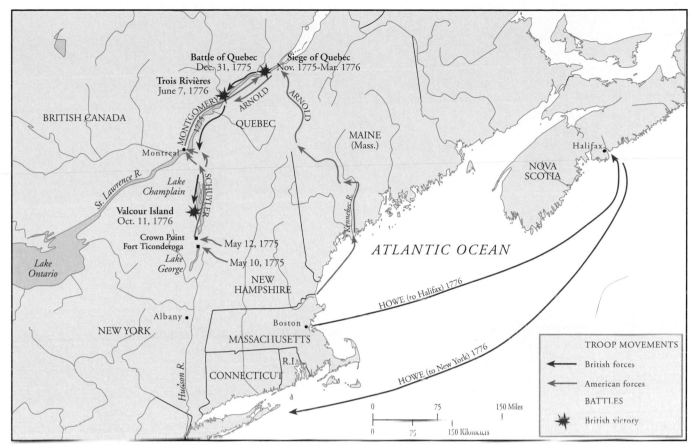

THE REVOLUTION IN THE NORTH, 1775–1776 After initial battles in and around Boston, the British forces left Massachusetts and (after a brief stay in Halifax, Canada) moved south to New York. ◆ *Why would the British have considered New York a better base than Boston?* In the meantime, American forces moved north in an effort to capture British strongholds in Montreal and Quebec, with little success.

For an interactive version of this map go to www.mhhe.com/brinkley12ch5maps

British threat and win the Canadians to their cause. Benedict Arnold, the commander of a small American force, threatened Quebec in late 1775 and early 1776 after a winter march of incredible hardship. Richard Montgomery, coming to his assistance, combined his forces with Arnold's and took command of both. Montgomery died in the assault on the city; and although a wounded Arnold kept up the siege for a time, the Quebec campaign ended in frustration. Congress sent a civilian commission to Canada, headed by the seventy-year-old Benjamin Franklin. But Franklin also failed to win the allegiance of the northern colonists. Canada was not to become part of the new nation.

Invasion of Canada

The British evacuation of Boston in 1776 was not, therefore, so much a victory for the Americans as a reflection of changing English assumptions about the war. By the spring of 1776, it had become clear to the British that England must be prepared to fight a much larger conflict. The departure of the British, therefore, signaled the beginning of a new phase in the war.

The Second Phase: The Mid-Atlantic Region

The next phase of the war, which lasted from 1776 until early 1778, was when the British were in the best position to win. Indeed, had it not been for a series of blunders and misfortunes, they probably would have crushed the rebellion then. During this period the struggle became, for the most part, a traditional, conventional war. And in that, the Americans were woefully overmatched.

The British regrouped quickly after their retreat from Boston. During the summer of 1776, in the weeks immediately following the Declaration of Independence, the waters around New York City grew crowded with the most formidable military force Great Britain had ever sent abroad. Hundreds of men-of-war and troopships and 32,000 disciplined soldiers arrived, under the command of the affable William Howe. Howe felt no particular hostility toward the Americans. He hoped to awe them into submission rather than fight them, and he believed that

THE BATTLE OF BUNKER HILL, 1775 British troops face Patriot forces outside Boston on June 17, 1775, in the first great battle of the American Revolution. The British ultimately drove the Americans from their positions on Breed's Hill and Bunker Hill, but only after suffering enormous casualties. General Gage, the British commander, reported to his superiors in London after the battle: "These people show a spirit and conduct against us they never showed against the French." This anonymous painting reveals the array of British troops and naval support and also shows the bombardment and burning of Charlestown from artillery in Boston. *(Gift of Edgar William and Bernice Chrysler Garbisch, © 1998 Board of Trustees, National Gallery of Art, Washington)*

most of them, if given a chance, would show their loyalty to the king. In a meeting with commissioners from Congress, he offered them a choice between submission with royal pardon and a battle against overwhelming odds.

To oppose Howe's impressive array, Washington could muster only about 19,000 poorly armed and trained soldiers, even after combining the Continental army with state militias; he had no navy at all. Even so, the Americans quickly rejected Howe's offer and chose to continue the war—a decision that led inevitably to a succession of rapid defeats. The British pushed the defenders off Long Island, compelled them to abandon Manhattan, and then drove them in slow retreat over the plains of New Jersey, across the Delaware River, and into Pennsylvania.

For eighteenth-century Europeans, warfare was a seasonal activity. Fighting generally stopped in cold weather. The British settled down for the winter at various points in New Jersey, leaving an outpost of Hessians (German mercenaries) at Trenton on the

British Take New York

Delaware River. But Washington did not sit still. On Christmas night 1776, he boldly recrossed the icy river, surprised and scattered the Hessians, and occupied the town. Then he advanced to Princeton and drove a British force from their base in the college there. But Washington was unable to hold either Princeton or Trenton, and he finally took refuge for the rest of the winter in the hills around Morristown, New Jersey.

For their campaigns of 1777 the British devised a strategy to cut the United States in two. Howe would move north from New York City up the Hudson to Albany, while another British force would come south from Canada to meet him. One of the younger British officers, the dashing John Burgoyne, secured command of this northern force and planned a two-pronged attack along both the Mohawk and the upper Hudson approaches to Albany.

Britain's Strategy

But after setting this plan in motion, Howe himself abandoned it. He decided instead to launch an assault on the rebel capital Philadelphia—an assault that would, he hoped, discourage the Patriots, rally the

THE REVOLUTION IN THE MIDDLE COLONIES, 1776–1778 These maps illustrate the major campaigns of the Revolution in the middle colonies—New York, New Jersey, and Pennsylvania—between 1776 and 1778. The large map on the left shows the two prongs of the British strategy: first, a movement of British forces south from Canada into the Hudson Valley; and second, a movement of other British forces, under General William Howe, out from New York. The strategy was designed to trap the American army in between the two British movements. ◆ *What movements of Howe helped thwart that plan?* The two smaller maps on the right show a more detailed picture of some of the major battles. The upper ones reveal the surprising American victory at Saratoga. The lower ones show a series of inconclusive battles between New York and Philadelphia in 1777 and 1778.

For an interactive version of this map go to www.mhhe.com/brinkley12ch5maps

Loyalists, and bring the war to a speedy conclusion. He removed the bulk of his forces from New York by sea, landed at the head of the Chesapeake Bay, brushed Washington aside at the Battle of Brandywine Creek on September 11, and proceeded north to Philadelphia, which he was able to occupy with little resistance. Meanwhile, Washington, after an unsuccessful October 4 attack at Germantown (just outside Philadelphia), went into winter quarters at Valley Forge. The Continental Congress, now dislodged from its capital, reassembled at York, Pennsylvania.

Howe's move to Philadelphia left Burgoyne to carry out the campaign in the north alone. Burgoyne sent Colonel Barry St. Leger up the St. Lawrence River toward Lake Ontario and the headwaters of the Mohawk, while Burgoyne himself advanced directly down the upper Hudson Valley. He got off to a flying start. He seized Fort Ticonderoga easily and with it an enormous store of powder and supplies; this caused such dismay in Congress that the delegates removed General Philip Schuyler from command of American forces in the north and replaced him with Horatio Gates.

By the time Gates took command, Burgoyne had already experienced two staggering defeats. In one of them—at Oriskany, New York, on August 6—a Patriot band of German farmers led by Nicholas Herkimer held off a force of Indians and Tories commanded by St. Leger. That gave Benedict Arnold time to go to the relief of Fort Stanwix and close off the Mohawk Valley to St. Leger's advance.

In the other battle—at Bennington, Vermont, on August 16—New England militiamen under the Bunker Hill veteran John Stark severely mauled a British detachment that Burgoyne had sent out to seek supplies. Short of materials, with all help cut off, Burgoyne fought several costly engagements and then withdrew to Saratoga, where Gates surrounded him. On October 17, 1777, Burgoyne ordered what was left of his army, nearly 5,000 men, to surrender to the Americans.

To the Patriots and peoples watching from around the world, the New York campaign was a remarkable victory. The British surrender at Saratoga became a major turning point in the war—above all, perhaps, because it led directly to an alliance between the United States and France.

> Patriot Victory at Saratoga

The British failure to win the war during this period, a period in which they had overwhelming advantages, was in large part a result of their own mistakes. And in assessing them, the role of William Howe looms large. He abandoned his own most important strategic initiative—the northern campaign—leaving Burgoyne to fight alone. And even in Pennsylvania, where he chose to engage the enemy, he refrained from moving in for a final attack on the weakened Continental army, even though he had several opportunities. Instead, he repeatedly allowed Washington to retreat and regroup; and he permitted the American army to spend a long winter unmolested in Valley Forge, where—weak and hungry—they might have been easy prey for British attack. Some believed that Howe did not want to win the war, that he was secretly in sympathy with the American cause. His family had close ties to the colonies, and he himself was linked politically to those forces within the British government that opposed the war. Others pointed to personal weaknesses: Howe's apparent alcoholism, his romantic attachment (he spent the winter of 1777–1778 in Philadelphia with his mistress when many were urging him to move elsewhere). But the most important problem, it seems clear, was his failure to understand the nature of the war that he was fighting—or even to understand that it was truly a war.

> British Blunders

The Iroquois and the British

The campaign in upstate New York was not just a British defeat. It was a setback for the ambitious efforts of several Iroquois leaders, who hoped to involve Indian forces in the English military effort, believing that a British victory would help stem white movement onto tribal lands. The Iroquois Confederacy had declared itself a neutral in the war in 1776, but not all its members were content to remain passive in the northern campaign. Among those who worked to expand the Native American role in the war were a Mohawk brother and sister, Joseph and Mary Brant. Both were people of stature within the Mohawk nation: Joseph was a celebrated warrior; Mary was a magnetic woman and the widow of Sir William Johnson, the British superintendent of Indians, who had achieved wide popularity among the tribes. The Brants persuaded their own tribe to contribute to the British cause and attracted the support of the Seneca and Cayuga as well. They played an important role in Burgoyne's unsuccessful campaigns in the north.

But the alliance was also a sign of the growing divisions within the Iroquois Confederacy. Only three of the six nations of the Confederacy supported the British. The Oneida and the Tuscarora backed the Americans; the Onondaga split into several factions. The three-century-old Confederacy, weakened by the aftermath of the French and Indian War, continued to unravel.

> Divisions in the Iroquois Confederacy

The alliance had other unhappy consequences for the Iroquois. A year after Oriskany, Indians joined British troops in a series of raids on outlying white settlements in upstate New York. Months later, Patriot forces under the command of General John Sullivan harshly retaliated, wreaking such destruction on tribal settlements that large groups of Iroquois fled north into Canada to seek refuge. Many never returned.

Securing Aid from Abroad

The failure of the British to crush the Continental army in the mid-Atlantic states, combined with the stunning American victory at Saratoga, was a turning point in the war. It transformed the conflict and ushered it into a new and final phase.

Central to this transformation of the war was American success in winning support from abroad—indirect support from several European nations, and direct support from France. Even before the Declaration of Independence, Congress dispatched representatives to the capitals of Europe to negotiate commercial treaties with the governments there; if America was to leave the British Empire, it would need to cultivate new trading partners. Such treaties would, of course, require European governments to recognize the United States as an independent nation. John Adams called the early American representatives abroad "militia diplomats." Unlike the diplomatic regulars of Europe, they had little experience with the formal art and etiquette of Old World diplomacy. Since transatlantic communication was slow and uncertain (it took from one to three months for a message to cross the Atlantic), they had to interpret the instructions of Congress very freely and make crucial decisions entirely on their own.

> Militia Diplomats

The most promising potential ally for the United States was France. King Louis XVI, who had come to the throne in 1774, and his astute foreign minister, the Count de Vergennes, were eager to see Britain lose a crucial part of its empire. Through a series of covert bargains, facilitated by the creation of a fictional trading firm and the use of secret agents on both sides (among them the famed French dramatist Caron de Beaumarchais), France began supplying the Americans large quantities of much-needed supplies. But the French government remained reluctant to provide the United States with what it most wanted: diplomatic recognition.

Finally, Benjamin Franklin himself went to France to represent the United States. A natural diplomat, Franklin became a popular hero among the French—aristocrats and common people alike. His popularity there greatly helped the American cause. Of even greater help was the news of the American victory at Saratoga, which arrived in London on December 2, 1777, and in Paris two days later. On February 6, 1778—in part to forestall a British peace offensive that Vergennes feared might persuade the Americans to abandon the war—France formally recognized the United States as a sovereign nation and laid the groundwork for greatly expanded assistance to the American war effort.

France's intervention made the war an international conflict. In the course of the next two years, France, Spain, and the Netherlands all | **Pivotal French Aid** | drifted into another general war with Great Britain in Europe, and all contributed both directly and indirectly to the ultimate American victory. But France was America's truly indispensable ally. Not only did it furnish the new nation with most of its money and munitions; it also provided a navy and an expeditionary force that proved invaluable in the decisive phase of the revolutionary conflict.

The Final Phase: The South

The last phase of the military struggle in America was very different from either of the first two. The British government had never been fully united behind the war in the first place; after the defeat at Saratoga and the intervention of the French, it imposed new limits on its commitment to the conflict. Instead of a full-scale military struggle against the American army, therefore, the British decided to try to enlist the support of those elements of the American population—a majority, they continued to believe—who were still loyal to the crown; in other words, they would work to undermine the Revolution from within. Since the British believed Loyalist sentiment was strongest in the southern colonies (despite their earlier failure to enlist Loyalist support in North Carolina), the main focus of their effort shifted there; and so it was in the South, for the most part, that the final stages of the war occurred.

The new strategy was a dismal failure. British forces spent three years (from 1778 to 1781) moving through the South, fighting small battles and large, and attempting to neutralize the territory through which they traveled. All such efforts ended in frustration. The British badly overestimated the extent of Loyalist sentiment. There were many Tories in Georgia and the Carolinas, some of them disgruntled members of the Regulator movement. But there were also many more Patriots than the British had believed. In Virginia, support for independence was as fervent as in Massachusetts. And even in the lower South, Loyalists often refused to aid the British because they feared reprisals from the Patriots around them. The British also harmed their own cause by encouraging southern slaves to desert their owners in return for promises of emancipation. Many slaves (perhaps 5 percent of the total) took advantage of this offer, despite the great difficulty of doing so. But white southerners were aghast; and even many who might otherwise have been inclined to support the crown now joined the Patriot side, which posed no such threat to slavery. The British also faced severe logistical problems in the South. Patriot forces could move at will throughout the region, living off the resources of the countryside, blending in with the civilian population and leaving the British unable to distinguish friend from foe. The British, by contrast, suffered all the disadvantages of an army in hostile territory.

It was this phase of the conflict that made the war truly "revolutionary"—not only because it introduced a new kind of combat, but also because it had the effect of mobilizing and politicizing large groups of the population who had previously remained aloof from the struggle. With the war expanding into previously isolated communities, with many civilians forced to involve themselves whether they liked it or not, the political climate of the United States grew more heated than ever. And support for independence, far from being crushed as the British had hoped, greatly increased.

That was the context in which the important military encounters of the last years of the war occurred. In the North, where significant numbers of British troops remained, the fighting settled into a relatively quiet stalemate. Sir Henry | **Revolutionary Consequences of the Southern Campaign** | Clinton replaced the hapless William Howe in 1778 and moved what had been Howe's army from Philadelphia back to New York. There the British troops stayed for more than a year, with Washington using his army to keep watch around them. The American forces in New York did so little fighting in this period that Washington sent some troops west to fight hostile Indians who had been attacking white settlers. In that same winter, George Rogers Clark, under orders from the state of Virginia—not from either Washington or Congress—led a daring expedition over the mountains and captured settlements in the Illinois country from the British and their Indian allies.

THE REVOLUTION IN THE SOUTH, 1778–1781 The final phase of the American Revolution occurred largely in the South, which the British thought would be a more receptive region for their troops. ♦ *Why did they believe that?* This map reveals the many, scattered military efforts of the British and the Americans in those years, none of them conclusive. It also shows the final chapter of the Revolution around the Chesapeake Bay and the James River. ♦ *What errors led the British to their surrender at Yorktown?*

OLC For an interactive version of this map go to www.mhhe.com/brinkley12ch5maps

During this period of relative calm, General Benedict Arnold shocked the American forces—and Washington in particular—by becoming a traitor. Arnold had been one of the early heroes of the war, but now, convinced that the American cause was hopeless, he conspired with British agents to betray the Patriot stronghold at West Point on the Hudson River. The scheme unraveled before Arnold could complete it, and he fled to the safety of the British camp, where he spent the rest of the war.

In the meantime, decisive fighting was in progress in the South. The British did have some significant military

successes during this period. On December 29, 1778, they captured Savannah, on the coast of Georgia; and on May 12, 1780, they took the port of Charleston, South Carolina. They also inspired some Loyalists to take up arms and advance with them into the interior. But although the British were able to win conventional battles, they were constantly harassed as they moved through the countryside by Patriot guerrillas led by such resourceful fighters as Thomas Sumter, Andrew Pickens, and Francis Marion, the "Swamp Fox."

Moving inland to Camden, South Carolina, Lord Cornwallis (Clinton's choice as British commander in the

THE BRITISH ON THE HUDSON, 1776 In one of the largest troop movements of the Revolution, English commanders sent 13,000 British and Hessian troops up the Hudson River to drive George Washington and his Patriot army from strongholds in the palisades above the river. The British took nearly 3,000 prisoners when the Patriots surrendered on November 16, 1776. Thomas Davies painted this watercolor of the British landing at the time *(Emmet Collection. Miriam & Ira D. Wallach Division of Art, Prints & Photographs, The New York Public Library, Astor, Lenox and Tilden Foundations)*

South) met and crushed a Patriot force under Horatio Gates on August 16, 1780. Congress recalled Gates, and Washington gave the southern command to Nathanael

Nathanael Greene

Greene, a Quaker and a former blacksmith from Rhode Island and probably the ablest of all the American generals of the time next to Washington himself.

Even before Greene joined the southern army, the tide of battle began to turn against Cornwallis. At King's Mountain (near the North Carolina–South Carolina border) on October 7, 1780, a band of Patriot riflemen from the backwoods killed, wounded, or captured an entire force of 1,100 New York and South Carolina Tories that Cornwallis was using as auxiliaries. Once Greene arrived, he confused and exasperated Cornwallis further by dividing the American forces into small, fast-moving contingents and refraining from a showdown in open battle. One of the contingents inflicted what Cornwallis admitted was "a very unexpected and severe blow" at Cowpens on January 17, 1781. Finally, after receiving reinforcements, Greene combined all his forces and maneuvered to meet the British on ground of his own choosing, at Guilford Court House, North Carolina. After a hard-fought battle there on March 15, 1781, Greene withdrew from the field; but Cornwallis had lost so many men that he decided at last to abandon the Carolina campaign.

Cornwallis withdrew to the port town of Wilmington, North Carolina, to receive supplies being sent to him by sea; later he moved north to launch raids in the interior of Virginia. But Clinton, concerned for the army's safety, ordered him to take up a position on the peninsula between the York and James Rivers and wait for ships to carry his troops to New York or Charleston. So Cornwallis retreated to Yorktown and began to build fortifications there.

George Washington—along with the Count Jean Baptiste de Rochambeau, commander of the French expeditionary force in America, and Admiral François Joseph Paul de Grasse, commander of the French fleet in American waters—set out

Yorktown

to trap Cornwallis at Yorktown. Washington and Rochambeau marched a French-American army from New York to join other French forces under Lafayette in Virginia, while de Grasse sailed with additional troops for Chesapeake Bay and the York River.

THE AGE OF REVOLUTIONS

The American Revolution was a result of specific tensions and conflicts between imperial Britain and its colonies along the Atlantic coast of North America. But it was also a part, and a cause, of what historians have come to call an "age of revolutions," which spread through much of the world in the last decades of the eighteenth century and the first decades of the nineteenth.

The modern idea of revolution—the overturning of old systems and regimes and the creation of new ones—was a product to a large degree of the ideas of the Enlightenment. Among those ideas was the notion of popular sovereignty, articulated by the English philosopher John Locke and others. It introduced the idea that political authority did not derive from the divine right of kings or the inherited authority of aristocracies but from the consent of the governed. A related Enlightenment idea was the concept of individual freedom, which challenged the traditional belief that governments had the right to prescribe the way people act, speak, and even think. Champions of individual freedom in the eighteenth century—among them the French philosopher Voltaire—advocated religious toleration (an end to discrimination against those who did not embrace a nation's dominant or official religion) and freedom of thought and expression. The Swiss-French Enlightenment theorist Jean Jacques Rousseau helped spread the idea of political and legal equality for all people—the end of special privileges for aristocrats and elites, the right of all

STORMING THE BASTILLE This painting portrays the storming of the great Parisian fortress and prison, the Bastille, on July 14, 1789. The Bastille was a despised symbol of royal tyranny to many of the French, because of the arbitrarily arrested and imprisoned people who were sent there. The July assault was designed to release the prisoners, but in fact the revolutionaries found only seven people in the vast fortress. Even so, the capture of the Bastille—which marked one of the first moments in which ordinary Frenchmen joined the Revolution—became one of the great moments in modern French history. The anniversary of the event, "Bastille Day," remains the French national holiday. *(Giraudon/Art Resource, NY)*

These joint operations, perfectly timed and executed, caught Cornwallis between land and sea. After a few shows of resistance, he capitulated on October 17, 1781 (four years to the day after the surrender of Burgoyne at Saratoga). Two days later, as a military band played the old tune "The World Turn'd Upside Down," Cornwallis, claiming to be ill, sent a deputy who formally surrendered the British army of more than 7,000 men.

Except for a few skirmishes, the fighting was now over; but the United States had not yet won the war. British forces continued to hold the seaports of Savannah, Charleston, Wilmington, and New York. Before long, a British fleet met and defeated Admiral de Grasse's fleet in the West Indies, ending Washington's hopes for further French naval assistance. For more than a year, although there was no significant further combat between British and American forces, it remained possible that the war might resume and the struggle for independence might still be lost.

Winning the Peace

Cornwallis's defeat provoked outcries in England against continuing the war. Lord North resigned as prime minister; Lord Shelburne emerged from the political wreckage to succeed him; and British emissaries appeared in France to talk informally with the American diplomats there, of whom the three principals were Benjamin Franklin, John Adams, and John Jay.

The Americans were under instructions to cooperate fully with France in their negotiations with England. But Vergennes insisted that France could not agree to any settlement of the war with England until its ally Spain had achieved its principal war aim: winning back citizens to participate in the formation of policies and laws. Together, these Enlightenment ideas formed the basis for challenges to existing social orders in many parts of the western world, and eventually beyond it.

The American Revolution was the first and in many ways most influential of the Enlightenment-derived uprisings against established orders. It served as an inspiration to people in other lands who were trying to find a way to oppose unpopular regimes. In 1789, a little over a decade after the beginning of the American Revolution, revolution began in France—at first through a revolt by the national legislature against the king and then through a series of increasingly radical challenges to established authority. The monarchy was abolished (and the king and queen publicly executed in 1793), the authority of the Catholic church was challenged and greatly weakened, and at the peak of revolutionary chaos during the Jacobin period (1793–1794), over 40,000 suspected enemies of the revolution were executed and hundreds of thousands of others imprisoned. The radical phase of the revolution came to an end in 1799, when Napoleon Bonaparte, a young general, seized power and began to build a new French empire. But France's *ancien regime* of king and aristocracy never wholly revived.

Together, the French and American revolutions helped inspire uprisings in many other parts of the Atlantic world. In 1791, a major slave uprising began in Haiti and soon attracted over 100,000 rebels. The slave army defeated both the white settlers of the island and the French colonial armies sent to quell their rebellion. Under the leadership of Toussaint L'Ouverture, they began to agitate for independence; and on January 1, 1804, a few months after Toussaint's death, Haiti established its independence and became the first black republic in the Americas.

The ideas of these revolutions spread next into Spanish and Portuguese colonies in the Americas, particularly among the so-called *creoles*, people of European ancestry born in America. In the late eighteenth century, they began to resist the continuing authority of colonial officials sent from Spain and Portugal and to demand a greater say in governing their own lands. When Napoleon invaded Spain and Portugal in 1807, the French armies weakened the ability of the European regimes to sustain authority over their American colonies. In the years that followed, revolutions swept through much of Latin America and established independent nations throughout the New World. Mexico became an independent nation in 1821 and provinces of Central America that had once been

part of Mexico (Guatemala, El Salvador, Honduras, Nicaragua, and Costa Rica) established their independence three years later. Simon Bolivar, modeling his efforts on those of George Washington, led a great revolutionary movement that won independence for Brazil in 1822 and also helped lead revolutionary campaigns in Venezuela, Ecuador, and Peru—all of which won their independence in the 1820s. At about the same time, Greek patriots—drawing from the examples of other revolutionary nations—launched a movement to win their independence from the Ottoman empire, which finally succeeded in 1830.

The age of revolutions left many new, independent nations in its wake. It did not, however, succeed in establishing the ideals of popular sovereignty, individual freedom, and political equality in all the nations it affected. Slavery survived in the United States and in many areas of Latin America. New forms of aristocracy and even monarchy emerged in France, Mexico, Brazil, and elsewhere. Women—many of whom had hoped the revolutionary age would win new rights for them—made few legal or political gains in this era. But the ideals that the revolutionary era introduced to the Western world continued to shape the histories of nations throughout the nineteenth century and beyond.

Gibraltar from the British. There was no real prospect of that happening soon, and the Americans began to fear that the alliance with France might keep them at war indefinitely. As a result, Franklin, Jay, and Adams began proceeding on their own, without informing Vergennes, and signed a preliminary treaty with Great Britain on November 30, 1782. Franklin, in the meantime, skillfully pacified Vergennes and avoided an immediate rift in the French-American alliance.

The British and Americans reached a final settlement— the Treaty of Paris—on September 3, 1783, when both Spain and France agreed to end hostilities. It was, on the whole, remarkably favorable to the United States in granting a clear-cut recognition of its independence and a generous, though ambiguous cession of territory—from the southern boundary of Canada to the northern boundary

Treaty of Paris

of Florida and from the Atlantic to the Mississippi. With good reason Americans celebrated in the fall of 1783 as the last of the British occupation forces embarked from New York and General Washington, at the head of his troops, rode triumphantly into the city.

WAR AND SOCIETY

Historians have long debated whether the American Revolution was a social as well as a political revolution. Some have argued that the colonists were struggling not only over the question of home rule, but over "who should rule at home." Others claim that domestic social and economic concerns had little to do with the conflict. (See "Where Historians Disagree," pp. 130–131.) Whatever the motivations of Americans, however, there can be little doubt that the War for Independence had important effects on the nature of American society.

Loyalists and Minorities

The losers in the American Revolution included not only the British but also American Loyalists. There is no way to be sure how many Americans remained loyal to England during the Revolution, but it is clear that there were many—at least a fifth (and some estimate as much as a third) of the white population. Their motivations were varied. Some were officeholders in the imperial government, who stood to lose their positions as a result of the Revolution. Others were merchants engaged in trade closely tied to the imperial system. (Most merchants, however, supported the Revolution.) Still others were people who lived in relative isolation and who thus had not been exposed to the wave of discontent that had turned so many Americans against Britain; they had simply retained their traditional loyalties. There were cultural and ethnic minorities who feared that an independent America would not offer them sufficient protection. There were settled, cautious people who feared social instability. And there were those who, expecting the British to win the war, were simply currying favor with the anticipated victors.

What happened to these men and women during the war is a turbulent and at times tragic story. Hounded by Patriots in their communities, harassed by legislative and judicial actions, the position of many Loyalists became intolerable. Up to 100,000 fled the country. Those who could afford to—for example, the hated Tory governor of Massachusetts, Thomas Hutchinson—moved to England, where many lived in difficult and lonely exile. Others of more modest means moved to Canada, establishing the first English-speaking community in the province of Quebec. Some returned to America after the war and, as the earlier passions and resentments faded, managed to reenter the life of the nation. Others remained abroad for the rest of their lives.

The Loyalists' Plight

Most Loyalists were people of average means, but a substantial minority consisted of men and women of wealth. They left behind large estates and vacated important positions of social and economic leadership. Even some who remained in the country saw their property confiscated and their positions forfeited. The result was new opportunities for Patriots to acquire land and influence, a situation that produced significant social changes in many communities.

It would be an exaggeration, however, to claim that the departure of the Loyalists was responsible for anything approaching a social revolution or that the Revolution created a general assault on the wealthy and powerful in America. When the war ended, those who had been wealthy at its beginning were, for the most part, still wealthy. Most of those who had wielded social and political influence continued to wield it. Indeed, the distribution of wealth and power changed more rapidly after the war than it had changed during it.

The war had a significant effect on other minorities as well, and on certain religious groups in particular. No sect suffered more than the Anglicans, many of whose members were Loyalists. In Virginia and Maryland, where the colonial governments had recognized Anglicanism as the official religion and had imposed

Disestablishment of the Anglican Church

a tax for its maintenance, the new Revolutionary regimes disestablished the church and eliminated the subsidy. By the time the fighting ended, many Anglican parishes no longer even had clergymen, for there were few ministers to take the place of those who had died or who had left the country as Loyalist refugees. Anglicanism survived in America, but the losses during the Revolution permanently weakened it. The Revolution weakened the Quakers in Pennsylvania and elsewhere. They incurred widespread unpopularity because of their pacifism, which destroyed much of the social and political prestige they had once enjoyed.

While the war was weakening the Anglicans and the Quakers, it was improving the position of the Roman Catholic Church. On the advice of Charles Carroll of Carrollton, a Maryland statesman and Catholic lay leader, most American Catholics supported the Patriot cause during the war. The French alliance brought Catholic troops and chaplains to the country, and the gratitude with which most Americans greeted them did much to erode old and bitter hostilities toward Catholics. The church did not greatly increase its numbers as a result of the Revolution, but it did gain considerable strength as an institution. Not long after the end of the war, the Vatican provided the United States with its own Catholic hierarchy. (Until then, Catholic bishops in Europe had controlled the American church.) Father John Carroll (also of Maryland) was named head of Catholic missions in America in 1784 and, in 1789, the first American bishop. In 1808 he became archbishop of Baltimore.

The War and Slavery

For the largest of America's minorities—the African-American population—the war had limited, but nevertheless profound, significance. For some, it meant freedom, because many slaves took advantage of the British presence in the South in the final years of the war to escape. The British enabled many of them to leave the country—not out of any principled commitment to emancipation, but as a way of disrupting the American war effort. In South Carolina, for example, nearly a third of all slaves defected during the war. Africans had constituted over 60 percent of the population in 1770; by 1790, that figure had declined to about 44 percent.

For other African Americans, the Revolution meant an increased exposure to the concept, although seldom to the reality, of liberty. Most black Americans could not

African American Desire for Freedom

read, but few could avoid the new and exciting ideas circulating through the towns and cities, and even at times on the plantations. The results included incidents in several communities in which African Americans engaged in open resistance to white control. In Charleston, South Carolina, for example, Thomas Jeremiah, a free black, was executed in 1775 after Patriot leaders accused him of conspiring to smuggle British guns to South Carolina slaves. It also produced some eloquent efforts by black writers (mostly in the North) to articulate the lessons of the revolution for their people. "Liberty is a jewel which was handed Down to man from the cabinet of heaven," the black New Englander Lemuel Hayes wrote in 1776. "Even an African has Equally good a right to his Liberty in common with Englishmen. . . . Shall a man's Couler Be the Decisive Criterion wherby to Judg of his natural right?"

That was one reason why in South Carolina and Georgia—where slaves constituted half or more of the population—there was great ambivalence about the revolution. Slaveowners opposed British efforts to emancipate their slaves, but they also feared that the revolution itself would foment slave rebellions. The same fears helped prevent English colonists in the Caribbean islands (who were far more greatly outnumbered by African slaves) from joining with the continental Americans in the revolt against Britain. In much of the North, the combination of revolutionary sentiment and evangelical Christian fervor helped spread antislavery sentiments widely through society. But in the South, white support for slavery survived. Southern churches rejected the antislavery ideas of the North and worked instead to develop a rationale for slavery—in part by reinforcing ideas about white superiority, in part by encouraging slaveowners to make slavery more humane.

As in so many other periods of American history, the Revolution exposed the continuing tension between the nation's commitment to liberty and its commitment to slavery. To people in our time, and even to some people in revolutionary times, it seems obvious that liberty and slavery are incompatible with one another. But to many white Americans in the eighteenth century, especially in the South, that did not seem obvious. Many white southerners believed, in fact, that enslaving Africans—whom they considered inferior and unfit for citizenship—was the best way to ensure liberty for white people. They feared the impact of free black people living alongside

Tension between Liberty and Slavery

whites. They also feared that without slaves, it would be necessary to recruit a servile white workforce in the South, and that the resulting inequalities would jeopardize the survival of liberty. One of the

ironies of the American Revolution, therefore, was that white Americans were fighting both to secure freedom for themselves and to preserve slavery for others.

Native Americans and the Revolution

Most Indians viewed the American Revolution with considerable uncertainty. The American Patriots tried to persuade them to remain neutral in the conflict, which they described as a "family quarrel" between the colonists and Britain that had nothing to do with the tribes. The British, too, generally sought to maintain Indian neutrality, fearing that native allies would prove unreliable and uncontrollable. Most tribes ultimately chose to stay out of the war.

To some Indians, however, the Revolution threatened to replace a ruling group in which they had developed at least some measure of trust (the British) with one they considered generally hostile to them (the Patriots). The British had consistently sought to limit the expansion of white settlement into Indian land (even if unsuccessfully); the Americans had spearheaded the encroachments. Thus some Native Americans, among them those Iroquois who participated in the Burgoyne campaign in upper New York, chose to join the English cause. Still others took advantage of the conflict to launch attacks of their own.

In the western Carolinas and Virginia, a Cherokee faction led by Dragging Canoe attacked outlying white settlements in the summer of 1776. Patriot militias responded with overwhelming force, ravaging Cherokee lands and forcing Dragging Canoe and many of his followers to flee west across the Tennessee River. Those Cherokee who remained behind agreed to a new treaty by which they gave up still more land. Not all Native American military efforts were so unsuccessful. Some Iroquois, despite the setbacks at Oriskany, continued to wage war against white Americans in the West and caused widespread destruction in large agricultural areas of New York and Pennsylvania—areas whose crops were of crucial importance to the Patriot cause. And although the retaliating United States armies inflicted heavy losses on the Indians, the attacks continued throughout the war.

In the end, however, the Revolution generally weakened the position of Native Americans in several ways. The Patriot victory increased the white demand for western lands; many American whites associated restrictions on settlement with British oppression and expected the new nation to remove the obstacles. At the same time, white attitudes toward the tribes, seldom friendly in the best of times, took a turn for the worse. Many

Taking Sides

whites deeply resented the assistance the Mohawk and other Indian nations had given the British and insisted on treating them as conquered people. Others adopted a paternalistic view of the tribes that was only slightly less dangerous to them. Thomas Jefferson, for example, came to view the Native Americans as "noble savages" uncivilized in their present state but redeemable if they were willing to adapt to the norms of white society.

Among the tribes themselves, the Revolution both revealed and increased the deep divisions that made it difficult for them to form a common front to resist the growing power of whites. In 1774, for example, the Shawnee Indians in western Virginia had attempted to lead an uprising against white settlers moving into the lands that would later become Kentucky. They attracted virtually no allies and (in a conflict known as Lord Dunmore's War) were defeated by the colonial militia and forced to cede more land to white settlers. And the Iroquois, whose power had been eroding since the end of the French and Indian War, were similarly unable to act in unison in the Revolution.

Growing Divisions among the Indians

Nor did the conclusion of the Revolutionary War end the fighting between white Americans and Indians. Bands of Native Americans continued to launch raids against white settlers on the frontier. White militias, often using such raids as pretexts, continued to attack Indian tribes who stood in the way of expansion. Perhaps the most vicious massacre of the era occurred in 1782, after the British surrender, when white militias slaughtered a peaceful band of Delaware Indians at Gnadenhuetten in Ohio. They claimed to be retaliating for the killing of a white family several days before, but few believed this band of Delaware (who were both Christian converts and pacifists) had played any role in the earlier attack. The white soldiers killed ninety-six people, including many women and children. Such massacres did not become the norm of Indian-white relations. But they did reveal how little the Revolution had done to settle the basic conflict between the two peoples.

Women's Rights and Women's Roles

The long Revolutionary War, which touched the lives of almost every region, naturally had a significant effect on American women. The departure of so many men to fight in the Patriot armies left wives, mothers, sisters, and daughters in charge of farms and businesses. Other women whose husbands or fathers went off to war did not have even a farm or shop to fall back on. Many cities and towns developed significant populations of impoverished women, who on occasion led popular protests against price increases. On a few occasions, hungry women rioted and looted for food. Elsewhere (in New Jersey and Staten Island), women launched attacks on occupying British troops, whom they were required to house and feed at considerable expense.

Not all women, however, stayed behind when the men went off to war. Sometimes by choice, but more often out of economic necessity or because they had been driven from their homes by the enemy (and by the smallpox and dysentery the British army carried with it), women flocked in increasing numbers to the camps of the Patriot armies to join their male relatives. George Washington looked askance at these female "camp followers," convinced that they were disruptive and distracting (even though his own wife, Martha, spent the winter of 1778–1779 with him at Valley Forge). Other officers were even more hostile, voicing complaints that reflected a high level of anxiety over this seeming violation of traditional gender roles (and also, perhaps, over the generally lower-class backgrounds of the camp women). One described them in decidedly hostile terms: "their hair falling, their brows beady with the heat, their belongings slung over one shoulder, chattering and yelling in sluttish shrills as they went." In fact, however, the women were of significant value to the new army. It had not yet developed an adequate system of supply and auxiliary services, and it profited greatly from the presence of women, who increased army morale and performed such necessary tasks as cooking, laundry, and nursing.

Women of the Army

But female activity did not always remain restricted to "women's" tasks. In the rough environment of the camps, traditional gender distinctions proved difficult to maintain. Considerable numbers of women became involved, at least intermittently, in combat—including the legendary Molly Pitcher (so named because she carried pitchers of water to soldiers on the battlefield). She watched her husband fall during one encounter and immediately took his place at a field gun. A few women even disguised themselves as men so as to be able to fight.

After the war, of course, the soldiers and the female camp followers returned home. The experience of combat had little visible impact on how society (or on how women themselves) defined female roles in peacetime. The Revolution did, however, call certain assumptions about women into question in other ways. The emphasis on liberty and the "rights of man" led some women to begin to question their position in society as well. "By the way," Abigail Adams wrote to her husband John Adams in 1776, "in the new code of laws which I suppose it will be necessary for you to make, I desire you would remember the ladies and be more generous and favorable to them than your ancestors."

Adams was calling for a very modest expansion of women's rights. She wanted new protections against abusive and tyrannical men. A few women, however, went further. Judith Sargent Murray, one of the leading essayists of the late eighteenth century, wrote in 1779 that women's minds were as good as men's and that

THE BRITISH INFANTRY The world's greatest military power raised its armies in almost haphazard fashion. Command of a British regiment was a favor to well-positioned gentlemen, who received a cash reward for every man they enlisted. With that incentive, they were hardly picky, and the foot soldiers of the British army were mostly men who could be persuaded (or tricked) into enlisting through a combination of liquor and cash. Even so, the rough-and-ready quality of the British infantry made them good soldiers on the whole. This drawing portrays a British encampment during the American Revolution. As with the colonial armies, the British troops attracted women, seen at left, some of whom served as "camp followers," doing chores to help the soldiers. The soldiers themselves wore highly ornamental uniforms that were in many ways very impractical. To keep himself properly groomed and attired could take a soldier up to three hours a day. (*Anne S. K. Brown Military Collection, Brown University Library*)

girls as well as boys therefore deserved access to education.

Some political leaders—among them Benjamin Franklin and Benjamin Rush—also voiced support for the education of women and for other

Calls for Women's Rights

feminist reforms. Yale students in the 1780s debated the question "Whether women ought to be admitted into the magistracy and government of empires and republics." And there was for a time wide discussion of the future role of women in a new republic that had broken with so many other traditions already. But few concrete reforms became either law or common social practice.

In colonial society, under the doctrines of English common law, an unmarried woman had some legal rights (to own property, to enter contracts, and others), but a married woman had virtually no rights at all. She could own no property and earn no independent wages; everything she owned and everything she earned belonged to her husband. She had no legal authority over her children; the father was, in the eyes of the law, the autocrat of the family. Because a married woman had no property rights, she could not engage in any legal transactions (buying or selling, suing or being sued, writing wills). She could not vote. Nor could she obtain

a divorce in most states; that, too, was a right reserved mostly for men, although in much of the South men could not obtain divorces either. These restrictions were what Abigail Adams (who herself enjoyed a very happy marriage) was describing when she appealed to her husband not to put "such unlimited power into the hands of the Husbands."

The Revolution did little to change any of these legal customs. In some states, it did become easier for women to obtain divorces. And in New Jersey, women obtained the right to vote (although that right was repealed in 1807). Otherwise, there were few advances and some setbacks—including widows' loss of the right to regain their dowries from their husbands' estates. That change left many widows without any means of support and was one of the reasons for the increased agitation for female education: such women needed a way to support themselves.

The Revolution, in other words, far from challenging the patriarchal structure of American society, actually confirmed and strengthened it. Few American women challenged the belief that they occupied a special sphere distinct from men. Most accepted that their place remained in the family. Abigail Adams, in the same letter in which she asked her husband to "remember the ladies," urged him to "regard us then as Beings placed by providence under your protection and in imitation of the Supreme Being make use of that power only for our happiness." Nevertheless, the revolutionary experience did contribute to a subtle but important alteration of women's expectations of their status within the family. In the past, they had often been little better than servants in their husbands' homes; men and women both had generally viewed the wife as a clear subordinate, performing functions in the family of much less importance than those of the husband. But the Revolution encouraged people of both genders to reevaluate the contribution of women to the family and the society.

One reason for this was the participation of women in the revolutionary struggle itself. And part was a result of the reevaluation of American life during and after the revolutionary struggle. As the republic searched for a cultural identity for itself, it began to place additional value on the role of women as mothers. The new nation was, many Americans liked to believe, producing a new kind of citizen, steeped in the principles of liberty. Mothers had a particularly important task, therefore, in instructing their children in the virtues the republican citizenry was expected now to possess. Wives were still far from equal partners in marriage, but their ideas, interests, and domestic roles received increased respect.

A Strengthened Patriarchal Structure

The War Economy

Inevitably, the Revolution produced important changes in the structure of the American economy. After more than a century of dependence on the British imperial system, American trade suddenly found itself on its own. No longer did it have the protection of the great British navy; on the contrary, English ships now attempted to drive American vessels from the seas. No longer did American merchants have access to the markets of the empire; those markets were now hostile ports—including, of course, the most important source of American trade: England itself.

Yet while the Revolution disrupted traditional economic patterns, in the long run it strengthened the American economy. Well before the war was over, American ships had learned to evade the British navy with light, fast, easily maneuverable vessels. Indeed, the Yankees began to prey on British commerce with hundreds of privateers. For many shipowners, privateering proved to be more profitable than ordinary peacetime trade. More important in the long run, the end of imperial restrictions on American shipping opened up enormous new areas of trade to the nation. Colonial merchants had been violating British regulations for years, but the rules of empire had nevertheless inhibited American exploration of many markets. Now, enterprising merchants in New England and elsewhere began to develop new commerce in the Caribbean and in South America. By the mid-1780s, American merchants were developing an important new pattern of trade with Asia; and by the end of that decade, Yankee ships were regularly sailing from the eastern seaboard around Cape Horn to the Pacific coast of North America, there exchanging manufactured goods for hides and furs, and then proceeding across the Pacific to barter for goods in China. There was also a substantial increase in trade among the American states.

When English imports to America were cut off—first by the prewar boycott, then by the war itself—there

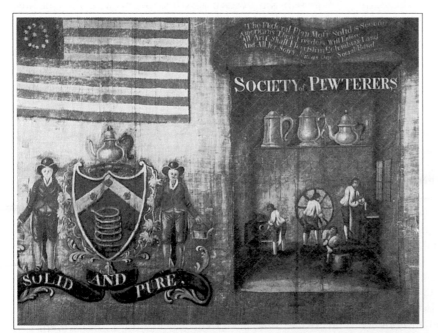

BANNER OF THE SOCIETY OF PEWTERERS Members of the American Society of Pewterers carried this patriotic banner when they marched in a New York City parade in July 1788. Its inscription celebrates the adoption of the new federal Constitution and predicts a future of prosperity and freedom in "Columbia's Land." The banner also suggests the growing importance of American manufacturing, which had received an important boost during the Revolution when British imports became unavailable. *(Collection of the New-York Historical Society)*

were desperate efforts throughout the states to stimulate domestic manufacturing of
New Patterns of Trade
certain necessities. No great
industrial expansion resulted, but there were several
signs of the economic growth that was to come in the
next century. Americans began to make their own
cloth—"homespun," which became both patriotic and
fashionable—to replace the now unobtainable British
fabrics. It would be some time before a large domestic
textile industry would emerge, but the nation was never
again to rely exclusively on foreign sources for its cloth.
There was, of course, pressure to build factories for the
manufacture of guns and ammunition. And there was a
growing general awareness that America need not
forever be dependent on other nations for manufactured goods.

The war stopped well short of revolutionizing the
American economy; not until the nineteenth century
would that begin to occur. But it did serve to release a
wide range of entrepreneurial energies that, despite the
temporary dislocations, encouraged growth and diversification.

THE CREATION OF STATE GOVERNMENTS

At the same time that Americans were struggling to win their independence on the battlefield, they
were also struggling to create new institutions of government to replace the British system they had repudiated. That struggle continued for more than fifteen years,
but its most important phase occurred during the war
itself, at the state level.

The Assumptions of Republicanism

If Americans agreed on nothing else when they began
to build new governments for themselves, they agreed
that those governments would
Importance of Civic Virtue
be republican. To them, that
meant a political system in
which all power came from the people, rather than from
some supreme authority (such as a king). The success of
such a government depended on the nature of its citizenry. If the population consisted of sturdy, independent
property owners imbued with civic virtue, then the
republic could survive. If it consisted of a few powerful
aristocrats and a great mass of dependent workers, then
it would be in danger. From the beginning, therefore, the
ideal of the small freeholder (the independent
landowner) was basic to American political ideology.

Another crucial part of that ideology was the concept
of equality. The Declaration of Independence had given
voice to that idea in its most ringing phrase: "All men are
created equal." It was a belief that stood in direct
contrast to the old European assumption of an inherited

aristocracy. The innate talents and energies of individuals, not their positions at birth, would determine their
roles in society. Some people would inevitably be wealthier and more powerful than others. But all people would
have to earn their success. There would be no equality
of condition, but there would be equality of opportunity.

In reality, of course, the United States was never a
nation in which all citizens were independent property
holders. From the beginning, there was a sizable dependent labor force—the white members of which were
allowed many of the privileges
Persistent Inequality
of citizenship, the black mem-
bers of which were allowed virtually none. American
women remained both politically and economically subordinate. Native Americans were systematically exploited
and displaced. Nor was there ever full equality of opportunity. American society was more open and more fluid
than that of most European nations, but the condition of
a person's birth was almost always a crucial determinant
of success.

Nevertheless, in embracing the assumptions of republicanism, Americans were adopting a powerful, even revolutionary, ideology, and their experiment in statecraft
became a model for many other countries. It made the
United States for a time the most admired and studied
nation on earth.

The First State Constitutions

Two states—Connecticut and Rhode Island—already had
governments that were republican in all but name even
before the Revolution. They simply deleted references to
England and the king from their charters and adopted
them as constitutions. The other eleven states, however,
produced new documents.

The first and perhaps most basic decision was that
the constitutions were to be written down, because
Americans believed the vagueness of England's unwrit-
ten constitution had produced corruption. The second
decision was that the power of
the executive, which Americans
Written Constitutions and Strong Legislatures
believed had grown too great in
England, must be limited. Pennsylvania eliminated the
executive altogether. Most other states inserted provisions limiting the power of governors over appointments, reducing or eliminating their right to veto bills,
and preventing them from dismissing the legislature.
Most important, every state forbade the governor or any
other executive officer from holding a seat in the legislature, thus ensuring that, unlike in England, the two
branches of government would remain wholly separate.

But the new constitutions did not embrace direct
popular rule. In Georgia and Pennsylvania, the legislature
consisted of one popularly elected house. But in every
other state, there was an upper and a lower chamber,
and in most cases, the upper chamber was designed to

represent the "higher orders" of society. There were property requirements for voters—some modest, some substantial—in all states.

Revising State Governments

By the late 1770s, Americans were growing concerned about the apparent divisiveness and instability of their new state governments, which were having trouble accomplishing anything at all. Many believed the problem was one of too much democracy. As a result, most of the states began to revise their constitutions to limit popular power. Massachusetts, which waited until 1780 to ratify its first constitution, was the first to act on the new concerns.

Two changes in particular differentiated the Massachusetts and later constitutions from the earlier ones. The first was a change in the process of constitution writing itself. Most of the first documents had been written by state legislatures and thus could easily be amended (or violated) by them. Massachusetts, and later other states, sought a way to protect the constitutions from ordinary politics and created the constitutional convention: a special assembly of the people that would meet only for the purpose of writing the constitution and that would never (except under extraordinary circumstances) meet again.

The second change was a significant strengthening of the executive, a reaction to what many believed was the instability of the original state governments that had weak governors. The 1780 Massachusetts constitution made the governor one of the strongest in any state. He

Shift to Strong Executives

was to be elected directly by the people; he was to have a fixed salary (in other words, he would not be dependent on the good will of the legislature each year for his wages); he would have significant appointment powers and a veto over legislation. Other states followed. Those with weak or nonexistent upper houses strengthened or created them. Most increased the powers of the governor. Pennsylvania, which had no executive at all at first, now produced a strong one. By the late 1780s, almost every state had either revised its constitution or drawn up an entirely new one in an effort to produce stability in government.

Toleration and Slavery

The new states moved far in the direction of complete religious freedom. Most Americans continued to believe that religion should play some role in government, but they did not wish to give special privileges to any par-

Statute of Religious Liberty

ticular denomination. The privileges that churches had once enjoyed were now largely stripped away. In 1786, Virginia enacted the Statute of Religious Liberty, written by Thomas Jefferson, which called for the complete separation of church and state.

More difficult to resolve was the question of slavery. In areas where slavery was already weak—in New England, where there had never been many slaves, and in Pennsylvania, where the Quakers opposed slavery—it was abolished. Even in the South, there were some pressures to amend or even eliminate the institution; every state but South Carolina and Georgia prohibited further importation of slaves from abroad, and South Carolina banned the slave trade during the war. Virginia passed a law encouraging manumission (the freeing of slaves).

Nevertheless, slavery survived in all the southern and border states. There were several reasons: racist assumptions among whites about the inferiority of blacks; the enormous economic investments many white southerners had in their slaves; and the inability of even such men as Washington and Jefferson, who had moral misgivings about slavery, to envision any alternative to it. If slavery were abolished, what would

A FREE BLACK MAN John Singleton Copley, the great American portraitist of the Revolutionary age, painted this picture of a young African American in 1777-78. He was probably a worker on New England fishing boats who appeared in another Copley painting ("Watson and the Shark"). It is one of a relatively small number of portrayals of the free blacks in the North in this era, and one of even a smaller number that portrays them realistically and seriously. (Head of a Negro, 1777-1778. *By John Singleton Copley. Oil on canvas, 53.3 × 41.3 cm. Founders Society Purchase, Gibbs-Williams Fund. Photograph © 1986 The Detroit Institute of Arts*)

happen to the black people in America? Few whites believed blacks could be integrated into American society as equals. In maintaining slavery, Jefferson once remarked, Americans were holding a "wolf by the ears." However unappealing it was to hold on to it, letting go would be even worse.

THE SEARCH FOR A NATIONAL GOVERNMENT

Americans were much quicker to agree on state institutions than they were on the structure of their national government. At first, most believed that the central government should remain a relatively weak and unimportant force and that each state would be virtually a sovereign nation. It was in response to such ideas that the Articles of Confederation emerged.

The Confederation

The Articles of Confederation, which the Continental Congress had adopted in 1777, provided for a national government much like the one already in place. Congress remained the central—indeed the only—institution of national authority. Its powers expanded to give it authority to conduct wars and foreign relations and to appropriate, borrow, and issue money. But it did not have power to regulate trade, draft troops, or levy taxes directly on the people. For troops and taxes it had to make formal requests to the state legislatures, which could—and often did—refuse them. There was no separate executive; the "president of the United States" was merely the presiding officer at the sessions of Congress. Each state had a single vote in Congress, and at least nine of the states had to approve any important measure. All thirteen state legislatures had to approve any amendment of the Articles.

Limited Power of the National Government

During the process of ratifying the Articles of Confederation (which required approval by all thirteen states), broad disagreements over the plan became evident. The small states had insisted on equal state representation, but the larger states wanted representation to be based on population. The smaller states prevailed on that issue. More important, the states claiming western lands wished to keep them, but the rest of the states demanded that all such territory be turned over to the national government. New York and Virginia had to give up their western claims before the Articles were finally approved. They went into effect in 1781.

The Confederation, which existed from 1781 until 1789, was not a complete failure, but it was far from a success. It lacked adequate powers to deal with interstate issues or to enforce its will on the states, and it had little stature in the eyes of the world.

Diplomatic Failures

Evidence of the low esteem in which the rest of the world held the Confederation was its difficulty in persuading Great Britain (and to a lesser extent Spain) to live up to the terms of the peace treaty of 1783.

Postwar Disputes with Britain and Spain

The British had promised to evacuate American territory, but British forces continued to occupy a string of frontier posts along the Great Lakes within the United States. Nor did the British honor their agreement to make restitution to slaveowners whose slaves the British army had confiscated. There were also disputes over the northeastern boundary of the new nation and over the border between the United States and Florida, which Britain had ceded back to Spain in the treaty. Most American trade remained within the British Empire, and Americans wanted full access to British markets; England, however, placed sharp restrictions on that access.

In 1784, Congress sent John Adams as minister to London to resolve these differences, but Adams made no headway with the English, who were never sure whether he represented a single nation or thirteen different ones. Throughout the 1780s, the British government refused even to send a diplomatic minister to the American capital.

Confederation diplomats agreed to a treaty with Spain in 1786. The Spanish accepted the American interpretation of the Florida boundary. In return the Americans recognized the Spanish possessions in North America and accepted limits on the right of United States vessels to navigate the Mississippi for twenty years. Southern states, incensed at the idea of giving up their access to the Mississippi, blocked ratification, further weakening the government's standing in world diplomacy.

Regional Differences over Diplomatic Policy

The Confederation and the Northwest

The Confederation's most important accomplishment was its resolution of some of the controversies involving the western lands. When the Revolution began, only a few thousand whites lived west of the Appalachian divide; by 1790 their numbers had increased to 120,000. The Confederation had to find a way to include these new settlements in the political structure of the new nation. The landed states began to yield their claims to the national government in 1781, and by 1784 the Confederation controlled enough land to permit Congress to begin making policy for the national domain.

The Ordinance of 1784, based on a proposal by Thomas Jefferson, divided the western territory into ten self-governing districts, each of which could petition Congress for statehood when its population

The Ordinances of 1784 and 1785

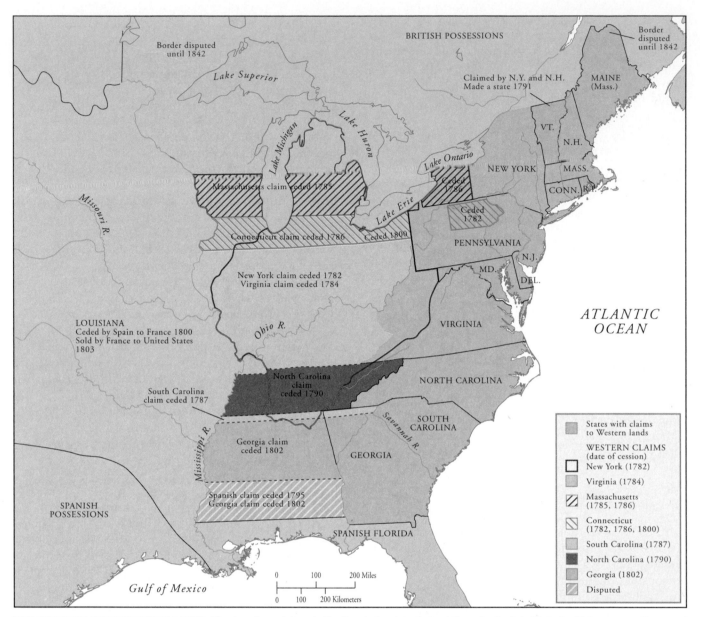

THE CONFLICT OVER WESTERN LANDS The American victory in the Revolution transformed the colonies into "states" within a new nation whose central government claimed at least some sovereignty over the individual units. An early conflict between national and state power took place over the state claims to western lands—claims established during the colonial period. This map shows the extensive western lands claimed by most of the original thirteen colonies to land in the West, and it illustrates the shifting nature of those claims over time—as colonies and then states transferred land to one another. The new national government gradually persuaded the states to give it control of the western lands, and in 1784 and 1785 it issued ordinances governing the process of settling those lands. ◆ *Why did the national government consider it important for the states to give up their claim to these territories?*

equaled the number of free inhabitants of the smallest existing state. The provision that these reorganized territories would eventually become states reflected the desire of the revolutionary generation to avoid creating second-class citizens in subordinate territories. Their model for the unhappiness they assumed such citizens would feel was their own experience as colonists under the British. Then, in the Ordinance of 1785, Congress created a system for surveying and selling the western lands. The territory north of the Ohio River was to be surveyed and marked off into

neat rectangular townships, each divided into thirty-six identical sections. In every township four sections were to be set aside for the United States; the revenue from the sale of one of the other sections was to support creation of a public school. Sections were to be sold at auction for no less than one dollar an acre.

Among the many important results of the Ordinance of 1785 was the establishment of an enduring pattern of dividing up land for human use. Many such systems have emerged

The Grid

THE GRID, ILLINOIS   Starting at the point where the Ohio River crosses the Pennsylvania-Ohio border, government surveyors applied the Land Ordinance of 1785 to most parts of the United States. The uniform checkerboard pattern of the national grid is visible to any traveler who flies or drives across this terrain. *(Comstock)*

throughout history. Some have relied on natural boundaries (rivers, mountains, and other topographical features). Some have reflected informal claims of landlords over vast but vaguely defined territories. Some have rested on random allocations of acres, to be determined by individual landholders. But many Enlightenment thinkers began in the eighteenth century to imagine more precise, even mathematical, forms of land distribution, which required both careful surveying and a clear method for defining boundaries. The result was the method applied in 1785 in the Northwest Territory, which came to be known as the grid— the division of land into carefully measured and evenly divided squares or rectangles. This pattern of land distribution eventually became the norm for much of the land west of the Appalachians. It also became a model for the organization of towns and cities, which distributed land in geometrical patterns within rectangular grids defined by streets. Although older land-distribution systems survive within the United States, the grid has become the most common form by which Americans impose human ownership and use on the landscape.

The original ordinances proved highly favorable to land speculators and less so to ordinary settlers, many of whom could not afford the price of the land. Congress compounded the problem by

Northwest Ordinance

selling much of the best land to the Ohio and Scioto Companies before making it available to anyone else. Criticism of these policies led to the passage in 1787 of another law governing western settlement—legislation that became known as the "Northwest Ordinance." The 1787 Ordinance abandoned the ten districts established in 1784 and created a single Northwest Territory out of the lands north of the Ohio; the territory could be divided subsequently into

between three and five territories. It also specified a population of 60,000 as a minimum for statehood, guaranteed freedom of religion and the right to trial by jury to residents of the Northwest, and prohibited slavery throughout the territory.

The western lands south of the Ohio River received less attention from Congress, and development was more chaotic there. The region that became Kentucky and Tennessee developed rapidly in the late 1770s, and in the 1780s speculators and settlers began setting up governments and asking for recognition as states. The Confederation Congress was never able to resolve the conflicting claims in that region successfully.

Indians and the Western Lands

On paper at least, the western land policies of the Confederation created a system that brought order and stability to the process of white settlement in the Northwest. But in reality, order and stability came slowly and at great cost, because much of the land the Confederation was neatly subdividing and offering for sale consisted of territory claimed by the Indians of the region. Congress tried to resolve that problem in 1784, 1785, and 1786 by persuading Iroquois, Choctaw, Chickasaw, and Cherokee leaders to sign treaties ceding substantial western lands in the North and South to the United States. But those agreements proved ineffective. In 1786, the leadership of the Iroquois Confederacy repudiated the treaty it had signed two years earlier and threatened to attack white settlements in the disputed lands. Other tribes had never really accepted the treaties affecting them and continued to resist white movement into their lands.

Violence between whites and Indians on the Northwest frontier reached a crescendo in the early 1790s. In

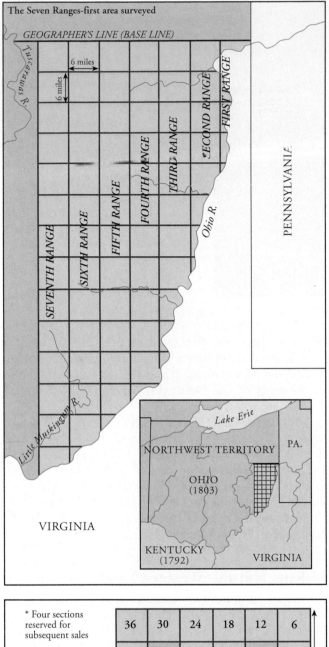

The Seven Ranges-first area surveyed

GEOGRAPHER'S LINE (BASE LINE)

6 miles

6 miles

FIRST RANGE
SECOND RANGE
THIRD RANGE
FOURTH RANGE
FIFTH RANGE
SIXTH RANGE
SEVENTH RANGE

Tuscarawas R.

Ohio R.

Little Muskingum R.

PENNSYLVANIA

VIRGINIA

Lake Erie

NORTHWEST TERRITORY

PA.

OHIO
(1803)

KENTUCKY
(1792)

VIRGINIA

* Four sections
reserved for
subsequent sales

Section 16
reserved for
school funds

36	30	24	18	12	6
35	29*	23	17	11*	5
34	28	22	16	10	4
33	27	21	15	9	3
32	26*	20	14	8*	2
31	25	19	13	7	1

A

B
C
D E

6 miles

1 mile

One Section = 640 acres (1 mile square)
A Half section = 320 acres
B Quarter section =160 acres
C Half-quarter section = 80 acres
D & E Quarter-quarter section = 40 acres

One township (six miles square)

1790 and again in 1791, a group of tribes led by the famed Miami warrior Little Turtle defeated United States forces in two major battles near what is now the western border **Battle of Fallen Timbers** of Ohio; in the second of those battles, on November 4, 1791, 630 white Americans died in fighting at the Wabash River (the greatest military victory Indians had ever or would ever achieve in their battles with whites). Efforts to negotiate a settlement failed because of the Miami's insistence that no treaty was possible unless it forbade white settlement west of the Ohio River. Negotiations did not resume until after General Anthony Wayne led 4,000 soldiers into the Ohio Valley in 1794 and defeated the Indians in the Battle of Fallen Timbers.

A year later, the Miami signed the Treaty of Greenville, ceding substantial new lands to the United States (which was now operating under the Constitution of 1789) in exchange for a formal acknowledgment of their claim to the territory they had managed to retain. In doing so, the United States was affirming that Indian lands could be ceded only by the tribes themselves. That hard-won assurance, however, proved a frail protection against the pressure of white expansion westward in later years.

Debts, Taxes, and Daniel Shays

The postwar depression, which lasted from 1784 to 1787, increased the perennial American problem of an inadequate money supply, a problem that weighed particu- **Postwar Depression** larly heavily on debtors. In dealing with this problem, Congress most clearly demonstrated its weakness.

The Confederation itself had an enormous outstanding debt that it had accumulated at home and abroad during the Revolutionary War, and few means with which to pay it, having no power to tax. It could only make requisitions of the states, and it received only about one-sixth of the money it requisitioned. The fragile new nation was faced with the grim prospect of defaulting on its obligations.

This alarming possibility brought to the fore a group of leaders who would play a crucial role in the shaping of the republic for several decades. Committed nationalists, they sought ways to increase the powers of the central government and to meet its financial obligations. Robert Morris, the head of the Confederation's treasury;

LAND SURVEY: ORDINANCE OF 1785 In the Ordinance of 1785, the Congress established a new system for surveying and selling western lands. These maps illustrate the way in which the lands were divided in an area of Ohio. Note the highly geometrical grid pattern that the Ordinance imposed on these lands. Each of the squares in the upper map was subdivided into 36 sections, as illustrated in the lower map. ◆ *Why was this grid pattern so appealing to the planners of the western lands?*

DANIEL SHAYS AND JOB SHATTUCK Shays and Shattuck were the principal leaders of the 1786 uprising by poor farmers in Massachusetts demanding relief from their indebtedness. Shattuck led an insurrection in the east, which collapsed when he was captured on November 30. Shays organized the rebellion in the west, which continued until finally dispersed by state militia in late February 1787. The following year, state authorities pardoned Shays; even before that, the legislature responded to the rebellion by providing some relief to the impoverished farmers. These drawings are part of a hostile account of the rebellion published in 1787 in a Boston almanac. *(National Portrait Gallery, Smithsonian Institution/Art Resource, NY)*

LITTLE TURTLE Little Turtle led the Miami confederacy in its wars with the United States in what is now Ohio and Indiana in the early 1790s. For a time he seemed almost invincible, but in 1794 Little Turtle was defeated in the Battle of Fallen Timbers. In this sketch (a rough copy of a painting attributed to Gilbert Stuart), Little Turtle wears a medal bearing the likeness of George Washington, awarded him by the United States after the signing of the Treaty of Greenville. *(Bettmann/Corbis)*

Alexander Hamilton, his young protégé; James Madison of Virginia; and others called for a "continental impost"—a 5 percent duty on imported goods to be levied by Congress and used to fund the debt. Many Americans, however, feared that the impost plan would concentrate too much financial power in the hands of Morris and his allies in Philadelphia. Congress failed to approve the impost in 1781 and again in 1783. Angry and discouraged, the nationalists largely withdrew from any active involvement in the Confederation.

Political Disputes over Economic Issues

The states had war debts, too, and they generally relied on increased taxation to pay them. But poor farmers, already burdened by debt and now burdened again by new taxes, considered such policies unfair, even tyrannical. They demanded that the state governments issue paper currency to increase the money supply and make it easier for them to meet their obligations. Resentment was especially high among farmers in New England, who felt that the states were squeezing them to enrich already wealthy bondholders in Boston and other towns.

Throughout the late 1780s, therefore, mobs of distressed farmers rioted periodically in various parts of New England. Dissidents in the Connecticut Valley and the Berkshire Hills of Massachusetts, many of them Revolutionary veterans, rallied behind Daniel Shays, a former captain in the Continental army. Shays issued a set of demands that included paper money, tax relief, a moratorium on debts, the relocation of the state capital from Boston to the interior, and the abolition of imprisonment for debt. During the summer of 1786, the Shaysites concentrated on preventing the collection of debts, private or public, and used force to keep courts from sitting and sheriffs from selling confiscated property. In Boston, members of the legislature, including Samuel Adams, denounced Shays and his men as rebels and traitors. When winter came, the rebels advanced on Springfield, hoping to seize weapons from the arsenal there. An army of state militiamen, financed by a loan from wealthy merchants, set out from Boston to confront them. In January 1787, this army met Shays's band and dispersed his ragged troops.

Shays's Rebellion

As a military enterprise, Shays's Rebellion was a failure, although it produced some concessions to the aggrieved farmers. Shays and his lieutenants, at first sentenced to death, were later pardoned, and Massachusetts offered the protesters some tax relief and a postponement of debt payments. The rebellion had more important consequences for the future of the United States, for it added urgency to a movement already gathering support throughout the new nation—the movement to produce a new, national constitution.

CONCLUSION

Between a small, inconclusive battle on a village green in New England in 1775 and a momentous surrender at Yorktown in 1781, the American people fought a great and terrible war against the mightiest military nation in the world. No one outside America, and few within it, would have predicted in 1775 that the makeshift armies of the colonies could withstand the armies and navies of the British empire. But a combination of luck, brilliance, determination, and timely aid from abroad allowed the Patriots, as they began to call themselves, to make full use of the advantages of fighting on their home soil and to frustrate British designs time and again.

The war was not just a historic military event. It was also a great political one, for it propelled the colonies to unite, to organize, and—in July 1776—to declare their independence. Having done so, they fought with even greater determination, defending now not just a set of principles, but an actual, fledgling nation. By the end of the war, they had created new governments at both the state and national level and had begun experimenting with new political forms that would distinguish the United States from any previous nation in history.

The war was also important for its effects on American society—for the way it shook (although never overturned) the existing social order; for the way it caused women to question (although seldom openly to challenge) their place in society; and for the way it spread notions of liberty and freedom throughout a society that in the past had often been rigidly hierarchical and highly deferential. Even African-American slaves absorbed some of the ideas of the Revolution, although it would be many years before they would be in any position to make very much use of them.

Victory in the American Revolution solved many of the problems of the new nation, but it also produced others. What should the United States do about its relations with the Indians and with its neighbors to the north and south? What should it do about the distribution of western lands? What should it do about slavery? How should it balance its commitment to liberty with its need for order? These questions bedeviled the new national government in its first years of existence and ultimately led Americans to create a new political order.

INTERACTIVE LEARNING

The *Primary Source Investigator CD-ROM* offers the following materials related to this chapter:

- A short documentary movie, **Daughters of Liberty,** examining the important role women played in the fight for American independence (D3).

- Interactive map: **The American Revolution** (M6).

- Documents, images, and maps related to the American Revolution and its immediate aftermath, including a selection from Thomas Paine's important work, *Common Sense;* several Drafts of the Declaration of

Independence, showing its gradual evolution; a March 31, 1776, letter from Abigail Adams to John Adams; and an engraving portraying "Molly Pitcher" at the Battle of Monmouth.

Online Learning Center (www.mhhe.com/brinkley12)

For quizzes, Internet resources, references to additional books and films, and more, consult this book's Online Learning Center.

FOR FURTHER REFERENCE

Robert Middlekauf, *The Glorious Cause: The American Revolution, 1763–1789* (1985), a volume in the Oxford History of the United States, is a thorough, general history of the Revolution. Edward Countryman, *The American Revolution* (1985) is a useful, briefer overview. Gordon Wood, *The Radicalism of the American Revolution* (1992) emphasizes the profound political change that the Revolution produced. Charles Royster, *A Revolution-* *ary People at War: The Continental Army and American Character* (1979) suggests the importance of military service for American men. David Hackett Fisher, *Washington's Crossing* (2004) uses this famous event to illuminate the meaning of the Revolution. Robert Gross, *The Minutemen and Their World* (1976) is an excellent social history of Revolutionary Concord. Mary Beth Norton, *Liberty's Daughters: The Revolutionary Experience of American Women, 1750–1800* (1980) demonstrates that the Revolution had a significant impact on the lives of American women as well. Eric Foner, *Tom Paine and Revolutionary America* (1976) connects the leading pamphleteer of the Revolution with urban radicalism in Philadelphia. Pauline Maier, *American Scripture* (1997) is a penetrating study of the making of the Declaration of Independence, and of its impact on subsequent generations of Americans. Colin Calloway, *The American Revolution in Indian Country*

(1995) is a new and important study on an often neglected aspect of the war. Sylvia R. Frey, *Water from the Rock: Black Resistance in a Revolutionary Age* (1991), argues that the American Revolution was a major turning point in the history of slavery in the American South. *Liberty* (1997), is a compelling six-hour PBS documentary film history of the American Revolution, from its early origins in the 1760s.

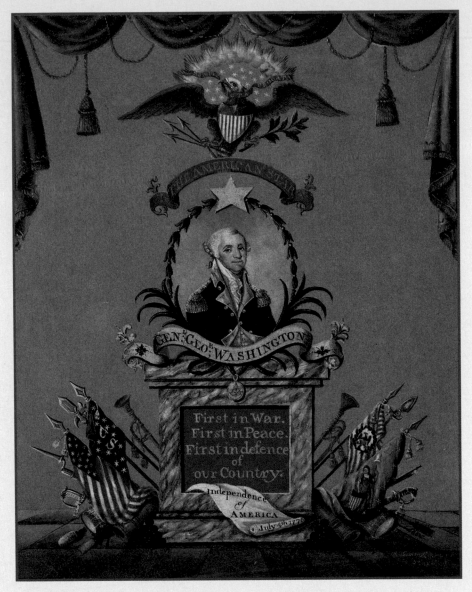

THE AMERICAN STAR Frederick Kemmelmeyer painted this tribute to George Washington sometime in the 1790s. It was one of many efforts by artists and others to create an iconography for the new republic. *(Metropolitan Museum of Art)*

SIGNIFICANT EVENTS

1783 ▶ Confederation Congress leaves Philadelphia

1785 ▶ Confederation Congress settles in New York

1786 ▶ Annapolis Conference meets

1787 ▶ Constitutional Convention in Philadelphia meets

▶ Constitution adopted (September 17)

1787–1788 ▶ States ratify Constitution

1789 ▶ First elections held under Constitution

▶ New government assembles in New York

▶ Washington becomes first president

▶ Bill of Rights adopted by Congress

CHAPTER 6

The Constitution and the New Republic

By the late 1780s, most Americans had grown deeply dissatisfied with the deficiencies of the Confederation: with the government's apparent inability to deal with factiousness and instability;

Deficiencies of the Confederation Government

with its failure to handle economic problems effectively; and perhaps most of all with the frightening powerlessness it had displayed in the face of Shays's Rebellion. A decade earlier, Americans had deliberately avoided creating a genuine national government, fearing that it would encroach on the sovereignty of the individual states. Now they reconsidered. In 1787, they created a new government defined by the Constitution of the United States.

The American Constitution derived most of its principles from the state documents that had preceded it. But it was also a remarkable achievement in its own right. Out of the contentious atmosphere of a fragile new nation, Americans fashioned a system of government that has survived for more than two centuries as one of the stablest and most successful in the world. William Gladstone, the great nineteenth-century British statesman, once called the Constitution the "most wonderful work ever struck off at a given time by the brain and purpose of man." The American people in the years to come generally agreed. Indeed, to them the Constitution took on some of the characteristics of a sacred document, a holy mystery. Later generations viewed its framers as men almost godlike in their wisdom. And while the framers of the Constitution were far from perfect, they included men of unusual talent and brilliance—among them Benjamin Franklin, the senior statesman of the Revolutionary generation; James Madison, the intellectual leader of the framers; and George Washington, whose reputation and character gave legitimacy to the project. Many considered the Constitution's provisions an unassailable "fundamental law," from which all public policies, all political principles, all solutions of controversies must spring. Few of the framers attributed such power to the document.

The adoption of the Constitution did not complete the creation of the republic. It only defined the terms in which debate over the future of government would continue. Americans may have agreed that the Constitution was a nearly perfect document, but they disagreed—at times fundamentally—on what that document meant. They still do. Out of such disagreements emerged the first great political battles of the new nation.

- Judiciary Act of 1789 is passed
- French Revolution begins
- 1791 Hamilton issues "Report on Manufactures"
- First Bank of the United States chartered
- Vermont becomes fourteenth state
- 1792 Washington reelected without opposition
- Kentucky becomes fifteenth state
- 1793 Citizen Genet affair challenges American neutrality
- 1794 Whiskey Rebellion quelled in Pennsylvania
- Jay's Treaty signed

- 1795 Pinckney's Treaty signed
- 1796 John Adams elected president
- Tennessee becomes sixteenth state
- 1798 XYZ Affair precipitates state of quasi war with France
- Alien and Sedition Acts passed
- Virginia and Kentucky Resolutions passed
- 1800 Jefferson and Burr tie vote in electoral college
- 1801 Jefferson becomes president after Congress confirms election
- Judiciary Act of 1801 passed

FRAMING A NEW GOVERNMENT

So unpopular and ineffectual had the Confederation Congress become by the mid-1780s that it began to lead an almost waiflike existence. In 1783, its members timidly withdrew from Philadelphia to escape from the clamor of army veterans demanding back pay. They

A Weak Central Government

took refuge for a while in Princeton, New Jersey, then moved to Annapolis, and in 1785 settled in New York. Through all of this, the delegates were often conspicuous largely by their absence. Only with great difficulty did Congress secure a quorum to ratify the treaty with Great Britain ending the Revolutionary War. Eighteen members, representing only eight states, voted on the Confederation's most important piece of legislation, the Northwest Ordinance. In the meantime, a major public debate was beginning over the future of the Confederation.

Advocates of Centralization

Weak and unpopular though the Confederation was, it had for a time satisfied a great many—probably a majority—of the people. They believed they had fought the Revolutionary War to avert the danger of what they considered remote and tyrannical authority; now they wanted to keep political power centered in the states, where they could carefully and closely control it.

But during the 1780s, some of the wealthiest and most powerful groups in the country began to clamor for a more genuinely national government capable of dealing with the nation's prob- **Supporters of a Strong National Government** lems—particularly the economic problems that most directly afflicted them. Some military men, many of them members of the exclusive and hereditary Society of the Cincinnati (formed by Revolutionary army officers in 1783), were disgruntled at the refusal of Congress to fund their pensions. They began aspiring to influence and invigorate the national government; some even envisioned a form of military dictatorship and flirted briefly (in 1783, in the so-called Newburgh Conspiracy) with a direct challenge to Congress, until George Washington intervened and blocked the potential rebellion.

American manufacturers—the artisans and "mechanics" of the nation's cities and towns—wanted to replace the various state tariffs with a uniformly high national duty. Merchants and shippers wanted to replace the

GEORGE WASHINGTON AT MOUNT VERNON Washington was in his first term as president in 1790 when an anonymous folk artist painted this view of his home at Mount Vernon, Virginia. Washington appears in uniform, along with members of his family, on the lawn. After he retired from office in 1797, Washington returned happily to his plantation and spent the two years before his death in 1799 "amusing myself in agricultural and rural pursuits." He also played host to an endless stream of visitors from throughout the country and Europe. *(Gift of Edgar William and Bernice Chrysler Garbisch, © 1998 Board of Trustees, National Gallery of Art, Washington)*

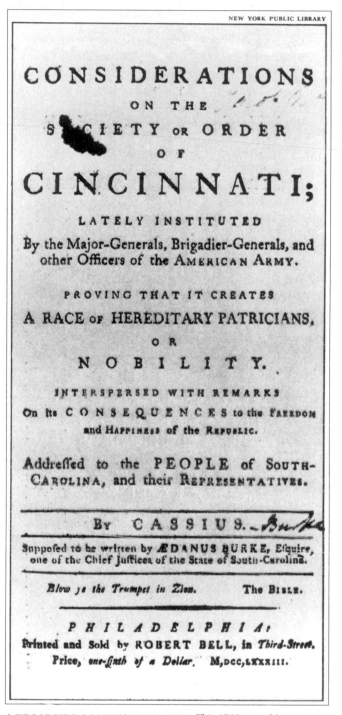

CONSIDERATIONS

ON THE

S CIETY or ORDER

OF

CINNATI;

LATELY INSTITUTED

By the Major-Generals, Brigadier-Generals, and other Officers of the AMERICAN ARMY.

PROVING THAT IT CREATES

A RACE of HEREDITARY PATRICIANS,

O R

N O B I L I T Y.

INTERSPERSED WITH REMARKS

On its CONSEQUENCES to the FREEDOM and HAPPINESS of the REPUBLIC.

Addressed to the PEOPLE of SOUTH-CAROLINA, and their REPRESENTATIVES.

By CASSIUS._Burke

Suppofed to be written by ÆDANUS BURKE, Efquire, one of the Chief Juftices of the State of South-Carolina.

Blow ye the Trumpet in Zion.   The BIBLE.

P H I L A D E L P H I A :

Printed and Sold by ROBERT BELL, in *Third-Street.*

Price, one-fixth of a Dollar. M,DCC,LXXXIII.

A BROADSIDE AGAINST "NOBILITY" This 1783 pamphlet was one of many expressions of the broad democratic sentiment that the Revolution unleashed in American society. The Society of the Cincinnati was an organization created shortly after the Revolution by men who had served as high-ranking officers in the Patriot Army. To many Americans, however, the Society—membership in which was to be hereditary—looked suspiciously like the inherited aristocracies of England. This pamphlet, printed in Philadelphia but intended for South Carolinians, warns of the dangers the Society supposedly posed to the "Freedom and Happiness of the Republic." *(New York Public Library)*

thirteen different (and largely ineffective) state commercial policies with a single, national one. Land speculators wanted the "Indian menace" finally removed from their western tracts. People who were owed money wanted to stop the states from issuing paper money, which would lower the value of what they received in payment. Investors in Confederation securities wanted the government to fund the debt and thus enhance the value of their securities. Large property owners looked for protection from the threat of mobs, a threat that seemed particularly menacing in light of such episodes as Shays's Rebellion. This fear of disorder and violence expressed a tension between the resolute defense of individual rights, which was a core principle of the Revolution and found reflection in the Bill of Rights, and the public concern for safety and security, which the occasional chaos of the Confederation period had reinforced. Frequent conflicts between liberty and order became, and remain, a central feature of American democracy.

By 1786, these diverse demands had grown so powerful that the issue was no longer whether the Confederation should be changed but how drastic the changes should be. Even the defenders of the existing system reluctantly came to agree that the government needed strengthening at its weakest point—its lack of power to tax.

The most resourceful of the reformers was Alexander Hamilton, political genius, New York lawyer, one-time military aide to General Washington, and illegitimate son of a Scottish merchant in the West Indies. From the beginning, Alexander Hamilton Hamilton had been unhappy with the Articles of Confederation and the weak central government they had created. He now called for a national convention to overhaul the entire document. He found an important ally in James Madison of Virginia, who persuaded the Virginia legislature to convene an interstate conference on commercial questions. Only five states sent delegates to the meeting, held in Annapolis, Maryland, in 1786; but the delegates approved a proposal drafted by Hamilton (who was representing New York) recommending that Congress call a convention of special delegates from all the states to gather in Philadelphia the next year and consider ways to "render the constitution of the Federal government adequate to the exigencies of the union."

At that moment, in 1786, there seemed little possibility that the Philadelphia convention would attract any more interest than the meeting at Annapolis had attracted. Only by winning the support of George Washington, the centralizers believed, could they hope to prevail. But Washington at first showed little interest in joining the cause. Then, early in 1787, the news of Shays's Rebellion spread throughout the nation. Thomas Jefferson, then the American minister in Paris, was not alarmed. "I hold," he confided in a letter to James Madison, "that a little rebellion, now and then, is a good thing, and as necessary in the political world as storms in the physical." But Washington took the news less calmly. In May, he left his home at Mount Vernon in Virginia for the Constitutional Convention in Philadelphia. His support gave the meeting immediate credibility.

A Divided Convention

Fifty-five men, representing all the states except Rhode Island, attended one or more sessions of the convention that sat in the Philadelphia State House from May to September 1787. These "Founding Fathers," as they would later become known, were on the whole relatively young men; their average age was forty-four, and only one delegate (Benjamin Franklin, then eighty-one) was of advanced age. They were well educated by the standards of their time. Most represented the great propertied interests of the country, and many feared what one of them called the "turbulence and follies" of democracy. Yet all were also products of the American Revolution and retained the Revolutionary suspicion of concentrated power.

The convention unanimously chose Washington to preside over its sessions and then closed its business to the public and the press. The members then ruled that each state delegation would have a single vote. Major decisions would not require unanimity, as they did in Congress, but only a simple majority. Virginia, the most populous state, sent the best-prepared delegation to Philadelphia. James Madison (thirty-six years old) was its intellectual leader. He had devised a detailed plan for a new "national" government, and the Virginians used it to control the agenda from the moment the convention began.

Edmund Randolph of Virginia began the discussion by proposing that "a national government ought to be established, consisting of a supreme Legislative, Executive, and Judiciary." Despite its vagueness, it was a drastic proposal. It called for the creation of a government very different from the existing Confederation, which, among other things, had no executive branch. But so committed were the delegates to fundamental reform that they approved this resolution after only perfunctory debate. Then Randolph introduced the details of Madison's plan.

The Virginia Plan (as it came to be known) called for a new national legislature consisting of two houses. In the lower house, the states would be represented in proportion to their population; thus the largest state (Virginia) would have about ten times as many representatives as the smallest (Delaware). Members of the upper house were to be elected by the lower house under no rigid system of representation; thus some of the smaller states might at times have no members at all in the upper house.

The proposal aroused immediate opposition among delegates from Delaware, New Jersey, and other small states. Some responded by arguing that Congress had called the convention "for the sole and express purpose of revising the Articles of Confederation" and had no authority to do more than that. Eventually, however, William Paterson of New Jersey submitted a substantive alternative to the Virginia Plan, a proposal for a "federal" as opposed to a "national" government. The New Jersey Plan preserved the existing one-house legislature, in which each state had equal representation, but it gave Congress expanded powers to tax and to regulate commerce. The delegates voted to table Paterson's proposal, but not without taking note of the substantial support for it among small-state representatives.

The Virginia Plan remained the basis for discussion. But its supporters realized they would have to make concessions to the small states if the convention was ever to reach a general agreement. They soon conceded an important point by agreeing to permit the members of the upper house to be elected by the state legislatures rather than by the lower house of the national legislature. Thus each state would be sure of always having at least one member in the upper house.

But many questions remained. Would the states be equally represented in the upper house, or would the large states have more members than the small ones? Would slaves (who could not vote) be counted as part of the population in determining the size of a state's representation in Congress, or were they to be considered simple property? Delegates from states with large and apparently permanent slave populations—especially those from South Carolina—wanted to have it both ways. They argued that slaves should be considered persons in determining representation. But they wanted slaves to be considered property if the new government were to levy taxes on each state on the basis of population. Representatives from states where slavery had disappeared or was expected soon to disappear argued that slaves should be included in calculating taxation but not representation. No one argued seriously for giving slaves citizenship or the right to vote.

Compromise

The delegates bickered for weeks. By the end of June, as both temperature and tempers rose to uncomfortable heights, the convention seemed in danger of collapsing. Benjamin Franklin, who remained a calm voice of conciliation through the summer, warned that if they failed, the delegates would "become a reproach and by-word down to future ages. And what is worse, mankind may hereafter, from this unfortunate instance, despair of establishing governments by human wisdom, and leave it to chance, war and conquest." Partly because of Franklin's soothing presence, the delegates refused to give up.

Finally, on July 2, the convention agreed to create a "grand committee," with a single delegate from each state (and with Franklin as chairman), to resolve the disagreements. The committee produced a proposal that

The Great Compromise

became the basis of the "Great Compromise." Its most important achievement was resolving the difficult problem of representation. The proposal called for a legislature in which the states would be represented in the lower house on the basis of population, with each slave counted as three-fifths of a free person in determining the basis for both representation and direct taxation. (The three-fifths formula was based on the false assumption that a slave was three-fifths as productive as a free worker and thus contributed only three-fifths as much wealth to the state.) The committee proposed that in the upper house, the states should be represented equally with two members apiece. The proposal broke the deadlock. On July 16, 1787, the convention voted to accept the compromise.

Over the next few weeks, the convention as a whole agreed to another important compromise on the explosive issue of slavery. The representatives of the southern states feared that the power to regulate trade might interfere with their agrarian economy, which relied heavily on sales abroad, and with slavery. In response, the convention agreed that the new legislature would not be permitted to tax exports; Congress would also be forbidden to impose a duty of more than $10 a head on imported slaves, and it would have no authority to stop the slave trade for twenty years. To those delegates who viewed the continued existence of slavery as an affront to the principles of the new nation, this was a large and difficult concession. They agreed to it because they feared that without it the Constitution would fail.

The convention disposed of other differences of opinion it was unable to harmonize by evasion or omission—leaving important questions alive that would surface again in later years. The Constitution provided no definition of citizenship. Most important was the absence of a list of individual rights, which would restrain the powers of the national government in the way that bills of rights restrained the state governments. Madison opposed the idea, arguing that specifying rights that were reserved to the people would, in effect, limit those rights. Others, however, feared that without such protections the national government might abuse its new authority.

The Constitution of 1787

Many people contributed to the creation of the American Constitution, but the single most important of them was

James Madison

James Madison—the most creative political thinker of his generation. Perhaps Madison's most important achievement was in helping resolve two important philosophical

"THE GRAND CONVENTION" The engraver John Norman created this imagined view of the Constitutional convention in 1787 for the *Weatherwise's Federal Almanack*, whose title suggested its pro-Constitution political leanings. Norman was familiar with the interior of the hall in Philadelphia where the convention took place, which gave this engraving a sense of reality—even though Norman never attended a session of the convention.

questions that had served as obstacles to the creation of an effective national government: the question of sovereignty and the question of limiting power.

The question of sovereignty had been one of the chief sources of friction between the colonies and Great Britain, and it continued to trouble Americans as they attempted to create their own government. How could both the national government and the

The Question of Sovereignty

state governments exercise sovereignty at the same time? Where did ultimate sovereignty lie? The answer, Madison

The Background of the Constitution

The Constitution—America's most powerful symbol of national identity and the nation's most important source of authority—has inspired debate from the moment it was drafted. Today, as throughout American national history, views of the Constitution reflect the political views of those who seek to interpret it. Some argue that the Constitution is a flexible document intended to evolve in response to society's evolution. Others argue that it has a fixed meaning, rooted in the "original intent" of the framers and that to move beyond that is to deny its value.

Historians, too, disagree about why the Constitution was written and what it meant; and their debate has also reflected contemporary beliefs about what the Constitution should mean. To some scholars, the creation of the federal system was an effort to preserve the ideals of the Revolution by eliminating the disorder and contention that threatened the new nation; it was an effort to create a strong national government capable of exercising real authority. To others, the Constitution was an effort to protect the economic interests of existing elites, even at the cost of betraying the principles of the Revolution. And to still others, the Constitution was designed to protect individual freedom and to limit the power of the federal government.

The first influential exponent of the heroic view of the Constitution as the culmination of the Revolution was John Fiske, whose book *The Critical Period of American History* (1888) painted a grim picture of political life under the Articles of Confederation.

The nation, Fiske argued, was reeling under the impact of a business depression; the weakness and ineptitude of the national government; the threats to American territory from Great Britain and Spain; the inability of either the Congress or the state governments to make good their debts; the interstate jealousies and barriers to trade; the widespread use of inflation-producing paper money; and the lawlessness that culminated in Shays's Rebellion. Only the timely adoption of the Constitution, Fiske claimed, saved the young republic from disaster.

Fiske's view met with little dissent until 1913, when Charles A. Beard published a powerful challenge to it in *An Economic Interpretation of the Constitution of the United States,* which became one of the most influential works of American history in the twentieth century. According to Beard,

the 1780s had been a "critical period" not for the nation as a whole but only for certain conservative business interests who feared that the decentralized political structure of the republic imperiled their financial position. Such men, he claimed, wanted a government able to promote industry and trade, protect private property, and perhaps most of all, make good the public debt—much of which was owed to them. The Constitution was, Beard claimed, "an economic document drawn with superb skill by men whose property interests were immediately at stake" and who won its ratification over the opposition of a majority of the people. Were it not for their impatience and determination, he argued in a later book (1927), the Articles of Confederation might have formed a perfectly satisfactory, permanent form of government.

Beard's view of the Constitution influenced more than a generation of historians. As late as the 1950s, for example, Merrill Jensen argued in *The New Nation* (1950) that the 1780s were not years of chaos and despair, but a time of hopeful striving. He agreed with Beard that only the economic interests of a small group of wealthy men could account for the creation of the Constitution. To them, the Constitution was notable chiefly for the way it abridged the democratic possibilities of the new nation.

But in the 1950s—in the aftermath of a great world crisis that many scholars believed called into question the desirability of giving free reign to popular passions—a series of powerful

and his contemporaries decided, was that all power, at all levels of government, flowed ultimately from the people. Thus neither the federal government nor the state governments were truly sovereign. All of them derived their authority from below. The opening phrase of the Constitution (devised by Robert Morris) was "We the people of the United States"—an expression of the belief that the new government derived its power not from the states but from its citizens.

Resolving the problem of sovereignty made possible one of the distinctive features of the Constitution—its

distribution of powers between the national and state governments. It was, Madison wrote at the time, "in strictness, neither a national nor a federal Constitution, but a composition of both." The Constitution and the government it created were to be the "supreme law" of the land; no state would have the authority to defy it. The federal government was to have broad powers, including the power to tax, to regulate commerce, to control the currency, and to pass such laws as would be "necessary and proper" for carrying out its other responsibilities. Gone was the stipulation of the Articles that challenges to the Beard thesis emerged. The Constitution, many scholars now began to argue, was not an effort to preserve property, but an enlightened effort to ensure stability and order. Robert E. Brown, for example, argued in 1956 that "absolutely no correlation" could be shown between the wealth of the delegates to the Constitutional Convention and their position on the Constitution. Forrest McDonald, in *We the People* (1958), looked beyond the convention itself to the debate between the Federalists and the Antifederalists and concluded similarly that there was no consistent relationship between wealth and property and support for the Constitution. Instead, opinion on the new system was far more likely to reflect local and regional interests. Areas suffering social and economic distress were likely to support the Constitution; states that were stable and prosperous were likely to oppose it. There was no intercolonial class of monied interests operating in concert to produce the Constitution. The cumulative effect of these attacks greatly weakened Beard's argument; few historians any longer accepted his thesis without reservation.

In the 1960s, a new group of scholars began to revive an economic interpretation of the Constitution—one that differed from Beard's in important ways but that nevertheless emphasized social and economic factors as motives for supporting the federal system. Jackson Turner Main argued, in *The Anti-federalists* (1961), that supporters of the Constitution, while not perhaps the united creditor class that Beard

described, were nevertheless economically distinct from critics of the document. The Federalists, he argued, were "cosmopolitan commercialists," eager to advance the economic development of the nation; the Antifederalists, by contrast, were "agrarian localists," fearful of centralization. Gordon Wood's important study, *The Creation of the American Republic* (1969), de-emphasized economic grievances but nevertheless suggested that the debate over the state constitutions in the 1770s and 1780s reflected profound social divisions and that those same divisions helped shape the argument over the federal Constitution. The Federalists, he suggested, were largely traditional aristocrats. They had become deeply concerned by the instability of life under the Articles of Confederation and were particularly alarmed by the decline in popular deference toward social elites. The creation of the Constitution was part of a larger search to create a legitimate political leadership based on the existing social hierarchy; it reflected the efforts of elites to contain what they considered the excesses of democracy.

In more recent years, as contemporary debates over the Constitution have intensified, historians have continued to examine the question of "intent." Did the framers intend a strong, centralized political system; or did they intend to create a decentralized system with a heavy emphasis on individual rights? The answer, according to Jack Rakove's *Original Meanings* (1996), is both—and many other things as well. The Constitution, he

argues, was not the product of a single intelligence or of a broad consensus. It was the result of a long and vigorous debate through which the views of many different groups found their way into the document. James Madison, generally known as the father of the Constitution, was a strong nationalist, who believed that only a powerful central government could preserve stability in a large nation and keep narrow factionalism in check. Alexander Hamilton, Madison's ally in the battle, also saw the Constitution as a way to protect order and property, as a way to defend the nation against the dangers of too much liberty. But if Madison and Hamilton feared too much liberty, they also feared too little. And that made them receptive to the vigorous demands of the "anti-Federalists" for protections of individual rights, which culminated in the Bill of Rights. The framers differed as well in their views of the proper relationship between the federal government and the state governments. Madison favored unquestioned federal supremacy, and even tried to insert a clause in the Constitution giving Congress the right to invalidate state laws. Many others involved in the debate wanted to preserve the rights of the states and saw in the federal system—and in its unusual division of sovereignty among different levels and branches of government—a guarantee against too much national power. The Constitution is not, Rakove argues, "infinitely malleable," But neither does it have a fixed meaning that can be a reliable guide to how we interpret it today.

"each State shall retain every power, jurisdiction, and right not expressly delegated to the United States in Congress assembled." On the other hand, the Constitution accepted the existence of separate states and left important powers in their hands.

In addition to solving the question of sovereignty, the Constitution produced a solution to a problem that was particularly troubling to Americans: the problem of concentrated authority. Nothing so frightened the leaders of the new nation as the prospect of creating a tyrannical government. Indeed, that fear had been one of the chief

obstacles to the creation of a national government at all. Drawing from the ideas of the French philosopher Baron de Montesquieu, most Americans had long believed that the best way, perhaps the only way, to avoid tyranny was to keep government close to the people. A republic, they thought, must remain confined to a relatively small area; a large nation would breed corruption and despotism because the rulers would be so distant from most of the people that there would be no way to control them. In the first years of the new American nation, these assumptions had led to the belief that the individual states must remain sovereign and that a strong national government would be dangerous.

Madison, however, helped break the grip of these assumptions by arguing that a large republic would be less, not more, likely to produce tyranny, because it would contain so many different factions that no single group would ever be able to dominate it. (In this, he drew from—among other sources—the Scottish philosopher David Hume.) This idea of many centers of power "checking each other" and preventing any single, despotic authority from emerging not only made possible the idea of a large republic, but also helped shape the internal structure of the federal government. The Constitution's most distinctive feature was its "separation of powers" within the government, its creation of "checks and balances" among the legislative, executive, and judicial branches. The array of forces within the government would constantly compete with (and often frustrate) one another. Congress would have two chambers, the Senate and the House of Representatives, each with members elected in a different way and for different terms, and each checking the other, since both would have to agree before any law could be passed. The president would have the power to veto acts of Congress. The federal courts would have protection from both the executive and the legislature because judges and justices, once appointed by the president and confirmed by the Senate, would serve for life.

The "federal" structure of the government, which divided power between the states and the nation, and the system of "checks and balances," which divided power among various elements within the national government itself, were designed to protect the United States from the kind of despotism Americans believed had emerged in England. But they were also designed to protect the nation from another kind of despotism, perhaps equally menacing: the tyranny of the people. Fear of the "mob," of an "excess of democracy," was at least as important to the framers as fear of a single tyrant. Shays's Rebellion had been only one example, they believed, of what could happen if a nation did not defend itself against the unchecked exercise of popular will. Thus in the new government, only the members of the House of Representatives would be elected directly by the people. Senators, the president, and federal judges would be insulated in varying degrees from the public.

On September 17, 1787, thirty-nine delegates signed the Constitution, doubtless sharing the feelings that Benjamin Franklin expressed at the end: "Thus I consent, Sir, to this Constitution, because I expect no better, and because I am not sure it is not the best."

Federalists and Antifederalists

The delegates at Philadelphia had greatly exceeded their instructions from Congress and the states. Instead of making simple revisions to the Articles of Confederation, they had produced a plan for a completely different form of government. They feared, therefore, that the Constitution might never be ratified under the rules of the Articles of Confederation, which required unanimous approval by the state legislatures. So the convention changed the rules. The Constitution specified that the new government would come into existence among the ratifying states when any nine of the thirteen had

FEDERALIST #1 The Federalist Papers, gathered together here in a book distributed to the people of New York, began as essays, letters, and articles published in newspapers throughout America during the debate over the Constitution. Its authors—James Madison, Alexander Hamilton, and John Jay—were defenders of the new Constitution and wrote these essays to explain its value and importance. They remain today one of the most important American contributions to political theory. *(The Granger Collection)* ratified it. The delegates recommended to Congress that special state conventions, not state legislatures, consider the document. They were required to vote "yes" or "no" on the document. They could make no changes until after the Constitution was ratified by the required number of states, at which point the Constitution's amendment process could be used (as it was for the Bill of Rights).

The old Confederation Congress, now overshadowed by the events in Philadelphia, passively accepted the convention's work and submitted it to the states for approval. All the state legislatures except Rhode Island's elected delegates to ratifying conventions, most of which began meeting by early 1788. Even before the ratifying conventions convened, however, a great national debate on the new Constitution had begun—in the state legislatures, in mass meetings, in the columns of newspapers, and in ordinary conversations. Occasionally, passions rose to the point that opposing factions came to blows. In at least one place—Albany, New York—such clashes resulted in injuries and death.

Supporters of the Constitution had a number of advantages. They were better organized than their opponents, and they had the support of the two most eminent men in America, Franklin and Washington. And

The Federalist Papers

they seized an appealing label for themselves: "Federalists"— the term that opponents of centralization had once used to describe themselves—thus implying that they were less committed to a "nationalist" government than in fact they were. The Federalists also had the support of the ablest political philosophers of their time: Alexander Hamilton, James Madison, and John Jay. Those three men, under the joint pseudonym "Publius," wrote a series of essays—widely published in newspapers throughout the nation—explaining the meaning and virtues of the Constitution. They did so in an effort to counter the powerful arguments that those opposed to the Constitution—those who became known as the Anti-federalists—were making. Without a powerful defense of the new Constitution, they feared, the Anti-federalists might repeal in several crucial states, and most notably in New York. The essays were later issued as a book, and they are known today as The Federalist Papers. They are among the greatest American contributions to political theory.

The Federalists called their critics "Antifederalists," implying that their rivals had nothing to offer except opposition and chaos. But the

The Antifederalists

Antifederalists had serious and intelligent arguments of their own. They presented themselves as the defenders of the true principles of the Revolution. The Constitution, they believed, would betray those principles by establishing a strong, potentially tyrannical, center of power in the new national government. The new government, they claimed, would increase taxes, obliterate the states, wield dictatorial powers, favor the "well born" over the common people, and put an end to individual liberty. But their biggest complaint was that the Constitution lacked a bill of rights, a concern that revealed one of the most important sources of their opposition: a basic mistrust of human nature and of the capacity of human beings to wield power. The Antifederalists argued that any government that centralized authority would inevitably produce despotism. Their demand for a bill of rights was a product of this belief: no government could be trusted to protect the liberties of its citizens; only by enumerating the natural rights of the people could there be any assurance that those rights would be preserved.

At its heart, then, the debate between the Federalists and the Antifederalists was a battle between two fears. The Federalists were afraid, above all, of disorder, anarchy, chaos; they feared the unchecked power of the masses, and they sought in the Constitution to create a government that would function at some distance from popular passions. The Antifeder-

Debating the Constitution

alists were not anarchists. They too recognized the need for an effective government. But they were much more concerned about the dangers of concentrated power than about the dangers of popular will. They opposed the Constitution for some of the same reasons the Federalists supported it: because it placed obstacles between the people and the exercise of power.

Despite the Antifederalist efforts, ratification proceeded quickly (although not without occasional difficulty) during the winter of 1787–1788. The Delaware convention was the first to act, when it ratified the Constitution unanimously. The New Jersey and Georgia conventions did the same. In the larger states of Pennsylvania and Massachusetts, the Antifederalists put up a more determined struggle but lost in the final vote. New Hampshire ratified the document in June 1788—the ninth state to do so. It was now theoretically possible for the Constitution to go into effect.

A new government could not hope to flourish, however, without the participation of Virginia and New York, the two biggest states, whose conventions remained closely divided. By the end of June, first Virginia and then New York had consented to the Constitution by narrow margins. The New York convention yielded to expediency—even some of the most staunchly Antifederalist delegates feared that the state's commercial interests would suffer if, once the other states gathered under the "New Roof," New York were to remain outside. Massachusetts, Virginia, and New York all ratified, on the assumption that a bill of rights would be added to the Constitution. The North Carolina convention adjourned without taking action, waiting to see what happened to the amendments. Rhode Island, whose leaders had opposed the Constitution almost from the start, did not even call a convention to consider ratification.

Completing the Structure

The first elections under the Constitution took place in the early months of 1789. Almost all the newly elected congressmen and senators had favored ratification, and many had served as delegates to the Philadelphia convention. There was never any real doubt about who would be the first president. George Washington had presided at the Constitutional Convention, and many who had favored ratification did so only because they expected him to preside over the new government as well. Washington received the votes of all the presidential electors. John Adams, a leading Federalist, became vice president. After a journey from Mount Vernon marked by elaborate celebrations along the way, Washington was inaugurated in New York—the national capital for the time being—on April 30, 1789.

The first Congress served in many ways almost as a continuation of the Constitutional Convention, because its principal responsibility was filling in the various gaps in the Constitution. Its most important task was drafting a bill of rights. By early 1789, even Madison had come to agree that some sort of bill of rights was essential to legitimize the new government in the eyes of its opponents. Congress approved twelve amendments on September 25, 1789; ten of them were ratified by the states by the end of 1791. What we know as the Bill of Rights is these first ten amendments to the Constitution. Nine of them placed limitations on Congress by forbidding it to infringe on certain basic rights: freedom of religion, speech, and the press; immunity from arbitrary arrest; trial by jury; and others. The Tenth Amendment reserved to the states all powers except those specifically withheld from them or delegated to the federal government.

The Bill of Rights

On the subject of the federal courts, the Constitution said only: "The judicial power of the United States shall be vested in one Supreme Court, and in such inferior courts as the Congress may from time to time ordain and establish." It was left to Congress to determine the number of Supreme Court judges to be appointed and the kinds of lower courts to be organized. In the Judiciary Act of 1789, Congress provided for a Supreme Court of six members, with a chief justice and five associate justices; thirteen district courts with one judge apiece; and three circuit courts of appeal, each to consist of one of the district judges sitting with two of the Supreme Court justices. In the same act, Congress gave the Supreme Court the power to make the final decision in cases involving the constitutionality of state laws.

The Constitution referred indirectly to executive departments but did not specify what or how many there should be. The first Congress created three such departments—state, treasury, and war—and also established the offices of the attorney general and postmaster general.

The Cabinet

To the office of secretary of the treasury, Washington appointed Alexander Hamilton of New York, who at age thirty-two was an acknowledged expert in public finance. For secretary of war he chose a Massachusetts Federalist, General Henry Knox. As attorney general he named Edmund Randolph of Virginia, sponsor of the plan on which the Constitution had been based. As secretary of state he chose another Virginian, Thomas Jefferson, who had recently served as minister to France.

FEDERALISTS AND REPUBLICANS

The resolution of these initial issues, however, did not resolve the deep disagreements about the nature of the new government. On the contrary, for the first twelve years under the Constitution, American politics was characterized by a level of acrimony seldom matched in any period since. The framers of the Constitution had dealt with many disagreements not by solving them but by papering them over with a series of vague compromises; as a result, the conflicts survived to plague the new government.

At the heart of the controversies of the 1790s was the same basic difference in philosophy that had been at the heart of the debate over the Constitution. On one side stood a powerful group that believed America required a strong, national government: that the country's mission was to become a genuine nation-state, with centralized authority, a complex commercial economy, and a proud standing in world affairs. On the other side stood another group—a minority at first, but one that gained strength during the decade—that envisioned a far more modest central government. American society should not, this group believed, aspire to be highly commercial or urban. It should remain predominantly rural and agrarian, and it should have a central government of modest size and powers that would leave most power in the hands of the states and the people. The centralizers became known as the Federalists and gravitated to the leadership of Alexander Hamilton. Their opponents took the name Republicans and gathered under the leadership of James Madison and Thomas Jefferson.

Competing Visions

Hamilton and the Federalists

For twelve years, control of the new government remained firmly in the hands of the Federalists. That was in part because George Washington had always envisioned a strong national government and as president had quietly supported those who were attempting to create one. His enormous prestige throughout the nation was one of the Federalists' greatest assets. But Washington also believed that the presidency should remain above political

BANK NOTE How to create a stable currency was one of the greatest challenges facing the new American nation. This fifty dollar bank note illustrates the principal form paper money assumed in the early republic. It was issued in 1797 by a bank in Philadelphia, and its value was directly tied to the stability of the bank itself. Only many years later did the national government assume control of printing and distributing currency. *(Eric P. Newman Numismatic Education Society)*

controversies, and so he avoided any personal involvement in the deliberations of Congress. As a result, the dominant figure in his administration became his talented secretary of the treasury, Alexander Hamilton, who exerted more influence on domestic and foreign policy than anyone else both during his term of office and, to an almost equal extent, after his resignation in 1794.

Of all the national leaders of his time, Hamilton was one of the most aristocratic in personal tastes and political philosophy—ironically, perhaps, since his own origins as an illegitimate child in the Caribbean had been so humble. Far from embracing the republican ideals of the virtue of the people, he believed that a stable and effective government required an enlightened ruling class. Thus, the new government needed the support of the wealthy and powerful; and to get that support it needed to give those elites a stake in its success. Hamilton proposed, therefore, that the new government take responsibility for the existing public debt. Many of the miscellaneous, uncertain, depreciated certificates of indebtedness that the old Congress had issued during and after the Revolution were now in the hands of wealthy speculators; the government should call them in and exchange them for uniform, interest-bearing bonds, payable at definite dates. (This policy was known as "funding" the debt.) He also recommended that the federal government "assume" (or take over) the debts the states had accumulated during the Revolution; this assumption policy would encourage state as well as federal bondholders to look to the central government for eventual payment. Hamilton did not, in other words, envision paying off and thus eliminating the debt. He wanted instead to create a large and permanent national debt, with new bonds being issued as old ones were paid off. The result, he believed, would be that creditors—the wealthy classes most likely to lend money to the government—would have a permanent stake in seeing the government survive.

Hamilton also wanted to create a national bank. At the time, there were only a few banks in the country,

Assuming the Debt

located principally in Boston, Philadelphia, and New York. A new, national bank would help fill the void that the absence of a well-developed banking system had created. It would provide loans and currency to businesses. It would give the government a safe place to deposit federal funds. It would help collect taxes and disburse the government's expenditures. It would keep up the price of government bonds through judicious bond purchases. The bank would be chartered by the federal government, would have a monopoly of the government's own banking business, and would be controlled by directors, of whom one-fifth would be appointed by the government. It would provide a stable center to the nation's small and feeble banking system.

The funding and assumption of debts would require new sources of revenue, since the government would now have to pay interest on the loans it was accepting. Up to now, most government revenues had come from the sale of public lands in the West. Hamilton proposed two new kinds of taxes. One was an excise to be paid by distillers of alcoholic liquors, a tax that would fall most heavily on the whiskey distillers of the backcountry, especially in Pennsylvania, Virginia, and North Carolina—small farmers who converted part of their corn and rye crop into whiskey. The other was a tariff on imports, which not only would raise revenue but would also protect American manufacturing from foreign competition. In his famous "Report on Manufactures" of 1791, he laid out a grand scheme for stimulating the growth of industry in the United States and wrote glowingly of the advantages to the nation of a healthy manufacturing base.

Hamilton's Report on Manufacturing

The Federalists, in short, offered more than a vision of how to stabilize the new government. They offered a vision of the sort of nation America should become—a nation with a wealthy, enlightened ruling class, a vigorous, independent commercial economy, and a thriving industrial sector; a nation able to play a prominent role in world economic affairs.

Enacting the Federalist Program

Few members of Congress objected to Hamilton's plan for funding the national debt, but many did oppose his

Debating Hamilton's Program

proposal to accept the debt "at par," that is at face value. The old certificates had been issued to merchants and farmers in payment for war supplies during the Revolution, or to officers and soldiers of the Revolutionary army in payment for their services. But many of these original holders had sold their bonds during the hard times of the 1780s to speculators, who had bought them at a fraction of their face value. Many members of Congress believed if the federal government was to assume responsibility for these bonds, some of them should be returned to the original purchasers. James Madison, now a representative from Virginia, proposed dividing the federally funded bonds between the original purchasers and the speculators. But Hamilton's allies insisted that such a plan was impractical and that the honor of the government required that it pay the bondholders themselves, not the original lenders who had sold their bonds of their own accord. Congress finally passed the funding bill Hamilton wanted.

Hamilton's proposal that the federal government assume the state debts encountered greater difficulty. His opponents argued that if the federal government took over the state debts, the people of states with few debts would have to pay taxes to service the larger debts of other states. Massachusetts, for example, owed far more money than did Virginia. Hamilton and his supporters struck a bargain with the Virginians to win passage of the bill.

The deal involved the location of the national capital. The capital had moved from New York back to Philadelphia in 1790. But the Virginians wanted a new capital near them in the South. Hamiton met with Thomas

Location of the Capital

Jefferson and agreed over dinner to provide northern support for placing the capital in the South in exchange for Virginia's votes for the assumption bill. The bargain called for the construction of a new capital city on the banks of the Potomac River, which divided Virginia and Maryland, on land to be selected by Washington himself. The government would move there by the beginning of the new century.

Hamilton's bank bill sparked the most heated debate, the first of many on this controversial issue. Hamilton argued that creation of a national bank was compatible

Bank of the United States

with the intent of the Constitution, even though the document did not explicitly authorize it. But Madison, Jefferson, Randolph, and others argued that Congress should exercise no powers that the Constitution had not clearly assigned it. Nevertheless, both the House and the Senate finally agreed to Hamilton's bill.

Washington displayed some uncertainty about its legality at first, but he finally signed it. The Bank of the United States began operations in 1791, under a charter that granted it the right to continue for twenty years.

Hamilton also had his way with the excise tax, although protests from farmers later forced revisions to reduce the burden on the smaller distillers. He won passage, too, of a new tariff in 1792, although it raised rates less than he had wished.

Once enacted, Hamilton's program had many of the effects he had intended and won the support of influential segments of the population. It quickly restored public credit; the bonds of the United States were soon selling at home and abroad at prices even above their par value. Speculators (among them many members of Congress) reaped large profits as a result. Manufacturers profited from the tariffs, and merchants in the seaports benefited from the new banking system.

Others, however, found the Hamilton program less appealing. Small farmers, who formed the vast majority of the population, complained that they had to bear a disproportionate tax burden. Not only did they have to pay property taxes to their state governments, but they bore the brunt of the excise tax on distilleries and, indirectly, the tariff. A feeling grew among many Americans that the Federalist program served the interests not of the people but of small, wealthy elites. Out of this feeling an organized political opposition arose.

The Republican Opposition

The Constitution had made no reference to political parties, and the omission was not an oversight. Most of the framers—and George Washington in particular—believed that organized parties were dangerous and should be avoided. Disagreement on particular issues was inevitable, but most of the founders believed that such disagreements need not and should not lead to the formation of permanent factions. "The public good is disregarded in the conflicts of rival parties," Madison had written in The Federalist Papers (in Number 10, perhaps the most influential of all the essays), "and . . . measures are too often decided, not according to the rules of justice and the rights of the minor party, but by the superior force of an interested and overbearing majority."

Yet within just a few years after ratification of the Constitution, Madison and others became convinced that Hamilton and his followers had become just such an "interested

Establishment of the Federalist Party

and overbearing majority." Not only had the Federalists enacted a program that many of these leaders opposed. More ominously, Hamilton himself had, in their eyes, worked to establish a national network of influence that embodied all the worst features of a party. The Federalists had used their control over appointments and the awarding of government franchises to

THE JEFFERSONIAN IDYLL American artists in the early nineteenth century were drawn to tranquil rural scenes, symbolic of the Jeffersonian vision of a nation of small, independent farmers. By 1822, when Francis Alexander painted this pastoral landscape, the simple agrarian republic it depicts was already being transformed by rapid economic growth *(Gift of Edgar William and Bernice Chrysler Garbisch, © 1998 Board of Trustees, National Gallery of Art, Washington)*

reward their supporters and win additional allies. They had encouraged the formation of local associations largely aristocratic in nature—to strengthen their standing in local communities. They were doing many of the same things, their opponents believed, that the corrupt British governments of the early eighteenth century had done.

Because the Federalists appeared to be creating such a menacing and tyrannical structure of power, their critics

Formation of the Republican Party

felt, there was no alternative but to organize a vigorous opposition. The result was the emergence of an alternative political organization, which called itself the Republican Party. (This first "Republican" Party is not a direct ancestor of the modern Republican Party, which was born in the 1850s.) By the late 1790s, the Republicans were going to even greater lengths than the Federalists to create an apparatus of partisan influence. In every state they formed committees, societies, and caucuses. Republican groups were corresponding with one another across state lines. They were banding together to influence state and local elections. And they were justifying their actions by claiming that they and they alone represented the true interests of the nation— that they were fighting to defend the people against a corrupt conspiracy by the Federalists. Just as Hamilton believed that the network of supporters he was creating represented the only legitimate interest group in the nation, so the Republicans believed that their party organization represented the best interests of the people. Neither side was willing to admit that it was acting as a party; neither would concede the right of the other to exist. This institutionalized factionalism is known to scholars as the "first party system."

From the beginning, the preeminent figures among the Republicans were Thomas Jefferson and James Madison. Indeed, the two men were such intimate collaborators with such similar political philosophies that it is sometimes difficult to distinguish the contributions of one from those of the other. But Jefferson, the more magnetic personality of the two, gradually emerged as the most prominent spokesman for the Republicans. Jefferson considered himself a farmer. (He was, in fact, a substantial planter; but he had spent relatively little time in recent years at his estate in Virginia.) He believed in an agrarian republic, most of whose citizens would be sturdy, independent farmer-citizens tilling their own soil.

Jefferson did not scorn commercial activity; he assumed farmers would market their crops in the national and even international markets. Nor did he oppose industry; he believed the United States should develop some manufacturing capacity. But he was suspicious of large cities, feared urban mobs as "sores upon the body politic," and opposed the development of an advanced industrial economy because it would, he feared, increase the number of propertyless workers packed in cities. In short, Jefferson envisioned a decentralized society, dominated by small property owners engaged largely in agrarian activities.

The difference between the Federalist and Republican social philosophies was visible in, among other things, reactions to the French Revolution. As that revolution grew increasingly radical in the 1790s, with its attacks on organized religion, the overthrow of the monarchy, and eventually the execution of the king and queen, the Federalists expressed horror. But the Republicans generally applauded the democratic, anti-aristocratic spirit they believed the French Revolution embodied. Some even imitated the French radicals (the Jacobins) by cutting their hair short, wearing pantaloons, and addressing one another as "Citizen" and "Citizeness."

Differences over the French Revolution

Although both parties had supporters in all parts of the country and among all classes, there were regional and economic differences. The Federalists were most numerous in the commercial centers of the Northeast and in such southern seaports as Charleston; the Republicans were most numerous in the rural areas of the South and the West.

As the 1792 presidential election—the nation's second—approached, both Jefferson and Hamilton urged Washington to run for another term. The president reluctantly agreed. But while most Americans considered Washington above the partisan battle, he was actually much more in sympathy with the Federalists than with the Republicans. And during his presidency, Hamilton remained the dominant figure in government.

ESTABLISHING NATIONAL SOVEREIGNTY

The Federalists consolidated their position—and attracted wide public support for the new national government—by dealing effectively with two problems the old Confederation had been unable fully to resolve. They helped stabilize the nation's western lands, and they strengthened America's international position.

Securing the Frontier

Despite the Northwest Ordinance, the Confederation Congress had largely failed to tie the outlying western areas of the country firmly to the government. Farmers in western Massachusetts had risen in revolt; settlers in Vermont, Kentucky, and Tennessee had toyed with the idea of separating from the Union. At first, the new government under the Constitution faced similar problems.

In 1794, farmers in western Pennsylvania raised a major challenge to federal authority when they refused to pay a whiskey excise tax and began terrorizing the tax collectors (much as colonists had done at the time of the Stamp Act). But the federal government did not leave settlement of the so-called Whiskey Rebellion to Pennsylvania, as the Confederation Congress had left Shays's Rebellion to Massachusetts. At Hamilton's urging, Washington called out the militias of three states, raised an army of nearly 15,000 (a larger force than he had commanded against the British during most of the Revolution), and personally led the troops into Pennsylvania. As the militiamen approached Pittsburgh, the center of the resistance, the rebellion quickly collapsed.

Whiskey Rebellion

The federal government won the allegiance of the whiskey rebels by intimidating them. It won the loyalties of other frontier people by accepting their territories as new states in the Union. The last of the original thirteen colonies joined the Union once the Bill of Rights had been appended to the Constitution—North Carolina in 1789 and Rhode Island in 1790. Then Vermont, which had had its own state government since the Revolution, became the fourteenth state in 1791 after New York and New Hampshire finally agreed to give up their claims to it. Next came Kentucky, in 1792, when Virginia gave up its claim to that region. After North Carolina finally ceded its western lands to the Union, Tennessee became first a territory and, in 1796, a state.

Native Americans and the New Nation

The new government faced a greater challenge, inherited from the Confederation, in the more distant areas of the Northwest and the Southwest, where Indians (occasionally in alliance with the British and Spanish) continued to challenge the republic's claim to tribal lands. The ordinances of 1784–1787 had produced a series of border conflicts with Indian tribes resisting white settlement in their lands. Although the United States eventually defeated virtually every Indian challenge (if often at great cost), it was clear that the larger question of who was to control the lands of the West—the United States or the Indian nations—remained unanswered.

These clashes revealed another issue the Constitution had done little to resolve: the place of the Indian nations within the new federal structure. The Constitution barely mentioned Native Americans. Article I excluded "Indians not taxed" from being counted in the population totals that determined the number of seats states would receive in the House of Representatives; and it gave Congress the power to "regulate Commerce with foreign Nations, and among the several States, and with the Indian tribes." Article VI bound the new government to respect treaties negotiated by the Confederation, most of which had been with the tribes. But none of this did very much to clarify the precise legal standing of Indians or Indian nations within the United States.

Indians and the Constitution

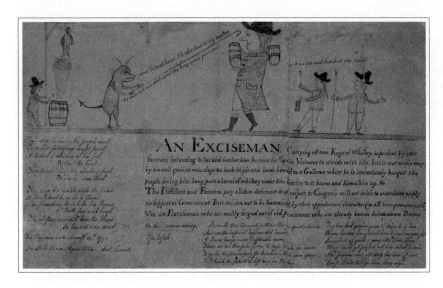

On the one hand, the Constitution seemed to recognize the existence of the tribes as legal entities. On the other hand, it made clear that they were not "foreign Nations" (in the same sense that European countries were); nor were their members citizens of the United States. The tribes received no direct representation in the new government. Above all, the Constitution did not address the major issue that would govern relations between whites and Indians: land. Indian nations lived within the boundaries of the United States, yet they claimed (and the white government at times agreed) that they had some measure of sovereignty within their own lands. But neither the Constitution nor common law offered any clear guide to the rights of a "nation within a nation" or to the precise nature of tribal sovereignty, which ultimately depended on control of land. Thus, the relationship between the tribes and the United States remained to be determined by a series of treaties, agreements, and judicial decisions in a process that has continued for two centuries.

Maintaining Neutrality

Not until 1791—eight years after the end of the Revolution—did Great Britain send a minister to the United States, and then only because Madison and the Republicans were threatening to place special trade restrictions on British ships. That was one of many symbols of the difficulty the new government had in establishing its legitimacy in the eyes of the British. Another crisis in Anglo-American relations emerged in 1793 when the new French government, created by the revolution of 1789, went to war with Great Britain and its allies. Both the president and Congress took steps to establish American neutrality in that conflict. But the neutrality quickly encountered severe tests.

The first challenge to American neutrality came from revolutionary France and its first diplomatic representative to America, the brash and youthful Edmond Genet. Instead of landing at Philadelphia and presenting himself immediately to the president, Genet disembarked at Charleston. There he made plans to use American ports to outfit French warships, encour-aged American shipowners to serve as French privateers, and commissioned the aging George Rogers Clark to lead a military expedition against Spanish lands to the south. (Spain was at the time an ally of Great Britain and an enemy of France.) In all of this, Genet was brazenly ignoring Washington's policies and flagrantly violating the Neutrality Act. His conduct infuriated Washington (who provided "Citizen Genet," as he was known, with an icy reception in Philadelphia) and the Federalists; it also embarrassed all but the most ardent admirers of the French Revolution among the Republicans. Washington eventually demanded that the French government recall him, but by then Genet's party was out of power in France. (The president granted him political asylum in the United States, and he settled with his American wife on a Long Island farm.) The neutrality policy had survived its first serious test.

Citizen Genet

A second and even greater challenge came from Great Britain. Early in 1794, the Royal Navy began seizing hundreds of American ships engaged in trade in the French West Indies, outraging public opinion in the United States. Anti-British feeling rose still higher at the report that the governor general of Canada had delivered a warlike speech to the Indians on the northwestern frontier. Hamilton was deeply concerned. War would mean an end to imports from England, and most of the revenue for maintaining his financial system came from duties on those imports.

Jay's Treaty and Pinckney's Treaty

This was, Hamilton believed, no time for ordinary diplomacy. He did not trust the State Department to reach a settlement with Britain. Jefferson had resigned as secretary of state in 1793 to devote more time to his political activities, but his successor, Edmund Randolph, was even more ardently pro-French than Jefferson had been. So Hamilton persuaded Washington to name a special commissioner to England: John Jay, chief justice of the United States Supreme Court and a staunch New York Federalist. Jay was instructed to secure compensation for the recent British assaults on American shipping, to demand withdrawal of British forces from the frontier posts, and to negotiate a new commercial treaty.

The long and complex treaty Jay negotiated in 1794 failed to achieve these goals. But it was not without merit. It settled the conflict with Britain and helped prevent what had seemed likely to become a war between the two nations. It established undisputed American sovereignty over the entire Northwest. And it produced a

Jay's Treaty

reasonably satisfactory commercial relationship with Britain, whose trade was important to the United States. Nevertheless, when the terms became public in America, there were bitter public denunciations of it for having failed to extract enough promises from the British. Jay himself was burned in effigy in various parts of the country. Opponents of the treaty—nearly all the Republicans and even some Federalists, encouraged by agents of France—went to extraordinary lengths to defeat it in the Senate. The American minister to France, James Monroe, and even the secretary of state, Edmund Randolph, joined the desperate attempt to prevent ratification. But in the end the Senate ratified what was by then known as Jay's Treaty.

Among other things, the treaty made possible a settlement of America's conflict with the Spanish, because it raised fears in Spain that the British and the Americans might now join together to challenge Spanish possessions in

Pinckney's Treaty

North America. When Thomas Pinckney arrived in Spain as a special negotiator, he had no difficulty in gaining nearly everything the United States had sought from the Spaniards for more than a decade. Under Pinckney's Treaty (signed in 1795), Spain recognized the right of Americans to navigate the Mississippi to its mouth and to deposit goods at New Orleans for reloading on ocean-going ships; agreed to fix the northern boundary of Florida where Americans always had insisted it should be, along the 31st parallel; and required Spanish authorities to prevent the Indians in Florida from launching raids across the border.

THE DOWNFALL OF THE FEDERALISTS

The Federalists' impressive triumphs did not ensure their continued dominance in the national government. On the contrary, success seemed to produce problems of its own—problems that eventually led to their downfall.

Since almost all Americans in the 1790s agreed that there was no place in a stable republic for an organized opposition, the emergence of the Republicans as powerful contenders for popular favor seemed to the Federalists a grave threat to national stability. Beginning in the late 1790s, when major international perils confronted the government as well, the Federalists could not resist the temptation to move forcefully against the opposition. Facing what they believed was a stark choice between respecting individual liberties and preserving stability, the Federalists chose stability. The result was political disaster. After 1796, the Federalists never won another election. The popular respect for the institutions of the federal government, which they had worked so hard to produce among the people, survived. But the Federalists themselves gradually vanished as an effective political force.

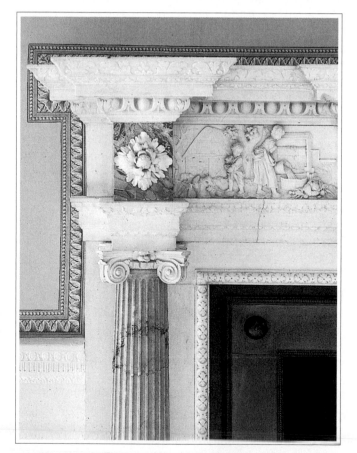

MOUNT VERNON George and Martha Washington lavished enormous attention to their home at Mount Vernon, importing materials and workmen from Europe to create a house that they hoped would rival some of the elegant country homes of England. This detail from a mantle suggests the degree to which they—like many wealthy planters and merchants of their time—strove to bring refinement and gentility to their lives. *(Paul Rocheleau/Rebus, Inc.)*

The Election of 1796

Despite strong pressure from his many admirers to run for a third term as president, George Washington insisted on retiring from office in 1797. In a "Farewell Address" to the American people (actually a long letter, composed in part by Hamilton and published in a Philadelphia newsletter), he reacted sharply to the Republicans. His reference to the "insidious wiles of foreign influence" was not just an abstract warning against international entanglements; it was also a specific denunciation of those Republicans who had been conspiring with the French to frustrate the Federalist diplomatic program.

Washington's Farewell Address

With Washington out of the running, no obstacle remained to an open expression of the partisan rivalries that had been building over the previous eight years. Jefferson was the uncontested candidate of the Republicans in 1796. The Federalists faced a more difficult choice. Hamilton, the personification of Federalism, had created too many enemies to be a credible candidate. So Vice President John Adams, who had been directly associated with none of the unpopular Federalist measures, became his party's nominee for president.

The Federalists were still clearly the dominant party, and there was little doubt of their ability to win a majority of the presidential electors. But without Washington to mediate, they fell victim to fierce factional rivalries that almost led to their undoing. Hamilton and many other Federalists (especially in the South) were not reconciled to Adams's candidacy and favored his running mate Thomas Pinckney instead. And when, as expected, the Federalists elected a majority of the presidential electors, some of these Pinckney supporters declined to vote for Adams; he managed to defeat Jefferson by only three electoral votes. Because a still larger number of Adams's supporters declined to vote for Pinckney, Jefferson finished second in the balloting and became vice president. (Until the Twelfth Amendment was adopted in 1804, the Constitution provided for the candidate receiving the second highest number of electoral votes to become vice president—hence the awkward result of men from different parties serving in the nation's two highest elected offices.)

Adams thus assumed the presidency under inauspicious circumstances. He presided over a divided party, which faced a strong and resourceful Republican opposition committed to its extinction. Adams himself was not even the dominant figure in his own party; Hamilton remained the most influential Federalist, and Adams was never able to challenge him effectively. The new president was one of the country's most accomplished and talented diplomats, but he had few skills as a politician. Austere, rigid, aloof, he had little talent at conciliating differences, soliciting support, or inspiring enthusiasm. He was a man of enormous, indeed intimidating rectitude, and he seemed to assume that his own virtue and the correctness of his positions would alone be enough to sustain him. He was usually wrong.

Divided Federalists

The Quasi War with France

American relations with Great Britain and Spain improved as a result of Jay's and Pinckney's Treaties. But the nation's relations with revolutionary France quickly deteriorated. French vessels captured American ships on the high seas and at times imprisoned the crews. When the South Carolina Federalist Charles Cotesworth Pinckney, brother of Thomas Pinckney, arrived in France, the government refused to receive him as the official representative of the United States.

Some of President Adams's advisers favored war, most notably Secretary of State Thomas Pickering, a stern New Englander who detested France. But Hamilton recommended conciliation, and Adams agreed. In an effort to stabilize relations, Adams appointed a bipartisan commission—consisting of Charles Cotesworth Pinckney,

JOHN ADAMS Adams's illustrious career as Revolutionary leader, diplomat, and president marked the beginning of four generations of public distinction among members of his family. His son, John Quincy Adams, served as secretary of state and president. His grandson, Charles Francis Adams, was one of the great diplomats of the Civil War era. His great-grandson, Henry Adams, was one of America's most distinguished historians and writers. *(Adams National Historic Site, Quincy, Massachusetts)*

THE XYZ AFFAIR The sensational "XYZ Affair" of 1798 is the subject of this American political cartoon. The five-headed figure in the center represents the Directory of the French government; he is demanding "money, money, money" from the three diplomats at left who were in Paris representing the United States. The monster at the top right is operating a guillotine—a symbol of the violence and terror of the later stages of the French Revolution. *(The Granger Collection, New York)*

the recently rejected minister; John Marshall, a Virginia Federalist, later chief justice of the Supreme Court; and Elbridge Gerry, a Massachusetts Republican but a personal friend of the president—to negotiate with France. When the Americans arrived in Paris in 1797, three agents of the French foreign minister, Prince Talleyrand, demanded a loan for France and a bribe for French officials before any negotiations could begin. Pinckney responded succinctly and angrily: "No! No! Not a sixpence!"

When Adams heard of the incident, he sent a message to Congress denouncing the French insults and urging preparations for war. He then turned the report of the

The XYZ Affair

American commissioners over to Congress, after deleting the names of the three French agents and designating them only as "Messrs. X, Y, and Z." When the report was published, it created widespread popular outrage at France's actions and strong support for the Federalists' response. For nearly two years after the "XYZ Affair," as it became known, the United States found itself engaged in an undeclared war with France.

Adams persuaded Congress to cut off all trade with France and to authorize American vessels to capture French armed ships on the high seas. In 1798, Congress

The Quasi War

created a Department of the Navy and appropriated money for the construction of new warships. The navy soon won a number of duels with French vessels and captured a total of eighty-five ships, including armed merchantmen. The United States also began cooperating closely with the British and became virtually an ally of Britain in the war with France.

In the end, France chose to conciliate the United States before the conflict grew. Adams sent another commission to Paris in 1800, and the new French government (headed now by "first consul" Napoleon Bonaparte) agreed to a treaty with the United States that canceled the old agreement of 1778 and established new commercial arrangements. As a result, the "quasi war" came to a reasonably peaceful end.

Repression and Protest

The conflict with France helped the Federalists increase their majorities in Congress in 1798. Armed with this new strength, they began to con-

Alien and Sedition Acts

sider ways to silence the Republican opposition. The result was some of the most controversial legislation in American history: the Alien and Sedition Acts.

The Alien Act placed new obstacles in the way of foreigners who wished to become American citizens, and it strengthened the president's hand in dealing with aliens. The Sedition Act allowed the government to prosecute those who engaged in "sedition" against the government. In theory only libelous or treasonous activities were subject to prosecution; but since such activities were subject to widely varying definitions, the law made it possible for the federal government to stifle virtually any opposition. The Republicans interpreted the new laws as part of a Federalist campaign to destroy them and fought back.

President Adams signed the new laws but was cautious in implementing them. He did not deport any

CONGRESSIONAL BRAWLERS This cartoon lampoons a celebrated fight on the floor of the House of Representatives in 1798 between Matthew Lyon, a Republican from Vermont, and Roger Griswold, a Federalist from Connecticut. The conflict began when Griswold insulted Lyon by attacking his military record in the Revolutionary War. Lyon replied by spitting in Griswold's face. Two weeks later, Griswold attacked Lyon with his cane, and Lyon seized a pair of fire tongs and fought back. That later scene is depicted (and ridiculed) here. Other members of Congress are portrayed as enjoying the spectacle. On the wall is a picture entitled "Royal Sport," showing animals fighting. *(New York Public Library)*

aliens, and he prevented the government from launching a major crusade against the Republicans. But the legislation had a significant repressive effect nevertheless. The Alien Act helped discourage immigration and encouraged some foreigners already in the country to leave. And the administration made use of the Sedition Act to arrest and convict ten men, most of them Republican newspaper editors whose only crime had been to criticize the Federalists in government.

Republican leaders pinned their hopes for a reversal of the Alien and Sedition Acts on the state legislatures.

Virginia and Kentucky Resolutions

(The Supreme Court had not yet established its sole right to nullify congressional legislation, and there were many who believed that the states had that power too.) The Republicans laid out a theory for state action in two sets of resolutions in 1798–1799, one written (anonymously) by Jefferson and adopted by the Kentucky legislature and the other drafted by Madison and approved by the Virginia legislature. The Virginia and Kentucky Resolutions, as they were known, used the ideas of John Locke to argue that the federal government had been formed by a "compact" or contract among the states and possessed only certain delegated powers. Whenever it exercised any undelegated powers, its acts were "unauthoritative, void, and of no force." If the parties to the contract, the states, decided that the central government had exceeded those powers, the Kentucky Resolution claimed, they had the right to "nullify" the appropriate laws. (Such claims emerged again in the South in the decades before the Civil War.)

The Republicans did not win wide support for nullification; only Virginia and Kentucky declared the congressional statutes void. The Republicans did, however, succeed in elevating their dispute with the Federalists to the level of a national crisis. By the late 1790s, the entire nation was as deeply and bitterly divided politically as it would ever be in its history. State legislatures at times resembled battlegrounds. Even the United States Congress was plagued with violent disagreements. In one celebrated incident in the chamber of the House of Representatives, Matthew Lyon, a Republican from Vermont, responded to an insult from Roger Griswold, a Federalist from Connecticut, by spitting in Griswold's eye. Griswold attacked Lyon with his cane. Lyon fought back with a pair of fire tongs, and the two men ended up wrestling on the floor.

The "Revolution" of 1800

These bitter controversies shaped the 1800 presidential election. The presidential candidates were the same as four years earlier: Adams for the Federalists, Jefferson for the Republicans. But the campaign of 1800 was very different from the one preceding it. Indeed, it may have been the ugliest in American history. Adams and Jefferson themselves displayed reasonable dignity, but their supporters showed no such restraint. The Federalists accused Jefferson of being a dangerous radical and his followers of being wild men who, if they should come to power, would bring on a reign of terror comparable to that of the French Revolution. The Republicans portrayed Adams as a tyrant conspiring to become king, and they accused the Federalists of plotting to subvert human liberty and impose slavery on the people.

The Election of 1800

There was considerable personal invective as well. For example, it was during this campaign that the story of Jefferson's romantic involvement with a slave woman on his plantation was first widely aired.

The election was close, and the crucial contest was in New York. There, Aaron Burr had mobilized an organization of Revolutionary War veterans, the Tammany Society, to serve as a Republican political machine. And through Tammany's efforts, the Republicans carried the city by a large majority, and with it the state. Jefferson was, apparently, elected.

But an unexpected complication soon jeopardized the Republican victory. The Constitution called for each elector to "vote by ballot for two persons." The normal practice was for an elector to cast one vote for his party's presidential candidate and another for the vice presidential candidate. To avoid a tie between Jefferson and Aaron Burr (the Republican vice presidential candidate in 1800), the Republicans had intended for one elector to refrain from voting for Burr. But the plan went awry. When the votes were counted, Jefferson and Burr each had 73. No candidate had a majority. According to the Constitution the House of Representatives had to choose between the two leading candidates when no one had a majority; in this case, that meant deciding between Jefferson and Burr. Each state delegation would cast a single vote.

The new Congress, elected in 1800 with a Republican majority, was not to convene until after the inauguration of the president, so it was the Federalist Congress that had to decide the question. Some Federalists hoped to use the situation to salvage the election for their party; others wanted to strike a bargain with Burr and elect him. But after a long deadlock, several leading Federalists, most prominent among them Alexander Hamilton, concluded that Burr (whom many suspected of having engineered the deadlock in the first place) was too unreliable to trust with the presidency. On the thirty-sixth ballot, Jefferson was elected.

After the election of 1800, the only branch of the federal government left in Federalist hands was the judiciary. The Adams administration spent its last months in office taking steps to make the party's hold on the courts secure. By the Judiciary Act of 1801, passed by the lame duck Congress, the **The Judiciary Act of 1801** Federalists reduced the number of Supreme Court justiceships by one but greatly increased the number of federal judgeships as a whole. Adams quickly appointed Federalists to the newly created positions. Indeed, there were charges that he stayed up until midnight on his last day in office to finish signing the new judges' commissions. These officeholders became known as the "midnight appointments."

Even so, the Republicans viewed their victory, incorrectly, as almost complete. The nation, they believed, had been saved from tyranny. A new era could now begin, one in which the true principles on which America had been founded would once again govern the land. The exuberance with which the victors viewed the future—and the importance they attributed to the Federalists' defeat—was evident in the phrase Jefferson himself later used to describe his election. He called it the "Revolution of 1800." It remained to be seen how revolutionary it would really be.

CONCLUSION

The writing of the Constitution of 1787 was the single most important political event in the history of the United States, and a notable event in the political history of the modern world. In creating a "federal" system of dispersed and divided authority—authority divided among national and state governments, authority divided among an executive, a legislature, and a judiciary—the young nation sought to balance its need for an effective central government against its fear of concentrated and despotic power. The ability of the delegates to the Constitutional Convention to compromise again and again to produce the ultimate structure gave evidence of the deep yearning among them for a stable political system. The same willingness to compromise allowed the greatest challenge to the ideals of the new democracy—slavery—to survive intact.

The writing and ratifying of the Constitution settled some questions about the shape of the new nation. The first twelve years under the government created by the Constitution solved others. And yet by the year 1800, a basic disagreement about the future of the nation—a disagreement personified by the differences between committed nationalist Alexander Hamilton and the self-proclaimed champion of democracy Thomas Jefferson—remained unresolved and was creating bitter divisions and conflicts within the political world. The election of Thomas Jefferson to the presidency that year opened a new chapter in the nation's public history. It also brought to a close, at least temporarily, savage political conflicts that had seemed to threaten the nation's future.

INTERACTIVE LEARNING

The *Primary Source Investigator CD-ROM* offers the following materials related to this chapter:

- Interactive map: **U.S. Elections (M7).**
- Documents, images, and maps related to the creation of the Constitution and the early years of the New Republic. Highlights include the text of the Northwest Ordinance and several key documents from this era, including

the U.S. Constitution; several excerpts from *The Federalist Papers* arguing for ratification of the new Constitution; and early Quaker antislavery tracts.

Online Learning Center (www.mhhe.com/brinkley12)

For quizzes, Internet resources, references to additional books and films, and more, consult this book's Online Learning Center.

FOR FURTHER REFERENCE

Charles Beard, *An Economic Interpretation of the Constitution of the United States* (1913) is one of the seminal works of modern American historical inquiry, although its interpretation is no longer widely accepted. Gordon Wood, *The Creation of the American Republic* (1969) is the leading analysis of the intellectual path from the Declaration of Independence to the American Constitution. Jack Rakove, *Original Meanings: Politics and Ideas in the Making of the Constitution* (1996) connects the politics of the 1780s with the political ideas embedded in the Constitution. Stanley Elkins and Eric McKitrick, *The Age of Federalism* (1993) provides a detailed overview of political and economic development in the 1790s. Joyce Appleby, *Capitalism and a New Social Order: The Republican Vision of the 1790s* (1984) highlights liberal and capitalist impulses unleashed after the ratification of the Constitution. Drew McCoy, *The Elusive Republic: Political Economy in Jeffersonian America* (1980) is an elegant account of the politics of the era of the Constitution. Joseph Ellis is the author of several highly regarded books on the founders: *After the Revolution: Profiles of Early American Culture* (1979), which examines some of the framers of the new nation; *American Sphinx: The Character of Thomas Jefferson* (1997); *Founding Brothers: The Revolutionary Generation* (2000); and *Passionate Sage: The Character and Legacy of John Adams* (1993). David McCullough, *John Adams* (2001) is a vivid, sympathetic, and outstandingly popular biography. Ron Chernow, *Alexander Hamilton* (2004) is another excellent biography of an important founder, as is Edmund Morgan, *Benjamin Franklin* (2002).

THE BURNING OF WASHINGTON This dramatic engraving somewhat exaggerates the extent of the blazes in Washington when the British occupied the city in August 1814. But the invaders did set fire to the Capitol, the White House, and other public buildings in retaliation for the American burning of the Canadian capital at York. *(Bettmann/Corbis)*

SIGNIFICANT EVENTS

1769 ▶ James Watt patents steam engine

1778 ▶ Phillips Academy founded in Andover, Massachusetts

1779 ▶ Universalist Church founded

1781 ▶ Phillips Exeter Academy founded in New Hampshire

1782 ▶ Unitarian Church founded in Boston

1784 ▶ Judith Sargent Murray publishes essay on rights of women

▶ Methodist Church formally established

1789 ▶ Massachusetts public schools admit female students

1790 ▶ Samuel Slater builds textile mill, first modern factory in America, in Pawtucket, Rhode Island

1792 ▶ Toll road constructed from Philadelphia to Lancaster

1793 ▶ Eli Whitney invents cotton gin

1794–1796 ▶ Thomas Paine's *The Age of Reason* published

1800 ▶ United States capital moves to Washington, D.C.

▶ Gabriel Prosser's plans for slave rebellion foiled

1801 ▶ Second Great Awakening begins

▶ John Marshall appointed chief justice

1801–1805 ▶ Conflict with Tripoli

1802 ▶ Jefferson abolishes all internal federal taxes

▶ United States Military Academy founded at West Point

1803 ▶ Napoleonic Wars escalate in Europe

▶ Louisiana Territory purchased from French

▶ Supreme Court establishes power of judicial review in *Marbury* v. *Madison*

1804 ▶ Aaron Burr kills Alexander Hamilton in duel

▶ Thomas Jefferson reelected president

1804–1806 ▶ Lewis and Clark, and Zebulon Pike, explore Louisiana Territory

1805 ▶ British defeat French at Trafalgar

CHAPTER 7

The Jeffersonian Era

Thomas Jefferson and his followers assumed control of the national government in 1801 as the champions of a distinctive vision of America. They envisioned a

The Jeffersonian Vision

society of sturdy, independent farmers, happily free from the workshops, the industrial towns, and the city mobs of Europe. They favored a system of universal education that would introduce all Americans to the scientific rationalism of the Enlightenment. They promoted a cultural outlook that emphasized localism and republican simplicity. And they proposed a federal government of sharply limited power, with most authority remaining at the level of the states.

Almost nothing worked out as they planned, for during their years in power the young republic was developing in ways that made much of their vision obsolete. The American economy in the period of Republican ascendancy became steadily more diversified and complex. Growing cities, surging commerce, and expanding industrialism made the ideal of a simple, agrarian society impossible to maintain. The quest for universal education floundered, and the nation's institutions of learning remained largely the preserve of privileged elites. American cultural life, far from reflecting localism and simplicity, reflected a vigorous and ambitious nationalism

reminiscent of (and often encouraged by) the Federalists. And although American religion began, as the Jeffersonians had hoped, to confront and adjust to the spread of Enlightenment rationalism, the new skepticism did not survive unchallenged. A great wave of revivalism, beginning early in the century, ultimately almost submerged the new rational philosophy.

The Republicans did manage to translate some of their political ideals into reality. Jefferson dismantled much of the bureaucratic power structure that the Federalists had erected in the 1790s, and he helped ensure that in many respects the federal government would remain a relatively unimportant force in American life. Yet he also frequently encountered situations that required him to exercise strong national authority. On occasion, he used his power more forcefully and arbitrarily than his Federalist predecessors had used theirs.

The Republicans did not always like these nationalizing and modernizing trends, and on occasion they resisted them. For the most part, however, they had the sense to recognize what they could not change. In adjusting to the new realities, they began to become agents of the very transformation of American life they had once resisted.

1806 ▶ Burr charged with conspiracy
1806–1807 ▶ Napoleon issues Berlin and Milan decrees
1807 ▶ Fulton and Livingston launch the first steamboat
▶ Burr tried and acquitted for conspiracy
▶ *Chesapeake-Leopard* incident with Great Britain
▶ Embargo begins
1808 ▶ Economy plunges into depression
▶ Madison elected president
1809 ▶ Embargo Act repealed
▶ Non-Intercourse Act passed
▶ Tecumseh establishes tribal confederacy
1810 ▶ Macon's Bill No. 2 reopens trade with Britain and France
▶ United States annexes West Florida
1811 ▶ Harrison is victorious in Battle of Tippecanoe
1812 ▶ United States declares war on Great Britain (June 18)
▶ Madison reelected president

▶ Louisiana admitted to Union as a state
1813 ▶ British erect naval blockade
▶ American forces burn York (Toronto), Canadian capital
▶ Perry defeats British fleet at Put-In Bay on Lake Erie
▶ Harrison defeats British and Tecumseh
1814 ▶ Jackson, at Battle of Horseshoe Bend, slaughters Creek Indians
▶ British troops capture and burn Washington
▶ Francis Scott Key writes "The Star-Spangled Banner"
▶ Americans win Battle of Plattsburgh
▶ Hartford Convention meets
▶ Treaty of Ghent signed
1815 ▶ Jackson wins Battle of New Orleans
▶ Naval war fought with Algiers
1828 ▶ Webster's *American Dictionary of the English Language* published

THE RISE OF CULTURAL NATIONALISM

In many respects, American cultural life in the early nineteenth century seemed to reflect the Republican vision of the nation's future. Opportunities for education increased; the nation's literary and artistic life began to free itself from European influences; and American religion began to confront and adjust to the spread of Enlightenment rationalism. In other respects, however, the new culture was posing a serious challenge to Republican ideals.

Patterns of Education

Central to the Republican vision of America was the concept of a virtuous and enlightened citizenry. Jefferson himself called emphatically for a national "crusade against ignorance." Republicans believed, therefore, in the creation of a nationwide system of public schools to create the educated electorate they believed a republic required. All male citizens (the nation's prospective voters) should, they argued, receive free education. Although they were unable to realize that dream, their efforts sustained a vision that in later years would produce much more substantial results.

Importance of a Virtuous Citizenry

Some states endorsed the principle of public education for all in the early years of the republic, but none actually created a working system of free schools. A Massachusetts law of 1789 reaffirmed the colonial laws by which each town was obligated to support a school, but there was little enforcement. In Virginia, the state legislature ignored Jefferson's call for universal elementary education and for advanced education for the gifted. As late as 1815, not a single state had a comprehensive public school system.

Instead, schooling became primarily the responsibility of private institutions, most of which were open only to those who could afford to pay for them. In the South and in the mid-Atlantic states, religious groups ran most of the schools. In New England and elsewhere, private academies were usually more secular, many of them modeled on schools founded by the Phillips family at Andover, Massachusetts, in 1778, and at Exeter, New Hampshire, three years later. By 1815, there were thirty such private secondary schools in Massachusetts, thirty-seven in New York, and several dozen more scattered throughout the country. Many were frankly aristocratic in outlook, training their students to become members of the nation's elite. There were a few schools open to the poor, but not nearly enough to accommodate everyone, and the education they offered was usually clearly inferior to that provided at more exclusive schools.

Private Schooling

Private secondary schools such as those in New England, and even many public schools, accepted only male students. The Republicans, like most of their contemporaries, clung to a paternal vision of society, in which virtuous white men presided benevolently over a world in which all other groups—including women—were dependents. Yet the early nineteenth century did see some important advances in female education.

In the eighteenth century, women had received very little education of any kind, and the female illiteracy rate at the time of the Revolution was very high—at least 50 percent. At the same time, however, Americans had begun to place a new value on the contribution of the "republican mother" to the training of the new generation. That raised an important question: If mothers remained ignorant, how could they raise their children to be enlightened? Beginning as early as the 1770s and accelerating thereafter, such concerns led to the creation of a network of female academies throughout the nation (usually for the daughters of affluent families). In 1789, Massachusetts required that its public schools serve females as well as males. Other states, although not all, soon followed.

New Educational Opportunities for Women

MORAVIAN BOYS' SCHOOL, C. 1800 This drawing illustrates the interior of a boys' school in North Carolina, run by Moravian Germans. The Moravians were a German Protestant sect many of whose members emigrated to America in the 1750s. One large group founded Bethlehem, Pennsylvania, and another established settlements in western North Carolina. Their belief in social improvement contributed to their interest in education and also to the creation of several short-lived Utopian communities. *(Courtesy of Moravian Archives, Winston-Salem, North Carolina)*

But there were strict limits to this new belief in education for women. Most men, at least, assumed that female education should serve only to make women better wives and mothers. Women therefore had no need for advanced or professional training; there was no reason for colleges and universities to make space for female students. Some women, however, aspired to more. In 1784, Judith Sargent Murray published an essay defending women's rights to education, a defense set in terms very different from those used by most men. Men and women were equal in intellect and potential, Murray argued. Women, therefore, should have precisely the same educational opportunities as men. What was more, they should have opportunities to earn their own living, to establish a role for themselves in society apart from their husbands and families. Murray's ideas became an inspiration to later generations of women, but during most of her own lifetime (1751–1820) they attracted relatively little support.

Reformers who believed in the power of education to reform and redeem ignorant and "backward" people spurred a growing interest in Indian education. Because Jefferson and his followers liked to think of Native Americans as "noble savages" (uncivilized, but unlike their view of African Americans, not necessarily innately inferior), they hoped that schooling the Indians in white culture would tame and "uplift" the tribes. Although white governments did little to promote Indian education, missionaries and mission schools proliferated among the tribes.

Indian Education

Almost no white people in the early nineteenth century believed that there was a need to educate African Americans, almost all of whom were still slaves. In a few northern states, some free black children attended segregated schools. In the South, slaveowners generally tried to prevent their black workers from learning to read or write, fearful that knowledge would make them unhappy with their condition. Some African Americans managed to acquire some education despite these obstacles, by teaching themselves and their own children. But the numbers of literate slaves remained very small.

Higher education was even less widely available than education at lower levels, despite republican hopes for a wide dispersion of advanced knowledge. (Jefferson himself founded the University of Virginia to promote that ideal.) The number of colleges and universities in America grew from nine at the start of the Revolution to twenty-two by 1800 and continued to increase thereafter. None of the new schools, however, was truly public. Even those established by state legislatures (in Georgia, North Carolina, Vermont, Ohio, and South Carolina, for example) relied on private contributions and on tuition fees. Scarcely more than one white man in a thousand (and no women, blacks, or Indians at all) had access to any college education, and those few who did attend universities were almost without exception members of prosperous, propertied families.

Higher Education

The education that the colleges provided was, moreover, exceedingly limited—narrow training in the classics and a few other areas and intensive work in theology. Indeed, the clergy was the only profession for which college training was generally a prerequisite. A few institutions attempted to provide their students advanced training in other fields. The College of William and Mary in Virginia, the University of Pennsylvania, and Columbia College in New York all created law schools before 1800, but most lawyers continued to train for their profession simply by apprenticing themselves to practicing attorneys.

Medicine and Science

The University of Pennsylvania created the first American medical school in the eighteenth century. In the early nineteenth century, however, most doctors studied medicine by working with an established practitioner. Some American physicians believed in applying new scientific methods to medicine and struggled against age-old prejudices and superstitions. Efforts to teach anatomy, for example, encountered strong public hostility because of the dissection of cadavers that the study required. Municipal authorities had virtually no understanding of medical science and almost no idea of what to do in the face of the severe epidemics that so often swept their populations; only slowly did they respond to the warnings of Benjamin Rush, a pioneering Philadelphia physician, and others that lack of adequate sanitation programs was to blame for disease.

Individual patients often had more to fear from their doctors than from their illnesses. Even the leading advocates of scientific medicine often embraced useless and dangerous treatments. Benjamin Rush, for example, was an advocate of the new and supposedly scientific techniques of bleeding and purging, and many of his patients died. George Washington's death in 1799 was probably less a result of the minor throat infection that had afflicted him than of his physicians' efforts to cure him by bleeding and purging.

Benjamin Rush

The medical profession also used its newfound commitment to the "scientific" method to justify expanding its own control to kinds of care that had traditionally been outside its domain. Most childbirths, for example, had been attended by female midwives. In the early nineteenth century, physicians began to handle deliveries themselves and to demand restrictions on the role of midwives. Among the results of that change was a narrowing of opportunities for women (midwifery was an important female occupation) and a restriction of access to childbirth care for poor mothers (who could have afforded midwives, but who could not pay the higher physicians' fees).

Decline of Midwifery

Education and professional training in the early republic—in medicine and in many other fields—thus fell

THE PENNSYLVANIA HOSPITAL As the ideas of the Enlightenment spread through American culture in the eighteenth and nineteenth centuries, encouraging the belief that every individual was a divine being and could be redeemed from even the most miserable condition, hospitals and asylums—such as this institution in Pennsylvania—began to emerge to provide settings for the redemption of the poor, the ill, and the deviant. *(Library Company of Philadelphia)*

far short of the Jeffersonian vision. Indeed, efforts to promote education and increase professionalism often had the effect of strengthening existing elites rather than eroding them. Nevertheless, the ideal of equal educational opportunity survived, and in later decades it would become a vital force behind universal public education.

Cultural Aspirations in the New Nation

Many Americans in the Jeffersonian era may have repudiated the Federalist belief in political and economic centralization, but most embraced another form of nationalism with great fervor. Having won political independence from Europe, they aspired now to a form of cultural independence. In the process, they dreamed of an American literary and artistic life that would rival the greatest achievements of Europe. As a popular "Poem on the Rising Glory of America" had predicted as early as 1772, Americans believed that their "happy land" was destined to become the "seat of empire" and the "final stage" of civilization, with "glorious works of high invention and of wond'rous art." The United States, another eighteenth-century writer had proclaimed, would serve as "the last and greatest theatre for the improvement of mankind."

Such nationalism found expression, among other places, in early American schoolbooks. The Massachusetts geographer Jedidiah Morse, author of *Geography Made Easy* (1784), said the country must have its own textbooks to prevent the aristocratic ideas of England from infecting the people. The Connecticut schoolmaster and lawyer Noah Webster argued similarly that the American students should be educated as patriots, their minds filled with nationalistic, American thoughts.

Establishment of a National Culture

To encourage a distinctive American culture and help unify the new nation, Webster insisted on a simplified and Americanized system of spelling—"honor" instead of "honour," for example. His *American Spelling Book,* first published in 1783 and commonly known as the "blue-backed speller," eventually sold over 100 million copies, to become the best-selling book (except for the Bible) in the history of American publishing. In addition, his school dictionary, issued in 1806, was republished in many editions and was eventually enlarged to become (in 1828) *An American Dictionary of the English Language.* His speller and his dictionary established a national standard of words and usages. Although Webster's Federalist political views fell into disfavor in the early nineteenth century, his cultural nationalism remained popular and influential.

Noah Webster

Those Americans who aspired to create a more elevated national literary life faced a number of obstacles. There was, to be sure, a large potential audience for a national literature—a substantial reading public, created in part by the wide circulation of newspapers and political pamphlets during the Revolution. But there were few opportunities for would-be American authors to get their work before the public. Printers preferred to publish popular works by English writers (for which they had to pay no royalties); magazine publishers filled their pages largely with items clipped from British periodicals. Only those American writers willing to pay the cost and bear the risk of publishing their own works could compete for public attention.

Even so, a growing number of American authors struggled to create a strong native literature so that, as the poet Joel Barlow wrote, "true ideas of glory may be implanted in the minds of men here, to take the place of the false and destructive ones that have degraded the species in other countries." Barlow himself, one of a group of Connecticut writers known as the "Hartford Wits," published an epic poem, *The Columbiad,* in 1807, in an effort to convey the special character of American civilization. The acclaim it received helped to encourage other native writers.

Among the most ambitious was the Philadelphian Charles Brockden Brown. Like many Americans, he was attracted to the relatively new literary form of the novel, which had become popular in England in the late eighteenth century and had been successfully imported to America. But Brown sought to do more than simply imitate the English forms; he tried to use his novels to give voice to distinctively American themes, to convey the "soaring passions and intellectual energy" of the new nation. His obsession with originality led him to produce a body of work characterized by a fascination with horror and deviant behavior. Perhaps as a result, his novels failed to develop a large popular following.

Much more successful was Washington Irving, a resident of New York State who won wide acclaim for his satirical histories of early American life and his powerful fables of society in the New World. His popular folk tales, recounting the adventures of such American rustics as Ichabod Crane and Rip Van Winkle, made him the widely acknowledged leader of American literary life in his era and one of the few writers of that time whose works would continue to be read by later generations.

Washington Irving

Perhaps the most influential works by American authors in the early republic were not poems, novels, or stories, but works of history that glorified the nation's past. Mercy Otis Warren, who had been an influential playwright and agitator during the 1770s, continued her literary efforts with a three-volume *History of the Revolution,* published in 1805 and emphasizing the heroism of the American struggle. Mason Weems, an Anglican clergyman, published a eulogistic *Life of Washington* in 1806, which became one of the best-selling books of the era. Weems had little interest in historical accuracy. He portrayed the aristocratic former president as a homespun man possessing simple republican virtues. (He also invented, among other things, the famous story of Washington and the cherry tree.) History, like literature, was serving as a vehicle for instilling a sense of nationalism in the American people.

Religious Skepticism

The American Revolution weakened traditional forms of religious practice by detaching churches from government and by elevating ideas of individual liberty and reason that challenged many ecclesiastical traditions. By the 1790s, only a small proportion of white Americans (perhaps as few as 10 percent) were members of formal churches, and ministers were complaining often about the "decay of vital piety." Religious traditionalists were particularly alarmed about the emergence of new, "rational" theologies that reflected modern, scientific attitudes and de-emphasized the role of God in the world.

Some Americans, including Jefferson and Franklin, embraced "deism," which had originated among Enlightenment philosophers in France. Deists accepted the existence of God, but considered Him a remote being who, after having created the universe, had withdrawn from direct involvement with the human race and its sins. Books and articles attacking religious "superstitions" attracted wide readerships and provoked much discussion, among them Thomas Paine's *The Age of Reason,* published in parts between 1794 and 1796. Paine once declared that Christianity was the "strangest religion ever set up," for "it committed a murder upon Jesus in order to redeem mankind from the sin of eating an apple."

Deism

Religious skepticism also produced the philosophies of "universalism" and "unitarianism," which emerged at first as dissenting views within the New England Congregational Church. Disciples of these new ideas rejected the Calvinist belief in predestination, arguing that salvation was available to all. They rejected, too, the idea of the Trinity. Jesus was only a great religious teacher, they claimed, not the Son of God. So wide was the gulf between these dissenters and the Congregationalist establishment that it finally became a permanent schism. James Murray (who later married Judith Sargent Murray) founded the Universalist Church as a separate denomination in Gloucester, Massachusetts, in 1779; the Unitarian Church was established in Boston three years later.

Some Americans believed that the spread of rationalism marked the end of traditional, evangelistic religion in the new nation. But quite the contrary was true. In fact, most Americans continued to hold strong religious beliefs. What had declined was their commitment to organized churches and denominations, which many considered too formal and traditional for their own zealous religious faith. Deism, Universalism, Unitarianism, and other "rational" religions seemed more powerful than they actually were because for a time traditional evangelicals were confused and disorganized. But beginning in 1801, traditional religion staged a dramatic comeback in the form of a wave of revivalism known as the Second Great Awakening.

The Second Great Awakening

The origins of the Second Awakening lay in the efforts of conservative theologians of the 1790s to fight the spread of religious rationalism, and in the efforts of church establishments to revitalize their organizations.

Leaders of several different denominations participated in the evangelizing efforts that drove the revival. Presbyterians tried to arouse the faithful on the western fringe of white settlement, and conservatives in the church became increasingly militant in response to so-called New Light dissenters (people who had altered their religious views to make them more compatible with the world of scientific rationalism). Methodism, which John Wesley had founded in England, spread to America in the 1770s and became a formal denomination in 1784 under the leadership of Francis Asbury. Authoritarian and hierarchical in structure, the Methodist Church sent itinerant preachers throughout the nation to win recruits; it soon became the fastest-growing denomination in America. Almost as successful were the Baptists, who were themselves relatively new to America; they found an especially fervent following in the South.

By 1800, the revivalist energies of all these denominations were combining to create the greatest surge of evangelical fervor since the first Great Awakening sixty years before. Beginning among Presbyterians in several eastern colleges (most notably at Yale, under the leadership of President Timothy Dwight), the new awakening soon spread rapidly throughout the country, reaching its greatest heights in the western regions. In only a few years, a large proportion of the American people were mobilized by the movement, and membership in those churches embracing the revival—most prominently the Methodists, the Baptists, and the Presbyterians—was mushrooming. At Cane Ridge, Kentucky, in the summer of 1801, a group of evangelical ministers presided over the nation's first "camp meeting"—an extraordinary revival that lasted several days and impressed all who saw it with its size (some estimated that 25,000 people attended) and its fervor. Such events became common in subsequent years, as the Methodists in particular came to rely on them as a way to "harvest" new members. The Methodist circuit-riding preacher Peter Cartwright won national fame as he traveled from region to region exhorting his listeners to embrace the church. Even Cartwright, however, was often unprepared for the results of his efforts—a religious frenzy that at times produced convulsions, fits, rolling in the dirt, and the twitching "holy jerks."

Cane Ridge

The message of the Second Great Awakening was not entirely consistent, but its basic thrust was clear. Individuals must readmit God and Christ into their daily lives, must embrace a fervent, active piety, and must reject the skeptical rationalism that threatened traditional beliefs. Even so, the wave of revivalism did not serve to restore the religious ideas of the past. Few of the revivalist denominations any longer accepted the idea of predestination; and the belief that a person could affect his or her own destiny, rather than encouraging irreligion as many had feared, added intensity to the individual's search for salvation. The Awakening, in short, combined a more active piety with a belief in God as an active force in the world whose grace could be attained through faith and good works.

The Second Awakening also accelerated the growth of different sects and denominations and helped create a broad popular acceptance of the idea that men and women could belong to different Protestant churches and still be committed to essentially the same Christian faith. Finally, the new evangelicalism—by spreading religious fervor into virtually every area of the nation, including remote regions where no formal church had ever existed—provided a vehicle for establishing a sense of order and social stability in communities still searching for an identity.

Message of the Great Awakening

One of the most striking features of the Second Great Awakening was the preponderance of women (and particularly young women) within it. In some areas, church membership became overwhelmingly female as a result. One reason for this was that women were more numerous in certain regions than men. Adventurous young men often struck out on their own and moved west; women, for the most part, had no such options. Their marriage prospects thus diminished and their futures plagued with uncertainty, some women discovered in religion a foundation on which to build their lives. But even where there was no shortage of men, women flocked to the revivals in enormous numbers, which suggests that they were responding to their changing economic roles as well. The movement of industrial work out of the home (where women had often contributed to the family economy through spinning and weaving) and into the factory—a process making rapid strides in the early nineteenth century (see pp. 188–190)—robbed older women, in particular, of one of their most important social roles. Religious enthusiasm helped compensate for the losses and adjustments these transitions produced; it also provided access to a new range of activities associated with the churches—charitable societies ministering to orphans and the poor, missionary organizations, and others—in which women came to play important roles.

Although revivalism was most widespread within white society, it penetrated other cultures as well. In some areas of the country, revivals were open to people of all races, and many blacks not only attended but eagerly embraced the new religious fervor. Out of these revivals, in fact, emerged a substantial group of black preachers, who became important figures within the slave community. Some of them translated the apparently egalitarian religious message of the Second Awakening—that salvation was available to all—into a similarly egalitarian message for blacks in the present world. For example, out of black revival

African Americans and the Revivals

METHODIST CAMP MEETING, 1837 Camp (or revival) meetings were popular among some evangelical Christians in America as early as 1800. By the 1820s, there were approximately 1,000 meetings a year, most of them in the South and the West. After one such meeting in 1806, a participant wrote: "Will I ever see anything more like the day of Judgement on this side of eternity—to see the people running, yes, running from every direction to the stand, weeping, shouting, and shouting for joy ... O! Glorious day they went home singing shouting." This lithograph, dated 1837, suggests the degree to which women predominated at many revivals. *(The Granger Collection, New York)*

meetings in Virginia arose an elaborate plan in 1800 (devised by Gabriel Prosser, the brother of a black preacher) for a slave rebellion and attack on Richmond. The plan was discovered and the rebellion forestalled by whites, but revivalism continued to stir racial unrest in the South.

The spirit of revivalism was also particularly strong in these years among Native Americans, although very different in its origins and expression from revivalism in white or black society. It drew heavily from earlier tribal experiences. In the 1760s, the Delaware prophet Neolin had sparked a widespread revival in the Old Northwest with a message combining Christian and Indian imagery and bringing to Native American religion a vision of a personal God, intimately involved in the affairs of man. Neolin had also called for Indians to rise up in defense of their lands and had denounced the growth of trade and other relationships with white civilization. His vehement statements had helped stimulate the Indian military efforts of 1763 and beyond.

The dislocations and military defeats Indians suffered

Indians and the Second Great Awakening

in the aftermath of the American Revolution created a sense of crisis among many of the eastern tribes in particular; as a result, the 1790s and early 1800s became another era of Indian religious fervor and

prophecy. Presbyterian and Baptist missionaries were active among the southern tribes and sparked a great wave of conversions. But the most important revivalism came from the efforts of another great prophet: Handsome Lake, a Seneca whose seemingly miraculous "rebirth" after years of alcoholism helped give him a special stature within his tribe. Handsome Lake, like Neolin before him, called for a revival of traditional Indian ways. (He claimed to have met Jesus, who instructed him to "tell your people they will become lost when they follow the ways of the white man.") Handsome Lake's message spread through the scattered Iroquois communities that had survived the military and political setbacks of previous decades and inspired many Indians to give up whiskey, gambling, and other destructive customs derived from white society.

But the revival did not, in fact, lead to a true restoration of traditional Iroquois culture. Instead, Handsome Lake encouraged Christian missionaries to become active within the tribes, and he urged Iroquois men to abandon their roles as hunters (partly because so much of their hunting land had been seized by whites) and become sedentary farmers instead. Iroquois women, who had traditionally done the farming, were to move into more domestic roles. When some women resisted the change, Handsome Lake denounced them as witches.

The Second Great Awakening also had important

Freethinkers

effects on those Americans who did not accept its teachings. The rational "freethinkers," whose skeptical philosophies had done so much to produce the revivals, were in many ways victims of the new religious fervor. They did not disappear after 1800, but their influence rapidly declined, and for many years they remained a small and defensive minority within American Christianity. Instead, the dominant religious characteristic of the new nation became a fervent evangelicalism, which would survive into the mid-nineteenth century and beyond.

STIRRINGS OF INDUSTRIALISM

Despite the hopes of Jefferson and his followers that the United States would remain a simple agrarian republic, the nation took its first, tentative steps in these years toward its transformation into exactly the sort of urban, industrial society the early Republicans had warned against. Americans of the Jeffersonian era were welcoming a series of technological advances that would ultimately help ensure that the United States too would be transformed.

Technology in America

Americans imported some of these technological advances from England. (See "America in the World," pp. 190–191.) The British government attempted to protect the nation's manufacturing preeminence by preventing the export of textile machinery or the emigration of skilled mechanics. Despite such efforts, immigrants arrived in the United States with advanced knowledge of English technology, eager to introduce the new machines to America. Samuel Slater, for example, used the knowledge he had acquired before leaving England to build a spinning mill for the Quaker merchant Moses Brown in Pawtucket, Rhode Island, in 1790. It was the first modern factory in America.

America in the early nineteenth century also produced several important inventors of its own. Among them was Oliver Evans, of Delaware, who devised a number of ingenious new machines: an automated flour mill, a card-making machine, and others. He made several important improvements in the steam engine, and in 1795 he published America's first textbook of mechanical engineering: *The Young Mill-Wright's and Miller's Guide*. His own flour mill, which began operations in 1787, required only two men to operate: one of them emptying a bag of wheat into the machinery, another putting the lid on the barrels of flour and rolling them away.

THE COTTON GIN Eli Whitney's cotton gin revolutionized the cotton economy of the South by making the processing of short-staple cotton simple and economical. These 1794 drawings are part of Whitney's application for a federal patent on his device. *(National Archives)*

Even more influential for the future of the nation were the inventions of the Massachusetts-born, Yale-educated Eli Whitney, who revolutionized both cotton production and weapons manufacturing. The growth of the textile industry in England had created an enormous demand for cotton, a demand that planters in the American South were finding impossible to meet. Their greatest obstacle was separating the seeds from cotton fiber—a difficult and time-consuming process that was essential before cotton could be sold. Long-staple, or Sea Island, cotton, with its smooth black seeds and long fibers, was easy to clean, but it grew successfully only along the Atlantic coast or on the offshore islands of Georgia and South Carolina. There was not nearly enough of it to satisfy the demand. Short-staple cotton, by contrast, could grow inland through vast areas of the South. But its sticky green seeds were extremely difficult to remove. A skilled worker could clean no more than a few pounds a day by hand. Then, in 1793, Whitney, who was working at the time as a tutor on the Georgia plantation of General Nathanael Greene's widow, invented a machine that performed the arduous task quickly

Eli Whitney's Cotton Gin

and efficiently. It was dubbed the cotton gin ("gin" was an abbreviation for "engine"), and it transformed the life of the South.

Mechanically, the gin was very simple. A toothed roller caught the fibers of the cotton boll and pulled them between the wires of a grating. The grating caught the seeds while a revolving brush removed the lint from the roller's teeth. With the device, a single operator could clean as much cotton in a few hours as a group of workers had once needed a whole day to do. The results were profound. Soon cotton growing spread into the upland South, and within a decade the total crop increased eightfold. African-American slavery, which with the decline of tobacco production some had considered a dwindling institution, regained its importance, expanded, and became more firmly fixed upon the South.

The cotton gin not only changed the economy of the

The Cotton Gin's Impact on the North

South, it also helped transform the North. The large supply of domestically produced fiber was a strong incentive to entrepreneurs in New England and elsewhere to develop an American textile industry. Few

northern states could hope to thrive on the basis of agriculture alone; by learning to turn cotton into yarn and thread, they could become industrially prosperous instead. The manufacturing preeminence of the North, which emerged with the development of the textile industry in the 1820s and 1830s, helped drive a wedge between the nation's two most populous regions—one becoming increasingly industrial, the other more firmly wedded to agriculture—and ultimately contributed to the coming of the Civil War. It also helped ensure the eventual Union victory.

Whitney also made a major contribution to the development of modern warfare and in the process made a contribution to other industrial techniques. During the two years of undeclared war with France (1798 and 1799), Americans were deeply troubled by their lack of sufficient armaments for the expected hostilities. Production of muskets—each carefully handcrafted by a skilled gunsmith—was discouragingly slow. Whitney devised a machine to make each part of a gun according to an exact pattern. Tasks could thus be divided among several workers, and one laborer could assemble a weapon out of parts made by several others. Before long,

PAWTUCKET BRIDGE AND FALLS One reason for the growth of the textile industry in New England in the early nineteenth century was that there were many sources of water power in the region to run the machinery in the factories. That was certainly the case with Slater's Mill, one of the first American textile factories, which was located in Pawtucket, Rhode Island, alongside a powerful waterfall, demonstrating the critical importance of water power to early American industry. This view was painted by an anonymous artist in the 1810s. *(Rhode Island Historical Society)*

The Global Industrial Revolution

While Americans were engaged in a revolution to win their independence, they were also taking the first steps toward an at least equally important revolution—one that was already in progress in England and Europe. It was the emergence of modern industrialism. Historians differ over precisely when the industrial revolution began, but it is clear that by the end of the eighteenth century it was well underway in many parts of the world. By the end of the nineteenth century, the global process of industrialization had transformed the societies of Britain, most of continental Europe, Japan, and the United States. Its social and economic consequences were complex and profound, and continue today to shape the nature of global society.

For Americans, the industrial revolution was largely a product of rapid changes in Great Britain, the nation with which they had the closest relations. Britain was the first nation to develop significant industrial capacity. The factory system took root in England in the late eighteenth century, revolutionizing the manufacture of cotton thread and cloth. One invention followed another in quick succession. Improvements in weaving drove improvements in spinning, and these changes created a demand for new devices for carding (combing and straightening the fibers for the spinner). Water, wind, and animal power continued to be important in the textile industry; but

more important was the emergence of steam power—which began to proliferate after the appearance of James Watt's advanced steam engine (patented in 1769). Cumbersome and inefficient by modern standards, Watt's engine was nevertheless a major improvement over the earlier "atmospheric" engine of Thomas Newcomen. England's textile industry quickly became the most profitable in the world and it helped encourage comparable advances in other fields of manufacturing as well. Despite the efforts of the British government to prevent the export of English industrial technology, knowledge of the new machines reached other nations quickly, usually through the emigration of people who had learned the technology in British factories.

America benefited the most from English technology, because it received more immigrants from Great Britain than from any other country. But English technology spread quickly to the nations of continental Europe as well. Belgium was the first, developing a significant coal, iron, and armaments industry in the early nineteenth century. France—profiting from the immigration of approximately fifteen thousand British workers with advanced technological skills—had created a substantial industrial capacity in textiles and metals by the end of the 1820s, which in turn contributed to a great boom in railroad construction later in the century. German industrialization progressed rapidly

after 1840, beginning with coal and iron production and then, in the 1850s, moving into large-scale railroad construction. By the late nineteenth century, Germany had created some of the world's largest industrial corporations. In Japan, the sudden intrusion of American and European traders helped cause the so-called Meiji reforms of the 1880s, and 1890s, which launched a period of rapid industrialization there as well.

Industrialization changed not just the world's economies, but also its societies. First in England, and then in Europe, America, and Japan, social systems underwent wrenching changes. Hundreds of thousands of men and women moved from rural areas into cities to work in factories, where they experienced both the benefits and the costs of industrialization. The standard of living of the new working class, when objectively quantified, was usually significantly higher than that of the rural poor. Many of those who moved from farm to factory experienced some improvement in nutrition and other material circumstances, and even in their health. But there were psychological costs to being suddenly uprooted from one way of life and thrust into another, fundamentally different. Those costs could outweigh the material gains. There was little in most workers' prior experience to prepare them for the nature of industrial labor. It was disciplined, routinized work with a fixed

manufacturers of sewing machines, clocks, and many other complicated products were using the same system.

The new technological advances were relatively isolated phenomena during the early years of the nineteenth century. Not until at least the 1840s did the nation begin to develop a true manufacturing economy. But the inventions of this period were crucial in making the eventual transformation possible.

Transportation Innovations

One of the prerequisites for industrialization is an efficient system for transporting raw materials to factories and finished goods to markets. The United States had no such system in the early years of the republic. But work

was under way that would ultimately remove the transportation obstacle.

There were several ways to solve the problem of the small American market. One was to look for customers overseas, and American merchants continued their efforts to do that. Among the first acts of the new Congress when it met in 1789 were two tariff bills giving preference to American ships in American ports, helping to stimulate an expansion of domestic shipping. More important—indeed the principal reason for the growth of American trade in this period—was the outbreak of war in Europe in the 1790s, allowing Yankee merchant vessels to take over most of the carrying trade between Europe and the Western Hemisphere. As early as 1793, the young republic had a merchant marine and

and rigid schedule, a sharp contrast to the varying, seasonal work pattern of the rural economy. Nor were many factory workers prepared for life in the new industrial towns and expanding cities. Industrial workers experienced, too, a fundamental change in their relationship with their employers. Unlike rural landlords and local aristocrats, factory owners and managers—the new class of industrial capitalists, many of them accumulating unprecedented wealth—were usually remote and inaccessible figures. They dealt with their workers impersonally and the result was a growing schism between the two classes—each lacking access to or understanding of the other. Working men and women throughout the globe began thinking of themselves as a distinct class, with common goals and interests. And their efforts simultaneously to adjust to their new way of life and to resist its most damaging aspects sometimes created great social turbulence. Battles between workers and employers became a characteristic feature of industrial life throughout the world.

Life in industrial nations changed at every level. Populations in industrial countries grew rapidly, and people began to live longer. At the same time, industrial cities began to produce great increases in pollution, crime, and—until modern sanitation systems emerged—infectious disease. Around the industrial world, middle classes

THE ENGLISH CANAL AGE Industrialization in England contributed, as it did in America, to the building of new transportation facilities to serve the growing commercial markets of the new economy. Among the most popular such facilities were canals, among them the Regent's Canal in London, pictured here in the 1820s. *(Guildhall Library, Corporation of London/The Bridgeman Art Library)*

expanded and came, in varying degrees, to dominate the economy (although not always the culture or the politics) of their nations.

Not since the agrarian revolution thousands of years earlier, when many humans had turned from hunting to farming for sustenance, had there been an economic change of a magnitude comparable to the industrial revolution. Centuries of traditions, of social patterns, and of cultural and religious assumptions were challenged and often shattered. The tentative stirrings of industrial activity in the United States in the early nineteenth century, therefore, were part of a vast movement that over the course of the next century was to transform much of the globe.

---

a foreign trade larger than those of any country except England. In proportion to its population, the United States had more ships and international commerce than any country in the world. And the shipping business was growing fast. Between 1789 and 1810, the total tonnage of American vessels engaged in overseas traffic rose from less than 125,000 to nearly 1 million. American ships had carried only 30 percent of the country's exports in 1789; they were carrying over 90 percent in 1810. The figures for imports increased even more dramatically, from 17.5 percent to 90 percent in the same period.

Another solution to the problem of limited markets was to develop new markets at home, by improving transportation between the states and into the interior of the continent. Progress was slower here than in international shipping, but some improvements were occurring nevertheless. In river transportation, a new era began with the development of the steamboat. A number of inventors began experimenting with steam-powered craft in the late eighteenth century; John Fitch exhibited a forty-five-foot vessel with paddles operated by steam to some of the delegates at the Constitutional Convention in 1787. But the real breakthrough was Oliver Evans's development of a high-pressure engine, lighter and more efficient than James Watt's, which made steam more feasible for powering boats (and, eventually, the locomotive) as well as mill machinery.

Rapid Growth of American Shipping

A SCENE OF THE ROAD The watercolorist George Tattersall painted this image of a stagecoach negotiating the rough roads and bridges that were beginning to link together the disparate regions of early nineteenth-century America. *(Museum of Fine Arts, Boston, Gift of Maxim Karolik, 56.400.11. Photograph © 2007 Museum of Fine Arts, Boston)*

The inventor Robert Fulton and the promoter Robert R. Livingston were principally responsible for perfecting the steamboat and bringing it to the attention of the nation. Their *Clermont,* equipped with paddle wheels and an English-built engine, sailed up the Hudson in the summer of 1807, demonstrating the practicability of steam navigation (even though it took the ship thirty hours to go 150 miles). In 1811, a partner of Livingston's, Nicholas J. Roosevelt (a remote ancestor of Theodore Roosevelt), introduced the steamboat to the West by sending the *New Orleans* from Pittsburgh down the Ohio and Mississippi. The next year, this vessel began a profitable career of service between New Orleans and Natchez.

Robert Fulton's Steamboat

Meanwhile, what was to become known as the "turnpike era" had begun. In 1792, a corporation constructed a toll road running the sixty miles from Philadelphia to Lancaster, with a hard-packed surface of crushed rock. This venture proved so successful that several other companies laid out similar turnpikes (so named from the

The Turnpike Era

kind of tollgate frequently used) from other cities to neighboring towns. Since the turnpikes had to produce profits for the companies that built them, construction costs had to be low enough and the prospective traffic heavy enough to ensure an early and ample return. As a result these roads, radiating from eastern cities, ran comparatively short distances and through thickly settled areas. No private operators were willing to build similar highways over the mountains and into the less populated interior. State governments and the federal government eventually had to finance them.

The Rising Cities

Despite all the changes and all the advances, America in the early nineteenth century remained an overwhelmingly rural and agrarian nation. Only 3 percent of the non-Indian population lived in towns of more than 8,000 at the time of the second census in 1800. Ten percent lived west of the Appalachian Mountains, far from what urban centers there were. Much of the country remained a wilderness. Even the nation's largest cities could not

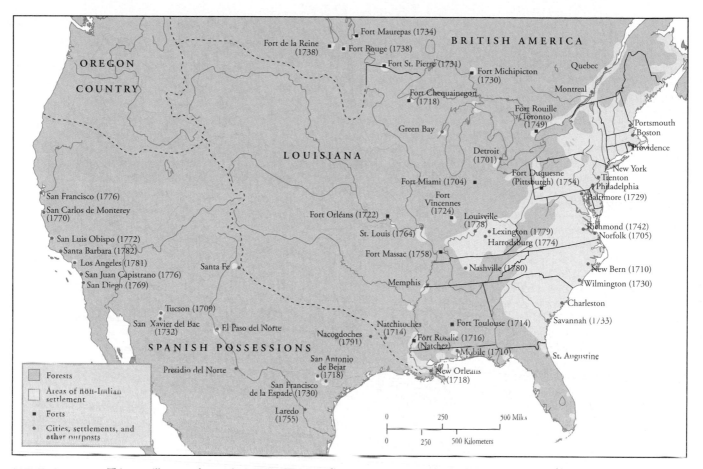

AMERICA IN 1800 This map illustrates how substantially the non-Indian settlement of British North America (much of it by 1800 the United States) had expanded since 1700. On p. 66, a similar map shows a tiny fringe of settlement along the Atlantic seaboard. Note the new areas of settlement here: west of the orginal thirteen colonies—including, in Kentucky, an area that reaches almost to the Mississippi River. Significant settlements are also now visible along the Gulf Coast, especially in the territory around New Orleans. Scattered non-Indian settlements are visible in the Southwest and along the coast of California, as well as in southern Canada (where the settlements were largely forts). ◆ *How does this map help explain the spread of settlement south from Pittsburgh into western Virginia and Kentucky?*

OLC For an interactive version of this map go to www.mhhe.com/brinkley12ch7maps

Black Jacks

begin to compare, either in size or in cultural sophistication, with such European capitals as London and Paris.

Yet here too there were signs of change. The leading American cities might not yet have become world capitals, but they were large and complex enough to rival the important secondary cities of Europe. Philadelphia, with 70,000 residents, and New York, with 60,000, were becoming major centers of commerce and learning. They were developing a distinctively urban culture. So too were the next largest cities of the new nation: Baltimore (26,000 in 1800), Boston (24,000), and Charleston (20,000).

People living in towns and cities lived differently from

Urban Life

the vast majority of Americans who continued to work as farmers. Among other things, urban life produced affluence, and affluent people sought amenities that would not have entered the imaginings of all but the wealthiest farmers. They sought increasing elegance and refinement in their homes, their grounds, and their dress.

They also looked for diversions—music, theater, dancing, and, for many people, one of the most popular entertainments of all, horse racing. (See "Patterns of Popular Culture," pp. 194–195.)

Much remained to be done before this small and still half-formed nation would become a complex modern society. It was still possible in the early nineteenth century to believe that those changes might not ever occur. But forces were already at work that, in time, would lastingly transform the United States. And Thomas Jefferson, for all his commitment to the agrarian ideal, found himself obliged as president to confront and accommodate them.

JEFFERSON THE PRESIDENT

Privately, Thomas Jefferson may well have considered his victory over John Adams in 1800 to be what he later termed it: a revolution "as real . . . as that of 1776." Publicly, however, he was restrained and conciliatory as

Horse Racing

There were few respites from the daily struggle for survival for the first European settlers in North America. Men and women attended church and celebrated major religious holidays, but there was little in most of their lives that twentieth-century Americans would recognize as leisure or popular culture. For relatively affluent colonists, however, one sport emerged very early as an enduringly popular form of entertainment: horse racing.

It was natural, perhaps, that horse racing would become so appealing in the seventeenth and eighteenth centuries, when horses were, for most people, the only source of transportation over land other than walking. Those who could afford to own horses considered them part of the essential equipment of life. But people also formed attachments to their horses and prided themselves on their beauty and speed. Eventually, such attachments led to the creation of a spectator sport in which that beauty and speed were the central attractions.

Informal horse racing began almost as soon as Europeans settled the English colonies. Formal racing followed quickly. The first race track in North America—New Market (named for a popular race course in England)—was established in 1665 near the site of present-day Garden City, on Long Island in New York. It was, from the beginning, a showcase for horses bred in America by Americans, and in 1751 the track's authorities decreed that no imported horses could race there. For a time, New Market (and other horse racing sites) were dominated by English military officers stationed in the colonies. But tracks quickly developed a much wider appeal, and soon horse racing had spread up and down the Atlantic coast. By the time of the American Revolution, it was popular in almost every colony. It had a particularly avid following in Maryland, Virginia, and South Carolina; and it was moving as well into the newly settled areas of the Southwest. Andrew Jackson was a founder of the first racing track in Nashville, Tennessee, in the early nineteenth century. Kentucky—whose native bluegrass was early recognized as ideal for grazing horses—had eight tracks by 1800.

Like almost everything else in the life of early America, the world of horse racing was bounded by lines of class and race. For many years, it was considered the exclusive preserve of "gentlemen," so much so that in 1674 a court in Virginia fined James Bullocke, a tailor, for proposing a race, "it being contrary to Law for a Labourer to make a race, being a sport only for Gentlemen." But while white aristocrats retained control of racing, they were not the only people who participated in it. Southern aristocrats often trained young male slaves as jockeys for their horses, just as northern horse owners employed the services of free blacks as riders. In the North and the South, African Americans eventually emerged as some of the most talented and experienced trainers of racing horses. And despite social and legal

OAKLAND HOUSE AND RACE COURSE This 1840 painting by Robert Brammer and August. A. Von Smith portrays an early race course in Louisville, Kentucky, which provided entertainment to affluent white southerners. *(Oakland House and Race Course, Louisville, 1840. By Robert Brammer and August A. Von Smith. Collection of The Speed Art Museum, Louisville, Kentucky. Purchase, Museum Art Fund, 56.19)*

he assumed office, attempting to minimize the differences between the two parties and to calm the passions that the bitter campaign had aroused. "We are all republicans, we are all federalists," he said in his inaugural address. And during his eight years in office, he did much to prove those words correct. There was no complete repudiation of Federalist policies, no true "revolution." Indeed, at times Jefferson seemed to outdo the Federalists at their own work—most notably in overseeing a remarkable expansion of the territory of the United States.

The Federal City and the "People's President"

Symbolic of the relative unimportance of the federal government during the Jeffersonian era was the character of the newly founded national capital, the city of Washington. The French architect Pierre L'Enfant had designed the capital on a grand scale, with broad avenues radiating out from the uncompleted Capitol building, set on one of the area's highest hills.

The District of Columbia

THE ECLIPSE-HENRY MATCH RACE "Match races" between famous horses were a popular feature of early nineteenth-century horse racing. This famous 1823 race on Long Island, New York, pitted prize-winning horses from the North and the South against one another. American Eclipse, the northern entry, won. *(Private collection)*

pressures, free blacks and poor whites often staged their own, informal races, which proved highly popular among lower-class men and women and which helped give racing a slightly disreputable image among more conservative white aristocrats.

Racing also began early to reflect the growing sectional rivalry between the North and the South. In 1824, the Union Race Course on Long Island established an astounding $24,000 purse for a race between two famous thoroughbreds: American Eclipse (from the North) and Sir Henry (from the South). American Eclipse won two of the three heats, but a southern racehorse prevailed in another such celebrated contest in 1836. These inter-sectional races, which drew enormous crowds and created tremendous publicity, continued into the 1850s, until the North-South rivalry began to take a more deadly form.

Horse racing remained popular after the Civil War, but two developments changed its character considerably. One was the successful effort to drive African Americans out of the sport. At least until the 1890s, black jockeys and trainers remained central to racing. At the first Kentucky Derby in 1875, fourteen of the fifteen horses had African-American riders. One black man, Isaac Murphy, became one of the greatest jockeys of all time, the winner of three Kentucky Derbys and a remarkable 44 percent of all races in which he rode. Gradually, however, the same social dynamics that enforced racial segregation on so many other areas of American life in this era penetrated racing as well. By the beginning of the twentieth century, through a combination of harassment, intimidation, and formal discrimination, white jockeys and the organized jockey clubs had driven almost all

black riders, and many black trainers, out of the sport.

The second change was the introduction of formalized betting to the sport. Informal wages had been part of racing almost from the beginning, but in the late nineteenth century race tracks themselves began creating betting systems as a way to lure customers to the races. At the same time that the breeding of racehorses was moving into the hands of enormously wealthy families (many of them the beneficiaries of new industrial fortunes), the audience for racing was becoming increasingly working class and lower middle class. The people who now came to tracks were mostly white men, and some white women, lured to the races not by a love of horses—which were coming now to play a less central role in their everyday lives—but by the usually futile hope of quick and easy riches through gambling.

Washington was, many Americans believed, to become the Paris of the United States.

In reality, however, throughout Jefferson's presidency—and indeed through most of the nineteenth century—Washington remained little more than a straggling, provincial village. Although the population increased steadily from the 3,200 counted in the 1800 census, it never rivaled that of New York, Philadelphia, or the other major cities of the nation. The city remained a raw, inhospitable community with few public buildings of any consequence. Members of Congress viewed Washington not

as a home but as a place to visit briefly during sessions of the legislature and leave as quickly as possible. Most lived in a cluster of simple boardinghouses in the vicinity of the Capitol. It was not unusual for a member of Congress to resign his seat in the midst of a session to return home if he had an opportunity to accept the more prestigious post of member of his state legislature.

Jefferson set out as president to act in a spirit of democratic simplicity in keeping with the frontier-like character of the unfinished federal city. He was a wealthy and aristocratic planter by background, the owner of

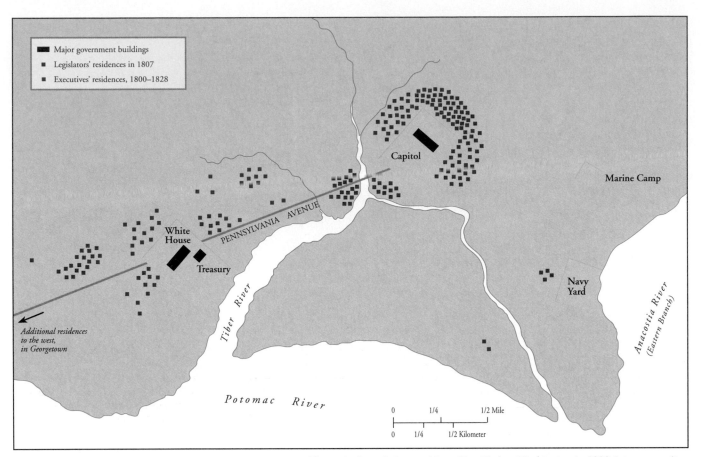

WASHINGTON, D.C. IN THE EARLY NINETEENTH CENTURY The nation's capital moved from New York to Washington in 1800, into a new city designed on a grand scale by the French planner Pierre L'Enfant. But in the early eighteenth century, it remained little more than a village in a marshy tract of land, which helped create hot, humid summers. This map shows the location of the principal government buildings in the early Republic, and also the sites of the homes of members of the executive and legislative branches. Note how the homes of executive officials clustered around the White House and the Treasury, while those of legislators clustered around the Capitol. ◆ *How did the geography of the city help shape the relationship between the executive and legislative branches?*

more than 100 slaves, and a man of rare cultivation and sophistication; but he conveyed to the public an image of plain, almost crude disdain for pretension. He walked like an ordinary citizen to and from his inauguration at the Capitol. In the presidential mansion, which had not yet acquired the name "White House," he disregarded the courtly etiquette of his predecessors (in part, no doubt, because as a widower he had no first lady to take charge of social affairs). At state dinners, he let his guests scramble pell-mell for places at the table. He did not always bother to dress up, once prompting the fastidious British ambassador to complain of being received by the president in coat and pantaloons that were "indicative of utter slovenliness and indifference to appearances."

Yet Jefferson managed nevertheless to impress most of those who knew him. He was a brilliant conversationalist, a gifted writer, and one of the nation's most intelligent and creative men, with perhaps a wider range of interests and accomplishments than any public figure in American history. In addition to politics and diplo-

macy, he was an active architect, educator, inventor, scientific farmer, and philosopher-scientist.

Jefferson was, above all, a shrewd and practical politician. On the one hand, he went to great lengths to eliminate the aura of majesty surrounding the presidency that he believed his predecessors had created. At the same time, however, Jefferson worked hard to exert influence as the leader of his party, giving direction to Republicans in Congress by quiet and sometimes even devious means. Although the Republicans had objected strenuously to the efforts of their Federalist predecessors to build a network of influence through patronage, Jefferson, too, used his powers of appointment as an effective political weapon. By the end of his first term about half the government jobs, and by the end of his second term practically all of them, were in the hands of loyal Republicans.

When Jefferson ran for reelection in 1804, he won overwhelmingly. The Federalist presidential nominee, Charles C. Pinckney, could not even carry most of the party's New England strongholds. Jefferson won 162 electoral votes to

Jefferson the Politician

WASHINGTON CITY, 1821 This 1821 painting by a French artist shows one of Washington's most significant vistas; looking across Lafayette Park at the North Facade of the White House. The painting suggests both the grandeur to which the new capital aspired and the relative crudeness and simplicity of the city as it then existed. *(I.N. Phelps Stokes Collection, Miriam and Ira D. Wallach Division of Art, Prints and Photographs, The New York Public Library, Astor, Lenox and Tilden Foundations)*

THOMAS JEFFERSON This 1805 portrait by the noted American painter Rembrandt Peale shows Jefferson at the beginning of his second term as president. It also conveys (through the simplicity of dress and the slightly unkempt hair) the image of democratic simplicity that Jefferson liked to project. *(New-York Historical Society)*

JEFFERSON THE ARCHITECT Among his many other accomplishments, Thomas Jefferson was one of the most gifted architects in early America. This rotunda is the centerpiece of the central campus of the University of Virginia, which Jefferson designed near the end of his life. Earlier, he designed his own home near Charlottesville, Monticello; and his proposal for a president's mansion in Washington placed second in a blind competition. *(University of Virginia Library)*

Pinckney's 14, and the Republican majorities in both houses of Congress increased.

Dollars and Ships

Under Washington and Adams, the Republicans believed, the government had been needlessly extravagant. Yearly federal expenditures had nearly tripled between 1793 and 1800. Hamilton had, as he had intended, increased the public debt and created an extensive system of internal taxation, including the hated whiskey excise tax.

The Jefferson administration moved deliberately to reverse the trend. In 1802, it persuaded Congress to abolish all internal taxes, leaving customs duties and the sale of western lands as the only sources of revenue for the government. Meanwhile, Secretary of the Treasury Gallatin drastically reduced government spending, cutting the already small staffs of the executive departments to minuscule levels. Although Jefferson was unable to retire the entire national debt as he had hoped, he did cut it almost in half (from $83 million to $45 million) during his presidency.

Limiting the Federal Government

Jefferson also scaled down the armed forces. He reduced the tiny army of 4,000 men to 2,500. He cut the navy from twenty-five ships to seven and reduced the number of officers and sailors accordingly. Anything but the smallest of standing armies, he argued, might menace civil liberties and civilian control of government. And a large navy, he feared, might promote overseas commerce, which Jefferson believed should remain secondary to agriculture. Yet Jefferson was not a pacifist. At the same time that he was reducing the size of the army and navy, he was helping to establish the United States Military Academy at West Point, founded in 1802. And when trouble began brewing overseas, he began again to build up the fleet.

Such trouble appeared first in the Mediterranean, off the coast of northern Africa. For years the Barbary states of North Africa—Morocco, Algiers, Tunis, and Tripoli (now part of Libya)—had been demanding protection money from all nations whose ships sailed the Mediterranean. Even Great Britain gave regular contributions to the pirates. During the 1780s and 1790s the United States agreed to treaties providing for annual tribute to the Barbary states, but Jefferson was reluctant to continue this policy of appeasement. "Tribute or war is the usual alternative of these Barbary pirates," he said. "Why not build a navy and decide on war?"

Challenging the Barbary Pirates

In 1801, the pasha of Tripoli forced Jefferson's hand. Unsatisfied by the American response to his extortionate demands, he ordered the flagpole of the American consulate chopped down—a symbolic declaration of war. Jefferson responded cautiously, building up the American fleet in the region over the next several years. Finally, in 1805, the United States reached an agreement with the pasha that ended American payments of tribute to Tripoli but required the United States to pay a substantial (and humiliating) ransom of $60,000 for the release of American prisoners seized by Barbary pirates.

Conflict with the Courts

Having won control of the executive and legislative branches of government, the Republicans looked with suspicion on the judiciary, which remained largely in the hands of Federalist judges. Soon after Jefferson's first inauguration, his followers in Congress launched an attack on this last preserve of the opposition. Their first step was the repeal of the Judiciary Act of 1801, thus eliminating the judgeships to which Adams had made his "midnight appointments."

The debate over the courts led to one of the most important judicial decisions in the history of the nation. Federalists had long maintained that the Supreme Court had the authority to nullify acts of Congress (although the Constitution said nothing specifically to support the claim), and the Court itself had actually exercised the power of judicial review in 1796 when it upheld the validity of a law passed by the legislature. But the Court's authority in this area would not be secure, it was clear, until it actually declared a congressional act unconstitutional.

Judicial Review

In 1803, in the case of *Marbury* v. *Madison* it did so. William Marbury, one of Adams's "midnight appointments," had been named a justice of the peace in the District of Columbia. But his commission, although signed and sealed, had not been delivered to him before Adams left office. Once Jefferson became president, the new secretary of state, James Madison, was responsible for transmitting appointments. He had refused to hand over the commission. Marbury applied to the Supreme Court for an order directing Madison to perform his official duty. In its historic ruling, the Court found that Marbury had a right to his commission but that the Court had no authority to order Madison to deliver it. On the surface, therefore, the decision was a victory for the administration. But of much greater importance than the relatively insignificant matter of Marbury's commission was the Court's reasoning in the decision.

Marbury v. Madison

The original Judiciary Act of 1789 had given the Court the power to compel executive officials to act in such matters as the delivery of commissions, and it was on that basis that Marbury had filed his suit. But the Court ruled that Congress had exceeded its authority in creating that statute: that the Constitution had defined the powers of the judiciary, and that the legislature had no right to expand them. The relevant section of the 1789 act was therefore void. In seeming to deny its own authority, the Court was in fact radically enlarging it.

WEST POINT Creating a professional military was an important task for the leaders of the early republic. Without an army, they realized, it would be difficult for the United States to win respect in the world. The establishment of the United States Military Academy at West Point (whose parade ground is pictured here) was, therefore, an important event in the early history of the republic. *(U.S. Military Academy, West Point)*

The justices had repudiated a relatively minor power (the power to force the delivery of a commission) by asserting a vastly greater one (the power to nullify an act of Congress).

The chief justice of the United States at the time of the ruling (and until 1835) was John Marshall, one of the

John Marshall

towering figures in the history of American law. A leading Federalist and prominent Virginia lawyer, he had served John Adams as secretary of state. (It had been Marshall, ironically, who had neglected to deliver Marbury's commission in the closing hours of the administration.) In 1801, just before leaving office, Adams had appointed him chief justice, and almost immediately Marshall established himself as the dominant figure on the Court, shaping virtually all its most important rulings—including, of course, *Marbury* v. *Madison.* Through a succession of Republican administrations, he established the judiciary as a branch of government coequal with the executive and the legislature—a position that the founders of the republic had never clearly indicated it should occupy.

Jefferson recognized the threat that an assertive judiciary could pose to his policies. Even while the Marbury case was still pending, he was preparing for a renewed assault on this last Federalist stronghold. He urged Congress to impeach obstructive judges, and Congress attempted to oblige him. After successfully removing from office a district judge, John Pickering of New Hampshire (on the perhaps specious grounds that he was insane and thus unfit for office), the Republicans targeted a justice of the Supreme Court itself: Justice Samuel Chase, a highly partisan Federal-

Impeachment of Samuel Chase

ist. Chase had certainly been injudicious; he had, for example, delivered stridently partisan speeches from the bench. But he had committed no crime. Some Republicans argued, however, that impeachment was not merely a criminal proceeding. Congress could properly impeach a judge for political reasons—for obstructing the other branches of the government and disregarding the will of the people.

At Jefferson's urging, the House impeached Chase and sent him to trial before the Senate early in 1805. But Republican leaders were unable to get the necessary two-thirds' vote for conviction in the Senate. Chase's acquittal helped establish that impeachment would not become a routine political weapon, that something more than partisan disagreement should have to underlie the process, a precedent that Congress only occasionally violated in future years. Marshall remained secure in his position as chief justice. And the judiciary survived as a powerful force within the government—more often than not ruling on behalf of the centralizing, expansionary policies that the Republicans had been trying to reverse.

DOUBLING THE NATIONAL DOMAIN

In the same year that Jefferson became president of the United States, Napoleon Bonaparte made himself ruler of France with the title of first consul. In the year that Jefferson was reelected, Napoleon named himself emperor. The two men had little in common. Yet for a time they were of great help to each other in international politics—until Napoleon's ambitions moved from Europe to America and created conflict and estrangement.

Jefferson and Napoleon

Having failed in a grandiose plan to seize India from the British Empire, Napoleon began turning his imperial ambitions in a new direction: he began to dream of restoring French power in the New World. The territory east of the Mississippi, which France had ceded to Great Britain in 1763, was now mostly part of the United States and lost to France forever. But Napoleon wanted to regain the lands west of the Mississippi, which now belonged to Spain, over which Napoleon now exercised heavy influence. Under the secret Treaty of San Ildefonso of 1800 between the French and the Spanish, France regained title to Louisiana, which included almost the whole of the Mississippi Valley to the west of the river, plus New Orleans near its mouth. The Louisiana Territory would, Napoleon hoped, become the heart of a great French empire in America.

Also part of Napoleon's empire in the New World were the sugar-rich and strategically valuable West Indian islands that still belonged to France—Guadeloupe, Martinique, and above all Santo Domingo. But unrest among the Caribbean slaves posed a threat to Napoleon's hopes for the islands. Africans in Santo Domingo (inspired by the French Revolution as some American slaves had been inspired by the American Revolution) revolted and created a republic of their own, under the remarkable black leader Toussaint L'Ouverture. Taking advantage of a truce in his war with England, Napoleon sent an army to the West Indies. It crushed the insurrection and restored French authority; but the incident was an early sign of the problems Napoleon would have in realizing his ambitions in America.

Toussaint L'Ouverture

Jefferson was unaware at first of Napoleon's imperial ambitions in America, and for a time he pursued a foreign policy that reflected his well-known admiration for France. He appointed as American minister to Paris the ardently pro-French Robert R. Livingston. He worked to secure ratification of the Franco-American settlement of 1800 and began observing the terms of the treaty even before it was ratified. The Adams administration had joined with the British in recognizing and supporting the rebel regime of Toussaint L'Ouverture in Santo Domingo; Jefferson assured the French minister in Washington that the American people, especially those of the slaveholding states, did not approve of the black revolutionary, who was setting a bad example for their own slaves. He even implied that the United States might join with France in putting down the rebellion (although nothing ever came of the suggestion).

Jefferson began to reconsider his position toward France when he heard rumors of the secret transfer of Louisiana.

Jefferson was even more alarmed when, in the fall of 1802, he learned that the Spanish intendant at New Orleans (who still governed the city, since the French had not yet taken formal possession of the region) had announced a disturbing new regulation. American ships sailing the Mississippi River had for many years been accustomed to depositing their cargoes in New Orleans for transfer to oceangoing vessels. The intendant now forbade the practice—even though Spain had guaranteed Americans that right in the Pinckney Treaty of 1795—thus effectively closing the lower Mississippi to American shippers.

Westerners demanded that the federal government do something to reopen the river. The president faced a dilemma. If he yielded to the frontier clamor and tried to change the policy by force, he would run the risk of a major war with France. If he ignored the westerners' demands, he might lose political support. But Jefferson saw another solution. He instructed Robert Livingston, the American ambassador in Paris, to negotiate the purchase of New Orleans. Livingston on his own authority proposed that the French sell the United States the vast western part of Louisiana as well.

In the meantime, Jefferson persuaded Congress to appropriate funds for an expansion of the army and the construction of a river fleet, and he deliberately gave the impression that American forces might soon descend on New Orleans and that the United States might form an alliance with Great Britain if the problems with France were not resolved. Perhaps that was why Napoleon suddenly decided to accept Livingston's proposal and offer the United States the entire Louisiana Territory.

Napoleon's Offer

Napoleon had good reasons for the decision. His plans for an American empire had already gone seriously awry, partly because a yellow fever epidemic had wiped out much of the French army in the New World and partly because the expeditionary force Napoleon wished to send to reinforce them and take possession of Louisiana had been frozen into a Dutch harbor through the winter of 1802–1803. By the time the harbor thawed in the spring of 1803, Napoleon was preparing for a renewed war in Europe. He would not, he realized, have the resources now to secure an American empire.

The Louisiana Purchase

Faced with Napoleon's startling proposal, Livingston and James Monroe, whom Jefferson had sent to Paris to assist in the negotiations, had to decide first whether they should even consider making a treaty for the purchase of the entire Louisiana Territory, since they had not been authorized by their government to do so. But fearful that Napoleon might withdraw the offer, they decided to pro-

ceed without further instructions from home. After some haggling over the price Livingston and Monroe signed the agreement on April 30, 1803.

By the terms of the treaty, the United States was to pay a total of 80 million francs ($15 million) to the French government. The United States was also to grant certain exclusive commercial privileges to France in the port of New Orleans and was to incorporate the residents of Louisiana into the Union with the same rights and privileges as other citizens. The boundaries of the purchase were not clearly defined; the treaty simply specified that Louisiana would occupy the

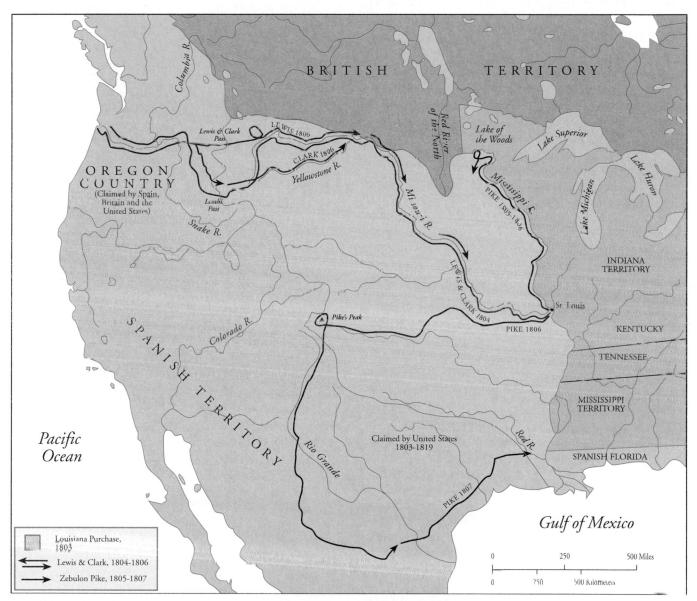

EXPLORING THE LOUISIANA PURCHASE, 1804-1807 When Jefferson purchased the Louisiana territory from France in 1803, he doubled the size of the nation. But few Americans knew what they had bought. The Lewis and Clark Expedition set out in 1804 to investigate the new territories, and this map shows their route, along with that of another inveterate explorer Zebulon Pike. Note the vast distances the two parties covered (including, in both cases, a great deal of land outside the Louisiana Purchase). Note, too, how much of this enormous territory lay outside the orbit of even these ambitious explorations. ◆ *How did the American public react to the addition of these new territories?*

For an interactive version of this map go to www.mhhe.com/brinkley12ch7maps

"same extent" as it had when France and Spain had owned it.

Jefferson's Quandary

In Washington, the president was both pleased and embarrassed when he received the treaty. He was pleased with the terms of the bargain but uncertain whether the United States had authority to accept it, since he had always insisted that the federal government could rightfully exercise only those powers explicitly assigned to it. Nowhere did the Constitution say anything about the acquisition of new territory. But Jefferson's advisers persuaded him that his treaty-making power under the Constitution would justify the purchase of Louisiana. The president finally agreed, trusting, as he said, "that the good sense of our country will correct the evil of loose construction when it shall produce ill effects." The Republican Congress promptly approved the treaty and appropriated money to implement its provisions. Finally, late in 1803, the French assumed formal control of Louisiana from Spain just long enough to turn the territory over to General James Wilkinson, the commissioner of the United States.

The government organized the Louisiana Territory much as it had organized the Northwest Territory, with the assumption that its various territories would eventually become states. The first of these was admitted to the Union as the state of Louisiana in 1812.

Lewis and Clark Explore the West

Meanwhile, several ambitious explorations were revealing the geography of the far-flung new territory to white Americans, few of whom had ever ventured much beyond the Mississippi River. In 1803, even before Napoleon's offer to sell Louisiana, Jefferson helped plan an expedition that was to cross the continent to the Pacific Ocean, gather geographical facts, and investigate prospects for trade with the Indians. He named as its leader his private secretary and Virginia neighbor, the thirty-two-year-old Meriwether Lewis, a veteran of Indian wars skilled in the ways of the wilderness. Lewis chose as a colleague the twenty-eight-year-old William Clark, who—like George Rogers Clark, his older brother—was an experienced frontiersman and Indian fighter. In the spring of 1804, Lewis and Clark, with a company of four dozen men, started up the Missouri River from St. Louis. With the Shoshone woman Sacajawea as their guide, they eventually crossed the Rocky Mountains, descended the Snake and Columbia Rivers, and in the late autumn of 1805 camped on the Pacific coast. In September 1806, they were back in St. Louis with elaborate records of the geography and the Indian civilizations they had observed along the way, and a lengthy diary recounting their experiences.

While Lewis and Clark were still on their journey, Jefferson dispatched other explorers to other parts of the Louisiana Territory. Lieu-

Zebulon Pike

tenant Zebulon Montgomery

THE JOURNAL OF LEWIS AND CLARK This page is from the journal the explorers Meriwether Lewis and William Clark kept on their famous journey through the territory the United States had acquired in the Louisiana Purchase—and beyond. Shown here is one of the rough maps they drew to describe the lands they had seen. *(British Museum)*

Pike, twenty-six years old, led an expedition in the fall of 1805 from St. Louis into the upper Mississippi Valley. In the summer of 1806, he set out again up the valley of the Arkansas River and into what later became Colorado, where he encountered (but failed in his attempt to climb) the peak that now bears his name. His account of his western travels created an enduring (and inaccurate) impression among many Americans in the East that the land between the Missouri River and the Rockies was an uninhabitable, uncultivable desert.

The Burr Conspiracy

Jefferson's triumphant reelection in 1804 suggested that most of the nation approved the new territorial acquisition. But some New England Federalists raged against it. They realized that the more the West grew and the more new states joined the Union, the less power the Federalists and their region would retain. In Massachusetts, a

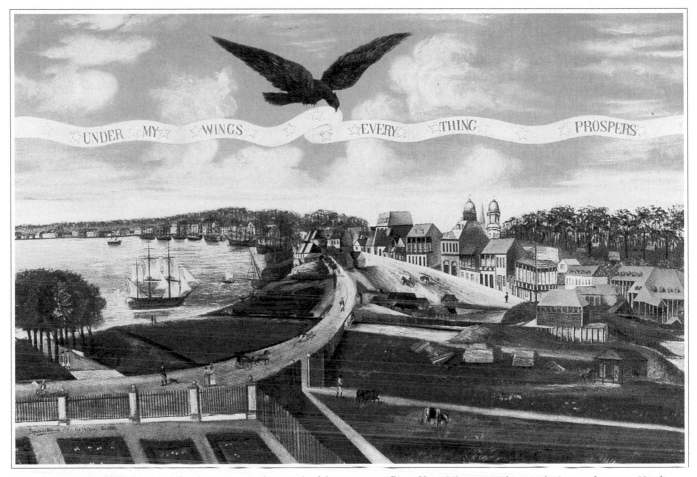

UNDER MY WINGS EVERY THING PROSPERS

NEW ORLEANS IN 1803 Because of its location near the mouth of the Mississippi River, New Orleans was the principal port of western North America in the early nineteenth century. Through it, western farmers shipped their produce to markets in the east and Europe. This 1803 painting celebrates the American acquisition of the city from France as part of the Louisiana Purchase. *(Chicago Historical Society)*

Essex Junto

group of the most extreme Federalists, known as the Essex Junto, concluded that the only recourse for New England was to secede from the Union and form a separate "Northern Confederacy." If this confederacy was to have any hope for lasting success, the Federalists believed, it would have to include New York and New Jersey as well. But the leading Federalist in New York, Alexander Hamilton, refused to support the secessionist scheme. "Dismemberment of our empire," he wrote, "will be a clear sacrifice of great positive advantages without any counterbalancing good, administering no relief to our real disease, which is democracy."

Federalists in New York then turned to Hamilton's greatest political rival: Vice President Aaron Burr, a politician without prospects in his own party, because Jefferson had never forgiven him for the 1800 election deadlock. Burr accepted a Federalist proposal that he become their candidate for governor of New York in 1804, and there were rumors (unsupported by any evidence) that

Hamilton and Burr

he had also agreed to support the Federalist plans for secession.

Hamilton accused Burr of plotting treason and made numerous private remarks, widely reported in the press, about Burr's "despicable" character. When Burr lost the election, he blamed his defeat on Hamilton's malevolence. "These things must have an end," Burr wrote. He challenged Hamilton to a duel.

Dueling had by then already fallen into some disrepute in America, but many people still considered it a legitimate institution for settling matters of "honor." Hamilton feared that refusing Burr's challenge would brand him a coward. And so, on a July morning in 1804, the two men met at Weehawken, New Jersey. Hamilton was mortally wounded; he died the next day.

The resourceful and charismatic Burr was now a political outcast who had to flee New York to avoid an indictment for murder. He found new outlets for his ambitions in the West. Even before the duel, he had begun corresponding with prominent white settlers in the Southwest, especially with General James Wilkinson, now governor of the Louisiana Territory. Burr and Wilkinson, it seems clear, hoped to lead an expedition that would capture Mexico from the Spanish. "Mexico glitters in all our eyes," Burr wrote; "the word is all we wait for." But there were also rumors that they wanted to separate the Southwest from the United States and create a western empire that Burr would rule. There is little evidence that these rumors were true.

Whether the rumors were true or not, many of Burr's opponents—including, ultimately, Jefferson himself—chose to believe them. When Burr led a group of armed followers down the Ohio River by boat in 1806, disturbing reports flowed into Washington (the most alarming from Wilkinson, who had suddenly turned against Burr and who now informed the president that treason was afoot) that an attack on New Orleans was imminent. Jefferson ordered Burr and his men arrested as traitors. Burr was brought to Richmond for trial. Determined to win a conviction, Jefferson carefully managed the government's case from Washington. But Chief Justice Marshall, presiding over the trial on circuit duty, limited the evidence the government could present and defined the charge in such a way that the jury had little choice but to acquit him.

The Burr "conspiracy" was in part the story of a single man's soaring ambitions and flamboyant personality. But it was also a symbol of the larger perils still facing the new nation. With a central government that remained deliberately weak, with vast tracts of land only nominally controlled by the United States, with ambitious political leaders willing, if necessary, to circumvent normal channels in their search for power, the legitimacy of the federal government, and indeed the existence of the United States as a stable and united nation, remained to be fully established.

EXPANSION AND WAR

Two very different conflicts were taking shape in the later years of Thomas Jefferson's presidency that would, together, draw the United States into a difficult and frustrating war. One was the continuing tension in Europe, which in 1803 escalated once again into a full-scale conflict (the Napoleonic Wars). As the fighting escalated, both the British and the French took steps to prevent the United States from trading with (and thus assisting) the other.

The other conflict was in North America itself, a result of the ceaseless westward expansion of white settlement, which was now stretching to the Mississippi River and beyond, colliding again with Native American populations committed to protecting their lands and their trade from intruders. In both the North and the South, the threatened tribes mobilized to resist white encroachments. They began as well to forge connections with British forces in Canada and Spanish forces in Florida. The Indian conflict on land therefore became intertwined with the European conflict on the seas, and ultimately

The Napoleonic Wars

helped cause the War of 1812, an unpopular conflict with ambiguous results.

Conflict on the Seas

The early nineteenth century saw a dramatic expansion of American shipping in the Atlantic. Britain retained significant naval superiority, but the British merchant marine was preoccupied with commerce in Europe and Asia and devoted little energy to trade with America. Thus the United States stepped effectively into the void and developed one of the most important merchant marines in the world, which soon controlled a large proportion of the trade between Europe and the West Indies.

In 1805, at the Battle of Trafalgar, a British fleet virtually destroyed what was left of the French navy. Because France could no longer challenge the British at sea, Napoleon now chose to pressure England through economic rather than naval means. The result was what he called the Continental System, designed to close the European continent to British trade. Napoleon issued a series of decrees barring British ships and neutral ships that had called at British ports from landing their cargoes at any European port controlled by France or its allies. The British government replied to Napoleon's decrees by establishing—through a series of "orders in council"—a blockade of the European coast. The blockade required that any goods being shipped to Napoleon's Europe be carried either in British vessels or in neutral vessels stopping at British ports—precisely what Napoleon's policies forbade.

American ships were caught between Napoleon's decrees and Britain's orders in council. If they sailed directly for the European continent, they risked being captured by the British navy; if they sailed by way of a British port, they risked seizure by the French. Both of the warring powers were violating America's rights as a neutral nation. But most Americans considered the British, with their greater sea power, the worse offender. British ships pounced on Yankee merchantmen all over the ocean; the French could do so only in European ports. Particularly infuriating to Americans, British vessels stopped United States ships on the high seas and seized sailors off the decks, making them victims of "impressment."

America's Predicament

Impressment

The British navy—with its floggings, low pay, and terrible shipboard conditions—was known as a "floating hell" to its sailors. Few volunteered. Most had to be "impressed" (forced) into the service. At every opportunity they deserted. By 1807, many of these deserters had joined the American merchant marine or the American navy. To check this loss of vital manpower, the British claimed the right to stop and search American merchant ships (although at first not naval vessels) and reimpress

PROTECTION FROM IMPRESSMENT To protect American sailors from British impressment, the federal government issued official certificates of United States citizenship—known as "protection papers." But British naval officers, aware that such documents were often forged, frequently ignored them. *(Peabody Essex Museum, Salem, Massachusetts)*

deserters. They did not claim the right to take native-born Americans, but they did claim the right to seize naturalized Americans born on British soil. In practice, the British navy often made no such distinctions, impressing British deserters and native-born Americans alike into service.

In the summer of 1807, the British went to more provocative extremes in an incident involving a vessel of the American navy. Sailing from Norfolk, with several alleged deserters from the British navy among the crew, the American naval frigate *Chesapeake* encountered the British ship *Leopard.* When the American commander, James Barron, refused to allow the British to search the *Chesapeake,* the *Leopard* opened fire. Barron had no choice but to surrender, and a boarding party from the *Leopard* dragged four men off the American frigate.

Chesapeake-Leopard Incident

When news of the *Chesapeake-Leopard* incident reached the United States, there was great popular clamor for revenge. If Congress had been in session, it might have declared war. But Jefferson and Madison tried to maintain the peace. Jefferson expelled all British warships from American waters, to lessen the likelihood of future incidents. Then he sent instructions to his minister in England, James Monroe, to demand that the British government renounce impressment. The British government disavowed the action of the officer responsible for the *Chesapeake-Leopard* affair and recalled him; it offered compensation for those killed and wounded in the incident; and it promised to return three of the captured sailors (one of the original four had been hanged). But the British refused to renounce impressment.

"Peaceable Coercion"

In an effort to prevent future incidents that might bring the nation again to the brink of war, Jefferson presented—and Republican legislators promptly enacted—a drastic measure known as the Embargo, and it became one of the most controversial political issues of its time. The Embargo prohibited American ships from leaving the United States for any foreign port anywhere in the world. (If it had specified only British and French ports, Jefferson reasoned, it could have been evaded by means of false clearance papers.) Congress also passed a "force act" to give the government power to enforce the Embargo.

The Embargo

The law was widely evaded, but it was effective enough to create a serious depression through most of the nation. Hardest hit were the merchants and shipowners of the Northeast, most of them Federalists. Their once lucrative shipping business was at a virtual standstill, and they were losing money every day. They became convinced that Jefferson had acted unconstitutionally.

The election of 1808 came in the midst of the Embargo-induced depression. James Madison, Jefferson's secretary of state and political ally, won the presidency. But the Federalists ran much more strongly than they had in 1804. The Embargo was clearly a growing political liability, and Jefferson decided to back down. A few days before leaving office, he approved a bill ending his experiment with what he called "peaceable coercion."

To replace the Embargo, Congress passed the Non-Intercourse Act just before Madison took office. The new law reopened trade with all nations but Great Britain and France. A year later, in 1810, Congress allowed the Non-Intercourse Act to expire and replaced it with Macon's Bill No. 2, which reopened free commercial relations with Britain and France, but authorized the president to prohibit commerce with either belligerent if one should continue violating neutral shipping after the other had stopped. Napoleon thus announced that France would no longer interfere with American shipping, and Madison announced that an embargo against Great Britain alone would automatically go into effect early in 1811

Non-Intercourse Act

THE TREATY OF GREENVILLE An unknown member of General Anthony Wayne's staff painted this scene of Indians and U.S. officers signing a treaty in Greenville, Ohio, in 1795, by which twelve tribes agreed to surrender the southern half of the territory to the United States in exchange for payment of about 1/8 cent per acre. *(Chicago Historical Society)*

unless Britain renounced its restrictions on American shipping.

Although less well enforced than the earlier one had been, the new limited embargo hurt the economy of England enough that the government repealed its blockade of Europe. But the repeal came too late to prevent war. In any case, naval policies were only part of the reason for tensions between Britain and the United States.

The "Indian Problem" and the British

Given the ruthlessness with which white settlers in North America had dislodged Indian tribes to make room for expanding settlement, it was hardly surprising that ever since the Revolution many Native Americans had continued to look to England—which had historically attempted to limit western expansion—for protection. The British in Canada, for their part, had relied on the tribes as partners in the lucrative fur trade and as potential military allies.

The 1807 war crisis following the *Chesapeake-Leopard* incident revived the conflict between Indians and white settlers. Two important (and very different) leaders emerged to oppose one

William Henry Harrison

another in the conflict: William Henry Harrison and Tecumseh.

The Virginia-born Harrison, already a veteran Indian fighter at age twenty-six, went to Washington as the congressional delegate from the Northwest Territory in 1799. He was a committed advocate of growth and development in the western lands, and he was largely responsible for the passage in 1800 of the so-called Harrison Land Law, which enabled white settlers to acquire farms from the public domain on much easier terms than before.

In 1801, Jefferson appointed Harrison governor of the Indiana Territory to administer the president's proposed solution to the "Indian problem." Jefferson offered the Native Americans a choice: they could convert themselves into settled farmers and assimilate—become a part of white society; or they could migrate to the west of the Mississippi. In either case, they would have to give up their claims to their tribal lands in the Northwest.

Jefferson's Offer

Jefferson considered the assimilation policy a benign alternative to continuing conflict between Indians and white settlers, conflict he assumed the tribes were destined to lose. But to the tribes, the new policy seemed far from benign, especially given the bludgeonlike efficiency with which Harrison set out to implement it. He played off one tribe against another and used threats, bribes, trickery, and whatever other tactics he felt would help him conclude treaties. By 1807, the United States had extracted from reluctant tribal leaders treaty rights to eastern Michigan, southern Indiana, and most of Illinois. Meanwhile, in the Southwest, white Americans were taking millions of acres from other tribes in Georgia, Tennessee, and Mississippi. The Indians wanted desperately to resist, but the separate tribes were helpless by themselves against the power of the United States. They might have accepted their fate passively but for the emergence of two new factors.

One factor was the policy of the British authorities in Canada. After the *Chesapeake* incident and the surge of anti-British feeling throughout the United States, the British colonial authorities began to expect an American invasion of Canada and took desperate measures for their own defense. Among those measures were efforts to renew friendship with the Indians and provide them with increased supplies.

Tecumseh and the Prophet

The second, and more important, factor intensifying the border conflict was the rise of two remarkable Native American leaders. One was Tens-

The Prophet's Message

kwatawa, a charismatic religious leader and orator known as the Prophet. He had experienced a mystical awakening in the process of recovering from alcoholism. Having freed himself from what he considered the evil effects of white culture, he began to speak to his people of the superior virtues of Indian civilization and the sinfulness and corruption of the white world. In the process, he inspired a religious revival that spread through numerous tribes and helped unite them. Like Neolin before him, and like his contemporary to the east,

Handsome Lake, Tenskwatawa demonstrated the power of religious leaders to mobilize Indians behind political and military objectives. The Prophet's headquarters at the confluence of Tippecanoe Creek and the Wabash River (known as Prophetstown) became a sacred place for people of many tribes and attracted thousands of Indians from throughout the Midwest. Out of their common religious experiences, they began to consider joint political and military efforts as well.

The Prophet's brother Tecumseh—"the Shooting Star," chief of the Shawnees—emerged as the leader of these more secular efforts. Tecumseh understood, as few other Indian leaders had, that only through united action could

Tecumseh's Strategy

the tribes hope to resist the advance of white civilization. Beginning in 1809, after tribes in Indiana had ceded vast lands to the United States, he set out to unite all the Indians of the Mississippi Valley, north and south. Together, he promised, they would halt white expansion, recover the whole Northwest, and make the Ohio River the boundary between the United States and the Indian country. He maintained that Harrison and others, by negotiating treaties with individual tribes, had obtained no real title to land. The land belonged to all the tribes; none of them could rightfully cede any of it without the consent of the others.

In 1811, Tecumseh left Prophetstown and traveled down the Mississippi to visit the tribes of the South and persuade

Battle of Tippecanoe

them to join the alliance. During his absence, Governor Harrison saw a chance to destroy the growing influence of the two Native American leaders. He camped near Prophetstown with 1,000 soldiers, and on November 7, 1811, he provoked a fight. Although the white forces suffered losses as heavy as those of the natives, Harrison drove off the Indians and burned the town. The Battle of

TECUMSEH Tecumseh's efforts to unite the tribes of the Mississippi Valley against further white encroachments on their lands led him ultimately into an alliance with the British after the Battle of Tippecanoe in 1811. In the War of 1812, he was commissioned a brigadier general by the British and fought against the United States in the Battle of the Thames. He is shown in this painting (by the daughter of an English officer stationed near Detroit) wearing British military trousers. *(Fort Malden National Historical Park)*

JAMES AND DOLLEY MADISON James Madison may have been the most brilliant of the early leaders of the republic, but he was also one of the most serious and humorless, as this grim portrait suggests. His wife (born Dolley Payne in North Carolina and raised a Quaker in Virginia) was twenty-six when she married the forty-three-year-old Madison in 1794. Her charm and social grace made her one of her husband's greatest political assets. She acted as hostess for Thomas Jefferson, a widower, while her husband was secretary of state. And she presided over a lively social life during her eight years in the White House as first lady. *(New-York Historical Society)*

Tippecanoe (named for the creek near the fighting) disillusioned many of the Prophet's followers, who had believed that his magic would protect them. Tecumseh returned to find the confederacy in disarray. But there were still many warriors eager for combat, and by the spring of 1812 they were active along the frontier, from Michigan to Mississippi, raiding white settlements and terrifying white settlers.

The bloodshed along the western borders was largely a result of the Indians' own initiative, but Britain's agents in Canada had encouraged and helped supply the uprising. To Harrison and most white residents of the regions, there seemed only one way to make the West safe for Americans. That was to drive the British out of Canada and annex that province to the United States—a goal that many westerners had long cherished for other reasons as well.

Florida and War Fever

While white "frontiersmen" in the North demanded the conquest of Canada, those in the South wanted the United States to acquire Spanish Florida, a territory that included the present state of Florida and the southern areas of what are now Alabama, Mississippi, and Louisiana. The territory was a continuing threat to whites in the southern United States. Slaves escaped across the Florida border; Indians launched frequent raids north into white settlements from Florida. But white southerners also coveted Florida because through it ran rivers that could provide residents of the Southwest with access to valuable ports on the Gulf of Mexico.

In 1810, American settlers in West Florida (an area that is part of Mississippi and Louisiana today) seized the Spanish fort at Baton Rouge and asked the federal government to annex the territory to the United States. President Madison happily agreed and then began planning to get the rest of Florida, too. The desire for Florida became yet another motivation for war with Britain. Spain was Britain's ally, and a war with Britain might provide a pretext for taking Spanish territory.

By 1812, war fever was growing on both the northern and southern borders of the United States. In the congressional elections of 1810, voters from these regions elected a large number of representatives of both parties eager for war with Britain. They became known as the "war hawks."

War Hawks

Some of them were ardent nationalists fired by passion for territorial expansion—among them two men who would play a great role in national politics for much of the next four decades: Henry Clay of Kentucky and John C. Calhoun of South Carolina. Others were men impassioned in their defense of Republican values. Together, they formed a powerful coalition in favor of war.

Clay became Speaker of the House in 1811, and he filled committees with those who shared his eagerness for war. He appointed Calhoun to the crucial Committee on Foreign Affairs, and both men began agitating for the conquest of Canada. Madison still hoped for peace. But he shared the concerns of other Republicans about the dangers to American trade, and he was losing control of Congress. On June 18, 1812, he gave in to the pressure and approved a declaration of war against Britain.

THE WAR OF 1812

Preoccupied with their struggle against Napoleon in Europe, the British were not eager for an open conflict with the United States. Even after the Americans declared war, Britain largely ignored them for a time. But in the fall of 1812, Napoleon launched a catastrophic campaign against Russia that left his army in disarray and his power in Europe diminished. By late 1813, with the French Empire on its way to final defeat, Britain was able to turn its military attention to America.

Battles with the Tribes

Americans entered the War of 1812 with great enthusiasm, but events on the battlefield soon cooled their ardor. In the summer of 1812, American forces invaded Canada through Detroit. They soon had to retreat back to Detroit and in August surrendered the fort there. Other invasion efforts also failed. In the meantime, Fort Dearborn (Chicago) fell before an Indian attack.

Things went only slightly better for the United States on the seas. At first, American frigates won some spectacular victories over British warships, and American privateers destroyed or captured many British merchant ships, occasionally braving the coastal waters of the British Isles themselves and burning vessels within sight of the shore. But by 1813, the British navy—now less preoccupied with Napoleon—was counterattacking effectively, driving the American frigates to cover and imposing a blockade on the United States.

Early Defeats

The United States did, however, achieve significant early military successes on the Great Lakes. First, the Americans took command of Lake Ontario, which permitted them to raid and burn York (now Toronto), the capital of Canada. American forces then seized control of Lake Erie, mainly through the work of the youthful Oliver Hazard Perry, who engaged

Put-In-Bay

and dispersed a British fleet at Put-In-Bay on September 10, 1813. This made possible, at last, another invasion of Canada by way of Detroit, which Americans could now reach easily by water. William Henry Harrison, the American commander in the West, pushed up the river Thames into upper Canada and on October 5, 1813, won a victory notable for the death of Tecumseh, who was serving as a brigadier general in the British army. The Battle of the Thames weakened and disheartened the Native Americans of the Northwest and greatly diminished their ability to defend their claims to the region.

In the meantime, another white military leader was striking an even harder blow at the tribes of the Southwest. The Creeks, whom Tecumseh had aroused on a visit to the South and whom the Spanish had supplied with weapons, had been attacking white settlers near the Florida border. Andrew Jackson, a wealthy Tennessee planter and a general in the state militia, temporarily abandoned plans for an invasion of Florida and set off in pursuit of them. On March 27, 1814, in the Battle of Horseshoe Bend, Jackson's men took terrible revenge on the Indians—slaughtering women and children along with warriors—and broke the resistance of the Creeks. The tribe agreed to cede most of its lands to the United States and retreated westward, farther into the interior. The battle also won Jackson a commission as major general in the United States Army, and in that capacity he led his men farther south into Florida and, on November 7, 1814, seized the Spanish fort at Pensacola.

Battles with the British

The victories over the tribes were not enough to win the war. After the surrender of Napoleon in 1814, England prepared to invade the United States. A British armada sailed up the Patuxent River from Chesapeake Bay and landed an army that marched a short distance overland to Bladensburg, on the outskirts of Washington, where it dispersed a poorly trained force of American militiamen. On August 24, 1814, the British troops entered Washington and set fire to several public buildings, including the White House, in retaliation for the earlier American burning of the Canadian capital at York. This was the low point of American fortunes in the war.

The British Invasion

Leaving Washington in partial ruins, the invading army proceeded up the bay toward Baltimore. But Baltimore harbor, guarded by Fort McHenry, was prepared. To block the approaching fleet, the American garrison had sunk several ships to clog the entry to the harbor, thus forcing the British to bombard the fort from a distance. Through the night of September 13, Francis Scott Key, a Washington lawyer who was on board one of the British ships trying to secure the release of an American prisoner, watched the bombardment. The next morning, "by the dawn's early light," he could see the

NAVAL AND TROOP MOVEMENTS

→ British forces
→ American forces
▲▲▲ British blockade

BATTLES

✴ British victory
✴ American victory
✴ Indian battles

Lake Superior

BRITISH AMERICA

Quebec

MAINE (Mass.)

Halifax

Montreal

Machias
Eastport

Lake Huron

Bangor
Waterville

VT.

Castine
Sept. 1814

Fort Mackinac
surrendered to
British
July 1812

Kingston

Fort
Ticonderoga

N.H.

Portland

Lake Ontario

Sacketts
Harbor

MICHIGAN
TERRITORY

NEW
YORK

MASS.

Boston

Lake Erie

CONN.

R.I.

Fort Dearborn
surrendered to
British
August 1812

PENNSYLVANIA

New York

INDIANA
TERRITORY

N.J.

Philadelphia

ILLINOIS
TERRITORY

OHIO

Pittsburgh

MD.

DEL.

Tippecanoe
Nov. 7, 1811

HARRISON
1811

VIRGINIA

1814

Wabash R.

Norfolk

**ATLANTIC
OCEAN**

MISSOURI
TERRITORY

KENTUCKY

TENNESSEE

NORTH CAROLINA

Wilmington

MISSISSIPPI
TERRITORY

SOUTH CAROLINA

Talladega
Nov. 9, 1813

GEORGIA

Charleston

Fort Jackson

Horseshoe Bend
Mar. 27, 1814

JACKSON
1813

Savannah

Vicksburg

LOUISIANA

Natchez

Fort Mims
Massacre
Aug. 30, 1813

JACKSON
1814-1815

Pensacola
Nov. 7, 1814

Fort Bowyer
Sept. 15, 1814

SPANISH
FLORIDA

New Orleans
Jan. 8, 1815

Gulf of Mexico

0   100   200 Miles

0   100   200 Kilometers

1814

PENNSYLVANIA

MARYLAND

Godly Wood
Sept. 12, 1814

Baltimore

Fort McHenry
bombardment
Sept. 13-14, 1814

Washington
burned
Aug. 24, 1814

Chesapeake Bay

DELAWARE

VIRGINIA

Lake Huron

PREVOST-DOWNIE 1814

MICHIGAN
TERRITORY

St. Lawrence R.

Châteaugay
Oct. 23, 1813

Lake
Michigan

Chrysler's Farm
Nov. 11, 1813

LaColle Mill
March 1814

York (Toronto)
April 27, 1813

DEARBORN 1813

Fort Detroit
surrendered to British
July 1812

Battle of the Thames
Oct. 5, 1813

Lake Ontario

Plattsburgh
Sept. 11, 1814

Frenchtown
Jan. 22, 1813

BROCK 1812

Lundy's Lane
July 25, 1814

MAINE
(Mass.)

WINCHESTER
1812-1813

Lake Erie

Stoney
Creek
June 6, 1813

The Chippewa
July 5, 1814

VERMONT

PERRY 1813

Fort
Stephenson

Put-In-Bay
Sept. 10, 1813

NEW YORK

NEW
HAMPSHIRE

INDIANA
TERRITORY

OHIO

PENNSYLVANIA

MASSACHUSETTS

ATLANTIC
OCEAN

THE WAR OF 1812 These three maps illustrate the military maneuvers of the British and the Americans during the War of 1812. The large map at top shows all the theaters of the war, from New Orleans to southern Canada. The detail at bottom shows the extended land and water battle along the Canadian border and in the Great Lakes. The detail in the bottom right corner of the upper map shows the fighting around Washington and Baltimore. Note how in all these theaters, there are about the same number of British and American victories. ◆ *What brought this inconclusive war finally to an end?*

OLC **For an interactive version of this map go to www.mhhe.com/brinkley12ch7maps**

THE BOMBARDMENT OF FORT MCHENRY The British bombardment of Fort McHenry in Baltimore harbor in September 1814 was of modest importance to the outcome of the War of 1812. It is remembered as the occasion for Francis Scott Key to write his poem "The Star-Spangled Banner," which recorded his sentiments at seeing an American flag still flying over the fort "by the dawn's early light." *(I.N. Phelps Stokes Collection of American Historical Prints, The New York Public Library)*

flag on the fort still flying; he recorded his pride in the moment by scribbling a poem—"The Star-Spangled Banner"—on the back of an envelope. The British withdrew from Baltimore, and Key's words were soon set to the tune of an old English drinking song. In 1931, "The Star-Spangled Banner" became the official national anthem.

Meanwhile, American forces repelled another British invasion in northern New York at the Battle of Plattsburgh, on September 11, 1814, which turned back a much larger British naval and land force and secured the northern border of the United States. In the South, a formidable array of battle-hardened British veterans, fresh from the campaign against the French in Spain, Battle of New Orleans landed below New Orleans and prepared to advance north up the Mississippi. Awaiting the British was Andrew Jackson with a motley collection of Tennesseans, Kentuckians, Creoles, blacks, pirates, and regular army troops behind earthen fortifications. On January 8, 1815, the British advanced, but their exposed forces were no match for Jackson's well-protected men. After the Americans had repulsed several waves of attackers, the British finally retreated, leaving behind 700 dead (including their commander, Sir Edward Pakenham), 1,400 wounded, and 500 prisoners. Jackson's losses were eight killed and thirteen wounded. Only later did news reach North America that the United States and Britain had signed a peace treaty several weeks before the Battle of New Orleans.

The Revolt of New England

With a few notable exceptions, such as the Battles of Put-In-Bay and New Orleans, the military operations of the United States between 1812 and 1815 consisted of a series of humiliating failures. As a result, the American government faced increasing popular opposition as the contest dragged on. In New England, opposition both to the war and to the Republican government that was waging it was so extreme that some Federalists celebrated British victories. In Congress, in the meantime, the Republicans had continual trouble with the Federalist opposition, led by a young congressman from New Hampshire, Daniel Webster, who missed no opportunity to embarrass the administration.

By now the Federalists were a minority in the country as a whole, but they were still the majority party in New England. Some of them began to dream again of creating a separate nation in that region, which they could dominate and in which they could escape what they saw as the tyranny of slaveholders and backwoodsmen. Talk of secession revived and reached a climax in the winter of 1814–1815.

On December 15, 1814, delegates from the New England states met in Hartford, Connecticut, to discuss their Hartford Convention grievances. Those who favored secession at the Hartford Convention were outnumbered by a comparatively moderate majority. But while the convention's report only hinted at secession, it reasserted the right of nullification and proposed seven amendments to the Constitution (presumably as the condition of New England's remaining in the Union)—amendments designed to protect New England from the growing influence of the South and the West.

Because the war was going badly and the government was becoming desperate, the New Englanders assumed that the Republicans would have to agree to their demands. Soon after the convention adjourned, however, the news of Jackson's smashing victory at New Orleans reached the cities of the Northeast. A day or two later, reports arrived from abroad of a negotiated peace. In the euphoria of this apparent triumph, the Hartford Convention and the Federalist party came to seem futile, irrelevant, even treasonable. The failure of the secession effort was a virtual death blow to the Federalist Party.

ATTACKING THE FEDERALISTS A Republican cartoonist derided the secession efforts of New England Federalists at the Hartford Convention in this cartoon. It portrays timid men representing Massachusetts, Connecticut, and Rhode Island preparing to leap into the arms of George III. *(Library of Congress)*

The Peace Settlement

Peace talks between the United States and Britain had begun even before fighting in the War of 1812 began. John Quincy Adams, Henry Clay, and Albert Gallatin led the American delegation.

Realizing that, with the defeat of Napoleon in Europe, the British would no longer have much incentive to

> Treaty of Ghent

interfere with American commerce, the Americans gave up their demand for a British renunciation of impressment and for the cession of Canada to the United States. Exhausted and in debt from their prolonged conflict with Napoleon and eager to settle the lesser dispute in North America, the British abandoned their call for the creation of an Indian buffer state in the Northwest and made other, minor territorial concessions. The negotiators referred other disputes to arbitration. Hastily drawn up, the treaty was signed on Christmas Eve 1814.

Other settlements followed the Treaty of Ghent and

> Rush Bagot Agreement

contributed to a long-term improvement in Anglo-American relations. A commercial treaty in 1815 gave Americans the right to trade freely with England and much of the British Empire. The Rush-Bagot agreement of 1817 provided for mutual disarmament on the Great Lakes; eventually (although not until 1872) the Canadian-American boundary became the longest "unguarded frontier" in the world.

For the other parties to the War of 1812, the Indian tribes east of the Mississippi, the Treaty of Ghent was of no lasting value. It required the United States to restore to the tribes lands seized by white Americans in the fighting, but those provisions were never enforced. Ultimately, the war was another disastrous blow to the capacity of Native Americans to resist white expansion. Tecumseh, their most important leader, was dead. The British, their most important allies, were gone from the Northwest. The alliance that Tecumseh and the Prophet had forged was in disarray. And the end of the war spurred a great new drive by white settlers deeper into the West, into land the Indians were less than ever able to defend.

CONCLUSION

Thomas Jefferson called his election to the presidency the "Revolution of 1800," and his supporters believed that his victory would bring a dramatic change in the character of the nation—a retreat from Hamilton's dreams of a powerful, developing nation with great stature in the world; a return to an ideal of a simple agrarian republic happily isolated from the corruption and intrigue of Europe.

But American society was changing rapidly in the early nineteenth century, making it virtually impossible for the Jeffersonian dream to prevail. The nation's population was expanding and diversifying. Its cities were growing, and its commercial life was becoming ever more important. In 1803, Jefferson himself made one of the most important contributions to the growth of the

United States: the Louisiana Purchase, which dramatically expanded the physical boundaries of the nation—and which began extending white settlement deeper into the continent. In the process, it greatly widened the battles between Europeans and Native Americans.

The growing national pride and commercial ambitions of the United States gradually created another serious conflict with Great Britain: the War of 1812, a war that went badly for the Americans on the whole, but that was settled finally in 1814 on terms at least mildly favorable to the United States. By then, the bitter party rivalries that had characterized the first years of the republic had to some degree subsided, and the nation was poised to enter what became known as the "Era of Good Feelings." It was to be an era in which good feelings did not last for very long.

INTERACTIVE LEARNING

The *Primary Source Investigator CD-ROM* offers the following materials related to this chapter:

- A short documentary movie, **Black Jacks**, about African-American sailors (D4).

- Interactive maps: **U.S. Elections** (M7); **Exploration of the Far West** (M8); **Indian Expulsion** (M9); and **The War of 1812** (M10).

- Documents, images, and maps related to the Jeffersonian Era, the rise of cultural nationalism, and the

War of 1812. Some highlights include the resolutions of the secessionist Hartford Convention, the text of the treaty between the United States and Algiers that ended the Barbary Wars, and maps depicting the War of 1812.

Online Learning Center (www.mhhe.com/brinkley12)

For quizzes, Internet resources, references to additional books and films, and more, consult this book's Online Learning Center.

FOR FURTHER REFERENCE

Joseph J.Ellis, *American Sphinx: The Character of Thomas Jefferson* (1997) is a perceptive study of the man. Henry Adams, *History of the United States During the Administration of Jefferson and Adams*, 9 vols. (1889-1891) is one of the great literary achievements of early American historiography. Frank Bergon, ed., *The Journals of Lewis and Clark* (1989) is a concise abridgement of these fascinating accounts of their explorations. James Ronda, *Lewis and Clark Among the Indians* (1984) examines the exploration from a Native American perspective. Thomas C.Cochran, *Frontiers of Change: Early Industrialization in America* (1981) summarizes economic development in the early republic. Jeanne Boydston, *Home and Work: Housework, Wages, and the Ideology of Labor in the Early Republic* (1990) argues that the cultural status of women declined as the market revolution

began to transform the American economy. Drew McCoy, *The Elusive Republic: Political Economy in Jeffersonian America* (1980) traces the Jeffersonian struggle to keep the United States free from European-style corruption and decay. Paul Finkleman, *Slavery and the Founders: Race and Liberty in the Age of Jefferson* (1996) considers the problem of slavery in the early Republic. Gary Wills, *James Madison* (2002) is an interpretive essay on this important early president. Donald Hickey, *The War of 1812: A Forgotten Conflict* (1989) is an account of the war. J.C.A. Stagg, *Mr. Madison's War: Politics, Diplomacy, and Warfare in the Early American Republic, 1783-1830* (1983) argues that James Madison led the United States to war against Great Britain in order to preserve vital American commercial interests, but that he underestimated New England opposition to the war.

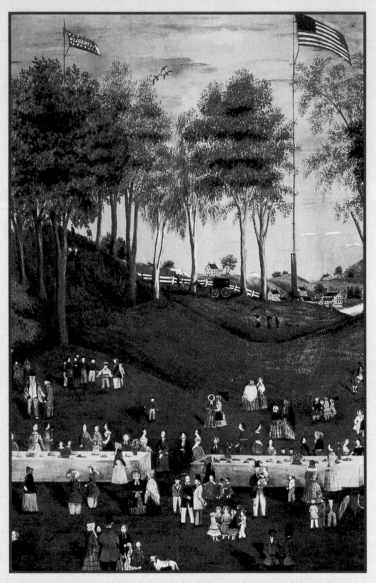

FOURTH OF JULY PICNIC AT WEYMOUTH LANDING (C.1845), BY SUSAN MERRETT Celebrations of Independence Day, like this one in eastern Massachusetts, became major festive events throughout the United States in the early nineteenth century, a sign of rising American nationalism. *(Art Institute of Chicago)*

SIGNIFICANT EVENTS

1813 ▶ Francis Lowell establishes textile factories in Waltham, Massachusetts

1815 ▶ U.S. signs treaties with tribes taking western lands from Indians

1816 ▶ Second Bank of the United States chartered

    ▶ Monroe elected president

    ▶ Tariff protects textile industry from foreign competition

    ▶ Indiana enters Union

1817 ▶ Madison vetoes internal improvements bill

    ▶ Mississippi enters Union

1818 ▶ Jackson invades Florida, ends first Seminole War

    ▶ Illinois enters Union

CHAPTER 8

Varieties of American Nationalism

Like a "fire bell in the night," as Thomas Jefferson put it, the issue of slavery arose after the War of 1812 to threaten the unity of the nation. The debate began when the territory of Missouri applied for admission to the Union, raising the question of whether it would be a free or a slaveholding state. But the larger issue, one that would arise again and again to plague the republic, was whether the vast new western regions of the United States would ultimately move into the orbit of the North or the South.

The Growing Crisis over Slavery

The Missouri crisis, which Congress settled by compromise in 1820, was significant at the time not only because it was a sign of the sectional crises to come but because it stood in such sharp contrast to the rising American nationalism of the years following the war. Whatever forces might be working to pull the nation apart, stronger ones were acting for the moment to draw it together. The American economy was experiencing remarkable growth. The federal government was acting in both domestic and foreign policy to assert a vigorous nationalism. Above all, perhaps, a set of widely (although never universally) shared sentiments and ideals worked to bind the nation together: the memory of the Revolution, the veneration of the Constitution and its framers, the belief that America had a special destiny in the world. These beliefs combined to produce among many Americans a vibrant, even romantic, patriotism.

Every year, Fourth of July celebrations reminded Americans of their common struggle for independence, as fife-and-drum corps and flamboyant orators appealed to patriotism and nationalism. When the Marquis de Lafayette, the French general who had aided the United States during the Revolution, traveled through the country in 1824, crowds in every region and of every party cheered him in frenzied celebration.

And on July 4, 1826—the fiftieth anniversary of the adoption of the Declaration of Independence—an event occurred which to many seemed to confirm that the United States was a nation specially chosen by God. On that remarkable day, Americans were to learn, two of the greatest of the country's founders and former presidents—Thomas Jefferson, author of the Declaration, and John Adams, whom Jefferson had called "its ablest advocate and defender"—died within hours of each other. Jefferson's last words, those at his bedside reported, were "Is it the Fourth?" And Adams comforted those around him moments before his death by saying, "Thomas Jefferson still survives."

For a time, it was possible for many Americans to overlook the very different forms their nationalism took—and to ignore the large elements of their population who were excluded from the national self-definition altogether. But the vigorous economic and territorial expansion this exuberant nationalism produced ultimately brought those differences to the fore.

1819 ▸ Commercial panic destabilizes economy

▸ Spain cedes Florida to United States in Adams-Onís Treaty

▸ Supreme Court hears *Dartmouth College* v. *Woodward* and *McCulloch* v. *Maryland*

▸ Alabama enters Union

1819–1820 ▸ Stephen H. Long explores Kansas, Nebraska, and Colorado

1820 ▸ Missouri Compromise enacted

▸ Monroe reelected president without opposition

1821 ▸ Mexico wins independence from Spain

▸ William Becknell opens trade between U.S. territories and New Mexico

1822 ▸ Rocky Mountain Fur Company established

1823 ▸ Monroe Doctrine proclaimed

1824 ▸ John Quincy Adams wins disputed presidential election

▸ Supreme Court rules in *Gibbons* v. *Ogden*

1826 ▸ Thomas Jefferson and John Adams die on July 4

1827 ▸ Creek Indians cede lands to Georgia

1828 ▸ "Tariff of abominations" passed

▸ Andrew Jackson elected president

A GROWING ECONOMY

The end of the War of 1812 allowed the United States to resume the economic growth and territorial expansion that, despite the Republicans' hopes for a simple agrarian society, had characterized the first decade of the nineteenth century. A vigorous postwar boom led to a disastrous bust in 1819. Brief though it was, the collapse was evidence that the United States continued to lack some of the basic institutions necessary to sustain long-term growth. In the years to follow, there were strenuous efforts to introduce stability to the expanding economy.

Banking, Currency, and Protection

The War of 1812 may have stimulated the growth of manufacturing by cutting off imports, but it also produced chaos in shipping and banking, and it exposed dramatically the inadequacy of the existing transportation and financial systems. The aftermath of the war, therefore, saw the emergence of a series of political issues connected with national economic development: reestablishing the Bank of the United States, protecting the new industries, and providing a nationwide network of roads and waterways.

Postwar Issues

The wartime experience underlined the need for another national bank. After the expiration of the first Bank's charter in 1811, a large number of state banks had begun operations. They issued vast quantities of bank notes but did not always bother to retain enough reserves of gold or silver to redeem the notes on demand. The notes passed from hand to hand more or less as money, but their actual value depended on the reputation of the bank that issued them. Thus there was a wide variety of notes, of widely differing value, in circulation at the same time. The result was a confusion that made honest business difficult and counterfeiting easy.

Congress dealt with the currency problem by chartering a second Bank of the United States in 1816. It was essentially the same institution Hamilton had founded in 1791 except that it had more capital than its predecessor. The national bank could not forbid state banks from issuing currency, but its size and power enabled it to dominate the state banks. It could compel them to issue only sound notes or risk being forced out of business.

Second Bank of the United States

Congress also acted to promote the already burgeoning manufacturing sector of the nation's economy. Manufactured goods had been so scarce during the conflict that, even with comparatively unskilled labor and inexperienced management, new factories could start operations virtually assured of quick profits.

The American textile industry had experienced a particularly dramatic growth. Between 1807 and 1815, the total number of cotton spindles increased more than fifteenfold, from 8,000 to 130,000. Until 1814, the textile factories—most of them in New England—produced only yarn and thread; families operating hand-looms at home did the actual weaving of cloth. Then the Boston merchant Francis Cabot Lowell, after examining textile machinery in England, developed a power loom that was better than its English counterpart. In 1813, Lowell organized the Boston Manufacturing Company and, at Waltham, Massachusetts, founded the first mill in America to carry on the processes of spinning and weaving under a single roof. Lowell's company was an important step in revolutionizing American manufacturing and in shaping the character of the early industrial work force. (See pp. 274–278.)

Growth of the Textile Industry

But the end of the war suddenly dimmed the prospects for American industry. British ships—determined to recapture their lost markets—swarmed into American

AN EARLY MILL IN NEW ENGLAND This early folk painting of about 1814 shows the small town of East Chelmsford, Massachusetts—still primarily agrarian, with its rural houses, open fields, and grazing livestock, but with a small textile mill already operating along the stream, at right. A little more than a decade later, the town had been transformed into a major manufacturing center and renamed for the family that owned the mills: Lowell. *(Part of the Town of Chelmsford. By Miss Warren. Abby Aldrich Rockefeller Folk Art Museum, Colonial Williamsburg Foundation, Williamsburg, VA)*

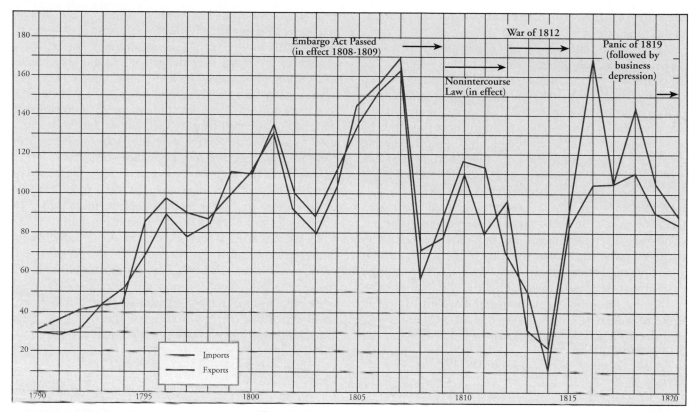

AMERICAN IMPORTS AND EXPORTS, 1790–1820 This chart shows the pattern of goods imported to and exported from the United States—the level of foreign trade, and the balance between goods bought and goods sold. Americans were heavily dependent on Britain and Europe for "finished" or "manufactured" goods in these years; and as you can see, imports grew as rapidly as, and often even more rapidly than, exports. Note how the nation's disputes with European powers depressed both exports and imports from about 1808 to 1814. ◆ *How does this chart help explain Congress's passage of a protective tariff law in 1816?*

ports and unloaded cargoes of manufactured goods, many priced below cost. As one English leader explained to Parliament, it was "well worth while to incur a loss upon the first exportation, in order, by the glut, to stifle in the cradle those rising manufactures in the United States." The "infant industries" cried out for protection against these tactics, arguing that they needed time to grow strong enough to withstand the foreign competition.

In 1816, protectionists in Congress won passage of a

A Protective Tariff

tariff law that effectively limited competition from abroad on a wide range of items, among the most important of which was cotton cloth. There were objections from agricultural interests, who would have to pay higher prices for manufactured goods as a result. But the nationalist dream of creating an important American industrial economy prevailed.

Transportation

The nation's most pressing economic need in the aftermath of the war was for a better transportation system. Without one, manufacturers would not have access to the raw materials they needed or to domestic markets. So an

old debate resumed: Should the federal government help to finance roads and other "internal improvements"?

The idea of using government funds to finance road building was not a new one.

Government-Funded Roads

When Ohio entered the Union in 1803, the federal government agreed that part of the proceeds from the government's sale of public lands there should finance road construction. In 1807, Jefferson's secretary of the treasury, Albert Gallatin, proposed that revenues from the Ohio land sales should help finance a National Road from the Potomac River to the Ohio River. Both Congress and the president approved. After many delays, construction of the National Road finally began in 1811 at Cumberland, Maryland, on the Potomac; and by 1818, this highway—with a crushed stone surface and massive stone bridges—ran as far as Wheeling, Virginia, on the Ohio River. Meanwhile the state of Pennsylvania gave $100,000 to a private company to extend the Lancaster pike westward to Pittsburgh. Over both of these roads a heavy traffic soon moved: stagecoaches, Conestoga wagons, private carriages, and other vehicles, as well as droves of cattle. Despite high tolls, the roads made transportation costs across the mountains lower than ever before. Manufactures, particularly textiles, moved from the Atlantic seaboard to the Ohio Valley in unprecedented quantities.

At the same time, on the rivers and the Great Lakes, steam-powered shipping was expanding rapidly. The development of steamboat lines was already well underway before the War of 1812, thanks to the technological advances introduced by Robert Fulton and others. The war had retarded expansion for a time, but by 1816, river steamers were beginning to journey up and down the Mississippi to the Ohio River, and up the Ohio as far as Pittsburgh. Within a few years, steamboats were carrying far more cargo on the Mississippi than all the earlier forms of river transport—flatboats, barges, and others—combined. They stimulated the agricultural economy of the West and the South, by providing much readier access to markets at greatly reduced cost. They enabled eastern manufacturers to send their finished goods west.

Steamboats

Despite the progress with steamboats and turnpikes, there remained serious gaps in the nation's transportation network, as the War of 1812 had shown. Once the British blockade cut off Atlantic shipping, the coastal roads became choked by the unaccustomed volume of north-south traffic. Long lines of wagons waited for a chance to use the ferries that were still the only means of crossing most rivers. Oxcarts, pressed into emergency service, took six or seven weeks to go from Philadelphia to Charleston. In some areas there were serious shortages of goods that normally traveled by sea, and prices rose to new heights. Rice cost three times as much in New York as in Charleston, flour three times as much in Boston as in Richmond—all because of the difficulty of transportation. There were military consequences, too. On the northern and western frontiers, the absence of good roads had frustrated American campaigns.

In 1815, with this wartime experience in mind, President Madison called the attention of Congress to the "great importance of establishing throughout our country the roads and canals which can be best executed under the national authority," and suggested that a constitutional amendment would resolve any doubts about Congress's authority to provide for their construction.

DECK LIFE ON THE *PARAGON*, 1811–1812 The *North River Steamboat Clermont*, launched in 1806 by the inventor Robert Fulton and propelled by an engine he had developed, traveled from Manhattan to Albany (about 150 miles) in thirty-two hours. That was neither the longest nor the fastest steam voyage to date, but the *Clermont* proved to be the first steam-powered vessel large enough and reliable enough to be commercially valuable. Within a few years Fulton and his partner Robert R. Livingston had several steamboats operating profitably around New York. The third vessel in their fleet, the *Paragon,* shown here in a painting by the Russian diplomat and artist Pavel Petrovich Svinin, could carry 150 people and contained an elegant dining salon fitted with bronze, mahogany, and mirrors. Svinin called it "a whole floating town," and Fulton told a friend that the *Paragon* "beats everything on the globe, for made as you and I are we cannot tell what is in the moon." *(Metropolitan Museum of Art)*

Representative John C. Calhoun promptly introduced a bill that would have used the funds owed the government by the Bank of the United States to finance internal improvements. "Let us, then, bind the republic together with a perfect system of roads and canals," Calhoun urged. "Let us conquer space."

Congress passed Calhoun's internal improvements bill, but President Madison, on his last day in office

Vetoing Internal Improvements

(March 3, 1817), vetoed it. He supported the purpose of the bill, he explained, but he still believed that Congress lacked authority to fund the improvements without a constitutional amendment. And so on the issue of internal improvements, at least, the nationalists fell short of their goals. It remained for state governments and private enterprise to undertake the tremendous task of building the transportation network necessary for the growing American economy.

EXPANDING WESTWARD

One reason for the growing interest in internal improvements was the sudden and dramatic surge in westward expansion in the years following the War of 1812. "Old America seems to be breaking up and moving westward," wrote an English observer at the time. By the time of the census of 1820, white settlers had pushed well beyond the Mississippi River, and the population of the western regions was increasing more rapidly than that of the nation as a whole. Almost one of every four white Americans lived west of the Appalachians in 1820; ten years before, only one in seven had resided there.

The Great Migrations

The westward movement of the white American population was one of the most important developments of the nineteenth century. It had a profound effect on the nation's economy, bringing vast new regions into the emerging capitalist system. It had great political ramifications, which ultimately became a major factor

Reasons for Westward Expansion

in the coming of the Civil War. And like earlier movements west, it thrust peoples of different cultures and traditions into intimate (and often disastrous) association with one another.

There were several important reasons for this expansion. The pressures driving white Americans out of the East came in part from the continued growth of the nation's population—both through natural increase and through immigration. Between 1800 and 1820, the population nearly doubled—from 5.3 million to 9.6 million. The growth of cities absorbed some of that increase, but most Americans were still farmers. The agricultural lands of the East were by now largely occupied, and some of

them were exhausted. In the South, the spread of the plantation system, and of a slave labor force, limited opportunities for new settlers.

Meanwhile, the West itself was becoming increasingly attractive to white settlers. The War of 1812 had helped diminish (although it did not wholly eliminate) one of the traditional deterrents to western expansion: Native American opposition. And in the aftermath of the war, the federal government continued its policy of pushing the remaining tribes farther and farther west. A series of treaties in 1815 wrested more land from the Indians. In the meantime, the government was erecting a chain of stockaded forts along the Great Lakes and the upper Mississippi to protect the frontier. It also created a

The Factor System

"factor" system, by which government factors (or agents) supplied the tribes with goods at cost. This not only worked to drive Canadian traders out of the region, it also helped create a situation of dependency that made Native Americans themselves easier to control.

FORT SNELLING This is an 1838 sketch of Fort Snelling (at the juncture of the Minnesota and Mississippi Rivers), containing instructions for reaching it from St. Louis. It was one of a string of fortifications built along the western edge of European settlement along the Great Lakes and the upper Mississippi in the first three decades of the nineteenth century. The forts were designed to protect the new white communities from hostile Indians. Fort Snelling stands today in Minnesota as a "living history" site. *(Minnesota Historical Society)*

Now that fertile lands were secure for white settlement, migrants from throughout the East flocked to what was then known as the Old Northwest (now called part of the Midwest). The Ohio and Monongahela Rivers were the main routes westward, until the completion of the Erie Canal in 1825. Once on the Ohio, they floated downstream on flatboats bearing all their possessions, then left the river (often at Cincinnati, which was becoming one of the region's—and the nation's—principal cities) and pressed on overland with wagons, handcarts, packhorses, cattle, and hogs.

The Plantation System in the Southwest

In the Southwest, the new agricultural economy emerged along different lines. The principal attraction there was cotton. The cotton lands in the uplands of the Old South had lost much of their fertility through overplanting and erosion. But the market for cotton continued to grow, so there was no lack of ambitious farmers seeking fresh soil in a climate suitable for the crop. In the Southwest, around the end of the Appalachian range, stretched a broad zone within which cotton could thrive. That zone included what was to become known as the Black Belt of central Alabama and Mississippi, a vast prairie with a dark, productive soil of rotted limestone.

The advance of southern settlement meant the spread of cotton, plantations, and slavery. The first arrivals in an uncultivated region were usually ordinary people like the settlers farther north, small farmers who made rough clearings in the forest. But wealthier planters soon followed. They bought up the cleared or partially cleared land, while the original settlers moved farther west and started over again.

Cotton and the Expansion of Slavery

The large planters made the westward journey in a style quite different from that of the first pioneers. Over the alternately dusty and muddy roads came great caravans consisting of herds of livestock, wagonloads of household goods, long lines of slaves, and—bringing up the rear—the planter's family riding in carriages. Success in the wilderness was by no means assured, even for the wealthiest settlers. But many planters soon expanded small clearings into vast cotton fields. They replaced the cabins of the early pioneers with more sumptuous log dwellings and ultimately with imposing mansions that symbolized the emergence of a newly rich class. In later years, these western planters would assume the airs of a longstanding aristocracy. But by the time of the Civil War, few planter families in the Southwest had been there for more than one or two generations.

The rapid growth of the Northwest and Southwest resulted in the admission of four new states to the Union in the immediate aftermath of the War of 1812: Indiana in 1816, Mississippi in 1817, Illinois in 1818, and Alabama in 1819.

Trade and Trapping in the Far West

Not many Anglo-Americans yet knew much about or were much interested in the far western areas of the continent. But a significant trade nevertheless began to develop between these western regions and the United States early in the nineteenth century, and it grew steadily for decades.

Mexico, which continued to control Texas, California, and much of the rest of the Southwest, won its independence from Spain in 1821. Almost immediately, it opened its northern territories to trade with the United States, hoping to revive an economy that had grown stagnant during its war with Spain. American traders poured into the region—overland into Texas and New Mexico, by sea into California. Merchants from the United States quickly displaced both the Indian traders who had dominated trade with Mexico in some areas of the Southwest and some of the same Mexicans who had hoped this new commerce would improve their fortunes. In New Mexico, for example, the Missouri trader William Becknell began in 1821 to offer American manufactured goods for sale, priced considerably below the inferior Mexican goods that had dominated the market in the past. Mexico effectively lost its markets in its own colony, and a steady traffic of commercial wagon trains was moving back and forth along the Santa Fe Trail between Missouri and New Mexico.

Becknell and those who followed him diverted an established trade from Mexico to the United States. Fur traders created a wholly new commerce with the West. Before the War of 1812, John Jacob Astor's American Fur Company had established Astoria as a trading post at the mouth of the Columbia River in Oregon. But when the war came, Astor sold his suddenly imperiled interests to the Northwestern Fur Company, a British concern operating out of Canada. After the war Astor centered his own operations in the Great Lakes area, from which he eventually extended them westward to the Rockies. Other companies carried on operations up the Missouri and its tributaries and into the Rocky Mountains.

Astor's American Fur Company

At first, fur traders did most of their business by purchasing pelts from the Indians. But increasingly, white trappers entered the region and began to hunt beaver on their own. Substantial numbers of Anglo-Americans and French Canadians moved deep into the Great Lakes region and beyond to join the Iroquois and other Indians in pursuit of furs.

As the trappers, or "mountain men," moved west from the Great Lakes region, they began to establish themselves in what is now Utah and in parts of New Mexico.

THE RENDEZVOUS The annual rendezvous of fur trappers and traders was a major event in the lives of the lonely men who made their livelihoods gathering furs. It was also a gathering of representatives of the many cultures that mingled in the Far West, among them Anglo-Americans, French Canadians, Indians, and Hispanics. *(Denver Public Library)*

In 1822, Andrew Henry and William Ashley founded the Rocky Mountain Fur Company and recruited white trappers to move permanently into the Rockies in search of furs, which were becoming increasingly scarce farther east. Henry and Ashley dispatched supplies annually to their trappers in exchange for furs and skins. The arrival of the supply train became the occasion for a gathering of scores of mountain men, some of whom lived much of the year in considerable isolation.

But however isolated their daily lives, these mountain men were closely bound up with the expanding market economy of the United States. Some were employees of the Rocky Mountain Fur Company (or some other, similar enterprise), earning a salary in return for providing a steady supply of furs. Others were nominally independent but relied on the companies for credit; they were almost always in debt and hence economically bound to the companies. Some trapped entirely on their own and simply sold their furs for cash, but they too depended on merchants from the East for their livelihoods. And it was to those merchants that the bulk of the profits from the trade flowed.

Many trappers and mountain men lived peacefully and successfully with the Native Americans and Mexicans whose lands they came to share. Perhaps two-thirds of the white trappers married Indian or Hispanic women while

The Fur Trade and the Market Economy

living in the West. But some did not. Jedediah S. Smith, a trapper who became an Ashley partner, led a series of forays deep into Mexican territory that ended in disastrous battles with the Mojaves and other tribes. Four years after an 1827 expedition to Oregon in which sixteen members of his party of twenty had died, he set out for New Mexico and was killed by Comanches, who took the weapons he was carrying and sold them to Mexican settlers.

Eastern Images of the West

Americans in the East were only dimly aware of the world the trappers were entering and helping to reshape. Smith and others became the source of dramatic (and often exaggerated) popular stories. But the trappers themselves did not often write of their lives or draw maps of the lands they explored.

More important in increasing eastern awareness of the West were explorers, many of them dispatched by the United States government with instructions to chart the territories they visited. In 1819 and 1820, with instructions from the War Department to find the sources of the Red River, Stephen H. Long led nineteen soldiers on a journey up the Platte and South Platte Rivers through what is now Nebraska and eastern

Stephen Long's Expedition

PLATTE RIVER CROSSING The trails to the West, along which hundreds of thousands of white, English-speaking people migrated in the antebellum period, were filled with hardships: steep hills, rugged mountains with narrow passes through them, broad deserts, and rivers—some broad, some rapid—that had to be crossed, in the absence of bridges, with makeshift rafts and barges. Joseph Goldsborough Bruff, who traveled to California along the Overland trail, sketched this crossing on the Platte River, which runs from Nebraska into the Missouri River. *(Reproduced by permission of The Huntington Library, San Marino, California)*

Colorado (where he discovered a peak that would be named for him), and then returned eastward along the Arkansas River through what is now Kansas. He failed to find the headwaters of the Red River. But he wrote an influential report on his trip, including an assessment of the region's potential for future settlement and development that echoed the dismissive conclusions of Zebulon Pike fifteen years before. On the published map of his expedition, he labeled the Great Plains the "Great American Desert."

THE "ERA OF GOOD FEELINGS"

The expansion of the economy, the growth of white settlement and trade in the West, the creation of new states—all reflected the rising spirit of nationalism that was permeating the United States in the years following the War of 1812. That spirit found reflection for a time in the character of national politics.

The End of the First Party System

Ever since 1800, the presidency seemed to have been the special possession of Virginians. After two terms in office Jefferson chose his secretary of state, James Madison of Virginia, to succeed him, and after two more terms, Madison secured

The Virginia Dynasty

the presidential nomination for his secretary of state, James Monroe, also of Virginia. Many in the North were expressing impatience with the so-called Virginia Dynasty, but the Republicans had no difficulty electing their candidate in the listless campaign of 1816. Monroe received 183 ballots in the electoral college; his Federalist opponent, Rufus King of New York, received only 34—from Massachusetts, Connecticut, and Delaware.

Monroe was sixty-one years old when he became president. In the course of his long career, he had served as a soldier in the Revolution, as a diplomat, and most recently as a cabinet officer. He entered office under what seemed to be remarkably favorable circumstances.

THE TRIUMPHANT TOUR OF JAMES MONROE After James Monroe's enormously successful tour of the northern and eastern states in 1818, midway through his first term as president, there was widespread self-congratulation through much of the United States for the apparent political unity that had gripped the nation. Only a few years earlier, the northeast had been the bastion of Federalist party opposition to the Republican governments of the early nineteenth century. At one point, some Federalist leaders had even proposed secession from the United States. But now a Virginia Republican president had been greeted as a hero in the former Federalist strongholds. This book, published in 1820 (when Monroe ran virtually unopposed for re-election), is an account of the president's triumphant tour and a short account of his life—an early version of the now familiar campaign biography. *(Collection of David J. and Janice L. Frent)*

With the decline of the Federalists, his party faced no serious opposition. With the conclusion of the War of 1812, the nation faced no important international threats. American politicians had dreamed since the first days of the republic of a time in which partisan divisions and factional disputes might come to an end. In the prosperous postwar years, Monroe attempted to use his office to realize that dream.

He made that clear, above all, in the selection of his cabinet. For secretary of state, he chose the New Englander and former Federalist John Quincy Adams. Jefferson, Madison, and Monroe had all served as secretary of state before becoming president; Adams, therefore, immediately became the heir apparent, suggesting that the "Virginia Dynasty" would soon come to an end. Speaker of the House Henry Clay declined an offer to be secretary of war, so Monroe named John C. Calhoun instead. In his other appointments, too, Monroe took pains to include both northerners and southerners, easterners and westerners, Federalists and Republicans.

Soon after his inauguration, Monroe did what no president since Washington had done: he made a goodwill tour through the country. In New England, so recently

Monroe's Goodwill Tour

the scene of rabid Federalist discontent, he was greeted everywhere with enthusiastic demonstrations. The *Columbian Centinel*, a Federalist newspaper in Boston, commenting on the "Presidential Jubilee" in that city, observed that an "era of good feelings" had arrived. And on the surface, at least, the years of Monroe's presidency did appear to be an "era of good feelings." In 1820, Monroe was reelected without opposition. For all practical purposes, the Federalist Party had now ceased to exist.

John Quincy Adams and Florida

Like his father, the second president, John Quincy Adams had spent much of his life in diplomatic service. And even before becoming secretary of state, he had become one of the great diplomats in American history. He was also a committed nationalist, and he considered his most important task to be the promotion of American expansion.

His first challenge was Florida. The United States had already annexed West Florida, but that claim was in dispute. Most Americans, moreover, still believed the nation should gain possession of the entire peninsula. In 1817, Adams began negotiations with the Spanish minister, Luis de Onís, in hopes of resolving the dispute and gaining the entire territory for the United States.

In the meantime, however, events were taking their own course in Florida itself. Andrew Jackson, now in command of American troops along the Florida frontier,

The Seminole War

had orders from Secretary of War Calhoun to "adopt the necessary

SEMINOLE DANCE This 1838 drawing by a U.S. military officer portrays a dance by Seminole Indians near Fort Butler in Florida. It was made in the midst of the prolonged Second Seminole War, which ended in 1842 with the removal of most of the tribe from Florida to reservations west of the Mississippi. *(Reproduced by permission of The Huntington Library, San Marino, California)*

measures" to stop continuing raids on American territory by Seminole Indians south of the border. Jackson used those orders as an excuse to invade Florida, seize the Spanish forts at St. Marks and Pensacola, and order the hanging of two British subjects on the charge of supplying and inciting the Indians. The operation became known as the Seminole War.

Instead of condemning Jackson's raid, Adams urged the government to assume responsibility for it. The United States, he told the Spanish, had the right under international law to defend itself against threats from across its borders. Since Spain was unwilling or unable to curb those threats, America had simply done what was necessary. Jackson's raid demonstrated to the Spanish that the United States could easily take Florida by force. Adams implied that the nation might consider doing so.

Onís realized, therefore, that he had little choice but to come to terms with the Americans. Under the provisions of the Adams-Onís Treaty of 1819, Spain ceded all of Florida to the United States and gave up its claim to territory

Adams-Onís Treaty

north of the 42nd parallel in the Pacific Northwest. In return, the American government gave up its claims to Texas.

The Panic of 1819

But the Monroe administration had little time to revel in its diplomatic successes, for the nation was falling victim to a serious economic crisis: the Panic of 1819. It followed a period of high foreign demand for American farm goods and thus of exceptionally high prices for American farmers (all as a result of the disruption of European agriculture caused by the Napoleonic Wars). The rising prices for farm goods had stimulated a land boom in the western United States. Fueled by speculative investments, land prices soared.

The availability of easy credit to settlers and speculators—from the government (under the land acts of 1800 and 1804), from state banks and wildcat banks, even for a time from the rechartered Bank of the United States—fueled the land boom. Beginning in 1819, however, new management at the national bank began tightening credit, calling in loans, and foreclosing mortgages. This precipitated a series of failures by state banks, and the result was a financial panic, which many Americans,

particularly those in the West, blamed on the national bank. Thus began a process that would eventually make the Bank's existence one of the nation's most burning political issues. Six years of depression followed.

Boom and Bust

Some Americans saw the Panic of 1819 and the widespread distress that followed as a warning that rapid economic growth and territorial expansion would destabilize the nation and threaten its survival. But by 1820 most Americans were irrevocably committed to the idea of growth and expansion. Public debate in the future would revolve less around whether growth was good or bad than around how to encourage and control it.

SECTIONALISM AND NATIONALISM

For a brief but alarming moment in 1819–1820, the increasing differences between the North and the South threatened the unity of the United States—until the Missouri Compromise averted a sectional crisis for a

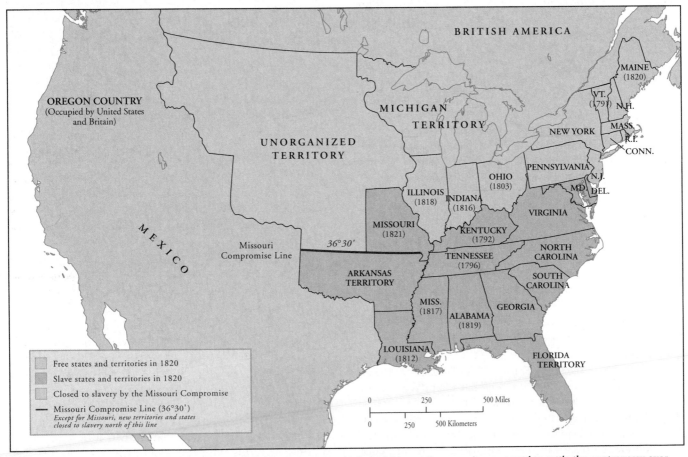

THE MISSOURI COMPROMISE, 1820 This map illustrates the way in which the Missouri Compromise proposed to settle the controversy over slavery in the new western territories of the United States. The compromise rested on the virtually simultaneous admission of Missouri and Maine to the Union, one a free state and the other a slave one. Note the red line extending beyond the southern border of Missouri, which in theory established a permanent boundary between areas in which slavery could be established and areas where it could not be. ◆ *What precipitated the Missouri Compromise?*

 For an interactive version of this map go to www.mhhe.com/brinkley12 ch8maps

time. The forces of nationalism continued to assert themselves, and the federal government began to assume the role of promoter of economic growth.

The Missouri Compromise

When Missouri applied for admission to the Union as a state in 1819, slavery was already well established there. Even so, Representative James Tallmadge, Jr. of New York proposed an amendment to the Missouri statehood bill that would prohibit the further introduction of slaves into Missouri and provide for the gradual emancipation of those already there. The Tallmadge Amendment provoked a controversy that was to rage for the next two years.

Tallmadge Amendment

Since the beginning of the republic, partly by chance and partly by design, new states had come into the Union more or less in pairs, one from the North, another from the South. In 1819, there were eleven free states and eleven slave states; the admission of Missouri would upset that balance and increase the political power of the North over the South. Hence the controversy over slavery and freedom in Missouri.

Complicating the Missouri question was the application of Maine (previously the northern part of Massachusetts) for admission as a new (and free) state. Speaker of the House Henry Clay informed northern members that if they blocked Missouri from entering the Union as a slave state, southerners would block the admission of Maine. But Maine ultimately offered a way out of the impasse, as the Senate agreed to combine the Maine and Missouri proposals into a single bill. Maine would be admitted as a free state, Missouri as a slave state. Then Senator Jesse B. Thomas of Illinois proposed an amendment prohibiting slavery in the rest of the Louisiana Purchase territory north of the southern boundary of Missouri (the 36° 30´ parallel). The Senate adopted the Thomas Amendment, and Speaker Clay, with great difficulty, guided the amended Maine-Missouri bill through the House.

Missouri Compromise

Nationalists in both North and South hailed this settlement—which became known as the Missouri Compromise—as a happy resolution of a danger to the Union. But the debate over it had revealed a strong undercurrent of sectionalism that was competing with—although at the moment failing to derail—the powerful tides of nationalism.

Marshall and the Court

John Marshall served as chief justice of the United States for almost thirty-five years, from 1801 to 1835, and he dominated the Court more fully than anyone else before or since. More than anyone but the framers themselves, he molded the development of the Constitution: strengthening the judicial branch at the expense of the executive and legislative branches, increasing the power of the federal government at the expense of the states, and advancing the interests of the propertied and commercial classes.

Committed to promoting commerce, the Marshall Court staunchly defended the inviolability of contracts. In *Fletcher* v. *Peck* (1810), which arose out of a series of notorious land frauds in Georgia, the Court had to decide whether the Georgia legislature of 1796 could repeal the act of the previous legislature granting lands under shady circumstances to the Yazoo Land Companies. In a unanimous decision, Marshall held that a land grant was a valid contract and could not be repealed even if corruption was involved.

JOHN MARSHALL The imposing figure in this early photograph is John Marshall, the most important chief justice of the Supreme Court in American history. A former secretary of state, Marshall served as chief justice from 1801 until his death in 1835 at the age of 80. Such was the power of his intellect and personality that he dominated his fellow justices throughout that period, regardless of their previous party affiliations or legal ideologies. Marshall established the independence of the Court, gave it a reputation for nonpartisan integrity, and established its powers, which were only vaguely described by the Constitution. *(National Archives and Records Administration)*

Dartmouth College v. *Woodward* (1819) further expanded the meaning of the contract clause of the Constitution. Having gained control of the New Hampshire state government, Republicans tried to revise Dartmouth College's charter (granted by King George III in 1769) to convert the private college into a state university. Daniel Webster, a Dartmouth graduate and brilliant orator, argued the college's case. The Dartmouth charter, he insisted, was a contract, protected by the same doctrine that the Court had already upheld in *Fletcher* v. *Peck*. Then, according to legend, he brought some of the justices to tears with an irrelevant passage that concluded: "It is, sir,... a small college. And yet there are those who love it." The Court ruled for Dartmouth, proclaiming that corporation charters such as the one the colonial legislature had granted the college were contracts and thus inviolable. The decision placed important restrictions on the ability of state governments to control corporations.

Dartmouth College v. Woodward

In overturning the act of the legislature and the decisions of the New Hampshire courts, the justices also implicitly claimed for themselves the right to override the decisions of state courts. But advocates of states' rights, especially in the South, continued to challenge its right to do so. In *Cohens* v. *Virginia* (1821), Marshall explicitly affirmed the constitutionality of federal review of state court decisions. The states had given up part of their sovereignty in ratifying the Constitution, he explained, and their courts must submit to federal jurisdiction; otherwise, the federal government would be prostrated "at the feet of every state in the Union."

Meanwhile, in *McCulloch* v. *Maryland* (1819), Marshall confirmed the "implied powers" of Congress by upholding the constitutionality of the Bank of the United States. The Bank had become so unpopular in the South and the West that several of the states tried to drive branches out of business by outright prohibition or by confiscatory taxes. This case presented two constitutional questions to the Supreme Court: Could Congress charter a bank? And if so, could individual states ban it or tax it? Daniel Webster, one of the Bank's attorneys, argued that establishing such an institution came within the "necessary and proper" clause of the Constitution and that the power to tax involved a "power to destroy." If the states could tax the Bank at all, they could tax it to death. Marshall adopted Webster's words in deciding for the Bank.

Confirming Implied Powers

In the case of *Gibbons* v. *Ogden* (1824), the Court strengthened Congress's power to regulate interstate commerce. The state of New York had granted the steamboat company of Robert Fulton and Robert Livingston the exclusive right to carry passengers on the Hudson River to New York City. Fulton and Livingston then gave Aaron Ogden the business of carrying passengers across the river between New York and New Jersey. But Thomas Gibbons, with a license granted under an act of Congress, began competing with Ogden for the ferry traffic. Ogden brought suit against him and won in the New York courts. Gibbons appealed to the Supreme Court. The most important question facing the justices was whether Congress's power to give Gibbons a license to operate his ferry superseded the state of New York's power to grant Ogden a monopoly. Marshall claimed that the power of Congress to regulate interstate commerce (which, he said, included navigation) was "complete in itself" and might be "exercised to its utmost extent." Ogden's state-granted monopoly, therefore, was void.

The decisions of the Marshall Court established the primacy of the federal government over the states in regulating the economy and opened the way for an increased federal role in promoting economic growth. They protected corporations and other private economic institutions from local government interference. They were, in short, highly nationalistic decisions, designed to promote the growth of a strong, unified, and economically developed United States.

Establishing Federal Primacy

The Court and the Tribes

The nationalist inclinations of the Marshall Court were visible as well in a series of decisions concerning the legal status of Indian tribes within the United States. But these decisions did not simply affirm the supremacy of the United States; they also carved out a distinctive position for Native Americans within the constitutional structure.

The first of the crucial Indian decisions was in the case of *Johnson* v. *McIntosh* (1823). Leaders of the Illinois and Pinakeshaw tribes had sold parcels of their land to a group of white settlers (including Johnson) but had later signed a treaty with the federal government ceding territory that included those same parcels to the United States. The government proceeded to grant homestead rights to new white settlers (among them McIntosh) on the land claimed by Johnson. The Court was asked to decide which claim had precedence. Marshall's ruling, not surprisingly, favored the United States. But in explaining it, he offered a preliminary definition of the place of Indians within the nation. The tribes had a basic right to their tribal lands, he said, that preceded all other American law. Individual American citizens could not buy or take land from the tribes; only the federal government—the supreme authority—could do that.

Even more important was the Court's 1832 decision in *Worcester* v. *Georgia,* in which the Court invalidated Georgia laws that attempted to regulate access by U.S. citizens

Worcester v. Georgia

to Cherokee country. Only the federal government could do that, Marshall claimed, thus taking another important step in consolidating federal authority over the states (and over the tribes). In doing so, he further defined the nature of the Indian nations. The tribes, he explained, were sovereign entities in much the same way Georgia was a sovereign entity—"distinct political communities, having territorial boundaries within which their authority is exclusive." In defending the power of the federal government, he was also affirming, indeed expanding, the rights of the tribes to remain free from the authority of state governments.

The Marshall decisions, therefore, did what the Constitution itself had not done: they defined a place for Indian tribes within the American political system. The tribes had basic property rights. They were sovereign entities not subject to the authority of state governments. But the federal government, like a "guardian" governing its "ward," had ultimate authority over tribal affairs—even if that authority was, according to the Court, limited by the government's obligation to protect Indian welfare. These provisions were seldom enough to

defend Indians from the steady westward march of white civilization, but they formed the basis of what legal protections they had.

The Latin American Revolution and the Monroe Doctrine

Just as the Supreme Court was asserting American nationalism in the shaping of the country's economic life, so the Monroe administration was asserting nationalism in foreign policy. As always, American diplomacy was principally concerned with Europe. But in the 1820s, dealing with Europe forced the United States to develop a policy toward Latin America.

Americans looking southward in the years following the War of 1812 beheld a gigantic spectacle: the Spanish Empire in its death throes, a | **Revolution in Latin America** |
whole continent in revolt, new nations in the making. Already the United States had developed a profitable trade with Latin America and was rivaling Great Britain as the principal trading nation there. Many

CHEROKEE LEADERS Sequoyah, left (who also used the name George Guess), was a mixed-blood Cherokee who translated his tribe's language into writing through an elaborate alphabet of his own invention, pictured here. He opposed Indian assimilation into white society and saw the preservation of the Cherokee language as a way to protect the culture of his tribe. He moved to Arkansas in the 1820s and became a chief of the western Cherokee tribes. Major George Lowery, shown on the right, was also a mixed-blood Cherokee and served as assistant principal chief of the Cherokee from 1828 to 1838. He supported acculturation but remained a Cherokee nationalist. He wears a U.S. presidential medal around his neck. (Left, *National Portrait Gallery, Smithsonian Institute/Art Resource, NY;* Right, *From the collection of the Gilcrease Museum, Tulsa, Oklahoma*)

believed the success of the anti-Spanish revolutions would further strengthen America's position in the region.

In 1815, the United States proclaimed neutrality in the wars between Spain and its rebellious colonies, implying a partial recognition of the rebels' status as nations. Moreover, the United States sold ships and supplies to the revolutionaries, a clear indication that it was not genuinely neutral but was trying to help the insurgents. Finally, in 1822, President Monroe established diplomatic relations with five new nations—La Plata (later Argentina), Chile, Peru, Colombia, and Mexico—making the United States the first country to recognize them.

In 1823, Monroe went further and announced a policy that would ultimately be | The Monroe Doctrine | known (beginning some thirty years later) as the "Monroe Doctrine," even though it was primarily the work of John Quincy Adams. "The American continents," Monroe declared, ". . . are henceforth not to be considered as subjects for future colonization by any European powers." The United States would consider any foreign challenge to the sovereignty of existing American nations an unfriendly act. At the same time, he proclaimed, "Our policy in regard to Europe . . . is not to interfere in the internal concerns of any of its powers."

The Monroe Doctrine emerged directly out of America's relations with Europe in the 1820s. Many Americans feared that Spain's European | American Fears | allies (notably France) would assist Spain in an effort to retake its lost empire. Even more troubling to Adams (and many other Americans) was the fear that Great Britain had designs on Cuba. Adams wanted to keep Cuba in Spanish hands until it fell (as he believed it ultimately would) to the Americans.

The Monroe Doctrine had few immediate effects, but it was important as an expression of the growing spirit of nationalism in the United States in the 1820s. And it established the idea of the United States as the dominant power in the Western Hemisphere.

THE REVIVAL OF OPPOSITION

After 1816, the Federalist Party offered no presidential candidate and soon ceased to exist as a national political force. The Republican Party (which considered itself not a party at all but an organization representing the whole of the population) was the only organized force in national politics.

By the late 1820s, however, partisan divisions were emerging once again. In some respects, the division | New Political Divisions | mirrored the schism that had produced the first party system in the 1790s. The Republicans had in many ways come to resemble the early Federalist regimes in their promotion of economic growth and centralization. And the opposition, like the opposition in the 1790s, objected to the federal government's expanding role in the economy. There was, however, a crucial difference. At the beginning of the century, the opponents of centralization had also often been opponents of economic growth. Now, in the 1820s, the controversy involved not whether but how the nation should continue to expand.

The "Corrupt Bargain"

Until 1820, when the Federalist Party effectively ceased operations and James Monroe ran for reelection unopposed, presidential candidates were | End of the Caucus System | nominated by caucuses of the two parties in Congress. But in 1824, "King Caucus" was overthrown. The Republican caucus nominated William H. Crawford of Georgia, the secretary of the treasury and the favorite of the extreme states' rights faction of the party. But other candidates received nominations from state legislatures and won endorsements from irregular mass meetings throughout the country.

One of them was Secretary of State John Quincy Adams, who held the office that was the traditional stepping-stone to the presidency. But as he himself ruefully understood, he was a man of cold and forbidding manners, with little popular appeal. Another contender was Henry Clay, the Speaker of the House. He had a devoted personal following and a definite and coherent program: the "American System," which proposed creating a great home market for factory and farm producers by raising the protective tariff, strengthening the national bank, and financing internal improvements. Andrew Jackson, the fourth major candidate, had no significant political record—even though he had served briefly as a representative in Congress and was now a new member of the United States Senate. But he was a military hero and had the help of shrewd political allies from his home state of Tennessee.

Jackson received more popular and electoral votes than any other candidate, but not a majority. He had 99 electoral votes to Adams's | Election of 1824 | 84, Crawford's 41, and Clay's 37. The Twelfth Amendment to the Constitution (passed in the aftermath of the contested 1800 election) required the House of Representatives to choose among the three candidates with the largest numbers of electoral votes. Crawford was seriously ill and not a plausible candidate. Clay was out of the running, but he was in a strong position to influence the result. Jackson was Clay's most dangerous political rival in the West, so Clay supported Adams, in part because, alone among the candidates, he was an ardent nationalist and a likely supporter of the American System. With Clay's endorsement, Adams won election in the House.

The Jacksonians believed their large popular and electoral pluralities entitled their candidate to the presidency, and they were enraged when he lost. But they grew angrier still when Adams named Clay his secretary of state. The State Department was the well-established route to the presidency, and Adams thus appeared to be naming Clay as his own successor. The outrage the Jacksonians expressed at what they called a "corrupt bargain" haunted Adams throughout his presidency.

The Second President Adams

Throughout Adams's term in the White House, the political bitterness arising from the "corrupt bargain" charges thoroughly frustrated his policies. Adams proposed an ambitiously nationalist program reminiscent of Clay's American System. But Jacksonians in Congress blocked most of it.

Adams also experienced diplomatic frustrations. He appointed delegates to an international conference that the Venezuelan liberator, Simón Bolívar, had called in Panama in 1826. But Haiti was one of the participating nations, and southerners in Congress opposed the idea of white Americans mingling with the black delegates. Congress delayed approving the Panama mission so long that the American delegation did not arrive until after the conference was over.

Adams also lost a contest with the state of Georgia, which wished to remove the remaining Creek and Cherokee Indians from the state to gain additional soil for cotton planters. The United States government, in a 1791 treaty, had guaranteed that land to the Creeks; but in 1825, white Georgians had extracted a new treaty from William McIntosh, the leader of one faction in the tribe and a longtime advocate of Indian cooperation with the United States. Adams believed the new treaty had no legal force, since McIntosh clearly did not represent the wishes of the tribe; and he refused to enforce the treaty, setting up a direct conflict between the president and the state. The governor of Georgia defied the president and proceeded with plans for Indian removal. Adams found no way to stop him.

Even more damaging to the administration was its support for a new tariff on imported goods in 1828. This measure originated with the demands of Massachusetts and Rhode Island woolen manufacturers, who complained that the British were dumping textiles on the American market at artificially low prices. But to win

Tariff of Abominations

JOHN QUINCY ADAMS This photograph of the former president was taken shortly before his death in 1848—almost twenty years after he had left the White House—when he was serving as a congressman from Massachusetts. During his years as president, he was—as he had been throughout his life—an intensely disciplined and hard-working man. He rose at four in the morning and made a long entry in his diary for the previous day. He wrote so much that his right hand at times became paralyzed with writer's cramp, so he taught himself to write with his left hand as well. *(Brown Brothers)*

support from middle and western states, the administration had to accept duties on other items. In the process, it antagonized the original New England supporters of the bill; the benefits of protecting their manufactured goods from foreign competition now had to be weighed against the prospects of having to pay more for raw materials. Adams signed the bill, earning the animosity of southerners, who cursed it as the "tariff of abominations."

Jackson Triumphant

By the time of the 1828 presidential election, a new two-party system had begun to emerge out of the divisions among the Republicans. On one side stood the supporters

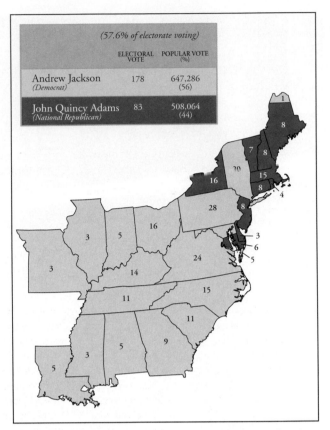

(57.6% of electorate voting)		
	ELECTORAL VOTE	POPULAR VOTE (%)
Andrew Jackson (Democrat)	178	647,286 (56)
John Quincy Adams (National Republican)	83	508,064 (44)

THE ELECTION OF 1828 As this map shows, Andrew Jackson's victory over John Quincy Adams was one of the most decisive in American history for a challenger facing an incumbent president.
♦ *What accounts for this decisive repudiation of President Adams?*

 For an interactive version of this map go to www.mhhe.com/brinkley12ch8maps

of John Quincy Adams, who called themselves the National Republicans and who supported the economic nationalism of the preceding years. Opposing them were the followers of Andrew Jackson, who took the name Democratic Republicans and who called for an assault on privilege and a widening of opportunity. Adams attracted the support of most of the remaining Federalists; Jackson appealed to a broad coalition that opposed the "economic aristocracy."

But issues seemed to count for little in the end, as the campaign degenerated into a war of personal invective. The Jacksonians charged that Adams as president had been guilty of gross waste and extravagance and had used public funds to buy gambling devices (a chess set and a billiard table) for the White House. Adams's supporters hurled even worse accusations at Jackson. They called him a murderer and distributed a "coffin handbill," which listed, within coffin-shaped outlines, the names of militiamen whom Jackson was said to have shot in cold blood during the War of 1812. (The men had been deserters who were legally executed after sentence by a court-martial.) And they called his wife a bigamist. Jackson had married his beloved Rachel at a time when the pair incorrectly believed her first husband had divorced her. (When Jackson's wife first read of the accusations against her shortly after the election, she collapsed, and a few weeks later, died; not without reason, Jackson blamed his opponents for her death.)

Jackson's victory was decisive, but sectional. He won 56 percent of the popular vote and an electoral majority of 178 votes to 83. Adams swept virtually all of New England and **Jackson Triumphant** showed significant strength in the mid-Atlantic region. Nevertheless, the Jacksonians considered their victory as complete and as important as Jefferson's in 1800. Once again, the forces of privilege had been driven from Washington. Once again, a champion of democracy would occupy the White House and restore liberty to the people and to the economy. America had entered, some Jacksonians claimed, a new era of democracy, the "era of the common man."

CONCLUSION

In the aftermath of the War of 1812, a vigorous nationalism came increasingly to characterize the political and popular culture of the United States. In all regions of the country, white men and women celebrated the achievements of the early leaders of the republic, the genius of the Constitution, and the success of the nation in withstanding serious challenges both from without and within. Party divisions faded to the point that James Monroe, the fifth president, won reelection in 1820 without opposition.

But the broad nationalism of the so-called era of good feelings disguised some deep divisions within the United States. Indeed, the character of American nationalism differed substantially from one region, and one group, to another. Battles continued between those who favored a strong central government committed to advancing the economic development of the nation and those who wanted a decentralization of power to open opportunity to more people. Battles continued as well over the role of slavery in American life—and in particular over the place of slavery in the new western territories that the United States was rapidly populating (and wresting from the tribes). The Missouri Compromise of 1820 postponed the day of reckoning on that issue—but only for a time, as Andrew Jackson would discover soon after becoming president in 1829.

INTERACTIVE LEARNING

The *Primary Source Investigator CD-ROM* offers the following materials related to this chapter:

- Interactive maps: **U.S. Elections** (M7) and **Exploration of the Far West** (M8).

- Documents, images, and maps related to westward expansion, the rise of sectionalism and the Missouri Compromise, and the revival of political opposition in the 1820s. Highlights include a patent diagram of the cotton gin, an original land advertisement, and an 1804 map of the Louisiana Purchase.

**Online Learning Center
(www.mhhe.com/brinkley12)**

For quizzes, Internet resources, references to additional books and films, and more, consult this book's Online Learning Center.

FOR FURTHER REFERENCE

Frederick Jackson Turner, *The Frontier in American History* (1920), is the classic statement of American exceptionalism. Turner argued that the western frontier endowed the United States with a distinctive, individualist, and democratic national character. John Mack Faragher, *Women and Men on the Overland Trail* (1979) was an early and influential book in the "new western history" that challenged Turner; his *Sugar Creek* (1987) portrays the society of the Old Northwest in the early nineteenth century. Robert V. Remini, *Andrew Jackson and the Course of American Empire: 1767–1821* (1977) emphasizes Andrew Jackson's importance in American territorial expansion in the South prior to 1821 and in the development of American nationalism. Morton J. Horwitz, *The Transformation of American Law, 1780–1865* (1977), an important work in American legal history, connects changes in the law to changes in the American economy. Ernest R. May, *The Making of the Monroe Doctrine* (1975) presents the history of a leading principle of American foreign policy.

DETAIL FROM *THE VERDICT OF THE PEOPLE* (1855), BY GEORGE CALEB BINGHAM This scene of an election-day gathering is peopled almost entirely by white men. Women and blacks were barred from voting, but among white males political rights expanded substantially in the 1830s and 1840s. *(Bank of America)*

SIGNIFICANT EVENTS

1820–1840 ▶ State constitutions revised

1823 ▶ Nicholas Biddle becomes president of Bank of the United States

1826 ▶ William Morgan's disappearance inflames Anti-Masonry

1828 ▶ Calhoun's South Carolina Exposition and Protest outlines nullification doctrine

1829 ▶ Andrew Jackson inaugurated

1830 ▶ Webster and Hayne debate

▶ Jackson vetoes Maysville Road Bill

▶ Indian Removal Act passed

1830–1838 ▶ Indians expelled from Southeast

1831 ▶ Anti-Mason party established

▶ Supreme Court rules in *Cherokee Nation* v. *Georgia*

1832 ▶ Democrats hold first national party convention

▶ Jackson vetoes bill to recharter Bank of the United States

▶ Jackson reelected president

1832–1833 ▶ Nullification crisis erupts

1833 ▶ Jackson and Taney remove federal deposits from Bank of the United States

▶ Commercial panic disrupts economy

CHAPTER 9

Jacksonian America

When the French aristocrat Alexis de Tocqueville visited the United States in 1831, one feature of American society struck him as "fundamental": the "general equality of condition among the people." Unlike older societies, in which privilege and wealth passed from generation to generation within an entrenched upper class, America had no rigid distinctions of rank. "The government of democracy," he wrote in his classic study *Democracy in America* (1835–1840), "brings the notion of political rights to the level of the humblest citizens, just as the dissemination of wealth brings the notion of property within the reach of all the members of the community."

De Tocqueville

Yet Tocqueville also wondered how long the fluidity of American society could survive in the face of the growth of manufacturing and the rise of the factory system. Industrialism, he feared, would create a large class of dependent workers and a small group of new aristocrats. For, as he explained it, "at the very moment at which the science of manufactures lowers the class of workmen, it raises the class of masters."

Americans, too, pondered the future of their democracy in these years of economic and territorial expansion. Some feared that the nation's rapid growth would produce social chaos and insisted that the country's first priority must be to establish order and a clear system of authority. Others argued that the greatest danger facing the nation was privilege and that society's goal should be to eliminate the favored status of powerful elites and make opportunity more widely available. Advocates of this latter vision seized control of the federal government in 1829 with the inauguration of Andrew Jackson.

Jackson and his followers were not egalitarians. They did nothing to challenge the existence of slavery; they supervised one of the harshest assaults on American Indians in the nation's history; and they accepted the necessity of economic inequality and social gradation. Jackson himself was a frontier aristocrat, and most of those who served him were people of wealth and standing. They were not, however, usually aristocrats by birth. They had, they believed, risen to prominence on the basis of their own talents and energies, and their goal in public life was to ensure that others like themselves would have the opportunity to do the same.

The "democratization" of government over which Andrew Jackson presided was accompanied by a lofty rhetoric of equality and aroused the excitement of working people. To the national leaders who promoted that democratization, however, its purpose was not to

Equality of Opportunity

aid farmers and laborers. Still less was it to assist the truly disenfranchised: African Americans (both slave and free), women, Native Americans. It was to challenge the power of eastern elites for the sake of the rising entrepreneurs of the South and the West.

1834 ▶ Indian Trade and Intercourse Act renewed

1835 ▶ Roger Taney succeeds Marshall as chief justice of the Supreme Court

▶ Federal debt retired

1835–1840 ▶ Tocqueville publishes *Democracy in America*

1835–1842 ▶ Seminole War

1836 ▶ Jackson issues "specie circular"

▶ Martin Van Buren elected president

1837 ▶ Supreme Court rules in *Charles River Bridge* case

1837–1842 ▶ Commercial panic and depression

1838 ▶ "Aroostook War" fought in Maine and Canada

1839 ▶ Whigs hold their first national convention

1840 ▶ William Henry Harrison elected president

▶ Independent Treasury Act passed

1841 ▶ Harrison dies

▶ John Tyler becomes president

1842 ▶ Dorr Rebellion hastens reform in Rhode Island

▶ Webster-Ashburton Treaty signed

THE RISE OF MASS POLITICS

On March 4, 1829, an unprecedented throng—thousands of Americans from all regions of the country, including farmers, laborers, and others of modest social rank—crowded before the Capitol in Washington, D.C., to witness the inauguration of Andrew Jackson. After the ceremonies, the boisterous crowd poured down Pennsylvania Avenue, following their hero to the White House. There, at a public reception open to all, they filled the state rooms to overflowing, trampling one another, soiling the carpets, ruining elegantly upholstered sofas and chairs in their eagerness to shake the new president's hand. "It was a proud day for the people," wrote Amos Kendall, one of Jackson's closest political associates. "General Jackson is their own President." To other observers, however, the scene was less appealing. Justice of the Supreme Court Joseph Story, a friend and colleague of John Marshall, looked on the inaugural levee, as it was called, and remarked with disgust: "The reign of King 'Mob' seems triumphant."

Jackson's Inauguration

The Expanding Electorate

What some have called the "age of Jackson" did not much advance the cause of economic equality. The distribution of wealth and property in America was little different at the end of the Jacksonian era than it was at the start. But it did mark a transformation of American politics that extended the right to vote widely to new groups.

Until the 1820s, relatively few Americans had been permitted to vote. Most states restricted the franchise to white males who were property owners or taxpayers or both, effectively barring an enormous number of the less affluent from the voting rolls. But beginning even before Jackson's election, the rules governing voting began to expand. Changes came first in Ohio and other new states of the West, which, on joining the Union, adopted constitutions that guaranteed all adult white males the right to vote and gave all voters the right to hold public office. Older states, concerned about the loss of their population to the West and thinking that extending the franchise might encourage some residents to stay, began to grant similar political rights to their citizens, dropping or reducing their property ownership or taxpaying requirements. Eventually, every state democratized its electorate to some degree, although some much later and less fully than others.

Broadening the Franchise

Change provoked resistance, and at times the democratic trend fell short of the aims of the more radical reformers, as when Massachusetts held its constitutional convention in 1820. Reform-minded delegates complained that in the Massachusetts government the rich were better represented than the poor, both because of restrictions on voting and officeholding and because of

ANDREW JACKSON This portrait suggests something of the fierce determination that characterized Andrew Jackson's military and political careers. Shattered by the death of his wife a few weeks after his election as president—a death he blamed (not entirely without reason) on the attacks his political opponents had leveled at her—he entered office with a steely determination to live by his own principles and give no quarter to his adversaries. *(New-York Historical Society)*

PARTICIPATION IN PRESIDENTIAL ELECTIONS, 1824–1860
This chart reveals the remarkable increase in popular participation in presidential elections in the years after 1824. Participation almost doubled between 1824 and 1828, and it increased substantially again beginning in 1840 and continuing through and beyond the Civil War.
♦ *What accounts for this dramatic expansion of the electorate? Who remained outside the voting population in these years?*

a peculiar system by which members of the state senate represented property rather than simply people. But Daniel Webster, one of the conservative delegates, opposed democratic changes on the grounds that "power naturally and necessarily follows property" and that "property as such should have its weight and influence in political arrangement." Webster and the rest of the conservatives could not prevent the reform of the rules for representation in the state senate; nor could they prevent elimination of the property requirement for voting. But, to the dismay of the radicals, the new constitution required that every voter be a taxpayer and that the governor be the owner of considerable real estate.

More often, however, the forces of democratization prevailed in the states. In the New York convention of 1821, for example, conservatives led by James Kent insisted that a taxpaying requirement for suffrage was not enough and that, at least in the election of state senators, the property qualification should survive. But reformers, citing the Declaration of Independence, maintained that life, liberty, and the pursuit of happiness, not property, were the main concerns of society and government. The property qualification was abolished.

The wave of state reforms was generally peaceful, but in Rhode Island democratization efforts created considerable instability. The Rhode Island constitution (which was still basically the old colonial charter) barred more than half the adult males of the state from voting. The conservative legislature, chosen by this restricted electorate, consistently blocked all efforts at reform. In 1840, the lawyer and activist Thomas L. Dorr and a group of his followers formed a "People's party," held a convention, drafted a new constitution, and submitted it to a popular vote. It was overwhelmingly approved. The existing legislature, however, refused to accept the Dorr document and submitted a new constitution of its own to the voters. It was narrowly defeated. The Dorrites, in the meantime, had begun to set up a new government, under their own constitution, with Dorr as governor; and so, in 1842, two governments were claiming legitimacy in Rhode Island. The old state government proclaimed that Dorr and his followers were rebels and began to imprison them. Meanwhile, the Dorrites made a brief and ineffectual effort to capture the state arsenal. The Dorr Rebellion, as it was known, quickly failed. Dorr himself surrendered and was briefly imprisoned. But the episode helped pressure the old guard to draft a new constitution, which greatly expanded the suffrage.

The democratization process was far from complete. In much of the South, election laws continued to favor the planters and politicians of the older counties and to limit the influence of more newly settled western areas. Slaves, of course, were disenfranchised by definition; they were not considered citizens and were believed to have no legal or political rights. Free blacks could not

The Dorr Rebellion

THE DORR REBELLION The democratic sentiments that swept much of the nation in the 1830s and 1840s produced, among many other things, the Dorr Rebellion (as its opponents termed it) in Rhode Island. Thomas Dorr was one of many Rhode Islanders who denounced the state's constitution, which limited voting rights to a small group of property owners known as "freeholders." The dissidents crafted a new constitution and submitted it to a vote; a majority of the state's citizens approved it. But the legislature refused to acknowledge its legitimacy, and the result was two separate elections in 1842 for the same state offices. Dorr ran for governor under the new constitution, and was elected by a majority of the people. This "ticket" was what his supporters placed in ballot boxes as they cast their votes. Another candidate, Samuel King, ran under the old constitution, and was elected by the freeholders. Both men were inaugurated, and not until President Tyler threatened federal intervention on behalf of King did the Dorr movement crumble. A year later, however, the state ratified a new constitution extending the franchise. *(Courtesy The Rhode Island Historical Society, RHi X5 304)*

vote anywhere in the South and hardly anywhere in the North. Pennsylvania, in fact, amended its state constitution in 1838 to strip blacks of the right to vote they had previously enjoyed. In no state could women vote. Nowhere was the ballot secret, and often voters had to cast a spoken vote rather than a written one, which meant that political bosses could, and often did, bribe and intimidate them.

Despite the persisting limitations, however, the number of voters increased far more rapidly than did the population as a whole. Indeed, one of the most striking political trends of the early nineteenth century was the change

Democratic Reforms

The "Age of Jackson"

To many Americans in the 1820s and 1830s, Andrew Jackson was a champion of democracy, a symbol of a spirit of anti-elitism and egalitarianism that was sweeping American life. In the twentieth century, however, historians have disagreed sharply not only in their assessments of Jackson himself, but in their portrayal of American society in his era.

The "progressive" historians of the early twentieth century tended to see the politics of Jackson and his supporters as a forerunner of their own generation's battles against economic privilege and political corruption. Frederick Jackson Turner encouraged scholars to see Jacksonianism as the product of the democratic West: a protest by the people of the frontier against the conservative aristocracy of the East, which they believed restricted their own freedom and opportunity. Jackson represented those who wanted to make government responsive to the will of the people rather than to the power of special interests. The culmination of this progressive interpretation of Jacksonianism was the publication in 1945 of Arthur M. Schlesinger, Jr.'s *The Age of Jackson.* Schlesinger was less interested in the regional basis of Jacksonianism than

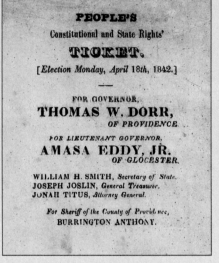

PEOPLE'S
Constitutional and State Rights'
TICKET.

[*Election Monday, April 18th, 1842.*]

FOR GOVERNOR,
THOMAS W. DORR,
OF PROVIDENCE.

FOR LIEUTENANT GOVERNOR,
AMASA EDDY, JR.
OF GLOCESTER.

WILLIAM H. SMITH, *Secretary of State.*
JOSEPH JOSLIN, *General Treasurer.*
JONAH TITUS, *Attorney General.*

For Sheriff of the County of Providence,
BURRINGTON ANTHONY.

(Courtesy The Rhode Island Historical Society, RHi X5 304)

Turner's disciples had been. He saw support for Jackson not just among western farmers, but also among urban laborers in the East. Jacksonian democracy, he argued, was the effort "to control the power of the capitalist groups, mainly Eastern, for the benefit of non-capitalist groups, farmers and laboring men, East, West, and South." He portrayed Jacksonianism as an early version of modern reform efforts (in the

progressive era and the New Deal) to "restrain the power of the business community."

Richard Hofstadter, in an influential 1948 essay in *The American Political Tradition,* sharply disagreed. He argued that Jackson was the spokesman of rising entrepreneurs—aspiring businessmen who saw the road to opportunity blocked by the monopolistic power of eastern aristocrats. The Jacksonians opposed special privileges only to the extent those privileges blocked their own road to success. They were less sympathetic to the aspirations of those below them. Similarly, Bray Hammond, writing in 1957, argued that the Jacksonian cause was "one of enterpriser against capitalist," of rising elites against entrenched ones. Other historians, exploring the ideological origins of the movement saw Jacksonianism less as a democratic reform movement than as a nostalgic effort to restore a lost (and largely imagined) past. Marvin Meyer's *The Jacksonian Persuasion* (1957) argued that Jackson and his followers looked with misgivings on the new industrial society emerging around them and yearned instead for a restoration of the agrarian, republican virtues of an earlier time.

in the method of choosing presidential electors and the dramatic increase in popular participation in the process. In 1800, the legislature had chosen the presidential electors in ten of the states, and the people in only six. By 1828, electors were chosen by popular vote in every state but South Carolina. In the presidential election of 1824, fewer than 27 percent of adult white males had voted. In the election of 1828, the figure rose to 58 percent and in 1840 to 80 percent.

The Legitimization of Party

The high level of voter participation was only partly the result of an expanded electorate. It was also the result of a growing interest in politics and a strengthening of party organization and, perhaps equally important, party loyalty. Although party competition was part of American politics almost from the beginning of the republic, acceptance of the idea of party was not. For more than thirty years, most Americans who had opinions about

the nature of government considered parties evils to be avoided and thought the nation should seek a broad consensus in which permanent factional lines would not exist. But in the 1820s and 1830s, those assumptions gave way to a new view: that permanent, institutionalized parties were a desirable part of the political process, that indeed they were essential to democracy.

The elevation of the idea of party occurred first at the state level, most prominently in New York. There Martin Van Buren led a dissident political faction (known as the "Bucktails" or the "Albany Regency"). In the years after the War of 1812, this group began to challenge the established political leadership—led by the aristocratic governor, De Witt Clinton—that had dominated the state for years. Factional rivalries were not new, of course. But the nature of Van Buren's challenge was. Refuting the traditional view of a political party as undemocratic, they argued that only an institutionalized party, based in the populace at large, could ensure genuine democracy. The alternative was the sort of closed elite that Clinton had created.

Historians of the 1960s began examining Jacksonianism in entirely new ways: looking less at Jackson himself, less at the rhetoric and ideas of his supporters, and more at the nature of American society in the early nineteenth century. Lee Benson's *The Concept of Jacksonian Democracy* (1961)—a pathbreaking work of quantitative history—emphasized the role of religion and ethnicity in determining political divisions in the 1830s. If there was an egalitarian spirit alive in America in those years, it extended well beyond the Democratic Party and the followers of Jackson. Edward Pessen's *Jacksonian America* (1969) revealed that the democratic rhetoric of the age disguised the reality of an increasingly stratified society, in which inequality was growing more, not less, severe. Richard McCormick (1963) and Glyndon Van Deusen (1963) similarly emphasized the pragmatism of Jackson and the Democrats and deemphasized clear ideological and partisan divisions.

Scholars in more recent years have also paid relatively little attention to Jackson and the Democratic Party and instead have focused on a series of broad social changes occurring in the early and mid-nineteenth century

which some have called a "market revolution." Those changes had profound effects on class relations, and the political battles of the era reflected only a part of their impact. Sean Wilentz, in *Chants Democratic* (1984), identified the rise in the 1820s of a powerful class identity among workers in New York, who were attracted less to Jackson himself than to the idea that power in a republic should be widely dispersed. John Ashworth, in *"Agrarians"* and *"Aristocrats"* (1983), and Harry Watson, in *Liberty and Power* (1990), have also seen party politics as a reflection of much larger social changes. The party system was an imperfect reflection of a struggle between people committed to unrestricted opportunities for all white men and those committed to advancing the goals of capitalists, in part through government action.

Recent scholarship may have turned the focus of discussion away from Jackson and the Democratic Party and toward the larger society. But its success in revealing inequality and oppression in antebellum America has produced some withering reassessments of Jackson himself. In *Fathers and Children: Andrew Jackson and*

the Subjugation of the American Indian (1975), Michael Rogin portrays Jackson as a man obsessed with escaping from the imposing shadow of the revolutionary generation. He would lead a new American revolution, not against British tyranny but against those who challenged the ability of white men to control the continent. He displayed special savagery toward American Indians, whom he pursued, Rogin argued, with an almost pathological violence and intensity. Alexander Saxton, in *The Rise and Fall of the White Republic* (1990), likewise points to the contradiction between the image of the age of Jackson as a time of expanding democracy and the reality of constricted rights for women, blacks, and Indians. The Democratic Party, he argues, was committed above all to defending slavery and white supremacy.

But the portrayal of Jackson as a champion of the common man has not vanished from scholarly life. The leading Jackson biographer of the postwar era, Robert V. Remini, has noted the flaws in Jackson's concept of democracy; but within the context of his time, Remini claims, Jackson was a genuine "man of the people."

In the new kind of party the Bucktails proposed, ideological commitments would be less important than loyalty to the party itself. Preservation of the party as an institution—through the use of favors, rewards, and patronage—would be the principal goal of the leadership. Above all, for a party to survive, it must have a permanent opposition. Competing parties would give each political faction a sense of purpose; they would force politicians to remain continually attuned to the will of the people; and they would check and balance each other in much the same way that the different branches of government checked and balanced one another.

By the late 1820s, this new idea of party was spreading beyond New York. The election of Jackson in 1828, the result of a popular movement that seemed to stand apart from the usual political elites, seemed further to legitimize the idea of party as a popular, democratic institution. "Parties of some sort must exist," said a New York newspaper. "'Tis in the nature and

The Second Party System

genius of our government." Finally, in the 1830s, a fully formed two-party system began to operate at the national level, with each party committed to its own existence as an institution and willing to accept the legitimacy of its opposition. The anti-Jackson forces began to call themselves Whigs. Jackson's followers called themselves Democrats (no longer Democratic Republicans), thus giving a permanent name to what is now the nation's oldest political party.

"President of the Common Man"

Unlike Thomas Jefferson, Jackson was no democratic philosopher. The Democratic Party, much less than Jefferson's Republicans, embraced no clear or uniform ideological position. But Jackson himself did embrace a distinct, if simple, theory of democracy. It should offer "equal protection and equal benefits" to all its white male citizens and favor no region or class over another. In practice, that meant an assault on what Jackson and his associates

ELECTION SCENE Frequent and often boisterous campaign rallies were characteristic of electoral politics in the 1840s, when party loyalties were high and political passions intense—as this 1845 drawing by Alfred Jacob Miller of a rally in Catonsville, Maryland, suggests. *(Museum of Fine Arts, Boston, Gift of Maxim Karolik for the proposed M. and M. Karolik Collection of American Watercolors, Drawings, and Prints, 1800–1875, 51.2537. Photograph © 2007 Museum of Fine Arts, Boston.)*

considered the citadels of the eastern aristocracy and an effort to extend opportunities to the rising classes of the West and the South. It also meant a firm commitment to the continuing subjugation of African Americans and Indians (and, although for different reasons, women), for the Jacksonians believed that only by keeping these "dangerous" elements from the body politic could the white-male democracy they valued be preserved.

Jackson's first targets were the entrenched office-holders in the federal government, many of whom had been in place for a generation or more. Official duties, he believed, could be made "so plain and simple that men of intelligence may readily qualify themselves for their performance." Offices belonged to the people, he argued, not to the entrenched officeholders. Or, as one of his henchmen, William L. Marcy of New York, more cynically put it, "To the victors belong the spoils."

In the end, Jackson removed a total of no more than one-fifth of the federal officeholders during his eight years in office, many of them less

The Spoils System

for partisan reasons than because they had misused government funds or engaged in other corruption. Proportionally, Jackson dismissed no more jobholders than Jefferson had dismissed during his presidency. But by embracing the philosophy of the "spoils system," a system already well entrenched in a number of state governments, the Jackson administration helped make the right of elected officials to appoint their own followers to public office an established feature of American politics.

Jackson's supporters also worked to transform the process by which presidential candidates won their party's nominations. They had long resented the con-gressional caucus, a process they believed worked to restrict access to the office to those favored by entrenched elites and a process Jackson himself had avoided in 1828. In 1832, the president's followers staged a national party convention to renominate him for the presidency—one year after the Anti-Masons (see p. 249) became the first party to hold such a meeting. In later generations, some would see the party convention as a source of corruption and political exclusivity. But those who created it in the 1830s considered it a great triumph for democracy. Through the convention, they believed, power would arise directly from the people, not from aristocratic political institutions such as the caucus.

The spoils system and the political convention did serve to limit the power of two entrenched elites—permanent officeholders and the exclusive party caucus. Yet neither really trans-ferred power to the people. Appointments to office almost

Limited Nature of Democratic Reform

always went to prominent political allies of the president and his associates. Delegates to national conventions were less often common men than members of local party organizations. Political opportunity within the party was expanding, but much less so than Jacksonian rhetoric suggested.

"OUR FEDERAL UNION"

Jackson's commitment to extending power beyond entrenched elites led him to want to reduce the functions of the federal government. A concentration of power in Washington would, he believed, restrict opportunity to people with political connections. But Jackson also believed in forceful presidential leadership and was strongly committed to the preservation of the Union. Thus at the same time that Jackson was promoting an economic program to reduce the power of the national government, he was asserting the supremacy of the Union in the face of a potent challenge. For no sooner had he entered office than his own vice president—John C. Calhoun—began to champion a controversial (and, in Jackson's view, dangerous) constitutional theory: nullification.

Calhoun and Nullification

Calhoun was forty-six years old in 1828, with a distinguished past and an apparently promising future. But the smoldering issue of the tariff created a dilemma for him. Once he had been an outspoken protectionist and had strongly supported the tariff of 1816. But by the late 1820s, many South Carolinians had come to believe that the "tariff of abominations" was responsible for the stagnation of their state's economy—even though

JOHN C. CALHOUN This photograph, by Matthew Brady, captured Calhoun toward the end of his life, when he was torn between his real commitment to the ideals of the Union and his equally fervent commitment to the interests of the South. The younger generation of southern leaders, who would dominate the politics of the region in the 1850s, were less idealistic and more purely sectional in their views. *(Library of Congress)*

the stagnation was largely a result of the exhaustion of South Carolina's farmland, which could no longer compete effectively with the newly opened and fertile lands of the Southwest. Some exasperated Carolinians were ready to consider a drastic remedy—secession.

Calhoun's future political hopes rested on how he met this challenge in his home state. He did so by developing a theory that he believed offered a more moderate alternative to secession: the theory of nullification. Drawing from the ideas of Madison and Jefferson and their Virginia and Kentucky Resolutions of 1798-1799 and citing the Tenth Amendment to the Constitution, Calhoun argued that since the federal government was a creation of the states, the states—not the courts or Congress—were the final arbiters of the constitutionality of federal laws. If a state concluded that Congress had passed an unconstitutional law, then it could hold a special convention and declare the federal law null and void within the state. The nullification doctrine—and the idea of using it to nullify the 1828 tariff—quickly attracted broad support in South Carolina. But it did nothing to help Calhoun's standing within the new administration, in part because he had a powerful rival in Martin Van Buren.

Calhoun's Theory of Nullification

The Rise of Van Buren

Van Buren was about the same age as Calhoun and equally ambitious. He had won election to the governorship of New York in 1828 and then resigned in 1829 when Jackson appointed him secretary of state. Alone among the figures in the Jackson administration, Van Buren soon established himself as a member both of the official cabinet and of the president's unofficial circle of political allies, known as the "Kitchen Cabinet" (which included such Democratic newspaper editors as Isaac Hill of New Hampshire and Amos Kendall and Francis P. Blair of Kentucky). Van Buren's influence with the president was unmatched and grew stronger still as a result of a quarrel over etiquette that drove a wedge between the president and Calhoun.

Martin Van Buren

Peggy O'Neale was the attractive daughter of a Washington tavern keeper with whom both Andrew Jackson and his friend John H. Eaton had taken lodgings while serving as senators from Tennessee. O'Neale was married, but rumors circulated in Washington in the mid-1820s that she and Senator Eaton were having an affair. O'Neale's husband died in 1828, and she and Eaton were soon married. A few weeks later, Jackson named Eaton secretary of war and thus made the new Mrs. Eaton a cabinet wife. The rest of the administration wives, led by Mrs. Calhoun, refused to receive her. Jackson (remembering the effects of public slander directed against his own late wife) was furious and demanded that the

MARTIN VAN BUREN As leader of the so-called Albany Regency in New York in the 1820s, Van Buren helped create one of the first modern party organizations in the United States. Later, as Andrew Jackson's secretary of state and (after 1832) vice president, he helped bring party politics to the national level. So it was ironic that in 1840, when he ran for reelection to the presidency, he lost to William Henry Harrison, whose Whig Party made effective use of many of the techniques of mass politics that Van Buren himself had pioneered. *(Library of Congress)*

DANIEL WEBSTER The great Civil War photographer Matthew Brady took this portrait of Daniel Webster shortly before Webster's death in 1852. It conveys something of Webster's intensity of purpose—an intensity that was perhaps most famously visible in his dramatic 1830 debate with South Carolina Senator Robert Y. Hayne. In his response to Hayne, he spoke words that became a rallying cry in the North and deeply associated with Webster's name: "Liberty and Union, now and forever, one and inseparable." During his long political career, Webster was one of the giants of American politics, a man of much greater stature than many of the presidents who were his contemporaries. *(Library of Congress, LC-USZ62-15233)*

members of the cabinet accept her into their social world. Calhoun, under pressure from his wife, refused. Van Buren, a widower, befriended the Eatons and thus ingratiated himself with Jackson. By 1831, partly as a result of the Peggy Eaton affair, Jackson had chosen Van Buren to succeed him in the White House, apparently ending Calhoun's dreams of the presidency.

The Webster-Hayne Debate

In January 1830, as the controversy over nullification grew more intense, a great debate occurred in the United States Senate over another sectional controversy. In the midst of a routine debate over federal policy toward western lands, a senator from Connecticut suggested that all land sales and surveys be temporarily discontinued. Robert Y. Hayne, a young senator from South

Carolina, responded, charging that slowing down the growth of the West was a way for the East to retain its political and economic power. Although he had no real interest in western lands, he hoped his stance would attract support from westerners in Congress for South Carolina's drive to lower the tariff. Both the South and the West, he argued, were victims of the tyranny of the Northeast. He hinted that the two regions might combine to defend themselves against that tyranny.

Daniel Webster, now a senator from Massachusetts and a nationalistic Whig, answered Hayne the next day. He attacked Hayne, and through him Calhoun, for what he considered their challenge to the integrity of the Union—in effect, challenging Hayne to a debate not on public lands and the tariff but on the issue of states' rights versus national power. Hayne, coached by Calhoun, responded with a defense of the theory of nullification. Webster then spent two full afternoons delivering what became known as his "Second Reply to Hayne," a speech that northerners quoted and revered

States' Rights versus National Power

CHARLESTON, 1831 The little-known South Carolina artist S. Bernard painted this view of Charleston's East Battery in 1831. Then, as now, residents and vistors liked to stroll along the battery and watch the activity in the city's busy harbor. But Charleston in the 1830s was a less important commercial center than it had been a few decades earlier. By then, overseas traders were increasingly avoiding southern ports and doing more and more business in New York. *(Yale University Art Gallery)*

for years to come. He concluded with the ringing appeal: "Liberty and Union, now and for ever, one and inseparable!"

Both sides now waited to hear what President Jackson thought of the argument. The answer became clear at the annual Democratic Party banquet in honor of Thomas Jefferson. After dinner, guests delivered a series of toasts. The president arrived with a written text in which he had underscored certain words: "Our Federal Union—It must be preserved." While he spoke, he looked directly at Calhoun. The diminutive Van Buren, who stood on his chair to see better, thought he saw Calhoun's hand shake and a trickle of wine run down his glass as he responded to the president's toast with his own: "The Union, next to our liberty most dear." The two most important figures in government had drawn sharp lines between themselves.

The Nullification Crisis

In 1832, finally, the controversy over nullification produced a crisis when South Carolinians responded angrily to a congressional tariff bill that offered them no relief from the 1828 "tariff of abominations." Almost immediately, the legislature summoned a state convention, which voted to nullify the tariffs of 1828 and 1832 and to forbid the collection of duties within the state. At the same time, South Carolina elected Hayne to serve as

governor and Calhoun (who resigned as vice president) to replace Hayne as senator.

Jackson insisted that nullification was treason and that those implementing it were traitors. He strengthened the federal forts in South Carolina and ordered a warship and several revenue ships to Charleston. When Congress convened early in 1833, Jackson proposed a force bill authorizing the president to use the military to see that acts of Congress were obeyed. Violence seemed a real possibility.

Calhoun faced a predicament as he took his place in the Senate. Not a single state had come to South Carolina's support. Even South Carolina itself was divided and could not hope to prevail in a showdown with the federal **Compromise** government. But the timely intervention of Henry Clay, newly elected to the Senate, averted a crisis. Clay devised a compromise by which the tariff would be lowered gradually so that, by 1842, it would reach approximately the same level as in 1816. The compromise and the force bill were passed on the same day, March 1, 1833. Jackson signed them both. In South Carolina, the convention reassembled and repealed its nullification of the tariffs. But unwilling to allow Congress to have the last word, the convention nullified the force act—a purely symbolic act, since the tariff toward which the force act was directed had already been repealed. Calhoun and his followers claimed a victory for nullification, which had, they insisted, forced the revision of the tariff. But the episode taught Calhoun and his allies that no state could defy the federal government alone.

THE REMOVAL OF THE INDIANS

There had never been any doubt about Andrew Jackson's attitude toward the Indian tribes that continued to live in the eastern states and territories of the United States. He wanted them to move west, beyond the Mississippi, out of the way of expanding white settlement. Jackson's antipathy toward the Native Americans had a special intensity because of his own earlier experiences leading military campaigns against tribes along the Southern border. But in most respects, his views were little different from those of most other white Americans.

White Attitudes Toward the Tribes

In the eighteenth century, many white Americans had

Changing Attitudes Toward the Indians

considered the Indians "noble savages," peoples without real civilization but with an inherent dignity that made civilization possible among them. By the first decades of the nineteenth century, this vaguely paternalistic attitude (the attitude of Thomas Jefferson, among others) was giving way to a more hostile one, particularly among the whites in the western states and territories whom Jackson came to represent. Such whites were coming to view Native Americans simply as "savages," not only uncivilized but uncivilizable. Whites, they believed, should not be expected to live in close proximity to the tribes.

White westerners favored removal as well because they feared that continued contact between the expanding white settlements and the Indians would produce endless conflict and violence. Most of all, however, they favored Indian removal because of their own insatiable desire for territory. The tribes possessed valuable land in the path of expanding white settlement. Whites wanted it.

Legally, only the federal government had authority to negotiate with the Indians over land, a result of Supreme Court decisions that established the tribes as, in effect, "nations within the nation." The tribal nations that the Court identified were not, however, securely rooted in Native American history. The large tribal aggregations with which white Americans dealt were, in fact, relatively new entities. Most Indians were accustomed to thinking in much more local terms. They created these larger tribes when they realized they would need some collective strength to deal with whites; but as new and untested political entities, the tribes were often weak and divided. The Marshall Court had seemed to acknowledge this in declaring the tribes not only sovereign

nations, but also dependent ones, for whom the federal government must take considerable responsibility. Through most of the nineteenth century, the government interpreted that responsibility as finding ways to move the Native Americans out of the way of expanding white settlement.

The Black Hawk War

In the Old Northwest, the long process of expelling the woodland Indians culminated in a last battle in 1831–1832, between white settlers in Illinois and an alliance of Sauk (or Sac) and Fox Indians under the fabled and now aged warrior Black Hawk. An earlier treaty had ceded tribal lands in Illinois to the United States; but Black Hawk and his followers refused to recognize the legality of the agreement, which a rival tribal faction had signed. Hungry and resentful, a thousand of them crossed the river and reoccupied vacant lands in Illinois. White settlers in the region feared that the resettlement was the beginning of a substantial invasion, and they assembled the Illinois state militia and federal troops to repel the "invaders."

The Black Hawk War, as it became known, was notable chiefly for the viciousness of the white military efforts. White leaders in western Illinois

Sauk and Fox Indians Defeated

vowed to exterminate the "bandit collection of Indians" and attacked them even when Black Hawk attempted to surrender. The Sauks and Foxes, defeated and starving,

BLACK HAWK AND WHIRLING THUNDER After his defeat by white settlers in Illinois in 1832, the famed Sauk warrior Black Hawk and his son, Whirling Thunder, were captured and sent on a tour by Andrew Jackson, displayed to the public as trophies of war. They showed such dignity through the ordeal that much of the white public quickly began to sympathize with them. This portrait, by John Wesley Jarvis, was painted on the tour's final stop, in New York City. Black Hawk wears the European-style suit, while Whirling Thunder wears native costume to emphasize his commitment to his tribal roots. Soon thereafter, Black Hawk returned to his tribe, wrote a celebrated autobiography, and died in 1838. *(Bettman/Corbis)*

retreated across the Mississippi into Iowa. White troops (and some bands of Sioux whom they encouraged to join the chase) pursued them as they fled and slaughtered most of them. United States troops captured Black Hawk himself and sent him on a tour of the East, where Andrew Jackson was one of many curious whites who arranged to meet him. (Abraham Lincoln served as a captain of the militia, but saw no action, in the Black Hawk War; Jefferson Davis was a lieutenant in the regular army.)

The "Five Civilized Tribes"

More troubling to the government in the 1830s were the

Agrarian Tribes of the South

tribes remaining in the South. In western Georgia, Alabama, Mississippi, and Florida lived what were known as the "Five Civilized Tribes"—the Cherokee, Creek, Seminole, Chickasaw, and Choctaw—most of whom had established settled agricultural societies with successful economies. The Cherokees in Georgia had formed a particularly stable and sophisticated culture, with their own written language and a formal constitution (adopted in 1827) that created an independent Cherokee Nation. They were more closely tied to their lands than many of the more nomadic tribes to the north.

Even some whites argued that the Cherokees, unlike other tribes, should be allowed to retain their eastern lands, since they had become such a "civilized" society and had, under pressure from missionaries and government agents, given up many of their traditional ways. Cherokee men had once been chiefly hunters and had left farming mainly to women. By now the men had given up most of their hunting and (like most white men) took over the farming themselves; Cherokee women, also like their white counterparts, restricted themselves largely to domestic tasks.

The federal government worked steadily to negotiate

Removal Act

treaties with the southern Indians that would remove them to the West and open their lands for white settlement. But the negotiating process often did not proceed fast enough to satisfy the region's whites. The State of Georgia's independent effort to dislodge the Creeks, over the objection of President Adams, was one example of this impatience. That same impatience became evident early in Jackson's administration, when the legislatures in Georgia, Alabama, and Mississippi began passing laws to regulate the tribes remaining in their states. They received assistance in these efforts from Congress, which in 1830 passed the Removal Act (with Jackson's approval), which appropriated money to finance federal negotiations with the southern tribes aimed at relocating them to the West. The president quickly dispatched federal officials to negotiate nearly a hundred new treaties with the remaining

tribes. Thus, the southern tribes faced a combination of pressures from both the state and federal governments. Most tribes were too weak to resist, and they ceded their lands in return for only token payments. Some, however, balked.

In Georgia, the Cherokees tried to stop the white encroachments (which were actively encouraged by Jackson) by appealing to the Supreme Court. The Court's decisions in *Cherokee Nation* v. *Georgia*, and *Worcester* v. *Georgia* in 1831 and 1832 (see pp. 226–227) seemed at least partially to vindicate the tribe. But Jackson's longtime hostility toward Native Americans left him with little sympathy for the Cherokees and little patience with the Court. He was eager to retain the support of white southerners and westerners in the increasingly bitter partisan battles in which his administration was becoming engaged. His reaction to Marshall's rulings reflected his belief that the justices were using the issue to express their hostility to the larger aims of his presidency. When the chief justice announced the decision in *Worcester* v. *Georgia*, Jackson reportedly responded with contempt. "John Marshall has made his decision," he was reported to have said. "Now let him enforce it." The decision was not enforced.

In 1835, the federal government extracted a treaty from a minority faction of the

Cherokee Resistance

Cherokees, none of them a chosen representative of the Cherokee Nation. The treaty ceded the tribe's land to Georgia in return for $5 million and a reservation west of the Mississippi. The great majority of the 17,000 Cherokees did not recognize the treaty as legitimate and refused to leave their homes. But Jackson would not be thwarted. He sent an army of 7,000 under General Winfield Scott to round them up and drive them westward at bayonet point.

Trails of Tears

About 1,000 Cherokee fled across the state line to North Carolina, where the federal government eventually provided a small reservation for them in the Smoky Mountains, which survives today. But most of the rest made the long,

Cherokee Removal

forced trek to "Indian Territory" (which later became Oklahoma) beginning in the winter of 1838. Along the way, a Kentuckian observed: "Even aged females, apparently nearly ready to drop in the grave, were travelling with heavy burdens attached to their backs, sometimes on frozen ground and sometimes on muddy streets, with no covering for their feet."

Thousands, perhaps an eighth or more of the emigrés, perished

Indian Removal

before or soon after reaching their unwanted destination. In the harsh new reservations in which they were now forced to live, the survivors never forgot the hard journey. They called their route "The Trail Where They

Cried," the Trail of Tears. Jackson claimed that the "remnant of that ill-fated race" was now "beyond the reach of injury or oppression," apparently trying to convince himself or others that he had supported removal as a way to protect the tribes.

The Cherokees were not alone in experiencing the hardships of the Trail of Tears. Between 1830 and 1838, virtually all the "Five Civilized Tribes" were expelled from the southern states and forced to relocate in the new Indian Territory, which Congress had officially created by the Indian Intercourse Act of 1834. The Choctaws of Mississippi and western Alabama were the first to make the trek, beginning in 1830. The army moved out the Creeks of eastern Alabama and western Georgia in 1836. The Chickasaw in northern Mississippi began the long march westward a year later, and the Cherokees, finally, a year after that. The government thought the Indian Territory was safely distant from existing white settlements and consisted of land that most whites con-

sidered undesirable. It had the additional advantage, the government believed, of being on the eastern edge of what earlier white explorers had christened the "Great American Desert," land unfit for habitation. It seemed unlikely that whites would ever seek to settle along the western borders of the Indian Territory; and thus the prospect of whites surrounding the reservation and producing further conflict seemed remote.

Only the Seminoles in Florida managed to resist the pressures to relocate, and even their success was limited. Like other tribes, the Seminoles had agreed under pressure to a settlement (the 1832–1833 treaties of Payne's Landing), by which they ceded their lands to the government and agreed to move to Indian Territory within three years. Most did move west, but a substantial minority, under the leadership of the chieftain Osceola, refused to leave and staged an uprising beginning in 1835 to defend their lands. (Joining the Indians in their struggle was a group of runaway black slaves who had been living

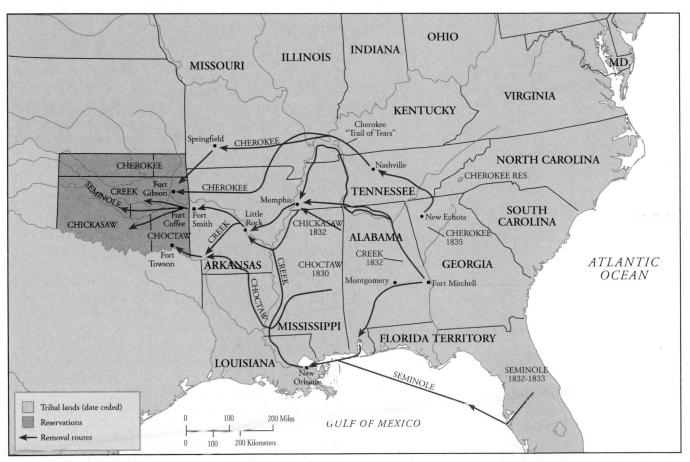

THE EXPULSION OF THE TRIBES, 1830–1835 Andrew Jackson was famous well before he became president for his military exploits against the tribes. Once in the White House, he ensured that few Indians would remain in the southern states of the nation, now that white settlement was increasing there. The result was a series of dramatic "removals" of Indian tribes out of their traditional lands and into new territories west of the Mississippi—mostly in Oklahoma. Note the very long distance many of these tribes had to travel. ◆ *Why was the route of the Cherokees, shown in the upper portion of the map, known as the "Trail of Tears"?*

 For an interactive version of this map go to www.mhhe.com/brinkley12ch9maps

AN INTER-TRIBAL NEGOTIATION
The devastating policies of the Jackson administration—which forced thousands of Native Americans to relocate from their lands—produced a wide range of desperate responses among the Indians themselves. Some tried to ally themselves with the American government, among them a group of Iroquois shown in this painting in "white man's clothes," negotiating on Washington's behalf with Shawnee, Miami, and other western tribes. Red Jacket, the Iroquois leader shown in the center, made little progress. The western Indians jeered at him for the failure of the Iroquois to defend their lands, and Red Jacket left humiliated. *(Smithsonian American Art Museum, Washington, DC/Art Resource, NY)*

The Seminole War

with the tribe.) The Seminole War dragged on for years. Jackson sent troops to Florida, but the Seminoles with their African-American associates were masters of guerrilla warfare in the jungly Everglades. Even after Osceola had been treacherously captured by white troops while under a flag of truce and had died in prison; even after white troops had engaged in a systematic campaign of extermination against the resisting Indians and their black allies; even after 1,500 white soldiers had died and the federal government had spent $20 million on the struggle—even then, followers of Osceola remained in Florida. Finally, in 1842, the government abandoned the war. By then, many of the Seminoles had been either killed or forced westward. But the relocation of the Seminoles, unlike the relocation of most of the other tribes, was never complete.

The Meaning of Removal

By the end of the 1830s, almost all the important Indian societies east of the Mississippi had been removed to the West. The tribes had ceded over 100 million acres of eastern land to the federal government; they had received in return about $68 million and 32 million acres in the far less hospitable lands west of the Mississippi between the Missouri and Red Rivers. There they lived, divided by tribe into a series of carefully defined reservations, in a territory surrounded by a string of United States forts to keep them in (and to keep most whites out), in a region whose climate and topography bore little relation to anything they had known before. Eventually, even this forlorn enclave would face incursions from white civilization.

What were the alternatives to the removal of the eastern Indians? There was probably never any realistic possibility that the government could stop white expansion westward. White people had already been penetrating the West for nearly two centuries, and such penetrations were certain to continue. But did that expansion really require removal?

There were, in theory at least, several alternatives to the brutal removal policy. There were many examples in the West of white settlers and native tribes living side by side and creating a shared (if not necessarily equal) world. In the pueblos of New Mexico, in the fur trading posts of the Pacific Northwest, in parts of Texas and California, settlers from Mexico, Canada, and the United States had created societies in which Indians and whites were in intimate contact with each other. Even during the famous Lewis and Clark expedition, white explorers had lived with western Indians on terms of such intimacy that many of them contracted venereal disease from Indian sexual partners. Sometimes these close contacts between whites and Indians were beneficial to both sides, even reasonably equal. Sometimes they were cruel and exploitive. But the early multiracial societies of the West did not separate whites and Indians. They demonstrated ways in which the two cultures could interact, each shaping the other.

Alternatives to Removal

By the mid-nineteenth century, however, white Americans had adopted a different model as they contemplated westward expansion. Much as the early British settlers along the Atlantic coast had established "plantations," from which natives were, in theory, to be excluded, so the westward-moving whites of later years came to imagine the territories they were entering as virgin land, with no preexisting civilization. Native Americans, they believed, could not be partners—either equal or subordinate—in the creation of new societies in the West. They were obstacles, to be removed and, as far as possible, isolated. Indians, Andrew Jackson once said, had "neither the intelligence, the industry, the moral habits, nor the desire of improvement" to be fit partners in the project of extending white civilization westward. By dismissing Native American cultures in that way, white Americans justified to themselves a series of harsh policies that they believed (incorrectly) would make the West theirs alone.

JACKSON AND THE BANK WAR

Jackson was quite willing to use federal power against rebellious states and Indian tribes. On economic issues, however, he was consis-

Jackson's Opposition to Concentrated Power

tently opposed to concentrating power either in the federal government or in powerful and, in his view, aristocratic institutions associated with it. An early example of his skeptical view of federal power was his 1830 veto of a congressional measure providing a subsidy to the proposed Maysville Road in Kentucky. The bill was unconstitutional, Jackson argued, because the road in question lay entirely within Kentucky and was not, therefore, a part of "interstate commerce." But the bill was also unwise, he believed, because it committed the government to what Jackson considered extravagant expenditures.

Jackson's opposition to federal power and aristocratic privilege lay behind the most celebrated episode of Jackson's presidency: the war against the Bank of the United States.

Biddle's Institution

The Bank of the United States in the 1830s was a mighty institution indeed, and it is not surprising that it would attract Jackson's wrath. Its stately headquarters in Philadelphia seemed to symbolize its haughty image of

Nicholas Biddle

itself. It had branches in twenty-nine other cities, making it the most powerful and far-flung financial institution in the nation. By law, the Bank was the only place that the federal government could deposit its own funds; the government, in turn, owned one-fifth of the bank's stock. The Bank did a tremendous business in general banking. It provided credit to growing enterprises; it issued bank notes, which served as a dependable medium of exchange throughout the country; and it exercised a restraining effect on the less well-managed state banks. Nicholas Biddle, who served as president of the Bank from 1823 on, had done much to put the institution on a sound and prosperous basis. Nevertheless, Andrew Jackson was determined to destroy it.

Opposition to the Bank came from two very different groups: the "soft-money" faction and the "hard-money" faction. Advocates of soft money—people who wanted more currency in circulation and believed that issuing bank notes unsupported by gold and silver was the best way to circulate more currency—consisted largely of state bankers and their allies.

Hard and Soft Money

They objected to the Bank of the United States because it restrained the state banks from issuing notes freely. The hard-money people believed that gold and silver were the only basis for money. They condemned all banks that issued bank notes, including the Bank of the United States. The soft-money advocates were believers in rapid economic growth and speculation; the hard-money forces embraced older ideas of "public virtue" and looked with suspicion on expansion and speculation.

Jackson himself supported the hard-money position. Many years before, he had been involved in some grandiose land and commercial speculations based on paper credit. His business had failed, and he had fallen deeply into debt as a result of the Panic of 1797. After that, he was suspicious of all banks and all paper currency. But as president he was also sensitive to the complaints of his many soft-money supporters in the West and the South. He made it clear that he would not favor renewing the charter of the Bank of the United States, which was due to expire in 1836.

A Philadelphia aristocrat, unaccustomed to politics, Biddle nevertheless began granting financial favors to influential men who he thought might help him preserve the bank. In particular, he turned to Daniel Webster and cultivated a close personal friendship with him. He named Webster the Bank's legal counsel and director of its Boston branch; Webster was also a frequent, heavy borrower from the Bank. Perhaps unsurprisingly, he helped Biddle win the support of other important figures, among them Henry Clay.

Clay, Webster, and other advisers persuaded Biddle to apply to Congress in 1832 for a bill to renew the Bank's charter. That was four years ahead of the date the original charter was scheduled to expire. But forcing a vote now would allow the Bank to become a major issue in the 1832 national elections. Congress passed the recharter bill; Jackson, predictably,

Jackson's Veto

vetoed it; and the Bank's supporters in Congress failed to override the veto. Just as Clay had hoped, the 1832 campaign now centered on the future of the Bank.

Clay himself ran for president that year as the unanimous choice of the National Republicans, who held a nominating convention in Baltimore late in 1831. But the bank war failed to provide him with the winning issue for which he had hoped. Jackson, with Van Buren as his running mate, overwhelmingly defeated Clay (and several minor party candidates) with 55 percent of the popular

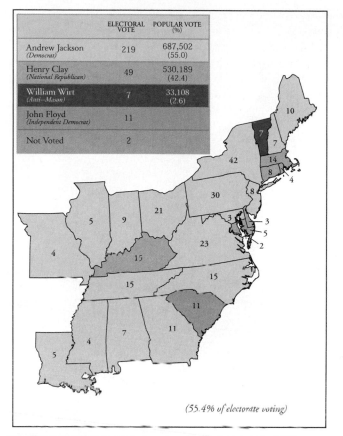

	ELECTORAL VOTE	POPULAR VOTE (%)
Andrew Jackson *(Democrat)*	219	687,502 (55.0)
Henry Clay *(National Republican)*	49	530,189 (42.4)
William Wirt *(Anti-Mason)*	7	33,108 (2.6)
John Floyd *(Independent Democrat)*	11	
Not Voted	2	

(55.4% of electorate voting)

THE ELECTION OF 1832 Jackson's re-election victory in 1832 was almost as decisive as his earlier victory in 1828. ◆ *What changes are visible in party loyalties since the previous election?*

 For an interactive version of this map go to www.mhhe.com/brinkley12ch9maps

vote and 219 electoral votes (more than four times as many as Clay received). These results were a defeat not only for Clay, but also for Biddle.

The "Monster" Destroyed

Jackson was now more determined than ever to destroy the "monster" Bank as quickly as possible. He could not legally abolish the institution before the expiration of its charter. Instead, he tried to weaken it. He decided to remove the government's deposits from the Bank. His secretary of the treasury believed that such an action would destabilize the financial system and refused to give the order. Jackson fired him and appointed a new one. When the new secretary similarly balked, Jackson fired him too and named a third, more compliant secretary: Attorney General Roger B. Taney, his close friend and loyal ally. Taney began placing the government's deposits not in the Bank of the United States, as it had in the past, but in a number of state banks (which Jackson's enemies called "pet banks").

Removal of Government Deposits

Nicholas Biddle, whom Jacksonians derisively called "Czar Nicholas," did not give in without a fight. "This worthy President," he wrote sarcastically, "thinks that because he has scalped Indians and imprisoned Judges, he is to have his way with the Bank. He is mistaken." When the administration began to transfer funds directly from the Bank of the United States to the pet banks (as opposed to the initial practice of simply depositing new funds in those banks), Biddle called in loans and raised interest rates, explaining that without the government deposits the Bank's resources were stretched too thin. He realized his actions were likely to cause financial distress. He hoped a short recession would persuade Congress to recharter the Bank. "Nothing but the evidence of suffering," he told a colleague, would "produce any effect in Congress." By now, the struggle had become not just a conflict over policy and principle, but a bitter and even petulant personal battle between two proud men—both of them acting recklessly in an effort to humiliate and defeat the other.

As financial conditions worsened in the winter of 1833–1834, supporters of the Bank blamed Jackson's policies for the recession. They organized meetings around the country and sent petitions to Washington urging a rechartering of the Bank. But the Jacksonians blamed the recession on Biddle and refused to budge. When distressed citizens appealed to the president for help, he dismissively answered, "Go to Biddle."

Finally, Biddle contracted credit too far even for his own allies in the business community, who began to fear that in his effort to save his own bank he was threatening their interests. Some of them did "go to Biddle." A group of New York and Boston merchants protested. To appease the business community, Biddle at last reversed himself and began to grant credit in abundance and on reasonable terms. His vacillating and unpopular tactics ended his chances of winning a recharter of the Bank.

Jackson had won a considerable political victory. But when the Bank of the United States died in 1836, the country lost a valuable, albeit flawed, financial institution and was left with a fragmented and chronically unstable banking system that would plague the economy for more than a century.

Jackson Victorious

The Taney Court

In the aftermath of the Bank War, Jackson moved against the most powerful institution of economic nationalism of all: the Supreme Court. In 1835, when John Marshall died, the president appointed as the new chief justice his trusted ally Roger B. Taney. Taney did not bring a sharp break in constitutional interpretation, but he gradually helped modify Marshall's vigorous nationalism.

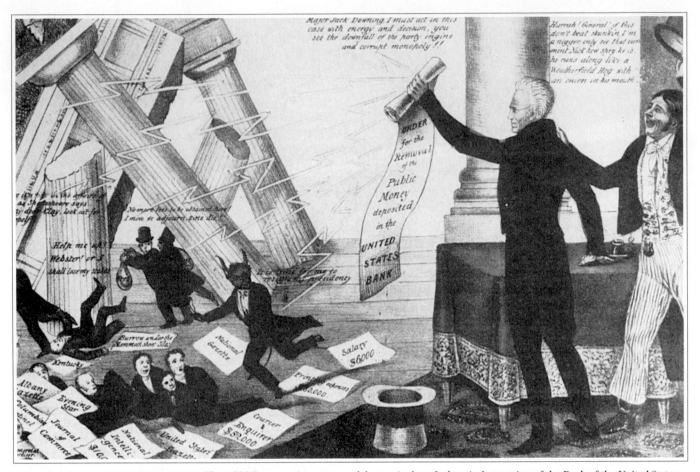

"THE DOWNFALL OF MOTHER BANK" This 1832 Democratic cartoon celebrates Andrew Jackson's destruction of the Bank of the United States. The president is shown here driving away the Bank's corrupt supporters by ordering the withdrawal of government deposits. *(New-York Historical Society)*

Perhaps the clearest indication of the new judicial mood was the celebrated case of *Charles River Bridge* v. *Warren Bridge* of 1837. The case involved a dispute between two Massachusetts companies over the right to build a bridge across the Charles River between Boston and Cambridge. One company had a longstanding charter from the state to operate a toll bridge and claimed that this charter guaranteed it a monopoly of the bridge traffic. Another company had applied to the legislature for authorization to construct a second, competing bridge that would—since it would be toll free—greatly reduce the value of the first company's charter.

Charles River Bridge v. Warren Bridge

The first company contended that in granting the second charter the legislature was engaging in a breach of contract and noted that the Marshall Court, in the *Dartmouth College* case and other decisions, had ruled that states had no right to abrogate contracts. But now Taney, speaking for the Democratic majority on the Court, supported the right of Massachusetts to award

the second charter. The object of government, Taney maintained, was to promote the general happiness, an object that took precedence over the rights of contract and property. A state, therefore, had the right to amend or abrogate a contract if such action was necessary to advance the well-being of the community. Such an abrogation was clearly necessary in the case of the Charles River Bridge, he argued, because the original bridge company, by exercising a monopoly, was benefiting from unjustifiable privilege. (It did not help the first company that its members were largely Boston aristocrats closely associated with Harvard College; the challenging company, by contrast, consisted largely of newer, aspiring entrepreneurs—the sort of people with whom Jackson and his allies instinctively identified.) The decision reflected one of the cornerstones of the Jacksonian ideal: that the key to democracy was an expansion of economic opportunity, which would not occur if older corporations could maintain monopolies and choke off competition from newer companies.

THE CHANGING FACE OF AMERICAN POLITICS

Jackson's forceful—some claimed tyrannical—tactics in crushing first the nullification movement and then the Bank of the United States helped galvanize a growing opposition coalition that by the mid-1830s was ready to assert itself in national politics. Denouncing the president as "King Andrew I," they began to refer to themselves as Whigs, after the party in England that had traditionally worked to limit the power of the king. With

| Birth of the Whig Party |

the emergence of the Whigs, the nation once again had two competing political parties. What scholars now call the "second party system" had begun what turned out to be its relatively brief life.

Democrats and Whigs

The two parties were different from one another in their philosophies, in their constituencies, and in the character of their leaders. But they became increasingly alike in the way they approached the process of electing their followers to office.

Democrats in the 1830s envisioned a future of steadily expanding economic and political opportunities for

| Democrats' Emphasis on Opportunity |

white males. The role of government should be limited, they believed, but it should include efforts to remove obstacles to opportunity and to avoid creating new ones. That meant defending the Union, which Jacksonians believed was essential to the dynamic economic growth they favored. It also meant attacking centers of corrupt privilege. As Jackson himself said in his farewell address, the society of America should be one in which "the planter, the farmer, the mechanic, and the laborer, all know that their success depends on their own industry and economy," in which artificial privilege would stifle no one's opportunity. Among the most radical members of the party—the so-called Locofocos, mainly workingmen and small businessmen and professionals in the Northeast—sentiment was strong for a vigorous, perhaps even violent assault on monopoly and privilege far in advance of anything Jackson himself ever contemplated.

The political philosophy that became known as

| Whigs' Call for Economic Union |

Whiggery was very different. It favored expanding the power of the federal government, encouraging industrial and commercial development, and knitting the country together into a consolidated economic system. Whigs embraced material progress enthusiastically; but unlike the Democrats, they were cautious about westward expansion, fearful that rapid territorial growth would produce instability. Their vision of America was of a nation embracing the industrial future and rising to world greatness as a commercial and manufacturing

power. Thus while Democrats were inclined to oppose legislation establishing banks, corporations, and other modernizing institutions, Whigs generally favored such measures.

To some extent, the constituencies of the two major parties reflected these diffuse philosophies. The Whigs were strongest among the more substantial merchants and manufacturers of the Northeast; the wealthier planters of the South (those who favored commercial development and the strengthening of ties with the North); and the ambitious farmers and rising commercial class of the West—usually migrants from the Northeast—who advocated internal improvements, expanding trade, and rapid economic progress. The Democrats drew more support from smaller merchants and the workingmen of the Northeast; from southern planters suspicious of industrial growth; and from westerners—usually with southern roots—who favored a predominantly agrarian economy and opposed the development of powerful economic institutions in their region. Whigs tended to be wealthier than Democrats, to have more aristocratic backgrounds, and to be more commercially ambitious.

But Whigs and Democrats alike were more interested in winning elections than in maintaining philosophical purity. And both parties made frequent adjustments in their public postures to attract the largest possible number of voters. In New York, for example, the Whigs worked to develop a popular following by making a connection

| Anti-Masons |

to a movement known as Anti-Masonry. The Anti Mason movement had emerged in the 1820s in response to widespread resentment against the secret, exclusive, and hence supposedly undemocratic, Society of Freemasons. Such resentments greatly increased in 1826 when a former Mason, William Morgan, mysteriously disappeared (and was assumed to have been murdered) from his home in Batavia, New York, shortly before he was scheduled to publish a book purporting to expose the secrets of Freemasonry. Whigs seized on the Anti-Mason frenzy to launch harsh attacks on Jackson and Van Buren (both Freemasons), implying that the Democrats were part of the antidemocratic conspiracy. In the process, the Whigs presented themselves as opponents of aristocracy and exclusivity. They were, in other words, attacking the Democrats with the Democrats' own issues.

Religious and ethnic divisions also played an important role in determining the constituencies of the two parties. Irish and German Catholics, among the largest of the recent immigrant groups, tended to support the Democrats, who appeared to share their own vague aversion to commercial development and entrepreneurial progress

| Cultural Issues |

and who seemed to respect their family- and community-centered values and habits. Evangelical Protestants gravitated toward the Whigs because they associated the party with constant development and improvement, goals their own faith embraced. These and other ethnic, religious, and cultural tensions were often more influential in determining party alignments than any concrete political or economic proposals.

The Whig Party was more successful at defining its positions and attracting a constituency than it was in uniting behind a national leader. No single person was ever able to command the loyalties of the party in the way Andrew Jackson did the Democrats. Instead, Whigs tended to divide their loyalties among three figures, each of whom was so substantial a figure that together they became known as the "Great Triumvirate": Henry Clay, Daniel Webster, and John Calhoun.

Clay won support from many of those who favored

Clay's American System

his program for internal improvements and economic development, what he called the American System; but his image as a devious operator and his identification with the West proved serious liabilities. He ran for president three times and never won. Daniel Webster, the greatest orator of his era, won broad support with his passionate speeches in defense of the Constitution and the Union; but his close connection with the Bank of the United States and the protective tariff, his reliance on rich men for financial support, and his excessive and often embarrassing fondness for brandy prevented him from developing enough of a national constituency to win him the office he so desperately wanted. John C. Calhoun, the third member of what became known as the Great Triumvirate, never considered himself a true Whig, and his identification with the nullification controversy in effect disqualified him from national leadership in any case. But he had tremendous strength in the South, supported a national bank, and shared with Clay and Webster a strong animosity toward Andrew Jackson.

The problems that emerged from this divided leadership became particularly

Election of 1836

clear in 1836. The Democrats were united behind Andrew Jackson's personal choice for president, Martin Van Buren. The Whigs could not even agree on a single candidate. Instead, they ran several candidates, hoping to profit from the regional strength of each. Webster represented the party in New England; Hugh Lawson White of Tennessee ran in the South; and the former Indian fighter and hero of the War of 1812 from Ohio, William Henry Harrison, was the candidate in the middle states and the West. Party leaders hoped the three candidates together might draw enough votes from Van Buren to prevent his getting a majority and throw the election to the House of Representatives, where the Whigs might be able to elect one of their own leaders. In the end, however, Van Buren won easily, with 170 electoral votes to 124 for all his opponents.

Van Buren and the Panic of 1837

Andrew Jackson retired from public life in 1837, the most beloved political figure of his age. Martin Van Buren was very different from his predecessor and far less fortunate. He was never able to match Jackson's personal popularity, and his administration encountered economic difficulties that devastated the Democrats and helped the Whigs.

Van Buren's success in the 1836 election was a result in part of a nationwide economic boom that was reaching its height in that year. Canal and railroad builders were at a peak of activity. Prices were rising, money was plentiful, and credit was easy as banks increased their loans and notes with little regard to their reserves of cash. The land business, in particular, was booming. Between 1835 and 1837, the government sold nearly 40 million acres of public land, nearly three-fourths of it to speculators, who purchased large tracts in hopes of reselling them at a profit. These land sales, along with revenues the government received from the tariff of 1833, created a series of substantial federal budget surpluses and made possible a steady reduction of the national debt (something Jackson had always advocated). From 1835 to 1837, the government for the first and only time in its history was out of debt, with a substantial surplus in the Treasury.

Congress and the administration now faced the question of what to do with the Treasury surplus. Reducing the tariff

Distribution Act

was not an option, since no one wanted to raise that thorny issue again. Instead, support grew for returning the federal surplus to the states. In 1836, Congress passed a "distribution" act requiring the federal government to pay its surplus funds to the states each year in four quarterly installments as interest-free, unsecured loans. No one expected the "loans" to be repaid. The states spent the money quickly, mainly to encourage construction of highways, railroads, and canals. The distribution of the surplus thus gave further stimulus to the economic boom. At the same time, the withdrawal of federal funds strained the state (or "pet") banks in which they had been deposited by the government; they had to call in their own loans to make the transfer of funds to the state governments.

Congress did nothing to check the speculative fever, with which many congressmen themselves were badly infected. Webster, for one, was buying up thousands of acres in the West. But Jackson, always suspicious of paper currency, was unhappy that the government was selling good land and receiving in return various state bank notes worth no more than the credit of the issuing bank.

In 1836, not long before leaving office, he issued a presidential order, the "specie circular." It provided that in payment for public lands the government would only

"THE TIMES," 1837 This savage caricature of the economic troubles besetting the United States in 1837 illustrates, among other things, popular resentment of the hard-money orthodoxies of the time. A sign on the Custom House reads: "All bonds must be paid in Specie." Next door, the bank announces: "No specie payments made here." Women and children are shown begging in the street, while unemployed workers stand shoeless in front of signs advertising loans and "grand schemes." *(New-York Historical Society)*

accept gold or silver coins or currency securely backed by gold or silver. Jackson was right to fear the speculative fever but wrong in thinking the specie circular would cure it. On the contrary, it produced a financial panic that began in the first months of Van Buren's presidency. Hundreds of banks and businesses failed. Unemployment grew. Bread riots broke out in some of the larger cities. Prices fell, especially the price of land. Many railroad and canal projects failed. Several of the debt-burdened state governments ceased to pay interest on their bonds, and a few repudiated their debts, at least temporarily. It was the worst depression in American history to that point, and it lasted for five years. It was a political catastrophe for Van Buren and the Democrats.

Panic of 1837

Both parties bore some responsibility for the panic. The distribution of the Treasury surplus, which had weakened the state banks and helped cause the crash, had been a Whig measure. Jackson's specie circular, which had started a run on the banks as land buyers rushed to trade in their bank notes for specie, was also to blame. But the depression was only partly a result of federal policies. England and western Europe were facing panics of their own, which caused European (and especially English) investors to withdraw funds from America, putting an added strain on American banks. A succession of crop failures on American farms reduced the purchasing power of farmers and required increased imports of food, which sent more money out of the country. But whatever its actual causes, the Panic of 1837 occurred during a Democratic administration, and the Democrats paid the political price for it. The Van Buren administration, which strongly opposed government intervention in the economy, did little to fight the depression. Some of the steps it took—borrowing money to pay government debts and accepting only specie for payment of taxes—may have made things worse. Van Buren did succeed in establishing a ten-hour workday on all federal projects, by presidential order, but he had only a few legislative achievements.

The most important and controversial of them was the creation of a new financial system to replace the Bank of the United States. Under Van Buren's plan, known as the

Independent Treasury

"independent treasury" or "subtreasury" system, the government would place its funds in an independent treasury at Washington and in subtreasuries in other cities. No private banks would have the government's money or name to use as a basis for speculation; the government and the banks would be "divorced."

Van Buren called a special session of Congress in 1837 to consider the proposal, which failed in the House. In 1840, the last year of Van Buren's presidency, the administration finally succeeded in driving the measure through both houses of Congress.

The Log Cabin Campaign

As the campaign of 1840 approached, the Whigs realized that they would have to settle on one candidate for president this time if they were to have any hope of winning. As a result, they held their first national nominating convention in Harrisburg, Pennsylvania, in December 1839. Passing over the controversial Henry Clay, who had expected the nomination, the convention chose William Henry Harrison and, for vice president, John Tyler of Virginia. Harrison was a descendant of the Virginia aristocracy but had spent his adult life in the Northwest. He was a renowned soldier, a famous Indian fighter, and a popular national figure. The Democrats nominated Van Buren. But because they were not much more united than the Whigs, they failed to nominate a vice presidential candidate, leaving the choice of that office to the electors.

The 1840 campaign was the first in which the new popular "penny press" carried news of the candidates to a large audience of workers and tradespeople. It also illustrated how fully the concept of party competition, the subordination of ideology to immediate political needs, had established itself in America. The Whigs—who had emerged as a party largely because of their opposition to Andrew Jackson's common-man democracy, who in most regions | New Techniques of Political Campaigning | represented the more affluent elements of the population, and who favored government policies that would aid business—presented themselves in 1840 as the party of the common people. So, of course, did the Democrats. Both parties used the same techniques of mass voter appeal, the same evocation of simple, rustic values. What mattered now was not the philosophical purity of the party but its ability to win votes. The Whig campaign was particularly effective in portraying William Henry Harrison, a wealthy member of the frontier elite with a considerable estate, as a simple man of the people who loved log cabins and hard cider. They accused Van Buren of being an aloof aristocrat who used cologne, drank champagne, and ate from gold plates. The Democrats had no defense against the combination of these campaign techniques and the effects of the depression. Harrison won the election with 234 electoral votes to 60 for Van Buren and with a popular vote majority of 53 percent.

HARRISON AND REFORM This hand-colored engraving was made for a brass brooch during the 1840 presidential campaign and served the same purposes that modern campaign buttons do. It conveys Harrison's presumably humble beginnings in a log cabin. In reality, Harrison was a wealthy, aristocratic man; but the unpopularity of the aristocratic airs of his opponent, President Martin Van Buren, persuaded the Whig Party that it would be good political strategy to portray Harrison as a humble "man of the people." *(Collection of David J. and Janice L. Frent)*

The Frustration of the Whigs

Despite their decisive victory, the Whigs found their four years in power frustrating and divisive ones. In large part, that was because their popular new president, "Old Tippecanoe," William Henry Harrison, died of pneumonia one month after taking office. Vice President Tyler succeeded him. Control of the administration thus fell to a man with whom the Whig party leadership had relatively weak ties. Harrison had generally deferred to Henry Clay and Daniel Webster, whom he named secretary of state. Under Tyler, things soon changed.

Tyler was a former Democrat who had left the party in reaction to what he considered Jackson's excessively egalitarian program and imperious methods. But there were still signs of his Democratic past in his approach to public policy. The president did agree to bills abolishing Van Buren's independent treasury system and raising tariff rates. But he refused to support Clay's attempt to recharter a Bank of the United States. And he vetoed several internal improvement bills that Clay and other congressional Whigs sponsored. Finally, a conference of

A BEAUTIFUL GOBLET OF WHITE·HOUSE CHAMPAGNE

AN UGLY MUG OF LOG·CABIN HARD CIDER

AN ATTACK ON VAN BUREN This "pull card," made during the 1840 presidential campaign, which Van Buren lost to William Henry Harrison, satirizes the president as an aristocratic dandy. The card displays Van Buren grinning while he drinks champagne in the White House. Pulling a tab on the card changes his champagne glass to a mug of hard cider (with Harrison's initials on it) and changes his expression from delight to revulsion. *(Division of Political History, American History Museum, Smithsonian Institution, Washington, D.C.)*

Whigs Break with Tyler congressional Whigs read Tyler out of the party. Every cabinet member but Webster resigned; five former Democrats took their places. When Webster, too, left the cabinet, Tyler appointed Calhoun, who had rejoined the Democratic Party, to replace him.

A new political alignment was emerging. Tyler and a small band of conservative southern Whigs were preparing to rejoin the Democrats. Joining the "common man's party" of Jackson and Van Buren was a faction with decidedly aristocratic political ideas, who thought that government had an obligation to protect and even expand the institution of slavery, and who believed in states' rights with almost fanatical devotion.

Whig Diplomacy

In the midst of these domestic controversies, a series of incidents in the late 1830s brought Great Britain and the United States once again to the brink of war. Residents of the eastern provinces of Canada launched a rebellion against the British colonial government in 1837, and some of the rebels chartered an American steamship, the *Caroline,* to ship supplies across the Niagara River to them from New York. British authorities in Canada seized the *Caroline* and burned it, killing one American in the process. The British government refused either to disavow the attack or to provide compensation for it, and resentment in the United States ran high. But the British soon had reasons for anger as well. Authorities in New York, attempting to exploit the *Caroline* affair, arrested a Canadian named Alexander McLeod and charged him with the murder of the American who had died in the incident. The British government, expressing majestic rage, insisted that McLeod could not be accused of murder because he had acted under official orders. The foreign secretary, the bellicose Lord Palmerston, demanded McLeod's release and threatened that his execution would bring "immediate and frightful" war.

The Caroline Affair

Webster as secretary of state did not think McLeod was worth a war, but he was powerless to release him. The prisoner was under New York jurisdiction and had to be tried in the state courts, a peculiarity of American

The Penny Press

On September 3, 1833, a small newspaper appeared in New York City for the first time: the *New York Sun,* published by a young former apprentice from Massachusetts named Benjamin Day. It was four pages long; it contained mostly trivial local news, with particular emphasis on sex, crime, and violence; and it sold for a penny. It launched a new age in the history of American journalism, the age of the "penny press."

Before the advent of the penny press, newspapers in America were produced almost entirely by and for

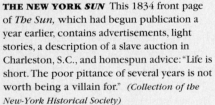

THE NEW YORK *SUN* This 1834 front page of *The Sun,* which had begun publication a year earlier, contains advertisements, light stories, a description of a slave auction in Charleston, S.C., and homespun advice: "Life is short. The poor pittance of several years is not worth being a villain for." *(Collection of the New-York Historical Society)*

the upper classes. Some published mainly business news; others worked to advance the aims of a political party. All were far too expensive for most ordinary citizens to buy. But several important changes in the business of journalism and the character of American society paved the way for Benjamin Day and others to challenge the established press. New technologies—the steam-powered cylinder printing press, new machines for making paper, railroads and canals for distributing issues to a larger market—made it possible to publish newspapers inexpensively and to sell them widely. A rising popular literacy rate, a result in part of the spread of public education, created a bigger reading public.

The penny press was also a response to the changing culture of the 1820s and 1830s. The spread of an urban, market economy contributed to the growth of the penny press by drawing a large population of workers, artisans, and clerks—the genesis of an industrial working class and a modern middle class—into large cities, where they became an important market for the new papers. The spirit of democracy—symbolized by the popularity of Andrew Jackson and the rising numbers of white male voters across the country—helped create an appetite for journalism that spoke to and for "the people," rather than the parties or the upper classes. Hence Benjamin Day's slogan for his new

paper: "It Shines for ALL." *The Sun,* and other papers like it, were self-consciously egalitarian. They were eager to tweak and embarrass the rich and powerful (through their popular gossip columns). They were also committed to feeding the appetites of the people of modest means, who constituted most of their readership. "Human interest stories" helped solidify their hold on the working public. Condescending stories about poor black men and women—ridiculing their subjects' illiteracy and their accents—were also popular among their virtually all-white readership.

Within six months of its first issue, the *Sun* had the largest circulation in New York—8,000 readers, more than twice its nearest competitors. Its success encouraged others to begin publishing penny papers of their own. James Gordon Bennett's *New York Herald,* which began publication in 1835, soon surpassed the *Sun* in popularity with its lively combination of sensationalism and local gossip and with its aggressive pursuit of national and international stories. The *Herald* pioneered a "letters to the editor" column. It was the first paper to have regular reviews of books and the arts. It even launched the first daily sports section. By 1860, it had the largest circulation of any daily newspaper in the world: more than 77,000.

Not all the new penny papers were as sensationalist as the *Sun* and the *Herald.* Both the *Philadelphia Public*

---

jurisprudence that the British did not seem to understand. A New York jury did what Webster could not: it defused the crisis by acquitting McLeod.

At the same time, tensions flared over the boundary between Canada and Maine, which had been in dispute since the Treaty of 1783. In 1838, groups of Americans and Canadians, mostly lumberjacks, began moving into the Aroostook River region in the disputed area, precipitating a violent brawl between the two groups that became known as the "Aroostook War."

Aroostook War

Several years later, there were yet more Anglo-American problems. In 1841, an American ship, the *Creole,* sailed from Virginia for New Orleans with more than 100 slaves

aboard. En route the slaves mutinied, took possession of the ship, and took it to the Bahamas. British officials there declared the slaves free, and the English government refused to overrule them. Many Americans, especially southerners, were furious.

At this critical juncture, a new government eager to reduce the tensions with the United States came to power in Great Britain. In the spring of 1842, it sent Lord Ashburton, an admirer of America, to negotiate an agreement on the Maine boundary and other matters. The result of his negotiations with Secretary of State Webster and representatives from Maine and Massachusetts was the Webster-Ashburton Treaty of 1842. Its

Webster-Ashburton Treaty

Ledger and the *Baltimore Sun,* founded in 1836 and 1837 respectively, strove to provide more serious coverage of the news. The *Baltimore Sun* even developed a Washington bureau, the first of the penny papers to do so. The *New York Tribune,* founded in 1841 by Horace Greeley (later a major antislavery leader and a Republican presidential candidate), hired some of the most important writers of the day—among them Charles A. Dana, Margaret Fuller, Henry James, and William Dean Howells—and prided itself on serious reporting and commentary. All of it was tinged with a conspicuous sympathy for socialism (Greeley once hired Karl Marx as a London correspondent) and for the aspirations of working people. As serious as the *Tribune,* but more sober and self-consciously "objective" in its reportage, was the *New York Times,* which Henry Raymond founded in 1851. "We do not mean to write as if we were in a passion—unless that shall really be the case," the *Times* huffily proclaimed in its first issue, in an obvious reference to Greeley and his impassioned reportage; "and we shall make it a point to get into a passion as rarely as possible."

But the *Times*'s dutiful restraint and self-conscious respectability was rare in the penny press. More typical was the front page of the June 4, 1836 *Herald,* devoted in its entirety to the sensational murder of a prostitute by a frequent patron of brothels. "Why is not the militia called?" Bennett's paper asked breathlessly at the beginning of the main story. "We give . . . testimony up to the latest hour . . . . The mystery of the bloody drama increases—increases—increases."

No papers in the 1830s had yet begun to use the large banner headlines of modern tabloids. None had photographs, and only a few—Bennett's *Herald* notable among them—ran drawings to accompany their stories with any regularity. But within their columns of unbroken newsprint lay the origins of the press we know today. They were the first papers to pay their reporters and thus began the process of turning journalism into a profession. They were the first to rely heavily on advertisements and often devoted up to half their space to paid advertising. They reached beyond the business world and the political clubs and communicated with a genuinely mass market. They were often sensationalist and usually opinionated. But they were often also aggressive in uncovering serious and important news—in police stations, courts, jails, streets, and private homes as well as in city halls, state capitals, Washington, and the world.

THE FIRST "EXTRA" This 1840 "special edition" of the *New York Sun* was innovative in two ways. It was probably the first "extra" edition of any daily newspaper in America. It was also one of the first examples of large and (in this case at least) lurid illustration in the daily press. This dramatic picture accompanies a story about the explosion of the ship. *(Print Collection Miriam and Ira D. Wallach Division. New-York Public Library, Astor, Lenox and Tilden Foundation)*

terms established a firm northern boundary between the United States and Canada along the Maine-New Brunswick border that survives to this day; the new border gave the United States a bit more than half of the previously disputed territory. Other, smaller provisions placated Maine and Massachusetts and protected critical trade routes in both the northern United States and southern Canada. In a separate exchange of notes, Ashburton eased the memory of the *Caroline* and *Creole* affairs by expressing regret and promising no future "officious interference" with American ships. The Webster-Ashburton treaty was generally popular in America, and in its aftermath Anglo-American relations substantially improved.

During the Tyler administration, the United States established its first diplomatic relations with China. In 1842, Britain forced China to open certain ports to foreign trade. Eager to share the new privileges, American mercantile interests persuaded Tyler and Congress to send a commissioner—Caleb Cushing—to China to negotiate a treaty giving the United States some part in the China trade. In the Treaty of Wang Hya, concluded in 1844, Cushing secured most-favored-nation provisions giving Americans the same privileges as the English. He also won for Americans the right of "extraterritoriality"—the right of Americans accused of crimes in China to be tried by American, not Chinese, officials.

Treaty of Wang Hya

In the next ten years, American trade with China steadily increased.

In their diplomatic efforts, at least, the Whigs were able to secure some important successes. But by the end of the Tyler administration, the party could look back on few other victories. In the election of 1844, the Whigs lost the White House. They were to win only one more national election in their history before a great sectional crisis arose that would shatter their party and, for a time, the Union.

CONCLUSION

The election of Andrew Jackson to the presidency in 1828 marked not only the triumph of a particular vision of government and democracy. It represented as well the

Jackson's Legacy

emergence of a new political world. Throughout the American nation, the laws governing political participation were loosening and the number of people permitted to vote (which eventually included most white males, but almost no one else) was increasing. Along with this expansion of the electorate was emerging a new spirit of party politics. Parties had once been reviled by American leaders as contributing to the spirit of faction. Now a new set of ideas was emerging that saw in institutionalized parties not a challenge, but a contribution to democracy. Party competition would be a way of containing and muting disagreements that might otherwise run amok. It would be another of the healthy restraints—another part of the system of checks and balances—that made American government work.

Andrew Jackson was a party man, and he set out as president to entrench his party, the Democrats, in power. He was also a fierce defender of his region, the West, and a sharp critic of what he considered the stranglehold of the aristocratic East on the nation's economic life. He sought to limit the role of the federal government in economic affairs, fearful that it would serve to entrench existing patterns of wealth and power. He worked to destroy the Bank of the United States, which he considered a corrupt vehicle of aristocratic influence. Jackson was, finally, a nationalist. And he confronted the greatest challenge to American unity yet to have emerged in the young nation— the nullification crisis of 1832–1833—with a strong assertion of the power and importance of the Union. These positions won him broad popularity and ensured his reelection in 1832 and the election of his designated successor, Martin Van Buren, in 1836.

But the Democrats were not the only ones to have learned the lessons of the age of parties. A new coalition of anti-Jacksonians, who called themselves the Whigs, launched a powerful new party that used much of the same anti-elitist rhetoric the Democrats had used to win support for their own much more nationalist program. Their emergence culminated in the campaign of 1840 with the election of the first Whig president.

INTERACTIVE LEARNING

The *Primary Source Investigator CD-ROM* offers the following materials related to this chapter:

- A short documentary movie, **Cherokee Removal,** on the federal government's forced removal of thousands of Native Americans to Indian Territory (Oklahoma) and the tragic results (D6).

- Interactive maps: **U.S. Elections** (M7) and **Indian Expulsion** (M9).

- Documents, images, and maps related to Jacksonian democracy, the forced removal of Native Americans to western territories, and the rise of the Whig Party. Highlights include a series of portraits of Andrew Jackson, a protest memorial about Cherokee removal, paintings of Native Americans, the Supreme Court decision *Cherokee Nation* v. *Georgia,* and a series of cartoons satirizing Jacksonian democracy.

 Online Learning Center (www.mhhe.com/brinkley12)

For quizzes, Internet resources, references to additional books and films, and more, consult this book's Online Learning Center.

FOR FURTHER REFERENCE

Arthur M. Schlesinger, Jr., *The Age of Jackson* (1945) represents Jacksonian politics as an eastern, urban democratic movement of working men and upper-class intellectuals. Bray Hammond, *Banks and Politics in America from the Revolution to the Civil War* (1957) challenges Schlesinger by arguing that the Bank War was essentially a struggle between different groups of capitalist elites. Harry L. Watson, *Liberty and Power: The Politics of Jacksonian America* (1990) provides an important newer synthesis of Jacksonian politics. Donald B. Cole, *Martin Van Buren and the American Political System* (1984) examines the emergence of modern notions of party through the career of Van Buren. Richard Hofstadter, *The Idea of a Party System: The Rise of Legitimate Opposition in the United States, 1740–1840* (1969) traces the growing acceptance of the idea of partisan competition. Daniel Walker Howe, *The Political Culture of the American Whigs* (1979) analyzes the careers of several leading Whig politicians including the Whig triumvirate of Calhoun, Clay, and Webster. William V. Freehling, *Prelude to Civil War: The Nullification Controversy in South Carolina* (1966) argues that South Carolina planters' anxiety over the fate of slavery was at the heart of the nullification crisis. Francis P. Prucha, *American Indian Policy in the Formative Years* (1962) is an overview of early Indian policy by the leading scholar of the subject. Michael Rogin, *Fathers and Children: Andrew Jackson and the Destruction of American Indians* (1975) offers a more radical and idiosyncratic perspective on Jackson's career as an Indian fighter using the methods of psychoanalysis. Sean Wilentz, *Chants Democratic: New York City and the Rise of the American Working Class, 1788–1850* (1984) is an important study of working-class ideology during the Jacksonian period.

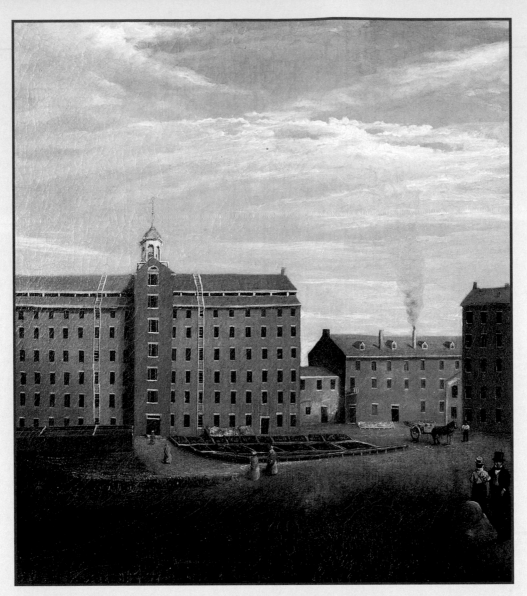

THE LOWELL MILLS Fifteen years earlier, Lowell, Massachusetts, had been a small farming village known as East Chelmsford. By the 1840s, when Fitzhugh Lane painted *The Middlesex Company Woolen Mills,* the town had become one of the most famous manufacturing centers in America and a magnet for visitors from around the world. Lane's painting shows female workers, who dominated the labor force in Lowell, entering the factory. *(American Textile History Museum, Lowell, Massachusetts)*

SIGNIFICANT EVENTS

1813 ▶ Lowell establishes textile mill at Waltham, Massachusetts

1817–1825 ▶ Erie Canal constructed

1830 ▶ Baltimore and Ohio becomes first American railroad to begin operations

1830s ▶ Major immigration from southern (Catholic) Ireland begins

▶ Factory system spreads in textile and shoe industries

▶ First national craft unions founded

1832 ▶ Cholera plague

1834 ▶ Women workers at Lowell mills stage strike

▶ Cyrus McCormick patents mechanical reaper

CHAPTER 10

America's Economic Revolution

When the United States entered the War of 1812, it was still an essentially agrarian nation. There were, to be sure, cities in America, several of substantial size. In some of them there was a flourishing mercantile economy, based largely on overseas trade. There was also modest but growing manufacturing activity, concentrated mainly in the Northeast. But the overwhelming majority of Americans were farmers and tradespeople, working within an economy that was still mainly local.

By the time the Civil War began in 1861, the United States had transformed itself. Most Americans were still rural people, to be sure. But even most American farmers

The Market Revolution

were now part of a national, and increasingly international, market economy. Above all, perhaps, the United States had developed a major manufacturing sector and was beginning to challenge the industrial nations of Europe for supremacy. The nation had experienced the first stage of its industrial revolution; and while the changes that revolution produced were far from complete, most Americans understood that their world had changed irrevocably.

These dramatic changes—changes that affected not just the economy, but society, culture, and politics—did not have the same impact everywhere. The Northeast, and its new economic ally the Northwest, were rapidly developing a complex, modern economy and society, increasingly dominated by large cities, important manufacturing, and profitable commercial farming. It was in many ways an unequal society, but it was also a fluid one, firmly committed to the ideal of free labor. Relatively few white Americans yet lived west of the Mississippi River, but parts of those western lands, too, were becoming part of large-scale commercial agriculture and other enterprises and were creating links to the capitalist economy of the Northeast.

In the South and Southwest, there were changes, too. Southern agriculture, particularly cotton farming,

Regional Divergences

flourished as never before in response to the growing demand from textile mills in New England and elsewhere. But while the southern states were becoming increasingly a part of the national and international capitalist world, they also remained much less economically developed than their northern counterparts. And as the North became ever more committed to the fluidity and mobility of its free-labor system, the South was becoming more and more resolute in its defense of slavery.

The industrial revolution, which was doing so much to draw the nation into a single, integrated economy, was also working to isolate—and, increasingly, to alarm—the residents of one of its regions. The economic revolution was transforming the nation. It was also dividing it.

1837 ▸ Native American Association begins efforts to restrict immigration

▸ Oberlin becomes first American coeducational college

▸ Mt. Holyoke College for women opens

1842 ▸ Massachusetts Supreme Court, in *Commonwealth* v. *Hunt*, declares unions and strikes legal

▸ P. T. Barnum opens American Museum in New York

1844 ▸ Samuel F. B. Morse sends first telegraph message

1845 ▸ Irish potato famine begins, spurring major emigration to America

▸ Native American Party formed to combat immigration

▸ Female Labor Reform Association established at Lowell

1846 ▸ Rotary press invented, making possible rapid printing of newspapers

▸ Associated Press organized

1847 ▸ John Deere begins manufacturing steel plows

1848 ▸ Failed revolution in Germany spurs emigration to America

▸ Wisconsin enters Union

1850 ▸ Nativists form Supreme Order of the Star-Spangled Banner to oppose immigration

1852 ▸ American Party (Know-Nothings) formed

THE CHANGING AMERICAN POPULATION

The American industrial revolution was a result of many factors. Before it could occur, the United States needed a population large enough both to grow its own food and to provide a work force for the industrial economy. It needed a transportation and communications system capable of sustaining commerce over a large geographical area. It needed the technology to permit manufacturing on a large scale. And it needed systems of business organization capable of managing large industrial enterprises. By 1860, the northern regions of the nation had acquired at least the beginnings of all those things.

The American Population, 1820–1840

Three trends characterized the American population between 1820 and 1840, all of them contributing in various ways to economic growth. The population was increasing rapidly; much of it was moving from the countryside into the industrializing cities of the Northeast and Northwest; and much of it was migrating westward.

The American population had stood at only 4 million in 1790. By 1820, it had reached 10 million; by 1830, nearly 13 million; and by 1840, 17 million. The United States was growing much more rapidly in population than Britain or Europe. One reason for this substantial

Reasons for Population Increase

population growth was improvements in public health. The number and ferocity of epidemics

(such as the great cholera plague of 1832)—which had periodically decimated urban and even rural populations in America—slowly declined, as did the nation's mortality rate as a whole. The population increase was also a result of a high birth rate. In 1840, white women bore an average of 6.14 children each, a decline from the very high rates of the eighteenth century but still substantial enough to produce rapid population increases, particularly since a larger proportion of children could expect to grow to adulthood than had been the case a generation or two earlier.

Immigration, choked off by wars in Europe and economic crises in America, contributed little to the American population in the first three decades of the nineteenth century but rapidly revived beginning in the 1830s. Of the total 1830 population of nearly 13 million, the foreign-born numbered fewer than 500,000. But the number of immigrants climbed by 60,000 in 1832 and nearly 80,000 in 1837. Reduced transportation costs and increasing economic opportunities helped stimulate the immigration boom, as did deteriorating economic conditions in some areas of Europe. The migrations introduced new groups to the United States. In particular, the number of immigrants arriving from the southern counties of Ireland began to grow, marking the beginning of a tremendous influx of Irish Catholics that was to continue through the three decades before the Civil War.

Much of this new European immigration flowed into the rapidly growing cities of the Northeast. But urban growth was a result of substantial internal migration as well. As the agricultural regions of New England and

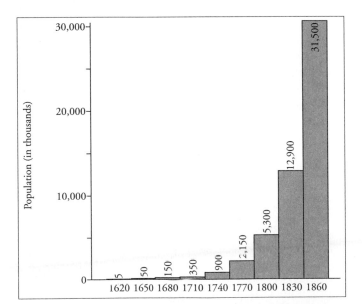

POPULATION GROWTH, 1620–1860 From its tiny beginnings in the seventeenth century, the American population grew rapidly and dramatically so that by 1860—with over 31 million people—the United States was one of the most populous countries in the world. ◆ *How did this growing population contribute to the nation's economic transformation?*

IMMIGRATION, 1820–1840 Among the sources of the nation's growing population in the nineteenth century was rapidly increasing immigration. This graph shows how rapidly immigration to the United States increased in the 1820s and 1830s. The 347,000 immigrants in the last half of the 1830s was almost nine times the number in the first half of the 1820s. ◆ *Where did most of these new immigrants settle?*

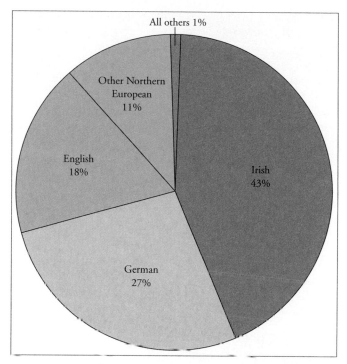

SOURCES OF IMMIGRATION, 1820–1840 This pie chart shows where the large numbers of immigrants portrayed in the previous chart came from. Note the very large number of Irish immigrants. ◆ *Why were the Irish among the most likely immigrant groups to become part of the industrial work force?*

other areas grew less profitable, more and more people picked up stakes and moved—some to more promising agricultural regions in the West, but many to eastern cities. In 1790, one person in thirty had lived in a city (defined as a community of 8,000 or more); in 1820, one in twenty; and in 1840, one in twelve.

The rise of New York City was particularly dramatic. By 1810 it was the largest city in the United States. That was partly a result of its superior natural harbor. It was also a result of the Erie Canal (completed in 1825), which gave the city unrivaled access to the interior, and of liberal state laws that made the city attractive for both foreign and domestic commerce.

Immigration and Urban Growth, 1840–1860

The growth of cities accelerated dramatically between 1840 and 1860. The population of New York, for example, rose from 312,000 to 805,000. (New York's population would have numbered 1.2 million in 1860 if Brooklyn, which was then a separate municipality, had been included in the total.) Philadelphia's population grew over the same twenty-year period from 220,000 to 565,000; Boston's from 93,000 to 177,000. By 1860, 26 percent of the population of the free states was living in towns (places of 2,500 people or more) or cities (8,000 people or more),

Rapid Urbanization

up from 14 percent in 1840. That percentage was even higher for the industrializing states of the Northeast. (In the South, by contrast, the increase of urban residents was only from 6 percent in 1840 to 10 percent in 1860.)

The booming agricultural economy of the western regions of the nation produced significant urban growth as well. Between 1820 and 1840, communities that had once been small western villages or trading posts became major cities: St. Louis, Pittsburgh, Cincinnati, Louisville. All of them benefited from strategic positions on the Mississippi River or one of its major tributaries. All of them became centers of the growing carrying trade that connected the farmers of the Midwest with New Orleans and, through it, the cities of the Northeast. After 1830, however, substantial shipping began from the Mississippi River to the Great Lakes, creating major new urban centers that gradually superseded the river ports. Among them were Buffalo, Detroit, Milwaukee, Cleveland, and—most important in the end—Chicago.

The enlarged urban population was in part simply a reflection of the growth of the national population as a whole, which rose by more than a third—from 23 million to over 31 million—in the decade of the 1850s alone. By 1860, the American population was larger than Britain's and quickly approaching that of France and Germany. Urban growth was also a result of the continuing, indeed increasing, flow of people into cities from the farms of the Northeast, which continued to decline because of competition from Europe and the American West (and because of the relative disadvantages of their own soil). Immigration from abroad continued to increase as well. The number of foreigners arriving in the United States in 1840—84,000—was the highest for any one year to that point in the nineteenth century. But in later years, even that number would come to seem insignificant. Between 1840 and 1850, more than 1.5 million Europeans moved to America, three times the number of arrivals in the 1830s; in the last years of that decade, average annual immigration was almost 300,000. Of the 23 million people in the United States in 1850, 2.2 million (almost 10 percent) were foreign-born. Still greater numbers arrived in the 1850s—over 2.5 million. Almost half the residents of New York City in the 1850s were recent immigrants. In St. Louis, Chicago, and Milwaukee, the foreign-born outnumbered those of native birth. Few immigrants settled in the South. Only 500,000 lived in the slave states in 1860, and a third of these were concentrated in Missouri, mostly in St. Louis.

Surging Immigration

The newcomers came from many different countries and regions: England, France, Italy, Scandinavia, Poland, and Holland. But the overwhelming majority came from Ireland and Germany. In 1850, the Irish constituted approximately 45 percent and the Germans over 20 percent of the foreign-born in America.

German and Irish Immigrants

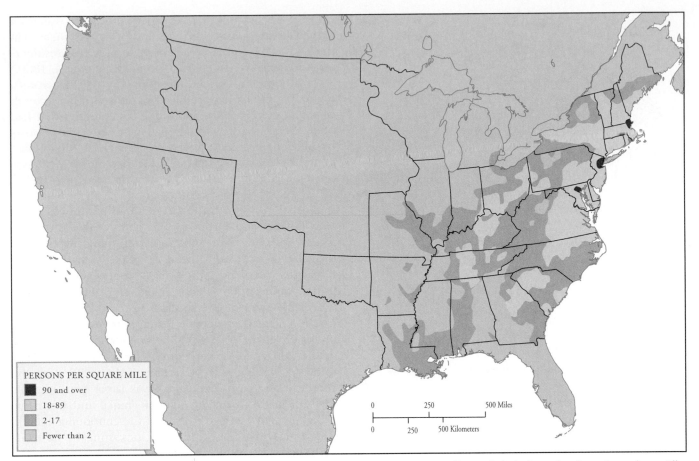

AMERICAN POPULATION DENSITY, 1820 The population of the United States in 1820 was still overwhelmingly rural and agrarian and was still concentrated largely in the original thirteen states, although settlement was growing in the Ohio River valley to the west. Note how few areas of the country were populated really densely: a small area in northeastern Massachusetts, the area around New York City, and the area in Maryland adjoining Baltimore. ◆ *What accounts for the density in these areas?*

BROADWAY IN 1836 This image of the area of New York City's Broadway in what is now lower Manhattan suggests the way in which New York was becoming an increasingly important center of trade and commerce—and a densely urban place—in the 1830s. *(The New York Public Library/Art Resource, NY)*

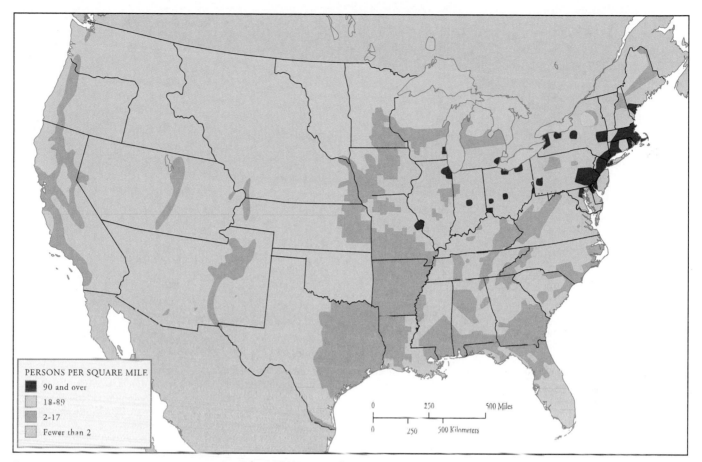

AMERICAN POPULATION DENSITY, 1860 By 1860, the population of the United States had spread much more evenly across the entire country. Communities that had once been small trading posts emerged as major cities. Among them were St. Louis, Pittsburgh, Cincinnati, and Louisville. In the meantime, the Erie Canal had opened up a large and prosperous market area for New York City. Note the larger and more numerous areas of dense population, including many in the Midwest. ◆ *What accounts for the growing population density in some areas of the deep South?*

By 1860, there were more than 1.5 million Irish-born and approximately 1 million German-born people in the United States. There were several reasons for this flood of immigration. In Germany, the economic dislocations of the industrial revolution had caused widespread poverty, and the collapse of the liberal revolution there in 1848 also persuaded many Germans to emigrate. In Ireland, the oppressiveness and unpopularity of English rule drove many people out. But these political factors were dwarfed in the mid-nineteenth century by the greatest disaster in Ireland's history: a catastrophic failure of the potato crop (and other food crops) that caused the devastating "potato famine" of 1845–1849. Nearly a million people died of starvation and disease. Well over a million more emigrated to the United States.

The Irish and German patterns of settlement in America were very different. The great majority of the Irish settled in the eastern cities, where they swelled the ranks of unskilled labor. Most Germans moved on to the Northwest, where they became farmers or went into business in the western towns. One reason for the difference was wealth: German immigrants generally

arrived with at least some money; the Irish had practically none. Another important reason was gender. Most German immigrants were members of family groups or were single men, for whom movement to the agricultural frontier was both possible and attractive. Many Irish immigrants were young, single women, for whom movement west was much less plausible. They were more likely to stay in the eastern cities, where factory and domestic work was available.

The Rise of Nativism

Some native-born Americans saw in the new immigration a source of great opportunity. Industrialists and other employers welcomed the arrival of a large supply of cheap labor, which they believed would help them keep wage rates low. Land speculators and others with investments in the sparsely populated West hoped that many of the immigrants would move into the region and help expand the population, and thus the market for land and goods, there. Political leaders in western states and territories hoped the immigrants would, by swelling their

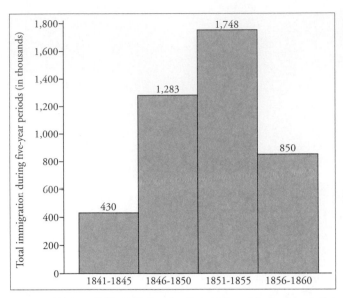

IMMIGRATION, 1840-1860 Immigration continued to increase in the forty years before the Civil War. This chart illustrates the much higher levels of growth than in the previous forty years. The low point in this era was the first half of the 1840s, in which 430,000 new immigrants entered the United States. That was significantly higher than the largest number of the previous twenty years. In the early 1850s, the number of immigrants grew to nearly two million. ♦ *What events in Europe contributed to this increase?*

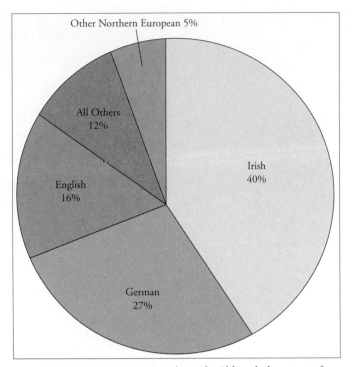

SOURCES OF IMMIGRATION, 1840-1860 Although the extent of immigration increased dramatically in the two decades after 1840, the sources of it remained remarkably stable. Note how closely the distribution of immigrant groups portrayed in this pie chart parallels that in the similar chart for the 1820–1840 period. ♦ *What were some of the differences between what German and Irish immigrants did once they arrived in America?*

population, also increase the political influence of the region. Wisconsin, for example, permitted foreign-born residents to become voters as soon as they had declared their intention of seeking citizenship and had resided in the state for a year; other western states soon followed its lead. In eastern cities, too, urban political organizations eagerly courted immigrant voters, hoping to enhance their own political strength.

Other Americans, however, viewed the growing foreign-born population with alarm. Their fears led to the rise of what is known as "nativism," a defense of native-born people and a hostility to the foreign-born, usually combined with a desire to stop or slow immigration. The emerging nativism took many forms. Some of it was a result of simple racism. Many nativists (conveniently overlooking their own immigrant heritage) argued that the new immigrants were inherently inferior to older-stock Americans. Some viewed them with the same contempt and prejudice—and the same low estimate of their potential abilities—with which they viewed African Americans. Many nativists avoided racist arguments but argued nevertheless that the newcomers were socially unfit to live alongside people of older stock, that they did not bring with them sufficient standards of civilization. Evidence for that, they claimed, was the wretched urban and sometimes rural slums in which they lived.

(Many nativists seemed to assume that such wretchedness was something immigrants chose, rather than the result of their extreme poverty.) Others—especially workers—complained that because foreigners were willing to work for low wages, they were stealing jobs from the native labor force. Protestants, observing the success of Irish Catholics in establishing footholds in urban politics, warned that the church of Rome was gaining a foothold in American government. Whig politicians were outraged because so many of the newcomers voted Democratic. Others complained that the immigrants corrupted politics by selling their votes. Many older-stock Americans of both parties feared that immigrants would bring new, radical ideas into national life.

Out of these tensions and prejudices emerged a number of new secret societies created to combat what nativists had come to call the "alien menace." Most of them originated in the Northeast. Some later spread to the West Native American Party and even to the South. The first of these, the Native American Association, began agitating against immigration in 1837. In 1845, nativists held a convention in Philadelphia and formed the Native American Party (unaware that the term they used to describe themselves would one day become a common label for American Indians). Many of the nativist groups combined in 1850

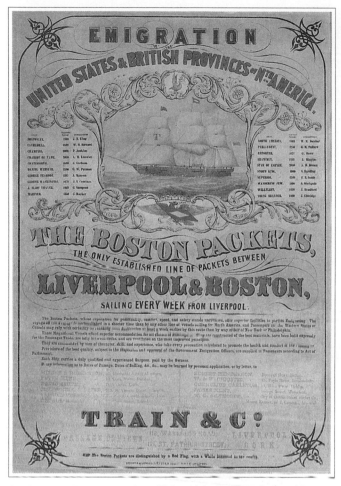

AN APPEAL TO EMIGRANTS   This widely distributed advertising card was one of many appeals to potential English and Irish travelers to America in the 1830s and 1840s. Like many such companies, it tried to attract both affluent passengers (by boasting of "superior accommodations") and working-class people of modest means. *(Courtesy of The Bostonian Society/Old State House)*

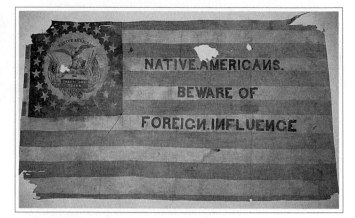

A "KNOW NOTHING" FLAG   The American Party, which began as a secret organization with the popular nickname "Know Nothings" (from their refusal to divulge any information about their activities), was in the forefront of antebellum campaigns against immigration—as this flag (which refers to the older-stock white members of the party as "Native Americans") suggests. The Know Nothings were particularly alarmed about the rising number of Catholic immigrants to the United States and warned that this "monster" (Catholicism) was "only waiting for the hour to approach to plant its flag of tyranny, persecution, and oppression among us." *(Photo Courtesy of Milwaukee County Historical Society)*

to form the Supreme Order of the Star-Spangled Banner. It endorsed a list of demands that included banning Catholics or the foreign-born from holding public office, more restrictive naturalization laws, and literacy tests for voting. The order adopted a strict code of secrecy, which included the secret password, used in lodges across the country, "I know nothing." Ultimately, members of the movement became known as the "Know Nothings."

Gradually, the Know-Nothings turned their attention to party politics, and after the election of 1852 they created a new political organization that they called the American Party. In the East, the new organization scored an immediate and astonishing success in the elections of 1854: the Know-Nothings cast a large vote in Pennsylvania and New York and won control of the state government in Massachusetts. Elsewhere, the progress of the Know-Nothings was more modest. Western members of the

> The Know-Nothings

party, because of the presence of many German voters in the area, found it expedient not to oppose naturalized Protestants. After 1854, the strength of the Know-Nothings declined. The Know-Nothing Party's most lasting impact was its contribution to the collapse of the existing party system (organized around the Whig and Democratic parties) and the creation of new national political alignments.

TRANSPORTATION, COMMUNICATIONS, AND TECHNOLOGY

Just as the industrial revolution needed a growing population, it also required an efficient system of transportation and communications. Such a system was essential in creating regional, national, and ultimately international markets. Progress in this area required not just significant investment, but also important advances in technological knowledge.

The Canal Age

From 1790 until the 1820s, the so-called turnpike era, Americans had relied largely on roads for internal transportation. But in a country as large as the United States was becoming, roads alone (and the mostly horse-drawn vehicles that used them) were not adequate for the nation's expanding needs. And so, in the 1820s and 1830s, Americans began to turn to other means of transportation as well.

"AMERICANS SHALL RULE AMERICA" Thomas Swann, a Maryland railroad magnate, was elected mayor of Baltimore in 1856 as the candidate of the American (or "Know-Nothing") Party after a campaign characterized by widespread violence and disorder and by a strident denunciation of immigrants. This cartoon lambasting the American Party's activities in Baltimore conveys the opponents' image of the Know-Nothings as a party of drunken hooligans. *(Maryland Historical Society)*

The larger rivers, especially the Mississippi and the Ohio, had been important transportation routes for years, but most of the traffic on them consisted of flat barges—little more than rafts—that floated downstream laden with cargo and were broken up at the end of their journeys because they could not navigate back upstream. To return north, shippers had to send goods by land or by agonizingly slow upstream vessels that sometimes took up to four months to travel the length of the Mississippi.

These rivers had become vastly more important by the 1820s, as steamboats grew in number and improved in design. The new riverboats carried the corn and wheat of northwestern farmers and the cotton and tobacco of southwestern planters to New Orleans in a fraction of the time of the old barges. From New Orleans, oceangoing ships took the cargoes on to eastern ports. Steamboats also developed a significant passenger traffic, and companies built increasingly lavish vessels to compete for this lucrative trade (even though most passengers could not afford the luxurious amenities and slept in the hold or on the deck).

Steamboats

But neither the farmers of the West nor the merchants of the East were wholly satisfied with this pattern of trade. Farmers would pay less to transport their goods (and eastern consumers would pay less to consume them) if they could ship them directly eastward to market, rather than by the roundabout river-sea route; and northeastern merchants, too, could sell larger quantities of their manufactured goods if they could transport their merchandise more directly and economically to the West. New highways across the mountains provided a partial solution to the problem. But the costs of hauling goods overland, although lower than before, were still too high for anything except the most compact and valuable merchandise. The thoughts of some merchants and entrepreneurs began, therefore, to turn to an alternative: canals.

A team of four horses could haul one and a half tons of goods eighteen miles a day on the turnpikes. But the same four horses, walking along the "towpaths" next to canals while yoked to barges, could draw a boatload of a hundred tons twenty-four miles a day. By the 1820s, the economic advantages of canals had generated a booming interest in expanding the water routes to the West. Canal building was too expensive for private enterprise, and the job of digging canals fell largely to the states. The ambitious state governments of the Northeast took the lead in constructing them. New York was the first to act. It had the natural advantage of a good land route between the Hudson River and Lake Erie through the only real break in the Appalachian chain. But the engineering tasks were still imposing. The distance was more than 350 miles, several times as long as any of the existing canals in America. The route was interrupted by high ridges and a wilderness of woods. After a long public debate over whether the scheme was practical, canal advocates prevailed when De Witt Clinton, a late but ardent convert to the cause, became governor in 1817. Digging began on July 4, 1817.

Economic Advantages of Canals

BUILDING THE ERIE CANAL This lithograph by Anthony Imbert suggests something of the enormous engineering challenges that the builders of the Erie Canal faced. This picture shows excavations at Lockport, New York, where a horse-powered crane and a large crew of Irish immigrant workers clear boulders from the channel. Imbert created these and other images to illustrate a book published in 1825 to celebrate the completion of the canal. *(Building the Erie Canal. Lithograph by Anthony Imbert. From Cadwallader Colden's Memoir on the Celebration of the Completion of the New York Canals. The Metropolitan Museum of Art, Harris Brisbane Dick Fund, 1941. (41.51))*

The building of the Erie Canal was the greatest construction project the United States had ever undertaken. The canal itself was simple: basically a ditch forty feet wide and four feet deep, with towpaths along the banks.

The Erie Canal — But hundreds of difficult cuts and fills, some of them enormous, were required to enable the canal to pass through hills and over valleys; stone aqueducts were necessary to carry it across streams; and eighty-eight locks, of heavy masonry with great wooden gates, were needed to permit ascents and descents. The Erie Canal was not just an engineering triumph, but an immediate financial success. It opened in October 1825, amid elaborate ceremonies and celebrations, and traffic was soon so heavy that within about seven years tolls had repaid the entire cost of construction. By providing a route to the Great Lakes, the canal gave New York direct access to Chicago and the growing markets of the West. New York could now compete with (and increasingly replace) New Orleans as a destination for agricultural goods (particularly wheat) and other products of the West, and as a source for manufactured goods to be sold in the region.

The system of water transportation—and the primacy of New York—extended farther when the states of Ohio and Indiana, inspired by the success of the Erie Canal, provided water connections between Lake Erie and the Ohio River. These canals helped connect them by an inland water route all the way to New York, although it was still necessary to transfer cargoes several times between canal, lake, and river craft. One of the immediate results of these new transportation routes was increased white settlement in the Northwest, because canals made it easier for migrants to make the westward journey and to ship their goods back to eastern markets.

Rival cities along the Atlantic seaboard took alarm at the prospect of New York's acquiring so vast a hinterland. But they had limited success in catching up. Boston, its way to the Hudson River blocked by the Berkshire Mountains, did not even try to connect itself to the West by canal; its hinterland would remain confined largely to New England. Philadelphia and Baltimore had the still more formidable Allegheny Mountains to contend with. They made a serious effort at canal building, nevertheless, but with discouraging results. Pennsylvania's effort

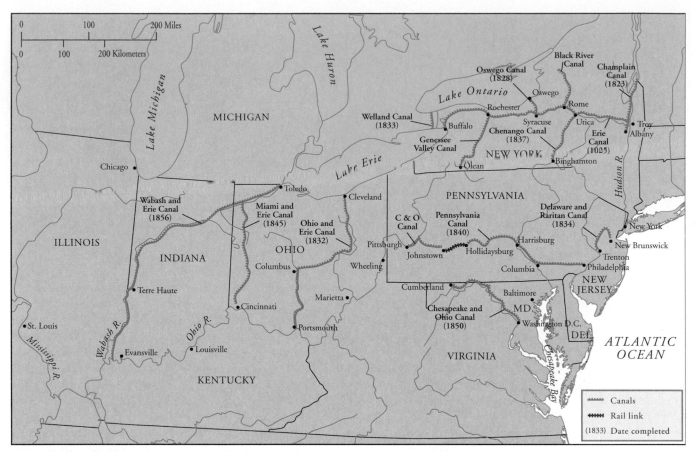

CANALS IN THE NORTHEAST, 1823–1860 The great success of the Erie Canal, which opened in 1825, inspired decades of energetic canal building in many areas of the United States, as this map illustrates. But none of the new canals had anything like the impact of the original Erie Canal, and thus none of New York's competitors—among them Baltimore, Philadelphia, and Boston—were able to displace it as the nation's leading commercial center. ◆ *What form of transportation ultimately displaced the canals?*

For an interactive version of this map go to www.mhhe.com/brinkley12ch10maps

ended in an expensive failure. Maryland constructed part of the Chesapeake and Ohio Canal beginning in 1828, but completed only the stretch between Washington, D.C., and Cumberland, Maryland, and thus never crossed the mountains. In the South, Richmond and Charleston also aspired to build water routes to the Ohio Valley, but never completed them.

In the end, canals did not provide a satisfactory route to the West for any of New York's rivals. Some cities, however, saw their opportunity in a different and newer means of transportation. Even before the canal age had reached its height, the era of the railroad was already beginning.

The Early Railroads

Railroads played no more than a secondary role in the nation's transportation system in the 1820s and 1830s, but railroad pioneers laid the groundwork in those years for the great surge of railroad building in midcentury. Eventually, railroads became the primary transportation

system for the United States, and they remained so until the construction of the interstate highway system in the mid-twentieth century.

Railroads emerged from a combination of technological and entrepreneurial innovations. The technological breakthroughs included the invention of tracks, the creation of steam-powered locomotives, and the development of railroad cars that could serve as public carriers of passengers and freight. By 1804, both English and American inventors had experimented with steam engines for propelling land vehicles. In 1820, John Stevens ran a locomotive and cars around a circular track on his New Jersey estate. And in 1825, the Stockton and Darlington Railroad in England opened a short length of track and became the first line to carry general traffic.

American entrepreneurs, especially in those northeastern cities that sought better communication with the West, quickly grew interested in the English experiment. The first company to begin actual operations was the

Technological Basis of the Railroad

RACING ON THE RAILROAD Peter Cooper, who in later years was best known as a philanthropist and as the founder of the Cooper Union in New York City, was also a successful iron manufacturer. Cooper designed and built the first steam-powered locomotive in America in 1830 for the Baltimore and Ohio railroad. On August 28 of that year, he raced his locomotive (the "Tom Thumb") against a horse-drawn railroad car. This sketch depicts the moment when Cooper's engine overtook the horsecar. *(Museum of the City of New York)*

Baltimore and Ohio, which opened a thirteen-mile stretch of track in 1830. In New York, the Mohawk and Hudson began running trains along the sixteen miles between Schenectady and Albany in 1831. By 1836, more than a thousand miles of track had been laid in eleven states.

But there was not yet a true railroad system. Even the longest of the lines was comparatively short in the 1830s, and most of them served simply to connect water routes, not to link one railroad to another. Even when two lines did connect, the tracks often differed in gauge (width), so that cars from one line often could not fit onto the tracks of another. Schedules were erratic, and wrecks were frequent. But railroads made some important advances in the 1830s and 1840s. The introduction of heavier iron rails improved the roadbeds. Steam locomotives became more flexible and powerful. Redesigned passenger cars became stabler, more comfortable, and larger.

Railroads and canals were soon competing bitterly.

Competition between Railroads and Canals For a time, the Chesapeake and Ohio Canal Company blocked the advance of the Baltimore and Ohio Railroad through the narrow gorge of the upper Potomac, which it controlled; and the state of New York prohibited railroads from hauling freight in competition with the Erie Canal and its branches. But railroads had so many advantages that when they were able to compete freely with other forms of transportation they almost always prevailed.

The Triumph of the Rails

After 1840, railroads gradually supplanted canals and all other modes of transport. In 1840, there were 2,818 miles of railroad tracks in the United States; by 1850, there were 9,021. An unparalleled burst of railroad construction followed in the 1850s, tripling the amount of trackage in just ten years. The most comprehensive and efficient system was in the Northeast, which had twice as much trackage per square mile as the Northwest and four times as much as the South. But the expansion of the rails left no region untouched. Railroads were even reaching west of the Mississippi, which was spanned at several points by great iron bridges. One line ran from Hannibal to St. Joseph on the Missouri River, and another was under construction between St. Louis and Kansas City.

An important change in railroad development—one that would profoundly affect the nature of sectional alignments—was the trend toward the consolidation of *Consolidation* short lines into longer lines (known as "trunk lines"). By 1853, four major railroad trunk lines had crossed the Appalachian barrier to connect the Northeast with the Northwest. Two, the New York Central and the New York and Erie, gave New York City access to the Lake Erie ports. The Pennsylvania railroad linked Philadelphia and Pittsburgh, and the Baltimore and Ohio connected Baltimore with the Ohio River at Wheeling. From the terminals of these lines, other railroads into the interior touched the Mississippi River at eight points. Chicago became the rail center of the West, served by fifteen lines and more than a hundred daily trains. The appearance of the great trunk lines tended to divert traffic from the main water routes—the Erie Canal and the Mississippi River. By lessening the dependence of the West on the Mississippi, the railroads helped weaken further the connection between the Northwest and the South.

Capital to finance the railroad boom came from many sources. Private American investors provided part of the necessary funding, and railroad companies borrowed large sums from abroad. But local governments—states,

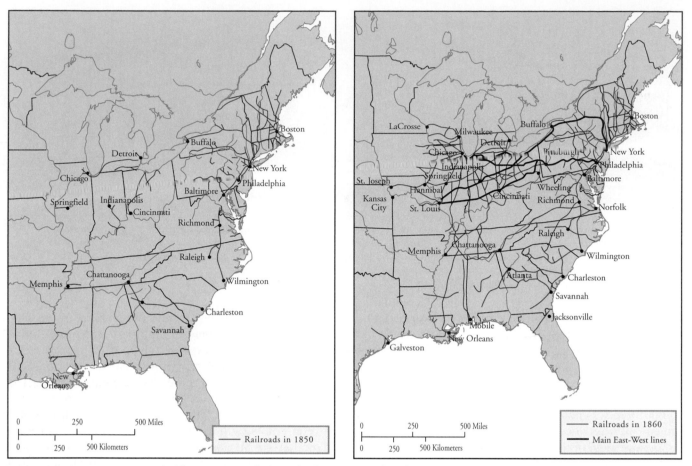

RAILROAD GROWTH, 1850-1860 These two maps illustrate the dramatic growth in the extent of American railroads in the 1850s. Note the particularly extensive increase in mileage in the upper Midwest (known at the time as the Northwest). Note too the relatively smaller increase in railroad mileage in the South. Railroads forged a close economic relationship between the upper Midwest and the Northeast, and weakened the Midwest's relationship to the South. ◆ *How did this contribute to the South's growing sense of insecurity within the Union?*

OLC For an interactive version of this map go to www.mhhe.com/brinkley12ch10maps

counties, cities, towns—also often contributed capital, because they were eager to have railroads serve them. This support came in the form of loans, stock subscriptions, subsidies, and donations of land for rights-of-way. The railroads obtained substantial additional assistance from the federal government in the form of public land grants. In 1850, Senator Stephen A. Douglas of Illinois and other railroad-minded politicians persuaded Congress to grant federal lands to aid the Illinois Central, which was building from Chicago toward the Gulf of Mexico. Other states and their railroad promoters demanded the same privileges, and by 1860, Congress had allotted over 30 million acres to eleven states to assist railroad construction.

Innovations in Communications and Journalism

Facilitating the operation of the railroads was an important innovation in communications: the magnetic telegraph. Telegraph lines extended along the tracks, connecting one

station with another and aiding the scheduling and routing of trains. But the telegraph had an importance to the nation's economic development beyond its contribution to the railroads. On the one hand, it permitted instant communication between distant cities, tying the nation together as never before. On the other hand, it helped reinforce the schism between the North and South. Like railroads, telegraph lines were far more extensive in the North than in the South, and they helped similarly to link the North to the Northwest (and thus to separate the Northwest further from the South).

The telegraph had burst into American life in 1844, when Samuel F. B. Morse, after several years of experimentation, succeeded in transmitting from Baltimore to Washington the news of James K. Polk's nomination for the presidency. The relatively low cost of constructing wire systems made the Morse telegraph system seem the ideal answer to the problems of long-distance communication. By 1860, more than 50,000 miles of wire connected most parts of the country; and a year later, the Pacific

The Telegraph

telegraph, with 3,595 miles of wire, opened between New York and San Francisco. By then, nearly all the independent lines had joined in one organization, the Western Union Telegraph Company.

New forms of journalism also drew communities together into a common communications system. In 1846, Richard Hoe invented the steam cylinder rotary press, making it possible to print newspapers rapidly and cheaply. The development of the **The Associated Press** telegraph, together with the introduction of the rotary press, made possible much speedier collection and distribution of news than ever before. In 1846, newspaper publishers from around the nation formed the Associated Press to promote cooperative news gathering by wire; no longer did they have to depend on the cumbersome exchange of newspapers for out-of-town reports.

Major metropolitan newspapers began to appear in the larger cities of the Northeast. In New York alone, there were Horace Greeley's *Tribune*, James Gordon Bennett's *Herald,* and Henry J. Raymond's *Times*. All gave serious attention to national and even international events and had substantial circulations beyond the city.

In the long run, journalism would become an important unifying factor in American **Fueling Sectional Discord** life. In the 1840s and 1850s, however, the rise of the new journalism helped to feed sectional discord. Most of the major magazines and newspapers were in the North, reinforcing the South's sense of subjugation. Southern newspapers tended to have smaller budgets and reported largely local news. Few had any impact outside their immediate communities. The combined circulation of the *Tribune* and the *Herald* exceeded that of all the daily newspapers published in the South put together. Above all, the news revolution—along with the revolutions in transportation and communications that accom-

panied it—contributed to a growing awareness within each section of how the other sections lived and of the deep differences that had grown up between the North and the South—differences that would ultimately seem irreconcilable.

COMMERCE AND INDUSTRY

By the middle years of the nineteenth century, the United States had developed the beginnings of a modern capitalist economy and an advanced industrial capacity. **Impact of the Market Economy** This emerging economy created enormous wealth and changed the face of all areas of the nation. But it did not, of course, affect everyone equally. Some classes and regions benefited from the economic development far more than others.

The Expansion of Business, 1820–1840

American business grew rapidly in the 1820s and 1830s, partly because of population growth and the transportation revolution, but also because of the daring, imagination, and ruthlessness of a new generation of entrepreneurs.

One important change came in the retail distribution of goods, which was becoming increasingly systematic and efficient. In the larger cities, stores specializing in groceries, dry goods, hardware, and other lines appeared, although residents of smaller towns and villages still depended on general stores (stores that did not specialize). In these less populous areas, many people did much of their business by barter.

The organization of business was also changing. Individuals or limited partnerships continued to operate most businesses, and the dominating figures were still the great merchant capitalists, who generally had sole ownership of their enterprises. In some larger businesses, however, the individual merchant capitalist was giving way to the corporation. Corporations began to develop particularly rapidly in the 1830s, when some legal obstacles **Advantages of the Corporation** to their formation were removed. Previously, a corporation could obtain a charter only by a special act of the state legislature—a cumbersome process that stifled corporate growth. By the 1830s, however, states were beginning to pass general incorporation laws, under which a group could secure a charter merely by paying a fee.

The new laws also permitted a system of limited liability, which meant that individual stockholders risked losing only the value of their own investment if a corporation should fail, and that they were not liable (as they had been in the past) for the corporation's larger losses. The rise of these new corporations made possible the accumulation of much greater amounts of capital and

THE CYLINDRICAL PRESS The revolving cylindrical press revolutionized newspaper (and other) publishing in the decades before the Civil War by making possible the printing of large numbers of papers relatively quickly. This ten-cylinder model dates from about 1850. *(Bettmann/Corbis)*

CHICAGO, 1858 This photograph of the busy freight depot and grain elevators of the Illinois Central Railroad illustrates the rapid growth of Chicago in the 1850s as the great trading center of the central part of the United States. *(Chicago Historical Society)*

hence made possible much larger manufacturing and business enterprises.

Investment alone, however, still provided too little capital to meet the demands of the most ambitious businesses.

Inadequate Credit

Such businesses relied heavily on credit, and their borrowing often created dangerous instability. Credit mechanisms remained very crude in the early nineteenth century. The government alone could issue official currency, but the official currency consisted only of gold and silver (or paper certificates backed literally by gold and silver), and there was thus too little of it to support the growing demand for credit. Under pressure from corporate promoters, many banks issued large quantities of bank notes—unofficial currency that circulated in much the same way that government currency did but was of much less stable value. But the notes had value only to the degree that the bank could sustain public confidence in their value; and some banks issued so many notes that their own reserves could not cover them. As a result, bank failures were frequent, and bank deposits were often insecure. The difficulty of obtaining credit for business investment remained, therefore, an impediment to economic growth.

The Emergence of the Factory

The most profound economic development in mid-nineteenth-century America was the rise of the factory. Before the War of 1812, most of what manufacturing there was in the United States took place within private households or in small, individually operated workshops. Men and women built or made products by hand, or with simple machines such as hand-operated looms. Gradually, however, improved technology and increasing demand produced a fundamental change. It came first in the New England textile industry. There, entrepreneurs were beginning to make use of new and larger machines driven by water power that allowed them to bring textile operations together under a single roof. This factory system, as it came to be known, spread rapidly in the 1820s and began to make serious inroads into the old home-based system of spinning thread and weaving cloth.

Factories also penetrated the shoe industry, concentrated in eastern Massachusetts. Shoes were still largely handmade, but manufacturers were beginning to employ workers who specialized in one or

Transformation of the Shoe Industry

another of the various tasks involved in production. Some factories began producing large numbers of identical shoes in ungraded sizes and without distinction as to rights and lefts. By the 1830s, factory production was spreading from textiles and shoes into other industries and from New England to other areas of the Northeast.

Between 1840 and 1860, American industry experienced even more dramatic growth as the factory system spread rapidly. In 1840, the total value of manufactured goods produced in the United States stood at $483 million; ten years later the figure had climbed to over $1 billion; and in 1860 it reached close to $2 billion. For the first time, the value of manufactured goods was approximately equal to that of agricultural products.

Of the approximately 140,000 manufacturing establishments in the country in 1860, 74,000 were located in the Northeast, including most of the larger enterprises. The Northeast had only a little more than half the

The Industrial Northeast

mills and factories in the United States; but the plants there were so large that the region produced more than two-thirds of the nation's manufactured goods. Of the 1,311,000 workers in manufacturing in the United States, about 938,000 were employed in the mills and factories of New England and the mid-Atlantic states.

Advances in Technology

Even the most highly developed industries were still relatively immature. American cotton manufacturers, for example, produced goods of coarse grade; fine items continued to come from England. But machine technology advanced more rapidly in the United States in the mid nineteenth century than in any other country in the world—partly because Americans were still catching up with the more advanced technologies of Europe and had to move quickly in order to compete; and partly because the American economy was growing so rapidly that the rewards of technological innovation were very great. Change was so rapid, in fact, that some manufacturers built their new machinery out of wood; by the time the wood wore out, they reasoned, improved technology would have made the machine obsolete. By the beginning of the 1830s, American technology had become so advanced—particularly in textile manufacturing—that industrialists in Britain and Europe were beginning to travel to the United States to learn new techniques, instead of the other way around.

Among the most important was in the manufacturing of machine tools—the tools used to make machinery parts. The government supported much of the research and development of machine tools, often in connection with supplying the military. For example, a government armory in Springfield, Massachusetts, developed two important tools—the turret lathe (used for cutting screws and other metal parts) and the universal milling machine (which replaced the hand chiseling of complicated parts and dies)—early in the nineteenth century. The precision grinding machine (which became critical to, among other things, the construction of sewing machines) was designed in the 1850s to help the United States Army produce standardized rifle parts. The federal armories such as those at Springfield and Harpers Ferry, Virginia, became the breeding ground for many technological discoveries, and a magnet for craftsmen and factory owners looking for ideas that could be of use to them. By the 1840s, the machine tools used in the factories of the Northeast were already better than those in most European factories.

One of the principal results of the creation of better machine tools was that the principle of interchangeable parts,

Interchangeable Parts

which Eli Whitney and Simeon North had tried to introduce into gun factories they had designed decades earlier, now found its way into many industries. Eventually, interchangeability would revolutionize watch and clock making, the manufacturing of locomotives and steam engines, and the making of many farm tools. It would also help make possible such newer devices as bicycles, sewing machines, typewriters, cash registers, and eventually the automobile.

Industrialization was also profiting from the introduction of new sources of energy. Coal was replacing wood and water power as fuel for many factories. The production of coal, most of it mined around Pittsburgh in western Pennsylvania, leaped from 50,000 tons in 1820 to 14 million tons in 1860. The new power source made it possible to locate mills away from running streams and thus permitted industry to expand still more widely.

The great technological advances in American industry owed much to American inventors, as the patent records of the time make clear. In 1830, the number of inventions patented was 544; by 1850,

Technological Innovations

the figure had risen to 993; and in 1860, it stood at 4,778. Several industries provide particularly vivid examples of how a technological innovation could produce a major economic change. In 1839, Charles Goodyear, a New England hardware merchant, discovered a method of vulcanizing rubber (treating it to give it greater strength and elasticity); by 1860, his process had found over 500 uses and had helped create a major American rubber industry. In 1846, Elias Howe of Massachusetts constructed a sewing machine; Isaac Singer made improvements on it, and the Howe-Singer machine was soon being used in the manufacture of ready-to-wear clothing.

For all the technological innovations that characterized the early factory system, most American industry remained wedded to the most traditional source of power: water. In the 1820s and 1830s, water power remained the most important source of power for manufacturing. The first important factory towns in New England—Lawrence, Lowell, and others—emerged where they did because of the natural waterfalls that could be channeled to provide power for the mills built along their banks. This sometimes required factories to close for periods in the winter when rivers were frozen. That was one reason why factory owners began to look for alternative forms of energy that could be used throughout the year, which led them by the late 1830s to rely more and more heavily on steam and other transportable forms of energy that could be fueled by wood, coal, or (later) petroleum.

Innovations in Corporate Organization

The merchant capitalists—entrepreneurs who were engaged primarily in foreign and domestic trade and who at times invested some of their profits in small-scale manufacturing ventures—remained figures of importance in the 1840s. In such cities as New York, Philadelphia, and Boston, influential mercantile groups operated shipping lines to southern ports—carrying off cotton, rice, and sugar—or dispatched fleets of trading vessels to the ports of Europe and Asia. Among their vessels were the famous clippers, the fastest (and most beautiful) sailing ships afloat. In their heyday in the late 1840s and early 1850s, the clippers could average 300 miles a day, which compared favorably with the best time of contemporary steamships.

But merchant capitalism was declining by the middle of the century. This was partly because British competitors were stealing much of America's export trade. But the more important reason for the decline was the discovery by the merchants themselves that there were greater opportunities for profit in manufacturing than in trade. That was one reason why industries developed first in the Northeast: an affluent merchant class already existed there and had the money and the will to finance them.

Decline of Merchant Capitalism

By the 1840s, the corporate form of organization was spreading rapidly, particularly in the textile industry. Ownership of American enterprise was gradually moving away from individuals and families and toward its highly dispersed modern form: many stockholders, each owning a relatively small proportion of the total. But whatever the form of business organization—and there continued to be many different forms—industrial capitalists soon became the new ruling class, the aristocrats of the Northeast, with far-reaching economic and political influence.

MEN AND WOMEN AT WORK

However sophisticated industrial firms became technologically and administratively, manufacturers still relied above all on a supply of labor. In the 1820s and 1830s, factory labor came primarily from the native-born population. After 1840, the growing immigrant population became the most important new source of workers.

Recruiting a Native Work Force

Recruiting a labor force was not an easy task in the early years of the factory system. Ninety percent of the American people in the 1820s still lived and worked on farms, and many urban residents were skilled artisans—independent craft workers who owned and managed their own shops as small businessmen; they were not likely to flock to factory jobs. The available unskilled workers were not numerous enough to form a reservoir from which the new industries could draw.

The beginnings of an industrial labor supply came instead from the transformation of American agriculture in the nineteenth century. The opening of vast, fertile new farmlands in the Midwest, the improvement of transportation systems, the development of new farm

Transformation of American Agriculture

WOMEN AT WORK This early photograph of female millworkers standing before their machines suggests something of the primitive quality of early factories—dimly lit, cramped, with conditions that offered little protection against accidents. All the women in this picture are wearing hair tightly pulled back, to prevent it from being caught in one of the machines. *(Courtesy George Eastman House)*

machinery—all combined to increase food production dramatically. New farming methods were also less labor intensive than the old ones; the number of workers required to produce large crops in the West was much smaller than the number required to produce smaller crops in the Northeast. No longer did each region have to feed itself entirely from its own farms; it could import food from other regions. As as result, farmers and their families began to abandon some of the relatively unprofitable farming areas of the East. In the Northeast, and especially in New England, where poor land had always placed harsh limits on farm productivity, rural people began leaving the land to work in the factories.

Two systems of recruitment emerged to bring this new labor supply to the expanding textile mills. One, common in the mid-Atlantic states (especially in such major manufacturing centers as New York and Philadelphia), brought whole families from the farm to the mill. Parents tended looms alongside their children, some of whom were no more than four or five years old. The second system,

common in Massachusetts, enlisted young women, mostly farmers' daughters in their late teens and early twenties. It was known as the Lowell or Waltham system, after the factory towns in which it first emerged. Many of these women worked for several years in the factories, saved their wages, and returned home to marry and raise children. Others married men they met in the factories or in town and remained part of the industrial world. But they often stopped working in the mills and took up domestic roles instead.

Labor conditions in these early years of the factory system were significantly better than those in English industry, better too than they would ultimately become in much of the United States. The employment of young children created undeniable hardships. But the misery was not as great as in European factories, since working children in America usually remained under the supervision of their parents. In England, by contrast, asylum authorities often hired out orphans to factory owners who showed little concern for their welfare and kept them in something close to slavery.

LOWELL, MASSACHUSETTS, 1832 Lowell was one of the leading manufacturing centers of New England in the 1830s, and one of the largest textile centers in America. Lowell relied heavily on women workers. Company owners—in deference to popular uneasiness about women working outside the home—created a paternalistic system of boarding houses for them, where they could be carefully supervised. This map shows the clusters of boarding houses adjacent to groups of factories. Note how concentrated the manufacturing center of the town was, and how the transportation system (rail and water) served the factories. Note also the many churches, which women workers were usually required to attend. ◆ *What happened to this labor system in the 1840s and 1850s?*

Even more different from the European labor pattern

The Lowell System

was the "Lowell System," which relied heavily, indeed almost exclusively, on young unmarried women. In England and other areas of industrial Europe, the conditions of work for women were often horrifyingly bad. A British parliamentary investigation revealed, for example, that women workers in the coal mines endured unimaginably wretched conditions. Some had to crawl on their hands and knees, naked and filthy, through cramped, narrow tunnels, pulling heavy coal carts behind them. It was little wonder that English visitors to America considered the Lowell mills a female paradise by contrast. The Lowell workers lived in clean boardinghouses and dormitories, which the factory owners maintained for them. They were well fed and carefully supervised. Because many New Englanders considered the employment of women to be vaguely immoral, the factory owners placed great emphasis on maintaining a proper environment for their employees, enforcing strict curfews and requiring regular church attendance. Employers quickly dismissed women suspected of immoral conduct. Wages for the Lowell workers were low, but generous by the standards of the time. The women even found time to write and publish a monthly magazine, the *Lowell Offering.*

Yet even these relatively well-treated workers often found the transition from farm life to factory work difficult,

Women Workers

even traumatic. Uprooted from everything familiar, forced to live among strangers in a regimented environment, many women suffered from severe loneliness and disorientation. Still more had difficulty adjusting to the nature of factory work—the repetition of fixed tasks hour after hour, day after day. That the women had to labor from sunrise to sunset was not in itself a new experience; many of them had worked similarly long days on the farm. But that they now had to spend those days performing tedious, unvarying chores, and that their schedules did not change from week to week or season to season, made the adjustment to factory work especially painful. But however uncomfortable women may have found factory work, they had few other options. They were barred from such manual labor as construction or from work as sailors or on the docks. Most of society considered it unthinkable for women to travel the country alone, as many men did, in search of opportunities. Work in the mills was in many cases virtually the only alternative to returning to farms that could no longer support them.

The paternalistic factory system of Lowell did not, in any case, survive for long. In the competitive textile

FOUR WOMEN WEAVERS This tintype shows four young women employed in the textile factories of Lowell, Massachusetts. Neatly dressed in matching uniforms, they conveyed the image the factory managers wanted the public to absorb: that women could work in the mills and still be protected from the rough and tumble world of industrialization. *(American Textile History Museum. Lowell, Massachusetts)* market as it developed in the 1830s and 1840s—a market prey to the booms and busts that afflicted the American economy as a whole—manufacturers found

Decline of the Lowell System

it difficult to maintain the high living standards and reasonably attractive working conditions with which they had begun. Wages declined; the hours of work lengthened; the conditions of the boardinghouses deteriorated as the buildings decayed and overcrowding increased.

In 1834, mill workers in Lowell organized a union—the Factory Girls Association—which staged a strike to protest a 25 percent wage cut. Two years later, the association struck again—against a rent increase in the boardinghouses. Both strikes failed, and a recession in 1837 virtually destroyed the organization. Eight years later the Lowell women, led by the militant Sarah Bagley, created the Female Labor Reform Association and began agitating for a ten-hour day and for improvements in conditions in the mills. The new association not only made demands of management; it also turned to state government and asked for legislative investigation of conditions in the mills. By then, however, the character of the factory work force was changing again. The mill girls were gradually moving into other occupations: teaching, domestic service, or marriage. And textile manufacturers were turning to a less contentious labor supply: immigrants.

The Immigrant Work Force

The rapidly increasing supply of immigrant workers after

Economic Advantages of Immigrant Labor

1840 was a boon to manufacturers and other entrepreneurs. At last they had access to a source of labor that was both large and inexpensive. These new workers, because of their vast numbers and their unfamiliarity with their new country, had even less leverage than the women they at times displaced. As a result, they often encountered far worse working conditions. Construction gangs, made up increasingly of Irish immigrants, performed the heavy, unskilled work on turnpikes, canals, and railroads under often intolerable conditions. Because most of these workers had no marketable skills and because of native prejudice against them, they received wages so low (and so intermittently, since the work was seasonal and uncertain) that they generally did not earn enough to support their families in even minimal comfort. Many of them lived in flimsy shanties, in grim conditions that endangered the health of their families (and reinforced native prejudices toward the "shanty Irish").

Irish workers began to predominate in the New England textile mills as well in the 1840s, and their arrival accelerated the deterioration of working conditions there. There was far less social pressure on owners

to provide a decent environment for Irish workers than there had been to provide the same for native women. Employers began paying piece rates (wages tied to how much a worker produced) rather than a daily wage and employed other devices to speed up production and use the labor force more profitably and efficiently. By the mid-1840s, Lowell—once a model for foreign visitors of enlightened industrial development—had become a squalid slum. Similarly miserable working-class neighborhoods were emerging in other northeastern cities.

Conditions were still not as bad as in most factory towns in England and Europe, but in almost all industrial areas, factories themselves were becoming large, noisy, unsanitary, and often dangerous places to work. The average

Harsh Work Conditions

workday was extending to twelve, often fourteen hours. Wages were declining, so that even skilled male workers could hope to earn only from $4 to $10 per week, while unskilled laborers were likely to earn only about $1 to $6 per week. Women and children, whatever their skills, also earned less than most men.

The Factory System and the Artisan Tradition

It was not only the mill workers who suffered from the transition to the modern factory system. It was also the skilled artisans whose trades the factories were displacing. The artisan tradition was as much a part of the older, republican vision of America as the tradition of sturdy, independent, yeoman farmers. Independent craftsmen considered themselves embodiments of the American ideal; they clung to a vision of economic life that was in some ways very different from that the new capitalist class was promoting. It was a vision based not just on the idea of individual, acquisitive success (although they were not, of course, averse to profits) but also on a sense of a "moral community." Skilled artisans valued their independence; they also valued the stability and relative equality within their economic world.

The factory system threatened that world with obsolescence. Some artisans made successful transitions into small-

Deskilling

scale industry. But others found themselves unable to compete with the new factory-made goods that sold for a fraction of the artisans' prices. In the face of this competition from industrial capitalists, craftsmen began early in the nineteenth century to form organizations—workingmen's political parties and the first American labor unions—to protect their endangered positions and to resist the new economic order. As early as the 1790s, printers and cordwainers (makers of high-quality boots and shoes) took the lead. The development of mass-production methods threatened their livelihoods; it also threatened their independence and their status in their communities. Members of other skilled trades—carpenters, joiners, masons, plasterers, hatters, and shipbuilders—felt similarly vulnerable.

In such cities as Philadelphia, Baltimore, Boston, and New York, the skilled workers of each craft formed societies for mutual aid. During the

National Trade Unions

1820s and 1830s, the craft societies began to combine on a citywide basis and set up central organizations known as trade unions. With the widening of markets, the economies of cities were interconnected, so workers soon realized there were advantages in joining forces and established national unions or federations of local ones. In 1834, delegates from six cities founded the National Trades' Union; and in 1836, the printers and the cordwainers set up their own national craft unions.

This early craft union movement fared poorly. Labor leaders struggled against the handicap of hostile laws and hostile courts. The common law, as interpreted by the courts in the industrial states, viewed a combination among workers as, in itself, an illegal conspiracy. The Panic of 1837, a dramatic financial collapse that produced a severe recession, weakened the movement further. Still, the failure of these first organizations did not end the efforts by workers—artisans and factory operatives alike—to gain some control over their productive lives.

Fighting for Control

Workers at all levels of the emerging industrial economy made continuous efforts to improve their lots. They tried, with little success, to persuade state legislatures to pass laws setting a maximum workday. Two states—New Hampshire in 1847 and Pennsylvania in 1848—actually passed ten-hour laws, limiting the workday unless the workers agreed to an "express contract" calling for more time on the job. Such measures were virtually without impact, however, because employers could simply require prospective employees to sign the "express contract" as a condition of hiring. Three states—Massachusetts, New Hampshire, and Pennsylvania—passed laws regulating child labor. But again, the results were minimal. The laws simply limited the workday to ten hours for children unless their parents agreed to something longer; employers had little difficulty persuading parents to consent to additional hours.

Perhaps the greatest legal victory of industrial workers came in Massachusetts in 1842, when the supreme

Commonwealth v. Hunt

court of the state, in *Commonwealth* v. *Hunt*, declared that unions were lawful organizations and that the strike was a lawful weapon. Other state courts gradually accepted the principles of the Massachusetts decision. On the whole, however, the union movement of the 1840s and 1850s remained generally

ineffective. Some workers were reluctant to think of themselves as members of a permanent laboring force and resisted joining unions. But even those unions that did manage to recruit significant numbers of industrial workers were usually not large enough or strong enough to stage strikes, and even less frequently strong enough to win them.

Artisans and skilled workers, despite their setbacks in the 1830s, had somewhat greater success than did factory workers. But their unions often had more in common with preindustrial guilds than with modern labor organizations. In most cases, their primary purpose was to protect the favored position of their members in the labor force by restricting admission to the skilled trades. The organizing effort that had floundered in the 1830s revived impressively in the 1850s. Among the new organizations skilled workers created were the National Typographical Union, founded in 1852, the Stone Cutters in 1853, the Hat Finishers in 1854, and the Molders and the Machinists, both in 1859.

Virtually all the early craft unions excluded women, even though female workers were numerous in almost every industry and craft. As a result, women began establishing their own protective unions

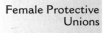

Female Protective Unions

by the 1850s, often with the support of middle-class female reformers. Like the male craft unions, the female protective unions had little power in dealing with employers. They did, however, serve an important role as mutual aid societies for women workers.

Despite these persistent efforts at organization and protest, the American working class in the 1840s and 1850s was notable for its relatively modest power. In England, workers were becoming a powerful, united, and often violent economic and political force. They were creating widespread social turmoil and helping to transform the nation's political structure. In America, nothing of the sort happened. Many factors combined to inhibit the growth of effective labor resistance. Among the most important was the flood of immigrant laborers into the country. The newcomers were usually willing to work for lower wages than native workers.

America's Divided Working Class

Because they were so numerous, manufacturers had little difficulty replacing disgruntled or striking workers with eager immigrants. Ethnic divisions and tensions—both between natives and immigrants and among the various immigrant groups themselves—often led workers to channel their resentments into internal bickering rather than into their shared grievances against employers. There was, too, the sheer strength of the industrial capitalists, who had not only economic but also political and social power and could usually triumph over even the most militant challenges.

PATTERNS OF INDUSTRIAL SOCIETY

The industrial revolution was making the United States—and particularly its more economically developed regions—dramatically wealthier by the year. It was also making society more unequal, and it was transforming social relationships and everyday life at almost every level—from the workplace to the family.

The Rich and the Poor

The commercial and industrial growth of the United States greatly elevated the average income of the American people. But what evidence there is—and it is admittedly sketchy—suggests that this increasing wealth was being distributed highly unequally. Substantial groups of the population, of course, shared hardly at all in the economic growth: slaves, Indians, landless farmers, and many of the unskilled workers on the fringes of the manufacturing system. But even among the rest of the population, disparities of income were marked. Wealth had always been unequally distributed in the United States, to be sure. Even in the era of the Revolution, according to some estimates, 45 percent of the wealth was concentrated in the hands of about 10 percent of the population. But by the mid-nineteenth century, that concentration had become far more pronounced. In Boston in 1845, for example, 4 percent of the citizens are estimated to have owned more than 65 percent of the wealth; in Philadelphia in 1860, 1 percent of the population possessed more than half the wealth. Among the American

Increasing Inequality in Wealth

people overall in 1860, according to scholarly estimates, 5 percent of the families possessed more than 50 percent of the wealth.

There had been wealthy classes in America almost from the beginning of European settlement. But the extent and character of wealth was changing in response to the commercial revolution of the mid-nineteenth century. Merchants and industrialists were accumulating enormous fortunes; and because there was now a significant number of rich people living in cities, a distinctive culture of wealth began to emerge. In large cities, people of great wealth gathered together in neighborhoods of astonishing opulence. They founded clubs and developed elaborate social rituals. They looked increasingly for ways to display their wealth—in the great mansions they built, the showy carriages in which they rode, the lavish household goods they accumulated, the clothes they wore, the elegant social establishments they patronized. New York, which had more wealthy families than anywhere else, developed a particularly elaborate high society. The construction of the city's great Central Park, which began in the 1850s, was in part a result of pressure from the members of high society, who wanted an elegant setting for their daily carriage rides.

There was also a significant population of genuinely destitute people emerging in the growing urban centers of the nation. These were people who were not merely poor, in the sense of having to struggle to sustain themselves—most Americans were poor in that sense. They were almost entirely without resources, often homeless,

The Urban Poor

THE SHOP AND WAREHOUSE OF DUNCAN PHYFE Duncan Phyfe was a celebrated and (as this watercolor by John Rubens Smith suggests) prosperous furniture maker in New York for many decades, serving the growing population of affluent households in search of refinement and display. The elegant Georgian details on Phyfe's shop on Fulton Street suggest how even places of business were adapting to the new conception of opulence. *(The Metropolitan Museum of Art, Rogers Fund, 1922(22.28.1) Photograph © 1982 The Metropolitan Museum of Art)*

CENTRAL PARK To affluent New Yorkers, the construction of the city's great Central Park was important because it provided them with an elegant setting for their daily carriage rides—an activity ostensibly designed to expose the riders to fresh air but that was really an occasion for them to display their finery to their neighbors. *(Museum of the City of New York)*

dependent on charity or crime or both for survival. Substantial numbers of people actually starved to death or died of exposure.

Some of these "paupers," as contemporaries called them, were recent immigrants who had failed to find work or to adjust to life in the New World. Some were widows and orphans, stripped of the family structures that allowed most working-class Americans to survive. Some were people suffering from alcoholism or mental illness, unable to work. Others were victims of native prejudice—barred from all but the most menial employment because of race or ethnicity. The Irish were particular victims of such prejudice.

Among the worst victims were free blacks. African-American communities in antebellum northern cities were small by later standards, but most major urban areas had significant black populations. Some of these African Americans were descendants of families that had lived in the North for generations. Others were former slaves who had escaped from the South or been released by their masters or had bought their freedom; some former slaves, once free, then worked to buy the freedom of relatives left behind. In material

African-American Poverty

terms, at least, life was not always much better for them in the North than it had been in slavery. Most had access only to very menial jobs, which usually paid too little to allow workers to support their families or educate their children; in bad times many had access to no jobs at all. In most parts of the North, blacks could not vote, could not attend public schools, indeed could not use any of the public services available to white residents. Most blacks preferred life in the North, however arduous, to life in the South because it permitted them at least some level of freedom. But that freedom did not bring anything approaching equality.

Social Mobility

One might expect the contrasts between conspicuous wealth and conspicuous poverty in antebellum America to have encouraged more class conflict than actually occurred. But a number of factors operated to quell resentments. For one thing, however much the relative economic position of American workers may have been declining, the absolute living standard of most laborers was improving. Life, in material terms at least, was usually better for factory workers than it had been on the farms or in the European societies from which they had migrated. They ate better, they were often better clothed and housed, and they had greater access to consumer goods.

There was also a significant amount of mobility within the working class, which helped to limit discontent. Opportunities for social mobility, for working one's way up the economic ladder, were relatively modest. A few workers did manage to move from poverty to riches by dint of work, ingenuity, and luck—a very small number, but enough to support the dreams of those who watched them. And a much larger number of workers managed to move at least one notch up the ladder—for example, becoming in the course of a lifetime a skilled, rather than an unskilled, laborer. Such people could envision their children and grandchildren moving up even further.

Social Mobility

More common than social mobility was geographical mobility, which was even more extensive in the United States than in Europe, where it was considerable. America had a huge expanse of uncultivated land in the West, much of it open for settlement for the first time in the 1840s and 1850s. Some workers saved money, bought land, and moved west to farm it. The historian Frederick Jackson Turner later referred to the availability of western lands as a "safety valve" for discontent, a basic explanation for the relative lack of social conflict in the antebellum United States. But few urban workers, and even fewer poor ones, could afford to make such a move or had the expertise to know how to work land even if they could. Much more common was the movement of laborers from one industrial town to another. Restless, questing, sometimes hopeful, sometimes despairing, these frequently moving people were often the victims of layoffs, looking for better opportunities elsewhere. Their search may seldom have led to a marked improvement in their circumstances, but the rootlessness of this large segment of the work force—one of the most distressed segments—made effective organization and protest far more difficult.

There was, finally, another "safety valve" for working-class discontent: politics. Economic opportunity may not have greatly expanded in the nineteenth century, but opportunities to participate in politics did. And to many white, male working people, access to the ballot seemed to offer a way to help guide their society and to feel like a significant part of their communities.

Middle-Class Life

For all the visibility of the very rich and the very poor in antebellum society, the fastest-growing group in America was the middle class. The expansion of the middle class was in part a result of the growth of the industrial economy and the increasing commercial life that accompanied it. Economic development opened many more opportunities for people to own or work in businesses, to own shops, to engage in trade, to enter professions, and to administer organizations. In earlier times, when ownership of land had been the only real basis of wealth, society had been divided between people with little or no land (people Europeans generally called peasants) and a landed gentry (which in Europe usually became an inherited aristocracy). Once commerce and industry became a source of wealth, these rigid distinctions broke down; and many people could become prosperous without owning land, but by providing valuable services to the new economy or by owning capital other than land.

Rapidly Expanding Middle Class

Middle-class life in the years before the Civil War rapidly established itself as the most influential cultural form of urban America. Middle-class families lived in solid and often substantial homes, which, like the wealthy, they tended to own. Workers and artisans were increasingly becoming renters—a relatively new phenomenon in American cities that spread widely in the early nineteenth century.

Middle-class women tended to remain in the home and care for the children and the household, although increasingly they were also able to hire servants—usually young, unmarried immigrant women who put in long hours of arduous work for very little money. One of the aspirations of middle class women in an age when doing the family's laundry could take an entire day was to escape from some of the drudgery of housework.

New household inventions altered, and greatly improved, the character of life in middle-class homes. Perhaps the most important was the invention of the cast-iron stove, which began to replace fireplaces as the principal vehicle for cooking and also as an important source of heat. These wood- or coal-burning devices were hot, clumsy, and dirty by the standards of the twentieth century; but compared to the inconvenience and danger of cooking on an open hearth, they seemed a great luxury. Stoves gave cooks more control over the preparation of food and allowed them to cook several things at once.

New Household Inventions

Middle-class diets were changing rapidly in the antebellum years, and not just because of the wider range of cooking the stove made possible. The expansion and diversification of American agriculture, and the ability of farmers to ship goods to urban markets by rail from distant regions greatly increased the variety of food available in cities. Fruits and vegetables were difficult to ship over long distances in an age with little refrigeration, but families had access to a greater variety of meats, grains, and dairy products than they had had in the past. A few households acquired iceboxes in the years before the Civil War, and the sight of wagons delivering large chunks of ice to wealthy and middle-class homes began to become a familiar part of urban life. Iceboxes allowed their owners to keep fresh meat and dairy products for as long as several days without spoilage. Most families, however, did not yet have any kind of refrigeration. Preserving food for them meant curing meat with salt and preserving fruits in sugar. Diets were generally much heavier and starchier than they are today, and middle-class people tended to be considerably stouter than would be fashionable in the twentieth century.

Middle-class homes came to differentiate themselves from those of workers and artisans in other ways as well.

Growing Class Distinctions

They were more elaborately decorated and furnished, with goods made available for the first time through factory production of household goods. Houses that had once had bare walls and floors now had carpeting, wallpaper, and curtains. The spare, simple styles of eighteenth-century homes gave way to the much more elaborate, even baroque household styles of the early Victorian era—styles increasingly characterized by crowded, even cluttered rooms, dark colors, lush fabrics, and heavy furniture and draperies. Middle-class homes also became larger. It became less common for children to share beds and for all family members to sleep in the same room. Parlors and dining rooms separate from the kitchen—once a luxury reserved largely for the wealthy—became the norm for the middle class as well. Some urban middle-class homes had indoor plumbing and indoor toilets by the 1850s—a significant advance over the outdoor wells and privies that had been virtually universal only a few years earlier (and that remained common among working-class people).

The Changing Family

The new industrializing society of the northern regions of the United States produced profound changes in the nature and function of the family. At the heart of the transformation was the movement of families from farms to urban areas, where jobs, not land, were the most valued commodities. The patriarchal system of the countryside, where fathers controlled their children's futures by controlling the distribution of land to them, could not survive the move to a city or town. Sons and daughters were much more likely to leave the family in search of work than they had been in the rural world.

Another important change was the shift of income-earning work out of the home and into the shop, mill, or factory. In the early decades of the nineteenth century (and for many years before that), the family itself had been the principal unit of economic activity. Family farms, family shops, and family industries were the norm throughout most of the United States. Men, women, and children worked together, sharing tasks and jointly earning the income that sustained the family. But as farming

spread to the fertile lands of the Northwest and as the size and profitability of farms expanded, agricultural work became more commercialized.

Declining Economic Role of the Family

Farm owners in need of labor began to rely less on their families (which often were not large enough to satisfy the demand) and more on hired male workers. These farmhands performed many of the tasks that on smaller farms had once been the jobs of the women and children of the family. As a result, farm women tended to work increasingly at domestic tasks—cooking, sewing, gardening, and dairying—a development that spared them from some heavy labor but that also removed them from the principal income-producing activities of the farm. Farm women in the new agricultural regions of the Northwest tended, therefore, to have a lower economic status within the family (and within the community) than their earlier counterparts in the East, who had been more crucial to the family economy. (See Chapter 11 for a discussion of family relations in the agrarian South.)

Similarly, in the industrial economy of the rapidly growing cities, there was an even more significant decline in the traditional economic function of the family. The urban household itself became less important as a center of production. Instead, most income earners left home each day to work elsewhere. A sharp distinction began to emerge between the public world of the workplace—the world of commerce and industry—and the private world of the family. The world of the family was now dominated not by production, but by housekeeping, child rearing, and other primarily domestic concerns. It was also a world dominated by women.

Accompanying (and perhaps in part caused by) the changing economic function of the family was a decline in the

Falling Birth Rates

birth rate. In 1800, the average American woman could be expected to give birth to approximately seven children during her childbearing years. By 1860, the average woman bore five children. The birth rate fell most quickly in urban areas and among middle-class women. Mid-nineteenth-century Americans had access to some birth control devices, which undoubtedly contributed in part to the change. There was also a significant rise in abortions, which remained legal in some states until after the Civil War and which, according to some estimates, may have terminated as many as 20 percent of all pregnancies in the 1850s. But the most important cause of the declining birth rate was almost certainly changes in sexual behavior—including increased abstinence.

The deliberate effort among middle-class men and women, in particular, to limit family size was a reflection of a much larger shift in the nature of society in the mid-nineteenth-century North. In a world in which the economy was becoming increasingly organized, in which production was moving out of the home, in which individuals were coming to expect more from the

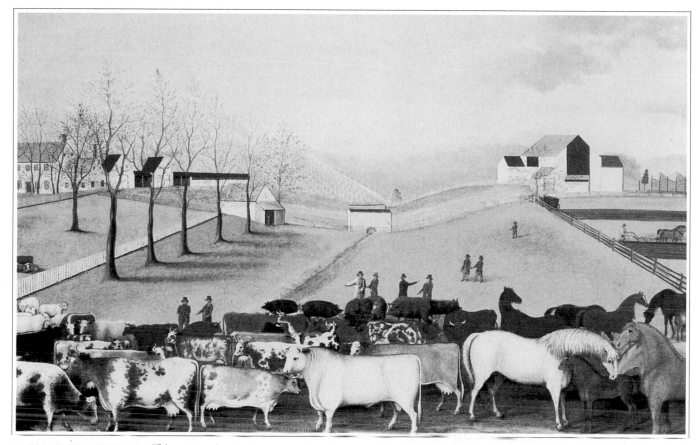

PASTORAL AMERICA, 1848 This painting by the American artist Edward Hicks suggests the degree to which Americans continued to admire the "Peaceable Kingdom" (the name of another, more famous Hicks work) of the agrarian world. Hicks entitled this work *An Indian Summer View of the Farm w. Stock of James C. Cornell of Northampton Bucks County Pennsylvania. That Took the Premium in the Agricultural Society, October the 12, 1848.* It portrays the diversified farming of a prosperous Pennsylvania family, shown here in the foreground with their cattle, sheep, and workhorses. In the background stretches a field ready for plowing and another ready for harvesting. *(Edward Hicks, The Cornell Farm. Photograph © Board of Trustees, National Gallery of Art, Washington)*

world, in which people placed more emphasis on calculations about the future, making careful decisions about bearing children seemed important. It expressed the increasingly secular, rationalized, and progressive orientation of the rapidly developing American North.

Women and the "Cult of Domesticity"

The emerging distinction between the public and private worlds, between the workplace and the home, accompanied (and helped cause) increasingly sharp distinctions between the social roles of men and women. Those distinctions affected not only factory workers and farmers, but members of the growing middle class as well. There had, of course, always been important differences between the male and female spheres in American society. Women had long been denied many legal and political rights enjoyed by men; within the family, the husband and father had traditionally ruled, and the wife and mother had generally bowed to his demands and desires. It had long been practically impossible for most women to obtain divorces, although divorces initiated by men were often easier to arrange. (Men were

also far more likely than women to win custody of children in case of a divorce.) In most states, husbands retained almost absolute authority over both the property and persons of their wives. Wife beating was illegal in only a few areas, and the law did not acknowledge that rape could occur within marriage. Women traditionally had very little access to the worlds of business or politics. Indeed, custom in most communities dictated that women never speak in public before mixed audiences.

Most women also had much less access to education than men, a situation that survived into the mid-nineteenth century. Although they were encouraged to attend school at the elementary level, they were strongly discouraged and in most cases effectively barred—from pursuing higher education. Oberlin in Ohio became the first college in America to accept female students; it permitted four to enroll in 1837, despite criticism that coeducation was a rash experiment approximating free love. Oberlin authorities were confident that "the mutual influence of the sexes upon each other is decidedly happy in the cultivation of both mind & manners." But few other institutions shared their

Female Education

NATHAN HAWLEY AND FAMILY Nathan Hawley, seated at center in this 1801 painting, was typical of many early-nineteenth-century fathers in having a very large family. Nine members are visible here. Hawley at the time was the warden of the Albany County jail in New York, and the painting was by William Wilkie, one of the inmates there. The painting suggests that Hawley was a man of modest but not great means. His family is fashionably dressed, and there are paintings on the walls—signs of style and affluence. But the house is very simply furnished, without drapes for the windows, with a simple painted floor cloth in the front room, and a bare floor in the back. *(Collection of the Albany Institute of History and Art)*

views. Coeducation remained extraordinarily rare until long after the Civil War; and only a very few women's colleges—such as Mount Holyoke, founded in Massachusetts by Mary Lyon in 1837—emerged.

However unequal the positions of men and women were in the preindustrial era, those positions were generally defined within the context of a household in which all members played crucial roles in generating family income. In the middle-class family of the new industrial society, however, the husband was assumed to be the principal, usually the only, income producer. The wife was now expected to remain in the home and to engage in largely domestic activities.

The result was an important shift in the middle-class concept of the woman's place within the family and of the family's place within the larger society, reflecting an emerging view of women as **New Roles for Women** guardians of the "domestic virtues." Their role as mothers, entrusted with the nurturing of the young, seemed more central to the family than it had in the past. And their role as wives—as companions and helpers to their husbands—grew more important as well. Middle-class women, no longer pro-

ducers, now became more important as consumers. They learned to place a high value on keeping a clean, comfortable, and well-appointed home, on entertaining, and on dressing elegantly and stylishly.

Occupying their own "separate sphere," some women began to develop a distinctive female culture. Friendships among women became increasingly intense; women began to form their own social **Women's Separate Sphere** networks (and, ultimately, to form female clubs and associations that were of great importance to the advancement of various reforms). A distinctive feminine literature began to emerge to meet the demands of middle-class women. There were romantic novels (many of them by female writers), which focused on the private sphere that women now inhabited. There were women's magazines, of which the most prominent was *Godey's Lady's Book,* edited after 1837 by Sarah Hale, who had earlier founded a women's magazine of her own. The magazine scrupulously avoided dealing with public controversies or political issues and focused instead on fashions, shopping and homemaking advice, and other purely domestic concerns. Politics and religion were inappropriate for the magazine, Hale explained in 1841, because "other subjects are more important for our sex and more proper for our sphere."

By the standards of a later era, the increasing isolation of women from the public world seems to be a form of oppression and discrimination. And it is true that few men considered women fit for business, politics, or the professions. On the other hand, most middle-class men—and many middle-class women as well—considered the new female sphere a vehicle for expressing special qualities that made women in some

Benefits and Costs

ways superior to men. Women were to be the custodians of morality and benevolence, just as the home—shaped by the influence of women—was to be a refuge from the harsh, competitive world of the marketplace. It was women's responsibility to provide religious and moral instruction to their children and to counterbalance the acquisitive, secular impulses of their husbands. Thus the "cult of domesticity," as some scholars have called it, brought both benefits and costs to middle-class women. It allowed them to live lives of greater material comfort than in the past, and it placed a higher value on their "female virtues" and on their roles as wife and mother. At the same time, it left women increasingly detached from the public world, with fewer outlets for their interests and energies.

The costs of that detachment were particularly clear among unmarried women of the middle class. By the 1840s, the ideology of domesticity had grown so powerful that few genteel women would any longer consider working (as many had in the past) in shops or mills, and few employers would consider hiring them. But unmarried women nevertheless required some income-producing activity. They had few choices. Some could become teachers or nurses, professions that seemed to call for the same female qualities that made women important within the home; and both those professions began in the 1840s and 1850s to attract significant numbers of women, although not until the Civil War did females begin to dominate them. Otherwise, unmarried females were largely dependent on the generosity of relatives.

Working Class Women

Middle-class people gradually came to consider work by women outside the household to be unseemly, something characteristic of the lower classes—as indeed it was. Working-class women could not afford to stay home and cultivate the "domestic virtues." They had to produce income for their families. They continued to work in factories and mills, but under conditions far worse than those that the original, more "respectable" women workers had enjoyed. They also frequently found employment in middle-class homes. Domestic service became one of the most frequent sources of female employment. In other words, now that production had moved outside the household, women who

needed to earn money had to move outside their own households to do so.

Leisure Activities

Leisure time was scarce for all but the wealthiest Americans in the mid-nineteenth century. Most people worked long hours. Saturday was a normal working day. Vacations—paid or unpaid—were rare. For most people, Sunday was the only respite from work and was generally reserved for religion and rest. Almost no commercial establishments did any business at all on Sunday, and even within the home most families frowned upon playing games or engaging in other kinds of entertainment on the Sabbath. For many working-class and middle-class people, therefore, holidays took on a special importance. That was one reason for the strikingly elaborate Fourth of July celebrations throughout the country. The celebrations were not just expressions of patriotism. They were a way of enjoying one of the few holidays from work available to most Americans.

In rural America, where most people still lived, the erratic pattern of farmwork gave many people some relief from the relentless working schedules of city residents. For urban people, however, leisure was something to be seized in what few free moments they had. Men gravitated to taverns for drinking, talking, and game-playing. Women gathered in one another's homes for conversation, card games, or to share work on such household tasks as sewing. For educated people, whose numbers were rapidly expanding, reading became one of the principal leisure activities. Newspapers and magazines proliferated rapidly, and books—novels, histories, autobiographies, biographies, travelogues, and others—became staples of affluent homes. Women were particularly avid readers, and women writers created a new genre of fiction specifically for females—the "sentimental novel," which often offered idealized visions of women's lives and romances (see pp. 334–335).

There was also a vigorous culture of public leisure, even if many families had to struggle to find time or means to participate in it. In larger cities, theaters were becoming increasingly popular; and while some of them catered to particular social groups, others attracted audiences that crossed class lines.

Minstrel Shows

Wealthy people, middle-class people, workers and their families: all could sometimes be found watching a performance of Shakespeare or a melodrama based on a popular novel or an American myth. Minstrel shows—in which white actors mimicked (and ridiculed) African-American culture—became increasingly popular (see pp. 422–423). Public sporting events—boxing, horse racing, cockfighting (already becoming controversial), and others—often attracted considerable crowds. Baseball—not yet organized into professional leagues—was beginning to attract large crowds when played in city parks or fields on the edges of towns (see pp. 384–385). A particularly exciting event in many communities was the arrival of the circus—a

Shakespeare in America

One of the characters Huckleberry Finn encountered in his journey down the Mississippi in Mark Twain's famous novel was a roguish traveling actor who called himself "the Duke of Bridgewater." The Duke improvised performances almost anywhere there was anyone willing to pay. One of his favorite encores, he claimed, was "Hamlet's soliloquy . . . the most celebrated thing in Shakespeare." He recited it with bravado, and with very little fidelity to the original text:

> To be, or not to be; that is the bare bodkin
> That makes calamity of so long life.

The events of Twain's novel were set in the years before the Civil War,

THE PARK THEATER This 1821 watercolor by John Searle shows the interior of the Park Theater in New York, which had recently been rebuilt after a fire. The play is a farce by the English playwright William T. Moncrieffe. The faces in the audience are all portraits of real New Yorkers at the time. (© *Collection of the New York Historical Society*)

when Shakespeare's work was familiar to Americans of all ages, classes, and regions. From elegant theaters in the great eastern cities, to makeshift stages and rickety "opera houses" in farming villages and mining towns in the West, Americans gathered to watch productions of Shakespeare's plays just as they gathered to watch now-forgotten comedies and melodramas written in their own time. Whether performed by famous actors or by hand-to-mouth hustlers like Twain's "Duke," Shakespeare was entertainment for the masses.

Performances of Shakespeare had begun in America as early as 1750, but public interest in his plays reached its peak in the 1830s, 1840s, and 1850s, when theater was the single most popular performing art throughout the United States, and Shakespeare the single most popular playwright. Many, perhaps most, performances of Shakespearean plays were irreverent, inaccurate, and romanticized. Tragedies were rewritten with happy endings. Comedies were interlaced with contemporary, regional humor. Texts were reworked with American dialect, and plays were abbreviated and sandwiched into programs containing other popular work of the time. So familiar were many Shakespearean plots that audiences took delight in seeing them parodied in productions such as "Julius Sneezer," "Hamlet and Egglet," and "Much Ado About a Merchant of Venice."

People from all walks of life went regularly to the theater and mingled with one another in ways that would become unusual in later eras. Seating was often divided by class—a tier of boxes for the wealthiest patrons, orchestra seats for the middle class, and balconies for those too poor to sit anywhere else (and for virtually all nonwhite members of the audience). But despite these distinctions, going to the theater was a vibrantly democratic

experience of a kind seldom visible in twentieth-century America except occasionally at sports events.

One result was that American audiences were often noisy, rambunctious, and—at least in the eyes of many actors—obnoxious. Men and women did not sit quietly in theaters as most do today. They shouted out reactions to the plays, taunted actors, and occasionally—as in an 1832 performance of *Richard III* in New York—climbed onto the stage and joined the performance, mingling with the actors during a battle scene and charging across the stage as if they were soldiers.

The leading Shakespearean actors of the antebellum era became figures of enormous public interest, and at times could spur great popular passion. Evidence of that came from events in New York City in 1849. The celebrated American actor Edwin Forrest—beloved by working-class audiences as a great patriot and a common man who had risen to greatness—gave a performance of *Macbeth* on the same evening that a renowned English actor, William Macready, was performing the same play elsewhere in the city. Many New Yorkers believed that the aloof, aristocratic Macready, and through him the city's wealthy elites, were attempting to humiliate Forrest. Forrest supporters crowded into Macready's performance and hooted him off the stage. Three days later, Macready tried again at the Astor Place Opera House. Ten thousand people, most of them Forrest enthusiasts, gathered outside and tried to force their way into the theater. Militia, called out for the occasion, fired into the crowd killing at least 22 and wounding more than 150. It was one of the bloodiest civil conflicts of the first half of the nineteenth century.

Shakespeare remained popular throughout the Civil War. In 1864

THE ASTOR PLACE RIOT This later watercolor of the Astor Place riot in 1849 conveys something of the violence and bedlam that the great rivalry between Edwin Forrest and William Macready produced. Here, anti-English mobs demonstrate outside the theater in which the English actor Macready was performing. During the rioting, they set the theater on fire, and the turmoil only subsided when the Seventh Regiment guard was called out. (*The Great Riot at the Astor Place Opera House, New York, Thursday Evening, May 10, 1849. Published by N. Currier, 1849. Museum of the City of New York, The Harry T. Peters Collection*)

THE BOOTHS IN *JULIUS CAESAR* The Booths were America's leading acting family in the 1860s, and this photograph by Matthew Brady captures a rare event: the appearance together in a play of Edwin Booth, the most famous and talented member of the family, and two of his acting brothers, John Wilkes (left, remembered today as Lincoln's assassin but well known at the time as a popular actor) and Junius Brutus Booth, Jr. (right). They are performing Shakespeare's *Julius Caesar* in New York. (*Library of Congress*)

enthusiastic crowds greeted a performance in New York of *Julius Caesar*, featuring three members of America's most celebrated theatrical family: William Junius Booth, an aging giant who had been the foremost tragic actor of his generation, and his two sons Edwin and John Wilkes. "No playgoer has seen Shakespere [sic] presented with attraction more likely to draw and charm the true lover of the drama since the days when Shakespere himself appeared in his own plays," the *New York Herald* editorialized in a fit of civic pride. "Only English cities could hope to rival us in this."

Edwin Booth went on to become America's most revered actor of the last half of the nineteenth century, renowned in particular for his performances of *Hamlet* and other great Shakespearean roles at the Booth Theater he founded in New York. His brother, John Wilkes, is best remembered leaping to the stage of Ford's Theater in Washington on April 14, 1865 after having fatally shot Abraham Lincoln. His famous exclamation at the time, "Sic semper tyrannis," was the motto of the state of Virginia. But it was better known as the phrase Brutus supposedly uttered after killing Julius Caesar, an event most familiar to nineteenth-century audiences—and to Booth himself—from performances of Shakespeare's play.

Huckleberry Finn was published in 1884, when the broad popularity of Shakespeare that Twain described was already beginning to fade. By the end of the nineteenth century, Shakespeare's work was beginning to be treated with much more gravity and was starting to be associated with the educated upper classes. The great Shakespearean actors of these later years had no large followings among workers and ordinary people. They were favorites of the aristocracy, who sought to protect them and the plays they performed from being debased by common audiences they considered incapable of understanding them. A clear distinction had grown up between "high culture," of which Shakespeare was now a part, and "lowbrow culture," from which Shakespeare was gradually excluded. That distinction has survived into our own time.

traveling entertainment with roots in the middle ages that continued to entertain, delight, and bamboozle children and adults alike.

Popular tastes in public spectacle tended toward the bizarre and the fantastic. Most men and women lived in a constricted world of familiar things. Relatively few people traveled; and in the absence of film, radio, television, or even much photography, they hungered for visions of unusual phenomena that contrasted with their normal experiences. People going to the theater or the circus or the museum wanted to see things that amazed and even frightened them. Perhaps the most celebrated provider of such experiences was the famous

P. T. Barnum

and unscrupulous showman P. T. Barnum, who opened the American Museum in New York in 1842—not a showcase for art or nature, but a great freak show populated by midgets (the most famous named Tom Thumb), Siamese twins, magicians, and ventriloquists. Barnum was a genius in publicizing his ventures with garish posters and elaborate newspaper announcements. Only later, in the 1870s, did he launch the famous circus for which he is still best remembered. But he was always a pioneer in exploiting public tastes for the wild and exotic.

One of the ways Barnum tried to draw visitors to his museum was by engaging lecturers. He did so because he understood that the lecture was one of the most popular forms of entertainment in nineteenth-century America. Men and women flocked in enormous numbers to lyceums (see pp. 360–361), churches, schools, and auditoriums to hear lecturers explain the latest advances in science, to describe their visits to exotic places, to provide vivid historical narratives, or to rail against the evils of alcohol or slavery. Messages of social uplift and reform attracted rapt audiences, particularly among women eager for guidance as they adjusted to the often jarring changes in the character of family life in the industrializing world.

THE AGRICULTURAL NORTH

Even in the rapidly urbanizing and industrializing Northeast, and more so in what nineteenth-century Americans called the Northwest (and what Americans today call the Midwest), most people remained tied to the agricultural world. But agriculture, like industry and commerce, was becoming increas-

Rise of Commercial Agriculture

ingly a part of the new capitalist economy, linked to the national and international market. Where agriculture could not compete in this new commercial world—as in much of the Northeast—it declined. Where it could compete—as in most of the Northwest—it simultaneously flourished and changed.

Northeastern Agriculture

The story of agriculture in the Northeast after 1840 is one of decline and transformation. The reason for the decline was simple: the farmers of the section could no longer compete with the new and richer soil of the Northwest. Centers of production were gradually shifting westward for many of the farm goods that had in the past been most important to northeastern agriculture: wheat, corn, grapes, cattle, sheep, and hogs.

Some eastern farmers responded to these changes by moving west themselves and establishing new farms. Still others moved to mill towns and became laborers. Some farmers, however, remained on the land and managed to hold their own. As the eastern urban centers increased in population, many farmers turned to the task of supplying food to the cities; they raised

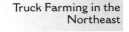
Truck Farming in the Northeast

vegetables (truck farming) or fruit and sold it in nearby towns. New York, for example, led all other states in apple production.

The rise of cities also stimulated the rise of profitable dairy farming. Approximately half the dairy products of the country were produced in the East; most of the rest came from the West, where Ohio was the leading dairy state. Partly because of the expansion of the dairy industry, the Northeast led other sections in the production of hay. New York was the leading hay state in the nation; Pennsylvania and New England grew large crops as well. The Northeast also exceeded other areas in producing potatoes.

But while agriculture in the region remained an important part of the economy, it was steadily becoming less important relative both to the agriculture of the Northwest and to the industrial growth of the Northeast itself. As a result, the rural population in many parts of the Northeast continued to decline.

The Old Northwest

There was some industry in the states of the Northwest, more than in the South; and in the two decades before the Civil War, the section experienced steady industrial growth. By 1860, it had 36,785 manufacturing establishments employing 209,909 workers. There was a flourishing industrial and commercial area along the shore of Lake Erie, with Cleveland at its center. Another manufacturing region was in the Ohio River valley; the meatpacking city of Cincinnati was its nucleus. Farther west, the rising city of Chicago, destined to become the great metropolis of the section, was

Industrialization in the Old Northwest

emerging as the national center of the agricultural machinery and meatpacking industries.

Most of the major industrial activities of the West either served agriculture (as in the case of farm machinery), or relied on agricultural products (as in flour milling, meatpacking, whiskey distilling, and the making of leather goods). As this suggests, industry was, on the whole, much less important in the Northwest than farming.

Some areas of the Northwest were not yet dominated by whites. Indians remained the most numerous inhabitants of much of the upper third of the Great Lakes states until after the Civil War. In those areas, hunting and fishing, along with some sedentary agriculture, remained the principal economic activities of both whites and Native Americans. But the tribes did not become integrated into the new commercialized economy that was emerging elsewhere in the Northwest.

For the white (and occasionally black) settlers who populated the lands farther south, the Northwest was primarily an agricultural region. Its rich and plentiful lands made farming a lucrative and expanding activity there, in contrast to the declining agrarian Northeast. Thus the typical citizen of the Northwest was not an industrial worker or poor, marginal farmer, but the owner of a reasonably prosperous family farm. The average size of western farms was 200 acres, the great majority of them owned by the people who worked them.

Rising farm prices around the world provided a strong incentive for these western farmers to engage in commercial agriculture: to concentrate on growing a single crop for market (corn, wheat, cattle, sheep, hogs, and others). In the early years of white settlement in the Northwest, farm prices rose because of the debilitation of European agriculture in the aftermath of the **Agricultural Specialization** Napoleonic Wars and the growing urban population (and hence the growing demand for food) of industrializing areas of Europe. The Northwest, with good water routes on the Mississippi for getting its crops to oceangoing vessels, profited from this international trade.

But industrialization, in both the United States and Europe, provided the greatest boost to agriculture. With the growth of factories and cities in the Northeast, the domestic market for farm goods increased dramatically. The growing national and worldwide demand for farm products resulted in steadily rising farm prices. For most farmers, the 1840s and early 1850s were years of increasing prosperity.

The expansion of agricultural markets had profound effects on sectional alignments in the United States. The **Growing Ties between Northeast and Northwest** Northwest sold most of its products to the residents of the Northeast and was thus dependent on eastern purchasing power. Eastern industry, in turn, found an important market for its products in the prospering West. Between the two sections a strong economic relationship was emerging that was profitable to both—and that was increasing the isolation of the South within the Union.

To meet the increasing demand for its farm products, residents of the Northwest worked strenuously, and often frantically, to increase their productive capacities. Many tried to take advantage of the large areas of still uncultivated land and to enlarge the area of white settlement during the 1840s. By 1850, the growing western population was moving into the prairie regions both east and west of the Mississippi: into areas of Indiana, Michigan, Illinois, Missouri, Iowa, and Minnesota. They cleared forest lands or made use of fields the Indians had cleared many years earlier. And they began to develop a timber industry to make use of the forests that remained. Wheat was the staple crop of the region, but other crops—corn, potatoes, and oats—and livestock were also important.

The Northwest increased production not only by expanding the area of settlement, but also by adopting new agricultural techniques that **New Agricultural Techniques** greatly reduced the labor necessary for producing a crop and slowed the exhaustion of the region's rich soil. Farmers began to cultivate new varieties of seed, notably Mediterranean wheat, which was hardier than the native type; and they imported better breeds of animals, such as hogs and sheep from England and Spain, to take the place of native stock. Most important were improved tools and farm machines, which American inventors and manufacturers produced in rapidly increasing numbers. During the 1840s, more efficient grain drills, harrows, mowers, and hay rakes came into wide use. The cast-iron plow, an earlier innovation, remained popular because its parts could be replaced when broken. An even better tool appeared in 1847, when John Deere established at Moline, Illinois, a factory to manufacture steel plows, which were more durable than those made of iron.

Two new machines heralded a coming revolution in grain production. The most important was the automatic reaper, the invention of Cyrus H. McCormick of Virginia. **McCormick Reaper** The reaper enabled a crew of six or seven men to harvest in a day as much wheat (or any other small grain) as fifteen men could harvest using older methods. McCormick, who had patented his device in 1834, established a factory at Chicago, in the heart of the grain belt, in 1847. By 1860, more than 100,000 reapers were in use on western farms. Almost as important to the grain grower was the thresher—a machine that separated the grain from the wheat stalks. Threshers appeared in large numbers after 1840. Before that, farmers generally flailed grain by hand (seven bushels a day was a good average for a farm) or used farm animals to tread it (twenty bushels a day on the average). A threshing machine, such as those manufactured by the Jerome I. Case factory in Racine, Wisconsin, could thresh twenty-five bushels or more in an hour.

The Northwest considered itself the most democratic section of the country. But its democracy was based on a defense of economic freedom and the rights of property—a white, middle-class vision of democracy that was becoming common in many other parts of the country as well. Abraham Lincoln, an Illinois Whig, voiced the economic opinions of many of the people of his section. "I take it that it is best for all to leave each man free to acquire property as fast as he can," said Lincoln. "Some will get wealthy. I don't believe in a law to prevent a man from getting rich; it would do more harm than good. . . . When one starts poor, as most do in the race of life, free society is such that he knows he can better his condition; he knows that there is no fixed condition of labor for his whole life."

Rural Life

Life for farming people was very different from life in towns and cities and also varied greatly from one farming region to another. In the more densely populated farm areas east of the Appalachians and in the easternmost areas of the Northwest, farmers were usually part of relatively vibrant communities and made extensive use of the institutions of those communities—the churches, schools, stores, and taverns. As white settlement moved further west, farmers became more isolated and had to struggle to find any occasions for contact with people outside their own families.

Although the extent of social interaction differed from one area to another, the forms of interaction—outside the South at least—were usually very similar. Religion drew farm communities together perhaps more than any other force, particularly since so many farm areas were populated by people of common ethnic

Importance of Religion in Rural Communities

(and therefore religious) backgrounds. Town or village churches were popular meeting places, both for services and for social events—most of them dominated by women. Even in areas with no organized churches, farm families—and, again, women in particular—gathered in one another's homes for prayer meetings, Bible readings, and other religious activities. Weddings, baptisms, and funerals also brought communities together in celebration or mourning.

But religion was only one of many reasons for interaction. Farm people joined together frequently to share tasks that a single family would have difficulty performing on its own; festive barn raisings were among the most frequent. Women prepared large suppers while the men worked on the barn and the children played. Large numbers of families also gathered together at harvest time to help bring in crops, husk corn, or thresh wheat. Women came together to share domestic tasks as well, holding "bees" in which groups of women joined together to make quilts, baked goods, preserves, and other products.

But despite the many social gatherings farm families managed to create, they lived in a world with much less contact with popular culture and public social life than people who lived in towns and cities. Rural people, often even more than urban ones, treasured their links to the outside world—letters from relatives and friends in distant places, newspapers and magazines from cities they had never seen, catalogs advertising merchandise that their local stores never had. Yet many also valued their separation from urban culture and cherished the relative autonomy that farm life gave them. One reason many rural Americans looked back nostalgically on country life once they moved to the city was that they sensed that in the urban world they did not have as much control over the patterns of their daily lives as they had once known.

CONCLUSION

Between the 1820s and the 1850s, the American economy experienced the beginnings of an industrial revolution—a change so profound that in the United States, as in Europe, it transformed almost every area of life in fundamental ways.

The American industrial revolution was a result of many things: population growth (through both natural increase and immigration), advances in transportation and communication, new technologies that spurred the development of factories capable of mass producing goods, the recruiting of a large industrial labor force, and the creation of corporate bodies capable of managing large enterprises. The new economy created great wealth, expanding the ranks of the wealthy and

helping to create a large new middle class. It also created high levels of inequality, which was particularly visible in the growth of a large industrial working class.

Culture in the industrializing areas of the North changed too, and there were important changes in the structure and behavior of the family, in the role of women, and in the way people used their leisure time and encountered popular culture. The changes were often alluring, often disorienting, and often both. They helped widen the gap in experience and understanding between the generation of the Revolution and the generation of the mid-nineteenth century. They also helped widen the gap between North and South.

INTERACTIVE LEARNING

The *Primary Source Investigator CD-ROM* offers the following materials related to this chapter:

- Interactive maps: **The Transportation Revolution** (M12) and **Lowell, MA** (M71).
- Documents, images, and maps related to industrial expansion in the early nineteenth century, and social patterns and economic changes in the northern United States. Some highlights include an image from

Godey's Lady's Book, a newspaper of the female factory workers in Lowell, Massachusetts, and a cartoon showing Irish immigration to America.

Online Learning Center (www.mhhe.com/brinkley12)

For quizzes, Internet resources, references to additional books and films, and more, consult this book's Online Learning Center.

FOR FURTHER REFERENCE

Charles G. Sellers, *The Market Revolution: Jacksonian America, 1815–1846* (1991) demonstrates the overwhelming impact of the market revolution on American social and political development. George R. Taylor, *The Transportation Revolution* (1951) is a classic account of economic development in the antebellum period. Christopher Clark, *The Roots of Rural Capitalism: Western Massachusetts, 1780–1860* (1990) is an examination of the impact of emerging capitalism on a rural area. Paul Johnson, *A Shopkeeper's Millennium: Society and Revivals in Rochester, New York, 1815–1837* (1978) explores the changing character of class relations in upstate New York in an age of rapid economic development. Alice Kessler-Harris, *Out to Work: A History of Wage-Earning Women in the United States* (1982) is a broad history of women in the wage labor force. Thomas Dublin, *Transforming Women's Work:*

New England Lives in the Industrial Revolution (1994) looks in particularly at the mill towns of the northeast. Mary Ryan, *Cradle of the Middle Class: The Family in Oneida County, New York, 1790–1865* (1981) demonstrates the relationship between the market revolution and the changing character of middle-class family structure. Christine Stansell, *City of Women: Sex and Class in New York, 1789–1860* (1983) explores the female world of antebellum New York City. John Bodnar, *The Transplanted: A History of Immigrants in America* (1985) is a useful survey. Paul W. Gates, *The Farmer's Age: Agriculture, 1815–1860* (1966) is an important overview. Alan Taylor, *William Cooper's Town: Power and Persuasion on the Frontier in the Early American Republic* (1995) examines the early years of Cooperstown, New York, and the impact on it of the rise of the market and of democratic politics.

THE OLD PLANTATION This painting, by an unidentified folk artist of the early nineteenth century, suggests the importance of music in the lives of plantation slaves in America. The banjo, which the black musician at right is playing, was originally an African instrument. *(Abby Aldrich Rockefeller Folk Art Museum, Colonial Williamsburg Foundation, Williamsburg, VA)*

SIGNIFICANT EVENTS

1800 ▶ Gabriel Prosser organizes unsuccessful slave revolt in Virginia

1808 ▶ Importation of slaves to United States banned

1820s ▶ Prolonged depression in tobacco prices begins

▶ English market for cotton textiles boosts prices and causes explosion in cotton production in the Southwest

CHAPTER 11

Cotton, Slavery, and the Old South

The South, like the North, experienced dramatic growth in the middle years of the nineteenth century. Southerners fanned out into the new territories of the Southwest and established new communities, new states, and new markets. The southern agricultural economy grew increasingly productive and increasingly prosperous. Trade in such staples as sugar, rice, tobacco, and above all cotton made the South a major force in international commerce and created substantial wealth within the region. It also tied the South securely to the emerging capitalist world of the United States and its European trading partners.

Southern society, southern culture, southern politics—all changed in response to these important demographic and economic changes. The South in the 1850s was a very different place from the South of the first years of the century.

Yet for all the expansion and all the changes, the South experienced a much less fundamental transformation in these years than did the North. It had begun the nineteenth

Growth without Development

century a primarily agricultural region; it remained overwhelmingly agrarian in 1860. It had begun the century with few important cities and little industry; so it remained sixty years later. In 1800, a plantation system dependent on slave labor had dominated the southern economy; by 1860, that system had only strengthened its grip on the region. One historian has written, "The South grew, but it did not develop." As a result, it became increasingly unlike the North and increasingly sensitive to what it considered to be threats to its distinctive way of life.

1822 ▶ Denmark Vesey thwarted in plans for slave rebellion in Charleston

1831 ▶ Nat Turner slave rebellion breaks out in Virginia

1833 ▶ John Randolph of Roanoke frees 400 slaves

1837 ▶ Cotton prices plummet

1846 ▶ *De Bow's Review* founded in New Orleans

1849 ▶ Rise in cotton prices spurs production boom

THE COTTON ECONOMY

The most important economic development in the mid-nineteenth-century South was the shift of economic power from the "upper South" (the original southern states along the Atlantic coast) to the "lower South" (the expanding agricultural regions in the new states of the Southwest). That shift reflected above all the growing dominance of cotton in the southern economy.

The Rise of King Cotton

Much of the upper South continued in the nineteenth century to rely, as it always had, on the cultivation of tobacco. But the market for that crop was notoriously unstable. Tobacco prices were subject to frequent depressions, including a prolonged one that began in the 1820s and extended into the 1850s. Tobacco also rapidly exhausted the land on which it grew; it was difficult for most growers to remain in business in the same place for very long. By the 1830s, therefore, many farmers in the old tobacco-growing regions of Virginia, Maryland, and North Carolina were shifting to other crops—notably wheat—while the center of tobacco cultivation was moving westward, into the Piedmont area.

Decline of the Tobacco Economy

The southern regions of the coastal South—South Carolina, Georgia, and parts of Florida—continued to rely on the cultivation of rice, a more stable and lucrative crop. Rice, however, demanded substantial irrigation and needed an exceptionally long growing season (nine months), so cultivation of that staple remained restricted to a relatively small area. Sugar growers along the Gulf Coast, similarly, enjoyed a reasonably profitable market for their crop. But sugar cultivation required intensive (and debilitating) labor and a long growing time. Only relatively wealthy planters could afford to engage in it, and they faced major competition from the great sugar plantations of the Caribbean. Sugar cultivation, therefore, did not spread much beyond a small area in southern Louisiana and eastern Texas. Long-staple (Sea Island) cotton was another lucrative crop, but like rice and sugar, it could grow only in a limited area—the coastal regions of the Southeast.

The decline of the tobacco economy in the upper South, and the inherent limits of the sugar, rice, and long-staple cotton economies farther south, might have forced the region to shift its attention in the nineteenth century to other nonagricultural pursuits, had it not been for the growing importance of a new product that soon overshadowed all else: short-staple cotton. This was a **Short-Staple Cotton** hardier and coarser strain of cotton that could grow successfully in a variety of climates and in a variety of soils. It was harder to process than the long-staple variety; its seeds were more difficult to remove from the fiber. But the invention of the cotton gin (see pp. 188–189) had largely solved that problem.

Demand for cotton was growing rapidly. The growth of the textile industry in Britain in the 1820s and 1830s, and in New England in the 1840s and 1850s, created an enormous new demand for the crop. As a result, ambitious men and women rapidly moved into previously uncultivated lands—many of them newly

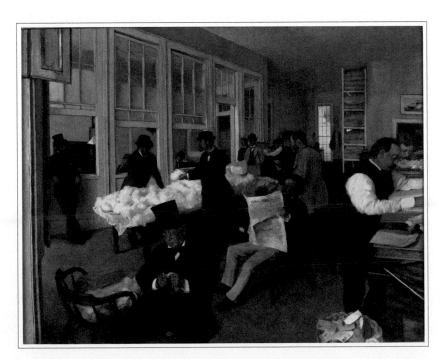

THE NEW ORLEANS COTTON EXCHANGE Edgar Degas, the great French impressionist, painted this scene of cotton traders examining samples in the New Orleans cotton exchange in 1873. By this time the cotton trade was producing less impressive profits than those that had made it the driving force of the booming southern economy of the 1850s. Degas's mother came from a Creole family of cotton brokers in New Orleans, and two of the artist's brothers (depicted here reading a newspaper and leaning against a window) joined the business in America. *(Giraudon/Art Resource)*

open to planter settlement after the relocation of the tribes in the 1820s and 1830s—to establish new cotton-growing regions.

Beginning in the 1820s, therefore, cotton production spread rapidly. From the western areas of South Carolina and Georgia, production moved steadily westward—first into Alabama and Mississippi, then into northern Louisiana, Texas, and Arkansas. By the 1850s, cotton had

Spread of Cotton Production

become the linchpin of the southern economy. In 1820, the South had produced about 500,000 bales of cotton. By 1850 it was producing nearly 3 million bales a year, and by 1860 nearly 5 million. There were periodic fluctuations in cotton prices, resulting generally from overproduction; periods of boom frequently gave way to abrupt busts. But the cotton economy continued to grow, even if in fits and starts. By the time of the Civil War, cotton constituted nearly two-thirds of the total export trade of the United States and was bringing in nearly $200 million a year. The annual value of the rice crop, in contrast, was $2 million. It was little wonder that southern politicians now proclaimed: "Cotton is king!"

Cotton production dominated the more recently settled areas of what came to be known as the "lower South" (or, in a later era, the "Deep South"). Some began to call this region the "Cotton Kingdom." Settlement of the area resembled in some ways the rush of gold seekers to a new strike. The prospect of tremendous profits from growing cotton drew white settlers to the lower South by the thousands. Some were wealthy planters from the older states who transferred their assets and slaves to a cotton plantation. Most were small slaveholders or slaveless farmers who hoped to move into the planter class.

A similar shift, if an involuntary one, occurred in the

Expansion of Slavery

slave population. Between 1820 and 1860, the number of slaves in Alabama leaped from 41,000 to 435,000, and in Mississippi from 32,000 to 436,000. In the same period, the increase in Virginia was only from 425,000 to 490,000. Between 1840 and 1860, according to some estimates, 410,000 slaves moved from the upper South to the cotton states—either accompanying masters who were themselves migrating to the Southwest, or (more often) sold to planters already there. Indeed, the sale of slaves to the Southwest became an important economic activity in the upper South and helped the troubled planters of that region compensate for the declining value of their crops.

Southern Trade and Industry

In the face of this booming agricultural expansion, other forms of economic activity developed slowly in the South. The business classes of the region—the manufacturers

and merchants—were not unimportant. There was growing activity in flour milling and in textile and iron manufacturing, particularly in the upper South. The Tredegar Iron Works in Richmond, for example, compared favorably with the best iron mills in the Northeast. But industry remained an insignificant force in comparison with the agricultural economy. The total value of southern textile manufactures in 1860 was $4.5 million—a threefold increase over the value of those goods twenty years before, but only about 2 percent of the value of the raw cotton exported that year.

Weak Manufacturing Sector

To the degree that the South developed a nonfarm commercial sector, it was largely to serve the needs of the plantation economy. Particularly important were the brokers, or "factors," who marketed the planters' crops. These merchants tended to live in such towns as New Orleans, Charleston, Mobile, and Savannah, where they worked to find buyers for cotton and other crops and where they purchased goods for the planters they served. The South had only a very rudimentary financial system, and the factors often also served the planters as bankers, providing them with credit. Planters frequently accumulated substantial debts, particularly during periods when cotton prices were in decline; and the southern merchant-bankers thus became figures of considerable influence and importance in the region. There were also substantial groups of professional people in the South—lawyers, editors, doctors, and others. In most parts of the region, however, they too were closely tied to and dependent on the plantation economy. However important manufacturers, merchants, and professionals might have been to southern society, they were relatively unimportant in comparison with the manufacturers, merchants, and professionals of the North, on whom southerners were coming more and more (and increasingly unhappily) to depend.

The primitive character of the region's banking system matched a lack of development in other basic services and structures necessary for industrial

Inadequate Regional Transportation System

development. Perhaps most notable was the South's inadequate transportation system. In the North in the antebellum period, enormous sums were invested in roads, canals, and above all railroads to knit the region together into an integrated market. In the South there were no such investments. Canals were almost nonexistent; most roads were crude and unsuitable for heavy transport; and railroads, although they expanded substantially in the 1840s and 1850s, failed to tie the region together effectively. Such towns as Charleston, Atlanta, Savannah, and Norfolk had direct connections with Memphis, and thus with the Northwest; and Richmond was connected, via the Virginia Central, with the Memphis and Charleston Railroad. In addition, several independent lines furnished a continuous connection

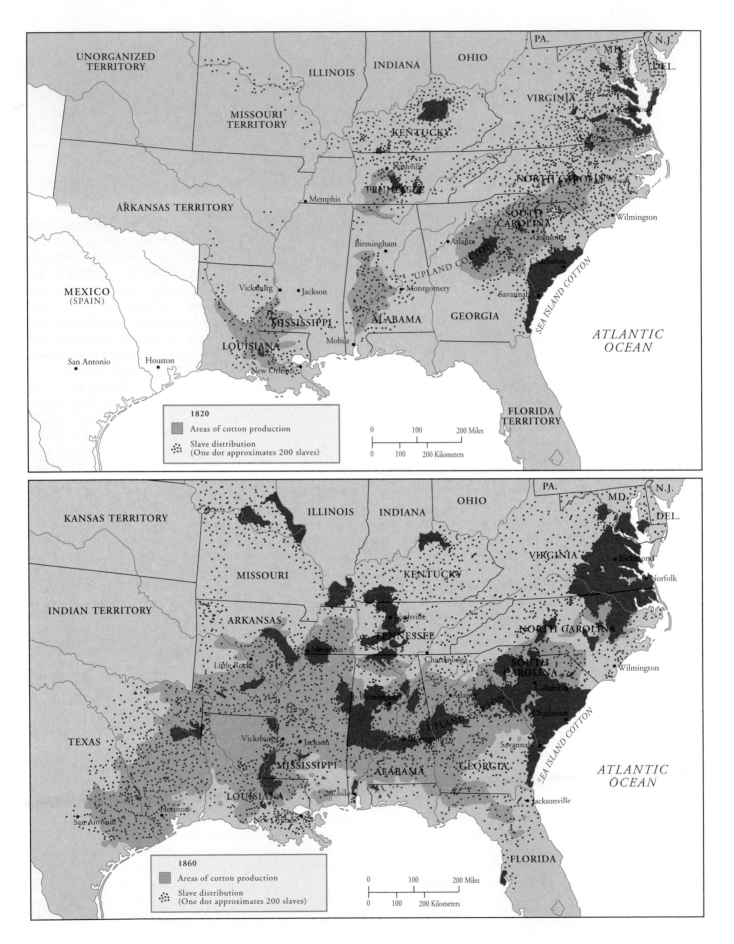

1820

■ Areas of cotton production

∴ Slave distribution
(One dot approximates 200 slaves)

| 0 | 100 | 200 Miles |
| 0 | 100 | 200 Kilometers |

1860

■ Areas of cotton production

∴ Slave distribution
(One dot approximates 200 slaves)

| 0 | 100 | 200 Miles |
| 0 | 100 | 200 Kilometers |

SLAVERY AND COTTON IN THE SOUTH, 1820 AND 1860 The two maps on the opposite page show the remarkable spread of cotton cultivation in the South in the decades before the Civil War. Both maps show the areas of cotton cultivation (the mustard-colored areas) as well as areas with large slave populations (the red-dotted areas). Note how in the top map, which represents 1820, cotton production is concentrated largely in the East, with a few areas scattered among Alabama, Mississippi, Louisiana, and Tennessee. Slavery is concentrated along the Georgia and South Carolina coast, areas in which long-staple cotton was grown, with only a few other areas of highly dense slave populations. By 1860, the South had changed dramatically. Cotton production had spread throughout the lower South, from Texas to northern Florida, and slavery had moved with it. Slavery was also much denser in the tobacco-growing regions of Virginia and North Carolina, which had also grown. *How did this economic shift affect the white South's commitment to slavery?*

 For an interactive version of this map go to www.mhhe.com/brinkley12ch11maps

between the Ohio River and New Orleans. Most of the South, however, remained unconnected to the national railroad system. Most lines in the region were short and local. The principal means of transportation was water. Planters generally shipped their crops to market along rivers or by sea; most manufacturing was in or near port towns.

Perceptive southerners recognized the economic subordination of their region to the North. "From the rattle with which the nurse tickles the ear of the child born in the South to the shroud that covers the cold form of the dead, everything comes to us from the North," the Arkansas journalist Albert Pike lamented. Perhaps the most prominent advocate of southern economic independence was James B. D. De Bow, a resident of New Orleans. He published a magazine advocating southern commercial and agricultural expansion, *De Bow's Review*, which survived from its founding in 1846 until 1880. De Bow made his journal into a tireless advocate

De Bow's Review

PLANTATIONS IN LOUISIANA, 1858 This map provides a detailed view of plantation lands along a stretch of the Mississippi River between New Orleans and Baton Rouge, Louisiana. Note the long, narrow shapes of these landholdings—known as "long lots." This system was designed to give as many planters as possible frontage on the river, which they needed to transport their crops to market and to receive goods in return. The river also deposited rich soil on the lands near its banks, which made cultivation of crops easier. Note how towns, stores, and churches all are near the riverbank, so planters and others living on plantations nearby could reach them easily by boat. ◆ *How is this landscape different from that of the newly opened federal lands in the West?*

of southern economic independence from the North, warning constantly of the dangers of the "colonial" relationship between the sections. One writer noted in the pages of his magazine: "I think it would be safe to estimate the amount which is lost to us annually by our vassalage to the North at $100,000,000. Great God!" Yet *De Bow's Review* was itself evidence of the dependency of the South on the North. It was printed in New York, because no New Orleans printer had facilities adequate for the task; it was filled with advertisements from northern manufacturing firms; and its circulation was always modest in comparison with those of northern publications. In Charleston, for example, it sold an average of 173 copies per issue; *Harper's Magazine* of New York, in contrast, regularly sold 1,500 copies to South Carolinians.

Sources of Southern Difference

Despite this growing concern about the region's "colonial dependency," the South made few serious efforts to build an economy that might challenge that dependency. An important question about antebellum southern history, therefore, is why the region did so little to develop a larger industrial and commercial economy of its own. Why did it remain so different from the North?

Part of the reason was the great profitability of the region's agricultural system, and particularly of cotton production. In the Northeast, many people had turned to manufacturing as the agricultural economy of the region declined. In the South, the agricultural economy was booming, and ambitious people eager to profit from the emerging capitalist economy had little incentive to look beyond it. Another reason was that wealthy southerners had so much capital invested in their land and, particularly, their slaves that they had little left for other investments. Some historians have suggested that the southern climate—with its long, hot, steamy summers—was less suitable for industrial development than the climate of the North. Still others have gone so far as to claim that southern work habits (perhaps a reflection of the debilitating effects of the climate) impeded industrialization; some white southerners appeared—at least to many northern observers—not to work very hard, to lack the strong work ethic that fueled northern economic development.

But the southern failure to create a flourishing commercial or industrial economy was also in part the result of a set of values distinctive to the South that discouraged the growth of cities and industry. Many white southerners liked to think of themselves as representatives of a special way of life: one based on traditional values of chivalry, leisure, and elegance. White southerners were, they argued, "cavaliers"—people happily free from the base, acquisitive instincts of the "yankees" to their north. Southern white people were, they believed, more concerned with a refined and gracious way of life than with rapid growth and development. Appealing as the "cavalier" image was to southern whites, however, it conformed to the reality of southern society in very limited ways.

WHITE SOCIETY IN THE SOUTH

Only a small minority of southern whites owned slaves. In 1850, when the total white population of the South was over 6 million, the number of slaveholders was only 347,525. In 1860, when the white population was just above 8 million, the number of slaveholders had risen to only 383,637. These figures are somewhat misleading, since each slaveholder was normally the head of a family averaging five members. But even with all members of slaveowning families included in the figures, those owning slaves still amounted to perhaps no more than one quarter of the white population. And of the minority of whites holding slaves, only a small proportion owned them in substantial numbers.

The Planter Class

How, then, did the South come to be seen—both by the outside world and by many southerners themselves—as a society dominated by great plantations and wealthy landowning planters? In large part, it was because the planter aristocracy—the cotton magnates, the sugar, rice, and tobacco nabobs, the whites who owned at least forty or fifty slaves and 800 or more acres—exercised power and influence far in excess of their numbers. They stood at the apex of society, determining the political, economic, and even social life of their region. Enriched by vast annual incomes, dwelling in palatial homes, surrounded by broad acres and many black servants, they became a class to which all others deferred. The wealthiest of them maintained homes in towns or cities and spent several months of the year there, engaged in a glittering social life. Others traveled widely, especially to Europe, as an antidote to the isolation of plantation life. And many used their plantations to host opulent social events.

White southerners liked to compare their planter class to the old upper classes of England and Europe: true aristocracies, long entrenched. In fact, however, the southern upper class was in most cases not at all similar to the landed aristocracies of the Old World. In some areas of the upper South—the Tidewater region of Virginia, for example—some of the great aristocrats were indeed people whose families had occupied positions of wealth and power for generations. In most of the South, however, a longstanding landed aristocracy, although central to the "cavalier" image, was largely a myth. Even the most important planters in the cotton-growing areas of the South were, typically, new to their wealth and power. As late as the 1850s, many of the great landowners in the lower South were still first-generation settlers, who had arrived with only modest resources, struggled for many years to clear land and develop a plantation in what was at first a rugged wilderness, and only relatively recently had started to live in the comfort and luxury for which they became famous. Large areas of the "Old South" (as Americans later called the South of the pre-Civil War era) had been settled and cultivated for less than two decades at the time of the Civil War.

Nor was the world of the planter nearly as leisured and genteel as the "cavalier" myth would suggest. Growing staple crops was a business that was in its own way just as competitive and just as risky as the industrial enterprises **Plantation Management** of the North. Planters had to supervise their operations carefully if they hoped to make a profit. They were, in many respects, just as much competitive capitalists as the

industrialists of the North whose lifestyles they claimed to hold in contempt. Even many affluent planters lived rather modestly, their wealth so heavily invested in land and slaves that there was little left for personal comfort. And white planters, even some substantial ones, tended to move frequently as new and presumably more productive areas opened up to cultivation.

Indeed, it may have been the very newness and precariousness of the plantation way of life, and the differences between the reality of that life and the image of it, that made many southern planters determined to portray themselves as genteel aristocrats. Having struggled so hard to reach and maintain their positions, they were all the more determined to defend them. Perhaps that was why the defense of slavery and of the South's "rights" was stronger in the new, booming regions of the lower South and weaker in the more established and less flourishing areas of the Tidewater.

Wealthy southern whites sustained their image of themselves as aristocrats in many ways. They avoided such **Aristocratic Values**

A GEORGIA PLANTATION This map of the Hopeton Plantation in South Carolina shows both how much plantations were connected to the national and world markets, and how much they tried to be self-sufficient. Note the large areas of land devoted to the growing of cotton, rice, and sugar cane, all of them crops for the market. ◆ *Why would a plantation in this part of the South be so much more diversified in the market crops it raised than the cotton plantations in the Mississippi Delta?* Note also the many crops grown for the local market or for consumption by residents of the plantation—potatoes, vegetables, corn, and others. The top left of the map shows the distribution of living quarters, with slaves' quarters grouped together very near the owner's residence. ◆ *Why would planters want their slaves living nearby? Why might slaves be unhappy about being so close to their owners?*

"coarse" occupations as trade and commerce; those who did not become planters often gravitated toward the military, a "suitable" career for men raised in a culture in which medieval knights (as portrayed in the novels of Walter Scott) were a powerful and popular image. The aristocratic ideal also found reflection in the definition of a special role for southern white women.

"Honor"

Above all perhaps white males adopted an elaborate code of chivalry, which obligated them to defend their "honor," often through dueling—which survived in the South long after it had largely vanished in the North. Southern white males placed enormous stock in conventional forms of courtesy and respect in their dealings with one another—perhaps as a way of distancing themselves from the cruelty and disrespect that were so fundamental to the slave system they controlled. Violations of such forms often brought what seemed to outsiders a disproportionately heated and even violent response.

The idea of honor in the South was only partly connected to the idea of ethical behavior and bravery. It was also tied to the importance among white males of the public appearance of dignity and authority—of saving face in the presence of others. Anything that seemed to challenge the dignity, social station, or "manhood" of a white southern male might be the occasion for a challenge to duel, or at least for a stern public rebuke. When the South Carolina congressman Preston Brooks strode into the chamber of the United States Senate and savagely beat Senator Charles Sumner of Massachusetts with a cane to retaliate for what he considered an insult to a relative, he was acting wholly in accord with the idea of southern honor. In the North, he was reviled as a savage. In the South, he became a popular hero. But Brooks was only the most public example of a code of behavior that many white southern men followed. Avenging insults was a social necessity in many parts of southern society, and avenging insults to white ~~Cult of Honor~~ southern women was perhaps the most important obligation of a white southern "gentleman."

ST. JOHN PLANTATION, LOUISIANA This Greek Revival "big house" of the St. John Plantation in St. Martin Parish, Louisiana, still stands today. In 1861, when the artist Adrien Persac painted this view of it, it occupied the center of a 5,000-acre sugar plantation and was the setting of the self-consciously elegant life of the planter and his family. To the right is a brick sugar factory and the cabins of the plantation's slaves, who performed the arduous work of sugar harvesting and production. *(Louisiana State University Museum of Art)*

The "Southern Lady"

In some respects, affluent white women in the South occupied roles very similar to those of middle-class white women in the North. Their lives generally centered in the home, where they served as companions to and hostesses for their husbands and as nurturing mothers for their children. Even less frequently than in the North did "genteel" southern white women engage in public activities or find income-producing employment.

But the life of the "southern lady" was also in many ways very different from that of her northern counterpart. For one thing, the cult of honor in the region meant in theory that southern white men gave particular importance to the "defense" of women. In practice, this generally meant that white men were even more dominant and white women even more subordinate in southern culture than they were in the North. George Fitzhugh, one of the South's most important social theorists, wrote in the 1850s: "Women, like children, have but one right, and that is the right to protection. The right to protection involves the obligation to obey."

Subordinate Status of Women

More important in determining the role of southern white women, however, were the social and economic realities in which they lived. The vast majority of females in the region lived on farms, relatively isolated from people outside their own families, with virtually no access to the "public world" and thus few opportunities to look beyond their roles as wives and mothers. Because the family was the principal economic unit on most farms, the dominance of husbands and fathers over wives and children was even greater than in those northern families in which income-producing activities had moved out of the home and into the factory or office. For many white women, living on farms of modest size meant a fuller engagement in the economic life of the family than was becoming typical for middle-class women in the North. These women engaged in spinning, weaving, and other production; they participated in agricultural tasks; they helped supervise the slave work force. On some of the larger plantations, however, even these limited roles were sometimes considered unsuitable for white women; and the "plantation mistress" became, in some cases, more an ornament for her husband than an active part of the economy or the society.

Southern white women also had less access to education than their northern counterparts. Nearly a quarter of all white women over twenty were completely illiterate; relatively few women had more than a rudimentary exposure to schooling. Even wealthy planters were not much interested in extensive schooling for their daughters. The few female "academies" in the South trained women primarily to be suitable wives.

Southern white women had other special burdens as well. The southern white birth rate remained nearly 20 percent higher than that of the nation as a whole, and infant mortality in the region remained higher than elsewhere; nearly half the children born in the South in 1860 died before they reached five years of age. The slave labor system had a mixed impact on white women. It helped spare many of them from certain kinds of arduous labor, but it also threatened their relationships with their husbands. Male slaveowners had frequent sexual relationships with the female slaves on their plantations; the children of those unions became part of the plantation labor force and served as a constant reminder to white women of their husbands' infidelity. Black women (and men) were obviously the most important victims of such practices. But white women suffered too.

Other Burdens

A few southern white women rebelled against their roles and against the prevailing assumptions of their region. Some became outspoken abolitionists and joined northerners in the crusade to abolish slavery. Some agitated for other reforms within the South itself. Most white women, however, found few outlets for whatever discontent they may have felt with their lives. Instead, they generally convinced themselves of the benefits of their position and—often even more fervently than southern white men—defended the special virtues of the southern way of life. Upper-class white women in the South were particularly energetic in defending the class lines that separated them from poorer whites.

CLEAR STARCHING IN LOUISIANA This 1837 etching by August Hervieu offers a strikingly unromanticized view of plantation women in the South. The white plantation mistress, soberly dressed, speaks harshly to two black household servants, presumably criticizing the way they are doing the laundry. The slaves cower, carefully hiding whatever resentment they might feel behind a submissive pose. Nothing in this picture suggests anything like the kind of ease and luxury often associated with plantation life in popular mythology at the time and since. *(General Research Division, New York Public Library, Astor, Lenox and Tilden Foundations)*

The Plain Folk

The typical white southerner was not a great planter and slaveholder, but a modest yeoman farmer. Some of these "plain folk," as they have become known, owned a few slaves, with whom they worked and lived far more closely than did the larger planters. Most (in fact, three-quarters of all white families) owned no slaves at all. Some plain folk, most of whom owned their own land, devoted themselves largely to subsistence farming; others grew cotton or other crops for the market, but usually could not produce enough to allow them to expand their operations or even get out of debt. During the 1850s, the number of nonslaveholding landowners increased much faster than the number of slaveholding landowners. While there were occasional examples of poor farmers moving into the ranks of the planter class, such cases were rare. Most yeomen knew that they had little prospect of substantially bettering their lot.

One reason was the southern educational system, which provided poor whites with few opportunities to learn and thus limited their chances of advancement. For the sons of wealthy planters, the region provided ample opportunities to gain an education. In 1860 there were 260 southern colleges and universities, public and private, with 25,000 students enrolled in them, or more than half the total number of students in the United States. But universities were only within the reach of the upper class. The elementary and secondary schools of the South were not only fewer but also inferior to those of the Northeast (although not much worse than the crude schools of the Northwest). The South had more than 500,000 illiterate whites, or over half the country's total.

Limited Educational Opportunities

That a majority of the South's white population consisted of modest farmers largely excluded from the dominant plantation society raises another important question about the antebellum South. Why did the plain folk have so little power in the public world of the Old South? Why did they not oppose the aristocratic social system in which they shared so little? Why did they not resent the system of slavery, from which they generally did not benefit?

Some nonslaveowning whites did oppose the planter elite, but for the most part in limited ways and in a relatively few, isolated areas. These were southern highlanders, the "hill people," who lived in the Appalachian ranges east of the Mississippi, in the Ozarks to the west of the river, and in other "hill country" or "backcountry" areas cut off from the more commercial world of the plantation system. Of all southern whites, they were the most isolated from the mainstream of the region's life. They practiced a simple form of subsistence agriculture, owned practically no slaves, and had a proud sense of seclusion. They were, in most respects, unconnected to the new commercial economy that dominated the great cotton-planting region of the South. They produced almost no surplus for the market, had little access to money, and often bartered for the goods they could not grow themselves.

Hill People

To such men and women, slavery was unattractive for many of the same reasons it was unappealing to workers and small farmers in the North: because it threatened their sense of their own independence. Upcountry farmers lived in a society of unusual individual personal freedom and unusual isolation from modern notions of property. They also held to older political ideals, which for many included the ideal of fervent loyalty to the nation as a whole.

Such whites frequently expressed animosity toward the planter aristocracy of the other regions of the South. The mountain region was the only part of the South to defy the trend toward sectional conformity, and it was the only part to resist the movement toward secession when it finally developed. Even during the Civil War itself, many refused to support the Confederacy; some went so far as to fight for the Union.

Far greater in number, however, were the nonslave-owning whites who lived in the midst of the plantation system. Many, perhaps most of them, accepted that system because they were tied to it in important ways. Small farmers depended on the local plantation aristocracy for many things: access to cotton gins, markets for their modest crops and their livestock, credit or other financial assistance in time of need. In many areas, there were also extensive kinship networks linking lower- and upper-class whites. The poorest resident of a county might easily be a cousin of the richest aristocrat. Taken together, these mutual ties helped mute what might otherwise have been pronounced class tensions.

Close Relations with the Plantation Aristocracy

Small farmers felt tied to the plantation society in other ways as well. For white men, at least, the South was an unusually democratic society, in the sense that participation in politics—both through voting and through attending campaign meetings and barbecues—was even more widespread than in the North, where participation was also high. Just as political participation gave workers in the North a sense of connection to the social order, so it did for farmers in the South—even though officeholders in the South, even more than in the North, were almost always members of the region's elites. In the 1850s, moreover, the boom in the cotton economy allowed many small farmers to improve their economic fortunes. Some bought more land, became slaveowners, and moved into at least the fringes of plantation society. Others simply felt more secure now in their positions as independent yeomen and hence more likely to embrace the fierce regional loyalty that was spreading throughout the white South in these years.

Small farmers, even more than great planters, were also committed to a traditional, male-dominated family structure. Their household-centered economies required the participation of all family members and, they believed, a stable system of gender relations to ensure

order and stability. Men were the unquestioned masters
of their homes; women and children, who were both family and work force, were firmly under
the master's control. As the northern attack on slavery increased in the 1840s and 1850s, it was easy for such farmers to believe—and easy for ministers, politicians, and other propagandists for slavery to persuade them—that an assault on one hierarchical system (slavery) would open the way to an assault on another such system (patriarchy).

There were other white southerners, however, who did not share in the plantation economy in even limited ways and yet continued to accept its premises. These were the members of a particularly degraded class—numbering perhaps a half-million in 1850—known variously as "crackers," "sand hillers," or "poor white trash." Occupying the infertile lands of the pine barrens, the red hills, and the swamps, they lived in miserable cabins amid genuine squalor. Many owned no land (or owned land on which virtually nothing could be grown) and supported themselves by foraging or hunting. Others worked at times as common laborers for their neighbors, although the slave system limited their opportunities. Their degradation resulted partly from dietary deficiencies and disease. They resorted at times to eating clay (hence the tendency of more affluent whites to refer to them disparagingly as "clay eaters"); and they suffered from pellagra, hookworm, and malaria. Planters and small farmers alike held them in contempt. They formed a true underclass. In some material respects, their plight was worse than that of the African-American slaves (who themselves often looked down on the poor whites).

Yet, even among these southerners—the true outcasts of white society in the region—there was no real opposition to the plantation system or slavery. In part, undoubtedly, this was because these men and women were so benumbed by poverty that they had little strength to protest. But their relative passivity resulted also from perhaps the single greatest unifying factor among the southern white population, the one force that was most responsible for reducing tensions among the various classes: their perception of race. However poor and miserable these white southerners might have been, they could still consider themselves members of a ruling race; they could still look down on the black population of the region and feel a bond with their fellow whites born of a determination to maintain their racial supremacy. As Frederick Law Olmsted, a northerner who visited the South and chronicled southern society in the 1850s, wrote: "From childhood, the one thing in their condition which has made life valuable to the mass of whites has been that the niggers are yet their inferiors."

Commitment to Paternalism

Limited Class Conflict

SLAVERY: THE "PECULIAR INSTITUTION"

White southerners often referred to slavery as the "peculiar institution." By that they meant not that the institution was odd, but that it was distinctive, special. The description was apt, for American slavery was indeed distinctive. The South in the mid-nineteenth century was the only area in the Western world—except for Brazil, Cuba, and Puerto Rico—where slavery still existed. Slavery, more than any other single factor, isolated the South from the rest of American society. And as that isolation increased, so did the commitment of southerners to defend the institution.

Within the South itself, the institution of slavery had paradoxical results. On the one hand, it isolated blacks from whites, drawing a sharp and inviolable racial line dividing one group of southerners from another. As a result, African Americans under slavery began to develop a society and culture of their own, one in many ways unrelated to the white civilization around them. On the other hand, slavery created a unique bond between blacks and whites—masters and slaves—in the South. The two groups may have maintained separate spheres, but each sphere was deeply influenced by, indeed dependent on, the other.

Varieties of Slavery

Slavery was an institution established and regulated in detail by law. The slave codes of the southern states forbade slaves to hold property, to leave their masters' premises without permission, to be out after dark, to congregate with other slaves except at church, to carry firearms, or to strike a white person even in self-defense. The codes prohibited whites from teaching slaves to read or write and denied to slaves the right to testify in court against white people. The laws contained no provisions to legalize slave marriages or divorces. If an owner killed a slave while punishing him, the act was generally not considered a crime. Slaves, however, faced the death penalty for killing or even resisting a white person and for inciting revolt. The codes also contained extraordinarily rigid provisions for defining a person's race. Anyone with even a trace of African ancestry was defined as black. And anyone even rumored to possess any such trace was presumed to be black unless he or she could prove otherwise— which was, of course, difficult to do.

Legal Basis of Slavery

These and dozens of other restrictions might seem to suggest that slaves lived under a uniformly harsh and dismal regime. Had the laws been rigidly enforced, that might have been the case. In fact, however, enforcement was spotty and uneven. Some slaves did acquire property, did learn to read and write, and did assemble with other slaves, in spite of laws to the contrary. Although the major slave offenses generally fell under the jurisdiction

HAULING THE WHOLE WEEK'S PICKING

HAULING THE WHOLE WEEK'S PICKING This watercolor by William Henry Brown, painted in approximately 1842, portrays a slave family loading cotton onto a wagon, presumably after a hard day of picking. Even young children participate in the chores. Brown was an artist known for his silhouettes, a form popular in the nineteenth century. (One of his later subjects was Abraham Lincoln.) This picture, however, is part of a five-foot cutout he made as a gift to a family he was visiting. *(Historic New Orleans Collection)*

of the courts (and thus of the slave codes), white owners handled most transgressions and inflicted widely varying punishments. In other words, despite the rigid provisions of law, there was in reality considerable variety within the slave system.

Reality of Slavery

Some blacks lived in almost prisonlike conditions, rigidly and harshly controlled by their masters. Many (probably most) others enjoyed some flexibility and (at least in comparison to the regimen prescribed by law) a striking degree of autonomy.

The nature of the relationship between masters and slaves depended in part on the size of the plantation. The typical master had a different image of slavery from that of the typical slave. Most masters possessed very few slaves, and their experience with (and image of) slavery was a reflection of the special nature of slavery on the small farm. White farmers with few slaves generally supervised their workers directly and often worked closely alongside them. On such farms, blacks and whites developed a form of intimacy unknown on larger plantations. The paternal relationship between such masters and their slaves could, like relationships between fathers and children, be warm and affectionate. It could also be tyrannical and cruel. In either case, it was a relationship based on the relative powerlessness of the slaves and the nearly absolute authority of their masters. In general, African Americans themselves preferred to live on larger plantations, where they had more privacy and a chance to build a cultural and social world of their own.

Although the majority of slaveowners were small farmers, the majority of slaves lived on plantations of medium or large size, with sizable slave work forces. Thus the relationship between master and slave was much less intimate for the typical slave than for the typical slaveowner. Substantial planters often hired overseers and even assistant overseers to represent them. "Head drivers," trusted and responsible slaves often assisted by several subdrivers, acted under the overseer as foremen.

Larger planters generally used one of two methods of assigning slave labor. One was the task system (most common

Task and Gang Systems

in rice culture), under which slaves were assigned a particular task in the morning, for example, hoeing one acre; after completing the job, they were free for the rest of the day. The other, far more common, was the gang system (employed on the cotton, sugar, and tobacco plantations), under which slaves were simply divided into groups, each of them directed by a driver, and compelled to work for as many hours as the overseer considered a reasonable workday.

Life Under Slavery

Slaves generally received at least enough necessities to enable them to live and work. Their masters usually furnished them with an adequate diet, consisting mainly of cornmeal, salt pork, molasses, and on special occasions fresh meat or poultry. Many slaves cultivated gardens for their own use. They received cheap clothing and shoes. They lived in crude cabins, called slave quarters, usually clustered together in a complex near the master's house. The plantation mistress or a doctor retained by the owner provided some medical care; but slave women themselves—as "healers" and midwives, or simply as mothers—were the more important source.

Special Position of Women

Slaves worked hard, beginning with light tasks as children; and their workdays were longest at harvest time. Slave women worked particularly hard. They generally labored in the fields with the men, and they assumed as well the crucial chores traditionally reserved for women—cooking, cleaning, and child rearing. Because slave families were often divided, with husbands and fathers frequently living on neighboring plantations (or, at times, sold to plantation owners far away), black women often found themselves acting in effect as single parents. Within the slave family, therefore, women had special burdens but also a special authority.

High Slave Mortality Rates

Slaves were, as a group, much less healthy than southern whites. After 1808, when the importation of slaves became illegal, the proportion of blacks to whites in the nation as a whole steadily declined. In 1820, there was one African American to every four whites; in 1840, one to every five. The slower increase of the black population was a result of its comparatively high death rate. Slave mothers had large families, but the enforced poverty in which virtually all African Americans lived ensured that fewer of their children would survive to adulthood than the children of white parents. Even those who did survive typically died at a younger age than the average white person.

Even so, according to some scholars, the actual material conditions of slavery may, in fact, have been better than those of many northern factory workers and considerably better than those of both peasants and industrial workers in nineteenth-century Europe. The conditions of American slaves were certainly less severe than those of slaves in the Caribbean and South America. That was in part because plantations in other parts of the Americas tended to grow crops that required more arduous labor; sugar production in the Caribbean islands, in particular, involved extraordinarily backbreaking work. In addition, Caribbean and South American planters continued to use the African slave trade well into the nineteenth century to replenish their labor supply, so they had less incentive than American planters (who no longer had much access to that trade) to protect their existing laborers. Working and living conditions in these other slave societies were arduous, and masters at times literally worked their slaves to death. Growing cotton, the principal activity for most slaves in the United States, was much less debilitating than growing sugar; and planters had strong economic incentives to maintain a healthy slave population. One result of this was that America became the only country where a slave population actually increased through natural reproduction (although it grew much more slowly than the white population).

Most masters did make some effort to preserve the health—and thus the usefulness—of their slaves. One example was the frequent practice of protecting slave children from hard work until early adolescence. Masters believed that doing so would make young slaves more loyal and would also ensure better health as adults. Another example was the use of hired labor, when available, for the most unhealthy or dangerous tasks. A traveler in Louisiana noted, for example, that Irishmen were employed to clear malarial swamps and to handle cotton bales at the bottom of chutes extending from the river bluff down to a boat landing. If an Irish worker died of disease or in an accident, a master could hire another for a dollar a day or less. But a master would lose an investment of perhaps $1,000 or more if a prime field hand died. Still, cruel masters might forget their pocketbooks in the heat of anger. Slaves were often left to the discipline of overseers, who had less of an economic stake in their well-being; overseers were paid in proportion to the amount of work they could get out of the slaves they supervised.

Household servants had a somewhat easier life—physically at least—than did field hands. On a small plantation, the same slaves might do both field work and

NURSING THE MASTER'S CHILD Louisa, a slave on a Missouri plantation owned by the Hayward family in the 1850s, is photographed here holding the master's infant son. Black women typically cared for white children on plantations, sometimes with great affection and sometimes—as this photograph may suggest—dutifully and without enthusiasm. *(Missouri Historical Society)*

The Character of Slavery

No issue in American history has produced a richer literature or a more spirited debate than the nature of American slavery. The debate began even before the Civil War, when abolitionists strove to expose slavery to the world as a brutal, dehumanizing institution, while southern defenders of slavery tried to depict it as a benevolent paternalistic system. That same debate continued for a time after the Civil War; but by the late nineteenth century, with white Americans eager for sectional conciliation, both northern and southern chroniclers of slavery began to accept a romanticized and unthreatening picture of the Old South and its "peculiar institution."

The first major scholarly examination of slavery was fully within this romantic tradition. Ulrich B. Phillips's *American Negro Slavery* (1918) portrayed slavery as an essentially benign institution in which kindly masters looked after submissive, childlike, and generally contented African Americans. Phillips's apologia for slavery remained the authoritative work on the subject for nearly thirty years.

In the 1940s, as concern about racial injustice increasingly engaged the attention of white Americans, challenges to Phillips began to emerge. In 1941, Melville J. Herskovits challenged Phillips's contention that black Americans retained little of their African cultural inheritance. In 1943, Herbert

(General Research Division, New York Public Library, Astor, Lenox and Tilden Foundations)

(Historic New Orleans Collection, 1975.93.2 (detail))

Aptheker published a chronicle of slave revolts as a way of challenging Phillips's claim that blacks were submissive and content.

A somewhat different challenge to Phillips emerged in the 1950s from historians who emphasized the brutality of the institution. Kenneth Stampp's *The Peculiar Institution* (1956) and, even more damningly, Stanley Elkins's *Slavery* (1959) described a labor system that did serious physical and psychological damage to its victims. Stampp and Elkins portrayed slavery as something like a prison, in which men and women had virtually no space in which to develop their own social and cultural lives. Elkins compared the system to Nazi concentration camps during World War II and likened the childlike "Sambo" personality of slavery to the distortions of character that many scholars believed the Holocaust had produced.

In the early 1970s, an explosion of new scholarship on slavery shifted the emphasis away from the damage the system inflicted on African Americans and toward the striking success of the slaves in building a culture of their own despite their enslavement. John Blassingame in 1973, echoing Herskovits's claims of thirty years earlier, argued that "the most remarkable aspect of the whole process of enslavement is the extent to which the American-born slaves were able to retain their ancestors' culture." Herbert Gutman, in *The Black Family in Slavery and Freedom* (1976) challenged the prevailing belief that slavery had weakened and even destroyed the African-American family. On the contrary, he argued, the black family survived slavery with

impressive strength, although with some significant differences from the prevailing form of the white family. Eugene Genovese's *Roll, Jordan, Roll* (1974) and other works revealed how African Americans manipulated the paternalist assumptions at the heart of slavery to build a large cultural space of their own within the system where they could develop their own family life, social traditions, and religious patterns. That same year, Robert Fogel and Stanley Engerman published their controversial *Time on the Cross,* a highly quantitative study that supported some of the claims of Gutman and Genovese about black achievement, but that went much further in portraying slavery as a successful and reasonably humane (if ultimately immoral) system. Slave workers, they argued, were better treated and lived in greater comfort than most northern industrial workers of the same era. Their conclusions produced a storm of criticism.

Some of the most important recent scholarship on slavery has focused on the role of women within it. Elizabeth Fox-Genovese's *Within the Plantation Household* (1988) examined the lives of both white and black women on the plantation. Rejecting the claims of some feminist historians that black and white women shared a common female identity born of their shared subordination to men, she portrayed slave women as defined by their dual roles as members of the plantation work force and anchors of the black family. Slave women, she argued, professed loyalty to their mistresses when forced to serve them as domestics; but their real loyalty remained to their own communities and families.

housework. But on a large estate, there would generally be a separate domestic staff: nursemaids, housemaids, cooks, butlers, coachmen. These people lived close to the master and his family, eating the leftovers from the family table and in some cases even sleeping in the "big house." Between the blacks and whites of such households affectionate, almost familial relationships might sometimes develop. More often, however, house servants resented their isolation from their fellow slaves and the lack of privacy that came with living in such close proximity to the master's family. Among other things, that proximity meant that their transgressions were more visible than those of field hands, and so they received punishments more often than did other slaves. When emancipation came after the Civil War, it was often the house servants who were the first to leave the plantations of their former owners.

| House Slaves |

Female household servants were especially vulnerable to sexual abuse by their masters and white overseers, who sometimes pressured them into supposedly consensual sexual relationships and sometimes literally raped them. In addition to unwanted sexual attention from white men, female slaves often received vindictive treatment from white women. Plantation mistresses naturally resented the sexual liaisons between their husbands and female slaves. Punishing their husbands was not usually possible, so they often punished the slaves instead – with arbitrary beatings, increased workloads, and various forms of psychological torment.

| Sexual Abuse |

Slavery in the Cities

The conditions of slavery in the cities differed significantly from those in the countryside. On the relatively isolated plantations, slaves had little contact with free blacks and lower-class whites, and masters maintained fairly direct and effective control; a deep and seemingly unbridgeable chasm yawned between slavery and freedom. In the city, however, a master often could not supervise his slaves closely and at the same time use them profitably. Even if they slept at night in carefully watched backyard barracks, slaves moved about during the day alone, performing errands of various kinds. Thus urban slaves gained numerous opportunities to mingle with free blacks and with whites. In the cities, the line between slavery and freedom became increasingly indistinct.

There was a considerable market in the South for common laborers, particularly since, unlike in the North, there were few European immigrants to perform menial chores. Even the poorest whites tended to prefer working on farms to doing ordinary labor, and so masters often hired out slaves for such tasks. Slaves on contract worked in mining and lumbering (often far

| Autonomy of Urban Slaves |

from cities); but others worked on the docks and on construction sites, drove wagons, and performed other unskilled jobs in cities and towns. Slave women and children worked in the region's few textile mills. Particularly skilled workers such as blacksmiths or carpenters were also often hired out.

Indeed, white southerners generally considered slavery to be incompatible with city life, and as southern cities grew the number of slaves in them declined, relatively if not absolutely. The reasons were social rather than economic. Fearing conspiracies and insurrections, urban slaveowners sold off much of their male property to the countryside. Remaining behind in the cities was a slave population in which black women outnumbered black men. The same cities also had more white men than women—a situation that helped account for the birth of many mulattoes. Even while slavery in the cities was declining, forced segregation of urban blacks, both free and slave, from white society increased. Segregation was a means of social control intended to make up for the loosening of the discipline of slavery itself in urban areas.

Free African Americans

There were about 250,000 free African Americans in the slaveholding states by the start of the Civil War, more than half of them in Virginia and Maryland. In some cases, they were slaves who had somehow earned money with which they managed to buy their own and their families' freedom, usually by developing a skill they could market independently of their masters. It was usually urban blacks, with their greater freedom of movement and activity, who could take that route. One example was Elizabeth Keckley, a slave woman who bought freedom for herself and her son with proceeds from sewing. She later became a seamstress, personal servant, and companion to Mary Todd Lincoln in the White House. But few masters had any incentive, or inclination, to give up their slaves, so this route was open to relatively few people.

Some slaves were set free by a master who had moral qualms about slavery, or by a master's will after his death—for example, the more than 400 slaves belonging to John Randolph of Roanoke, freed in 1833. From the 1830s on, however, state laws governing slavery became more rigid. That was in part a response to the fears Nat Turner's revolt (see p. 309) created among white southerners: free blacks, removed from close supervision by whites, might generate more violence and rebellion than slaves. It was also in part because the community of free blacks in southern cities was becoming larger and, to whites, more threatening—a dangerous example to blacks still in slavery. The rise of abolitionist agitation in the North—and the fear that it would inspire slaves to rebel—also persuaded southern whites to tighten their system.

| Tightened Restrictions on Free Blacks |

The new laws made it more and more difficult, and in some cases practically impossible, for owners to set free (or "manumit") their slaves; all southern states forbade free African Americans from entering. Arkansas even forced the freed slaves living there to leave.

A few free blacks (generally those on the northern fringes of the slaveholding regions) attained wealth and prominence. Some owned slaves themselves, usually relatives whom they had bought in order to ensure their ultimate emancipation. In a few cities—New Orleans, Natchez, Charleston—free black communities managed to flourish relatively unmolested by whites and with some economic stability. Most free blacks, however, lived in abject poverty, under conditions worse than those of blacks in the North. Law or custom closed many occupations to them, forbade them to assemble without white supervision, and placed numerous other restraints on them. They were only quasi-free, and yet they had all the burdens of freedom: the necessity to support themselves, to find housing, to pay taxes. Yet great as were the hardships of freedom, blacks usually preferred them to slavery.

The Slave Trade

The transfer of slaves from one part of the South to another was one of the most important consequences of the development of the Southwest. Sometimes slaves moved to the new cotton lands in the company of their original owners, who were migrating themselves. More often, however, the transfer occurred through the medium of professional slave traders. Traders transported

THE BUSINESS OF SLAVERY The offices of slave dealers were familiar sights on the streets of pre-Civil War southern cities and towns. They provide testimony to the way in which slavery was not just a social system, but a business, deeply woven into the fabric of southern economic life. *(Library of Congress)*

slaves over long distances on trains or on river or ocean steamers. On shorter journeys, the slaves moved on foot, trudging in coffles of hundreds along dusty highways— just as their ancestors had marched to the ports in Africa **Slave Markets** from which they had embarked to America. Eventually they arrived at some central market such as Natchez, New Orleans, Mobile, or Galveston, where purchasers gathered to bid for them. At the auction, the bidders checked the slaves like livestock, watching them as they were made to walk or trot, inspecting their teeth, feeling their arms and legs, looking for signs of infirmity or age. Some traders tried to deceive buyers by blacking gray hair, oiling withered skin, and concealing physical defects in other ways. A sound young field hand would fetch a price that, during the 1840s and 1850s, varied from $500 to $1,700, depending mainly on fluctuations in the price of cotton. An attractive, sexually desirable woman might bring much more.

The domestic slave trade, essential to the growth and prosperity of the whole system, was also one of its most horrible aspects. The trade dehumanized all who were involved in it. It separated children from parents, and parents from each other. Even families kept together by scrupulous masters might be broken up in the division of the estate after the master's death. Planters might deplore the trade, but they eased their consciences by holding the traders in contempt and assigning them a low social position.

The foreign slave trade was as bad or worse. Although federal law had prohibited the importation of slaves from 1808 on, some continued to be smuggled into the United States as late as the 1850s. The **The Foreign Slave Trade** numbers can only be estimated. There were not enough such imports to satisfy all planters, and the southern commercial conventions, which met annually to consider means of making the South economically independent, began to discuss the legal reopening of the trade. "If it is right to buy slaves in Virginia and carry them to New Orleans," William L. Yancey of Alabama asked his fellow delegates at the 1858 meeting, "why is it not right to buy them in Cuba, Brazil, or Africa and carry them there?" The convention that year voted to recommend the repeal of all laws against slave imports. Within the South, only the delegates from the states of the upper South, which profited from the domestic trade, opposed the foreign competition.

Slave Resistance

Few issues have sparked as much debate among historians as the effects of slavery on the blacks themselves. (See "Where Historians Disagree," pp. 306–307) Slaveowners, and many white Americans after emancipation, liked to argue that the slaves were generally content, "happy with their lot." That may well have been true in some cases. But it is clear that the vast majority of southern blacks were not

HARRIET TUBMAN WITH ESCAPED SLAVES Harriet Tubman (c. 1820–1913) was born into slavery in Maryland. In 1849, when her master died, she escaped to Philadelphia to avoid being sold out of state. Over the next ten years, she assisted first members of her own family and then up to 300 other slaves to escape from Maryland to freedom. During the Civil War, she served alternately as a nurse and as a spy for Union forces in South Carolina. She is shown here, on the left, with some of the slaves she had helped to free. *(Smith College Museum of Art)*

content with being slaves, that they yearned for freedom even though most realized there was little they could do to secure it. Evidence for that conclusion can be found, if nowhere else, from the reaction of slaves when emancipation finally came. Virtually all reacted to freedom with joy and celebration; relatively few chose to remain in the service of the whites who had owned them before the Civil War (although most blacks, of course, remained for many years subservient to whites in one way or another).

Rather than contented acceptance, the dominant response of blacks to slavery was a complex one: a combination of adaptation and resistance. At the extremes, slavery could produce two very different reactions, each of which served as the basis for a powerful stereotype in white society. One extreme was what became known as the "Sambo"—the shuffling, grinning, head-scratching, deferential slave who acted out the role that he recognized the white world expected of him. More often than not, the "Sambo" pattern of behavior was a charade, a facade assumed in the presence of whites. The other extreme was the slave rebel—the African American who could not bring himself or herself to either acceptance or accommodation but remained forever rebellious. Actual slave

revolts were extremely rare, but the knowledge that they were possible struck terror into the hearts of white southerners everywhere. In 1800, Gabriel Prosser gathered 1,000 rebellious slaves outside Richmond; but two Africans gave the plot away, and the Virginia militia stymied the uprising before it could begin. Prosser and thirty-five others were executed. In 1822, the Charleston free black Denmark Vesey and his followers—rumored to total 9,000—made preparations for revolt; but again word leaked out, and suppression and retribution followed.

Prosser and Turner Rebellions

In 1831, Nat Turner, a slave preacher, led a band of African Americans who armed themselves with guns and axes and, on a summer night, went from house to house in Southampton County, Virginia. They killed sixty white men, women, and children before being overpowered by state and federal troops. More than a hundred blacks were executed in the aftermath. Nat Turner's was the only actual large-scale slave insurrection in the nineteenth-century South, but fear of slave conspiracies and renewed violence pervaded the section as long as slavery lasted.

For the most part, however, resistance to slavery took other, less drastic forms such as running away. A small number managed to escape to the North or to Canada, especially after sympathetic whites began organizing the so-called underground railroad to assist them in flight. But the odds against a successful escape, particularly from the Deep South, were impossibly high. The hazards of distance and the slaves' ignorance of geography were serious obstacles. So were the white "slave patrols," which stopped wandering blacks on sight throughout the South demanding to see travel permits. Without such a permit, slaves were presumed to be runaways and were taken captive. Slave patrols often employed blood-hounds to track blacks who attempted to escape through the woods. Despite all the obstacles to success, however, blacks continued to run away from their masters in large numbers. Some did so repeatedly, unde-terred by the whippings and other penalties inflicted on them when captured.

But perhaps the most important method of resistance was simply a pattern of everyday behavior by which blacks defied their masters. That whites so often con-sidered blacks to be lazy and shiftless suggests one means of resistance: refusal to work hard.

Some slaves stole from their masters or from neigh-boring whites. Some performed isolated acts of sabotage: losing or breaking tools (southern planters gradually began to buy unusually heavy hoes because so many of the lighter ones got broken) or performing tasks improperly. For the most part, blacks resisted by building into their normal patterns of behavior subtle methods of rebellion.

Slave Resistance

THE CULTURE OF SLAVERY

Resistance was only part of the slave response to slavery. Another was an elaborate process of adaptation—a process that did not imply contentment with bondage but a recognition that there was no realistic alternative. One of the ways blacks adapted was by developing their own, separate culture, one that enabled them to sustain a sense of racial pride and unity.

Language and Music

In many areas, slaves retained a language of their own, sometimes incorporating African speech patterns into English. Having arrived in America speaking many dif-ferent African languages, the first generations of slaves had as much difficulty communicating with one another as they did with white people. To overcome these bar-riers, they learned a simple, common language (known to linguists as "pidgin"). It retained some African words, but it drew primarily, if selectively, from English. And while slave language grew more sophisticated as blacks spent more time in America—and as new generations grew up never having known African tongues—some features

Pidgin

of this early pidgin survived in black speech for many generations.

Music was especially important in slave society. In some ways, it was as important to African Americans as language. Again, the African heritage was an important influence. African music relied heavily on rhythm, and was usually intended as an accompaniment to dance in America. The banjo, an instrument original to Africa, became important to slave music. But most important were voices and song. Field workers

Importance of Slave Spirituals

often used songs to pass the time in the fields; since they sang them in the presence of whites, they usually attached relatively innocuous words to them. But African Americans also created more emotionally rich and polit-ically challenging music in the relative privacy of their religious services. It was there that the tradition of the spiritual emerged in the early nineteenth century. And through the spiritual, Africans in America not only expressed their religious faith, but also lamented their bondage and expressed continuing hope for freedom. Similar sentiments surfaced throughout slave religion.

African-American Religion

A separate slave religion was not supposed to exist. Almost all African Americans were Christians by the early nineteenth century. Some had converted voluntar-ily and some after coercion by their masters and Protes-tant missionaries who evangelized among them. Masters expected their slaves to worship under the supervision of white ministers. Indeed, autonomous black churches were banned by law; and many slaves became members of the same denominations as their owners—usually Baptist or Methodist. In the 1840s and 1850s, as slavery expanded in the South, missionary efforts increased. Vast numbers of blacks became members of Protestant churches in those years.

Nevertheless, blacks throughout the South developed their own version of Christianity, at times incorporating into it such practices as voodoo or other polytheistic reli-gious traditions of Africa. Or they simply bent religion to the special circumstances of bondage. Natural leaders emerging within the slave community rose to the rank of preacher.

African-American religion was often more emotional than its white counterparts and reflected the influence of African

Slave Religion

customs and practices. Slave prayer meetings routinely involved fervent chanting, spontaneous exclamations from the congregation, and ecstatic conversion experiences. Black religion was also more joyful and affirming than that of many white denominations. And above all, black reli-gion emphasized the dream of freedom and deliverance. In their prayers and songs and sermons, black Christians talked and sang of the day when the Lord would "call us

The Slaves' Music

For African Americans living as slaves on southern plantations, there was little leisure time—and little opportunity for the kinds of cultural activities that were beginning to appeal to other groups of Americans. But slaves managed nevertheless to create a culture of their own. And among its most distinctive and pervasive features was music.

Indeed to white observers at least, nothing was more striking about slave life than the role music played within it. African Americans sang frequently, sometimes alone, even more often in groups. They sang while they worked together in the fields, as they shucked corn, slaughtered hogs, or repaired fences. They sang whenever they had social gatherings—on Sundays or on the rare other holidays from work. They sang when they gathered for chores in the evenings. They sang during their religious services. And they sang with a passion, at times even an ecstasy, that was completely unfamiliar to whites—and sometimes troubling to them.

Their songs were rarely written down and often seemed entirely spontaneous; but much slave music was really derived from African and Caribbean traditions passed on through generations and from snatches of other songs the performers had heard before and from which they improvised variations. In its emotionalism, its pulsing rhythms, and its lack of conventional formal structure, it resembled nothing its white listeners had ever heard before.

Slaves sang whether or not there were any musical instruments to accompany them, but they often created instruments for themselves out of whatever materials were at hand. "Us take pieces of sheep's rib or cow's jaw or a piece of iron, with an old kettle or a hollow gourd and some horsehair to make the drum," one former slave recalled years later. "They'd take the buffalo horn and scrape it out to make the flute." When they could, they would build banjos, an instrument that had originated in Africa. Their masters sometimes gave them violins and guitars. When the setting permitted it, African Americans danced to their music—dances very different from and much more spontaneous

than the formal steps that nineteenth-century whites generally learned. They also used music to accompany one of their other important cultural traditions: storytelling. Black music on the plantations took a number of forms. The most common was religious songs, the precursors of modern gospel music, which expressed—in terms that their white masters, who usually did not listen to the words very carefully, usually found acceptable—a faith in their eventual freedom and salvation and often spoke of Africans as a chosen people waiting for redemption. At other times, the songs would express a bitterness toward white slaveholders. The great black abolitionist Frederick Douglass remembered one:

> We raise de wheat,
> Dey gib us de corn;
> We bake de bread,
> Dey gib us de crust;
> We sif the meal,
> Dey gib us de huss;
> We peel de meat,
> Dey gib us de skin;
> And dat's de way
> Dey take us in;
> We skim de pot,
> Dey gib us de liquor,
> And say dat's good enough for nigger.
> Your butter and the fat;
> Poor nigger, you can't ever get that.

To African Americans, in other words, music was a treasured avenue of escape from the hardships of slavery. It was also a vehicle through which they could express anger, resentment, and hope. Their masters generally tolerated their slaves' music—and even valued it, both because they often enjoyed listening to it and because the more intelligent understood that without this means of emotional and spiritual release, active resistance to slavery might be more frequent.

The powerful music that emerged from slavery helped shape the lives of African Americans on the plantations. It also helped lay the foundations for music that almost all Americans later embraced: gospel, blues, jazz, rhythm and blues, rock, and rap.

THE OLD PLANTATION This painting, by an unidentified folk artist of the early nineteenth century, suggests the importance of music in the lives of plantation slaves in America. The banjo, which the black musician at right is playing, was originally an African instrument. *(Abby Aldrich Rockefeller Folk Art Museum, Colonial Williamsburg Foundation, Williamsburg, VA)*

PLANTATION RELIGION A black preacher leads his fellow slaves, as well as the family of the master, in a Sunday service in the modest plantation chapel. African-American religious services were considerably less restrained when white people were not present—one reason why blacks withdrew so quickly from white churches after the Civil War and formed their own. *(Bettmann/Corbis)*

home," "deliver us to freedom," "take us to the Promised Land." And while their white masters generally chose to interpret such language merely as the expression of hopes for life after death, many blacks themselves used the images of Christian salvation to express their own dream of freedom in the present world. Christian images, and biblical injunctions, were central to Gabriel Prosser, Denmark Vesey, Nat Turner, and others who planned or engaged in open resistance to slavery.

In cities and towns in the South, some African Americans had their own churches, where free blacks occasionally worshiped alongside slaves. In the countryside, however, slaves usually attended the same churches as their masters—sometimes a chapel on the plantation itself, sometimes a church serving a larger farm community. Seating in such churches was usually segregated. Blacks sat in the rear or in balconies. They held their own services later, often in secret, usually at night.

The Slave Family

The slave family was the other crucial institution of black culture in the South. Like religion, it suffered from certain legal restrictions—most notably the lack of legal marriage. Nevertheless, what we now call the "nuclear family" consistently emerged as the dominant kinship model among African Americans.

Such families did not always operate according to white customs. Black women generally began bearing children at younger ages than most whites, often as early as age fourteen or fifteen. Slave communities did not condemn premarital pregnancy in the way white society did, and black couples would often begin liv-

ing together before marrying. It was customary, however, for couples to marry—in a ceremony involving formal vows—soon after conceiving a child. Often, marriages occurred between slaves living on neighboring plantations. Husbands and wives sometimes visited each other with the permission of their masters, but often such visits had to be in secret, at night. Family ties were no less strong than those of whites, and many slave marriages lasted throughout the course of long lifetimes.

Slave Marriages

When marriages did not survive, it was often because of circumstances over which blacks had no control. Up to a third of all black families were broken apart by the slave trade; an average slave might expect during a lifetime to see ten or more relatives sold. And that accounted for some of the other distinctive characteristics of the black family, which adapted itself to the cruel realities of its own uncertain future.

Importance of Kinship Networks

Extended kinship networks—which grew to include not only spouses and their children, but also aunts, uncles, grandparents, even distant cousins—were strong and important and often helped compensate for the breakup of nuclear families. A slave forced suddenly to move to a new area, far from his or her family, might create fictional kinship ties and become "adopted" by a family in the new community. Even so, the impulse to maintain contact with a spouse and children remained strong long after the breakup of a family. One of the most frequent causes of flight from the plantation was a slave's desire to find a husband, wife, or child who had been sent elsewhere.

It was not only by breaking up families through sale that whites intruded on black family life. Black women, usually powerless to resist the sexual advances of their masters, often bore the children of whites—children whom the whites almost never recognized as their own and who were consigned to slavery from birth.

In addition to establishing social and cultural institutions of their own, slaves adapted themselves to slavery by forming complex relationships with their masters. However much blacks resented their lack of freedom, they often found it difficult to maintain an entirely hostile attitude toward their owners. Not only were they dependent on whites for the material means of existence—food, clothing, and shelter; they also often derived from their masters a sense of security and protection.

Paternal Nature of Slavery

There was, in short, a paternal relationship between slave and master—sometimes harsh, sometimes kindly, but almost invariably important. That paternalism, in fact, became (even if not always consciously) a vital instrument of white control. By creating a sense of mutual dependence, whites helped reduce resistance to an institution that, in essence, served only the interests of the ruling race.

CONCLUSION

While the North was creating a complex and rapidly developing commercial-industrial economy, the South was expanding its agrarian economy without making many fundamental changes in its character. Great migrations took many southern whites, and even more African-American slaves, into new agricultural areas in the Deep South, where they created a booming "cotton kingdom" that raised crops for export around the world. The cotton economy created many great fortunes, and some modest ones. It also entrenched the planter class as the dominant force within southern society—both as owners of vast numbers of slaves, and as patrons, creditors, landlords, and marketers for the large number of poor whites who lived on the edge of the planter world.

The differences between the North and the South were a result of differences in natural resources, differences in social structure, differences in climate, and differences in culture. Above all, they were the result of the existence within the South of an unfree labor system that prevented the kind of social fluidity that an industrializing society usually requires and that kept a large proportion of the southern population in debilitating bondage.

INTERACTIVE LEARNING

The *Primary Source Investigator CD-ROM* offers the following materials related to this chapter:

- Interactive maps: **Slavery and Cotton** (M11) and **Barrow Plantation** (M18).

- Documents, images, and maps related to southern society, the importance of cotton, and the "peculiar institution" of slavery. Some highlights include an image of a whipped slave, a certificate of freedom for an African American, and an African-American sailor's protection certificate.

Online Learning Center
(www.mhhe.com/brinkley12)

For quizzes, Internet resources, references to additional books and films, and more, consult this book's Online Learning Center.

FOR FURTHER REFERENCE

Peter Kolchin, *American Slavery, 1619–1877* (1993) is an excellent synthesis of the history of slavery in the United States from the settlement of Virginia through Reconstruction. Ira Berlin, *Generations of Captivity* (2003) is another fine history of slavery. James Oakes, *Slavery and Freedom* (1990) provides an overview of southern politics and society in the antebellum period. Eugene Genovese's classic study, *Roll, Jordan, Roll: The World the Slaves Made* (1974) argues that masters and slaves forged a system of mutual obligations within a fundamentally coercive social system. Genovese's *The Political Economy of Slavery* (1965) argues that slavery blocked southern economic development. James Oakes, *The Ruling Race: A History of American Slaveholders* (1982) argues that slaveowners were hardheaded businessmen and capitalists. Frederick Douglass's *Narrative of the Life of Frederick Douglass,* first published in 1845, is a classic autobiography. Elizabeth Fox-Genovese, *Within the Plantation Household* (1988) argues against the idea that black and white women shared a community of interests on southern plantations. Charles Joyner, *Down by the Riverside: A South Carolina Slave Community* (1984) is a fine study of slavery in a single community. Charles C. Bolton, *Poor Whites of the Antebellum South: Tenants and Laborers in Central North and Northeast Mississippi* (1994) is a good study of a neglected group in the southern population. Bertram Wyatt-Brown, *Southern Honor: Ethics and Behavior in the Old South* (1982) argues that concepts of honor lay at the core of southern white identity in the antebellum period. Steven Hahn, *The Roots of Southern Populism: Yeomen Farmers and the Transformation of the Georgia Upcountry, 1850–1890* (1983) argues that white farmers in upcountry regions of the antebellum South maintained economically self-sufficient communities on the periphery of the market.

GIRLS' EVENING SCHOOL (C. 1840), ANONYMOUS Schooling for women, which expanded significantly in the mid-nineteenth century, included training in domestic arts (as indicated by the sewing table at right), as well as in reading, writing, and other basic skills. *(Museum of Fine Atrs, Boston, Gift of Maxim Karolik, 53.2431. Photograph ©2007 Museum of Fine Arts, Boston)*

SIGNIFICANT EVENTS

1817 ▶ American Colonization Society founded

1821 ▶ New York constructs first penitentiary

1823 ▶ Catharine Beecher founds Hartford Female Seminary

1825 ▶ Robert Owen founds New Harmony community in Indiana

1826 ▶ James Fenimore Cooper publishes *The Last of the Mohicans*

▶ American Society for the Promotion of Temperance founded

1829 ▶ David Walker publishes *Appeal . . . to the Colored Citizens*

1830 ▶ Joseph Smith publishes the Book of Mormon

▶ American Colonization Society helps create Liberia for emigrating American slaves

1831 ▶ William Lloyd Garrison begins publishing the *Liberator*

1833 ▶ American Antislavery Society founded

1834 ▶ Anti-abolitionist mob burns abolitionist headquarters in Philadelphia

1837 ▶ Horace Mann becomes first secretary of Massachusetts Board of Education

▶ Elijah Lovejoy killed by anti-abolitionist mob in Illinois

CHAPTER 12

Antebellum Culture and Reform

The United States in the mid-nineteenth century was a rapidly changing society. The nation was growing in geographical extent, in the size and diversity of its population, and in the dimensions and complexity of its economy. Like any people faced with such rapid and fundamental alterations in their surroundings, most Americans reacted with ambiguity. On the one hand, many were excited by the new possibilities that economic growth was providing. On the other hand, many were painfully aware of the dislocations that it was creating: the challenges to traditional values and institutions, the social instability, the increasing inequality, the uncertainty about the future.

One result of these conflicting attitudes was the emergence of a broad array of movements intended to adapt society to its new conditions, to "reform" the nation. These reform efforts took many different shapes, but in general they reflected one of two basic impulses, and at times elements of both. Many of these movements rested on an optimistic faith in human nature, a belief that within every individual resided a spirit that was basically good and that society should attempt to unleash.

This assumption—which spawned in both Europe and America

Romanticism a movement known, in its artistic aspects at least, as romanticism—stood in marked contrast to traditional Protestant assumptions of original sin, which humans needed to overcome through a disciplined, virtuous life. Instead, reformers now argued, individuals should strive to give full expression to the inner spirit, should work to unleash their innate capacity to experience joy and to do good.

A second impulse, which appeared directly to contradict the first but in practice often existed alongside it, was a desire for order and **Order and Control** control. With society changing so rapidly, with traditional values and institutions under assault and often eroding, many Americans yearned above all for a restoration of stability and discipline to their nation. Often, this impulse embodied a conservative nostalgia for better, simpler times. But it also inspired forward-looking efforts to create new institutions of social control, suited to the realities of the new age.

The reforms that flowed from these two impulses came in many guises and mobilized many different groups. Reformers were far more numerous and influential in the North and Northwest than in the South, but reform activity could be found in all areas of the nation. In the course of the 1840s, however, one issue—slavery—came to overshadow all others. And one group of reformers—the abolitionists—became the most visible of all. At that point, the reform impulse, which at first had been a force that tended to unify the sections, became another wedge between the North and the South.

1840 ▸ Garrison demands admission of women into American Antislavery Society, precipitating schism

▸ Liberty Party formed

1841 ▸ Brook Farm founded in Roxbury, Massachusetts

1842 ▸ Supreme Court, in *Prigg v. Pennsylvania*, rules states do not have to enforce return of fugitive slaves

1843 ▸ Amana Community founded

1844 ▸ Mormon leader Joseph Smith killed

1845 ▸ Frederick Douglass publishes autobiography

▸ Edgar Allan Poe publishes "The Raven"

▸ First professional teachers' association formed in Massachusetts

1847 ▸ Brook Farm dissolved

▸ Mormons found Salt Lake City

1848 ▸ Women's rights convention held at Seneca Falls, New York

▸ Oneida Community founded in New York

▸ Debate over women's rights causes schism in Society of Friends (Quakers)

1850 ▸ Nathaniel Hawthorne publishes *The Scarlet Letter*

1851 ▸ Herman Melville publishes *Moby Dick*

1852 ▸ Harriet Beecher Stowe publishes *Uncle Tom's Cabin*

1854 ▸ Henry David Thoreau publishes *Walden*

1855 ▸ Walt Whitman publishes *Leaves of Grass*

THE ROMANTIC IMPULSE

"In the four quarters of the globe," wrote the English wit Sydney Smith in 1820, "who reads an American

National Cultural Aspirations

book? or goes to an American play? or looks at an American picture or statue?" The answer, he assumed, was obvious: no one. American intellectuals were painfully aware of the low regard in which Europeans held their artistic and intellectual life, and in the middle decades of the nineteenth century they continued to work for both an elevation and a liberation of their nation's culture—for the creation of an American artistic world independent of Europe, one that would express their nation's special virtues.

At the same time, however, some of the nation's cultural leaders were beginning to strive for another kind of liberation, one that would gradually come almost to overshadow their self-conscious nationalism. That impulse—which was, ironically, largely an import from Europe—was the spirit of romanticism. In literature, in philosophy, in art, even in politics and economics, American intellectuals were committing themselves to the liberation of the human spirit.

Nationalism and Romanticism in American Painting

When Sydney Smith asked in 1820 who looked at an American painting, he was expressing the almost universal belief among European artists that they—and they alone—stood at the center of the world of art. But in the United States, a great many people were, in fact, looking at American paintings in the antebellum era—and they were doing so not because the paintings introduced them to the great traditions of Europe, but because they believed Americans were creating important new artistic traditions of their own.

The most important and popular American paintings of the first half of the nineteenth century set out to evoke the wonder of the nation's landscape. Unlike their European counterparts, American painters did not favor gentle scenes of carefully cultivated countrysides. They sought instead to capture the undiluted power of nature by portraying some of the nation's wildest and most spectacular areas—to evoke what many nineteenth-century people called the "sublime," the feeling of awe and wonderment and even fear of the grandeur of nature. The first great school of American painters

Hudson River School

emerged in New York. Frederic Church, Thomas Cole, Thomas Doughty, and Asher Durand—who were, along with others, known as the Hudson River School—painted the spectacular vistas of the rugged and still largely unsettled Hudson Valley. Like Emerson and Thoreau, whom many of the painters read and admired, they considered nature—more than civilization—the best source of wisdom and spiritual fulfillment. In portraying the Hudson Valley, they seemed to announce that in America, unlike in Europe, "wild nature" still existed; and that America, therefore, was a nation of greater promise than the played-out lands of the Old World. Yet there was also a sense of nostalgia in many of the Hudson River paintings, an effort to preserve and cherish a kind of nature that many Americans feared was fast disappearing.

In later years, some of the Hudson River painters traveled further west, in search of even more profound spiritual experiences in an even more rugged and spectacular natural world. Their enormous canvases of great natural wonders—the Yosemite Valley, Yellowstone, the Rocky Mountains—touched a passionate chord among the public. Some of the most famous of their paintings—particularly the works of Albert Bierstadt and Thomas Moran—traveled around the country attracting enormous crowds.

Literature and the Quest for Liberation

American readers in the first decades of the nineteenth century were relatively indifferent to the work of their nation's own writers. The most popular novelist in America in these years was the British writer Sir Walter Scott, whose swashbuckling historical novels set in eighteenth-century England and Scotland won him an impassioned readership in both Britain and America. When Americans read books written in their own country, many were more likely to turn to the large number of "sentimental novels," written mostly by and for women, than to what would ordinarily be considered serious literature. (See "Patterns of Popular Culture," pp. 334–335 [Sentimental Novels].)

But even during the heyday of Scott in the 1820s, the effort to create a distinctively American literature—which Washington Irving and others had advanced in the first decades of the century—made considerable progress with the emergence of the first great American novelist: James Fenimore Cooper. The author of over thirty novels in the space of three decades, Cooper was known to his contemporaries as a master of adventure and suspense. What most distinguished his work, however, was its evocation of the American wilderness. Cooper had grown up in central New York, at a time when the

Cooper and the American Wilderness

edge of white settlement was not far away; and he retained throughout his life a fascination with man's relationship to nature and with the challenges (and dangers) of America's expansion westward. His most important novels were known as the "Leatherstocking Tales." Among them were *The Last of the Mohicans* (1826) and *The Deerslayer* (1841). They explored the American frontiersman's experience with Indians, pioneers, violence, and the law.

Cooper's novels were a continuation, in many ways a culmination, of the early-nineteenth-century effort to produce a truly American literature. But they also served as a link to the concerns of later intellectuals. For in the "Leatherstocking Tales" could be seen not only a celebration of the American spirit and landscape but an evocation, through the central character of Natty Bumppo, of the ideal of the independent individual with a natural inner goodness. There was also evidence of another impulse that would motivate American reform: the fear of disorder. Many of Cooper's less savory characters illustrated the vicious, grasping nature of some of the nation's western settlers and suggested a need for social discipline even in the wilderness.

TITLE PAGE FOR WHITMAN'S LEAVES OF GRASS For more than thirty years after the publication of the original *Leaves of Grass* in 1855, Walt Whitman constantly revised and expanded the collection of poems and issued numerous subsequent editions. This sample title page, with notations by Whitman indicating changes and additions he wanted made, is for the final such edition, published in 1892, the year of Whitman's death. In a public announcement he prepared to announce publication, he said that "the book *Leaves of Grass,* which he has been working on at great intervals and partially issued for the past thirty-five or forty years, is now completed. . . . Faulty as it is, he decides it is by far his special and entire self-chosen poetic utterance." *(Rare Book and Special Collections Division, Library of Congress)*

Another group of important American writers emerged on the heels of Cooper. They displayed even more clearly the grip of romanticism on the nation's intellectual life. Walt Whitman, the self-proclaimed poet of American democracy, was the son of a Long Island carpenter and lived for many years roaming from place to place, doing odd jobs. Finally, in 1855, he hired a printer and published a first volume of work: *Leaves of Grass.* His poems were an unrestrained celebration of democracy, of the liberation of the individual, and of the pleasures of the flesh as well as of the spirit. They also expressed Whitman's personal yearning for emotional and physical release and personal fulfillment—a yearning perhaps rooted in part in his own experience as a homosexual living in a society profoundly intolerant of unconventional sexuality. In his large body of poems, Whitman not only helped liberate verse from traditional, restrictive conventions but also helped express the soaring spirit of individualism that characterized his age.

The new literary concern with the unleashing of human emotions did not always produce such optimistic works, **Herman Melville** as the work of Herman Melville suggests. Born in New York in 1819, Melville ran away to sea as a youth and spent years sailing the world before returning home to become the greatest American novelist of his era. The most important of his novels was *Moby Dick,* published in 1851. His portrayal of Ahab, the powerful, driven captain of a whaling vessel, was a story of courage and of the strength of individual will; but it was also a tragedy of pride and revenge. Ahab's maniacal search for Moby Dick, a great white whale that had maimed him, suggested how the search for personal fulfillment and triumph could not only liberate but destroy. The result of Ahab's great quest was his own annihilation, reflecting Melville's conviction that the human spirit was a troubled, often self-destructive force.

Similarly bleak were the works of one of the few southern writers of the time to embrace the search for the essence of the human spirit: Edgar Allan Poe. In the course of his short and unhappy life (he died in 1849 at the age of forty), Poe produced stories and poems that were primarily sad and macabre. His first book, *Tamerlane and Other Poems* (1827), received little recognition. But later works, including his most famous poem, "The Raven" (1845), established him as a major, if controversial, literary figure. Poe evoked images of individuals rising above the narrow confines of intellect and exploring the deeper world of the spirit and the emotions. Yet that world, he seemed to say, contained much pain and horror. Other American writers were contemptuous of Poe's work and his message, but he was ultimately to have a profound effect on European poets such as Baudelaire.

Literature in the Antebellum South

Poe, however, was something of an exception in the world of southern literature. Like the North, the South experienced a literary flowering in the mid-nineteenth century, and produced writers and artists who were concerned with defining the nature of American society and of the American nation. But white southerners tended to produce very different images of what that society was and should be.

Southern novelists of the 1830s (among them Beverly Tucker, William Alexander Caruthers, and John Pendleton Kennedy), some of them writers of great talent, many of them residents of Richmond, produced historical romances or romantic eulogies of the plantation system of the upper South. In the 1840s, the southern literary capital moved to Charleston, home of the most distinguished of the region's men of letters: William Gilmore Simms. For a time, his work expressed a broad nationalism that transcended his regional background; but by the 1840s he too had become a strong defender of southern institutions—especially slavery—against the encroachments of the North. There was, he believed, a unique quality to southern life that it was the duty of intellectuals to defend.

Southern Romanticism

One group of southern writers, however, produced works that were more broadly American and less committed to a glorification of the peculiarities of southern life. These were writers from the fringes of plantation society, who depicted the world of the backwoods rural areas. Augustus B. Longstreet, Joseph G. Baldwin, Johnson J. Hooper, and others focused not on aristocratic "cavaliers," but on ordinary people and poor whites. Instead of romanticizing their subjects, they were deliberately and sometimes painfully realistic. And they seasoned their sketches with a robust, vulgar humor that was new to American literature. These southern realists established a tradition of American regional humor that was ultimately to find its most powerful voice in Mark Twain.

The Transcendentalists

One of the outstanding expressions of the romantic impulse in America came from a group of New England writers and philosophers known as the transcendentalists. Borrowing heavily from German philosophers such as Kant, Hegel, and Schelling, and from the English writers Coleridge and Carlyle, the transcendentalists embraced a theory of the individual that rested on a distinction (first suggested by Kant) between what they called "reason" and "understanding"—words they used in ways that seem unfamiliar, even strange, to modern ears. Reason, as they defined it, had little to do with rationality. It was, rather, the individual's innate capacity to grasp beauty and truth through giving full expression to the instincts and emotions; and as such, it was the highest human faculty. Understanding, the transcendentalists argued, was the use of intellect in the narrow, artificial ways imposed by society; it involved the repression of instinct and the victory of externally imposed learning. Every person's goal, therefore, should be liberation from the confines of "understanding" and the cultivation of "reason." Each individual should strive to "transcend" the limits of the intellect and allow the emotions, the "soul," to create an "original relation to the Universe."

Transcendentalist philosophy emerged first among a small group of intellectuals centered in Concord, Massachusetts. Their leader and most eloquent voice was Ralph Waldo Emerson. A Unitarian minister in his youth, Emerson left the church in 1832 to devote himself entirely to writing and teaching the elements of transcendentalism. He was a dazzling figure to his contemporaries—a lecturer whose public appearances drew rapturous crowds; a conversationalist who drew intellectuals to his Concord home almost daily. He was the most important intellectual of his age.

Ralph Waldo Emerson

Emerson produced a significant body of poetry, but he was most renowned for his essays and lectures. In "Nature" (1836), one of his best-known essays, Emerson wrote that in the quest for self-fulfillment, individuals should work for a communion with the natural world: "in the woods, we return to reason and faith. . . . Standing on the bare ground—my head bathed by the blithe air, and uplifted into infinite space,—all mean egotism vanishes. . . . I am part and particle of God." In other essays, he was even more explicit in advocating a commitment of the individual to the full exploration of inner capacities. "Nothing is at last sacred," he wrote in "Self-Reliance" (1841), perhaps his most famous essay, "but the integrity of your own mind." The quest for self-reliance, he explained, was really a search for communion with the unity of the universe, the wholeness of God, the great spiritual force that he described as the "Oversoul." Each person's innate capacity to become, through his or her private efforts, a part of this essence was perhaps the classic expression of the romantic belief in the "divinity" of the individual.

Emerson was also a committed nationalist, an ardent proponent of American cultural independence. In a famous 1837 lecture, "The American Scholar," he boasted that "Our day of dependence, our long apprenticeship to the learning of other lands, draws to a close." His belief that truth and beauty could be derived as much from instinct as from learning suggested that Americans, lacking the rich cultural heritage of European nations, could still aspire to artistic and literary greatness. Artistic and intellectual achievement need not rely on tradition and history; it could come from the instinctive creative genius of individuals. "Let the single man plant himself indomitably on his instincts and there abide," Emerson once said, "and the huge world will come round to him."

Almost as influential as Emerson was another leading Concord transcendentalist, Henry David Thoreau. Thoreau went even further than his friend Emerson in repudiating the repressive forces of society, which produced, he said, "lives of quiet desperation." Individuals should work for self-realization by resisting pressures to conform to society's expectations and responding instead to their own instincts. Thoreau's own effort to free himself—immortalized in his most famous book, *Walden* (1854)—led him to build a small cabin in the Concord woods on the edge of Walden Pond, where he lived alone for two years as simply as he could. "I went to the woods," he explained, "because I wished to live deliberately, to front only the essential facts of life, and see if I could not learn what it had to teach, and not, when I came to die, discover that I had not lived." Living simply, he believed, was a desirable alternative to the rapidly modernizing world around him—a world, he believed, that the disruptive and intrusive railroad unhappily symbolized.

Thoreau's rejection of what he considered the artificial constraints of society extended as well to his relationship with government. In 1846, he went to jail (briefly) rather than agree to pay a poll tax. He would not, he insisted, give financial support to a government that permitted the existence of slavery. In his 1849 essay "Resistance to Civil Government," he explained his refusal by claiming that the individual's personal morality had the first claim on his or her actions, that a government which required violation of that morality had no legitimate authority. The proper response was "civil disobedience," or "passive resistance"—a public refusal to obey unjust laws.

Thoreau and Civil Disobedience

The Defense of Nature

As the tributes of Emerson and Thoreau to the power of nature suggest, a small but influential group of Americans in the mid- and late nineteenth century were uneasy with the rapid economic development of their age. They feared the impact of the new capitalist enthusiasms on the integrity of the natural world. "The mountains and cataracts, which were to have made poets and painters," wrote the essayist Oliver Wendell Holmes, "have been mined for anthracite and dammed for water power."

To the transcendentalists, as well as to others, nature was not just a setting for economic activity, as many farmers, miners, and others believed; and it was not simply a body of data to be catalogued and studied, as many scientists thought. It was the source of deep, personal human inspiration—the vehicle through which individuals could best realize the truth within their own souls. Genuine spirituality, they argued, did not come from formal religion, but through communion with the natural

world. As they watched the rapid march of industrialization, and the even more rapid race to exploit natural resources for economic gain, they expressed horror at the destruction of the wilderness and began to mount a defense of preservation. "In wildness is the preservation of the world," Thoreau once wrote. Humans separated from nature, he believed, would lose a substantial part of their humanity.

In making such claims, the transcendentalists were among the first Americans to anticipate the environmental movement of the twentieth century. They had no scientific basis for their defense of the wilderness, no knowledge of modern ecology, little sense of the twentieth-century notion of the interconnectedness of species. But they did believe in, and articulate, an essential unity between humanity and nature—a spiritual unity, they believed, without which civilization would be impoverished. They looked at nature, they said, "with new eyes," and with those eyes they saw that "behind nature, throughout nature, spirit is present."

Visions of Utopia

Although transcendentalism was above all an individualistic philosophy, it helped spawn the most famous of all nineteenth-century experiments in communal living: Brook Farm, which the Boston transcendentalist George Ripley established as an experimental community in West Roxbury, Massachusetts, in 1841. There, according to Ripley, individuals would gather to create a new form of social organization, one that would permit every member of the community full opportunity for self-realization. All residents would share equally in the labor of the community so that all could share too in the leisure, for it was leisure that was the first necessity for cultivation of the self. (Ripley was one of the first Americans to attribute positive connotations to the idea of leisure; most of his contemporaries equated it with laziness and sloth.) Participation in manual labor served another purpose as well: it helped individuals bridge the gap between the world of the intellect and learning, and the world of instinct and nature. The obvious tension between the ideal of individual freedom and the demands of a communal society took their toll on Brook Farm. Increasingly, individualism gave way to a form of socialism. Many residents became disenchanted and left; when a fire destroyed the central building of the community in 1847, the experiment dissolved.

Brook Farm

Among the original residents of Brook Farm was the writer Nathaniel Hawthorne, who expressed his disillusionment with the experiment and, to some extent, with transcendentalism in a series of notable novels. In *The Blithedale Romance* (1852), he wrote scathingly of Brook Farm itself, portraying the disastrous consequences of the experiment on the individuals who submitted to

NEW HARMONY New Harmony, Indiana, was home to several Utopian movements in the early and mid-nineteenth century. The best known of them was the short-lived community experiment of the British reformer Robert Owen, who created a settlement in New Harmony for a "cooperative" society. His design for the settlement is shown here. *(Library of Congress, LC-4USZ62-55096)*

OWEN'S PROPOSED VILLAGE.
From an old print.

it and describing the great fire that destroyed the community as a kind of liberation from oppression. In other novels—most notably *The Scarlet Letter* (1850) and *The House of Seven Gables* (1851)—he wrote equally passionately about the price individuals pay for cutting themselves off from society. Egotism, he claimed (in an indirect challenge to the transcendentalist faith in the self), was the "serpent" that lay at the heart of human misery.

The failure of Brook Farm did not, however, prevent the formation of other experimental communities. Some borrowed, as Ripley had done, from the ideas of the French philosopher Charles Fourier, whose ideas of socialist communities organized as cooperative "phalanxes" received wide attention in America. Others drew from the ideas of the Scottish industrialist and philanthropist Robert Owen. Owen himself founded an experimental community in Indiana in 1825, which he named New Harmony. It was to be a "Village of Cooperation," in which every resident worked and lived in total equality. The community was an economic failure, but the vision that had inspired it continued to enchant Americans. Dozens of other "Owenite" experiments began in other locations in the following years.

New Harmony

Redefining Gender Roles

One of the principal concerns of many of the new utopian communities (and of the new social philosophies on which they rested) was the relationship between men and women. Transcendentalism and other movements of this period fostered expressions of a kind of feminism that would not gain a secure foothold in American society until the late twentieth century.

One of those most responsible for drawing issues of gender into the larger discussion of individual liberation was Margaret Fuller. A leading transcendentalist and a close associate of Emerson, she suggested the important relationship between the discovery of the "self" that was so central to antebellum reform and the questioning of gender roles: "Many women are considering within themselves what they need and what they have not," she wrote in a famous feminist work, *Woman in the Nineteenth Century* (1844). "I would have Woman lay aside all thought, such as she habitually cherishes, of being taught and led by men." Fuller herself, before her premature death in a shipwreck in 1850, lived a life far different from the domestic ideal of her time. She had intimate relationships with many men; became a great admirer of European socialists and a great champion of the Italian revolution of 1848, which she witnessed during travels there; and established herself as an intellectual leader whose power came in part from her perspective as a woman.

A redefinition of gender roles was crucial to one of the most enduring of the utopian colonies of the nineteenth century: the Oneida Community, established in 1848 in upstate New York by John Humphrey Noyes. The Oneida "Perfectionists," as residents of the community called themselves, rejected traditional notions of family and marriage. All residents, Noyes declared, were "married" to all other residents; there were to be no permanent conjugal ties. But Oneida was not, as its horrified critics often claimed, an experiment in unrestrained "free love." It was a place where the community carefully monitored sexual behavior; where women were to be protected

Redefined Gender Roles at the Oneida Community

from unwanted childbearing; in which children were raised communally, often seeing little of their own parents. The Oneidans took special pride in what they considered the liberation of their women from the demands of male "lust" and from the traditional bonds of family.

The Shakers, even more than the Oneidans, made a redefinition of traditional sexuality and gender roles central to their society. Founded by "Mother" Ann Lee in the 1770s, the society of the Shakers survived throughout the nineteenth century and into the twentieth. (A tiny remnant survives today.) But the Shakers attracted a particularly large following in the antebellum period and established more than twenty communities throughout the Northeast and Northwest in the 1840s. They derived their name from a unique religious ritual, a sort of ecstatic dance, in which members of a congregation would "shake" themselves free of sin while performing a loud chant.

The most distinctive feature of Shakerism, however, was its commitment to complete celibacy—which meant, of course, that no one could be born to Shakerism; all Shakers had to choose the faith voluntarily. Shaker communities attracted about 6,000 members in

The Shakers

the 1840s, more women than men; and members lived in conditions in which contact between men and women was very limited. Shakers openly endorsed the idea of sexual equality; they even embraced the idea of a God who was not clearly male or female. Indeed, within the Shaker society as a whole, it was women who exercised the most power. Mother Ann Lee was succeeded as leader of the movement by Mother Lucy Wright. Shakerism, one observer wrote in the 1840s, was a refuge from the "perversions of marriage" and "the gross abuses which drag it down."

The Shakers were not, however, motivated only by a desire to escape the burdens of traditional gender roles. They were trying as well to create a society separated and protected from the chaos and disorder that they believed had come to characterize American life as a whole. They were less interested in personal freedom than in social discipline. And in that, they were like some other dissenting religious sects and utopian communities of their time. Another example was the Amana Community, founded by German immigrants in 1843; its members settled in Iowa in 1855. The Amanas attempted to realize Christian ideals by creating an ordered, socialist society.

The Mormons

Among the most important efforts to create a new and more ordered society within the old was that of the

Joseph Smith

Church of Jesus Christ of Latter Day Saints—the Mormons. Mormonism began in upstate New York as a result of the

efforts of Joseph Smith, a young, energetic, but economically unsuccessful man, who had spent most of his twenty-four years moving restlessly through New England and the Northeast. Then, in 1830, he published a remarkable document—the Book of Mormon, named for the ancient prophet who he claimed had written it. It was, he said, a translation of a set of golden tablets he had found in the hills of New York, revealed to him by an angel of God. The Book of Mormon told the story of an ancient and successful civilization in America, peopled by one of the lost tribes of Israel who had found their way to the New World centuries before Columbus. Its members waited patiently for the appearance of the Messiah, and they were rewarded when Jesus actually came to America after his resurrection. Subsequent generations, however, had strayed from the path of righteousness that Jesus had laid out for them. Ultimately, their civilization collapsed, and God punished the sinful by making their skin dark. These darkened people, Smith believed, were the descendants of the American Indians, although the modern tribes had no memory of their origins. But while the ancient Hebrew kingdom in America had ultimately vanished, Smith believed, its history as a righteous society could serve as a model for a new holy community in the United States.

In 1831, gathering a small group of believers around him, Smith began searching for a sanctuary for his new community of "saints," an effort that would continue unhappily for more than twenty years. Time and again, the Mormons attempted to establish their "New Jerusalem." Time and again, they met with persecution from surrounding communities suspicious of their radical religious doctrines—which included polygamy (the right of men to take several wives), a rigid form of social organization, and particularly damaging to their image, an intense secrecy, which gave rise to wild rumors among their critics of conspiracy and depravity.

Driven from their original settlements in Independence, Missouri, and Kirtland, Ohio, the Mormons moved on to the new town of Nauvoo, Illinois, which in the early 1840s became an imposing and economically successful community. In 1844, however, Joseph Smith was arrested, charged with treason (for allegedly conspiring against the government to win foreign support for a new Mormon colony in the Southwest), and imprisoned in Carthage, Illinois.

There an angry mob attacked the jail, forced Smith from his cell, and shot and killed him. The Mormons now abandoned Nauvoo and, under the leadership of Smith's successor, Brigham Young, traveled

Establishment of Salt Lake City

across the desert—a society of 12,000 people, in one of the largest single group migrations in American history—and established a new community in Utah, the present Salt Lake City. There, at last, the Mormons were able to create a permanent settlement.

JOSEPH SMITH REVIEWING HIS TROOPS After being driven from earlier homes in Missouri, Mormons under the leadership of the religion's founder Joseph Smith created a model city in Nauvoo, Illinois—where they also organized an army of over 4,000 men. This painting by the Mormon artist Carl Christensen portrays Smith, aboard the white horse in front, reviewing a vast array of troops—with the pastoral and productive landscape of Nauvoo arrayed in the background. The existence of this large private army aroused great alarm in surrounding non-Mormon communities and contributed to the clashes that led both to the murder of Smith himself and the expulsion of the Mormons from Illinois. (*Joseph Mustering the Nauvoo Legion by C.C.A. Christensen. Courtesy Brigham Young University Museum of Art. All Rights Reserved.*)

Like other experiments in social organization of the era, Mormonism reflected a belief in human perfectibility. God had once been a man, the church taught, and thus every man or woman could aspire to become—as Joseph Smith had become—a god. But unlike other new communities, the Mormons did not embrace the doctrine of individual liberty. Instead, they created a highly organized, centrally directed, almost militarized social structure, a refuge against the disorder and uncertainty of the secular world. They placed particular emphasis on the structure of the family. Mormon religious rituals even included a process by which men and women went through a baptism ceremony in the name of a deceased ancestor; as a result, they believed, they would be reunited with those ancestors in heaven. The intense Mormon interest in genealogy, which continues today, is a reflection of this belief in the possibility of reuniting present generations with those of the past.

The original Mormons were, for the most part, men and women who felt displaced in their rapidly changing society—economically marginal people left behind by the material growth and social progress of their era. In the new religion, they found genuine faith. In the society it created, they found security and order.

REMAKING SOCIETY

The simultaneous efforts to liberate the individual and impose order on a changing world also helped create a wide range of new movements to remake society—movements in which, to a striking degree, women formed the real rank and file and often the leadership as well. By the 1830s, such movements had taken the form of organized reform societies. "In no country in the world," Tocqueville had observed, "has the principle of association been more successfully used, or more unsparingly applied to a multitude of different objects, than in America."

The new organizations did indeed work on behalf of a wide range of goals: temperance; education; peace; the

New Reform
Movements

care of the poor, the handicapped, and the mentally ill; the treatment of criminals; the rights of women; and many more. Few eras in American history have witnessed as wide a range of reform efforts. And few eras have exposed more clearly the simultaneous attraction of Americans to the ideas of personal liberty and social order.

Revivalism, Morality, and Order

The philosophy of reform arose from two distinct sources. One was the optimistic vision of those who, like the transcendentalists, rejected Calvinist doctrines and preached the divinity of the individual. These included not only Emerson, Thoreau, and their followers, but a much larger group of Americans who embraced the doctrines of Unitarianism and Universalism and absorbed European romanticism.

The second, and in many respects more important, source was Protestant revivalism—the movement that had begun with the Second Great Awakening early in the century and had, by the 1820s, evolved into a powerful force for social reform. Although the New Light revivalists were theologically far removed from the transcendentalists and Unitarians, they had come to share the optimistic belief that every individual was capable of salvation. According to Charles Grandison Finney, an evangelistic Presbyterian minister who became the most influential revival leader of the 1820s and 1830s, traditional Calvinist doctrines of predestination and individual human helplessness were both obsolete and destructive. Each person, he preached, contained within himself or herself the capacity to experience spiritual rebirth and achieve salvation. A revival of faith need not depend on a miracle from God; it could be created by individual effort.

Finney enjoyed particular success in upstate New

Revivalism in the
Burned-Over District

York, where he helped launch a series of passionate revivals in towns along the Erie Canal—a region so prone to religious awakenings that it was known as the "burned-over district." It was no coincidence that the new revivalism should prove so powerful there, for this region of New York was experiencing—largely as a result of the construction of the canal—a major economic transformation. And with that transformation had come changes in the social fabric so profound that many men and women felt baffled and disoriented. (It was in roughly this same area of New York that Joseph Smith first organized the Mormon church.)

In Rochester, New York, the site of his greatest suc-

Finney's Doctrine of
Personal Regeneration

cess, Finney staged a series of emotionally wrenching religious meetings that aroused a large segment of the community. He had particular success in

mobilizing women, on whom he tended to concentrate his efforts—both because women found the liberating message of revivalism particularly appealing and because, Finney discovered, they provided him with access to their male relatives. Gradually, he developed a large following among the relatively prosperous citizens of the region, who were enjoying the economic benefits of the new commercial growth but who were also uneasy about some of the social changes accompanying it (among them the introduction into their community of a new, undisciplined pool of transient laborers). For them, revivalism became not only a means of personal salvation but a mandate for the reform (and control) of the larger society. Finney's revivalism became a call for a crusade against personal immorality. "The church," he maintained, "must take right ground on the subject of Temperance, the Moral Reform, and all the subjects of practical morality which come up for decision from time to time."

The Temperance Crusade

Evangelical Protestantism added major strength to one of the most influential reform movements of the era: the crusade against drunkenness. No social vice, argued some reformers (including, for example, many of Finney's converts in cities such as Rochester), was more responsible for crime, disorder, and poverty than the excessive use of alcohol. Women, who were particularly active in the temperance movement, claimed that alcoholism placed a special burden on wives: men spent money on alcohol that their families needed for basic necessities, and drunken husbands often abused their wives and children.

In fact, alcoholism was an even more serious problem in antebellum America than it has been in the twentieth and twenty-first centuries. The supply of alcohol was growing rapidly, particularly in the West; farmers there grew more grain than they could sell in the still-limited markets in this prerailroad era, so they distilled much of it into whiskey. But in the East, too, commercial distilleries and private stills were widespread. The appetite for alcohol was growing as well: in isolated western areas, where drinking provided a social pastime in small towns and helped ease the loneliness and isolation on farms; in pubs and saloons in eastern cities, where drinking was the principal leisure activity for many workers. The average male in the 1830s drank nearly three times as much alcohol as the average person does today. And as that figure suggests, many people drank habitually and excessively, with bitter consequences for themselves and others. Among the many supporters of the temperance movement were people who saw it as a way to overcome their own problems with alcoholism.

Although advocates of temperance had been active since the late eighteenth century, the new reformers

THE DRUNKARD'S PROGRESS This 1846 lithograph by Nathaniel Currier shows what temperance advocates argued was the inevitable consequence of alcohol consumption. Beginning with an apparently innocent "glass with a friend," the young man rises step by step to the summit of drunken revelry, then declines to desperation and suicide while his abandoned wife and child grieve. *(Library of Congress)*

American Society for the Promotion of Temperance

gave the movement an energy and influence it had never previously known. In 1826, the American Society for the Promotion of Temperance emerged as a coordinating agency among various groups; it attempted to use many of the techniques of revivalism in preaching abstinence. Then, in 1840, six reformed alcoholics in Baltimore organized the Washington Temperance Society and began to draw large crowds—in which workers (many of them attempting to overcome their own alcoholism) were heavily represented—to hear their impassioned and intriguing confessions of past sins. By then, temperance advocates had grown dramatically in numbers; more than a million people had signed a formal pledge to forgo hard liquor.

As the movement gained in strength, it also became divided in purpose. Some temperance advocates now urged that abstinence include not only liquor but beer and wine; not everyone agreed. Some began to demand state legislation to restrict the sale and consumption of alcohol (Maine passed such a law in 1851); others insisted that temperance must rely on the conscience of the individual. Whatever their disagreements by promoting abstinence, reformers were attempting to promote the moral self-improvement of individuals. They were also trying to impose discipline on society.

The latter impulse was particularly clear in the battle over prohibition laws, which pitted established Protestants against new Catholic immigrants, to many of whom drinking was an important

Cultural Divisions over Alcohol

social ritual and an integral part of the life of their community. The arrival of the immigrants was profoundly disturbing to established residents of many communities, and the restriction of alcohol seemed to them a way to curb the disorder they believed the new population was creating.

Health Fads and Phrenology

For some Americans, the search for individual and social perfection led to an interest in new theories of health and knowledge. Threats to public health were critical to the sense of insecurity that underlay many reform movements, especially after the terrible cholera epidemics of the 1830s and 1840s. Cholera is a severe bacterial infection of the intestines, usually a result of consuming contaminated food or water. In the nineteenth century, long before the discovery of antibiotics, fewer than half of those who contracted the disease normally survived. Thousands of people died of cholera during its occasional outbreaks, and in certain cities—New Orleans in 1833 and

"SPOUT BATH AT WARM SPRINGS" Among the many fads and theories about human health to gain currency in the 1830s and 1840s, one of the most popular was the idea that bathing in warm, sulphurous water was restorative. Visitors to "warm springs" all over the United States and Europe "took the baths," drank the foul-smelling water, and sometimes stayed for weeks as part of a combination vacation and "cure." This 1837 drawing is by Sophie Dupont, a visitor to a popular spa. She wrote to a friend that the water, "notwithstanding its odour of half spoiled eggs and its warmth, is not very nauseous to the taste." *(Courtesy of Hagley Museum and Library)*

PHRENOLOGY This lithograph illustrates some of the ideas of the popular "science" of phrenology in the 1830s. Drawing from the concepts of the German writer Johann Gaspar Spurzheim, American phrenologists promoted the belief that a person's character and talents could be understood by the formation of his or her skull; that the brain was, in fact, a cluster of autonomous organs, each controlling some aspect of human thought or behavior. In this diagram, the areas of the brain that supposedly control "identity," "acquisitiveness," "secretiveness," "marvelousness," and "hope" are clearly identified. The theory has no scientific basis. *(Library of Congress)*

St. Louis in 1849—the effects were truly catastrophic. Nearly a quarter of the population of New Orleans died in the 1833 epidemic. Many municipalities, pressured by reformers, established city health boards to try to find solutions to the problems of epidemics. But the medical profession of the time, unaware of the nature of bacterial infections, had no answers; and the boards therefore found little to do.

Instead, many Americans turned to nonscientific theories for improving health. Affluent men and, especially, women flocked to health spas for the celebrated "water cure," which purported to improve health through immersing people in hot or cold baths or wrapping them in wet sheets. Although the water cure in fact delivered few of the benefits its promoters promised, it did have some therapeutic value; some forms of hydrotherapy are still in use today. Other people adopted new dietary theories. Sylvester Graham, a Connecticut-born Presbyterian minister and committed reformer, won many followers with his prescriptions for eating fruits, vegetables, and bread made from coarsely ground flour—a prescription not unlike some dietary theories today—instead of meat. (The "Graham cracker" is made from a kind of flour named for him.) Graham accompanied his dietary prescriptions with moral warnings about the evils of excess and luxury.

Perhaps strangest of all to modern sensibilities was the widespread belief in the new "science" of phrenology, which | Phrenology | appeared first in Germany and became popular in the United States beginning in the 1830s through the efforts of Orson and Lorenzo Fowler, publishers of the *Phrenology Almanac*. Phrenologists argued that the shape of an individual's skull was an important indicator of his or her character and intelligence. They made elaborate measurements of bumps and indentations to calculate the size (and, they claimed, the strength) of different parts of the brain, each of which, they argued, controlled a specific kind of intelligence or behavior. For a time, phrenology seemed to many Americans an important vehicle for improving society. It provided a way of measuring an individual's fitness for various positions in life and seemed to promise an end to the arbitrary process by which people matched their talents to occupations and responsibilities. The theory is now universally believed to have no scientific value at all.

Medical Science

In an age of rapid technological and scientific advances, the science of medicine sometimes seemed to lag behind. In part, that was because of the greater difficulty of experimentation in medicine, which required human subjects as compared to other areas of science and technology that relied on inanimate objects. In part, it was because of the character of the medical profession, which—in the absence of any significant regulation—attracted many poorly educated people and many quacks, in addition to trained physicians. Efforts to regulate the profession were beaten back in the 1830s and 1840s by those who considered the licensing of physicians to be a form of undemocratic monopoly. The prestige of the profession, therefore, remained low, and it was for many people a career of last resort.

The biggest problem facing American medicine, however, was the absence of basic knowledge about disease. The great medical achievement of the eighteenth century—the development of a vaccination against smallpox by Edward Jenner—came from no broad theory of infection, but from a brilliant adaptation of folk practices among country people. The development of anesthetics came not from medical doctors at first, but from a New England dentist, William Morton, who was looking for ways to help his patients endure the extraction of teeth. Beginning in 1844, Morton began experimenting with using sulphuric ether. John Warren, a Boston surgeon, soon began using ether to sedate surgical patients. Even these advances met with stiff resistance from traditional physicians, some of whom continued to believe that all medical knowledge derived from timeless truths and ancient scholars and who mistrusted innovation and experimentation. Others rejected scientific advances because they became convinced of the power of new, unorthodox, and untested "medical" techniques popularized by entrepreneurs, many of them charlatans.

In the absence of any broad acceptance of scientific methods and experimental practice in medicine, it was very difficult for even the most talented doctors to make progress in treating disease. Even so, halting progress toward the discovery of the germ theory did occur in antebellum America. In 1843, the Boston essayist, poet, and physician Oliver Wendell Holmes published his findings from a study of large numbers of cases of "puerperal fever" (septicemia in children) and concluded that the

Discovery of Contagion

disease could be transmitted from one person to another. This discovery of contagion met with a storm of criticism, but was later vindicated by the clinical success of the Hungarian physician Ignaz Semmelweis, who noticed that the infection seemed to be spread by medical students who had been working with corpses. Once he began requiring students to wash their hands and disinfect their instruments, the infections virtually disappeared.

Reforming Education

One of the outstanding reform movements of the mid-nineteenth century was the effort to produce a system of universal public education. As of 1830, no state yet had such a system, although some states—such as Massachusetts—had supported a limited version for many years. In the 1830s, however, interest in public education grew rapidly. It was a reflection of the new belief in the innate capacity of every person and of society's obligation to tap that capacity; but it was a reflection, too, of the desire to expose students to stable social values as a way to resist instability.

The greatest of the educational reformers was Horace Mann, the first secretary of the Massachusetts Board of Education, which was established in 1837. To Mann and his followers, education was the only way to "counterwork this tendency to the domination of

Horace Mann's Reforms

capital and the servility of labor." It was also the only way to protect democracy, for an educated electorate was essential to the workings of a free political system. Mann reorganized the Massachusetts school system, lengthened the academic year (to six months), doubled teachers' salaries (although he did nothing to eliminate the large disparities between the salaries of male and female teachers), enriched the curriculum, and introduced new methods of professional training for teachers.

Other states experienced similar expansion and development. They built new schools, created teachers' colleges, and offered vast new groups of chil-

Rapid Growth of Public Education

dren access to education. Henry Barnard helped produce a new educational system in Connecticut and Rhode Island. Pennsylvania passed a law in 1835 appropriating state funds for the support of universal education. Governor William Seward of New York extended public support of schools throughout the state in the early 1840s. By the 1850s, the principle of tax-supported elementary schools had been accepted in all the states; and all, despite continuing opposition from certain groups, were making at least a start toward putting the principle into practice.

Yet the quality of the new education continued to vary widely. In some places—Massachusetts, for example, where Mann established the first American state-supported teachers' college in 1839 and where the first professional association of teachers was created in 1845—educators were usually capable men and women, often highly trained, and with an emerging sense of themselves as career professionals. In other areas, however, teachers were often barely literate, and limited funding for education restricted opportunities severely. In the newly settled regions of the West, where the white population was highly dispersed, many children had no access to schools at all. In the South, the entire black population was barred from formal education (although approximately 10 percent of the slaves managed to achieve literacy anyway), and only about a third of all white children of school age actually enrolled in schools in 1860. In the North the percentage was 72 percent, but even there, many students attended classes only briefly and casually.

The interest in education was visible too in the growing movement to educate American Indians in the antebellum period. Some reformers held racist assumptions about the unredeemability of nonwhite peoples; but even many who accepted that idea about African Americans continued to believe that Indians could be "civilized" if only they could be taught the ways of the white world. Efforts by missionaries and others to educate Native Americans and encourage them to assimilate were particularly prominent in such areas of the Far West as Oregon, where substantial numbers of whites were beginning to settle in the 1840s but where conflicts with the natives had not yet become acute. Nevertheless, the great majority of Native Americans remained outside the reach of educational reform, either by choice or by circumstance or both.

Despite limitations and inequities, the achievements of the school reformers were impressive by any standard. By the beginning of the Civil War, the United States had one of the highest literacy rates of any nation of the world: 94 percent of the population of the North and 83 percent of the white population of the South (58 percent of the total southern population).

Achievements of Educational Reform

The conflicting impulses that underlay the movement for school reform were visible in some of the different educational institutions that emerged. In New England, for example, the transcendentalist Bronson Alcott established a controversial experimental school in Concord that reflected his strong belief in the importance of complete self-realization. He urged children to learn from their own inner wisdom, not from the imposition of values by the larger society. Children were to teach themselves, rather than rely on teachers.

A similar emphasis on the potential of the individual sparked the creation of new institutions to help the handicapped, institutions that formed part of a great network of charitable activities known as the Benevolent Empire. Among them was the Perkins School for the Blind in Boston, the first such school in America. Nothing better exemplified the romantic impulse of the era than the belief of those who founded Perkins that even society's supposedly least-favored

The Benevolent Empire

members—the blind and otherwise handicapped—could be helped to discover inner strength and wisdom.

More typical of educational reform, however, were efforts to use schools to impose a set of social values on children—the values that reformers believed were appropriate for their new, industrializing society. These values included thrift, order, discipline, punctuality, and respect for authority. Horace Mann, for example, spoke frequently of the role of public schools in extending democracy and expanding individual opportunity. But he spoke, too, of their role in creating social order. "The unrestrained passions of men are not only homicidal, but suicidal," he said, suggesting a philosophy very different from that of Alcott and other transcendentalists, who emphasized instinct and emotion. "Train up a child in the way he should go, and when he is old he will not depart from it."

Rehabilitation

Similar impulses helped create another powerful movement of reform: the creation of "asylums" (as they now began to be called) for criminals and for the mentally ill. On the one hand, in advocating prison and hospital reform, Americans were reacting to one of society's most glaring ills. Criminals of all kinds, debtors unable to pay their debts, the mentally ill, even senile paupers—all were crowded together indiscriminately into prisons and jails, which in some cases were literally holes in the ground; one jail in Connecticut was an abandoned mine shaft. Beginning in the 1820s, numerous states replaced these antiquated facilities with new "penitentiaries" and mental institutions designed to provide a proper environment for inmates. New York built the first penitentiary at Auburn in 1821. In Massachusetts, the reformer Dorothea Dix began a national movement for new methods of treating the mentally ill. Imprisonment of debtors and paupers gradually disappeared, as did such traditional practices as legal public hangings.

The Asylum Movement

But the creation of "asylums" for social deviants was not simply an effort to curb the abuses of the old system. It was also an attempt to reform and rehabilitate the inmates. New forms of rigid prison discipline were designed to rid criminals of the "laxness" that had presumably led them astray. Solitary confinement and the imposition of silence on work crews (both adopted in Pennsylvania and New York in the 1820s) were meant to give prisoners opportunities to meditate on their wrongdoings. (Hence the term "penitentiary": a place for individuals to cultivate penitence.) Some reformers argued that the discipline of the asylum could serve as a model for other potentially disordered environments—for example, factories and schools. But penitentiaries and many mental hospitals soon fell victim to overcrowding, and the

Prison Reform

PERKINS SCHOOL FOR THE BLIND The Perkins School in Boston was the first school for the blind in the United States and was committed to the idea that the blind could be connected effectively to the world through the development of new skills, such as reading through the relatively new technique of Braille. This woodcut shows Perkins's main building in the mid-1850s, by which time the school was already over twenty years old. It continues to educate the blind today. *(Perkins School for the Blind History Museum)*

original reform ideal gradually faded. Many prisons ultimately degenerated into little more than warehouses for criminals, with scant emphasis on rehabilitation. The idea, in its early stages, had been more optimistic.

The "asylum" movement was not, however, restricted only to criminals and people otherwise considered "unfit." The idea that a properly structured institution could prevent moral failure or rescue individuals from failure and despair helped spawn the creation of new orphanages designed as educational institutions. Such institutions, reformers believed, would provide an environment in which children who might otherwise be drawn into criminality could be trained to become useful citizens. Similar institutions emerged to provide homes for "friendless" women—women without families or homes, but otherwise respectable, for whom the institutions might provide an opportunity to build a new life. (Such homes were in part an effort to prevent such women from turning to prostitution.) There were also new facilities for the poor: almshouses and workhouses, which created closely supervised environments for those who had failed to work their way up in society. Such an environment, reformers believed, would train them to live more productive lives.

The Indian Reservation

Some of these same beliefs underlay the emergence in the 1840s and 1850s of a new "reform" approach to the problems of Native Americans: the idea of the reservation. For several decades, the dominant thrust of U.S. policy toward the Indians in areas of white settlement had been relocation. The principal motive behind relocation had always been a simple one: getting the tribes out of the way of white civilization. But among some whites there had also been another, if secondary, intent: to move the Indians to a place where they would be protected from whites and allowed to develop to a point where assimilation might be possible. Even Andrew Jackson, whose animus toward Indians was legendary, once described the removals as part of the nation's "moral duty . . . to protect and if possible to preserve and perpetuate the scattered remnants of the Indian race."

It was a small step from the idea of relocation to the idea of the reservation: the idea of creating an enclosed region in which Indians would live in isolation from white society. Again, the reservations served white economic purposes above all—moving Native Americans out of good lands that white settlers wanted. But they were also supposed to serve a reform purpose. Just as prisons, asylums, and orphanages would provide society with an opportunity to train and uplift misfits and unfortunates within white society, so the reservations might provide a way to undertake what one official called "the great work of regenerating the Indian race." Native Americans on reservations, reformers argued, would learn the ways of civilization in a protected setting.

The Rise of Feminism

The reform ferment of the antebellum period had a particular meaning for American women. They played central roles in a wide range of reform movements and a particularly important role in the movements on behalf of temperance and the abolition of slavery. In the process, they expressed their awareness of the problems that women themselves faced in a male-dominated society. The result was the creation of the first important American feminist movement, one that laid the groundwork for more than a century of agitation for women's rights.

Women in the 1830s and 1840s suffered not only all the traditional restrictions imposed on members of their sex by society, but a new set of barriers that had emerged from the doctrine of "separate spheres" and the transformation of the family. Many women who began to involve themselves in reform movements in the 1820s and 1830s came to look on such restrictions with rising resentment. Some began to defy them. Sarah and Angelina Grimké, sisters born in South Carolina who had become active and outspoken abolitionists, ignored attacks by men who claimed that their activities were inappropriate for their sex. "Men and women were CREATED EQUAL," they argued. "They are both moral and accountable beings, and whatever is right for man to do, is right for women to do." Other reformers—Catharine Beecher, Harriet Beecher Stowe (her sister), Lucretia Mott, Elizabeth Cady Stanton, and Dorothea Dix—also chafing at the restrictions

Reform Movements and the Rise of Feminism

placed on them by men, similarly pressed at the boundaries of "acceptable" female behavior.

Finally, in 1840, the patience of several women snapped. A group of American female delegates arrived at a world antislavery convention in London, only to be turned away by the men who controlled the proceedings. Angered at the rejection, several of the delegates—notably Lucretia Mott and Elizabeth Cady Stanton—became convinced that their first duty as reformers should now be to elevate the status of women. Over the next several years, Mott, Stanton, Susan B. Anthony, and others began drawing pointed parallels between the plight of women and the plight of slaves; and in 1848, they organized a convention in Seneca Falls, New York, to discuss the question of women's rights. Out of the meeting emerged a "Declaration of Sentiments and Resolutions" (patterned on the Declaration of Independence), which stated that "all men and women are created equal," that women no less than men have certain inalienable rights. Their most prominent demand was for the right to vote, thus launching a movement for woman suffrage that would continue until 1920. But the document was in many ways more important for its rejection of the whole notion that men and women should be assigned separate "spheres" in society.

Seneca Falls

It should not be surprising, perhaps, that many of the women involved in these feminist efforts were Quakers. Quakerism had long embraced the ideal of sexual equality and had tolerated, indeed encouraged, the emergence of women as preachers and community leaders. Women taught to expect the absence of gender-based restrictions in their own communities naturally resented the restrictions they encountered when they moved outside them. Quakers had also been among the leaders of the antislavery movement, and Quaker women played a leading role within those efforts.

Not all Quakers went so far as to advocate full sexual equality in American society; but enough Quaker women coalesced around such demands to cause a schism in the yearly meeting of the Society of Friends in Genesee, New York, in 1848. That dissident faction formed the core of the group that organized the Seneca Falls convention. Of the women who drafted the Declaration of Sentiments there, all but Elizabeth Cady Stanton were Quakers.

Progress toward feminist goals was limited in the antebellum years, but certain individual women did manage to break the social barriers to advancement. Elizabeth Blackwell, born in England, gained acceptance and fame as a physician. Her sister-in-law Antoinette Brown Blackwell became the first ordained woman minister in the United States; and another sister-in-law, Lucy Stone, took the revolutionary step of retaining her maiden name after marriage (as did the abolitionist Angelina Grimké). Stone became a successful and influential lecturer on women's rights. Emma Willard, founder of the Troy

---

7

FREDERICK DOUGLASS, AMY POST, CATHARINE STEBBINS, and ELIZABETH C. STANTON, and was unanimously adopted, as follows :

DECLARATION OF SENTIMENTS.

When, in the course of human events, it becomes necessary for one portion of the family of man to assume among the people of the earth a position different from that which they have hitherto occupied, but one to which the laws of nature and of nature's God entitle them, a decent respect to the opinions of mankind requires that they should declare the causes that impel them to such a course.

THE "DECLARATION OF SENTIMENTS" Frederick Douglass joined female abolitionists in signing the famous "Declaration of Sentiments" that emerged out of the Women's Rights Convention at Seneca Falls, New York, in 1848—one of the founding documents of American feminism. This introduction to the declaration makes clear how closely it was modeled on the 1776 Declaration of Independence. *(National Park Service, U.S. Department of the Interior)*

Female Seminary in 1821, and Catharine Beecher, who founded the Hartford Female Seminary in 1823, worked on behalf of women's education. Some women expressed

Limited Progress for Women

their feminist sentiments even in their choice of costume—by wearing a distinctive style of dress (introduced in the 1850s) that combined a short skirt with full length pantalettes—an outfit that allowed freedom of movement without loss of modesty. Introduced by the famous actress Fanny Kemble, it came to be called the "bloomer" costume, after one of its advocates, Amelia Bloomer. (It provoked so much controversy that feminists finally abandoned it, convinced that the furor was drawing attention away from their more important demands.) Yet there was an irony in this rise of interest in the rights of women. Feminists benefited greatly from their association with other reform movements, most notably abolitionism; but they also suffered from them. For the demands of women were usually assigned—even by some women themselves—a secondary position to what many considered the far greater issue of the rights of slaves.

THE CRUSADE AGAINST SLAVERY

The antislavery movement was not new to the mid-nineteenth century. There had been efforts even before the Revolution to limit, and even eliminate, the institution. Those efforts had helped remove slavery from most of the North by the end of the eighteenth century. There were powerful antislavery movements in England and Europe that cried out forcefully against human bondage. But American antislavery sentiment remained relatively muted in the first decades after independence. Not until 1830 did it begin to gather the force that would ultimately enable it to overshadow virtually all other efforts at social reform.

Early Opposition to Slavery

In the early years of the nineteenth century, those who opposed slavery were, for the most part, a calm and genteel lot, expressing moral disapproval but engaging in few overt activities. To the extent that there was an organized antislavery movement, it centered on the concept of colonization—the effort to encourage the resettlement of African Americans in

American Colonization Society

Africa or the Caribbean. In 1817, a group of prominent white Virginians organized the American Colonization Society (ACS), which worked carefully to challenge slavery without challenging property rights or southern sensibilities. The ACS proposed a gradual manumission (or freeing) of slaves, with masters receiving compensation through funds raised by private charity or appropriated by state legislatures. The Society would then transport liberated slaves out of the country and help them to establish a new society of their own elsewhere.

The ACS was not without impact. It received some funding from private donors, some from Congress, some from the legislatures of Virginia and Maryland. And it arranged the shipment of several groups of African Americans out of the country, some of them to the west coast of Africa where in 1830 they established the nation of Liberia (which became an independent republic in 1846—its capital, Monrovia, was named for the American president who had presided over the initial settlement).

But the ACS was in the end a negligible force. Neither private nor public funding was nearly enough to carry out the vast projects its supporters envisioned. In the space of a decade, they managed to "colonize" fewer slaves than were born in the United States in a month. No

Failure of Colonization

amount of funding, in fact, would have been enough; there were far too many black men and women in America in the nineteenth century to be transported to Africa by any conceivable program. And in any case, the ACS met resistance from African Americans themselves, many of whom were now three or more generations removed from Africa and had no wish to move to a land of which they knew almost nothing. (The Massachusetts free black Paul Cuffe had met similar resistance from members of his race in the early 1800s when he proposed a colonization scheme of his own.)

By 1830, in other words, the early antislavery movement was rapidly losing strength. Colonization was proving not to be a viable method of attacking the institution, particularly since the cotton boom in the Deep South was increasing the commitment of planters to their "peculiar" labor system. Those opposed to slavery had reached what appeared to be a dead end.

Garrison and Abolitionism

It was at this crucial juncture, with the antislavery movement seemingly on the verge of collapse, that a new figure emerged to transform it into a dramatically different phenomenon. He was William Lloyd Garrison. Born in Massachusetts in 1805, Garrison was an assistant in the 1820s to the New Jersey Quaker Benjamin Lundy, who published the leading antislavery newspaper of the time—the *Genius of Universal Emancipation*—in Baltimore. Garrison shared Lundy's abhorrence of slavery, but he soon grew impatient with his employer's moderate tone and mild proposals for

Garrison and the *Liberator*

reform. In 1831, therefore, he returned to Boston to found his own weekly newspaper, the *Liberator.*

Garrison's simple philosophy was genuinely revolutionary. Opponents of slavery, he said, should view the institution from the point of view of the black man, not the white slaveowner. They should not, as earlier reformers had done, talk about the evil influence of slavery on white society; they should talk about the damage the system did to blacks. And they should, therefore, reject "gradualism" and demand the immediate, unconditional, universal abolition of slavery. Garrison spoke with particular scorn about the advocates of colonization. They were not emancipationists, he argued; on the contrary, their real aim was to strengthen slavery by ridding the country of those African Americans who were already free. The true aim of foes of slavery, he insisted, must be to extend to African Americans all the rights of American citizenship. As startling as the drastic nature of his proposals was the relentless, uncompromising tone with which he promoted them. "I am aware," he wrote in the very first issue of the *Liberator,* "that many object to the severity of my language; but is there not cause for severity? I will be as harsh as truth, and as uncompromising as justice. . . . I am in earnest—I will not equivocate—I will not excuse—I will not retreat a single inch—AND I WILL BE HEARD."

Garrison soon attracted a large group of followers throughout the North, enough to enable him to found the New England Antislavery Society in 1832 and a year later,

| American Antislavery Society |

after a convention in Philadelphia, the American Antislavery Society. Membership in the new organizations mushroomed. By 1835, there were more than 400 chapters of the societies; by 1838, there were 1,350 chapters, with more than 250,000 members. Antislavery sentiment was developing a strength and assertiveness greater than at any point in the nation's history.

This success was in part a result of the similarity between abolitionism and other reform movements of the era. Like reformers committed to other causes, abolitionists were calling for an unleashing of the individual human spirit, the elimination of artificial social barriers to fulfillment. Who, after all, was more in need of assistance in realizing individual potential than enslaved men and women?

Black Abolitionists

Abolitionism had a particular appeal to the free blacks of the North, who in 1850 numbered about 250,000, mostly concentrated in cities. They lived in conditions of poverty and oppression often worse than those of their slave counterparts in the South. An English traveler who had visited both sections of the country wrote in 1854 that he was "utterly at a loss to imagine the source of that prejudice which subsists against [African Americans] in the Northern states, a prejudice unknown in the South, where the relations between the Africans and the European [white American] are so much more intimate." This confirmed an earlier observation by Tocqueville that "the prejudice which repels the Negroes seems to increase in proportion as they are emancipated." Northern blacks were often victimized by mob violence; they had virtually no access to education; they could vote in only a few states; and they were barred from all but the most menial of occupations. Most worked either as domestic servants or as sailors in the American merchant marine, and their wages were such that they lived, for the most part, in squalor. Some were kidnapped by whites and forced back into slavery.

FUGITIVE SLAVE LAW CONVENTION Abolitionists gathered in Cazenovia, New York, in August 1850 to consider how to respond to the law recently passed by Congress requiring northern states to return fugitive slaves to their owners. Frederick Douglass is seated just to the left of the table in this photograph of some of the participants. The gathering was unusual among abolitionist gatherings in including substantial numbers of African Americans. *(Madison County Historical Society, Oneida, NY)*

For all their problems, however, northern blacks were aware of, and fiercely proud of, their freedom. And they remained acutely sensitive to the plight of those members

Free Blacks'
Commitment
to Abolition

of their race who remained in bondage, aware that their own position in society would remain precarious as long as slavery existed. Many in the 1830s came to support Garrison, to subscribe to his newspaper, and to sell subscriptions to it in their own communities. Indeed, the majority of the *Liberator*'s early subscribers were free blacks.

There were also important African-American leaders who expressed the aspirations of their race. One of the most militant was David Walker, a free black from Boston, who in 1829 published a harsh pamphlet: *Walker's Appeal . . . to the Colored Citizens*. In it he declared: "America is more our country than it is the whites'—we have enriched it with our blood and tears." He warned: "The whites want slaves, and want us for their slaves, but some of them will curse the day they ever saw us." Slaves should, he declared, cut their masters' throats, should "kill, or be killed!"

Most black critics of slavery, however, were less violent in their rhetoric. One of them was Sojourner Truth, a freed black who after spending several years involved in a strange religious cult in upstate New York, emerged as a powerful and eloquent spokeswoman for the abolition of slavery. The greatest African-American abolitionist of all—and one of the most electrifying orators of his time, black or white—was Frederick Douglass.

Frederick Douglass

Born a slave in Maryland, Douglass escaped to Massachusetts in 1838, became an outspoken leader of antislavery sentiment, and spent two years lecturing in England, where members of that country's vigorous antislavery movement lionized him. On his return to the United States in 1847, Douglass purchased his freedom from his Maryland owner and founded an antislavery newspaper, the *North Star*, in Rochester, New York. He achieved wide renown as well for his autobiography, *Narrative of the Life of Frederick Douglass* (1845), in which he presented a damning picture of slavery. Douglass demanded for African Americans not only freedom but full social and economic equality. Black abolitionists had been active for years before Douglass emerged as a leader of their cause; they had held their first national convention in 1830. But with Douglass's leadership, they became a more influential force; and they began, too, to forge alliances with white antislavery leaders such as Garrison.

Anti-Abolitionism

Abolitionism was a powerful force, but it provoked a powerful opposition as well. Almost all white southerners, of course, looked on the movement with fear and contempt. But so too did many northern whites. Indeed,

even in the North, abolitionists were never more than a small, dissenting minority.

To its critics, the abolitionist crusade was a dangerous and frightening threat to the existing social system. Some whites (including many substantial businessmen) warned that it would produce a destructive war between the sections. Others feared that it might lead to a great influx of free blacks into the North. The strident, outspoken movement seemed to many northern whites a sign of the disorienting social changes their society was experiencing, yet another threat to stability and order.

The result was an escalating wave of violence directed against abolitionists in the 1830s. When Prudence Crandall attempted to admit several African-American girls to her private school in Connecticut, local citizens had her arrested, threw filth into her well, and forced her to close down the school. A mob in Philadelphia attacked the abolitionist headquarters, the "Temple of Liberty," in 1834, burned it to the ground, and began a bloody race riot. Another mob seized Garrison on the streets of Boston in 1835 and threatened to hang him. Authorities saved him

Violent Reprisals

FREDERICK DOUGLASS Frederick Douglass, an escaped slave and active abolitionist, was one of the great orators of his age, widely admired among antislavery groups in the United States and Great Britain. So central did he become in the imaginations of antislavery men and women that he inspired tributes such as the "Fugitive's Song" published in Boston in 1845. *(Bettmann/Corbis)*

The Abolition of Slavery

The United States abolished slavery through the Thirteenth Amendment to the Constitution in 1865, in the aftermath of a great Civil War. But the effort to abolish slavery did not begin or end in North America. Emancipation in the United States was part of a worldwide antislavery movement that had begun in the late eighteenth century and continued through the end of the nineteenth.

The end of slavery, like the end of monarchies and aristocracies, was one of the ideals of the Enlightenment, which inspired new concepts of individual freedom and political equality. As Enlightenment ideas spread throughout the western world in the seventeenth and eighteenth centuries, introducing the idea of human rights and individual liberty to the concept of civilization, people on both sides of the Atlantic began to examine slavery anew and to ask whether it was compatible with these new ideas. Some Enlightenment thinkers, including some of the founders of the American Republic, believed that freedom was appropriate for white people, but not for people of color. But others came to believe that all human beings had an equal claim to liberty, and their views became the basis for an escalating series of antislavery movements.

Opponents of slavery first targeted the slave trade—the vast commerce in human beings that had grown up in the seventeenth and eighteenth centuries and had come to involve large parts of Europe, Africa, the Caribbean, and North and South America. In the aftermath of the revolutions in America, France, and Haiti in the late eighteenth and early nineteenth centuries, the attack on the slave trade quickly gained momentum. Its central figure was the English reformer William Wilberforce, who spent years attacking Britain's connection with the slave trade. He argued against it on moral and religious grounds, and eventually, after the Haitian revolution, he argued as well that the continuation of slavery would create more slave revolts. In 1807, he persuaded Parliament to pass a law ending the slave trade within the entire British empire. The British example—when combined with heavy political, economic, and even military pressure from London—persuaded many other nations to make the international slave trade illegal as well: the United States in 1808, France in 1814, Holland in 1817, and Spain in 1845. Trading in slaves continued within countries and colonies where slavery remained legal (including the United States), and some illegal slave trading continued throughout the Atlantic world. But the sale of slaves steadily declined after 1807. The last known shipment of slaves across the Atlantic—from Africa to Cuba—occurred in 1867.

Ending the slave trade was a great deal easier than ending slavery itself, in which many people had major investments and on which much agriculture, commerce, and industry depended. But pressure to abolish slavery grew steadily throughout the nineteenth century, with Wilberforce once more helping to lead the international outcry against the institution. In Haiti, the slave revolts that began in 1791 eventually abolished not only slavery but also French rule. In some parts of South America, slavery came to an end with the overthrow of Spanish rule in the 1820s. Simon Bolivar, the great leader of Latin American independence, considered abolishing slavery an important part of his mission. He freed those slaves who joined his armies, and he insisted on constitutional prohibitions of slavery in several of the constitutions he helped frame. In 1833, the British parliament passed a law abolishing slavery throughout the British empire and compensated slaveowners for freeing their slaves. France abolished slavery in its empire, after years of agitation from abolitionists within France, in 1848. In the Caribbean, Spain followed Britain in slowly eliminating slavery from its colonies. Puerto Rico abolished slavery in 1873 and Cuba became the last colony in the Caribbean to end slavery, in 1886, in the face of increasing slave resistance and the declining profitability of slave-based plantations. Brazil was the last nation in the Americas to end the system, in 1888. The Brazilian military began to turn against slavery after the valiant participation of slaves in Brazil's war with Paraguay in the late 1860s; eventually educated Brazilian civilians began to oppose the system too, arguing that it obstructed economic and social progress.

In the United States, the power of world opinion—and the example of Wilberforce's movement in England—became an important source of the abolitionist movement as it gained strength in the 1820s and 1830s. American abolitionism, in turn, helped reinforce the movements abroad. Frederick Douglass, the former slave turned abolitionist, became a major figure in the international antislavery movement and was a much-admired and much-sought after speaker in England and Europe in the 1840s and 1850s. No other nation paid such a terrible price for abolishing slavery as did the United States during its Civil War, but American emancipation was nevertheless a part of a worldwide movement toward ending legalized human bondage.

"AM I NOT A MAN AND A BROTHER" This bronze medallion commemorates the victory of British antislavery activists in extinguishing slavery from throughout the British empire in 1834. It also records the close links between their movement and the American abolitionist movement led by William Lloyd Garrison. The image on this medallion of a man in chains became a popular one in American antislavery circles in the following years. *(The Art Archive)*

Sentimental Novels

"America is now wholly given over to a damned mob of scribbling women," Nathaniel Hawthorne complained in 1855, "and I should have no chance of

"A SAD STORY" This nineteenth-century engraving shows a reader gazing sadly and wistfully away from a popular sentimental novel of the time. The magazine that published this picture wrote a disapproving story to accompany it, which began: "The young girl whose tender heart is so powerfully stirred with imaginative sorrow by the reading of some fictitious tale of distress might in our judgment have been provided by wise parents with a more wholesome form of entertainment." *(Culver Pictures, Inc.)*

success while the public taste is occupied with their trash." Hawthorne was one of the leading novelists of his time; and what he was complaining about was the most popular form of fiction in mid-nineteenth-century America—not his own dark and serious works, but the "sentimental novel," a genre of literature written and read mostly by middle-class women.

In an age when affluent women occupied primarily domestic roles, and in which finding a favorable marriage was the most important thing many women could do to secure or improve their lots in life, the sentimental novel gave voice to both female hopes and female anxieties. The heroines in such books were almost always beautiful, and often vaguely helpless—requiring special attention from and protection by men, and using their looks and charms to get it. The plots of sentimental novels were usually filled with character-improving problems and domestic trials, but most of them ended with the heroine securely and happily married. They were phenomenally successful, as Hawthorne lamented. Many of them sold over 100,000 copies each—far more than almost any other books of the time—and the more celebrated of such novels were the subject of rapt discussion

among middle-class women when they gathered for social occasions.

Sentimental heroines were not only beautiful. They were also endowed with specifically female qualities—"all the virtues," one novelist wrote, "that are founded in the sensibility of the heart: Pity, the attribute of angels, and friendship, the balm of life, delight to dwell in the female breast." Women were highly sensitive creatures, the sentimental writers believed, incapable of disguising their feelings, and subject to such emotional expressions as fainting, mysterious illnesses, trances, and, of course, tears—things rarely expected of men. But they were also capable of a kind of nurturing love and natural sincerity that was hard to find in the predominantly male public world. In Susan Warner's *The Wide, Wide World* (1850), for example, the heroine, a young girl named Ellen Montgomery, finds herself suddenly thrust into the "wide, wide world" of male competition after her father loses his fortune. She is unable to adapt to it, but she is saved in the end when she is taken in by wealthy relatives, who will undoubtedly prepare her for a successful marriage. They restore to her the security and comfort to which she had been born and without which she seemed unable to thrive.

Sentimental novels created idealized images of conventional female

---

from death only by locking him in jail. Elijah Lovejoy, the editor of an abolitionist newspaper in Alton, Illinois, was a repeated victim of mob violence. Three times angry whites invaded his offices and smashed his presses. Three times Lovejoy installed new machines and began publishing again. When a mob attacked his office a fourth time, late in 1837, he tried to defend his press. The attackers set fire to the building and, as Lovejoy fled, shot and killed him.

That so many men and women continued to embrace abolitionism in the face of such vicious opposition from within their own communities suggests much about the nature of the movement. Abolitionists were not people who made their political commitments lightly or casually. They were strong-willed, passionate crusaders, displaying enormous courage and moral strength, and displaying, too, at times a level of fervor that many of their con-

temporaries (and some later historians) found disturbing. Abolitionists were widely denounced, even by some who shared their aversion to slavery, as wild-eyed fanatics bent on social revolution. The anti-abolitionist mobs, in other words, were only the most violent expression of a sentiment that many other white Americans shared.

Abolitionism Divided

By the mid-1830s, the abolitionist crusade had become impossible to ignore. It had also begun to experience serious internal strains and divisions. One reason was the violence of the anti-abolitionists, which persuaded some members of the movement that a more moderate approach was necessary. Another reason was the growing radicalism of William Lloyd Garrison, who success. In doing so, they performed something of the same function that romance novels of the twentieth century perform today (although without the overt sexuality that is so central to modern romances). They accepted uncritically the popular assumptions about women's special needs and desires, and they offered stirring tales of how women satisfied them. But sentimental novels did not stop with romanticized images of female fulfillment through protection and marriage. They hinted as well at the increasing role of women in movements of social and moral reform. Many such books portrayed women dealing with problems of drunkenness, poverty, irreligion, and prostitution—and using their highly developed female sensibilities to help other women escape from their troubles. Women were particularly suitable for such reform work, the writers implied, because they were specially gifted at helping and nurturing others.

The most famous sentimental novelist of her day was Harriet Beecher Stowe. Most of her books—*The Minister's Wooing, My Wife and I, We and Our Neighbors,* and others—portrayed the travails and ultimate triumphs of women as they became wives, mothers, and hostesses. But Stowe was and remains best known for her 1852

antislavery novel *Uncle Tom's Cabin,* one of the most influential books ever published in America. As a story about slavery, and about an aging black man—Uncle Tom—who is unfailingly submissive to his white masters, it is in many

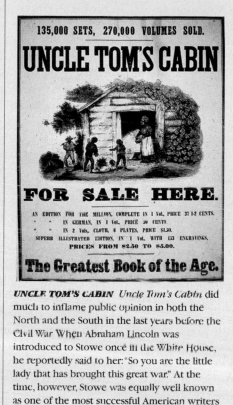

UNCLE TOM'S CABIN *Uncle Tom's Cabin* did much to inflame public opinion in both the North and the South in the last years before the Civil War. When Abraham Lincoln was introduced to Stowe once in the White House, he reportedly said to her: "So you are the little lady that has brought this great war." At the time, however, Stowe was equally well known as one of the most successful American writers of sentimental novels. *(Bettmann/Corbis)*

ways very different from her other novels. But *Uncle Tom's Cabin* is a sentimental novel, too. Stowe's critique of slavery is based on her belief in the importance of domestic values and family security. Slavery's violation of those values, and its denial of that security, is what made it so abhorrent to her. The simple, decent Uncle Tom faces many of the same dilemmas that the simple, decent female heroines of other sentimental novels encounter in their struggles to find security and tranquility in their lives.

Women were emerging from their domestic sphere in at least one other important way in the mid-nineteenth century. They were becoming consumers of the expanding products of America's industrializing economy. The female characters in sentimental novels, therefore, searched not just for love, security, and social justice. They also searched for luxury, and for the pleasure of buying some favored item. Susan Warner illustrated this aspect of the culture of the sentimental novel—and the desires of the women who read them—in *The Wide, Wide World,* in her description of the young Ellen Montgomery in an elegant bookstore, buying a Bible: "Such beautiful Bibles she had never seen; she pored in ecstasy over their varieties of type and binding, and was very evidently in love with them all."

shocked even many of his own allies (including Frederick Douglass) by attacking not only slavery but the government itself. The Constitution, he said, was "a covenant with death and an agreement with hell." The nation's churches, he claimed, were bulwarks of slavery. In 1840, finally, Garrison precipitated a formal division within the American Antislavery Society by insisting that women, who had always been central to the organization's work, be permitted to participate in the movement on terms of full equality. He continued after 1840 to arouse controversy with new and even more radical stands: an extreme pacifism that rejected even defensive wars; opposition to all forms of coercion—not just slavery but prisons and asylums; and finally, in 1843, a call for northern disunion from the South. The nation could, he suggested, purge itself of the sin of slavery by expelling the slave states from the Union.

From 1840 on, therefore, abolitionism moved in many channels and spoke with many different voices. The Garrisonians remained influential, with their uncompromising moral stance. Others operated in more moderate ways, arguing that abolition could be accomplished only as the result of a long, patient, peaceful struggle—"immediate abolition gradually accomplished," as they called it. At first, such moderates depended on "moral suasion." They would appeal to the conscience of the slaveholders and convince them that their institution was sinful. When that produced no results, they turned to political action, seeking to induce the northern states and the federal government to aid the cause wherever possible. They joined the Garrisonians in helping runaway slaves find refuge in the North or in Canada through the so-called underground railroad (although their efforts were never as

The *Amistad* Case highly organized as the term suggests). They helped fund the legal battle over the Spanish slave vessel, *Amistad*. Africans destined for slavery in Cuba had seized the ship from its crew in 1839 and tried to return it to Africa. But the U.S. navy had seized the ship and held the Africans as pirates. But with abolitionist support, legal efforts to declare the Africans free (because the international slave trade had been illegal in the United States since 1808) finally reached the Supreme Court, where the antislavery position was argued by former president John Quincy Adams. The court declared the Africans free in 1841 and antislavery groups funded their passage back to Africa. Later, after the Supreme Court (in *Prigg* v. *Pennsylvania*, 1842) ruled that states need not aid in enforcing the 1793 law requiring the return of fugitive slaves to their owners, abolitionists secured the passage of "personal liberty laws" in several northern states. These laws forbade state officials to assist in the capture and return of runaways. Above all, the antislavery societies petitioned Congress to abolish slavery in places where the federal government had jurisdiction—in the territories and in the District of Columbia—and to prohibit the interstate slave trade. But political abolitionism had severe limits. Few members of the movement believed that Congress could constitutionally interfere with a "domestic" institution such as slavery within the individual states themselves.

Although the abolitionists engaged in pressure politics, they never actually formed a political party. Antislavery sentiment underlay the formation in 1840 of the Liberty Party, which offered the Kentucky antislavery leader James G. Birney as its presidential candidate. But this party, and its successors, never campaigned for outright abolition (an illustration of the important fact that "antislavery" and "abolitionism" were not always the same thing). They stood instead for "free soil," for keeping slavery out of the territories. Some free-soilers were concerned about the welfare of African Americans; others cared nothing about the slaves but simply wanted to keep the West a country for whites. Garrison dismissed free-soilism as "white-manism." But the free-soil position would ultimately do what abolitionism never could accomplish: attract the support of large numbers, even a majority, of the white population of the North.

The frustrations of political abolitionism drove some critics of slavery to embrace more drastic measures. A few began to advocate violence; it was a group of prominent abolitionists in New England, for example, who funneled money and arms to John Brown for his bloody uprisings in Kansas and Virginia (see pp. 357, 362). Others attempted to arouse widespread public anger through propaganda. Abolitionist descriptions of slavery—for example, Theodore Dwight Weld and Angelina Grimké's *American Slavery as It Is: Testimony of a Thousand Witnesses* (1839)—presented what the authors claimed were careful, factual pictures of slavery, but what were in fact highly polemical, often wildly distorted images.

The most powerful document of abolitionist propaganda, however, was a work of fiction: Harriet Beecher Stowe's *Uncle Tom's Cabin*. It appeared first, in 1851–1852, as a serial in an antislavery weekly. Then, in 1852, it was published as a book. Harriet Beecher Stowe It rocked the nation, selling more than 300,000 copies within a year of publication and later issued again and again to become one of the most remarkable best-sellers in American history.

Stowe's novel emerged not just out of abolitionist politics, but also out of a popular tradition of sentimental novels written by, and largely for, women (see "Patterns of Popular Culture," pp. 334–335). Stowe combined the emotional conventions of the sentimental novel with the political ideas of the abolition movement, and to sensational effect. Her novel, by embedding the antislavery message within a familiar and popular literary form, succeeded in bringing the message of abolitionism to an enormous new audience—not only those who read the book but also those who watched dramatizations of its story by countless theater companies throughout the nation. The novel's emotional portrayal of good, kindly blacks victimized by a cruel system; of the loyal, trusting Uncle Tom; of the vicious overseer Simon Legree (described as a New Englander so as to prevent the book from seeming to be an attack on southern whites); of the escape of the beautiful Eliza; of the heart-rending death of Little Eva—all became a part of American popular legend. Reviled throughout the South, Stowe became a hero to many in the North. And in both regions, her novel helped to inflame sectional tensions to a new level of passion. Few books in American history have had so great an impact on the course of public events.

Even divided, therefore, abolitionism remained a powerful influence on the life of the nation. Only a relatively small number of people before Abolitionism's Enduring Influence the Civil War ever accepted the abolitionist position that slavery must be entirely eliminated in a single stroke. But the crusade that Garrison had launched, and that thousands of committed men and women kept alive for three decades, was a constant, visible reminder of how deeply the institution of slavery was dividing America.

CONCLUSION

The rapidly changing society of antebellum America produced a remarkable upsurge of cultural nationalism and reform. Writers, artists, intellectuals, and others drew heavily from new European notions of personal liberation—a set of ideas often known as romanticism. But they also strove to create a truly American culture, unbeholden to European models. The literary and artistic life of the nation expressed the rising interest in personal liberation—in giving individuals the freedom to explore their own souls and to find in nature a full expression of their divinity. It also called attention to some of the nation's glaring social problems.

Reformers, too, made use of the romantic belief in the divinity of the individual. They flocked to religious revivals, worked on behalf of such "moral" reforms as temperance, supported education, and stirred the beginnings of feminism. Above all, in the North, they rallied against slavery. Out of this growing antislavery movement emerged a new and powerful phenomenon: abolitionism, which rejected moderate reform and insisted on nothing less than immediate emancipation of the slaves. The abolitionist crusade galvanized much of the North. It also contributed greatly to the growing schism between North and South.

INTERACTIVE LEARNING

The *Primary Source Investigator CD-ROM* offers the following materials related to this chapter:

- Interactive map: U.S. Elections (M7).

- Documents, images, and maps related to culture and reform in the antebellum era, including excerpts from abolitionist newspapers *The North Star* and the *Liberator,* house plans from a utopian community, and a letter from Ralph Waldo Emerson to Walt Whitman praising Whitman's *Leaves of Grass.*

Online Learning Center (www.mhhe.com/brinkley12)

For quizzes, Internet resources, references to additional books and films, and more, consult this book's Online Learning Center.

FOR FURTHER REFERENCE

Steven Mintz, *Moralists and Moralizers: America's Pre-Civil War Reformers* (1995) and Ronald G. Walters, *American Reformers, 1815–1860* (1978) are good overviews. David Reynolds, *Walt Whitman's America* (1995) is both a cultural biography of Whitman and an evocation of the society Whitman celebrated. Leo Marx, *The Machine in the Garden* (1964) is an influential study of the tension between technological progress and the veneration of nature in the era of early industrialization. Nancy F. Cott, *The Bonds of Womanhood: "Woman's Sphere" in New England, 1780–1835* (1977) argues that nineteenth-century feminism emerged from the separation of home and work in the early nineteenth century. Klaus J. Hansen, *Mormonism and the American Experience* (1981) examines the emergence of the most important new religion in nineteenth-century America. Ellen C. Dubois, *Feminism and Suffrage: The Emergence of an Independent Women's Movement in America, 1848–1869* (1978) examines the origins of the suffrage movement. David Brion Davis, *The Problem of Slavery in the Age of Revolution, 1770–1823* (1975) is an influential study of the rise of antislavery sentiment in the western world. James Brewer Stewart, *Holy Warriors* (1976) is a good summary of the trajectory of abolitionism from the American Revolution through the emancipation. Ronald G. Walters, *The Antislavery Appeal: American Abolitionists After 1830* (1976) emphasizes the religious motivations of antebellum abolitionism.

"BLEEDING KANSAS" The battle over the fate of slavery in Kansas was one of the most turbulent events of the 1850s. This 1855 poster invites antislavery forces to a meeting to protest the actions of the "bogus" pro-slavery territorial legislature, which had passed laws that, among other things, made it illegal to speak or write against slavery. "Squatter sovereignty" was another term for "popular sovereignty," the doctrine that gave residents of a prospective state the power to decide the fate of slavery there. (*Bettmann/Corbis*)

SIGNIFICANT EVENTS

1818 ▶ United States and Great Britain sign treaty sharing rights to Oregon country

1822 ▶ Mexico wins independence from Spain

▶ Stephen F. Austin establishes first legal American settlement in Texas

1824 ▶ Mexico passes colonization law to attract American settlers to Texas

1826 ▶ American settlers in Texas revolt unsuccessfully against Mexican rule

1830 ▶ Mexican government bars further American immigration into Texas

1833 ▶ Mexico drops Texas immigration ban

1836 ▶ Texas declares independence from Mexico

▶ Battle of San Jacinto in Texas revolution

1844 ▶ James K. Polk elected president

1845 ▶ Texas admitted to Union

1846 ▶ Oregon boundary dispute settled

▶ United States declares war on Mexico

▶ Wilmot Proviso introduced in Congress

1848 ▶ Treaty of Guadalupe Hidalgo settles Mexican War

▶ Antislavery Free-Soil Party formed

▶ Zachary Taylor elected president

▶ Gold discovered in Sacramento Valley, California, sparking gold rush

CHAPTER 13

The Impending Crisis

$\mathcal{U}$ntil the 1840s, the tensions between the North and the South remained relatively contained. Had no new sectional controversies arisen, the United States might have avoided a civil war and the two sections might have resolved their differences peaceably over time. But new controversies did arise, all of them centered on slavery.

From the North came the increasingly powerful abolitionist movement, which rejected compromise and conciliation and attempted, with great success, to make the elimination of slavery a moral issue that would not be subject to compromise. As abolitionist sentiment spread through the North, it helped strengthen as well the opposition to other critics of slavery who had no such deep moral commitment to the cause.

From the South came an increasingly belligerent defense of slavery, responding directly to the absolutism of the abolitionist position with an absolutist position of its own. Slavery, its proponents argued, was not a necessary evil, as many southerners had once argued, but a positive good—the best possible system for white southerners, who needed a labor force, and the best possible system as well for black southerners, whom the defenders of slavery insisted needed the paternalistic supervision of white masters.

But it was the West that brought these differences to a head most forcefully. Ironically, the vigorous nationalism that was in some ways helping to keep the United States together was also producing a desire for territorial expansion that would tear the nation apart. As the nation annexed extensive new lands—Texas, the Southwest territories, California, Oregon country, and others—the question began to arise: What would be the status of slavery in the

Territorial Growth

territories? The Missouri Compromise, which had drawn a line across the Louisiana Purchase and had proclaimed that all the territories south of the line would permit slavery and all those north of it would not, failed to provide an acceptable basis for compromise as passions on both side of the issue intensified and as white settlement spread beyond the boundaries of the Louisiana Purchase. Two new compromises—one in 1850 and another in 1854—failed to contain the conflict. The result was a dangerous and persistent crisis that produced such bitterness, such anger, and such despair on both sides that it could no longer be contained. By the time of the election of Abraham Lincoln to the presidency in 1860, the nation was beginning to break apart and the momentum toward civil war becoming almost impossible to reverse.

1850 ▶ Compromise of 1850 enacted

▶ Taylor dies

▶ Millard Fillmore succeeds Taylor as president

▶ California admitted to Union

1852 ▶ Franklin Pierce elected president

▶ *The Pro-Slavery Argument* published

▶ Harriet Beecher Stowe publishes *Uncle Tom's Cabin*

1853 ▶ Gadsden Purchase

1854 ▶ Kansas-Nebraska Act passed

▶ Republican Party formed

1855–1856 ▶ Violence breaks out in "Bleeding Kansas"

1856 ▶ Preston Brooks canes Charles Sumner

▶ James Buchanan elected president

1857 ▶ George Fitzhugh publishes *Cannibals All*

▶ Supreme Court hands down *Dred Scott* decision

1858 ▶ Pro-slavery Lecompton constitution defeated by popular referendum in Kansas

▶ Lincoln and Douglas debate

1859 ▶ John Brown raids Harpers Ferry

1860 ▶ Democratic Party splits

▶ Lincoln elected president

▶ Process of secession begins

LOOKING WESTWARD

The United States acquired more than a million square miles of new territory in the 1840s—the greatest wave of expansion since the Louisiana Purchase nearly forty years before. By the end of the decade, the nation possessed all the territory of the present-day United States except Alaska, Hawaii, and a few relatively small areas acquired later through border adjustments. Many factors accounted for this great new wave of expansion, the most important of which were the hopes and ambitions of the many thousands of Americans who moved into or invested in these new territories. Advocates of expansion justified their goals with a carefully articulated set of ideas—an ideology known as "Manifest Destiny," which itself became one of the factors driving white Americans to look to the West.

Manifest Destiny

Manifest Destiny reflected both the burgeoning pride that characterized American nationalism in the mid-nineteenth century and the idealistic vision of social perfection that fueled so much of the reform energy of the time. It rested on the idea that America was destined—by God and by history—to expand its boundaries over a vast area, an area that included, but was not necessarily restricted to, the continent of North America. American expansion was not selfish, its advocates insisted; it was an altruistic attempt to extend American liberty to new realms. John L. O'Sullivan, the influential Democratic editor who gave the movement its name, wrote in 1845 that the American claim to new territory

> . . . is by the right of our manifest destiny to overspread and to possess the whole of the continent which Providence has given us for the development of the great experiment of liberty and federative self government entrusted to us.

Manifest Destiny represented more than pride in the nation's political system. Running throughout many of the arguments for expansion was an explicitly racial justification. Throughout the 1840s, many Americans defended the idea of westward expansion by citing the superiority of the "American race"—white people of northern European origins. The peoples of the territories into which American civilization was destined to spread, these advocates of

Racial Justification

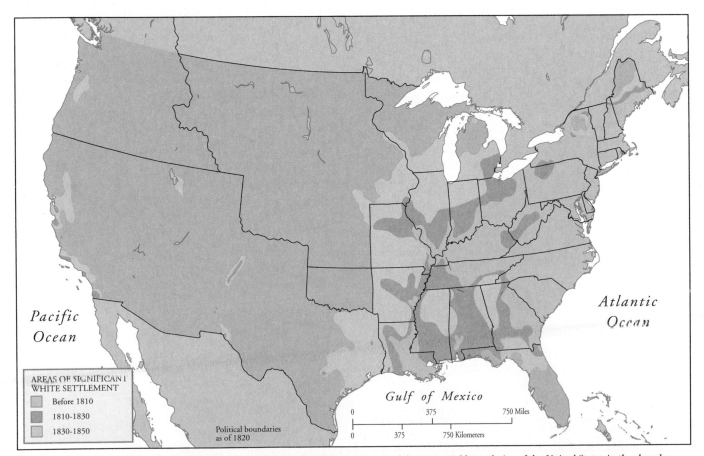

EXPANDING SETTLEMENT, 1810-1850 This map shows the dramatic expansion of the territorial boundaries of the United States in the decades after the Louisiana Purchase. By 1850, the nation had reached its present boundaries (with the exception of Alaska and Hawaii, which it acquired later). Much of this acquisition occurred in the 1840s. ◆ *What events contributed to the annexation of new land to the United States in those years?*

Manifest Destiny argued, could not be absorbed into the republican system. The Indians, the Mexicans, and others in the western regions were racially unfit to be part of an "American" community. Westward expansion was, therefore, a movement to spread both a political system and a racially defined society.

By the 1840s, the idea of Manifest Destiny had spread throughout the nation, publicized by the new "penny press" (inexpensive newspapers aimed at a mass audience), and fanned by the rhetoric of nationalist politicians. Advocates of Manifest Destiny disagreed, however, about how far and by what means the nation should expand. Some had relatively limited territorial goals; others envisioned a vast new "empire of liberty" that would include Canada, Mexico, Caribbean and Pacific islands, and ultimately, a few dreamed, much of the rest of the world. Some believed America should use force to achieve its expansionist goals, while others felt that the nation should expand peacefully or not at all.

Not everyone embraced the idea of Manifest Destiny. Henry Clay and other prominent
Opposition to Further Expansion
politicians feared, correctly as it turned out, that territorial expansion would reopen the painful controversy over slavery and threaten the stability of the Union. But their voices were barely audible over the clamor of enthusiasm for expansion in the 1840s, which began with the issues of Texas and Oregon.

THE LONE STAR FLAG Almost from the moment Texas won its independence from Mexico in 1836, it sought admission to the United States as a state. Controversies over the status of slavery in the territories prevented its admission until 1845, and so for nine years it was an independent republic. The tattered banner pictured here was one of the republic's original flags. *(Frank Lerner, from Showers-Brown Collection, Star of the Republic Museum)*

Americans in Texas

The United States had once claimed Texas—which until the 1830s was part of the Republic of Mexico—as a part of the Louisiana Purchase, but it had renounced the claim in 1819. Twice thereafter the United States had offered to buy Texas, only to meet with indignant Mexican refusals.

But in the early 1820s, the Mexican government launched an ill-advised experiment that would eventually cause it to lose its great northern province: it encouraged American immigration into Texas. The Mexicans hoped to strengthen the economy of the territory and increase their own tax revenues. They also liked the idea of the Americans sitting between Mexican settlement and the large and sometimes militant Indian tribes to the north. They convinced themselves, too, that settlers in Texas would serve as an effective buffer against United States expansion into the region; the Americans, they thought, would soon become loyal to the Mexican government. An 1824 colonization law designed to attract American settlers promised the newcomers cheap land and a four-year exemption from taxes.

Thousands of Americans, attracted by the rich soil in Texas, took advantage of Mexico's welcome. Since much of the available land was suitable for growing cotton, the great majority of the immigrants were southerners, many of whom brought slaves with them. By 1830, there were about 7,000 Americans living in Texas, more than twice the number of Mexicans there.

The Mexican government offered land directly to immigrants, but most of the settlers came to Texas through the efforts of American intermediaries, who received sizable land grants from Mexico in return for promising to bring settlers into the region. The most successful of them was Stephen F. Austin, a young immigrant from
Stephen Austin
Missouri who had established the first legal American settlement in Texas in 1822. Austin and other intermediaries were effective in recruiting American immigrants to Texas, but they also created centers of power in the region that competed with the Mexican government. In 1826, one of these American intermediaries led a revolt to establish Texas as an independent nation (which he proposed calling Fredonia). The Mexicans quickly crushed the revolt and, four years later, passed new laws barring any further American immigration into the region. They were too late. Americans kept flowing into the territory, and in 1833 Mexico dropped the futile immigration ban. By 1835 over 30,000 Americans, white and black, had settled in Texas.

Tensions Between the United States and Mexico

Friction between the American settlers and the Mexican government continued to grow, in part, from the continuing cultural and economic ties of the immigrants to the United States and their desire to create stronger bonds with their former home. It arose, too, from their desire to legalize slavery, which the Mexican government had made illegal in Texas (as it was in Mexico) in 1830. But the Americans were divided over how to address their unhappiness with Mexican rule. Austin and his followers wanted to reach a peaceful settlement that would give Texas more autonomy within the Mexican republic. Others wanted to fight for independence.

In the mid-1830s, instability in Mexico itself drove General Antonio Lopez de Santa Anna to seize power as a dictator and impose a new, more conservative and autocratic regime on the nation and its territories. A new law increased the powers of the national government of Mexico at the expense of the state governments, a measure that Texans from the United States assumed Santa Anna was aiming specifically at them. The Mexicans even imprisoned Stephen Austin in Mexico City for a time, claiming that he was encouraging revolts among his fellow Americans in Texas. Sporadic fighting between Americans and Mexicans in Texas began in 1835 and escalated as the Mexican government sent more troops into the territory. In 1836, the American settlers defiantly proclaimed their independence from Mexico.

Santa Anna led a large army into Texas, where the American settlers were having enormous difficulties organizing an effective defense of their new "nation." Several different factions claimed to be the legitimate government of Texas, and American soldiers could not even agree on who their commanders were. Mexican forces annihilated an American garrison at the Alamo mission in San Antonio after a famous, if futile, defense by a group of Texas "patriots," a group that included, among others, the renowned frontiersman and former Tennessee congressman Davy Crockett. Another garrison at Goliad suffered substantially the same fate when the Mexicans executed most of the force after it had surrendered. By the end of 1836, the rebellion appeared to have collapsed. Americans were fleeing east toward Louisiana to escape Santa Anna's army.

But General Sam Houston managed to keep a small force together. And on April 23, 1836, at the Battle of San Jacinto (near the present day city of Houston), he defeated the Mexican army and took Santa Anna prisoner. American troops then killed many of the Mexican soldiers in retribution for the executions at Goliad. Santa Anna, under pressure from his captors, signed a treaty giving Texas independence. And while the Mexican government repudiated the treaty, there were no further military efforts to win Texas back.

San Jacinto

A number of Mexican residents of Texas (*Tejanos*) had fought with the Americans in the revolution. But soon after Texas won its independence, their positions grew difficult. The Americans did not trust them, fearing that they were agents of the Mexican government, and in effect drove many of them out of the new republic. Most of those who stayed had to settle for a politically and economically subordinate status within the fledgling nation.

Above all, American Texans hoped for annexation by the United States. One of the first acts of the new president of Texas, Sam Houston, was to send a delegation to Washington with an offer to join the Union. There were supporters of expansion in the United States who welcomed these overtures; indeed, expansionists in the United States had been supporting and encouraging the revolt against Mexico for years. But there was also opposition. Many American northerners opposed acquiring a large new slave territory, and others opposed

Opposition to Annexation

AUSTIN, TEXAS, 1840 Four years after Texas declared its independence from Mexico, the new republic's capital, Austin, was still a small village most of whose buildings were rustic cabins, as this handcolored lithograph from the time suggests. The imposing house atop the hill at right was a notable exception. It was the residence of President Mirabeau Lamar. *(The Center for the American History, The University of Texas at Austin)*

increasing the southern votes in Congress and in the electoral college. Unfortunately for the Texans, one of the opponents was President Jackson, who feared annexation might cause a dangerous sectional controversy and even a war with Mexico. He therefore did not support annexation and even delayed recognizing the new republic until 1837. Presidents Martin Van Buren and William Henry Harrison also refrained from pressing the issue during their terms of office.

Spurned by the United States, Texas cast out on its own. Its leaders sought money and support from Europe. Some of them dreamed of creating a vast southwestern nation, stretching to the Pacific, that would rival the United States—a dream that appealed to European nations eager to counter the growing power of America. England and France quickly recognized and concluded trade treaties with Texas. In response, President Tyler persuaded Texas to apply for statehood again in 1844. But when Secretary of State Calhoun presented an annexation treaty to Congress as if its only purpose were to extend slavery, northern senators rebelled and defeated it. Rejection of the treaty only spurred advocates of Manifest Destiny to greater efforts toward their goal. The Texas question quickly became the central issue in the election of 1844.

Oregon

Control of what was known as Oregon country, in the Pacific Northwest, was another major political issue in the 1840s. Its half-million square miles included the present states of Oregon, Washington, and Idaho, parts of Montana and Wyoming, and half of British Columbia. Both Britain and the United States claimed sovereignty in the region—the British on the basis of explorations in the 1790s by George Vancouver, a naval officer; the Americans on the basis of simultaneous claims by Robert Gray, a fur trader. Unable to resolve their conflicting claims diplomatically, they agreed in an 1818 treaty to allow citizens of each country equal access to the territory. This arrangement, known as "joint occupation," continued for twenty years.

Disputed Claims

In fact, by the time of the treaty neither Britain nor the United States had established much of a presence in Oregon country. White settlement in the region consisted largely of American and Canadian fur traders, and the most significant white settlements were the fur trading post established by John Jacob Astor's company at Astoria and other posts built by the British Hudson Bay Company north of the Columbia River—where residents combined fur trading with farming and recruited Indian labor to compensate for their small numbers.

But American interest in Oregon grew substantially in the 1820s and 1830s. Missionaries considered the territory an attractive target for evangelical efforts, especially after the strange appearance of four Nez Percé and Flathead Indians in St. Louis in 1831. White Americans never discovered what had brought the Indians (who spoke no English) from Oregon to Missouri, and all four died before they could find out. But some missionaries considered the visit a divinely inspired invitation to extend their efforts westward. They were also motivated by a desire to counter the Catholic missionaries from Canada, whose presence in Oregon, many believed, threatened American hopes for annexation. The missionaries had little success with the tribes they attempted to convert, and some—embittered by Indian resistance to their efforts—began encouraging white immigration into the region, arguing that by repudiating Christianity the Indians had abdicated their right to the land. "When a people refuse or neglect to fill the designs of Providence, they ought not to complain of the results," said the missionary Marcus Whitman, who, with his wife Narcissa, had established an important, if largely unsuccessful, mission among the Cayuse Indians east of the Cascade Mountains.

Significant numbers of white Americans began emigrating to Oregon in the early 1840s, and they soon substantially outnumbered the British settlers there. They also devastated much of the Indian population, in part through a measles epidemic that spread through the Cayuse. The tribe blamed the Whitman mission for the plague, and in 1847 they attacked it and killed thirteen whites, including Marcus and Narcissa. But such resistance did little to stem the white immigration. By the mid-1840s, American settlements had spread up and down the Pacific coast; and the new settlers (along with advocates of Manifest Destiny in the East) were urging the United States government to take possession of the disputed Oregon territory.

Conflict between Settlers and Indians

The Westward Migration

The migrations into Texas and Oregon were part of a larger movement that took hundreds of thousands of white and black Americans into the far western regions of the continent between 1840 and 1860. Southerners flocked mainly to Texas. But the largest number of migrants came from the Old Northwest—white men and women, and a few blacks, who undertook arduous journeys in search of new opportunities. Most traveled in family groups, until the early 1850s, when the great gold rush attracted many single men (see pp. 351–353). Most were relatively young people. Most had undertaken earlier, if usually shorter, migrations in the past. Few were wealthy, but many were relatively prosperous. Poor people could not afford the expensive trip and the cost of new land. Those without money who wished to migrate usually had to do so by joining more established families or groups as laborers—men as farm or ranch hands,

PROMOTING THE WEST Cyrus McCormick was one of many American businessmen with an interest in the peopling of the American West. The reaper he invented was crucial to the cultivation of the new agricultural regions, and the rapid settlement of those regions was, in turn, essential to the health of his company. In this poster, the McCormick Reaper Company presents a romantic, idealized image of vast, fertile lands awaiting settlement, an image that drew many settlers westward. *(Chicago Historical Society)*

women as domestic servants, teachers, or, in some cases, prostitutes. The character of the migrations varied according to the destination of the migrants. Groups headed for areas where mining or lumbering was the principal economic activity consisted mostly of men. Those heading for farming regions traveled mainly as families.

All the migrants were in search of a new life, but they harbored many different visions of what the new life would bring. Some—particularly after the discovery of gold in California in 1848—hoped for quick riches. Others planned to take advantage of the vast public lands the federal government was selling at modest prices to acquire property for farming or speculation. Still others hoped to establish themselves as merchants and serve the new white communities developing in the West. Some (among them the Mormons) were on religious missions or were attempting to escape the epidemic diseases that were plaguing many cities in the East. But the vast majority of migrants were looking for economic opportunities. They formed a vanguard for the expanding capitalist economy of the United States. Perhaps not surprisingly, migrations were largest during boom times in the United States and dwindled during recessions.

Life on the Trail

Most migrants—about 300,000 between 1840 and 1860—traveled west along the great overland trails. They generally gathered in one of several major depots in Iowa and Missouri (Independence, St. Joseph, or Council Bluffs), joined a wagon train led by hired guides, and set off with their belongings piled in covered wagons, livestock trailing behind. The major route west was the 2,000-mile Oregon Trail, which stretched from Independence across the Great Plains and through the South Pass of the Rocky Mountains. From there, migrants moved north into Oregon or south (along the California trail) to the northern California coast. Other migrations moved along the Santa Fe Trail, southwest from Independence into New Mexico.

Oregon Trail

However they traveled, overland migrants faced considerable hardships—although the death rate for travelers was only slightly higher than the rate for the American population as a whole. The mountain and desert terrain in the later portions of the trip were particularly difficult. Most journeys lasted five or six months (from May to November), and there was always pressure to get through the Rockies before the snows began, not always an easy task given the very slow pace of most wagon trains (about fifteen miles a day). And although some migrants were moving west at least in part to escape the epidemic diseases of eastern cities, they were not immune from plagues. Thousands of people died on the trail of cholera during the great epidemic of the early 1850s.

In the years before the Civil War, fewer than 400 migrants (about one-tenth of 1 percent) died in conflicts with the tribes. In fact, Indians were usually more helpful than dangerous to the white migrants. They often served as guides through difficult terrain or aided travelers in crossing streams or herding livestock. They maintained an extensive trade with the white travelers in horses, clothing, and fresh food. But stories of the

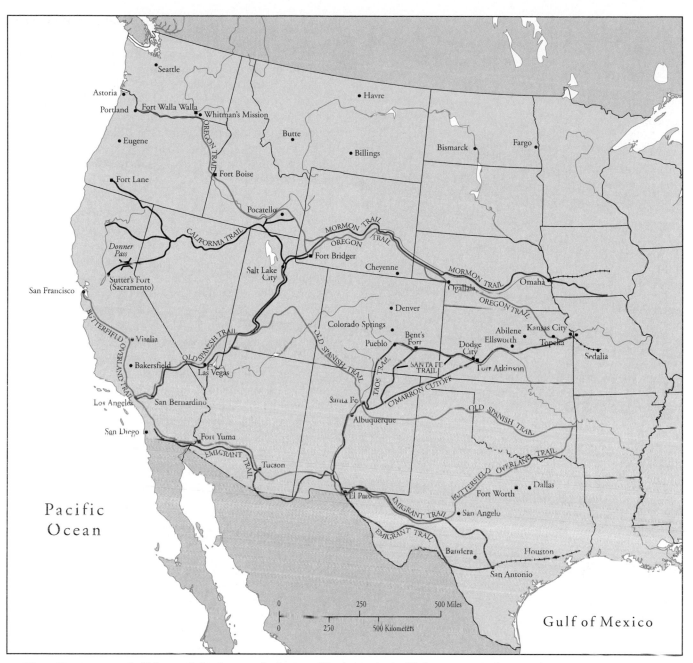

WESTERN TRAILS IN 1860 This map shows how much of western North America had little or no non-Indian population in 1800. As settlers began the long process of exploring and establishing farms and businesses in the West, major trails began to develop to facilitate travel and trade between the region and the more thickly settled areas to the East. Note how many of the trails lead to California and how few of them lead into any of the far northern regions of United States territory. Note too the important towns and cities that grew up along these trails. ◆ *What other, later forms of transportation performed the functions that these trails performed prior to the Civil War?*

occasional conflicts between migrants and Indians on the trail created widespread fear among white travelers, even though more Indians than white people (and relatively few of either) died in those conflicts.

Life on the trail was obviously very different from life on a farm or in a town. But the society of the trail recreated many of the patterns of conventional American society. Families divided tasks along gender lines: the

Life on the Trail

men driving and, when necessary, repairing the wagons or hunting game; the women cooking, washing clothes, and caring for children. Almost everyone, male or female, walked the great majority of the time, to lighten the load for the horses drawing the wagons; and so the women, many of whose chores came at the end of the day, generally worked much harder than the men, who usually rested when the caravan halted.

Despite the traditional image of westward migrants as rugged individualists, most travelers found the journey a highly collective experience. That was partly because

CROSSING THE PLAINS A long wagon train carries migrants across the Plains toward Montana in 1866. This photograph gives some indication of the rugged condition of even some of the most well-traveled trails. *(New-York Historical Society)*

many expeditions consisted of groups of friends, neighbors, or relatives who had decided to pull up stakes and move west together. And it was partly because of the intensity of the experience: many weeks of difficult travel with no other human contacts except, occasionally, with Indians. Indeed, one of the most frequent causes of disaster for travelers was the breakdown of the necessarily communal character of the migratory companies. Even so, it was a rare expedition in which there were not some internal conflicts before the trip was over.

EXPANSION AND WAR

The growing number of white Americans in the lands west of the Mississippi put great pressure on the government in Washington to annex Texas, Oregon, and other territory. And in the 1840s, these expansionist pressures helped push the United States into a war that—however dubious its origins—became a triumph for the advocates of Manifest Destiny.

The Democrats and Expansion

In preparing for the election of 1844, the two leading candidates—Henry Clay and former president Martin Van Buren—both tried to avoid taking a stand on the controversial issue of the annexation of Texas. Sentiment for expansion was mild within the Whig Party, and Clay had no difficulty securing the nomination despite his

noncommittal position. But many southern Democrats supported annexation, and the party passed over Van Buren to nominate a strong supporter of annexation, the previously unheralded James K. Polk.

Polk was not as obscure as his Whig critics claimed. He had represented Tennessee in the House of Representatives for fourteen years, four of them as Speaker, and had subsequently served as governor. But by 1844, he had been out of public office—and for the most part out of the public mind—for three years. What made his victory possible was his support for the position, expressed in the Democratic platform, "that the re-occupation of Oregon and the re-annexation of Texas at the earliest practicable period are great American measures." By combining the Oregon and Texas questions, the Democrats hoped to appeal to both northern and southern expansionists. Polk carried the election by 170 electoral votes to 105, although his popular majority was less than 40,000.

James K. Polk

Polk entered office with a clear set of goals and with plans for attaining them. John Tyler accomplished the first of Polk's goals for him. Interpreting the election returns as a mandate for the annexation of Texas, the outgoing president won congressional approval for it in February 1845. That December, Texas became a state.

Polk himself resolved the Oregon question. The British minister in Washington brusquely rejected a compromise Polk offered that would establish the United States–Canadian border at the 49th parallel; he did not even refer the proposal to London. Incensed, Polk again asserted the American claim to all of Oregon. There was loose talk of war on both sides of the Atlantic—talk that in the United States often took the form of the bellicose slogan "Fifty-four forty or fight!" (a reference to where the Americans hoped to draw the northern boundary of their part of Oregon). But neither country really wanted war. Finally, the British government accepted Polk's original proposal. On June 15, 1846, the Senate approved a treaty that fixed the boundary at the 49th parallel, where it remains today.

Compromise over Oregon

The Southwest and California

One of the reasons the Senate and the president had agreed so readily to the British offer to settle the Oregon question was that new tensions were emerging in the Southwest—tensions that ultimately led to a war with Mexico. As soon as the United States admitted Texas to statehood in 1845, the Mexican government broke diplomatic relations with Washington. Mexican-American relations grew still worse when a dispute developed over the boundary between Texas and Mexico. Texans claimed the Rio Grande as their western and southern border, a claim that would have

Texas Boundary in Dispute

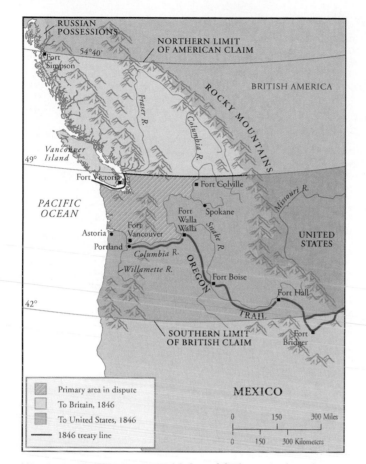

RUSSIAN POSSESSIONS

THE OREGON BOUNDARY, 1846 One of the last major boundary disputes between the United States and Great Britain involved the territory known as Oregon—the large region on the Pacific Coast north of California (which in 1846 was still part of Mexico). For years, America and Britain had overlapping claims on the territory. The British claimed land as far south as the present state of Oregon, while the Americans claimed land extending well into what is now Canada. Tensions over the Oregon border at times rose to the point that many Americans were demanding war, some using the slogan "54-40 or fight," referring to the latitude of the northernmost point of the American claim. ◆ *How did President James K. Polk defuse the crisis?*

added much of what is now New Mexico to Texas. Mexico, although still not conceding the loss of Texas, argued nevertheless that the border had always been the Nueces River, to the north of the Rio Grande. Polk accepted the Texas claim, and in the summer of 1845 he sent a small army under General Zachary Taylor to Texas to protect it against a possible Mexican invasion.

Part of the area in dispute was New Mexico, whose Spanish and Indian residents lived in a multiracial society that had by the 1840s endured for nearly a century and a half. In the 1820s, the Mexican government had invited American traders into the region (just as it invited American settlers into Texas), hoping to speed development of the province. And New Mexico, like Texas, soon began to become more American than Mexican. A flourishing commerce soon developed between Santa Fe and Independence, Missouri.

Americans were also increasing their interest in an even more distant province of Mexico: California. In this vast region lived members of several western Indian tribes and perhaps 7,000 Mexicans, mostly descendants of Spanish colonists. Gradually, however, white Americans began to arrive: first maritime traders and captains of Pacific whaling ships, who stopped to barter goods or buy supplies; then merchants, who established stores, imported merchandise, and developed a profitable trade with the Mexicans and Indians; and finally pioneering farmers, who entered California from the east, by land, and settled in the Sacramento Valley. Some of these new settlers began to dream of bringing California into the United States.

American Interests in California

President Polk soon came to share their dream and committed himself to acquiring both New Mexico and California for the United States. At the same time that he dispatched the troops under Taylor to Texas, he sent secret instructions to the commander of the Pacific naval squadron to seize the California ports if Mexico declared war. Representatives of the president quietly informed Americans in California that the United States would respond sympathetically to a revolt against Mexican authority there.

The Mexican War

Having appeared to prepare for war, Polk turned to diplomacy and dispatched a special minister, John Slidell, to try to buy off the Mexicans. But Mexican leaders rejected Slidell's offer to purchase the disputed territories. On January 13, 1846, as soon as he heard the news, Polk ordered Taylor's army in Texas to move across the Nueces River, where it had been stationed, to the Rio Grande. For months, the Mexicans refused to fight. But finally, according to disputed American accounts, some Mexican troops crossed the Rio Grande and attacked a unit of American soldiers. Polk now told Congress: "War exists by the act of Mexico herself." On May 13, 1846, Congress declared war by votes of 40 to 2 in the Senate and 174 to 14 in the House.

Failure of the Slidell Mission

The war had many opponents in the United States. Whig critics charged from the beginning (and not without some justification) that Polk had deliberately maneuvered the country into the conflict and had staged the border incident that had precipitated the declaration. Many argued that the hostilities with Mexico were draining resources and attention away from the more important issue of the Pacific Northwest; and when the United States finally reached its agreement with Britain on the Oregon question, opponents claimed that Polk had settled for less than he should have because he was preoccupied with Mexico. Opposition intensified as the war

Opposition to the War

America's First Foreign War

SACRAMENTO IN THE 1850S The busy river port of Sacramento served the growing agricultural and mining economies of north central California in the 1850s—years in which the new state began the dramatic population growth that a century later would make it the nation's largest. *(California State Library, Sacramento)*

continued and as the public became aware of the casualties and expense.

American forces did well against the Mexicans, but victory did not come as quickly as Polk had hoped. The president ordered Taylor to cross the Rio Grande, seize parts of northeastern Mexico, beginning with the city of Monterrey, and then march on to Mexico City itself. Taylor captured Monterrey in September 1846, but he let the Mexican garrison evacuate without pursuit. Polk now began to fear that Taylor lacked the tactical skill for the planned advance against Mexico City. He also feared that, if successful, Taylor would become a powerful political rival (as, in fact, he did).

In the meantime, Polk ordered other offensives against New Mexico and California. In the summer of 1846, a small army under Colonel Stephen W. Kearny captured Santa Fe with no opposition. Then Kearny proceeded to California, where he

Bear Flag Revolution

joined a conflict already in progress that was being staged jointly by American settlers, a well-armed exploring party led by John C. Frémont, and the American navy: the so-called Bear Flag Revolution. Kearny brought the disparate American forces together under his command, and by the autumn of 1846 he had completed the conquest of California.

The United States now controlled the two territories for which it had gone to war. But Mexico still refused to concede defeat. At this point, Polk and General Winfield Scott, the commanding general of the army and its finest soldier, launched a bold new campaign. Scott assembled an army at Tampico, which the navy transported down the Mexican coast to Veracruz. With an army that never numbered more than 14,000, Scott advanced 260 miles along the Mexican National Highway toward Mexico City, kept American casualties low, and never lost a battle before finally seizing the Mexican capital. A new Mexican government took power and announced its willingness to negotiate a peace treaty.

President Polk was now growing thoroughly unclear about his objectives. He continued to encourage those who demanded that the United States annex much of Mexico itself. At the same time, concerned about the approaching presidential election, he was growing anxious to get the war finished quickly. Polk had sent a special presidential envoy, Nicholas Trist, to negotiate a settlement. On February 2, 1848, he reached agreement with the new Mexican government on the Treaty of

Treaty of Guadalupe Hidalgo

Guadalupe Hidalgo, by which Mexico agreed to cede California and New Mexico to the United States and acknowledge the Rio Grande as the boundary of Texas. In return, the United States promised to assume any financial

THE MEXICAN WAR, 1846-1848 Shortly after the settlement of the Oregon border dispute with Britain, the United States entered a war with Mexico over another contested border. This map shows the movement of Mexican and American troops during the fighting, which extended from the area around Santa Fe south to Mexico City and west to the coast of California. Note the American use of its naval forces to facilitate a successful assault on Mexico City, and others on the coast of California. Note, too, how unsuccessful the Mexican forces were in their battles with the United States. Mexico won only one battle—a relatively minor one at San Pasqual near San Diego—in the war. ◆ *How did President Polk deal with the popular clamor for the United States to annex much of present-day Mexico?*

OLC For an interactive version of this map go to www.mhhe.com/brinkley12ch13maps

claims its new citizens had against Mexico and to pay the Mexicans $15 million. Trist had obtained most of Polk's original demands, but he had not satisfied the new, more expansive dreams of acquiring additional territory in Mexico itself. Polk angrily claimed that Trist had violated his instructions, but he soon realized that he had no choice but to accept the treaty to silence a bitter battle growing between ardent expansionists demanding the annexation of "All Mexico!" and antislavery leaders charging that the expansionists were conspiring to extend slavery to new realms. The president submitted the Trist treaty to the Senate, which approved it by a vote of 38 to 14. The war was over, and America had gained a vast new territory. But it had also acquired a new set of troubling and divisive issues.

STEPHEN KEARNY IN SANTA FE Colonel
Stephen Kearny led a small U.S. military party to
Santa Fe in 1846 and seized the town without
opposition. In this 1909 drawing (which the
artist Stephen Chapman acknowledged was not
entirely accurate), Kearny raises the American
flag over the "old palace" in Santa Fe. The image
appeared on a U.S. postage stamp in 1946.
(Museum of New Mexico)

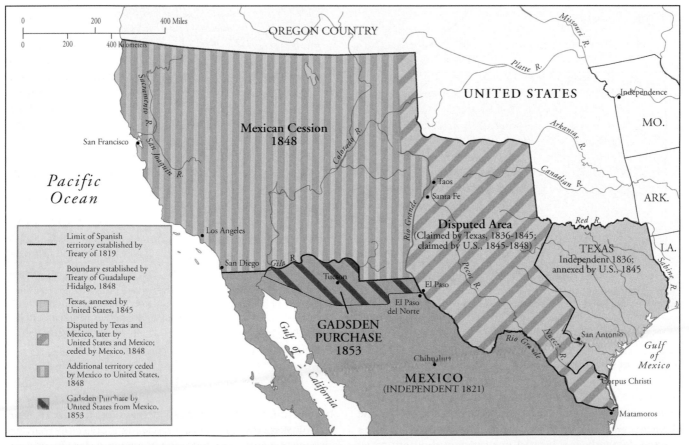

SOUTHWESTERN EXPANSION, 1845–1853 The annexation of much of what is now Texas in 1845, the much larger territorial gains won in the
Mexican War in 1848, and the purchase of additional land from Mexico in 1853 completed the present continental border of the United States.
◆ *What great event shortly after the Mexican War contributed to a rapid settlement of California by migrants from the eastern United States?*

OLC For an interactive version of this map go to www.mhhe.com/brinkley12ch13maps

THE SECTIONAL DEBATE

James Polk tried to be a president whose policies transcended sectional divisions. But conciliating the sections was becoming an ever more difficult task, and Polk gradually earned the enmity of northerners and westerners alike, who believed his policies (and particularly his enthusiasm for territorial expansion in the Southwest) favored the South at their expense.

Slavery and the Territories

In August 1846, while the Mexican War was still in progress, Polk asked Congress to appropriate $2 million for purchasing peace with Mexico. Representative David Wilmot of Pennsylvania, an antislavery Democrat, introduced an amendment to the appropriation bill prohibiting slavery in any territory acquired from Mexico. The so-called Wilmot Proviso passed the House but failed in the Senate. It would be called up, debated, and voted on repeatedly for years. Southern militants, in the meantime, contended that all Americans had equal rights in the new territories, including the right to move their "property" (slaves).

Wilmot Proviso

As the sectional debate intensified, President Polk supported a proposal to extend the Missouri Compromise line through the new territories to the Pacific coast, banning slavery north of the line and permitting it south of the line. Others supported a plan, originally known as "squatter sovereignty" and later by the more dignified phrase "popular sovereignty," which would allow the people of each territory (acting through their legislature) to decide the status of slavery there. The debate over these various proposals dragged on for many months, and the issue remained unresolved when Polk left office in 1849.

Competing Plans

The presidential campaign of 1848 dampened the controversy for a time as both Democrats and Whigs tried to avoid the slavery question. When Polk, in poor health, declined to run again, the Democrats nominated Lewis Cass of Michigan, a dull, aging party regular. The Whigs nominated General Zachary Taylor of Louisiana, hero of the Mexican War but a man with no political experience whatsoever. Opponents of slavery found the choice of candidates unsatisfying, and out of their discontent emerged the new Free-Soil Party, which drew from the existing Liberty Party and the antislavery wings of the Whig and Democratic Parties and which endorsed the Wilmot Proviso. Its candidate was former president Martin Van Buren.

Taylor won a narrow victory. But while Van Buren failed to carry a single state, he polled an impressive 291,000 votes (10 percent of the total), and the Free-Soilers elected ten members to Congress. The emergence of the Free-Soil Party as an important political force, like the

Free-Soil Party

emergence of the Know-Nothing and Liberty Parties before it, signaled the inability of the existing parties to contain the political passions slavery was creating. It was an important part of a process that would lead to the collapse of the second party system in the 1850s.

The California Gold Rush

By the time Taylor took office, the pressure to resolve the question of slavery in the far western territories had become more urgent as a result of dramatic events in California. In January 1848, James Marshall, a carpenter working on one of John Sutter's sawmills, found traces of gold in the foothills of the Sierra Nevadas. Sutter tried to suppress the news, fearing a gold rush would destroy his own substantial empire in the region. But by May, word of the discovery had reached San Francisco; by late summer, it had reached the east coast of the United States and much of the rest of the world. Almost immediately, hundreds of thousands of people from around the world began flocking to California in a frantic search for gold. The non-Indian population increased nearly twentyfold in four years: from 14,000 in 1848 to over 220,000 in 1852.

The atmosphere in California at the peak of the gold rush was one of almost crazed excitement and greed. For a short time San Francisco was almost completely depopulated as residents raced to the mountains to search for gold; the city's principal newspaper (which had been criticizing the gold mania) had to stop publication because it could no longer find either staff or readers. "Nothing but the introduction of insane asylums can effect a cure," one visitor remarked of the gold mania.

Most migrants to the Far West prepared carefully before making the journey. But the California migrants (known as "Forty-niners") threw caution to the winds. They abandoned farms, jobs, homes, families; they piled onto ships and flooded the overland trails—many carrying only what they could pack on their backs. The overwhelming majority of the Forty-niners (perhaps 95 percent) were men, and the society they created on their arrival in California was unusually fluid and volatile because of the almost total absence of women, children, or families.

Forty-niners

The gold rush also attracted some of the first Chinese migrants to the western United States. News of the discoveries created great excitement in China, particularly in impoverished areas, where letters from Chinese already in California and reports from Americans visiting in China spread the word. It was, of course, extremely difficult for a poor Chinese peasant to get to America; but many young, adventurous people (mostly men) decided to go anyway—believing that they could quickly become rich and then return to China. Emigration brokers loaned many migrants money for passage to California,

"MINERS WITH ROCKERS AND BLUE SHIRTS" Despite its romantic image, mining for gold during the great California Gold Rush was for most people hard, discouraging, and ultimately profitless work—as this photograph of a grim band of miners with their equipment suggests. Most of those who came to California in search of gold eventually either returned home with nothing to show for their efforts or remained in California to make their way in some other occupation. *(Collection of W. Bruce Lundberg. Photograph courtesy Oakland Museum of California)*

which the migrants paid off out of their earnings there. The migration was almost entirely voluntary (unlike the forced movement of kidnapped "coolies" to such places as Peru and Cuba at about the same time). The Chinese in California were, therefore, free laborers and merchants, looking for gold or, more often, hoping to profit from other economic opportunities the gold boom was creating.

The gold rush created a serious labor shortage in California, as many male workers left their jobs and flocked to the gold fields. This shortage created opportunities for many people who needed work (including Chinese immigrants). It also led to an overt exploitation of Indians that resembled slavery in all but name. At the same time that white vigilantes, who called themselves "Indian hunters," were hunting down and killing

Indian Slavery

thousands of Indians (contributing to the process by which the Native American population of California declined from

150,000 to 30,000 between the 1850s and 1870), a state law permitted the arrest of "loitering" or orphaned Indians and their assignment to a term of "indentured" labor.

The gold rush was of critical importance to the growth of California, but not for the reasons most of the migrants hoped. There was substantial gold in the hills of the Sierra Nevada, and many people got rich from it. But only a tiny fraction of the Forty-niners ever found gold, or even managed to stake a claim to land on which they could look for gold. Some disappointed migrants returned home after a while. But many stayed in California and swelled both the agricultural and urban populations of the territory. By 1856, for example, San Francisco—whose population had been 1,000 before the gold rush (and at one point declined to about 100 as people left for the mines)—was the home of over 50,000 people. By the early 1850s, California, which had always had a diverse population, had become remarkably heterogeneous. The

THE IMPENDING CRISIS 353

gold rush had attracted not just white Americans, but Europeans, Chinese, South Americans, Mexicans, free blacks, and slaves who accompanied southern migrants. Conflicts over gold intersected with racial and ethnic tensions to make the territory an unusually turbulent place. As a result, pressure grew to create a more stable and effective government. The gold rush, therefore, became another factor putting pressure on the United States to resolve the status of the territories—and of slavery within them.

Rising Sectional Tensions

Zachary Taylor believed statehood could become the solution to the issue of slavery in the territories. As long as the new lands remained territories, the federal government was responsible for deciding the fate of slavery within them. But once they became states, he thought, their own governments would be able to settle the slavery question. At Taylor's urging, California quickly adopted a constitution that prohibited slavery, and in December 1849 Taylor asked Congress to admit California as a free state. New Mexico, he added, should also be granted statehood as soon as it was ready and should, like California, be permitted to decide for itself what it wanted to do about slavery.

Congress balked, in part because of several other controversies concerning slavery that were complicating the debate. One was the effort of antislavery forces to abolish slavery in the District of Columbia, a movement bitterly resisted by southerners. Another was the emergence of personal liberty laws in northern states, which barred courts and police officers from helping to return runaway slaves to their owners. In response, southerners demanded a stringent law that would require northern states to return fugitive slaves to their owners. But the biggest obstacle to the president's program was the white South's fear that two new free states would be added to the northern majority. The number of free and slave states was equal in 1849—fifteen each. But the admission of California would upset the balance; and New Mexico, Oregon, and Utah might upset it further, leaving the South in a minority in the Senate, as it already was in the House.

Tempers were now rising to dangerous levels. Even many otherwise moderate south-

Sectional Conflict over Slavery in the Territories ern leaders were beginning to talk about secession from the Union. In the North, every state legislature but one adopted a resolution demanding the prohibition of slavery in the territories.

The Compromise of 1850

Faced with this mounting crisis, moderates and unionists spent the winter of 1849–1850 trying to frame a great compromise. The aging Henry Clay, who was spearheading the effort, believed that no compromise could last unless it settled all the issues in dispute between the sections. As a result, he took sev-

Clay's Proposed Solution

eral measures that had been proposed separately, combined them into a single piece of legislation, and presented it to the Senate on January 29, 1850. Among the bill's provisions were the admission of California as a free state; the formation of territorial governments in the rest of the lands acquired from Mexico, without restrictions on slavery; the abolition of the slave trade, but not slavery itself, in the District of Columbia; and a new and more effective fugitive slave law. These resolutions launched a debate that raged for seven months— both in Congress and throughout the nation. The debate occurred in two phases, the differences between which revealed much about how American politics was changing in the 1850s.

In the first phase of the debate, the dominant voices in Congress were those of old men—national leaders who still remembered Jefferson, Adams, and other founders—who argued for or against the compromise on the basis of broad ideals. Clay himself, seventy-three years old in 1850, appealed to shared national sentiments of nationalism. Early in March, another of the older leaders—John C. Calhoun, sixty-eight years old and so ill that he had to sit grimly in his seat while a colleague read his speech for him—joined the debate. He insisted that the North grant the South equal rights in the territories, that it agree to observe the laws concerning fugitive slaves, that it cease attacking slavery, and that it amend the Constitution to create dual presidents, one from the North and one from the South, each with a veto. Calhoun was making radical demands that had no chance of passage. But like Clay, he was offering what he considered a comprehensive, permanent solution to the sectional problem that would, he believed, save the Union. After Calhoun came the third of the elder statesmen, sixty-eight-year-old Daniel Webster, one of the great orators of his time. Still nourishing presidential ambitions, he delivered an eloquent address in the Senate, trying to rally northern moderates to support Clay's compromise.

But in July, after six months of this impassioned, nationalistic debate, Congress defeated the Clay proposal. And with that, the controversy moved into its second phase, in which a very different cast of characters predominated. Clay, ill and tired, left Washington to spend the summer resting in the mountains. Calhoun had died even before the vote in July. And Webster accepted a new appointment as secretary of state, thus removing himself from the Senate and from the debate.

In place of these leaders, a new, younger group now emerged. One spokesman was William H. Seward,

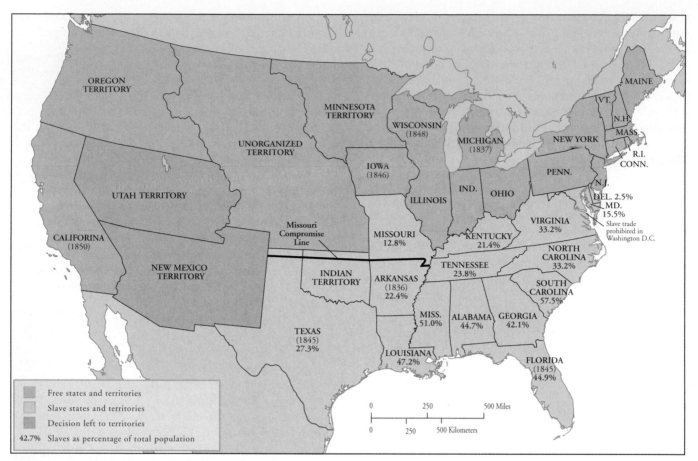

SLAVE AND FREE TERRITORIES UNDER THE COMPROMISE OF 1850 The acquisition of vast new western lands raised the question of the status of slavery in new territories organized for statehood by the United States. Tension between the North and South on this question led in 1850 to a great compromise, forged in Congress, to settle this dispute. The compromise allowed California to join the Union as a free state and introduced the concept of "popular sovereignty" for other new territories. ◆ *How well did the compromise of 1850 work?*

OLC For an interactive version of this map go to www.mhhe.com/brinkley12ch13maps

New Leadership

forty-nine years old, of New York, a wily political operator who staunchly opposed the proposed compromise. The ideals of Union were to him less important than the issue of eliminating slavery. Another was Jefferson Davis of Mississippi, forty-two years old, a representative of the new, cotton South. To him, the slavery issue was less one of principles and ideals than one of economic self-interest. Most important of all, there was Stephen A. Douglas, a thirty-seven-year-old Democratic senator from Illinois. A westerner from a rapidly growing state, he was an open spokesman for the economic needs of his section—and especially for the construction of railroads. His was a career devoted not to any broad national goals but frankly to sectional gain and personal self-promotion.

The new leaders of the Senate were able, as the old leaders had not been, to produce a compromise. One spur to the compromise was the disappearance of the most powerful obstacle to it: the president. Zachary Taylor had been adamant that only after California and possibly

New Mexico were admitted as states could other measures be discussed. But on July 9, 1850, Taylor suddenly died—the victim of a violent stomach disorder. He was succeeded by Millard Fillmore of New York—a dull, handsome, dignified man who understood the political importance of flexibility. He supported the compromise and used his powers of persuasion to swing northern Whigs into line.

The new leaders also benefited from their own pragmatic tactics. Douglas's first step, after the departure of Clay, was to break up the "omnibus bill" that Clay had envisioned as a great, comprehensive solution to the sectional crisis and to introduce instead a series of separate measures to be voted on one by one. Thus representatives of different sections could support those elements of the compromise they liked and oppose those they did not. Douglas also gained support with complicated backroom deals linking the compromise to such nonideological matters as the sale of government bonds and the construction of

Temporary Compromise

railroads. As a result of his efforts, by mid-September Congress had enacted and the president had signed all the components of the compromise.

The Compromise of 1850, unlike the Missouri Compromise thirty years before, was not a product of widespread agreement on common national ideals. It was, rather, a victory of self-interest. Still, members of Congress hailed the measure as a triumph of statesmanship; and Millard Fillmore, signing it, called it a just settlement of the sectional problem, "in its character final and irrevocable."

THE CRISES OF THE 1850s

For a few years after the Compromise of 1850, the sectional conflict seemed briefly to be forgotten amid booming prosperity and growth. But the tensions between North and South remained, and the crisis continued to smolder until—in 1854—it once more burst into the open.

The Uneasy Truce

Both major parties endorsed the Compromise of 1850 in 1852, and both nominated presidential candidates unidentified with sectional passions. The Democrats chose the obscure New Hampshire politician Franklin Pierce and the Whigs the military hero General Winfield Scott, a man of entirely unknown political views. But the sectional question was a divisive influence in the election anyway, and the Whigs were the principal victims. They suffered massive defections from antislavery members angered by the party's evasiveness on the issue. Many of them flocked to the Free-Soil Party, whose antislavery presidential candidate, John P. Hale, repudiated the Compromise of 1850. The divisions among the Whigs helped produce a victory for the Democrats in 1852.

Franklin Pierce, a charming, amiable man of no particular distinction, attempted to maintain party—and national—harmony by avoiding divisive issues, and particularly by avoiding the issue of slavery. But it was an impossible task. Northern opposition to the Fugitive Slave Act intensified quickly after 1850, when southerners began appearing occasionally in northern states to pursue people they claimed were fugitives. Mobs formed in some northern cities to prevent enforcement of the law, and several northern states also passed their own laws barring the deportation of fugitive slaves. White southerners watched with growing anger and alarm as the one element of the Compromise of 1850 that they had considered a victory seemed to become meaningless as a result of northern defiance.

Opposition to the Fugitive Slave Act

"Young America"

One of the ways Franklin Pierce hoped to dampen sectional controversy was through his support of a movement in the Democratic Party known as "Young America." Its adherents saw the expansion of American democracy throughout the world as a way to divert attention from the controversies over slavery. The great liberal and nationalist revolutions of 1848 in Europe stirred them to dream of a republican Europe with governments based on the model of the United States. They dreamed as well of expanding American commerce in the Pacific and acquiring new territories in the Western Hemisphere.

But efforts to extend the nation's domain could not avoid becoming entangled with the sectional crisis. Pierce had been pursuing unsuccessful diplomatic attempts to buy Cuba from Spain (efforts begun in 1848 by Polk). In 1854, however, a group of his envoys sent him a private document from Ostend, Belgium, making the case for seizing Cuba by force. When the Ostend Manifesto, as it became known, was leaked to the public, it enraged many antislavery northerners, who charged the administration with conspiring to bring a new slave state into the Union.

Ostend Manifesto

The South, for its part, opposed all efforts to acquire new territory that would not support a slave system. The kingdom of Hawaii agreed to join the United States in 1854, but the treaty died in the Senate because it contained a clause prohibiting slavery in the islands. A powerful movement to annex Canada to the United States—a movement that had the support of many Canadians eager for access to American markets—similarly foundered, at least in part because of slavery.

Slavery, Railroads, and the West

What fully revived the sectional crisis, however, was the same issue that had produced it in the first place: slavery in the territories. By the 1850s, the line of substantial white settlement had moved beyond the boundaries of Missouri, Iowa, and what is now Minnesota into a great expanse of plains, which many white Americans had once believed was unfit for cultivation. Now it was becoming apparent that large sections of this region were, in fact, suitable for farming. In the states of the Old Northwest, therefore, prospective settlers urged the government to open the area to them, provide territorial governments, and—despite the solemn assurance the United States had earlier given the Indians of the sanctity of their reservations—dislodge the tribes located there so as to make room for white settlers. There was relatively little opposition from any segment of white society to this proposed violation of Indian rights. But the interest in further settlement raised two issues that did prove highly divisive and that gradually became entwined with each other: railroads and slavery.

As the nation expanded westward, the problem of

Transcontinental Railroad and Slavery

communication between the older states and the areas west of the Mississippi River became more and more critical. As a result, broad support began to emerge for building a transcontinental railroad. The problem was where to place it—and in particular, where to locate the railroad's eastern terminus, where the line could connect with the existing rail network east of the Mississippi. Northerners favored Chicago, the rapidly growing capital of the free states of the Northwest. Southerners supported St. Louis, Memphis, or New Orleans—all located in slave states. The transcontinental railroad, in other words, had become part of the struggle between the North and the South.

Pierce's secretary of war, Jefferson Davis of Mississippi,

Gadsden Purchase

removed one obstacle to a southern route. Surveys indicated that a railroad with a southern terminus would have to pass through an area in Mexican territory. But in 1853 Davis sent James Gadsden, a southern railroad builder, to Mexico, where he persuaded the Mexican government to accept $10 million in exchange for a strip of land that today comprises part of Arizona and New Mexico. The so-called Gadsden Purchase only accentuated the sectional rivalry.

The Kansas-Nebraska Controversy

As a senator from Illinois, a resident of Chicago, and the acknowledged leader of northwestern Democrats, Stephen A. Douglas naturally wanted the transcontinental railroad for his own city and section. He also realized the strength of the principal argument against the northern route west of the Mississippi: that it would run mostly through country with a substantial Indian population. As a result, he introduced a bill in January 1854 to organize (and thus open to white settlement) a huge new territory, known as Nebraska, west of Iowa and Missouri.

Douglas knew the South would oppose his bill because it would prepare the way for a new free state; the proposed territory was in the area of the Louisiana Purchase north of the Missouri Compromise line (36°30') and hence closed to slavery. In an effort to make the measure acceptable to southerners, Douglas inserted a provision that the status of slavery in the territory would be determined by the territorial legislature—that is,

Kansas-Nebraska Act

according to "popular sovereignty." In theory, the region could choose to open itself to slavery (although few believed it actually would). When southern Democrats demanded more, Douglas agreed to an additional clause

explicitly repealing the Missouri Compromise. He also agreed to divide the area into two territories—Nebraska and Kansas—instead of one. The new, second territory (Kansas) was more likely to become a slave state. In its final form the measure was known as the Kansas-Nebraska Act. President Pierce supported the bill, and after a strenuous debate, it became law in May 1854 with the unanimous support of the South and the partial support of northern Democrats.

No piece of legislation in American history produced so many immediate, sweeping, and ominous consequences. It divided and destroyed the Whig Party, which disappeared almost entirely by 1856. It divided the northern Democrats (many of whom were appalled at the repeal of the Missouri Compromise, which they considered an almost sacred part of the fabric of the Union) and drove many of them from the party. Most important of all, it spurred the creation of a new party that was frankly sectional in composition and creed.

Birth of the Republican Party

People in both major parties who opposed Douglas's bill began to call themselves Anti-Nebraska Democrats and Anti-Nebraska Whigs. In 1854, they formed a new organization and named it the Republican Party. It instantly became a major force in American politics. In the elections of that year, the Republicans won enough seats in Congress to permit them, in combination with allies among the Know-Nothings, to organize the House of Representatives.

"Bleeding Kansas"

Events in Kansas itself in the next two years increased the political turmoil in the North. White settlers from both the North and the South began moving into the territory almost immediately after the passage of the Kansas-Nebraska Act. In the spring of 1855, elections were held for a territorial legislature. There were only about 1,500 legal voters in Kansas by then, but thousands of Missourians, some traveling in armed bands into Kansas, swelled the vote to over 6,000. The result was that pro-slavery forces elected a majority to the legislature, which immediately legalized slavery. Outraged free-staters elected their own delegates to a constitutional convention, which met at Topeka and adopted a constitution excluding slavery. They then chose their own governor and legislature and petitioned Congress for statehood. President Pierce denounced them as traitors and threw the full support of the federal government behind the pro-slavery territorial legislature. A few months later a pro-slavery federal marshal assembled a large posse, consisting mostly of Missourians, to arrest the free-state leaders, who had set up their headquarters in Lawrence. The posse sacked the town, burned the "governor's" house,

"BLEEDING KANSAS" During the bitter battles over slavery in 1856, the slave state of Missouri tried to prevent antislavery emigrants from passing through their territory en route to Kansas. Free-staters responded by organizing a large emigration through Iowa, circumventing Missouri. Those who entered Kansas by that route tended to arrive armed, some of them with large cannon—among them the one pictured here, which Free-staters brought with them to Topeka that year. *(Kansas State Historical Society)*

and destroyed several printing presses. Retribution came quickly.

Among the most fervent abolitionists in Kansas was John Brown, a grim, fiercely committed zealot who considered himself an instrument of God's will to destroy slavery. He had moved to Kansas with his sons so that they could fight to make it a free state. After the events in Lawrence, he gathered six followers (including four of his sons) and in one night murdered five pro-slavery settlers, leaving their mutilated bodies to discourage other supporters of slavery from entering Kansas. This terrible episode, known as the Pottawatomie Massacre, led to more civil strife in Kansas—irregular, guerrilla warfare conducted by armed bands, some of them more interested in land claims or loot than in ideologies. Northerners and southerners alike came to believe that the events in Kansas illustrated (and were caused by) the aggressive designs of the other section. "Bleeding Kansas" became a symbol of the sectional controversy.

Pottawatomie Massacre

Another symbol soon appeared, in the United States Senate. In May 1856, Charles Sumner of Massachusetts—a militant and passionately doctrinaire opponent of slavery—rose to give a speech entitled "The Crime Against Kansas." In it, he gave particular attention to Senator Andrew P. Butler of South Carolina, an outspoken defender of slavery. The South Carolinian was, Sumner claimed, the "Don Quixote" of slavery, having "chosen a mistress . . . who, though ugly to others, is always lovely to him, though polluted in the sight of the world, is chaste in his sight . . . the harlot slavery."

The pointedly sexual references and the general viciousness of the speech enraged Butler's nephew, Preston Brooks, a member of the House of Representatives from South Carolina. Several days after the speech, Brooks approached Sumner at his desk in the Senate chamber during a recess, raised a heavy cane, and began beating him repeatedly on the head and shoulders. Sumner, trapped in his chair, rose in agony with such strength that he tore the desk from the bolts holding it to the floor. Then he collapsed, bleeding and unconscious. So severe were his injuries that he was unable to return to the Senate for four years. Throughout the North, he became a hero—a martyr to the barbarism of the South. In the South, Preston Brooks became a hero, too. Censured by the House, he resigned his seat, returned to South Carolina, and stood successfully for reelection.

Preston Brooks and Charles Sumner

The Free-Soil Ideology

What had happened to produce such deep hostility between the two sections? In part, the tensions were reflections of the two sections' differing economic and territorial interests. But they were also reflections of a hardening of ideas in both North and South. As the nation expanded and political power grew more dispersed, each section became concerned with ensuring that its vision of America's future would be the dominant one.

In the North, assumptions about the proper structure of society came to center on the belief in "free soil" and "free labor." Although abolitionists generated some support for their argument that slavery was a moral evil and must be eliminated, most white northerners came to believe that the existence of slavery was

"Free Soil" Ideology

THE BATTLE FOR KANSAS The conflicts over Kansas eventually took on much of the character of a civil war, as this picture of a battle between free-soilers and pro-slavery forces at Hickory Point, Kansas, makes clear. *(Anne S. K. Brown Military Collection, Brown University Library)*

ANTI-ABOLITIONIST VIOLENCE This 1838 woodcut depicts the anti-abolitionist riot in Alton, Illinois, in which Elijah P. Lovejoy, publisher of an abolitionist newspaper, was slain on November 7, 1837. The death of Lovejoy aroused the antislavery movement throughout the United States. *(Library of Congress)*

dangerous not because of what it did to blacks but because of what it threatened to do to whites. At the heart of American democracy, they argued, was the right of all citizens to own property, to control their own labor, and to have access to opportunities for advancement.

According to this vision, the South was the antithesis of democracy—a closed, static society, in which slavery preserved an entrenched aristocracy and in which common whites had no opportunity to improve themselves. While the North was growing and prospering,

"Slave Power Conspiracy"

the South was stagnating, rejecting the values of individualism and progress. The South was, northern free-laborites further maintained, engaged in a conspiracy to extend slavery throughout the nation and thus to destroy the openness of northern capitalism and replace it with the closed, aristocratic system of the South. The only solution to this "slave power conspiracy" was to fight the spread of slavery and extend the nation's democratic (i.e., free-labor) ideals to all sections of the country.

This ideology, which lay at the heart of the new Republican Party, also strengthened the commitment of Republicans to the Union. Since the idea of continued growth and progress was central to the free-labor vision, the prospect of dismemberment of the nation—a diminution of America's size and economic power—was unthinkable.

The Pro-Slavery Argument

In the South, in the meantime, a very different ideology—entirely incompatible with the free-labor ideology—was emerging out of a rapid hardening of position among southern whites on the issue of slavery. It was a result of many things: the Nat Turner uprising in 1831, which terrified southern whites and made them more determined than ever to make slavery secure; the expansion of the cotton economy into the Deep South, which made slavery unprecedentedly lucrative; and the growth of the Garrisonian abolitionist movement, with its strident attacks on southern society. The popularity of Harriet Beecher Stowe's *Uncle Tom's Cabin* was perhaps the most glaring evidence of the success of those attacks, but other abolitionist writings had been antagonizing white southerners for years.

In response to these pressures, a number of white southerners produced a new intellectual defense of slavery. Professor Thomas R. Dew of the College of William and Mary helped begin that effort in 1832. Twenty years later, apologists for slavery summarized their views in an anthology that gave their ideology its name: *The Pro-Slavery Argument.* John C. Calhoun stated the essence of the case in 1837: Southerners should stop apologizing for slavery as a necessary evil and defend it as "a good—a positive good." It was good for the slaves, the southern apologists argued, because they enjoyed better conditions than industrial workers in the North. Slavery was good for southern society as a whole because it was the only way the two races could live together in peace. It was good for the entire country because the southern economy, based on slavery, was the key to the prosperity of the nation.

Above all, southern apologists argued, slavery was good because it served as the basis for the southern way of life—a way of life superior to any other in the United States, perhaps in the world. White southerners looking at the North saw a spirit of greed, debauchery, and destructiveness. "The masses of the North are venal, corrupt, covetous, mean and selfish," wrote one southerner. Others wrote with horror of the factory system and the crowded, pestilential cities filled with unruly immigrants. But the South, they believed, was a stable, orderly society, operating at a slow and human pace. It was free from the feuds between capital and labor plaguing the North. It protected the welfare of its workers. And it allowed the aristocracy to enjoy a refined and accomplished cultural life. It was, in short, an ideal social order in which all elements of the population were secure and content.

The defense of slavery rested, too, on increasingly elaborate arguments about the biological inferiority of African Americans, who were, white Southerners claimed, inherently unfit to take care of themselves, let alone exercise the rights of citizenship. And just as abolitionist arguments drew strength from Protestant theology in the North, the pro-slavery defense mobilized the Protestant clergy in the South to give the institution a religious and biblical justification.

Buchanan and Depression

In this unpromising climate, the presidential campaign of 1856 began. Democratic Party leaders wanted a candidate who, unlike President Pierce, was not closely associated with the explosive question of "Bleeding Kansas." They chose James Buchanan of Pennsylvania, a reliable party stalwart who as minister to England had been safely out of the country during the recent controversies. The Republicans, participating in their first presidential contest, denounced the Kansas-Nebraska Act and the expansion of slavery but also endorsed a Whiggish program of internal improvements, thus combining the idealism of antislavery with the economic aspirations of the North. As eager as the Democrats to present a safe candidate, the Republicans nominated John C. Frémont, who had made a national reputation as an explorer of the Far West and who had no political record. The Native American, or Know-Nothing, Party was beginning to break apart, but it nominated former president Millard Fillmore, who also received the endorsement of a sad remnant of the Whig Party.

After a heated, even frenzied campaign, Buchanan won a narrow victory over Frémont and Fillmore. A slight shift of votes in Pennsylvania and Illinois would have elected the Republican candidate. Particularly ominous was that Frémont had attracted virtually no votes at all in the South while outpolling all other candidates in the North. At the time of his inauguration, Buchanan was, at age sixty-five, the oldest president, except for

Lyceums

Two passions of the mid-nineteenth century—education and oratory—combined in the 1830s to create a movement that was both popular and, its creators believed, educational: the lyceum.

The lyceum was not a place, although some places were given its name (which came from a building in ancient Greece where Aristotle had taught). It was an idea. It was the brainchild of Josiah Holbrook, a Yale graduate and schoolteacher who dreamed of bringing knowledge to adults. Holbrook himself gave a series of lectures in Millbury, Massachusetts, in 1826 to an audience of "farmers and mechanics," offering "instruction in the sciences and other branches of useful knowledge." From that modest experiment, the "lyceum movement" quickly spread through Massachusetts, New England, and other parts of the American North and Northwest. (The movement had only a small impact in the South.)

Making use of public libraries, vacant schools, and other existing spaces, lyceum organizers recruited some of the leading scholars, politicians, and orators of their time to provide entertainment and instruction to adult audiences. The topics of lectures were as various as the speakers. The lyceum in Salem, Massachusetts, for example, sponsored lectures in 1838 on "Causes of the American Revolution," "The Sun," "The Legal Rights of Women," and "The Satanic School of Literature and Reform." At the Lowell Institute in Boston, founded in 1830 as "a perennial source of public good—a dispensation of sound science, of useful knowledge, of truth," there were lectures by the geologist Benjamin Silliman (who spoke there ninety-six times), the naturalist Louis Aggasiz, the Russian traveler George Kennan, and the writer Oliver Wendell Holmes (who appeared many times to give a popular lecture on "The Common Law"). Organizers estimated that 13,000 people attended the Lowell lectures in the 1837–1838 season alone. Lectures were open to all (for a small admission charge), but those who attended had to be "neatly dressed and of orderly behavior," and no one could leave the hall while a lecture was in progress. Lyceums may have entertained, but their purpose was to educate. Their founders considered them serious business and expected their audiences to do the same.

As the nation became increasingly preoccupied with sectional divisions and battles over slavery, the lyceums became important forums for discussion of public controversies. In Springfield, Illinois, in 1838, Abraham Lincoln spoke at the Young Men's Lyceum to denounce the lynchings of several slaves in Mississippi and an attack on a free black man in St. Louis—examples, he said, of the "mobocratic spirit" and a challenge to the "reverence for the laws" that should be the "political religion of the nation." In the years that followed, prominent abolitionists—William Lloyd Garrison, Wendell Phillips, Frederick Douglass, and others—became among the most popular lyceum orators in the North. Douglass, a former slave turned

---

William Henry Harrison, ever to have taken office. Whether because of age and physical infirmities or because of a more fundamental weakness of character, he was a painfully timid and indecisive president at a critical moment in history.

In the year Buchanan took office, a financial panic struck the country, followed by a depression that lasted several years. In the North, the depression strengthened the Republican Party because distressed manufacturers, workers, and farmers came to believe that the hard times were the result of the unsound policies of southern-controlled Democratic administrations. They expressed their frustrations by moving into an alliance with antislavery elements and thus into the Republican Party.

The *Dred Scott* Decision

On March 6, 1857, the Supreme Court of the United States projected itself into the sectional controversy with one of the most controversial and notorious decisions in its history—its ruling in the case of *Dred Scott*

v. *Sandford,* handed down two days after Buchanan was inaugurated. Dred Scott was a Missouri slave, once owned by an army surgeon who had taken Scott with him into Illinois and Wisconsin, where slavery was forbidden. In 1846, after the surgeon died, Scott sued his master's widow for freedom on the grounds that his residence in free territory had liberated him from slavery. The claim was well grounded in Missouri law, and in 1850 the circuit court in which Scott filed the suit declared him free. By now, John Sanford, the brother of the surgeon's widow, was claiming ownership of Scott, and he appealed the circuit court ruling to the state supreme court, which reversed the earlier decision. When Scott appealed to the federal courts, Sanford's attorneys claimed that Scott had no standing to sue because he was not a citizen, but private property.

The Supreme Court (which misspelled Sanford's name in its decision) was so divided that it was unable to issue a single ruling on the case. The thrust of the various rulings, however, was a

Taney's Sweeping Opinion

LYCEUM LECTURE, 1841 This drawing portrays an 1841 Lyceum lecture at Clinton Hall in New York City by James Pollard Espy, a meteorologist. "An army of men of talent," the New York *Mirror* commented at the time, observing the great popularity of the Lyceum series, "has held the town captive." *(Museum of the City of New York)*

antislavery orator, traveled widely speaking at lyceums as far-flung as central Ohio, the island of Nantucket, Massachusetts, and England (where he created a sensation within the British lyceum movement). Douglass mesmerized audiences with his scathing descriptions of life under slavery, and his lyceum lectures helped make him one of the best known and, in the North, most widely admired public figures of his time.

At their heart, lyceums always remained what they had been at the start: a place for men and women to educate and improve themselves by listening to knowledgeable speakers talk about what they knew. They both reflected, and helped strengthen, the growing interest in education in mid-nineteenth-century America. They helped drive the expansion and improvement of the public school system in many areas,

and they marked the beginning of many decades of efforts to extend the benefits of education to adults. They helped popularize the lecture system of instruction, which remains a staple of university education even today. In the fevered years preceding the Civil War, however, lyceums also helped spread explosive ideas about slavery, freedom, and union that fanned the popular passions of the age.

stunning defeat for the antislavery movement. Chief Justice Roger Taney, who wrote one of the majority opinions, declared that Scott could not bring a suit in the federal courts because he was not a citizen. Blacks had no claim to citizenship, Taney argued, and in fact virtually no rights at all under the Constitution. Slaves were property, and the Fifth Amendment prohibited Congress from taking property without "due process of law." Consequently, Taney concluded, Congress possessed no authority to pass a law depriving persons of their slave property in the territories. The Missouri Compromise, therefore, had always been unconstitutional.

The ruling did nothing to challenge the right of an individual state to prohibit slavery within its borders, but the statement that the federal government was powerless to act on the issue was a drastic and startling one. Few judicial opinions have ever created as much controversy. Southern whites were elated: the highest tribunal in the land had sanctioned parts of the most extreme southern argument. In the North, the decision produced widespread dismay. Republicans threatened that when

they won control of the national government, they would reverse the decision—by "packing" the Court with new members.

Deadlock over Kansas

President Buchanan timidly endorsed the *Dred Scott* decision. At the same time, he tried to resolve the controversy over Kansas by supporting its admission to the Union as a slave state. In response, the pro-slavery territorial legislature called an election for delegates to a constitutional convention. The free-state residents refused to participate, claiming that the legislature had discriminated against them in drawing district lines. As a result, the pro slavery forces won control of the convention, which met in 1857 at Lecompton, framed a constitution legalizing slavery, and refused to give voters a chance to reject it. When an election for a new territorial legislature was called, the antislavery groups turned out to vote and won a majority. The new legislature promptly submitted the Lecompton constitution to the voters, who rejected it by more than 10,000 votes.

Both sides had resorted to fraud and violence, but it was clear nevertheless that a majority of the people of Kansas opposed slavery. Buchanan, however, pressured Congress to admit Kansas under the Lecompton constitution. Stephen A. Douglas and other western Democrats refused to support the president's proposal, which died in the House of Representatives. Finally, in April 1858, Congress approved a compromise: The Lecompton constitution would be submitted to the voters of Kansas again. If it was approved, Kansas would be admitted to the Union; if it was rejected, statehood would be postponed. Again, Kansas voters decisively rejected the Lecompton constitution. Not until the closing months of Buchanan's administration in 1861, after several southern states had already withdrawn from the Union, did Kansas enter the Union—as a free state.

Lecompton Constitution Rejected

The Emergence of Lincoln

Given the gravity of the sectional crisis, the congressional elections of 1858 took on a special importance. Of particular note was the United States Senate election in Illinois, which pitted Stephen A. Douglas, the most prominent northern Democrat, against Abraham Lincoln, who was largely unknown outside Illinois but who quickly emerged as one of the most skillful politicians in the Republican Party.

Lincoln was a successful lawyer who had long been involved in state politics. He had served several terms in the Illinois legislature and one undistinguished term in Congress. But he was not a national figure like Douglas, and so he tried to increase his visibility by engaging Douglas in a series of debates. The Lincoln-Douglas debates attracted enormous crowds and received wide attention. By the time they ended, Lincoln's increasingly eloquent and passionate attacks on slavery had made him nationally prominent.

Lincoln-Douglas Debates

At the heart of the debates was a basic difference on the issue of slavery. Douglas appeared to have no moral position on the issue and, Lincoln claimed, did not care whether slavery was "voted up, or voted down." Lincoln's opposition to slavery was more fundamental. If the nation could accept that blacks were not entitled to basic human rights, he argued, then it could accept that other groups—immigrant laborers, for example—could be deprived of rights, too. And if slavery were to extend into the western territories, he argued, opportunities for poor white laborers to better their lots there would be lost. The nation's future, he argued (reflecting the central idea of the Republican Party), rested on the spread of free labor.

Lincoln believed slavery was morally wrong, but he was not an abolitionist. That was in part because he

THE HARPERS FERRY ARSENAL John Brown's famous raid on Harpers Ferry in 1859 centered on this arsenal, from which he and his followers tried, in vain, to foment slave rebellion throughout the South. *(National Park Service, Harper's Ferry. U.S. Department of the Interior)*

Lincoln's Position

could not envision an easy alternative to slavery in the areas where it already existed. He shared the prevailing view among northern whites that the black race was not prepared (and perhaps never would be) to live on equal terms with whites. He and his party would "arrest the further spread" of slavery—that is, prevent its expansion into the territories; they would not directly challenge it where it already existed, but would trust that the institution would gradually die out there of its own accord.

Douglas's position satisfied his followers sufficiently to win him reelection to the Senate, but it aroused little enthusiasm and did nothing to enhance his national political ambitions. Lincoln, by contrast, lost the election but emerged with a growing following both in and beyond the state. And outside Illinois, the elections went heavily against the Democrats, who lost ground in almost every northern state. The party retained control of the Senate but lost its majority in the House, with the result that the congressional sessions of 1858 and 1859 were bitterly deadlocked.

John Brown's Raid

The battles in Congress, however, were almost entirely overshadowed by a spectacular event that enraged and horrified the entire South and greatly hastened the rush toward disunion. In the fall of 1859, John Brown, the antislavery zealot whose bloody actions in Kansas had

John Brown's Raid

inflamed the crisis there, staged an even more dramatic episode, this time in the South itself. With private encouragement and financial aid from some prominent eastern abolitionists, he made elaborate plans to seize a mountain fortress in Virginia from which, he believed, he could foment a slave insurrection in the South. On October 16, he and a group of eighteen followers attacked and seized control of a United States arsenal in Harpers Ferry, Virginia. But the slave uprising Brown hoped to inspire did not occur, and he quickly found himself besieged in the arsenal by citizens, local militia companies, and before long United States troops under the command of Robert E. Lee. After ten of his men were killed, Brown surrendered. He was promptly tried in a Virginia court for treason against the state, found guilty, and sentenced to death. He and six of his followers were hanged.

No other single event did more than the Harpers Ferry raid to convince white southerners that they could not live safely in the Union. John Brown's raid, many southerners believed (incorrectly) had the support of the Republican Party, and it suggested to them that the North was now committed to producing a slave insurrection.

The Election of Lincoln

The presidential election of 1860 had the most momentous consequences of any in American history. It was also among the most complex.

The Democratic Party was torn apart by a battle between southerners, who demanded a strong endorsement of slavery, and westerners, who supported the idea of popular sovereignty. The party convention

Divided Democrats

met in April in Charleston, South Carolina. When the convention endorsed popular sovereignty, delegates from eight states in the lower South walked out. The remaining delegates could not agree on a presidential candidate and finally adjourned after agreeing to meet again in Baltimore in June. The decimated convention at Baltimore nominated Stephen Douglas for president. In the meantime, disenchanted southern Democrats met in Richmond and nominated John C. Breckinridge of Kentucky. Later, a group of conservative ex-Whigs met in Baltimore to form the Constitutional Union Party, with John Bell of Tennessee as their presidential candidate. They endorsed the Union and remained silent on slavery.

The Republican leaders, in the meantime, were trying to broaden their appeal so as to attract every major

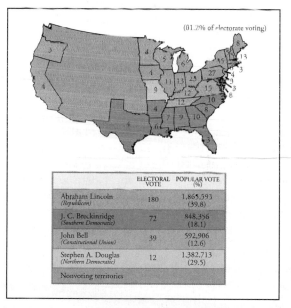

(81.2% of electorate voting)

	ELECTORAL VOTE	POPULAR VOTE (%)
Abraham Lincoln *(Republican)*	180	1,865,593 (39.8)
J. C. Breckinridge *(Southern Democratic)*	72	848,356 (18.1)
John Bell *(Constitutional Union)*	39	592,906 (12.6)
Stephen A. Douglas *(Northern Democratic)*	12	1,382,713 (29.5)
Nonvoting territories		

THE ELECTION OF 1860 The stark sectional divisions that helped produce the Civil War were clearly visible in the results of the 1860 presidential election. Abraham Lincoln, the antislavery Republican candidate, won virtually all the free states. Stephen Douglas, a northern Democrat with no strong position on the issue of slavery, won most of the border states. John Breckinridge, a strong pro-slavery southern Democrat, carried the entire South. Lincoln won under 40 percent of the popular vote, but because of the four-way division in the race, managed to win a slim majority of the electoral vote. ◆ *What impact did the election of Lincoln have on the sectional crisis?*

 For an interactive version of this map go to www.mhhe.com/ brinkley12ch13maps

interest group in the North that feared the South was blocking its economic aspirations. The platform endorsed such traditional Whig measures as a high tariff, internal improvements, a homestead bill, and a Pacific railroad to be built with federal financial assistance. It supported the right of each state to decide the status of slavery within its borders. But it also insisted that neither Congress nor territorial legislatures could legalize slavery in the territories. The Republican convention chose Abraham Lincoln as the party's presidential nominee. Lincoln was appealing because of his growing reputation for eloquence, because of his firm but moderate position on slavery, and because his relative obscurity ensured that he would have none of the drawbacks of other, more prominent (and therefore more controversial) Republicans. He was

a representative of the West, a considerable asset in a race against Douglas.

In the November election, Lincoln won the presidency with a majority of the electoral votes but only about two-fifths of the fragmented popular vote. The Republicans, moreover, failed to win a majority in Congress. Even so, the election of Lincoln became the final signal to many white southerners that their position in the Union was hopeless. And within a few weeks of Lincoln's victory, the process of disunion began—a process that would quickly lead to a prolonged and bloody war between two groups of Americans, each heir to more than a century of struggling toward nationhood, each now convinced that it shared no common ground with the other.

Disunion

CONCLUSION

In the decades following the War of 1812, a vigorous sense of nationalism pervaded much of American life, helping to smooth over the growing differences among the very different societies emerging in the regions of the United States. During the 1850s, however, the forces that had worked to hold the nation together in the past fell victim to new and much more divisive pressures that were working to split the nation apart.

Driving the sectional tensions of the 1850s was a battle over national policy toward the western territories, which were clamoring to become states of the Union—and over the place of slavery within them. Should slavery be permitted in the new states? And who should decide whether to permit it or not? There were strenuous efforts to craft compromises and solutions to this dilemma: the Compromise of 1850, the Kansas-Nebraska Act of 1854, and others. But despite these efforts, positions on slavery continued to harden in both the North and South until ultimately each region came to consider the other its enemy. Bitter battles in the territory of Kansas over whether to permit slavery there; growing agitation by

abolitionists in the North and pro-slavery advocates in the South; the Supreme Court's controversial *Dred Scott* decision in 1857; the popularity of *Uncle Tom's Cabin* throughout the decade; and the emergence of a new political party—the Republican party—openly and centrally opposed to slavery: all worked to destroy the hopes for compromise and push the South toward secession.

In 1860, all pretense of common sentiment collapsed when no political party presented a presidential candidate capable of attracting national support. The Republicans nominated Abraham Lincoln of Illinois, a little-known politician recognized for his eloquent condemnations of slavery in a Senate race two years earlier. The Democratic party split apart, with its northern and southern wings each nominating different candidates. A third party, devoted to the Constitution and the Union, forlornly nominated a candidate of its own who found almost no constituency at all. Lincoln won the election easily, but with less than forty percent of the vote. And almost immediately after his victory, the states of the South began preparing to secede from the Union.

INTERACTIVE LEARNING

The *Primary Source Investigator CD-ROM* offers the following materials related to this chapter:

- A short documentary movie, **America's First Foreign War**, exploring the controversial Mexican War (D7).

- Interactive maps: U.S. Elections (M7) and the Mexican War (M13).

- Documents, images, and maps related to the Mexican War and the growing national split over slavery in the 1850s. Highlights include a variety of historical evidence related to the birth of Texas and the outbreak

of the Mexican War, an image of slave pens where humans were held until their sale, the text of the Kansas-Nebraska Act, the text of the Supreme Court decision in the *Dred Scott* case, and images of the abolitionist John Brown.

 Online Learning Center (www.mhhe.com/brinkley12)

For quizzes, Internet resources, references to additional books and films, and more, consult the book's Online Learning Center.

FOR FURTHER REFERENCE

Richard White, *It's Your Misfortune and None of My Own: A History of the American West* (1991) is an excellent presentation of the social and economic history of the region. Anders Stephanson, *Manifest Destiny* (1995) briefly traces the origins of American expansion ideology. Robert M. Johannsen, *To the Halls of Montezuma: The Mexican War in the American Imagination* (1985) examines public attitudes toward the conflict. Paul D. Lack, *The Texas Revolutionary Experience: A Political and Social History, 1835–1836* (1992) chronicles Texas's route to independence from Mexico. Malcolm Rorabaugh, *Days of Gold: The California Gold Rush and the American Nation* (1997) is an account of this seminal event in the history of the West. Susan Lee Johnson, *Roaring Camp: The Social World of the Gold Rush* (2000) examines the experiences of men and women involved in the frenzy. David M. Pletcher, *The Diplomacy of Annexation: Texas, Oregon, and the Mexican War* (1973) is the standard work on war and diplomacy in the 1840s. Reginald Horsman, *Race and Manifest Destiny* (1981) is a seminal study of racial views in antebellum America. William W. Freehling, *The Road to Disunion, Vol. 1: Secessionists at Bay, 1776–1854* (1990) explores the successful containment of sectionalism prior to the 1850s. David Potter, *The Impending Crisis, 1848–1861* (1976) is a thorough summary of the decisive decade. Eric Foner, *Free Soil, Free Labor, Free Men* (1970) traces the emergence of the Republican Party. Michael Holt, *The Political Crisis of the 1850s* (1978) challenges Foner by emphasizing ethnic and religious alignment in northern politics. Don E. Fehrenbacher, *The Dred Scott Case* (1978) explains the Supreme Court's most infamous decision.

YOUNG SOLDIER This somber 1864 painting by Winslow Homer portrays a young Union soldier—perhaps a drummer boy. When they were not playing music, drummers and buglers performed other functions in camp, as barbers, valets, and members of burial teams. Boys as young as 12 and 13 sometimes joined the army and grew up quickly in the rough surroundings of the camps. *(Cooper-Hewitt Museum, Smithsonian Institution. Gift of Charles Savage Homer, 1912-12-110/Art Resource, NY)*

SIGNIFICANT EVENTS

1860 ▶ South Carolina secedes from Union

1861 ▶ Ten more Southern states secede

▶ Confederate States of America formed

▶ Jefferson Davis named president of Confederacy

▶ Conflict at Fort Sumter, South Carolina (April 12–14), begins Civil War

▶ George B. McClellan appointed commander of Army of the Potomac and army chief of staff

▶ Union blockades Confederate coast

▶ *Trent* affair imperils U.S. relations with Britain

▶ First Battle of Bull Run

1862 ▶ Battle of Shiloh (April 6–7)

▶ Union forces capture New Orleans (April 25)

▶ Second Battle of Bull Run (August 29–30)

▶ Battle of Antietam (September 17)

▶ Battle of Fredericksburg (December 13)

▶ McClellan removed as chief of staff and, later, from command of Army of the Potomac

▶ Robert E. Lee named commander of Confederate armies

▶ Homestead Act and Morrill Land Grant Act passed

▶ Union Pacific Railroad chartered

▶ Confederacy enacts military draft

CHAPTER 14

The Civil War

By the end of 1860, the cords that had once bound the Union together seemed to have snapped. The almost mystical veneration of the Constitution and its framers was no longer working to unite the nation; most residents of the North and South—particularly after the controversial *Dred Scott* decision—now differed fundamentally on their interpretations of the Constitution and what the framers had meant. The romantic vision of America's great national destiny had ceased to be a unifying force; the two sections now defined that destiny in different and apparently irreconcilable terms. The stable two-party system could not dampen sectional conflict any longer; that system had collapsed in the 1850s, to be replaced by a new one that accentuated, rather than muted, regional controversy. Above all, the federal government was no longer the remote, unthreatening presence it once had been; the need to resolve the status of the territories had made it necessary for Washington to deal with sectional issues in a direct and forceful way. And thus, the divisive forces that had always existed within the United States could no longer be counterbalanced by unifying forces.

The election of Abraham Lincoln in 1860—the result of a four-way race in which no candidate achieved close to a majority of the popular vote—was itself evidence of the growing divisions within the nation. That the victor was a man who was clearly from the antislavery camp (even if one of its more moderate members) made his election a powerful factor in the movement toward war. In the aftermath of Lincoln's victory, southern states began to proclaim their secession from the Union, and the new administration was faced with the fateful choice between letting the Union dissolve or engaging in war. Lincoln and his party did not hesitate to defend the Union and accept the necessity of war.

The conflict that followed was one of the most savage in the history of warfare to that point. More than 600,000 Americans died in the Civil War—a level of casualties almost equal to the total number of American deaths in all the nation's other wars combined. But the war had many other effects on the character of the nation. It helped strengthen the role of government. It accelerated the economic development of the North. It made the Republican party a powerful and enduring political force. It devastated the economy of the South and had far-reaching effects on its agricultural system and its politics. And perhaps most important of all, it produced the end of slavery in the United States—first through the Emancipation Proclamation of 1863 and then through the passage of the Thirteenth Amendment of 1865. The abolition of slavery did not lead to equality or justice for African Americans, but it did mark a major turning point in their—and the nation's—history.

▶ Republicans experience heavy losses in congressional elections

1863 ▶ Lincoln issues Emancipation Proclamation (January 1)

▶ Battle of Chancellorsville (May 1–5)

▶ Battle of Gettysburg (July 1–3)

▶ Vicksburg surrenders (July 4)

▶ Battle of Chattanooga (November 23–25)

▶ Union enacts military draft

▶ Antidraft riots break out in New York City

▶ South experiences food riots

▶ West Virginia admitted to Union

1864 ▶ Grant named commander of Union armies

▶ Battle of the Wilderness (May 5–7)

▶ Petersburg, Virginia, besieged

▶ Sherman captures Atlanta (September 2)

▶ Sherman's "March to the Sea" begins

▶ Lincoln reelected president

▶ Central Pacific Railroad chartered

1865 ▶ Lee surrenders to Grant at Appomattox Courthouse (April 9)

▶ Thirteenth Amendment, abolishing slavery, ratified

THE SECESSION CRISIS

Almost as soon as the news of Abraham Lincoln's election reached the South, the militant leaders of the region—the champions of the new concept of "Southern nationalism," men known both to their contemporaries and to history as the "fire-eaters"—began to demand an end to the Union.

"Southern Nationalism"

The Withdrawal of the South

South Carolina, long the hotbed of Southern separatism, seceded first. It called a special convention, which voted unanimously on December 20, 1860, to withdraw the state from the Union. By the time Lincoln took office, six other states—Mississippi (January 9, 1861), Florida (January 10), Alabama (January 11), Georgia (January 19), Louisiana (January 26), and Texas (February 1)—had seceded. In February 1861, representatives of the seven seceded states met at Montgomery, Alabama, and formed a new nation: the Confederate States of America. The response from the North was confused and indecisive. President James Buchanan told Congress in December 1860 that no state had the right to secede from the Union but suggested that the federal government had no authority to stop a state if it did.

Establishment of the Confederacy

The seceding states immediately seized the federal property—forts, arsenals, government offices—within their boundaries. But at first they did not have sufficient military power to seize two fortified offshore military installations: Fort Sumter, on an island in the harbor of Charleston, South Carolina, garrisoned by a small force under Major Robert Anderson; and Fort Pickens in the harbor of Pensacola, Florida. South Carolina sent commissioners to Washington to ask for the surrender of Sumter; but Buchanan, timid though he was, refused to yield it. Indeed, in January 1861 he ordered an unarmed merchant ship to proceed to Fort Sumter with additional troops and supplies. Confederate guns on shore fired at the vessel—the first shots between North and South—and turned it back. Still, neither section was yet ready to concede that war had begun. And in Washington, efforts began once more to forge a compromise.

The Failure of Compromise

Gradually, the compromise forces gathered behind a proposal first submitted by Senator John J. Crittenden of Kentucky and known as the Crittenden Compromise. It called for several constitutional amendments, which would guarantee the permanent existence of slavery in the slave states and would satisfy Southern demands on such issues as fugitive slaves and slavery in the District of Columbia. But the heart of Crittenden's plan was a proposal to reestablish the Missouri Compromise line in all present and future territory of the United States: Slavery would be prohibited north of the line and permitted south of it. The remaining southerners in the Senate seemed willing to accept the plan, but the Republicans were not. The compromise would have required the Republicans to abandon their most fundamental position: that slavery not be allowed to expand.

Crittenden Compromise

And so nothing had been resolved when Abraham Lincoln arrived in Washington for his inauguration—sneaking into the city in disguise on a night train to avoid assassination as he passed through the slave state of Maryland. In his inaugural address, which dealt directly with the secession crisis, Lincoln laid down several basic principles. Since the Union was older than the Constitution, no state could leave it. Acts of force or violence to support secession were insurrectionary. And the government would "hold, occupy, and possess" federal property in the seceded states—a clear reference to Fort Sumter.

Fort Sumter

Conditions at Fort Sumter were deteriorating quickly. Union forces were running short of supplies; unless they received fresh provisions the fort would have to be evacuated. Lincoln believed that if he surrendered Sumter, his commitment to maintaining the Union would no longer be credible. So he sent a relief expedition to the fort, carefully informing the South Carolina authorities that

AN EARLY CONFEDERATE FLAG This early Confederate naval flag was seized by Union forces when they captured New Orleans in April 1862. *(The Museum of the Confederacy, Richmond, Virginia. Photography by Katherine Wetzel)*

FORT SUMTER DURING THE BOMBARDMENT This graphic drawing shows the interior of Fort Sumter during its bombardment by Confederate forces in April 1861. Union forces faced the dual problem of heavy artillery and cannon fire, and dwindling supplies—since the Confederates had blockaded the Charleston harbor to prevent the North from resupplying the fort. (*National Geographic Society*)

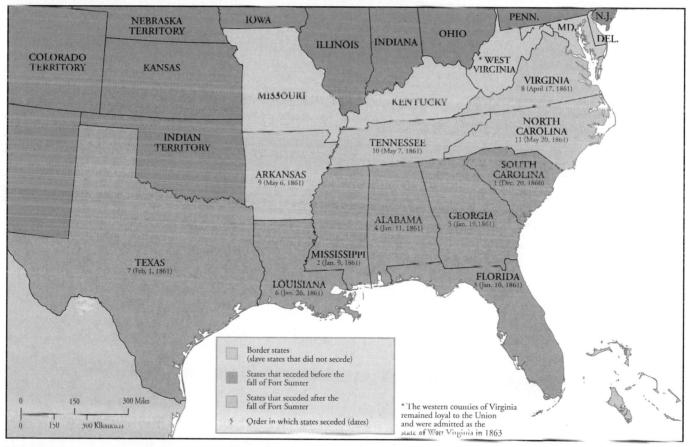

THE PROCESS OF SECESSION The election of Lincoln, the candidate of the antislavery Republican party, to the presidency had the immediate result of inspiring many of the states in the deep South to secede from the Union, beginning with South Carolina only a little more than a month after the November election. Other states nearer the northern border of the slaveholding region remained in the Union for a time, but the U.S. attempt to resupply Fort Sumter (and the bombardment of the fort by the new Confederate army) mobilized the upper South to secede as well. Only enormous pressure from the federal government kept the slaveholding states of Maryland, Kentucky, and Missouri in the Union. ◆ *What accounted for the creation of the state of West Virginia in 1861?*

For an interactive version of this map go to www.mhhe.com/brinkley12ch14maps

there would be no attempt to send troops or munitions unless the supply ships met with resistance.

The new Confederate government now faced a dilemma. Permitting the expedition to land would seem to be a tame submission to federal authority. Firing on the ships or the fort would seem (to the North at least) to be aggression. But Confederate leaders finally decided that to appear cowardly would be worse than to appear belligerent, and they ordered General P. G. T. Beauregard,

The War Begins commander of Confederate forces at Charleston, to take the island, by force if necessary. When Anderson refused to surrender the fort, the Confederates bombarded it for two days, April 12-13, 1861. On April 14, Anderson surrendered. The Civil War had begun.

Almost immediately, Lincoln began mobilizing the North for war. And equally promptly, four more slave states seceded from the Union and joined the Confederacy: Virginia (April 17, 1861), Arkansas (May 6), Tennessee (June 8), and North Carolina (May 20). The four remaining slave states—Maryland, Delaware, Kentucky, and Missouri—cast their lot with the Union (under heavy political and even military pressure from Washington).

Was there anything that Lincoln (or those before him) could have done to settle the sectional conflict peaceably? That question has preoccupied historians for more than a century without resolution (see "Where Historians Disagree," pp. 372-373). There were, of course, actions that might have prevented a war: if, for example, northern leaders had decided to let the South withdraw in peace. The real question, however, is not what hypothetical situations might have reversed the trend toward war but whether the preponderance of forces in the nation were acting to hold the nation together or to drive it apart. And by 1861, it seems clear that in both the North and the South, sectional antagonisms—whether justified or not—had risen to such a point that the existing terms of union had become untenable.

People in both regions had come to believe that two distinct and incompatible civilizations had developed in the United States and that those civilizations were incapable of living together in peace. Ralph Waldo Emerson, speaking for much of the North, said at the time: "I do not see how a barbarous community and a civilized community can constitute one state." And a slaveowner, expressing the sentiments of much of the South, said shortly after the election of Lincoln: "These [Northern] people hate us, annoy us, and would have us assassinated by our slaves if they dared. They are a different people from us, whether better or worse, and there is no love between us. Why then continue together?"

That the North and the South had come to believe these things helped lead to secession and war. Whether these things were actually true—whether the North and the South were really as different and incompatible as

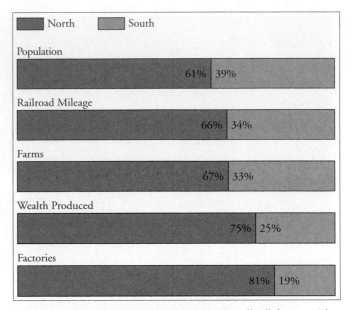

UNION AND CONFEDERATE RESOURCES Virtually all the material advantages—population, manufacturing, railroads, wealth, even agriculture—lay with the North during the Civil War, as this chart shows. ◆ *What advantages did the South have in the conflict?*

they thought—is another question, one that the preparations for and conduct of the war help to answer.

The Opposing Sides

As the war began, only one thing was clear: all the important material advantages lay with the North. Its population was more than twice as large as that of the South (and **Union Advantages** nearly four times as large as the nonslave population of the South), so the Union had a much greater manpower reserve both for its armies and its work force. The North had an advanced industrial system and was able by 1862 to manufacture almost all its own war materials. The South had almost no industry at all and, despite impressive efforts to increase its manufacturing capacity, had to rely on imports from Europe throughout the war.

In addition, the North had a much better transportation system than did the South, and in particular more and better railroads: twice as much trackage as the Confederacy, and a much better integrated system of lines. During the war, moreover, the already inferior Confederate railroad system steadily deteriorated and by the beginning of 1864 had almost collapsed.

But in the beginning the North's material advantages were not as decisive as they appear in retrospect. The South was, for the most part, fighting a defensive war on its own land and thus had the advantage of local support and familiarity with the territory. The Northern armies, on the other hand, were fighting mostly within the South, with long lines of communications, amid hostile local populations, and with access only to the South's own inadequate transportation system. The

WAR BY RAILROAD Union soldiers pose beside a mortar mounted on a railroad car in July 1864, during the siege of Petersburg, Virginia. Railroads played a critical role in the Civil War, and the superiority of the North's rail system was an important factor in its victory. It was appropriate, perhaps, that the battle for Petersburg, the last great struggle of the war, was over control of critical railroad lines. *(National Archives and Records Administration)*

commitment of the white population of the South to

Southern Advantages

the war was, with limited exceptions, clear and firm. In the North, opinion about the war was more divided and support for it remained shaky until very near the end. A major Southern victory at any one of several crucial moments might have proved decisive by breaking the North's will to continue the struggle. Finally, many Southerners believed that the dependence of the English and French textile industries on American cotton would require them to intervene on the side of the Confederacy.

THE MOBILIZATION OF THE NORTH

In the North, the war produced considerable discord, frustration, and suffering. But it also produced prosperity and economic growth by giving a major stimulus to both industry and agriculture.

Economic Measures

With Southern forces now gone from Congress, the Republican Party could exercise virtually unchallenged authority. During the war, it enacted an aggressively

The Causes of the Civil War

In his second inaugural address in March 1865, Abraham Lincoln looked back at the beginning of the Civil War four years earlier. "All knew," he said, that slavery "was somehow the cause of the war." Few historians in the decades since Lincoln spoke have doubted the basic truth of Lincoln's statement; no credible explanation of the causes of the Civil War can ignore slavery. But historians have, nevertheless, disagreed sharply about many things. Was the Civil War inevitable, or could it have been avoided? Was slavery the only, or even the principal, cause of the war? Were other factors equally or more important?

This debate began even before the war itself. In 1858, Senator William H. Seward of New York took note of two competing explanations of the sectional tensions that were then inflaming the nation. On one side, he claimed, stood those who believed the sectional hostility to be "accidental, unnecessary, the work of interested or fanatical agitators." Opposing them stood those (like Seward himself) who believed there to be "an irrepressible conflict between opposing and enduring forces." For at least a century, the division Seward described remained at the heart of scholarly debate.

The "irrepressible conflict" argument was the first to dominate historical discussion. In the first decades after the fighting, histories of the Civil War generally reflected the views of Northerners who had themselves participated in the conflict. To them, the war appeared to be a stark moral conflict in which the South was clearly to blame, a conflict that arose inevitably as a result of the militant immorality of slave society. Henry Wilson's *History of the Rise and Fall of the Slave Power* (1872–1877) was a particularly vivid version of this moral interpretation of the war, which argued that Northerners had fought to preserve the Union and a system of free labor against the aggressive designs of the South.

A more temperate interpretation, but one that reached generally the same conclusions, emerged in the 1890s, when the first serious histories of the war began to appear. Preeminent among them was the seven-volume *History of the United States from the Compromise of 1850 . . .* (1893–1900) by James Ford Rhodes. Like Wilson and others, Rhodes identified slavery as the central, indeed virtually the only, cause of the war. "If the Negro had not been brought to America," he wrote, "the Civil War could not have occurred." And because the North and South had reached positions on the issue of slavery that were both irreconcilable and unalterable, the conflict had become "inevitable."

Although Rhodes placed his greatest emphasis on the moral conflict over slavery, he suggested that the struggle also reflected fundamental differences between the Northern and Southern economic systems. In the 1920s, the idea of the war as an irrepressible economic, rather than moral, conflict received fuller expression from Charles and Mary Beard in *The Rise of American Civilization* (2 vols., 1927). Slavery, the Beards claimed, was not so much a social or cultural institution as an economic one, a labor system. There were, they insisted, "inherent antagonisms" between Northern industrialists and Southern planters. Each group sought to control the federal government so as to protect its own economic interests. Both groups used arguments over slavery and states' rights largely as smoke screens.

The economic determinism of the Beards influenced a generation of historians in important ways, but ultimately most of those who believed the Civil War to have been "irrepressible" returned to an emphasis on social and cultural factors. Allan Nevins argued as much in his great work, *The Ordeal of the Union* (8 vols., 1947–1971). The North and the South, he wrote, "were rapidly becoming separate peoples." At the root of these cultural differences was the "problem of slavery," but the "fundamental assumptions, tastes, and cultural aims" of the two regions were diverging in other ways as well.

More recent proponents of the "irrepressible conflict" argument have taken different views of the Northern and Southern positions on the conflict but have been equally insistent on the role of culture and ideology in creating them. Eric Foner, in *Free Soil, Free Labor, Free Men* (1970) and other writings, emphasized the importance

(*National Geographic Society*)

of the "free-labor ideology" to Northern opponents of slavery. The moral concerns of the abolitionists were not the dominant sentiments in the North, he claimed. Instead, most Northerners (including Abraham Lincoln) opposed slavery largely because they feared it might spread to the North and threaten the position of free white laborers. Convinced that Northern society was superior to that of the South, and increasingly persuaded of the South's intentions to extend the "slave power" beyond its existing borders, Northerners were embracing a viewpoint that made conflict almost inevitable. Eugene Genovese, writing of Southern slaveholders in *The Political Economy of Slavery* (1965), emphasized their conviction that the slave system provided a far more humane society than industrial labor, that the South had constructed "a special civilization built on the relation of master to slave." Just as Northerners were becoming convinced of a Southern threat to their economic system, so Southerners believed that the North had aggressive and hostile designs on the Southern way of life. Like Foner, therefore, Genovese saw in the cultural outlook of the section the source of an all but inevitable conflict.

Historians who argue that the conflict emerged naturally, even inevitably, out of a fundamental divergence between the sections have therefore disagreed markedly over whether moral, cultural, social, ideological, or economic issues were the primary causes of the Civil War. But they have been in general accord that the conflict between North and South was deeply embedded in the nature of the two societies, that slavery was somehow at the heart of the differences, and that the crisis that ultimately emerged was irrepressible. Other historians, however, have questioned that assumption and have argued that the Civil War might have been avoided, that the differences between North and South were not so fundamental as to have necessitated war. Like proponents of the "irrepressible conflict" school, advocates of the war as a "repressible conflict" emerged first in the nineteenth century. President James Buchanan, for example, believed that extremist agitators were to blame for the conflict,

(Library of Congress)

and many Southerners writing of the war in the late nineteenth century claimed that only the fanaticism of the Republican Party could account for the conflict.

The idea of the war as avoidable gained wide recognition among historians in the 1920s and 1930s, when a group known as the "revisionists" began to offer new accounts of the origins of the conflict. One of the leading revisionists was James G. Randall, who saw in the social and economic systems of the North and the South no differences so fundamental as to require a war. Slavery, he suggested, was an essentially benign institution; it was in any case already "crumbling in the presence of nineteenth century tendencies." Only the political ineptitude of a "blundering generation" of leaders could account for the Civil War, he claimed. Avery Craven, another leading revisionist, placed more emphasis on the issue of slavery than had Randall. But in *The Coming of the Civil War* (1942) he too argued that slave laborers were not much worse off than Northern industrial workers, that the institution was already on the road to "ultimate extinction," and that war could therefore have been averted had skillful and responsible leaders worked to produce compromise.

More recent students of the war have kept elements of the revisionist interpretation alive by emphasizing the role of political agitation and ethnocultural conflicts in the coming of the war. In 1960, for example, David Herbert Donald argued that the politicians of the 1850s were not unusually inept, but that they were operating in a society in which traditional restraints

were being eroded in the face of the rapid extension of democracy. Thus the sober, statesmanlike solution of differences was particularly difficult. Michael Holt, in *The Political Crisis of the 1850s* (1978), emphasized the role of political parties and especially the collapse of the second party system, rather than the irreconcilable differences between sections, in explaining the conflict, although he avoided placing blame on any one group.

Holt, however, also helped introduce another element to the debate. He was, along with Paul Kleppner, Joel Silbey, and William Gienapp, one of the creators of an "ethnocultural" interpretation of the war. The Civil War began, the ethnoculturalists argue, in large part because the party system—the most effective instrument for containing and mediating sectional differences—collapsed in the 1850s and produced a new Republican party that aggravated, rather than calmed, the divisions in the nation. But unlike other scholars, who saw the debate over slavery as the central factor in the collapse of the party system, the ethnoculturalists argue for other factors. For example, William Gienapp, in *The Origins of the Republican Party, 1852–1856* (1987) argues that the disintegration of the party system in the early 1850s was less a result of the debate over slavery in the territories than of such ethnocultural issues as temperance and nativism. The Republican Party itself, he argues, was less a product of antislavery fervor than of a sustained competition with the Know-Nothing Party over ethnic and cultural issues. Gienapp and the other ethnoculturalists would not entirely dispute Lincoln's claim that slavery was "somehow the cause of the war." But they do challenge the arguments of Eric Foner and others that the "free labor ideal" of the North—and the challenge slavery, and its possible expansion into the territories, posed to that ideal—was the principal reason for the conflict. Slavery became important, they suggest, less because of irreconcilable differences of attitude than because of the collapse of parties and other structures that might have contained the conflict.

nationalistic program to promote economic development, particularly in the West. The Homestead Act of 1862 permitted any citizen or prospective citizen to claim 160

Republican Economic Policy

acres of public land and to purchase it for a small fee after living on it for five years. The Morrill Land Grant Act of the same year transferred substantial public acreage to the state governments, which were to sell the land and use the proceeds to finance public education. This act led to the creation of many new state colleges and universities, the so-called land-grant institutions. Congress also passed a series of tariff bills that by the end of the war had raised duties to the highest level in the nation's history—a great boon to domestic industries eager for protection from foreign competition.

Congress also moved to complete the dream of a transcontinental railroad. It created two new federally chartered corporations: the Union Pacific Railroad Company, which was to build westward from Omaha, and the Central Pacific, which was to build eastward from California. The two projects were to meet in the middle and complete the link. The government provided free public lands and generous loans to the companies.

The National Bank Acts of 1863–1864 created a new national banking system. Existing or newly formed banks

National Bank Acts

could join the system if they had enough capital and were willing to invest one-third of it in government securities. In return, they could issue U.S. Treasury notes as currency. The new system eliminated much of the chaos and uncertainty in the nation's currency and created a uniform system of national bank notes.

More difficult than promoting economic growth was financing the war itself. The government tried to do so in three ways: by levying taxes, issuing paper currency, and borrowing. Congress levied new taxes on almost all goods and services; and in 1861 the government levied an income tax for the first time, with rates that eventually rose to 10 percent on incomes above $5,000. But taxation raised only a small pro-

Financing the War

portion of the funds necessary for financing the war, and strong popular resistance prevented the government from raising the rates. At least equally controversial was the printing of paper currency, or "greenbacks." The new currency was backed not by gold or silver, but simply by the good faith and credit of the government (much like today's currency). The value of the greenbacks fluctuated according to the fortunes of the Northern armies. Early in 1864, with the war effort bogged down, a greenback dollar was worth only 39 percent of a gold dollar. Even at the close of the war, it was worth only 67 percent of a gold dollar. Because of the difficulty of making purchases with this uncertain currency, the government used greenbacks sparingly. The Treasury issued only $450 million worth of paper currency—a small proportion of the cost of the war but enough to produce significant inflation.

By far the largest source of financing for the war was loans from the American people. In previous wars, the government had sold bonds only to banks and to a few wealthy investors. Now, however, the Treasury persuaded ordinary citizens to buy over $400 million worth of bonds—the first example of mass financing of a war in American history. Still, bond purchases by individuals constituted only a small part of the government's borrowing, which in the end totaled $2.6 billion. Most of the loans came from banks and large financial interests.

Raising the Union Armies

Over 2 million men served in the Union armed forces during the course of the Civil War. But at the beginning of 1861, the regular army of the United States consisted of only 16,000 troops, many of them stationed in the West to

SENDING THE BOYS OFF TO WAR In this painting by Thomas Nast, New York's Seventh Regiment parades down Broadway in April 1861, to the cheers of exuberant, patriotic throngs, shortly before departing to fight in what most people then assumed would be a brief war. Thomas Nast is better known for his famous political cartoons of the 1870s. *(Seventh Regiment Armory, New York City)*

protect white settlers from Indians. So the Union, like the Confederacy, had to raise its army mostly from scratch. Lincoln called for an increase of 23,000 in the regular army, but the bulk of the fighting, he knew, would have to be done by volunteers in state militias. When Congress convened in July 1861, it authorized enlisting 500,000 volunteers for three-year terms (as opposed to the customary three-month terms). This voluntary system of recruitment produced adequate forces only briefly. After the first flush of enthusiasm for the war, enlistments declined. By March 1863, Congress was forced to pass a national draft law. Virtually all young adult males were eligible to be drafted; but a man could escape service by hiring someone to go in his place or by paying the government a fee of $300. Only about 46,000 men were ever actually conscripted, but the draft greatly increased voluntary enlistments.

To a people accustomed to a remote and inactive national government, conscription was strange and ominous. Opposition to the law was widespread, particularly

Draft Riots

among laborers, immigrants, and Democrats opposed to the war (known as "Peace Democrats" or "Copperheads" by their enemies). Occasionally it erupted into violence. Demonstrators against the draft rioted in New York City for four days in July 1863, after the first names were selected for conscription. Over 100 people died. Irish workers were at the center of the violence. They were angry because black strikebreakers had been used against them in a recent longshoremen's strike; and they blamed African Americans generally for the war, which they thought was being fought for the benefit of slaves who would soon be competing with white workers for jobs. The rioters lynched a number of African Americans, burned down homes and businesses (mostly those of free blacks), and even destroyed an orphanage for African-American children. Only the arrival of federal troops subdued the rioters.

HANGING A NEGRO IN CLARKSON STREET.

THE NEW YORK CITY DRAFT RIOT, 1863 Opposition to the Civil War draft was widespread in the North and in July 1863 produced a violent four-day uprising in New York City in which as many as 100 people died. The riot began on July 13 with a march by 4,000 men, mostly poor Irish laborers, who were protesting the provisions by which some wealthy people could be exempted from conscription "Rich man's war, poor man's fight," the demonstrators cried (just as some critics of the war chanted at times in the South). Many New Yorkers also feared that the war would drive black workers north to compete for their jobs. The demonstration turned violent when officials began drawing names for the draft. The crowd burned the draft building and then split into factions. Some rioters attacked symbols of wealth such as exclusive shops and mansions. Others terrorized black neighborhoods and lynched some residents. This contemporary engraving depicts one such lynching. Only by transferring five regiments to the city from Gettysburg (less than two weeks after the great battle there) was the government able to restore order. *(The Granger Collection)*

Wartime Politics

When Abraham Lincoln arrived in Washington early in 1861, many politicians—noting his lack of national experience and his folksy, unpretentious manner—considered him a minor politician from the prairies, a man whom the real leaders of his party would easily control. But the new president moved quickly to establish his own authority. He assembled a cabinet representing every faction of the Republican Party and every segment of Northern opinion—men of exceptional prestige and influence and in some cases arrogance, several of whom believed that they, not Lincoln, should be president. Lincoln moved boldly as well to use the war powers of the presidency, ignoring inconvenient parts of the Constitution because, he said, it would be foolish to lose the whole by being afraid to disregard a part. He sent troops into battle without asking Congress for a declaration of war.

(Lincoln insisted on calling the conflict a domestic insurrection, which required no formal declaration of war; to ask for a declaration would, he believed, constitute implicit recognition of the Confederacy as an independent nation.) He increased the size of the regular army without receiving legislative authority to do so. He unilaterally proclaimed a naval blockade of the South.

Lincoln's greatest political problem was the widespread popular opposition to the war, mobilized by factions in the Democratic Party. The Peace Democrats feared that the agricultural Northwest was losing influence to the industrial East and that Republican nationalism was

Wartime Repression

eroding states' rights. Lincoln used extraordinary methods to suppress them. He ordered military arrests of civilian dissenters and suspended the right of habeas corpus (the right of an arrested person to a speedy trial). At first,

Lincoln used these methods only in sensitive areas such as the border states; but in 1862, he proclaimed that all persons who discouraged enlistments or engaged in disloyal practices were subject to martial law. In all, more than 13,000 persons were arrested and imprisoned for varying periods. The most prominent Copperhead in the country—Ohio congressman Clement L. Vallandigham—was seized by military authorities and exiled to the Confederacy after he made a speech claiming that the purpose of the war was to free the blacks and enslave the whites. Lincoln defied all efforts to curb his authority to suppress opposition, even those of the Supreme Court. When Chief Justice Taney issued a writ (*Ex parte Merryman*) requiring him to release an imprisoned Maryland secessionist leader, Lincoln simply ignored it. (After the war, in 1866, the Supreme Court ruled in *Ex parte Milligan* that military trials in areas where the civil courts existed were unconstitutional.)

The presidential election of 1864 occurred, therefore, in the midst of considerable political dissension. The Republicans had suffered heavy losses in the congressional elections of 1862, and in response leaders of the party tried to create a broad coalition of all the groups that supported the war. They called the new organization the Union Party, but in reality it was little more than the Republican Party and a small faction of War Democrats. The Union Party nominated Lincoln for another term as president and Andrew Johnson of Tennessee, a War Democrat who had opposed his state's decision to secede, for the vice presidency.

The Democrats nominated George B. McClellan, a celebrated former Union general who had been relieved of his command by Lincoln, and adopted a platform denouncing the war and calling for a truce. McClellan repudiated that demand, but the Democrats were clearly the peace party in the campaign, trying to profit from growing war weariness and from the Union's discouraging military position in the summer of 1864.

At this crucial moment, however, several Northern military victories, particularly the capture of Atlanta, Georgia, early in September, rejuvenated Northern morale and boosted Republican prospects. Lincoln won reelection comfortably, with 212 electoral votes to McClellan's 21; the president carried every state except Kentucky, New Jersey, and Delaware. But Lincoln's lead in the popular vote was a more modest 10 percent. Had Union victories not occurred when they did, and had Lincoln not made special arrangements to allow Union troops to vote, the Democrats might have won.

1864 Election

The Politics of Emancipation

Despite their surface unity in 1864 and their general agreement on most economic matters, the Republicans disagreed sharply on the issue of slavery. Radicals—led in Congress by such men as Representative Thaddeus Stevens of Pennsylvania and Senators Charles Sumner of Massachusetts and Benjamin Wade of Ohio—wanted to use the war to abolish slavery immediately and completely. Conservatives favored a slower, more gradual, and, they believed, less disruptive process for ending slavery; in the beginning, at least, they had the support of the president.

Despite Lincoln's cautious view of emancipation, momentum began to gather behind it early in the war. In 1861, Congress passed the Confiscation Act, which declared that all slaves used for "insurrectionary" purposes (that is, in support of the Confederate military effort) would be considered freed. Subsequent laws in the spring of 1862 abolished slavery in the District of Columbia and in the western territories, and compensated owners. In July 1862, the Radicals pushed through Congress the second Confiscation Act, which declared free the slaves of persons aiding and supporting the insurrection (whether or not the slaves themselves were doing so) and authorized the president to employ African Americans, including freed slaves, as soldiers. As the war progressed, much of the North seemed slowly to accept emancipation as a central war aim; nothing less, many believed, would justify the enormous sacrifices of the struggle. As a result, the Radicals increased their influence within the Republican Party—a development that did not go unnoticed by the president, who decided to seize the leadership of the rising antislavery sentiment himself.

Confiscation Acts

Free at Last!

On September 22, 1862, after the Union victory at the Battle of Antietam, the president announced his intention to use his war powers to issue an executive order freeing all slaves in the Confederacy. And on January 1, 1863, he formally signed the Emancipation Proclamation, which declared forever free slaves in all areas of the Confederacy except those already under Union control: Tennessee, western Virginia, and southern Louisiana. The proclamation did not apply to the border slave states, which had never seceded from the Union and therefore were not subject to the president's war powers.

Emancipation Proclamation

The immediate effect of the proclamation was limited, since it applied only to slaves still under Confederate control. But the document was of great importance nevertheless, because it clearly and irrevocably established that the war was being fought not only to preserve the Union but also to eliminate slavery. Eventually, as federal armies occupied much of the South, the proclamation became a practical reality and led directly to the freeing of thousands of slaves. Even in areas not directly affected by the proclamation, the antislavery impulse gained strength. By the end of the war, slavery had been abolished in two Union slave states—Maryland and Missouri—and in three Confederate states occupied by Union forces—Tennessee, Arkansas, and Louisiana. The final step came in 1865, when Congress approved and the necessary states ratified

AFRICAN-AMERICAN TROOPS Although most of the black soldiers who enlisted in the Union army during the Civil War performed noncombat jobs behind the lines, there were also black combat regiments—members of one of which are pictured here—who fought with great success and valor in critical battles. *(Library of Congress)*

the Thirteenth Amendment, abolishing slavery as an institution in all parts of the United States. After more than two centuries, legalized slavery finally ceased to exist in the United States.

African Americans and the Union Cause

About 186,000 emancipated blacks served as soldiers, sailors, and laborers for the Union forces, joining a significant number of free blacks from the North. The services of African Americans to the Union military were significant in many ways, not least because of the substantial obstacles many blacks had to surmount in order to enlist.

In the first months of the war, African Americans were largely excluded from the military. A few black regiments eventually took shape in some of the Union-occupied areas of the Confederacy, largely because they were a ready source of manpower in these defeated regions. But once Lincoln issued the Emancipation Proclamation, black enlistment increased rapidly and the Union military began actively to recruit African-American soldiers and sailors in both the North and, where possible, the South.

Black Enlistment

Some of these men were organized into fighting units, of which the best known was probably the Fifty-fourth Massachusetts infantry, which (like most black regiments) had a white commander: Robert Gould Shaw, a member of an aristocratic Boston family. Shaw and more than half his regiment died during a battle near Charleston, South Carolina, in the summer of 1863.

Most black soldiers, however, were assigned menial tasks behind the lines, such as digging trenches and transporting water. Even though fewer blacks than whites died in combat, the black mortality rate was actually higher than the rate for white soldiers because so many black soldiers died of disease from working long, arduous hours in unsanitary conditions. Conditions for blacks and whites were unequal in other ways as well. African-American soldiers were paid a third less than were white soldiers (until Congress changed the law in mid-1864). Black fighting men captured by the Confederates were, unlike white prisoners, not returned to the North in exchange for Southern soldiers being returned to the South. They were sent back to their masters (if they were escaped slaves) or often executed. In 1864, Confederate soldiers killed over 260 African Americans after capturing them in Tennessee.

Mistreatment of Black Soldiers

The War and Economic Development

The Civil War did not, as some historians used to claim, transform the North from an agrarian to an industrial society. Industrialization was already far advanced when the war began, and in some areas, the war actually retarded growth—by cutting manufacturers off from their Southern markets and sources of raw material, and by diverting labor and resources to military purposes.

On the whole, however, the war sped the economic development of the North. That was in part a result of the political dominance of the Republican Party and its promotion of nationalistic economic legislation. But it was also because the war itself required the expansion of certain sectors of the economy. Coal production increased by nearly 20 percent during the war. Railroad facilities improved—mainly through the adoption of a standard gauge (track width) on new lines. The loss of farm labor to the military forced many farmers to increase the mechanization of agriculture.

The war was a difficult experience for many American workers. Industrial laborers experienced a substantial loss of purchasing power, as prices in the North rose by more than 70 percent during the war while wages rose only about 40 percent. That was partly because liberalized immigration laws permitted a flood of new workers into the labor market and helped keep wages low. It was also because the increasing mechanization of production eliminated the jobs of many skilled workers. One result of these hardships was a substantial increase in union membership in many industries and the creation of several national unions, for coal miners, railroad engineers, and others—organizations bitterly opposed and rigorously suppressed by employers.

Hard Times for Workers

Women, Nursing, and the War

Responding not only to the needs of employers for additional labor, but to their own, often desperate, need for money, women found themselves, either by choice or by necessity, thrust into new and often unfamiliar roles during the war. They took over positions vacated by men and worked as teachers, retail sales clerks, office workers, and mill and factory hands.

Above all, women entered nursing, a field previously dominated by men. The U.S. Sanitary Commission, an organization of civilian volunteers led by Dorothea Dix, mobilized large numbers of female nurses to serve in field hospitals. By the end of the war, women were the dominant force in nursing; by 1900, nursing had become an almost entirely female profession. Female nurses not only cared for patients but performed other tasks considered appropriate for women: cooking, cleaning, and laundering.

U.S. Sanitary Commission

Female nurses encountered considerable resistance from male doctors, many of whom considered women too weak for medical work and who, in any case, found the sight of women taking care of strange men inappropriate. The Sanitary Commission tried to counter such arguments by attributing to nursing many of the domestic ideals that American society attributed to women's work in the home. Women as nurses were to play the same maternal, nurturing, instructive role they played as wives and mothers. "The right of woman to her sphere, which includes housekeeping, cooking, and nursing, has never been disputed," one Sanitary Commission official insisted. But not all women who worked for the commission were content with a purely maternal role; some challenged the dominance of men in the organization and even stood up against doctors whom they considered incompetent, increasing the resentment felt toward them by many men. In the end, though, the work of female nurses was so indispensable to the military that the complaints of male doctors were irrelevant.

Traditional Gender Roles Reinforced

Nurses, and many other women, found the war a liberating experience, in which (as one Sanitary Commission nurse later wrote) the American woman "had developed potencies and possibilities of which she had been unaware

THE U.S. SANITARY COMMISSION Mathew Brady took this photograph of female nurses and Union soldiers standing before an infirmary at Brandy Station, Virginia, near Petersburg, in 1864. The infirmary was run by the U.S. Sanitary Commission, the government-supported nursing corps that became indispensable to the medical care of wounded soldiers during the Civil War. *(National Archives and Records Administration)*

and which surprised her, as it did those who witnessed her marvelous achievement." Some women, especially those who had been committed to feminist causes earlier, came to see the war as an opportunity to win support for their own goals. Elizabeth Cady Stanton and Susan B. Anthony, who together founded the National Woman's Loyal League in 1863, worked simultaneously for the abolition of slavery and the awarding of suffrage to women. Clara Barton, who was active during the war in collecting and distributing medical supplies and who later became an important figure in the nursing profession (and a founder of the American Red Cross), said in 1888: "At the war's end, woman was at least fifty years in advance of the normal position which continued peace would have assigned her." That may have been a considerable exaggeration; but it captured the degree to which many women looked back on the war as a crucial moment in the redefinition of female roles and in the awakening of a sense of independence and new possibilities.

Whatever nursing may have done for the status of women, it had an enormous impact on the medical profession and on the treatment of wounded soldiers during the war. The U.S. Sanitary Commission not only organized women to serve at the front, it also funneled medicine and supplies to badly overtaxed field hospitals. The commission also (as its name suggests) helped spread ideas about the importance of sanitary conditions in hospitals and clinics and probably contributed to the relative decline of death by disease in the Civil War. Nevertheless, twice as many soldiers died of diseases—malaria, dysentery, typhoid, gangrene, and others—as died in combat during the war. Even minor injuries could lead to fatal infections.

Nursing and Medicine

THE MOBILIZATION OF THE SOUTH

Many Southerners boasted loudly of the differences between their new nation and the nation they had left. Those differences were real. But there were also important similarities between the Union and the Confederacy, which became particularly clear as the two sides mobilized for war: similarities in their political systems, in the methods they used for financing the war and conscripting troops, and in the way they fought.

The Confederate Government

The Confederate constitution was almost identical to the Constitution of the United States, with several significant exceptions: It explicitly acknowledged the sovereignty of the individual states (although not the right of secession), and it specifically sanctioned slavery and made its abolition (even by one of the states) practically impossible.

The constitutional convention at Montgomery named a provisional president and vice president: Jefferson Davis

of Mississippi and Alexander H. Stephens of Georgia, who were later chosen by the general electorate, without opposition, for six-year terms. Davis had been a moderate secessionist before the war; Stephens had argued against secession. The Confederate government, like the Union government, was dominated throughout the war by moderate leaders. Also like the Union, it was dominated less by the old aristocracy of the East than by the newer aristocrats of the West, of whom Davis was the most prominent example.

Davis was, in the end, an unsuccessful president. He was a reasonably able administrator and the dominating figure in his government, encountering little interference from the generally tame members of his unstable cabinet and serving as his own secretary of war. But he rarely provided genuinely national leadership. One shrewd Confederate official wrote: "All the revolutionary vigor is with the enemy. . . . With us timidity-hair splitting."

Davis's Leadership

There were no formal political parties in the Confederacy, but its congressional and popular politics were rife with dissension nevertheless. Some white Southerners (and of course most African Americans who were aware of the course of events) opposed secession and war altogether. Many white people in poorer "backcountry" and "upcountry" regions, where slavery was limited, refused to recognize the new Confederate government or to serve in the Southern army; some worked or even fought for the Union. Most white Southerners supported the war, but as in the North many were openly critical of the government and the military, particularly as the tide of battle turned against the South and the Confederate economy decayed.

Southern Divisions

Money and Manpower

Financing the Confederate war effort was a monumental and ultimately impossible task. It involved creating a national revenue system in a society unaccustomed to significant tax burdens. It depended on a small and unstable banking system that had little capital to lend. Because most wealth in the South was invested in slaves and land, liquid assets were scarce; and the Confederacy's only specie—seized from U.S. mints located in the South—was worth only about $1 million.

The Confederate Congress tried at first not to tax the people directly but to requisition funds from the individual states. But most of the states were also unwilling to tax their citizens and paid their shares, when they paid them at all, with bonds or notes of dubious worth. In 1863, therefore, the congress enacted an income tax—which planters could pay "in kind" (as a percentage of their produce). But taxation never provided the Confederacy with very much revenue; it produced only about 1 percent of the government's total income. Borrowing was not much more successful. The Confederate

Funding Problems

The Consolidation of Nations

The American Civil War was an event largely rooted in conditions particular to the United States. But it was also a part of a worldwide movement in the nineteenth century to create large, consolidated nations. America's expansion into the western regions of the continent—and its efforts to incorporate those areas into the nation—was one of the principal causes of the controversies over slavery that led to the Civil War. A commitment to preserving the Union—to consolidating, rather than dismantling, the nation—was one of the principal motives for the North's commitment to fighting a war against the seceding states. Similar efforts at expansion, consolidation, and unification were occurring in many other nations around the same time.

The consolidation of nation states was, of course, not new to the nineteenth century. Spain, Britain, Russia, and other nations had united disparate states and regions into substantial nations in the fifteenth, sixteenth, and seventeenth centuries. But nationalism took on new force in the nineteenth century. That was partly because of growing nationalist sentiment among peoples who shared language, culture, ethnicity, and tradition and who came to believe that a consolidated nation was the best vehicle for strengthening their common bonds. Nationalism was also a product of the centralization of governments in many areas of the world, and the development within

them of the ability to administer large territories from above. The revolutions in America and France in the late eighteenth century—and the subsequent strengthening of the French concept of nationhood under Napoleon in the early nineteenth century—inspired new nationalist enthusiasms in other parts of Europe.

In 1848, a wave of nationalist revolutions erupted in Italy, France, and Austria, challenging the imperial powers

THE UNIFICATION OF ITALY This painting shows a climactic moment in the history of Italian unification. Garibaldi, the great leader of independence forces in southern Italy, greets King Victor Emmanuel of the Piedmont, the leader of independence forces in the North. Garibaldi greeted him by saying, "Saluto il primo Re d'Italia" ("I hail the first king of Italy"). The moment was significant both practically—it demonstrated Garibaldi's willingness to accept Victor Emmanuel's authority—and symbolically, as the triumph of nationalist sentiment in this once decentralized country. *(Museo del Risorgimento, Milan/Index S.A.S.)*

government issued bonds in such vast amounts that the public lost faith in them and stopped buying them, and efforts to borrow money in Europe using cotton as collateral fared no better.

As a result the Confederacy had to pay for the war through the least stable, most destructive form of financing: paper currency, which it began issuing in 1861. By 1864, the Confederacy had issued the staggering total of $1.5 billion in paper money, more than twice what the Union had produced. And unlike the Union, the Confederacy did not establish a uniform currency system; the national government, states, cities, and private banks all issued their own notes, producing widespread chaos and confusion. The result was a disastrous inflation, far

worse than anything the North experienced. Prices in the North rose 80 percent in the course of the war; in the South they rose 9,000 percent, with devastating effects on the new nation's morale.

Like the United States, the Confederacy first raised a military by calling for volunteers. And as in the North, by the end of 1861 voluntary enlistments were declining. In April 1862, therefore, the congress enacted a Conscription Act, which subjected all white males between the ages of eighteen and thirty-five to military service for three years. As in the North, a draftee could avoid service if he furnished a substitute. But since the price of substitutes was high, the provision aroused

Raising the Confederate Army

that many Europeans believed were subjugating national cultures. Those revolutions failed, but they helped lay the groundwork for the two most important national consolidations of nineteenth-century Europe.

One of them occurred in Germany, which was divided into numerous small, independent states in the early nineteenth century but where popular sentiment for German unification had been growing for decades. It was spurred in part by new histories of the German *volk* (people) and by newly constructed images of German traditions, visible in such literature as Grimm's fairy tales—an effort to record and popularize German folk traditions and make them the basis of a shared sense of a common past. In 1862, King Wilhelm I of Prussia—the leader of one of the most powerful of the scattered German states—appointed an aristocratic landowner, Otto von Bismarck, as his prime minister. Bismarck exploited the growing nationalism throughout the various German states and helped develop a strong popular base for unification. He did so in part by launching Prussian wars against Denmark, Austria, and France—wars Prussia easily won, inspiring pride in German power that extended well beyond Prussia itself. The Franco-Prussian War of 1870 was particularly important, because Prussia fought it to take possession of the French provinces of Alsace and Lorraine—provinces the Prussians claimed were part of the German "national community" because its people, although legally French citizens, were ethnically and linguistically German. In 1871, capitalizing on the widespread nationalist sentiment the war had created throughout the German-speaking states, Bismarck persuaded the German king to proclaim himself emperor (or *Kaiser*) of a new empire that united all German peoples except those in Austria and Switzerland.

The second great European movement for national unification occurred in Italy, which had long been divided into small kingdoms, city-states, and regions controlled by the Vatican. Some areas of Italy were at one time or another dominated by the French, the Spanish, and the Austro-Hungarian empire.

Beginning in the early nineteenth century, Italian nationalists formed what became known as the Young Italy movement, under the leadership of Giuseppe Mazzini. The movement demanded an end of foreign control in Italy and the unification of the Italian people into a single nation. It promoted an idea of the nation as a kind of family, and of its territories as a family home. Peoples with common language, culture, and tradition, Mazzini believed, should be free to unite and govern themselves. More important than this growing popular nationalism as a cause of Italian unification were the efforts of powerful and ambitious leaders. The most powerful Italian state in the mid-nineteenth century was the kingdom of the Piedmont and Sardinia, in the northwestern part of the peninsula. Its king, Victor Emmanuel II, appointed his own version of Bismarck—Camillo di Cavour—as prime minister in 1852. Cavour joined forces with nationalists in other areas of Italy to drive the Spanish and the Austrians out of Italian territory. Having first won independence for northern Italy, Cavour joined forces with the southern nationalist leader Giuseppe Garibaldi, who helped win independence in the South and then agreed to a unification of the entire Italian nation under Victor Emmanuel in 1860.

Other nations in these years were also trying to create, preserve, and strengthen nation states. Some failed to do so—Russia, which despite the reform efforts of several tsars, never managed to create a stable nation-state from among its broad and diverse peoples; Austria, whose empire could never consolidate its claim over a similarly diverse group of national groups; Turkey, whose Ottoman empire (known as "the sick man of Europe") remained frail despite the efforts of leaders to strengthen it; and China, which likewise tried and failed to produce reforms that would consolidate its vast lands effectively. But others succeeded—Meiji Japan, for example, instituted a series of reforms in the 1880s and 1890s that created a powerful new Japanese nation-state.

In fighting and winning the Civil War, the nationalists of the northern parts of the United States not only preserved the unity of their nation. They also became part of a movement toward the consolidation of national cultures and national territories that extended through many areas of the globe.

such opposition from poorer whites that it was repealed in 1863. Even more controversial was the exemption from the draft of one white man on each plantation with twenty or more slaves, a provision that caused smaller farmers to complain: "It's a rich man's war but a poor man's fight." Many more white Southerners were exempted from military service than Northerners.

Even so, conscription worked for a time. At the end of 1862, about 500,000 men were in the Confederate military. (A total of approximately 900,000 served in the course of the entire war.) That number did not include the many slave men and women recruited by the military to perform such services as cooking, laundry, and manual labor, hence freeing additional white manpower for fighting. After 1862, however, conscription began producing fewer men—in part because the Union had by then begun to seize large areas of the Confederacy and thus had cut off much of the population from conscription or recruitment.

As 1864 opened, the government faced a critical manpower shortage. In a desperate move, the Confederate Congress began trying to draft men as young as seventeen and **Manpower Shortages** as old as fifty. But in a nation suffering from intense war weariness, where many had concluded that defeat was inevitable, nothing could attract or retain an adequate army any longer. In 1864–1865 there were 100,000 desertions. In a frantic final attempt to raise men, the

CONFEDERATE VOLUNTEERS Young Southern soldiers posed for this photograph in 1861, shortly before the first Battle of Bull Run. The Civil War was the first major military conflict in the age of photography, and it launched the careers of many of America's early photographers. *(Cook Collection, Valentine Richmond History Center)*

congress authorized the conscription of 300,000 slaves, but the war ended before the government could attempt this incongruous experiment.

States' Rights versus Centralization

The greatest source of division in the South, however, was not differences of opinion over the war, but the doctrine of states' rights. States' rights had become such a cult among many white Southerners that they resisted virtually all efforts to exert national authority, even those necessary to win the war. They restricted Davis's ability to impose martial law and suspend habeas corpus. They obstructed conscription. Recalcitrant governors such as Joseph Brown of Georgia and Zebulon M. Vance of North Carolina tried at times to keep their own troops apart from the Confederate forces and insisted on hoarding surplus supplies for their own states' militias.

But the Confederate government did make substantial strides in centralizing power in the South. By the end of the war, the Confederate bureaucracy was larger than its counterpart in Washington. The national government experimented, successfully for a time, with a "food draft"—which permitted soldiers to feed themselves by seizing crops from farms in their path. The government impressed slaves, often over the objections of their owners, to work

Centralization

as laborers on military projects. The Confederacy seized control of the railroads and shipping; it imposed regulations on industry; it limited corporate profits. States' rights sentiment was a significant handicap, but the South nevertheless took dramatic steps in the direction of centralization—becoming in the process increasingly like the region whose institutions it was fighting to escape.

Economic and Social Effects of the War

The war had a devastating effect on the economy of the South. It cut off Southern planters and producers from the markets in the North on which they had depended; it made the sale of cotton overseas much more difficult; it robbed farms and industries that did not have large slave populations of a male work force, leaving some of them unable to function effectively. While in the North production of all goods, agricultural and industrial, increased somewhat during the war, in the South it declined by more than a third.

Most of all, perhaps, the fighting itself wreaked havoc on the Southern economy. Almost all the major battles of the war occurred within the Confederacy; both armies spent most of their time on Southern soil. As a result of the savage fighting, the South's already inadequate railroad system was nearly destroyed; much of its most valuable farmland, and many of its most successful plantations, were ruined by Union troops (especially in the last year of the war).

Once the Northern naval blockade became effective, the South experienced massive shortages of almost everything. The region was overwhelmingly agricultural, but since it had concentrated so single-mindedly on producing cotton and other export crops, it did not grow enough food to meet its own needs. And despite the efforts of women and slaves to keep farms functioning, the departure of white male workers seriously diminished the region's ability to keep up what food production there had been. Large numbers of doctors were conscripted to serve the needs of the military, leaving many communities without any medical care. Blacksmiths, carpenters, and other craftsmen were similarly in short supply.

Economic Woes

As the war continued, the shortages, the inflation, and the suffering created increasing instability in Southern society. There were major food riots, some led by women, in Georgia, North Carolina, and Alabama in 1863, as well as a large demonstration in Richmond that quickly turned violent. Resistance to conscription, food impressment, and taxation increased throughout the Confederacy, as did hoarding and black-market commerce.

Despite the economic woes of the South, in other respects the war transformed Confederate society in many of the same ways that it was changing the society of the Union. It was particularly significant for Southern women. Because so many men left the farms and

ATLANTA AFTER THE BURNING General Sherman captured Atlanta on September 2, 1864, evacuated most of the population, and set fire to the city. This photograph shows the extent of the devastation. The destruction of Atlanta was the beginning of Sherman's famous "March to the Sea." It also signaled the beginning of a new kind of warfare, waged not just against opposing armies but against the economics and even the populations of the enemy. *(Corbis)*

plantations to fight, the task of keeping families together and maintaining agricultural production fell increasingly to women. Slaveowners' wives often became responsible for managing large slave work forces; the wives of more modest farmers learned to plow fields and harvest crops.

New Roles for Women
Substantial numbers of females worked as schoolteachers or in government agencies in Richmond. Even larger numbers chose nursing, both in hospitals and in temporary facilities set up to care for wounded soldiers.

The long-range results of the war for Southern women are more difficult to measure but equally profound. The experience of the 1860s almost certainly forced many women to question the prevailing Southern assumption that females were unsuited for certain activities, that they were not fit to participate actively in the public sphere. A more concrete legacy was the decimation of the male population and the creation of a major gender imbalance in the region. After the war, there were many thousands more women in the South than men. In Georgia, for example, women outnumbered men by 36,000 in 1870; in North Carolina by 25,000. The result, of course, was a large number of unmarried or widowed women who, both during and after the war, had no choice but to find

employment—thus, by necessity rather than choice, expanding the number of acceptable roles for women in Southern society.

Even before emancipation, the war had far-reaching effects on the lives of slaves. Confederate leaders were even more terrified of slave revolts during the war than they had been in peacetime, and they enforced slave codes and other regulations with particular severity. Even so, many slaves—especially those near the front—found ways to escape their masters and cross behind Union lines in search of freedom. Those who had no realistic avenue for escape seemed, to their owners at least, to be particularly resistant to authority during the war. That was in part because on many plantations, the masters and overseers for whom they were accustomed to working were away at war; they found it easier to resist the authority of the women and boys left behind to manage the farms.

STRATEGY AND DIPLOMACY

Militarily, the initiative in the Civil War lay mainly with the North, since it needed to defeat the Confederacy while the South needed only to avoid

Baseball and the Civil War

Long before the great urban stadiums, long before the lights and the cameras and the multimillion dollar salaries, long before the Little Leagues and the high school and college teams, baseball was the most popular game in America. And during the Civil War, it was a treasured pastime for soldiers, and for thousands of men (and some women) behind the lines, in both North and South.

Baseball was not invented by Abner Doubleday, who probably never even saw the game. The legend that it was came many years later from Albert G. Spalding, a patriotic sporting-goods manufacturer eager to prove that the game had purely American origins and to dispel the notion that it came from England. In fact, baseball was derived from a variety of earlier games, especially the English pastimes of cricket and rounders. American baseball took its own distinctive form beginning in the 1840s, when Alexander Cartwright, a shipping clerk, formed the New York Knickerbockers, laid out a diamond-shaped field with four bases, and declared that batters with three strikes were out and that teams with three outs were retired.

Cartwright moved west in search of gold in 1849, ultimately grew rich, and settled finally in Hawaii (where he brought the game to Americans in the Pacific). But the game did not languish in his absence. Henry Chadwick, an English-born journalist, developed his own passion for baseball in the late 1840s and spent much of the next decade popularizing the game (and regularizing its rules). "Our ambition," he said, was "that of endeavoring to establish a national game." It was also to keep baseball a sport for the "best classes," for gentlemen—a goal that was already lost before it was even uttered. By 1860, baseball was being played by college students and Irish workers, by urban elites and provincial farmers, by people of all classes and ethnic groups from New England to Louisiana. It was also attracting the attention of women. Students at Vassar College formed "ladies" teams in the 1860s. And in Philadelphia, free black men formed the first of what was to become a great network of African-American baseball teams, the Pythians. From the beginning, they were barred from playing against most white teams.

When young men donned their uniforms of blue and gray and marched off to war in 1861, some took their bats and balls with them. Almost from the start of the fighting, soldiers in both armies took advantage of idle moments to lay out baseball diamonds and organize games. There were games in prison camps; games on the White House lawn (where Union soldiers were sometimes billeted); and games on battlefields that were sometimes interrupted by gunfire and cannon. "It is astonishing how indifferent a person can become to danger," a soldier wrote home to Ohio in 1862. "The report of musketry is heard but a very little distance from us, . . . yet over there on the other side of the road is most of our company, playing Bat Ball." After a skirmish in Texas, another Union soldier lamented that, in addition to casualties, his company had lost "the only baseball in Alexandria, Texas."

An unlikely legend has it that in Hilton Head, South Carolina—occupied by Union soldiers very early in the war—two teams of New York volunteers played a game in front of more

---

defeat. Diplomatically, however, the initiative lay with the South. It needed to enlist the recognition and support of foreign governments; the Union wanted only to preserve the status quo.

The Commanders

The most important Union military commander was Abraham Lincoln, whose previous military experience

Lincoln's Leadership

consisted only of brief service in his state militia during the Black Hawk War. Lincoln was a successful commander in chief because he realized that numbers and resources were on his side, and because he took advantage of the North's material advantages. He realized, too, that the proper objective of his armies was the destruction of the Confederate armies and not the occupation of Southern territory. It was important that Lincoln had a good grasp of strategy, because many of his generals did not. The problem of finding adequate commanders for the troops in the field plagued him throughout the first three years of

the war. From 1861 to 1864, Lincoln tried time and again to find a chief of staff capable of orchestrating the Union war effort. He turned first to General Winfield Scott, the aging hero of the Mexican War. But Scott was unprepared for the magnitude of the new conflict and retired on November 1, 1861. Lincoln replaced him with the young George B. McClellan, commander of the Union armies in the East, the Army of the Potomac; but the proud, arrogant McClellan had a wholly inadequate grasp of strategy and in any case returned to the field in March 1862. For most of the rest of the year, Lincoln had no chief of staff at all. And when he finally appointed General Henry W. Halleck to the post, he found him an ineffectual strategist who left all substantive decision making to the president. Not until March 1864 did Lincoln finally find a general he trusted to command the war effort: Ulysses S. Grant, who shared Lincoln's belief in making enemy armies and resources, not enemy territory, the target of military efforts. Lincoln gave Grant a relatively free hand, but the general always submitted at least the broad outlines of his plans to the president for advance approval.

RIFLES AND BATS Union soldiers pose on the battlefield in full uniform and carrying their rifles, with a pile of baseball bats on the grass in front of them. Baseball was a popular recreation for troops on both sides of the Civil War. *(Dennis Goldstein, Atlanta)*

still the leading baseball city in the nation, games between local teams continued to draw crowds of ten or twenty thousand. The National Association of Baseball Players (founded in 1859) had recruited ninety-one clubs in ten northern states by 1865; a North Western Association of Baseball Players, organized in Chicago in 1865, indicated that the game was becoming well established in the West as well. And in Brooklyn during the war, William Cammeyer drained a skating pond on his property, built a board fence around it, and created the first enclosed baseball field in America—the Union grounds. He charged 10 cents admission. The professionalization of the game was underway.

But for all the commercialization and spectacle that came to be associated with baseball in the years after the Civil War, the game remained for many Americans what it was to millions of young men fighting in the most savage war in the nation's history—an American passion that at times, even if briefly, erased the barriers dividing groups from one another. "Officers and men forget, for a time, the differences in rank," a Massachusetts private wrote in 1863, "and indulge in the invigorating sport with a schoolboy's ardor."

than 40,000 spectators. Far from discouraging baseball, military commanders—and the United States Sanitary Commission, the Union army's medical arm—actively encouraged the game during the war. It would, they believed, help keep up the soldiers' morale.

Away from the battlefield, baseball continued to flourish (even if diminished by the departure of so many young men to the war). In New York,

Lincoln's (and later Grant's) handling of the war effort faced constant scrutiny from the Committee on the Conduct of the War, a joint investigative committee of the two houses of Congress and the most powerful voice the legislative branch has ever had in formulating war policies. Established in December 1861 and chaired by Senator Benjamin F. Wade of Ohio, it complained constantly of the insufficient ruthlessness of Northern generals, which Radicals on the committee attributed (largely inaccurately) to a secret sympathy among the officers for slavery. The committee's efforts often seriously interfered with the conduct of the war.

Southern command arrangements centered on President Davis, who unlike Lincoln was a trained professional soldier but who, also unlike Lincoln, failed ever to create an effective command system. Early in 1862, Davis named General Robert E. Lee as his principal military adviser. But in fact, Davis had no intention of sharing control of strategy with anyone. After a few months, Lee left Richmond to command forces in the field, and for the next two years Davis

Robert E. Lee

planned strategy alone. In February 1864, he named General Braxton Bragg as a military adviser; but Bragg never provided much more than technical advice. Not until February 1865 did the Confederate Congress create the formal position of general in chief. Davis named Lee to the post but made clear that he expected to continue to make all basic decisions. In any case, the war ended before this last command structure had time to take shape.

At lower levels of command, men of markedly similar backgrounds controlled the war in both the North and the South. Many of the professional officers on both sides were graduates of the United States Military Academy at West Point and the United States Naval Academy at Annapolis, and thus had been trained in similar ways. Many were closely acquainted, even friendly, with their counterparts on the other side. And all were imbued with the classic, eighteenth-century models of warfare that the service academies still taught. The most successful officers were those who, like Grant and William Tecumseh Sherman, were able to see beyond

ULYSSES S. GRANT One observer said of Grant (seen here posing for a photograph during the Wilderness campaign of 1864): "He habitually wears an expression as if he had determined to drive his head through a brick wall, and was about to do it." It was an apt metaphor for Grant's military philosophy, which relied on constant, unrelenting assault. One result was that Grant was willing to fight when other Northern generals held back. Another was that Grant presided over some of the worst carnage of the Civil War. *(Library of Congress)*

ROBERT E. LEE Lee was a moderate by the standards of Southern politics in the 1850s. He opposed secession and was ambivalent about slavery. But he could not bring himself to break with his region, and he left the U.S. army to lead Confederate forces beginning in 1861. He was (and remains) the most revered of all the white Southern leaders of the Civil War. For decades after his surrender at Appomattox, he was a symbol to white Southerners of the "Lost Cause." *(Bettmann/Corbis)*

their academic training and envision a new kind of warfare in which destruction of resources was as important as battlefield tactics.

Amateur officers played an important role in both armies as commanders of volunteer regiments. In both North and South, such men were usually economic or social leaders in their communities who appointed themselves officers and rounded up troops to lead. This system was responsible for recruiting considerable numbers of men into the armies of the two nations. Only occasionally, however, did it produce officers of real ability.

The Role of Sea Power

The Union had an overwhelming advantage in naval power, and it gave its navy two important roles in the war. One was enforcing a blockade of the Southern coast, which the president ordered on April 19, 1861. The other was assisting the Union armies in field operations.

The blockade of the South was never fully effective, but it had a major impact on the Confederacy nevertheless. The United States Navy could generally keep oceangoing ships out of Confederate ports. For a time, small blockade runners continued to slip through. But gradually, federal forces tightened the blockade by seizing the ports themselves. The last important port in Confederate hands—Wilmington, North Carolina—fell to the Union early in 1865.

The Union Blockade

The Confederates made bold attempts to break the blockade with new weapons. Foremost among them was an ironclad warship, constructed by plating with iron a former United States frigate, the *Merrimac,* which the Yankees had scuttled in Norfolk harbor when Virginia seceded. On March 8, 1862, the refitted *Merrimac,* renamed the *Virginia,* left Norfolk to attack a blockading squadron of wooden ships at nearby Hampton Roads. It destroyed two of the ships and scattered the rest. But the Union government had already built ironclads of its own. And

Ironclads

one of them, the *Monitor*, arrived off the coast of Virginia only a few hours after the *Virginia's* dramatic foray. The next day, it met the *Virginia* in the first battle between ironclad ships. Neither vessel was able to sink the other, but the *Monitor* put an end to the *Virginia's* raids and preserved the blockade. The Confederacy experimented as well with other naval innovations, such as small torpedo boats and hand-powered submarines. But despite occasional small successes with these new weapons, the South never managed to overcome the Union's naval advantages.

As a supporter of land operations, the Union navy was particularly important in the western theater of war—the vast region between the Appalachian Mountains and the Mississippi River—where the major rivers were navigable by large vessels. The navy transported supplies and troops and joined in attacking Confederate strong points. With no significant navy of its own, the South could defend only with fixed land fortifications, which proved no match for the mobile land-and-water forces of the Union.

Europe and the Disunited States

Judah P. Benjamin, the Confederate secretary of state for most of the war, was a clever and intelligent man, but he lacked strong convictions and confined most of his energy to routine administrative tasks. William Seward, his counterpart in Washington, gradually became one of the great American secretaries of state. He had invaluable assistance from Charles Francis Adams, the American minister to London, who had inherited the considerable diplomatic talents of his father, John Quincy Adams, and his grandfather, John Adams.

At the beginning of the war, the ruling classes of England and France, the two nations whose support was most crucial to both sides, were generally sympathetic to the Confederacy, for several reasons. The two nations imported much Southern cotton for their textile industries; they were eager to weaken the United States, an increasingly powerful commercial rival; and some admired the supposedly aristocratic social order of the South, which they believed resembled the hierarchical structures of their own societies. But France was unwilling to take sides in the conflict unless England did so first. And in England, the government was reluctant to act because there was powerful popular support for the Union. Important English liberals such as John Bright and Richard Cobden considered the war a struggle between free and slave labor and urged their followers to support the Union cause. The politically conscious but largely unenfranchised workers in Britain expressed their sympathy for the North frequently and unmistakably—in mass meetings, in resolutions, and through their champions in Parliament. After Lincoln issued the Emancipation Proclamation, these groups worked particularly avidly for the Union.

Southern leaders hoped to counter the strength of the British antislavery forces by arguing that access to Southern cotton was vital to the English and French textile industries. But this "King Cotton diplomacy," on which the Confederacy had staked so many of its hopes, was a failure. English manufacturers had a surplus of both raw cotton and finished goods on hand in 1861 and could withstand a temporary loss of access to American cotton. Later, as the supply of cotton began to diminish, both England and France managed to keep at least some of their mills open by importing cotton from Egypt, India, and other sources. Equally important, English workers, the people most seriously threatened by the cotton shortage, did not clamor to have the blockade broken. Even the 500,000 English textile workers thrown out of jobs as a result of mill closings continued to support the North. In the end, therefore, no European nation offered diplomatic recognition to the Confederacy or intervened in the war. No nation wanted to antagonize the United States unless the Confederacy seemed likely to win, and the South never came close enough to victory to convince its potential allies to support it.

King Cotton Diplomacy

Even so, there was considerable tension, and on occasion near hostilities, between the United States and Britain, beginning in the first days of the war. Great Britain declared itself neutral as soon as the fighting began, followed by France and other nations. The Union government was furious. Neutrality implied that the two sides to the conflict had equal stature, but Washington was insisting that the conflict was simply a domestic insurrection, not a war between two legitimate governments.

A more serious crisis, the so-called Trent affair, began in late 1861. Two Confederate diplomats, James M. Mason and John Slidell, had slipped through the then ineffective Union blockade to Havana, Cuba, where they boarded an English steamer, the *Trent*, for England. Waiting in Cuban waters was the American frigate *San Jacinto*, commanded by the impetuous Charles Wilkes. Acting without authorization, Wilkes stopped the British vessel, arrested the diplomats, and carried them in triumph to Boston. The British government demanded the release of the prisoners, reparations, and an apology. Lincoln and Seward, aware that Wilkes had violated maritime law and unwilling to risk war with England, spun out the negotiations until American public opinion had cooled off, then released the diplomats with an indirect apology. A second diplomatic crisis produced problems that lasted for years. Unable to construct large vessels itself, the Confederacy bought six ships, known as commerce destroyers, from British shipyards. The best known of them were the *Alabama*, the *Florida*, and the *Shenandoah*. The United States protested that this sale of military equipment to a belligerent violated the laws

Trent Affair

of neutrality, and the protests became the basis, after the war, of damage claims by the United States against Great Britain (see p. 416).

The American West and the War

Most of the states and territories of the American West, about which there had been so much controversy in the years leading up to the Civil War, were far removed from the major fighting. But they played a continuing political, diplomatic, and military part in the conflict nevertheless.

Except for Texas, which joined the Confederacy, all the western states and territories remained officially loyal to the Union—but not without controversy and conflict. Southerners and Southern sympathizers were active throughout the West. And, in some places, there was actual combat between Unionists and secessionists.

There was particularly vicious fighting in Kansas and Missouri, the scene of so much bitterness before the war. The same pro-slavery and free-state forces who had fought one another in the 1850s continued to do so, with even more deadly results. William C. Quantrill, an Ohio native who had spent much of his youth in the West, became a captain in the Confederate army after he organized a band of guerrilla fighters (mostly teenage boys) with which he terrorized areas around the Kansas-Missouri border. Quantrill and his band were an exceptionally murderous group, notorious for killing almost everyone in their path. Their most infamous act was a siege of Lawrence, Kansas, during which they slaughtered 150 civilians, adults and children alike. Quantrill finally died at the hands of Union troops shortly after the end of the war. Union sympathizers in Kansas, organized in bands known as the Jayhawkers, were only marginally less savage, as they moved across western Missouri exacting reprisals for the actions of Quantrill and other Confederate guerrillas. One Jayhawk unit was commanded by the son of John Brown and the brother of Susan B. Anthony, men who brought the fervor of abolitionists to their work. Even without a major battle, the border areas of Kansas and Missouri were among the bloodiest and most terrorized places in the United States during the Civil War.

Not long after the war began, Confederate agents tried to negotiate alliances with the Five Civilized Tribes living in Indian Territory (later Oklahoma), in hopes of recruiting their support against Union forces in the West. The Indians themselves were divided. Some wanted to support the South, both because they resented the way the United States government had treated them and because some tribal leaders were themselves slaveholders. But other Indians supported the North out of a general hostility to slavery (both in the South and in their own nation).

One result of these divisions was something of a civil war within Indian Territory itself. Another was that Indian regiments fought for both the Union and the Confederacy during the war. But the tribes themselves never formally allied themselves with either side.

THE COURSE OF BATTLE

In the absence of direct intervention by the European powers, the two contestants in America were left to resolve the conflict between themselves. They did so High Casualties in four long years of bloody combat that produced more carnage than any war in American history, before or since. More than 618,000 Americans died in the Civil War, far more than the 115,000 who perished in World War I or the 318,000 who died in World War II; more, indeed, than died in all other American wars prior to Vietnam combined. There were nearly 2,000 deaths for every 100,000 of population during the Civil War. In World War I, the comparable figure was 109 deaths; in World War II, 241 deaths.

Despite the gruesome cost, the Civil War has become the most romanticized and the most intently studied of all American wars. In part, that is because the conflict produced—in addition to terrible fatalities—a series of military campaigns of classic strategic interest and a series of military leaders who displayed unusual brilliance and daring.

The Technology of Battle

Much of what happened on the battlefield in the Civil War was a result of new technologies that transformed the nature of combat. The Civil War has often been called the first "modern" war and the first "total" war. Such descriptions are imprecise and debatable. But it is certainly true that the great conflict between the North and the South was unlike any war fought before it. It is also clear that it suggested a great deal about what warfare would be like in the future.

The most obvious change in the character of warfare in the 1860s was the nature of the armaments that both sides used in battle. Among the most important was the introduction of Repeating Weapons repeating weapons. Samuel Colt had patented a repeating pistol (the revolver) in 1835, but more important for military purposes was the repeating rifle, introduced in 1860 by Oliver Winchester. Also important were greatly improved cannons and artillery, a result of advances in iron and steel technology of the previous decades.

These devastating advances in the effectiveness of arms and artillery changed the way soldiers in the field fought. It was now impossibly deadly to fight battles as they had been fought for centuries, with lines of infantry soldiers standing erect in the field firing volleys at their opponents until one side withdrew. Fighting in that way now produced almost inconceivable slaughter, and soldiers quickly learned that the proper position for combat was staying low to the ground and behind cover.

For the first time in the history of organized warfare, therefore, infantry did not fight in formation, and the battlefield became a more chaotic place. Gradually, the deadliness of the new weapons encouraged armies on both sides to spend a great deal of time building elaborate fortifications and trenches to protect themselves from enemy fire. The sieges of Vicksburg and Petersburg, the defense of Richmond, and many other military events all produced the construction of vast fortifications around the cities and around the attacking armies. (They became the predecessors to the great network of trenches that became so central a part of World War I.)

Other weapons technologies were less central to the fighting of the war, but important nevertheless. There was sporadic use of the relatively new technology of hot-air balloons, employed intermittently to provide a view of enemy formations in the field. (During one battle, a Union balloonist took a telegraph line aloft with him in his balloon and tapped out messages about troop movements to the commanders below.) Ironclad ships such as the *Merrimac* (or *Virginia*) and the *Monitor,* torpedoes, and submarine technology all suggested the dramatic changes that would soon overtake naval warfare, although none played a major role in the Civil War.

Critical to the conduct of the war, however, were two other relatively new technologies: the railroad and the

Importance of the Railroad

telegraph. The railroad was particularly important in a war in which millions of soldiers were being mobilized and transferred to the front, and in which a single field army could number as many as 250,000 men. Transporting such enormous numbers of soldiers, and the supplies necessary to sustain them, by land or by horse and wagon would have been almost impossible. Railroads made it possible for these large armies to be assembled and moved from place to place. However, they also limited their mobility. Railroad lines and stations are, of course, in fixed positions. Commanders, therefore, were forced to organize their campaigns at least in part around the location of the railroads rather than on the basis of the best topography or most direct land route to a destination. The dependence on the rails—and the resulting necessity of concentrating huge numbers of men in a few places—also encouraged commanders to prefer great battles with large armies rather than smaller engagements with fewer troops.

The impact of the telegraph on the war was limited both by the scarcity of qualified telegraph operators and

The Telegraph

by the difficulty of bringing telegraph wires into the fields where battles were being fought. Things improved somewhat after the new U.S. Military Telegraph Corps, headed by Thomas Scott and Andrew Carnegie, trained and employed over 1,200 operators. Gradually, too, both the Union and Confederate armies learned to string telegraph wires along the routes of their troops (who, once they were off the railroads, generally moved slowly, on foot or horseback), so that field commanders were able to stay in close touch with one another during battles. Both the North and the South sent spies behind enemy lines who tried to tap the telegraph lines of their opponents and send important information back about troop movements and formations.

The Opening Clashes, 1861

The Union and the Confederacy fought their first major battle of the war in northern Virginia. A Union army of over 30,000 men under the command of General Irvin McDowell was stationed just outside Washington. About thirty miles away, at the town of Manassas, was a slightly smaller Confederate army under P. G. T. Beauregard. If the Northern army could destroy the Southern one, Union leaders believed, the war might end at once. In mid-July, McDowell marched his inexperienced troops toward Manassas. Beauregard moved his troops behind Bull Run, a small stream north of Manassas, and called for reinforcements, which reached him the day before the battle. The two armies were now approximately the same size.

On July 21, in the First Battle of Bull Run, or First Battle of Manassas, McDowell almost succeeded in dispersing the Confederate forces. But

First Battle of Bull Run

the Southerners stopped a last strong Union assault and then began a savage counterattack. The Union troops, exhausted after hours of hot, hard fighting, suddenly panicked. They broke ranks and retreated chaotically. McDowell was unable to reorganize them, and he had to order a retreat to Washington—a disorderly withdrawal complicated by the presence along the route of many civilians who had ridden down from the capital, picnic baskets in hand, to watch the battle from nearby hills. The Confederates, as disorganized by victory as the Union forces were by defeat, and short of supplies and transportation, did not pursue. The battle was a severe blow to Union morale and to the president's confidence in his officers. It also dispelled the illusion that the war would be a quick one.

Elsewhere in 1861, Union forces were achieving some small but significant victories. In Missouri, rebel forces gathered behind Governor Claiborne Jackson and other state officials who wanted to secede from the Union. Nathaniel Lyon, who commanded a small regular army force in St. Louis, moved his troops into southern Missouri to face the secessionists. On August 10, at the Battle of Wilson's Creek, he was

Wilson's Creek

defeated and killed—but not before he had seriously weakened the striking power of the Confederates. Union forces were subsequently able to hold most of the state.

Meanwhile, a Union force under George B. McClellan moved east from Ohio into western Virginia. By the end of 1861, it had "liberated" the anti-secession mountain people of the region. They created their own state government loyal to the Union and were admitted to the Union as West Virginia in 1863. The occupation of western Virginia was of limited military value, since the mountains cut the area off from the rest of Virginia. It was, however, an important symbolic victory for the North.

The Western Theater

After the battle at Bull Run, military operations in the East settled into a long and frustrating stalemate. The first decisive operations in 1862 occurred, therefore, in the western theater. Union forces were trying to seize control of the southern part of the Mississippi River, which would divide the Confederacy and give the North easy transportation into the heart of the South. Northern soldiers advanced on the southern Mississippi from both the north and south, moving downriver from Kentucky and upriver from the Gulf of Mexico toward New Orleans.

In April, a Union squadron of ironclads and wooden vessels commanded by David G. Farragut gathered in the Gulf of Mexico, then smashed past weak Confederate forts near the mouth of the Mississippi, and from there sailed up to New Orleans, which was virtually defenseless because the Confederate high command had expected the attack to come from the north. The city surrendered on April 25—the first major Union victory and an important turning point in the war. From then on, the mouth of the Mississippi was closed to Confederate trade; and the South's largest city and most important banking center was in Union hands.

| New Orleans Captured |

Farther north in the western theater, Confederate troops under the command of Albert Sidney Johnston were stretched out in a long defensive line centered at two forts in Tennessee, Fort Henry and Fort Donelson, on the Tennessee and Cumberland Rivers respectively. But the forts were located well behind the main Southern flanks, a fatal weakness that Union commanders recognized and exploited. Early in 1862, Ulysses S. Grant attacked Fort Henry, whose defenders, awed by the ironclad riverboats accompanying the Union army, surrendered with almost no resistance on February 6. Grant then moved both his naval and ground forces to Fort Donelson, where the Confederates put up a stronger fight but finally, on February 16, had to surrender. By cracking the Confederate center, Grant had gained control of river communications and forced Confederate forces out of Kentucky and half of Tennessee.

With about 40,000 men, Grant now advanced south along the Tennessee River to seize control of railroad lines vital to the Confederacy. From Pittsburg Landing, he marched to nearby Shiloh, Tennessee, where a force almost equal to his own, commanded by Albert Sidney Johnston and P. G. T. Beauregard, caught him by surprise. The result was the Battle of Shiloh, April 6–7. In the first day's fighting (during which Johnston was killed), the Southerners drove Grant back to the river. But the next day, reinforced by 25,000 fresh troops, Grant recovered the lost ground and forced Beauregard to withdraw. After the

| Shiloh |

narrow Union victory at Shiloh, Northern forces occupied Corinth, Mississippi, the hub of several important railroads, and established control of the Mississippi River as far south as Memphis.

Braxton Bragg, now in command of the Confederate army in the West, gathered his forces at Chattanooga, in eastern Tennessee, which the Confederacy still controlled. He hoped to win back the rest of the state and then move north into Kentucky. But first he had to face a Union army (commanded by Don Carlos Buell and later by William S. Rosecrans), whose assignment was to capture Chattanooga. The two armies maneuvered for advantage inconclusively in northern Tennessee and southern Kentucky for several months until they finally met, December 31–January 2, in the Battle of Murfreesboro, or Stone's River. Bragg was forced to withdraw to the south, his campaign a failure. By the end of 1862, Union forces had made considerable progress in the West. But the major conflict remained in the East, where they were having much less success.

The Virginia Front, 1862

Union operations were being directed in 1862 by George B. McClellan, commander of the Army of the Potomac and the most controversial general of the war. McClellan was a superb trainer of men, but he often appeared reluctant to commit his troops to battle. Opportunities for important engagements came and went, and McClellan seemed never to take advantage of them—claiming always that his preparations were not yet complete or that the moment was not right. During the winter of 1861–1862, McClellan concentrated on training his army of 150,000 men near Washington. Finally, he designed a spring campaign whose purpose was to capture the Confederate capital at Richmond. But instead of heading overland directly toward Richmond, McClellan chose a complicated, roundabout route that he thought would circumvent the Confederate defenses. The navy would carry his troops down the Potomac to a peninsula east of Richmond, between the York and James Rivers. The army would approach the city from there. It became known as the Peninsular campaign.

| George McClellan |

McClellan began the campaign with only part of his army. Approximately 100,000 men accompanied him down the Potomac. Another 30,000—under General Irvin McDowell—remained behind to protect Washington. McClellan insisted that Washington was safe as long as he was threatening Richmond, and finally persuaded Lincoln to promise to send him the additional men. But before the president could do so, a Confederate army under Thomas J. ("Stonewall") Jackson changed his plans. Jackson staged a rapid march north through the Shenandoah Valley, as if he were planning to cross the Potomac and attack Washington. Alarmed, Lincoln

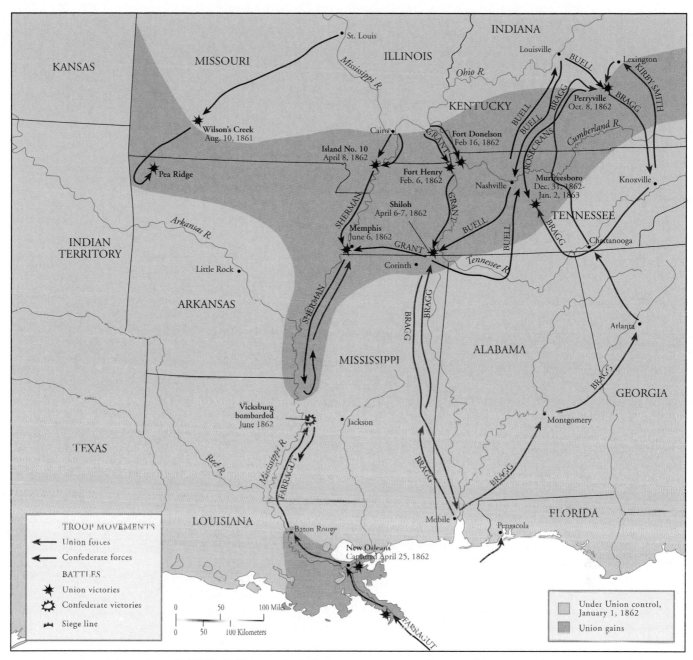

THE WAR IN THE WEST, 1861–1863 While the Union armies in Virginia were meeting with repeated frustrations, the Union armies in the West were scoring notable successes in the first two years of the war. This map shows a series of Union drives in the western Confederacy. Admiral David Farragut's ironclads led to the capture of New Orleans—a critical Confederate port—in April 1862, while forces further north under the command of Ulysses S. Grant drove the Confederate army out of Kentucky and western Tennessee. These battles culminated in the Union victory at Shiloh, which led to Union control of the upper Mississippi River. ◆ *Why was control of the Mississippi so important to both sides?*

For an interactive version of this map go to www.mhhe.com/brinkley12ch14maps

dispatched McDowell's corps to head off Jackson. In the brilliant Valley campaign of May 4–June 9, 1862, Jackson defeated two separate Union forces and slipped away before McDowell could catch him.

Meanwhile, Confederate troops under Joseph E. Johnston were attacking McClellan's advancing army outside Richmond. But in the

Seven Pines

two-day Battle of Fair Oaks, or Seven Pines (May 31–June 1), they could not repel the Union forces. Johnston, badly wounded, was replaced by Robert E. Lee, who then recalled Stonewall Jackson from the Shenandoah Valley. With a combined force of 85,000 to face McClellan's 100,000, Lee launched a new offensive, known as the Battle of the Seven Days (June 25–July 1). Lee wanted to cut McClellan off from his base on the York River and then destroy the isolated

THE VIRGINIA THEATER, 1861–1863 Much of the fighting during the first two years of the Civil War took place in what became known as the Virginia theater—although the campaigns in this region eventually extended north into Maryland and Pennsylvania. The Union hoped for a quick victory over the newly created Confederate army. But as these maps show, the southern forces consistently thwarted these hopes. The map at top left shows the battles of 1861 and the first half of 1862, almost all of them won by the Confederates. The map at lower left shows the last months of 1862, during which the southerners again defeated the Union in most of their engagements—although northern forces drove the Confederates back from Maryland in September. The large map on the right shows the troop movements that led to the climactic battle of Gettysburg in 1863. ◆ *Why were the Union forces unable to profit more from material advantages during these first years of the war?*

 For an interactive version of this map go to www.mhhe.com/brinkley12ch14maps

Union army. But McClellan fought his way across the peninsula and set up a new base on the James. There, with naval support, the Army of the Potomac was safe.

McClellan was now only twenty-five miles from Richmond, with a secure line of water communications,

and thus in a good position to renew the campaign. Time and again, however, he found reasons for delay. Instead of replacing McClellan with a more aggressive commander, Lincoln finally ordered the army to move to northern Virginia and join a smaller force under John

Pope. The president hoped to begin a new offensive against Richmond on the direct overland route that he himself had always preferred.

As the Army of the Potomac left the peninsula by water, Lee moved north with the Army of Northern Virginia to strike Pope before McClellan could join him. Pope was as rash as McClellan was cautious, and he attacked the approaching Confederates without waiting for the arrival of all of McClellan's troops. In the ensuing Second Battle of Bull Run, or Second Battle of Manassas (August 29–30), Lee threw back the assault and routed Pope's army, which fled to Washington. With hopes for an overland campaign against Richmond now in disarray, Lincoln removed Pope from command and put McClellan in charge of all the Union forces in the region.

Lee soon went on the offensive again, heading north through western Maryland, and McClellan moved out to meet him. McClellan had the good luck to get a copy of Lee's orders, which revealed that a part of the Confederate army, under Stonewall Jackson, had separated from the rest to attack Harpers Ferry. But instead of attacking quickly before the Confederates could recombine, McClellan stalled and gave Lee time to pull most of his forces together behind Antietam Creek, near the town of Sharpsburg. There, on September 17, in the bloodiest single-day engagement of the war, McClellan's 87,000-man army repeatedly attacked Lee's force of 50,000, with enormous casualties on both sides. Six thousand soldiers died, and 17,000 sustained injuries. Late in the day, just as the Confederate line seemed ready to break, the last of Jackson's troops arrived from Harpers Ferry to reinforce it. McClellan might have broken through with one more assault. Instead, he allowed Lee to retreat into Virginia. Technically, Antietam was a Union victory, but in reality, it was an opportunity squandered. In

Antietam

November, Lincoln finally removed McClellan from command for good.

McClellan's replacement, Ambrose E. Burnside, was a short-lived mediocrity. He tried to move toward Richmond by crossing the Rappahannock at Fredericksburg, the strongest defensive point on the river. There, on December 13, he launched a series of attacks against Lee, all of them bloody, all of them hopeless. After losing a large part of his army, Burnside withdrew to the north bank of the Rappahannock. He was relieved at his own request.

1863: Year of Decision

At the beginning of 1863, General Joseph Hooker was in command of the still formidable Army of the Potomac, whose 120,000 troops remained north of the Rappahannock, opposite Fredericksburg. But despite his reputation as a fighter (his popular nickname was "Fighting Joe"), Hooker showed little resolve as he launched his own campaign in the spring. Taking part of his army, Hooker crossed the river above Fredericksburg and moved toward the town and Lee's army. But at the last minute, he apparently lost his nerve and drew back to a defensive position in a desolate area of brush and scrub trees known as the Wilderness. Lee had only half as many men as Hooker did, but he boldly divided his forces for a dual assault on the Union army. In the Battle of Chancellorsville, May 1–5, Stonewall Jackson attacked the Union right and Lee himself charged the front. Hooker barely managed to escape with his army. Lee had defeated the Union objectives, but he had not destroyed the Union army. And his ablest officer, Jackson, was wounded during the battle and subsequently died of pneumonia.

Battle of Chancellorsville

While the Union forces were suffering repeated frustrations in the East, they were continuing to win

THE FIRST NEW YORK ARTILLERY
Photographed on an unidentified battlefield, the first New York Artillery stands posing before its array of cannon— and the stumps of trees cut down to allow them unimpeded shots at the enemy.
(US Army Military History Institute, Carlisle PA)

Vicksburg

important victories in the West. In the spring of 1863, Ulysses S. Grant was driving at Vicksburg, Mississippi, one of the Confederacy's two remaining strongholds on the southern Mississippi River. Vicksburg was well protected, surrounded by rough country on the north and low, marshy ground on the west, and with good artillery coverage of

the river itself. But in May, Grant boldly moved men and supplies—overland and by water—to an area south of the city, where the terrain was better. He then attacked Vicksburg from the rear. Six weeks later, on July 4, Vicksburg—whose residents were by then literally starving as a result of a prolonged siege—surrendered. At almost the same time, the other Confederate strong point on the river, Port Hudson, Louisiana, also surrendered—to a Union force that had moved north from New Orleans. The Union had achieved one of its basic military aims: control of the whole length of the Mississippi. The Confederacy was split in two, with Louisiana, Arkansas, and Texas cut off from the other seceded states. The victories on the Mississippi were one of the great turning points of the war.

Early in the siege of Vicksburg, Lee proposed an invasion of Pennsylvania, which would, he argued, divert Union troops north and remove the pressure on the lower Mississippi. Further, he argued, if he could win a major victory on Northern soil, England and France might come to the Confederacy's aid. The war-weary North might even quit the war before Vicksburg fell.

In June 1863, Lee moved up the Shenandoah Valley into Maryland and then entered Pennsylvania. The Union Army of the Potomac, commanded first by Hooker and then by George C. Meade, also moved north, parallel with the Confederates' movement, staying between Lee and Washington. The two armies finally encountered one another at the small town of Gettysburg, Pennsylvania. There, on July 1–3, 1863, they fought the most celebrated battle of the war.

Meade's army established a strong, well-protected position on the hills south of the town. The confident and combative Lee attacked, even though his army was outnumbered 75,000 to 90,000. His first assault on the Union forces on Cemetery Ridge failed. A day later he ordered a second, larger effort. In what is remembered as Pickett's Charge, a force of 15,000 Confederate soldiers advanced for almost a mile across open country while being swept by Union fire. Only about 5,000 made it up the ridge, and this remnant finally had to surrender or retreat. By now Lee had lost nearly a third of his army. On July 4, the same day as the surrender of Vicksburg, he withdrew from Gettysburg—another major turning point in the war. Never again were the weakened Confederate forces able to seriously threaten Northern territory.

Gettysburg

Before the end of the year, there was a third important turning point, this one in Tennessee. After occupying Chattanooga on September 9, Union forces under William Rosecrans began an unwise pursuit of Bragg's retreating Confederate forces. Bragg was waiting for them just across the Georgia line, with reinforcements from Lee's army. The two armies engaged in the Battle of Chickamauga (September 19–20), one of the few battles in which the Confederates enjoyed a numerical superiority (70,000 to 56,000). Union forces could not break the Confederate lines and retreated back to Chattanooga.

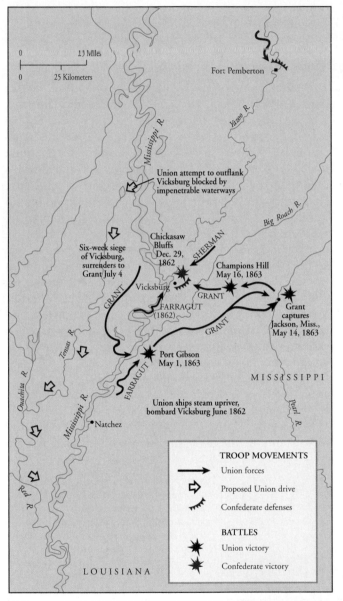

THE SIEGE OF VICKSBURG, MAY–JULY 1863 In the spring of 1863, Grant began a campaign to win control of the final piece of the Mississippi River still controlled by the Confederacy. To do that required capturing the southern stronghold at Vicksburg—a well-defended city sitting above the river. Vicksburg's main defenses were in the North, so Grant boldly moved men and supplies around the city and attacked it from the South. Eventually, he cut off the city's access to the outside world, and after a six-week siege, its residents finally surrendered. ◆ *What impact did the combined victories at Vicksburg and Gettysburg have on northern commitment to the war?*

For an interactive version of this map go to www.mhhe.com/ brinkley12ch14maps

GETTYSBURG, JULY 1-3, 1863 Gettysburg was the most important single battle of the Civil War. Had Confederate forces prevailed at Gettysburg, the future course of the war might well have been very different. The map on the right shows the distribution of Union and Confederate forces at the beginning of the battle, July 1, after Lee had driven the northern forces south of town. The map on the left reveals the pattern of the attacks on July 2 and 3. Note, in particular, Pickett's bold and costly charge, whose failure on July 3 was the turning point in the battle and, some have argued, the war. ◆ *Why did Robert E. Lee believe that an invasion of Pennsylvania would advance the Confederate cause?*

Bragg now began a siege of Chattanooga itself, seizing the heights nearby and cutting off fresh supplies to the Union forces. Grant came to the rescue. In the Battle of Chattanooga (November 23–25), the reinforced Union army drove the Confederates back into Georgia. Northern troops then occupied most of eastern Tennessee. Union forces had now achieved a second important objective: control of the Tennessee River. Four of the eleven Confederate states were now effectively cut off from the Southern nation. No longer could the Confederacy hope to win independence through a decisive military victory. They could hope to win only by holding on and exhausting the Northern will to fight.

The Last Stage, 1864–1865

By the beginning of 1864, Ulysses S. Grant had become general in chief of all the Union armies. At long last, the president had found a commander whom he could rely on to pursue the war doggedly and tenaciously. Grant was not a subtle strategic or tactical general; he believed in using the North's overwhelming advantage in troops

and material resources to overwhelm the South. He was not afraid to absorb massive casualties as long as he was inflicting similar casualties on his opponents.

Grant planned two great offensives for 1864. In Virginia, the Army of the Potomac (technically under Meade's command, but really now under Grant's) would advance toward Richmond and force Lee into a decisive battle. In Georgia, the western army, under William T. Sherman, would advance east toward Atlanta and destroy the remaining Confederate force further south, which was now under the command of Joseph E. Johnston. The northern campaign began when the Army of the Potomac, 115,000 strong, plunged into the rough, wooded Wilderness area of northwestern Virginia in pursuit of Lee's 75,000-man army. After avoiding an engagement for several weeks, Lee turned Grant back in the Battle of the Wilderness (May 5–7). But Grant was undeterred. Without stopping to rest or reorganize, he resumed his march toward Richmond. He met Lee again in the bloody, five-day Battle of Spotsylvania Court House, in which 12,000 Union troops and a large but unknown

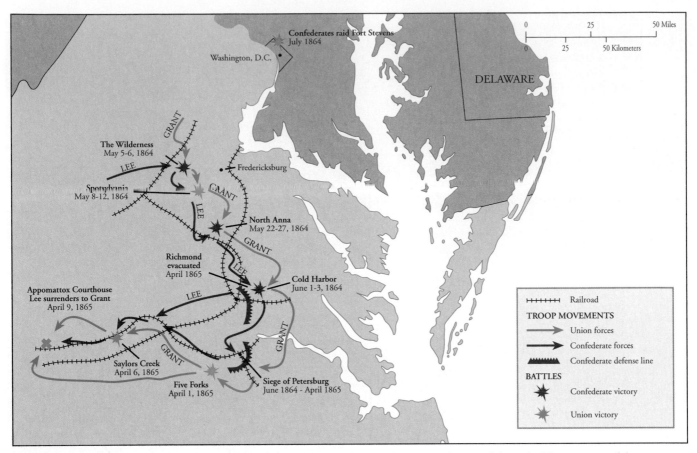

VIRGINIA CAMPAIGNS, 1864–1865 From the Confederate defeat at (and retreat from) Gettysburg until the end of the war, most of the eastern fighting took place in Virginia. By now, Ulysses S. Grant was commander of all Union forces and had taken over the Army of the Potomac. Although Confederate forces won a number of important battles during the Virginia campaign, the Union army grew steadily stronger and the southern forces steadily weaker. Grant believed that the Union strategy should reflect the North's greatest advantage: its superiority in men and equipment. ◆ *What effect did this decision have on the level of casualties?*

OLC For an interactive version of this map go to www.mhhe.com/brinkley12ch14maps

number of Confederates died or were wounded. Despite the enormous losses, Grant kept moving. But victory continued to elude him.

Lee kept his army between Grant and the Confederate capital and on June 1–3 repulsed the Union forces again, just northeast of Richmond, at Cold Harbor. The month-long Wilderness campaign had cost Grant 55,000 men (killed, wounded, and captured) to Lee's 31,000. And Richmond still had not fallen.

Grant now changed his strategy. He moved his army east of Richmond, bypassing the capital altogether, and headed south toward the railroad center at Petersburg. If he could seize Petersburg, he could cut off the capital's communications with the rest of the Confederacy. But Petersburg had strong defenses; and once Lee came to the city's relief, the assault became a prolonged siege, which lasted nine months. In Georgia, meanwhile, Sherman was facing a less ferocious resistance. With 90,000 men, he confronted Confederate forces of 60,000 under Johnston, who was unwilling to risk a direct engagement. As Sherman advanced, Johnston tried to

delay him by maneuvering. The two armies fought only one real battle—at Kennesaw Mountain, northwest of Atlanta, on June 27—where Johnston scored an impressive victory. Even so, he was unable to stop the Union advance toward Atlanta. President Davis replaced Johnston with the combative John B. Hood, who twice daringly attacked Sherman's army but accomplished nothing except seriously weakening his own forces. Sherman took Atlanta on September 2. News of the victory electrified the North and helped unite the previously divided Republican Party behind President Lincoln.

Capture of Atlanta

Hood now tried unsuccessfully to draw Sherman out of Atlanta by moving back up through Tennessee and threatening an invasion of the North. Sherman did not take the bait. But he did send Union troops to reinforce Nashville. In the Battle of Nashville on December 15–16, 1864, Northern forces practically destroyed what was left of Hood's army.

Meanwhile, Sherman had left Atlanta to begin his soon-to-be-famous March to the Sea. Living off the land,

MOBILE BAY, 1864 This painting by Robert Weir portrays a famous naval battle at the entrance to Mobile Bay between a Union Sloop-of-War, the *U.S.S. Richmond*, part of a fleet commanded by Admiral David Farragut, and a Confederate ironclad, the *C.S.S. Tennessee*. Although Confederate mines were scattered across the entrance to the harbor, Farragut ordered his ships into battle with the memorable command: "Damn the torpedoes! Full speed ahead!" The Union forces defeated the Confederate flotilla and three weeks later captured the forts defending the harbor—thus removing from Confederate control the last port on the Gulf Coast available to the blockade runners who were attempting to supply the South's war needs. *(Mariners' Museum, Newport News, Virginia)*

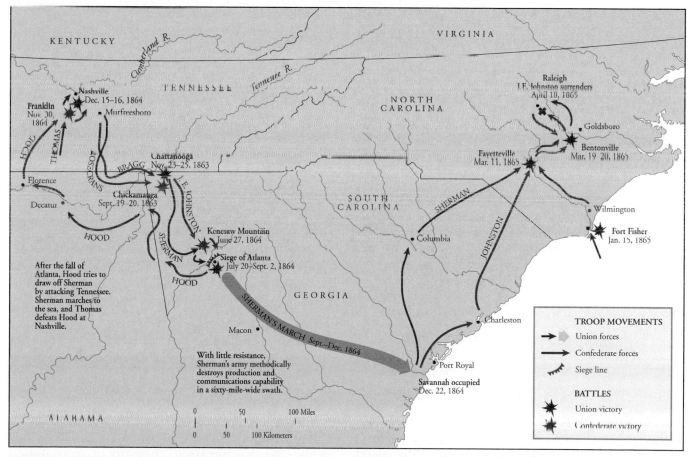

SHERMAN'S MARCH TO THE SEA, 1864-1865 While Grant was wearing Lee down in Virginia, General William Tecumseh Sherman was moving east across Georgia. After a series of battles in Tennessee and northwest Georgia, Sherman captured Atlanta and then marched unimpeded to Savannah, on the Georgia coast—deliberately devastating the towns and plantations through which his troops marched. Note that after capturing Savannah by Christmas 1864, Sherman began moving North through the Carolinas. A few days after Lee surrendered to Grant at Appomattox, Confederate forces further south surrendered to Sherman. ◆ *What did Sherman believe his devastating March to the Sea would accomplish?*

OLC For an interactive version of this map go to www.mhhe.com/brinkley12ch14maps

March to the Sea

destroying supplies it could not use, his army cut a sixty-mile-wide swath of desolation across Georgia. "War is all hell," Sherman had once said. By that he meant not that war is a terrible thing to be avoided, but that it should be made as horrible and costly as possible for the opponent. He sought not only to deprive the Confederate army of war materials and railroad communications but also to break the will of the Southern people, by burning towns and plantations along his route. By December 20, he had reached Savannah, which surrendered two days later. Sherman offered it to President Lincoln as a Christmas gift. Early in 1865, having left Savannah largely undamaged, Sherman continued his destructive march northward through South Carolina. He was virtually unopposed until he was well inside North Carolina, where a small force under Johnston could do no more than cause a brief delay.

In April 1865, Grant's Army of the Potomac—still engaged in the prolonged siege at Petersburg—finally captured a vital railroad junction southwest of the town. Without rail access to the South, cut off from other Confederate forces, Lee could no longer hope to defend Richmond. With the remnant of his army, now about 25,000 men, Lee began moving west in the forlorn hope of finding a way around the Union forces so he could head south and link up with Johnston in North Carolina. But the Union army pursued him and blocked his escape route. Finally recognizing that further bloodshed was futile, Lee arranged to meet Grant at a private home in the small town of Appomattox Courthouse, Virginia. There, on April 9, he surrendered what was left of his forces. Nine days later, near Durham, North Carolina, Johnston surrendered to Sherman.

Appomattox Courthouse

In military terms, at least, the long war was now effectively over, even though Jefferson Davis refused to accept defeat. He fled south from Richmond and was finally captured in Georgia. A few Southern diehards continued to fight, but even their resistance collapsed before long. Well before the last shot was fired, the difficult process of reuniting the shattered nation had begun.

A LETTER FROM THE FRONT Charles Wellington Reed, a nineteen-year-old soldier who was also a talented artist, sent illustrated letters to the members of his family throughout the war. In this 1863 letter to his mother, he portrays the Ninth Massachusetts Battery leaving Centreville, Virginia on its way to Gettysburg. Two weeks later, Reed fought in the famous battle and eventually received the Congressional Medal of Honor for his bravery there. "Such a shrieking, hissing, seathing I never dreamed was imaginable," he wrote of the fighting at the time. *(Manuscript Division, Library of Congress)*

CONCLUSION

The American Civil War began with high hopes and high ideals on both sides. In both the North and the South, thousands of men enthusiastically enlisted in local regiments; marched down the streets of their towns and cities dressed in uniforms of blue or gray to the cheers of family, friends, and neighbors; and went off to war. Four years later, over 600,000 of them were dead and many more maimed and traumatized for life. A fight for "principles" and "ideals"—a fight few people had thought would last more than a few months—had become one of the longest wars, and by far the bloodiest war, in American history, before or since.

During the first two years of fighting, the Confederate forces seemed to have all the advantages. They were fighting on their own soil. Their troops seemed more committed to the cause than those of the North. Their commanders were exceptionally talented, while Union forces were for a time erratically led. Gradually, however, the Union's advantages began to assert themselves. It had a stabler political system led by one of the greatest leaders in the nation's history (as opposed to the Confederacy's untested government led by a relatively weak president). It had a much larger population, a far more developed industrial economy, superior financial institutions, and a better railroad system. By the middle of 1863, the tide of war had changed; and over the next two years, Union forces gradually wore down the Confederate armies before finally triumphing in 1865.

The North's victory was not just a military one. The war strengthened the North's economy, giving a spur to

Impact of the North's Victory

industry and railroad development. It greatly weakened the South's, by destroying millions of dollars of property and depleting the region's young male population. Southerners had gone to war in part because of their fears of growing Northern dominance. The war itself, ironically, confirmed and strengthened

that dominance. There was no doubt by 1865 that the future of the United States lay in the growth of industry and commerce, which would occur for many years primarily outside the South.

But most of all, the Civil War was a victory for the millions of African-American slaves, over whose plight the conflict had largely begun in the first place. The war produced Abraham Lincoln's epochal Emancipation Proclamation and, later, the Thirteenth Amendment to the Constitution, which abolished slavery altogether. It also encouraged hundreds of thousands of slaves literally to free themselves, to desert their masters and seek refuge behind Union lines—at times to fight in the Union armies. The future of the freed slaves was not to be an easy one, but three and a half million people who had once lived in bondage emerged from the war as free men and women.

INTERACTIVE LEARNING

The *Primary Source Investigator CD-ROM* offers the following materials related to this chapter:

- A short documentary movie, **Free at Last!**, a study of President Lincoln's wartime decision to issue the Emancipation Proclamation (D9).

- Interactive map: **The Civil War** (M15).

- Documents, images, and maps related to the secession of the southern states and the American Civil War, including cartoons and letters showing how England

reacted to the Civil War, an image of contraband slaves, Mary Chesnut's diary on the war's end, and a letter from Charles Douglass to his father Frederick discussing life in the Union troops.

Online Learning Center (www.mhhe.com/brinkley12)

For quizzes, Internet resources, references to additional books and films, and more, consult this book's Online Learning Center.

FOR FURTHER REFERENCE

James McPherson, *Battle Cry of Freedom* (1988) is a fine general history of the Civil War. Shelby Foote, *The Civil War: A Narrative,* 3 vols. (1958–1974) recounts the military history of the war with great literary power. David Donald, *Lincoln* (1995) is the best modern biography of the sixteenth president. James M. McPherson, *Abraham Lincoln and the Second American Revolution* (1990) offers provocative reflections on the life and significance of Lincoln. Douglas Southall Freeman, *Robert E. Lee*, 4 vols. (1934–1935) and William McFeely, *Grant* (1981) are the leading biographies of the two most important Civil War generals. Philip Shaw Paludan, *"A People's Contest": The Union at War, 1861–1865* (1988) is a good account of the social impact of the war in the North. Iver Bernstein, *The New York City Draft Riots* (1990) examines an important event away from the battlefield. Alvin Josephy, *The Civil War in the West* (1992) remedies a long-neglected aspect of the war. Emory Thomas, *The Confederate Nation* (1979) is a fine one-volume history of the Confederacy. Drew Gilpin Faust, *Mothers of Invention* (1996) examines the lives of elite southern women

during the war. Ira Berlin et al., eds., *Free At Last: A Documentary History of Slavery, Freedom and the Civil War* (1992) is a superb compilation of primary sources from slaves and slaveowners relating to the demise of slavery during the Civil War years. Ira Berlin et al., *Slaves No More: Three Essays on Emancipation and the Civil War* (1992), the companion volume to the documents in *Free At Last,* argues that slaves and freedmen played an active role in destroying slavery and redefining freedom. Catherine Clinton and Nina Silber, *Divided Houses* (1992) is a collection of essays in the "new social history" from various historians demonstrating the importance of gender to the history of the Civil War. Edward L. Ayres, *In the Presence of Mine Enemies: War in the Heart of America* (2003) is an important social history of two neighboring communities—one in the Union, the other in the Confederacy—at war. Stephen Sears, *Gettysburg* (2003) is a good popular history of the decisive battle. *The Civil War* (1989), Ken Burns's outstandingly popular and award-winning, nine-hour epic documentary, has shaped the recent popular image of the conflict for many Americans.

THE GENIUS OF FREEDOM This 1874 lithograph portrays a series of important moments in the history of African Americans in the South during Reconstruction—among them the participation of black soldiers in the Civil War, a speech by a black representative in the North Carolina legislature, and the movement of African-American workers from slavery into a system of free labor. It also portrays some of the white leaders (among them Lincoln and Charles Sumner) who had promoted the cause of the freedmen. *(Chicago Historical Society)*

SIGNIFICANT EVENTS

1863 ▶ Lincoln announces preliminary Reconstruction plan

1864 ▶ Louisiana, Arkansas, and Tennessee readmitted to Union under Lincoln plan

▶ Wade-Davis Bill passed

1865 ▶ Lincoln assassinated (April 14); Andrew Johnson becomes president

▶ Johnson tries to readmit rest of Confederate states to Union

▶ Black Codes enacted in South

▶ Freedmen's Bureau established

▶ Congress reconvenes (December) and refuses to admit Southern representatives; creates Joint Committee on Reconstruction

1866 ▶ Freedmen's Bureau Act renewed

▶ Congress approves Fourteenth Amendment; most Southern states reject it

▶ Republicans gain in congressional elections

▶ *Ex parte Milligan* challenges Radicals' Reconstruction plans

▶ Ku Klux Klan formed in South

1867 ▶ Military Reconstruction Act (and two supplementary acts) outlines congressional plan of Reconstruction

▶ Tenure of Office Act and Command of the Army Act restrict presidential power

▶ Southern states establish Reconstruction governments under congressional plan

▶ U.S. purchases Alaska

1868 ▶ Most Southern states readmitted to Union under congressional plan

▶ Andrew Johnson impeached but not convicted

CHAPTER 15

Reconstruction and the New South

F ew periods in the history of the United States have produced as much bitterness or created such enduring controversy as the era of Reconstruction—the years following the Civil War when Americans attempted to reunite their shattered nation. Those who lived through Reconstruction viewed it in sharply different ways. To many white Southerners, it was a vicious and destructive experience—a time when vindictive Northerners inflicted humiliation and revenge on the prostrate South and unnecessarily delayed a genuine reunion of the sections. Northern defenders of Reconstruction, in contrast, argued that their policies were the only way to keep unrepentant Confederates from restoring Southern society as it had been before the war; without forceful federal intervention, it would be impossible to stop the re-emergence of a backward aristocracy and the continued subjugation of former slaves; there would be no way, in other words, to prevent the same sectional problems that had produced the Civil War in the first place.

To most African Americans at the time, and to many people of all races since, Reconstruction was notable for other reasons. Neither a vicious tyranny, as white Southerners charged, nor a thoroughgoing reform, as many Northerners claimed, it was, rather, a small but important first step in the effort by former slaves to secure civil rights and economic power. Reconstruction did not provide African Americans with either the legal protections or the material resources to assure them anything like real equality. And when it came to an end, finally, in the late 1870s—as a result of an economic crisis, a lack of political will in the North, and organized, at times violent, resistance by white Southerners—the freed slaves found themselves abandoned by the federal government to face a system of economic peonage and legal subordination alone. For the remainder of the nineteenth century, those blacks who continued to live in what came to be known as the New South were unable effectively to resist oppression. And yet for all its shortcomings, Reconstruction did help African Americans create institutions and legal precedents that they carried with them into the twentieth century and that became the basis for later efforts to win freedom and equality.

▶ Fourteenth Amendment ratified

▶ Ulysses S. Grant elected president

1869 ▶ Congress passes Fifteenth Amendment

▶ First "redeemer" governments elected in South

1870 ▶ Last Southern states readmitted to Union

▶ "Enforcement acts" passed

1871 ▶ *Alabama* claims settled

1872 ▶ Liberal Republicans defect

▶ Grant reelected president

1873 ▶ Commercial and financial panic disrupts economy

1875 ▶ Specie Resumption Act passed

▶ "Whiskey ring" scandal discredits Grant administration

1877 ▶ Rutherford B. Hayes elected president after disputed election

▶ Last federal troops withdrawn from South after Compromise of 1877

▶ Last Southern states "redeemed"

1879 ▶ Readjusters win control of Virginia legislature

1880 ▶ Joel Chandler Harris publishes *Uncle Remus*

1883 ▶ Supreme Court upholds segregation in private institutions

1890s ▶ "Jim Crow" laws passed throughout South

▶ Lynchings increase in South

1895 ▶ Booker T. Washington outlines Atlanta Compromise

1896 ▶ *Plessy* v. *Ferguson* upholds "separate but equal" racial facilities

1898 ▶ *Williams* v. *Mississippi* validates literacy tests for voting

THE PROBLEMS OF PEACEMAKING

In 1865, as it became clear that the war was almost over, no one in Washington knew quite what to do. Abraham Lincoln could not negotiate a treaty with the defeated government; he continued to insist that the Confederate government had no legal right to exist. Yet neither could he simply readmit the Southern states into the Union as if nothing had happened.

The Aftermath of War and Emancipation

What happened to the South in the Civil War was a catastrophe with no parallel in America's experience as a nation. Towns had been gutted, plantations burned, fields neglected, bridges and railroads destroyed. Many white Southerners, stripped of their slaves through emancipation and stripped of the capital they had invested in now worthless Confederate bonds and currency, had almost no personal property. Many families had to rebuild their fortunes without the help of adult males. Some white Southerners faced starvation and homelessness.

The Devastated South

More than 258,000 Confederate soldiers had died in the war—more than 20 percent of the adult white male population of the region; thousands more returned home wounded or sick. Almost all surviving white Southerners had lost people close to them in the fighting. A cult of ritualized mourning developed throughout the region in the late 1860s, particularly among white women—many of whom wore mourning clothes (and jewelry) for two years or longer. At the same time, white Southerners began to romanticize the "Lost Cause" and its leaders, and to look back nostalgically at the South as it had existed before the terrible disruptions of war. Such Confederate heroes as Robert E. Lee, Stonewall Jackson, and (later) Jefferson Davis were treated with extraordinary reverence, almost as religious figures. Communities throughout the South built elaborate monuments to their war dead in town squares. The tremendous sense of loss that pervaded the white South reinforced the determination of many whites to protect what remained of their now-vanished world.

Myth of the "Lost Cause"

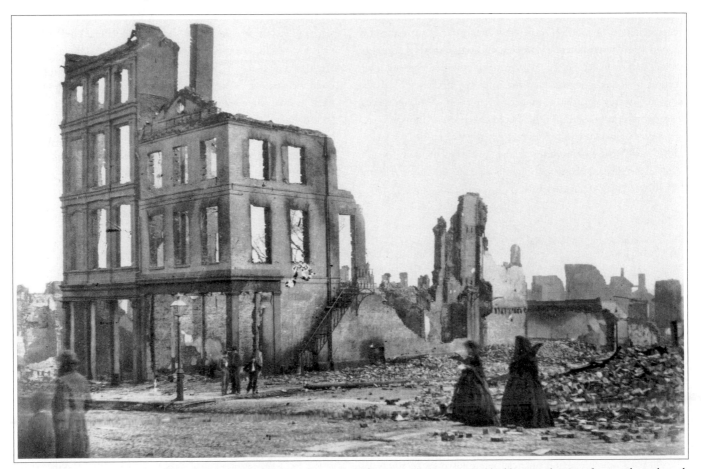

RICHMOND, 1865 By the time Union forces captured Richmond in early 1865, the Confederate capital had been under siege for months and much of the city lay in ruins, as this photograph reveals. On April 4, President Lincoln, accompanied by his son Tad, visited Richmond. As he walked through the streets of the shattered city, hundreds of former slaves emerged from the rubble to watch him pass. "No triumphal march of a conqueror could have equalled in moral sublimity the humble manner in which he entered Richmond," a black soldier serving with the Union army wrote. "It was a great deliverer among the delivered. No wonder tears came to his eyes." *(Library of Congress)*

A MONUMENT TO THE LOST CAUSE This monument in the town square of Monroe, Georgia, was typical of many such memorials erected all across the South after the Civil War. They served both to commemorate the Confederate dead and to remind white southerners of what was by the 1870s already widely known and romanticized as the "Lost Cause." (*©Lee Snider/Corbis*)

hoping for assistance. Others spent months, even years, searching for relatives from whom they had been separated. Virtually none, of course, owned any land or property. Most had no possessions except the clothes they wore.

In 1865, in short, Southern society was in disarray. Blacks and whites, men and women faced a future of great uncertainty. Yet people of both races faced this future with some very clear aspirations. For both blacks and whites, Reconstruction became a struggle to define the meaning of freedom. But the former slaves and the defeated whites had very different conceptions of what freedom meant.

Competing Notions of Freedom

For African Americans, freedom meant above all an end to slavery and to all the injustices and humiliation they associated with it. But it also meant the acquisition of rights and protections that would allow them to live as free men and women in the same way white people did. "If I cannot do like a white man," one African-American man told his former master, "I am not free."

Blacks differed with one another on how to achieve that freedom. Some demanded a redistribution of economic resources, especially land, because, as a convention of Alabama freedmen put it in a formal resolution, "The property which they hold was nearly Freedom for the Ex-slaves

all earned by the sweat of our brows." Others asked simply for legal equality, confident that given the same opportunities as white citizens they could advance successfully in American society. But whatever their particular demands, virtually all former slaves were united in their desire for independence from white control. Freed from slavery, blacks throughout the South began almost immediately to create autonomous African-American communities. They pulled out of white-controlled churches and established their own. They created fraternal, benevolent, and mutual aid societies. When they could, they began their own schools.

For most white Southerners, freedom meant something very different. It meant the ability to control their own destinies without interference from the North or the federal government. And in the immediate aftermath of the war, they attempted to exercise this version of freedom by trying to restore their society to its antebellum form. Slavery had been abolished in the former Confederacy by the Emancipation Proclamation, and everywhere else (as of December 1865) by the Thirteenth Amendment. But many white planters wanted to continue slavery in an altered form by keeping black workers legally tied to the plantations. When these white Southerners fought for what they considered freedom, they were fighting above all to preserve local and regional autonomy and white supremacy.

If conditions were bad for many Southern whites, they were far worse for most Southern blacks—the 4 million men and women emerging from bondage. Some of them had also seen service during the war—as servants to Confederate officers or as teamsters and laborers for the Southern armies. Nearly 200,000 had fought for the Union, and 38,000 had died. Others had worked as spies or scouts for Union forces in the South. Many more had flocked to the Union lines to escape slavery. Even before Emancipation, thousands of slaves in many parts of the South had taken advantage of wartime disruptions to leave their owners and move off in search of freedom. As soon as the war ended, hundreds of thousands more former slaves—young and old, healthy and sick—left their plantations. But most had nowhere to go. Many of them trudged to the nearest town or city, roamed the countryside camping at night on the bare ground, or gathered around Union occupation forces,

A FREEDMANS' BUREAU SCHOOL African-American students and teachers stand outside a school for former slaves, one of many run by the Freedman's Bureau throughout the defeated Confederacy in the first years after the war. *(U.S. Military History Institute, Carlisle, Pennsylvania. Photo by Jim Enos)*

The federal government kept troops in the South after the war to preserve order and protect the freedmen. In

The Freedman's Bureau

March 1865, Congress established the Freedmen's Bureau, an agency of the army directed by General Oliver O. Howard. The Freedmen's Bureau distributed food to millions of former slaves. It established schools staffed by missionaries and teachers who had been sent to the South by Freedmen's Aid Societies and other private and church groups in the North. It made modest efforts to settle blacks on lands of their own. (The bureau also offered considerable assistance to poor whites, many of whom were similarly destitute and homeless after the war.) But the Freedmen's Bureau was not a permanent solution. It had authority to operate for only one year; and in any case it was far too small to deal effectively with the enormous problems facing southern society. By the time the war ended, other proposals for reconstructing the defeated South were emerging.

Issues of Reconstruction

The terms by which the southern states rejoined the Union had important implications for both major political parties. The Republican victories in 1860 and 1864 had been a result in large part of the division of the Democratic Party and, later, the removal of the South from the electorate. Readmitting the South, leaders of both parties believed, would reunite the Democrats and weaken the Republicans. In addition, the Republican Party had taken advantage of the South's absence from Congress to pass a program of nationalistic economic legislation—railroad subsidies, protective tariffs, banking and currency reforms, and other measures to benefit northern business leaders and industrialists. Should the Democratic Party regain power with heavy southern support, these programs would be in jeopardy. Complicating these practical questions were emotional concerns. Many northerners believed the South should be punished in some way for the suffering and sacrifice its rebellion had caused. Many northerners believed, too, that the South should be transformed, made over in the North's urbanized image—its supposedly backward, feudal, undemocratic society civilized and modernized.

Even among the Republicans in Congress, there was considerable disagreement about the proper approach to Reconstruction—disagreement that reflected the same factional division that had created disputes over emancipation during the war. Conservatives insisted that the South accept the abolition of slavery,

Conservative and Radical Republicans

but proposed few other conditions for the readmission of the seceded states. The Radicals, led by Representative Thaddeus Stevens of Pennsylvania and Senator Charles Sumner of Massachusetts, urged that the civil and military leaders of the Confederacy be punished, that large numbers of Southern whites be disenfranchised, that the legal rights of blacks be protected, and that the property of wealthy white Southerners who had aided the Confederacy be confiscated and distributed among the freedmen. Some Radicals favored granting suffrage to the former slaves. Others hesitated, since few Northern states permitted blacks to vote. Between the Radicals and the Conservatives stood a faction of uncommitted Republicans, the Moderates, who rejected the punitive goals of the Radicals but supported extracting at least some concessions from the South on black rights.

Plans for Reconstruction

President Lincoln's sympathies lay with the Moderates and Conservatives of his party. He believed that a lenient Reconstruction policy would encourage southern unionists and other former Whigs to join the Republican Party and would thus prevent the readmission of the South from strengthening the Democrats. More immediately, the southern unionists could become the nucleus of new, loyal state governments in the South. Lincoln was not uninterested in the fate of the freedmen, but he was willing to defer questions about their future for the sake of rapid reunification.

Lincoln's Reconstruction plan, which he announced in December 1863, offered a general amnesty to white

Lincoln's 10% Plan southerners—other than high officials of the Confederacy—who would pledge loyalty to the government and accept the elimination of slavery. Whenever 10 percent of the number of voters in 1860 took the oath in any state, those loyal voters could set up a state government. Lincoln also hoped to extend suffrage to those blacks who were educated, owned property, and had served in the Union army. Three southern states—Louisiana, Arkansas, and Tennessee, all under Union occupation—reestablished loyal governments under the Lincoln formula in 1864.

The Radical Republicans were astonished at the mildness of Lincoln's program. They persuaded Congress to deny seats to representatives from the three "reconstructed" states and refused to count the electoral vote of those states in the election of 1864. But for the moment, the Radicals were uncertain about what form their own Reconstruction plan should take. Their first effort to **Wade-Davis Bill** resolve that question was the Wade-Davis Bill, passed by Congress in July 1864. It authorized the president to appoint a provisional governor for each conquered state. When a majority (not Lincoln's 10 percent) of the white males of the state pledged their allegiance to the Union, the governor could summon a state constitutional convention, whose delegates were to be elected by those who would swear (through the so-called Ironclad Oath) that they had never borne arms against the United States—another departure from Lincoln's plan. The new state constitutions would have to abolish slavery, disfranchise Confederate civil and military leaders, and repudiate debts accumulated by the state governments during the war. After a state had met these conditions, Congress would readmit it to the Union. Like the president's proposal, the Wade-Davis Bill left up to the states the question of political rights for blacks. Congress passed the bill a few days before it adjourned in 1864, and Lincoln disposed of it with a pocket veto. His action enraged the Radical leaders, and the pragmatic Lincoln became convinced he would have to accept at least some of the Radical demands. He began to move toward a new approach to Reconstruction.

The Death of Lincoln

What plan he might have produced no one can say. On the night of April 14, 1865, Lincoln and his wife attended a play at Ford's Theater in Washington. As they sat in the presidential box, John Wilkes Booth, a member of a distinguished family of actors and a man obsessed with aiding the Southern cause, entered the box from the rear and shot Lincoln in the head. The president was carried unconscious to a house across the street, where early the next morning, surrounded by family, friends, and political associates (among them a tearful Charles Sumner), he died.

ABRAHAM LINCOLN This haunting photograph of Abraham Lincoln, showing clearly the weariness and aging that four years as a war president had created, was taken in Washington only four days before his assassination in 1865. *(Library of Congress)*

The circumstances of Lincoln's death earned him immediate martyrdom. It also produced something close to hysteria throughout the North. There were accusations that Booth had acted as part of a great conspiracy—accusations that contained some truth. Booth did indeed have associates, one of whom shot and wounded Secretary of State Seward the night of the assassination, another of whom abandoned at the last moment a scheme to murder Vice President Johnson. Booth himself escaped on horseback into the Virginia countryside, where, on April 26, he was cornered by Union troops and shot to death in a blazing barn. A military tribunal convicted eight other people of participating in the conspiracy (at least two of them on the basis of virtually no evidence). Four were hanged.

To many Northerners, however, the murder of the president seemed evidence of an even greater conspiracy—one masterminded and directed by the unrepentant leaders of the defeated South. Militant Republicans exploited such suspicions relentlessly for months, ensuring that Lincoln's death would help doom his plans for a relatively easy peace.

Johnson and "Restoration"

Leadership of the Moderates and Conservatives fell to Lincoln's successor, Andrew Johnson, who was not well suited, either by circumstance or personality, for the task. A Democrat until he had joined the Union ticket with Lincoln in 1864, he became a Republican president at a moment when partisan passions were growing. Johnson himself was an intemperate and tactless man, filled with resentments and insecurities. He was also openly hostile to the freed slaves and unwilling to support any plans that guaranteed them civil equality or enfranchisement. He once declared, "White men alone must manage the South."

Andrew Johnson's Personality

Johnson revealed his plan for Reconstruction—or "Restoration," as he preferred to call it—soon after he took office, and he implemented it during the summer of 1865 when Congress was in recess. Like Lincoln, he offered amnesty to those Southerners who would take an oath of allegiance. (High-ranking Confederate officials and any white Southerner with land worth $20,000 or more would have to apply to the president for individual pardons. Johnson, a self-made man, apparently liked the thought of the great planter aristocrats humbling themselves before him.) In most other respects, however, his plan resembled that of the Wade-Davis Bill. For each state, the president appointed a provisional governor, who was to invite qualified voters to elect delegates to a constitutional convention. Johnson did not specify how many qualified voters were necessary, but he implied that he would require a majority (as had the Wade-Davis Bill). In order to win readmission to Congress, a state had to revoke its ordinance of secession, abolish slavery, ratify the Thirteenth Amendment, and repudiate the Confederate and state war debts. The final procedure before restoration was for a state to elect a state government and send representatives to Congress.

By the end of 1865, all the seceded states had formed new governments—some under Lincoln's plan, some under Johnson's—and were prepared to rejoin the Union as soon as Congress recognized them. But Radical Republicans vowed not to recognize the Johnson governments, just as they had previously refused to recognize the Lincoln regimes; for by now, northern opinion had become more hostile toward the South than it had been a year earlier when Congress passed the Wade-Davis Bill. Many northerners were disturbed by the apparent reluctance of some delegates to the southern conventions to abolish slavery, and by the refusal of all the conventions to grant suffrage to any blacks. They were astounded that states claiming to be "loyal" should elect prominent leaders of the recent Confederacy as state officials and representatives to Congress. Particularly hard to accept was Georgia's choice of Alexander H. Stephens, former Confederate vice president, as a United States senator.

Northern Attitudes Harden

RADICAL RECONSTRUCTION

Reconstruction under Johnson's plan—often known as "presidential Reconstruction"—continued only until Congress reconvened in December 1865. At that point, Congress refused to seat the representatives of the "restored" states and created a new Joint Committee on Reconstruction to frame a Reconstruction policy of its own. The period of "congressional" or "Radical Reconstruction had begun.

The Black Codes

Meanwhile, events in the South were driving Northern opinion in even more radical directions. Throughout the South in 1865 and early 1866, state legislatures were enacting sets of laws known as the Black Codes, designed to give whites substantial control over the former slaves. The codes authorized local officials to apprehend unemployed blacks, fine them for vagrancy, and hire them out to private employers to satisfy the fine. Some of the codes forbade blacks to own or lease farms or to take any jobs other than as plantation workers or domestic servants.

Congress first responded to the Black Codes by passing an act extending the life of the Freedmen's Bureau and widening its powers so that it could nullify work agreements forced on freedmen under the Black Codes. Then, in April 1866, Congress passed the first Civil Rights Act, which declared blacks to be citizens of the United States and gave the federal government power to intervene in state affairs to protect the rights of citizens. Johnson vetoed both bills, but Congress overrode him on each of them.

Johnson's Vetoes

The Fourteenth Amendment

In April 1866, the Joint Committee on Reconstruction proposed a new amendment to the Constitution, which Congress approved in early summer and sent to the states for ratification. Eventually, it became one of the most important of all the provisions in the Constitution.

The Fourteenth Amendment offered the first constitutional definition of American citizenship. Everyone born in the United States, and everyone naturalized, was automatically a citizen and entitled to all the "privileges and immunities" guaranteed by the Constitution, including equal protection of the laws by both the state and national governments. There could be no other requirements for citizenship. The amendment also imposed penalties—reduction of representation in Congress and in the electoral college—on states that denied suffrage to any adult male inhabitants. (The wording reflected the prevailing view in Congress and elsewhere that the franchise was properly restricted to men.) Finally, it prohibited former

Citizenship for Blacks

THE MEMPHIS RACE RIOT, 1866 Angry whites (shown here shooting down blacks) rampaged through the black neighborhoods of Memphis, Tennessee, during the first three days of May 1866, burning homes, schools, and churches and leaving forty-six people dead. Some claimed the riot was a response to strict new regulations protecting blacks that had been imposed on Tennessee by General George Stoneman, the military commander of the district; others argued that it was an attempt by whites to intimidate and control an African-American population that was trying to exercise its new freedom. Such riots were among the events that persuaded Radical Republicans in Congress to press for a harsher policy of Reconstruction. *(The Granger Collection)*

Congressional Radicals offered to readmit to the Union any state whose legislature ratified the Fourteenth Amendment. Only Tennessee did so. All the other former Confederate states, along with Delaware and Kentucky, refused, leaving the amendment temporarily without the necessary approval of three-fourths of the states.

But by now, the Radicals were growing more confident and determined. Bloody race riots in New Orleans and other Southern cities—riots in which African Americans were the principal victims—were among the events that strengthened their hand. In the 1866 congressional elections, Johnson actively campaigned for Conservative candidates, but he did his own cause more harm than good with his intemperate speeches. The voters returned an overwhelming majority of Republicans, most of them Radicals, to Congress. In the Senate, there were now 42 Republicans to 11 Democrats; in the House, 143 Republicans to 49 Democrats. (The South remained largely unrepresented in both chambers.) Congressional Republicans were now strong enough to enact a plan of their own even over the president's objections.

The Congressional Plan

The Radicals passed three Reconstruction bills early in 1867 and overrode Johnson's vetoes of all of them. These bills finally established, nearly two years after the end of the war, a coherent plan for Reconstruction.

Three Reconstruction Bills

members of Congress or other former federal officials who had aided the Confederacy from holding any state or federal office unless two-thirds of Congress voted to pardon them.

AMERICAN CITIZENS (TO THE POLLS) The artist T. W. Wood painted this watercolor of voters standing in line at the polls during the 1866 elections. A prosperous Yankee, a working-class Irishman, and a Dutch coach driver stand next to the newest addition to the American electorate: an African American, whose expression conveys his excitement at being able to join the community of voters. Wood meant this painting to celebrate the democratic character of American life after the Civil War. *(T. W. Wood Art Gallery, Vermont College, Montpelier)*

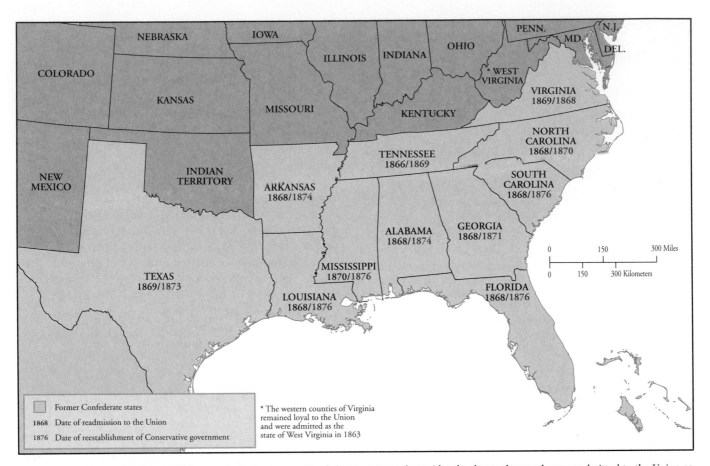

RECONSTRUCTION, 1866–1877 This map shows the former Confederate states and provides the dates when each was readmitted to the Union as well as a subsequent date when each state managed to return political power to traditional white, conservative elites—a process white southerners liked to call "redemption." ◆ *What had to happen for a state to be readmitted to the Union? What had to happen before a state could experience "redemption"?*

Under the congressional plan, Tennessee, which had ratified the Fourteenth Amendment, was promptly readmitted. But Congress rejected the Lincoln-Johnson governments of the other ten Confederate states and, instead, combined those states into five military districts. A military commander governed each district and had orders to register qualified voters (defined as all adult black males and those white males who had not participated in the rebellion). Once registered, voters would elect conventions to prepare new state constitutions, which had to include provisions for black suffrage. Once voters ratified the new constitutions, they could elect state governments. Congress had to approve a state's constitution, and the state legislature had to ratify the Fourteenth Amendment. Once that happened, and once enough states ratified the amendment to make it part of the Constitution, then the former Confederate states could be restored to the Union.

By 1868, seven of the ten former Confederate states (Arkansas, North Carolina, South Carolina, Louisiana, Alabama, Georgia, and Florida) had fulfilled these conditions (including ratification of the Fourteenth Amendment, which now became part of the Constitution) and were

readmitted to the Union. Conservative whites held up the return of Virginia and Texas until 1869 and Mississippi until 1870. By then, Congress had added an additional requirement for readmission—ratification of another constitutional amendment, the Fifteenth, which forbade the states **Fifteenth Amendment** and the federal government to deny suffrage to any citizen on account of "race, color, or previous condition of servitude."

To stop the president from interfering with their plans, the congressional Radicals passed two remarkable laws of dubious constitutionality in 1867. One, the Tenure of Office Act, forbade the president to remove civil officials, including members of his own cabinet, without the consent of the Senate. The principal purpose of the law was to protect the job of Secretary of War Edwin M. Stanton, who was cooperating with the Radicals. The other law, the Command of the Army Act, prohibited the president from issuing military orders except through the commanding general of the army (General Grant), who could not be relieved or assigned elsewhere without the consent of the Senate.

The congressional Radicals also took action to stop the Supreme Court from interfering with their plans. In 1866, the Court had declared in the case of *Ex parte Milligan* that military tribunals were unconstitutional in places where civil courts were functioning, a decision that seemed to threaten the system of military government the Radicals were planning for the South. Radicals in Congress immediately proposed several bills that would require two-thirds of the justices to support any decision overruling a law of Congress, would deny the Court jurisdiction in Reconstruction cases, would reduce its membership to three, and would even abolish it. The justices apparently took notice. Over the next two years, the Court refused to accept jurisdiction in any cases involving Reconstruction (and the congressional bills concerning the Court never passed).

The Impeachment of the President

President Johnson had long since ceased to be a serious obstacle to the passage of Radical legislation, but he was still the official charged with administering the Reconstruction programs. As such, the Radicals believed, he remained a serious impediment to their plans. Early in 1867, they began looking for a way to impeach him and remove him from office. Republicans found them, they believed, when Johnson dismissed Secretary of War Stanton despite Congress's refusal to agree, thus deliberately

Tenure of Office Act

violating the Tenure of Office Act in hopes of testing the law before the courts. Elated Radicals in the House quickly impeached the president and sent the case to the Senate for trial.

The trial before the Senate lasted throughout April and May 1868. The Radicals put heavy pressure on all the Republican senators, but the Moderates (who were

Johnson Acquitted

losing faith in the Radical program) vacillated. On the first three charges to come to a vote, seven Republicans joined the Democrats and independents to support acquittal. The vote was 35 to 19, one short of the constitutionally required two-thirds majority. After that, the Radicals dropped the impeachment effort.

THE SOUTH IN RECONSTRUCTION

When white Southerners spoke bitterly in later years of the effects of Reconstruction, they referred most frequently to the governments Congress helped impose on them—governments they claimed were both incompetent and corrupt, that saddled the region with enormous debts, and that trampled on the rights of citizens. When black Southerners and their defenders condemned Reconstruction, in contrast, they spoke of the failure of the national and state governments to go far enough to guarantee freedmen even the most elemental

rights of citizenship—a failure that resulted in a harsh new system of economic subordination. (See "Where Historians Disagree," pp. 418–419).

The Reconstruction Governments

In the ten states of the South that were reorganized under the congressional plan, approximately one-fourth of the white males were at first excluded from voting or holding office. That produced black majorities among voters in South Carolina, Mississippi, and Louisiana (states where blacks were also a majority of the population), and in Alabama and Florida (where they were not). But the government soon lifted most suffrage restrictions so that nearly all white males could vote. After that, Republicans maintained control only with the support of many Southern whites.

Critics called these Southern white Republicans "scalawags." Many were former Whigs who had never felt comfortable in the Democratic Party—some of them wealthy

"Scalawags"

THE BURDENED SOUTH This Reconstruction-era cartoon expresses the South's sense of its oppression at the hands of Northern Republicans. President Grant (whose hat bears Abraham Lincoln's initials) rides in comfort in a giant carpetbag, guarded by bayonet-wielding soldiers, as the South staggers under the burden in chains. More evidence of destruction and military occupations is visible in the background. *(Culver Pictures, Inc.)*

THE LOUISIANA CONSTITUTIONAL CONVENTION, 1868 This
lithograph commemorates the brief moment during which black voters
actually dominated the politics of Louisiana. When the state held a
constitutional convention in 1868, a majority of the delegates were
African Americans (many of them freeborn blacks who had moved to
Louisiana from the North). The Constitution they passed guaranteed
political and civil rights to black citizens. When white conservatives
regained control of the state several years later, they passed a new
constitution of their own, repealing most of those guarantees. *(Library
of Congress)*

(or once wealthy) planters or businessmen interested in
the economic development of the region. Others were
farmers who lived in remote areas where there had been
little or no slavery and who hoped the Republican program of internal improvements would help end their
economic isolation. Despite their diverse social positions, scalawags shared a belief that the Republican Party
would serve their economic interests better than the
Democrats.

White men from the North also served as Republican leaders in the South. Critics of Reconstruction
referred to them pejoratively as "carpetbaggers," which
conveyed an image of penniless adventurers who
arrived with all their posses-
sions in a carpetbag (a common

"Carpetbaggers"

kind of cheap suitcase covered with carpeting material). In fact, most of the so-called carpetbaggers were
well-educated people of middle-class origin, many of
them doctors, lawyers, and teachers. Most were veterans of the Union army who looked on the South as a
new frontier, more promising than the West. They had
settled there at war's end as hopeful planters, or as
business and professional people.

But the most numerous Republicans in the South
were the black freedmen, most of whom had no previous experience in politics and who tried, therefore, to
build institutions through which they could learn to
exercise their power. In several states, African-American
voters held their own conven-
tions to chart their future

Freedmen

course. One such "colored convention," as Southern
whites called them, assembled in Alabama in 1867 and
announced: "We claim exactly the same rights, privileges
and immunities as are enjoyed by white men—we ask
nothing more and will be content with nothing less." The
black churches freedmen created after emancipation also
helped give unity and political self-confidence to the former slaves. African Americans played a significant role in
the politics of the Reconstruction South. They served as
delegates to the constitutional conventions. They held
public offices of practically every kind. Between 1869 and
1901, twenty blacks served in the U.S. House of Representatives, two in the Senate (Hiram Revels of Mississippi
and Blanche K. Bruce of Mississippi). African Americans
served, too, in state legislatures and in various other state
offices. Southern whites complained loudly (both at the
time and for generations to come) about "Negro rule"
during Reconstruction, but no such thing ever actually
existed in any of the states. No black man was ever
elected governor of a southern state (although Lieutenant Governor P. B. S. Pinchback briefly performed
gubernatorial duties in Louisiana). Blacks never controlled any of the state legislatures, although they held a
majority in the lower house in South Carolina for a time.
In the South as a whole, the percentage of black officeholders was always far lower than the percentage of
blacks in the population. The record of the Reconstruction governments is mixed. Critics at the time and since
denounced them for corruption and financial extravagance, and there is some truth to both charges. Officeholders in many states enriched themselves through
graft and other illicit activities. State budgets expanded
to hitherto unknown totals, and state debts soared to
previously undreamed-of heights. In South Carolina, for
example, the public debt increased from $7 million to
$29 million in eight years.

But the corruption in the South, real as it was, was
hardly unique to the Reconstruction governments.
Corruption was at least as rampant in the northern states.
And in both North and South, it was a result of the same
thing: a rapid economic expansion of government

services (and revenues) that put new strains on (and new temptations before) elected officials everywhere. The end of Reconstruction did not end corruption in southern state governments. In many states, in fact, corruption increased.

And the state expenditures of the Reconstruction years were huge only in comparison with the meager budgets of the antebellum era. They represented an effort to provide the South with desperately needed services that antebellum governments had never offered: public education, public works programs, poor relief, and other costly new commitments. There were, to be sure, graft and extravagance in Reconstruction governments; there were also positive and permanent accomplishments.

Education

Perhaps the most important of those accomplishments was a dramatic improvement in southern education for both races. In the first years of Reconstruction, much of the impetus for educational reform in the South came from outside groups—from the Freedmen's Bureau, from Northern private philanthropic organizations, from many Northern women, black and white, who traveled to the South to teach in freedmen's schools—and from southern blacks themselves. Over the opposition of many southern whites, who feared that education would give blacks "false notions of equality," these reformers established a large network of schools for former slaves—4,000 schools by 1870, staffed by 9,000 teachers (half of them black), teaching 200,000 students (about 12 percent of the total school-age population of the freedmen). In the 1870s, Reconstruction governments began to build a comprehensive public school system in the South. By 1876, more than half of all white children and about 40 percent of all black children were attending schools in the South. Several black "academies," offering more advanced education, also began operating. Gradually, these academies grew into an important network of black colleges and universities, which included such distinguished schools as Fisk and Atlanta Universities and Morehouse College.

Already, however, southern education was becoming divided into two separate systems, one black and one white. Early efforts to integrate the schools of the region were a dismal failure. The Freedmen's Bureau schools, for example, were open to students of all races, but almost no whites attended them. New Orleans set up an integrated school system under the Reconstruction government; again, whites almost universally stayed away. The one federal effort to mandate school integration—the Civil Rights Act of 1875—had its provisions for educational desegregation removed before it was passed. As soon as the Republican governments of Reconstruction were

Segregated Schools

replaced, the new Southern Democratic regimes quickly abandoned all efforts to promote integration.

Landownership and Tenancy

The most ambitious goal of the Freedmen's Bureau, and of some Republican Radicals in Congress, was to make Reconstruction the vehicle for a fundamental reform of landownership in the South. The effort failed. In the last years of the war and the first years of Reconstruction, the Freedmen's Bureau did oversee the redistribution of substantial amounts of land to freedmen in a few areas—notably the Sea Islands of South Carolina and Georgia, and areas of Mississippi that had once

Failure of Land Redistribution

belonged to the family of Jefferson Davis. By June 1865, the Bureau had settled nearly 10,000 black families on their own land—most of it drawn from abandoned plantations—arousing dreams among former slaves throughout the South of "forty acres and a mule." By the end of that year, however, the experiment was already collapsing. Southern plantation owners were returning and demanding the restoration of their property, and President Johnson was supporting their demands. Despite the resistance of the Freedmen's Bureau, the government eventually returned most of the confiscated land to the original white owners. Congress, moreover, never had much stomach for the idea of land redistribution. Very few Northern Republicans believed that the federal government had the right to confiscate property. Even so, distribution of landownership in the South changed considerably in the postwar years. Among whites, there was a striking decline in landownership, from 80 percent before the war to 67 percent by the end of Reconstruction. Some whites lost their land because of unpaid debt or increased taxes; some left the marginal lands they had owned to move to more fertile areas, where they rented. Among blacks, during the same period, the proportion who owned land rose from virtually none to more than 20 percent. Many black landowners acquired their property through hard work or luck or both. But some relied on assistance from white-dominated financial or philanthropic institutions. One of them was the Freedman's Bank, established in 1865 by antislavery whites in an effort to promote landownership among blacks. They persuaded thousands of freedmen to deposit their modest savings in the bank, but then invested heavily in unsuccessful enterprises. It was ill prepared, therefore, for the national depression of the 1870s and it failed in 1874.

Still, most blacks, and a growing minority of whites, did not own their own land during Reconstruction; and some who acquired land in the 1860s had lost it by the 1890s.

Sharecropping

These people worked for others in one form or another. Many black agricultural laborers—perhaps 25 percent of

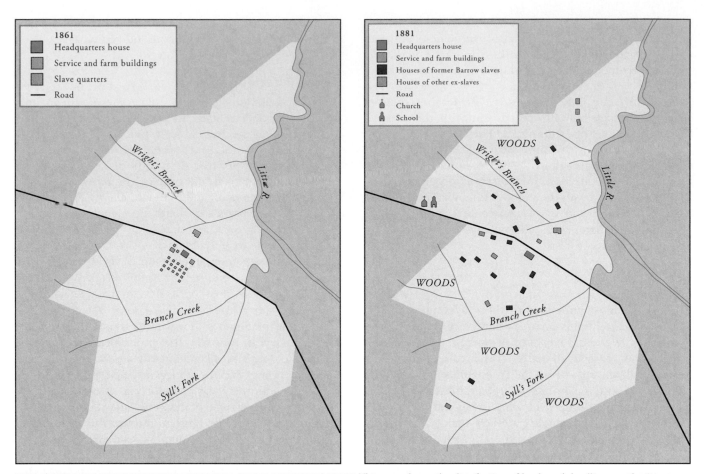

THE SOUTHERN PLANTATION BEFORE AND AFTER EMANCIPATION This map shows the distribution of lands and dwellings on the Barrow Plantation in Oglethorpe County, Georgia, before and after the emancipation of slaves at the close of the Civil War. The map on the left shows the plantation in 1861, as the war began. Like the Hopeton Plantation shown on p. 299, the Barrow plantation was highly centralized before the war, with slaves living all together in a complex of dwellings near the master's house. Twenty years later, as the map on the right shows, the same landscape was very differently divided. Housing was now widely dispersed, as former slaves became tenants or sharecroppers and began working their own small pieces of land and living more independently. Churches had sprung up away from the landowner's house as well. ◆ *Why did former slaves move so quickly to relocate their homes and churches away from their former masters?*

 For an interactive version of this map go to www.mhhe.com/brinkley12ch15maps

the total—simply worked for wages. Most, however, became tenants of white landowners—working their own plots of land and paying their landlords either a fixed rent or a share of their crop (see pp. 424–425).

The new system represented a repudiation by blacks of the gang-labor system of the antebellum plantation, in which slaves had lived and worked together under the direction of a master. As tenants and sharecroppers, blacks enjoyed at least a physical independence from their landlords and had the sense of working their own land, even if in most cases they could never hope to buy it. But tenantry also benefited landlords in some ways, relieving them of any responsibility for the physical well-being of their workers.

The Crop-Lien System

In some respects, the postwar years were a period of remarkable economic progress for African Americans. If the material benefits they had received under slavery are calculated as income, then prewar blacks had earned about a 22 percent share of the profits of the plantation system. By the end of Reconstruction, they were earning 56 percent. Measured another way, the per capita income of southern blacks rose 46 percent between 1857 and 1879, while the per capita income of southern whites declined 35 percent. This represented one of the most significant redistributions of income in American history.

But these figures are somewhat misleading. For one thing, while the black share of profits was increasing, the total profits of southern agriculture were declining—a result of the dislocations of the war and a reduction in the world market for cotton. For another thing, while blacks were earning a greater return on each hour of labor than they had under slavery, they were working fewer hours. Women and children were less likely to labor in the fields than in the past. Adult men tended to work shorter days. In all, the black labor force worked about one-third fewer hours during Reconstruction than it had been compelled to work under slavery—a reduction that brought the working schedule of blacks roughly into line with that of white farm laborers. Nor did the income redistribution of the postwar years lift many blacks out of poverty. Black per capita income rose from about one-quarter of white per capita income to about one-half in the first few years after the war. And after this initial increase, it rose hardly at all.

For blacks and poor whites alike, whatever gains there might have been as a result of land and income redistribution were often overshadowed by the ravages of the crop-lien system. Few of the traditional institutions of credit in the South—the

New System of Credit   "factors" and banks—returned
after the war. In their stead emerged a new system of credit, centered in large part on local country stores, some of them owned by planters, others by independent merchants. Blacks and whites, landowners and tenants—all depended on these stores for such necessities as food, clothing, seed, and farm implements. And since farmers did not have the same steady cash flow as other workers, customers usually had to rely on credit from these merchants in order to purchase what they needed. Most local stores had no competition (and went to great lengths to ensure that things stayed that way). As a result, they were able to set interest rates as high as 50 or 60 percent. Farmers had to give the merchants a lien (or claim) on their crops as collateral for the loans (thus the term "crop-lien system"). Farmers who suffered a few bad years in a row, as often happened, could become trapped in a cycle of debt from which they could never escape.

This burdensome credit system had a number of effects on the region, almost all of them unhealthy. One was that some blacks who had acquired land during the early years of Reconstruction gradually lost it as they fell into debt. So, to a lesser extent, did white small landowners. Another was that Southern farmers became almost wholly dependent on cash crops—and most of all on cotton—because only such marketable commodities seemed to offer any possibility of escape from debt. Thus Southern agriculture, never sufficiently diversified even in the best of times, became more one-dimensional than ever. The relentless planting of cotton, moreover, was contributing to an exhaustion of the soil. The crop-lien system, in other words, was not only helping to impoverish small farmers; it was also contributing to a general decline in the Southern agricultural economy.

The African-American Family in Freedom

One of the most striking features of the black response to Reconstruction was the effort to build or rebuild family structures and to protect them from the interference they had experienced under slavery. A major reason for the rapid departure of so many blacks from plantations was the desire to find lost relatives and reunite families. Thousands of African Americans wandered through the South—often over vast distances—looking for husbands, wives, children, or other relatives from whom they had been separated. In the few black newspapers that circulated in the South, there were many advertisements by people searching for information about their relatives. Former slaves rushed to have marriages, previously without legal standing, sanctified by church and law. Black families resisted living in the former slave quarters and moved instead to small cabins scattered widely across

A VISIT FROM THE OLD MISTRESS Winslow Homer's 1876 painting of an imagined visit by a southern white woman to a group of her former slaves was an effort to convey something of the tension in relations between the races in the South during Reconstruction. The women, once intimately involved in one another's lives, look at each other guardedly, carefully maintaining the space between them. White southerners attacked the painting for portraying white and black women on a relatively equal footing. Some black southerners criticized it for depicting poor rural African Americans instead of the more prosperous professional blacks who were emerging in southern cities. "There were plenty of well-dressed negroes if he would but look for them," one wrote. *(National Museum of American Art, Smithsonian Institution. Gift of William T. Evans/Art Resource, NY)*

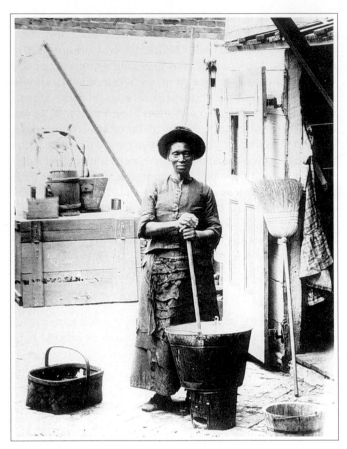

AFRICAN-AMERICAN WORK AFTER SLAVERY Black men and women engaged in a wide range of economic activities in the aftermath of slavery. But discrimination by white Southerners and the former slaves' own lack of education limited most of them to relatively menial jobs. Many black women (including this former slave) earned money for their families by working as "washer women," doing laundry for white people. *(Historic New Orleans Collection)*

the countryside, where they could enjoy at least some privacy. Within the black family, the definition of male and female roles quickly came to resemble that within white families. Many women and children ceased working in the fields. Such work, they believed, was a badge of slavery. Instead, many women restricted themselves largely to domestic tasks—cooking, cleaning, gardening, raising children, attending to the needs of their husbands. Some black husbands refused to allow their wives to work as servants in white homes. "When I married my wife I married her to wait on me," one freedman told a former master who was attempting to hire his wife as a servant. "She got all she can do right here for me and the children."

Still, middle-class notions of domesticity were often difficult to sustain in the impoverished circumstances of

Changing Gender Roles

most former slaves. Economic necessity required many black women to engage in income-producing activities, including activities that they and their husbands resisted because they reminded them of slavery: working as

domestic servants, taking in laundry, or helping in the field. By the end of Reconstruction, half of all black women over the age of sixteen were working for wages. And unlike white working women, most black female income-earners were married.

THE GRANT ADMINISTRATION

Exhausted by the political turmoil of the Johnson administration, American voters in 1868 yearned for a strong, stable figure to guide them through the troubled years of Reconstruction. They turned trustingly to General Ulysses S. Grant, the hero of the war and, by 1868, a revered national idol.

The Soldier President

Grant could have had the nomination of either party in 1868. But believing that Republican Reconstruction policies were more popular in the North, he accepted the Republican nomination. The Democrats nominated former governor Horatio Seymour of New York. The campaign was a bitter one, and Grant's triumph was surprisingly narrow. Without the 500,000 new black Republican voters in the South, he would have had a minority of the popular vote.

U. S. Grant

Grant entered the White House with no political experience, and his performance was clumsy and ineffectual from the start. Except for Hamilton Fish, whom Grant appointed secretary of state and who served for eight years with great distinction, most members of the cabinet were ill-equipped for their tasks. Grant relied chiefly, and increasingly, on established party leaders— the group most ardently devoted to patronage, and his administration used the spoils system even more blatantly than most of its predecessors, embittering reform-minded members of his party. Grant also alienated the many Northerners who were growing disillusioned with the Radical Reconstruction policies, which the president continued to support. Some Republicans suspected, correctly, that there was also corruption in the Grant administration itself.

By the end of Grant's first term, therefore, members of a substantial faction of the party—who referred to themselves as Liberal Republicans— had come to oppose what they called "Grantism." In 1872, hoping to prevent Grant's reelection, they bolted the party and nominated their own presidential candidate: Horace Greeley, veteran editor and publisher of the *New York Tribune*. The Democrats, somewhat reluctantly, named Greeley their candidate as well, hoping that the alliance with the Liberals would enable them to defeat Grant. But the effort was in vain. Grant won a substantial victory, polling 286 electoral votes to Greeley's 66, and nearly 56 percent of the popular total.

Liberal Republicans

The Grant Scandals

During the 1872 campaign, the first of a series of political scandals came to light that would plague Grant and the Republicans for years. It involved the French-owned Crédit Mobilier construction company, which had helped build the Union Pacific Railroad. The heads of Crédit Mobilier had used their positions as Union Pacific stockholders to steer large fraudulent contracts to their construction company, thus bilking the Union Pacific (and the federal government, which provided large subsidies to the railroad) of millions. To prevent investigations, the directors had given Crédit Mobilier stock to key members of Congress. But in 1872, Congress did conduct an investigation, which revealed that some highly placed Republicans—including Schuyler Colfax, now Grant's vice president—had accepted stock.

Crédit Mobilier

GRANT THE TRAPEZE ARTISTS This cartoon by the eminent cartoonist Joseph Keppler shows President Ulysses S. Grant swinging on a trapeze holding on the "whiskey ring" and the "Navy ring" (references to two of the many scandals that plagued his presidency). Using a strap labeled corruption, he holds aloft some of the most notorious figures in those scandals. The cartoon was published in 1880, when Grant was attempting to win the Republican nomination to run for another term as president. *(Library of Congress)*

One dreary episode followed another in Grant's second term. Benjamin H. Bristow, Grant's third Treasury secretary, discovered that some of his officials and a group of distillers operating as a "whiskey ring" were cheating the government out of taxes by filing false reports. Then a House investigation revealed that William W. Belknap, secretary of war, had accepted bribes to retain an Indian-post trader in office (the so-called Indian ring). Other, lesser scandals added to the growing impression that "Grantism" had brought rampant corruption to government.

The Greenback Question

Compounding Grant's, and the nation's, problems was a financial crisis, known as the Panic of 1873. It began with the failure of a leading investment banking firm, Jay Cooke and Company, which had invested too heavily in postwar railroad building. There had been panics before—in 1819, 1837, and 1857—but this was the worst one yet. The depression it produced lasted four years.

Panic of 1873

Debtors now pressured the government to redeem federal war bonds with greenbacks, paper currency of the sort printed during the Civil War, which would increase the amount of money in circulation. But Grant and most Republicans wanted a "sound" currency—based solidly on gold reserves—which would favor the interests of banks and other creditors. There was approximately $356 million in paper currency issued during the Civil War that was still in circulation. In 1873, the Treasury issued more in response to the panic. But in 1875, Republican leaders in Congress, in an effort to crush the greenback movement for good, passed the Specie Resumption Act. It provided that after January 1, 1879, the greenback dollars, whose value constantly fluctuated, would be redeemed by the government and replaced with new certificates, firmly pegged to the price of gold. The law satisfied creditors, who had worried that debts would be repaid in paper currency of uncertain value. But "resumption" made things more difficult for debtors, because the gold-based money supply could not easily expand.

In 1875, the "greenbackers," as the inflationists were called, formed their own political organization: the National Greenback Party. It was active in the next three presidential elections, but it failed to gain widespread support. It did, however, keep the money issue alive. The question of the proper composition of the currency was to remain one of the most controversial and enduring issues in late-nineteenth-century American politics.

National Greenback Party

Republican Diplomacy

The Johnson and Grant administrations achieved their greatest successes in foreign affairs. The accomplishments were the work not of the presidents themselves, who displayed little aptitude for diplomacy, but of two outstanding secretaries of state: William H. Seward, who had served Lincoln and who remained in office until 1869; and Hamilton Fish, who served throughout the two terms of the Grant administration.

An ardent expansionist, Seward acted with as much daring as the demands of Reconstruction politics and the Republican hatred of President Johnson would permit. Seward accepted a Russian offer to sell Alaska to the United States for $7.2 million, despite criticism from many who considered Alaska a frozen wasteland and derided it as "Seward's Folly." In 1867, Seward also engineered the American annexation of the tiny Midway Islands, west of Hawaii.

"Seward's Folly"

Hamilton Fish's first major challenge was resolving the longstanding controversy with England over the American claims that it had violated neutrality laws during the Civil War by permitting English shipyards to build ships (among them the *Alabama*) for the Confederacy. American demands that England pay for the damage these vessels had caused became known as the "*Alabama* claims." In 1871, after a number of failed efforts, Fish forged an agreement, the Treaty of Washington, which provided for international arbitration and in which Britain expressed regret for the escape of the *Alabama* from England.

Alabama Claims

THE ABANDONMENT OF RECONSTRUCTION

As the North grew increasingly preoccupied with its own political and economic problems, interest in Reconstruction began to wane. The Grant administration continued to protect Republican governments in the South, but less because of any interest in ensuring the position of freedmen than because of a desire to prevent the reemergence of a strong Democratic Party in the region. But even the presence of federal troops was not enough to prevent white Southerners from overturning the Reconstruction regimes. By the time Grant left office, Democrats had taken back (or, as white Southerners liked to put it, "redeemed") the governments of seven of the eleven former Confederate states. For three other states—South Carolina, Louisiana, and Florida—the end of Reconstruction had to wait for the withdrawal of the last federal troops in 1876, a withdrawal that was the result of a long process of political bargaining and compromise at the national level. (One former Confederate state, Tennessee, had never been part of the Reconstruction process.)

The Southern States "Redeemed"

In the states where whites constituted a majority—the states of the upper South—overthrowing Republican control was relatively simple. By 1872, all but a handful of Southern whites had regained suffrage. Now a clear majority of the electorate, they needed only to organize and vote for their candidates.

In other states, where blacks were a majority or the populations of the two races were almost equal, whites used intimidation and violence to undermine the Reconstruction regimes. Secret societies—the Ku Klux Klan, the Knights of the White Camellia, and others—used terrorism to frighten or physically bar blacks from voting or otherwise exercising citizenship. Paramilitary organizations—the Red Shirts and White Leagues—armed themselves to "police" elections and worked to force all white males to join the Democratic Party and to exclude all blacks from meaningful political activity.

The Ku Klux Klan was the largest and most effective of these organizations. Formed in 1866 and led by former Confederate General Nathan Bedford Forrest, it gradually absorbed many of the smaller terrorist organizations. Its leaders devised rituals, costumes, secret languages, and other airs of mystery to create a bond among its members and make it seem even more terrifying to those it was attempting to intimidate. The Klan's "midnight rides"—bands of men clad in white sheets and masks, their horses covered with white robes and with hooves muffled—created terror in black communities throughout the South.

Ku Klux Klan

Many white Southerners considered the Klan and the other secret societies and paramilitary groups proud, patriotic societies. Together such groups served, in effect, as a military force (even if a decentralized and poorly organized one) continuing the battle against Northern rule. They worked in particular to advance the interests of those with the most to gain from a restoration of white supremacy—above all the planter class and the Southern Democratic Party. Even stronger than the Klan in discouraging black political power, however, was the simple weapon of economic pressure. Some planters refused to rent land to Republican blacks; storekeepers refused to extend them credit; employers refused to give them work.

The Ku Klux Klan Acts

The Republican Congress tried for a time to turn back this new wave of white repression. In 1870 and 1871, they passed two Enforcement Acts, also known as the Ku Klux Klan Acts, which were in many ways the most radical measures of the era. The Enforcement Acts prohibited the states from discriminating against voters on the basis of race and gave the federal government power to supersede the state courts and prosecute violations of the law. It was the first time the federal government had ever claimed the power to prosecute crimes by individuals under federal law. Federal district attorneys were now

Enforcement Acts

empowered to take action against conspiracies to deny African Americans such rights as voting, holding office, and serving on juries. The new laws also authorized the president to use the military to protect civil rights and to suspend the right of habeas corpus when violations of the rights seemed particularly egregious. In October 1871, President Grant used this provision of the law when he declared a "state of lawlessness" in nine counties in South Carolina and sent in federal troops to occupy the area. Hundreds of suspected Klan members were arrested; some were held for long periods without trial; some were eventually convicted under the law and sent to jail.

The Enforcement Acts were seldom used as severely as they were in South Carolina, but they were effective in the effort by blacks and Northern whites to weaken the Klan. By 1872, Klan violence against blacks was in decline throughout the region.

> Decline of the Klan

Waning Northern Commitment

The Ku Klux Klan Acts marked the peak of Republican commitment to enforce the new rights Reconstruction was extending to black citizens. But that commitment did not last for very long. Southern blacks were gradually losing the support of many of their former backers in the North. As early as 1870, after the adoption of the Fifteenth Amendment, some reformers convinced themselves that their long campaign on behalf of black people was now over; that with the vote, blacks ought to be able to take care of themselves. Over the next several years, former Radical leaders such as Charles Sumner and Horace Greeley now began calling themselves Liberals, cooperating with Democrats, and at times outdoing even the Democrats in denouncing what they viewed as black and carpetbag misgovernment. Within the South itself, many white Republicans joined the Liberals and eventually moved into the Democratic Party.

The Panic of 1873 further undermined support for Reconstruction. This economic crisis spurred Northern industrialists and their allies to find an explanation for the poverty and instability around them. They found it in a new idea known as "Social Darwinism" (see p. 473), a harsh theory that argued that individuals who failed did so because of their own weakness and "unfitness." Those influenced by Social Darwinism came to view the large number of unemployed vagrants in the North—and poor blacks in the South—as irredeemable misfits. Social Darwinism also encouraged a broad critique of government intervention in social and economic life, which further weakened commitment to the Reconstruction program. Support for land redistribution, never great, and willingness to spend money from the depleted federal treasury to aid the freedmen, waned

> Impact of Social Darwinism

quickly after 1873. State and local governments also found themselves short of funds, and rushed to cut back on social services—which in the South meant the end of almost all services to the former slaves.

In the congressional elections of 1874, the Democrats won control of the House of Representatives for the first time since 1861. Grant took note of the changing temper of the North and made use of military force to prop up the Republican regimes that were still standing in the South. By the end of 1876, only three states were left in the hands of the Republicans—South Carolina, Louisiana, and Florida. In state elections that year, Democrats (after using terrorist tactics) claimed victory in all three. But the Republicans challenged the results and claimed victory as well, and they were able to remain in office because of the presence of federal troops. Without federal troops, it was now clear, the last of the Republican regimes would quickly fall.

The Compromise of 1877

Grant had hoped to run for another term in 1876, but most Republican leaders—shaken by recent Democrat successes, afraid of the scandals with which Grant was associated, and concerned about the president's failing health—resisted. Instead, they sought a candidate not associated with the problems of the Grant years, one who might entice Liberals back and unite the party again. They settled on Rutherford B. Hayes, a former Union army officer, governor, and congressman, champion of civil service reform. The Democrats united behind Samuel J. Tilden, the reform governor of New York who had been instrumental in overthrowing the corrupt Tweed Ring of New York City's Tammany Hall.

> Hayes versus Tilden

Although the campaign was a bitter one, there were few differences of principle between the candidates, both of whom were conservatives committed to moderate reform. The November election produced an apparent Democratic victory. Tilden carried the South and several large Northern states, and his popular margin over Hayes was nearly 300,000 votes. But disputed returns from Louisiana, South Carolina, Florida, and Oregon, whose total electoral vote was 20, threw the election in doubt. Tilden had undisputed claim to 184 electoral votes, only one short of a majority. But Hayes could still win if he managed to receive all 20 disputed votes.

The Constitution had established no method to determine the validity of disputed returns. It was clear that the decision lay with Congress, but it was not clear with which house or through what method. (The Senate was Republican, the House, Democratic.) Members of each party naturally supported a solution that would yield them the victory.

Finally, late in January 1877, Congress tried to break the deadlock by creating a special electoral commission

Reconstruction

Debate over the nature of Reconstruction—not only among historians, but among the public at large—has created so much controversy over the decades that one scholar, writing in 1959, described the issue as a "dark and bloody ground." Among historians, the passions of the debate have to some extent subsided since then; but in the popular mind, Reconstruction continues to raise "dark and bloody" images.

For many years, a relatively uniform and highly critical view of Reconstruction prevailed among historians, a reflection of broad currents in popular thought. By the late nineteenth century, most white Americans in both the North and the South had come to believe that few real differences any longer divided the sections, that the nation should strive for a genuine reconciliation. And most white Americans believed as well in the superiority of their race, in the inherent unfitness of blacks for political or social equality. Out of this mentality was born the first major historical interpretation of Reconstruction, through the work of William A. Dunning. In *Reconstruction, Political and Economic* (1907), Dunning portrayed Reconstruction as a corrupt outrage perpetrated on the prostrate South by a vicious and vindictive cabal of Northern Republican Radicals. Reconstruction governments were based on "bayonet rule." Unscrupulous and self-aggrandizing carpetbaggers flooded the South to profit from the misery of the defeated region. Ignorant, illiterate blacks were thrust into positions of power for which they were entirely

unfit. The Reconstruction experiment, a moral abomination from its first moments, survived only because of the determination of the Republican Party to keep itself in power. (Some later writers, notably Howard K. Beale, added an economic motive—to protect Northern business interests.) Dunning and his many students (who together formed what became known as the "Dunning school") compiled state-by-state evidence to show that the legacy of Reconstruction was corruption, ruinous taxation, and astronomical increases in the public debt.

The Dunning school not only shaped the views of several generations of historians. It also reflected and helped to shape the views of much of the public. Popular depictions of Reconstruction for years to come (as first the 1915 film *The Birth of a Nation* and then the 1936 book and 1939 movie *Gone With the Wind* illustrated) portrayed the era as one of tragic exploitation of the South by the North. Even today, many white southerners and many others continue to accept the basic premises of the Dunning interpretation. Among historians, however, the old view of Reconstruction has gradually lost credibility.

The great African-American scholar W. E. B. Du Bois was among the first to challenge the Dunning view in a 1910 article and, later, in a 1935 book, *Black Reconstruction*. To him, Reconstruction politics in the Southern states had been an effort on the part of the masses, black and white, to create a more democratic society. The misdeeds of the Reconstruction

(U.S. Military History Institute, Carlisle, Pennsylvania. Photo by Jim Enos)

governments, he claimed, had been greatly exaggerated, and their achievements overlooked. The governments had been expensive, he insisted, because they had tried to provide public education and other public services on a scale never before attempted in the South. But Du Bois's use of Marxist theory in his work caused many historians to dismiss his argument; and it remained for a group of less radical, white historians to shatter the Dunning image of Reconstruction.

In the 1940s, historians such as C. Vann Woodward, David Herbert Donald, Thomas B. Alexander, and others began to reexamine the Reconstruction governments in the South

Special Electoral Commission

to judge the disputed votes. The commission was to be composed of five senators, five representatives, and five justices of the Supreme Court. The congressional delegation would consist of five Republicans and five Democrats. The Court delegation would include two Republicans, two Democrats, and an independent. But the independent seat ultimately went to a justice whose real sympathies were with the Republicans. The commission voted along straight party

lines, 8 to 7, awarding every disputed vote to Hayes. Congress accepted their verdict on March 2. Two days later, Hayes was inaugurated.

Behind the resolution of the deadlock however, lay a series of elaborate compromises among leaders of both parties. When a Democratic filibuster threatened to derail the commission's report, Republican Senate leaders met secretly with Southern Democratic leaders to work out terms by which the Democrats would allow the election of Hayes. According to traditional accounts, Republicans and to suggest that their records were not nearly as bad as most historians had previously assumed. They also looked at the Radical Republicans in Congress and suggested that they had not been motivated by vindictiveness and partisanship alone. By the early 1960s, a new view of Reconstruction was emerging from these efforts, a view whose appeal to historians grew stronger with the emergence of the "Second Reconstruction," the civil rights movement. The revisionist approach was summarized by John Hope Franklin in *Reconstruction After the Civil War* (1961) and Kenneth Stampp in *The Era of Reconstruction* (1965), which claimed that the postwar Republicans had been engaged in a genuine, if flawed, effort to solve the problem of race in the South by providing much-needed protection to the freedmen. The Reconstruction governments, for all their faults, had been bold experiments in interracial politics. The congressional Radicals were not saints, but they had displayed a genuine concern for the rights of slaves. Andrew Johnson was not a martyred defender of the Constitution, but an inept, racist politician who resisted reasonable compromise and brought the government to a crisis. There had been no such thing as "bayonet rule" or "Negro rule" in the South. Blacks had played only a small part in Reconstruction governments and had generally acquitted themselves well. The Reconstruction regimes had, in fact, brought important progress to the South, establishing the region's first public school system and other important social changes. Corruption in the South had been no worse than corruption in the North at that time. What was tragic

EXTRACT from the Reconstructed Constitution OF THE
STATE OF LOUISIANA

WITH PORTRAITS of the Distinguished Members of the Convention & Assembly A.D. 1868.

(Library of Congress)

about Reconstruction, the revisionist view claimed, was not what it did to Southern whites but what it did not do for Southern blacks. By stopping short of the reforms necessary to ensure blacks genuine equality, Reconstruction had consigned them to more than a century of injustice and discrimination.

In recent years scholars have begun to question the revisionist view —not in an effort to revive the old Dunning interpretation, but in an attempt to draw attention to those things Reconstruction in fact achieved. Eric Foner, in *Nothing but Freedom* (1983) and *Reconstruction: America's Unfinished Revolution* (1988) concluded that what is striking about the American experience in this context is not how little was accomplished, but how far

the former slaves moved toward freedom and independence in a short time, and how large a role African Americans themselves played in shaping Reconstruction. During Reconstruction, blacks won a certain amount of legal and political power in the South; and even though they held that power only temporarily, they used it for a time to strengthen their economic and social positions and to win a position of limited but genuine independence. Through Reconstruction they won, if not equality, a measure of individual and community autonomy, building blocks of the freedom that emancipation alone had not guaranteed.

Historians writing from the perspective of African-American and women's history have made related arguments. Leon Litwack's *Been in the Storm So Long* (1979) maintained that former slaves used the relative latitude they enjoyed under Reconstruction to build a certain independence for themselves within Southern society. They strengthened their churches; they reunited their families; they refused to work in the "gang labor" system of the plantations and forced the creation of a new labor system in which they had more control over their own lives. Amy Dru Stanley and Jacqueline Jones have both argued that the freed slaves displayed considerable independence in constructing their households on their own terms and asserting their control over family life, reproduction, and work. Women in particular sought the opportunity, according to Jacqueline Jones in *Labor of Love, Labor of Sorrow* (1985), "to labor on behalf of their own families and kin within the protected spheres of household and community."

and Southern Democrats met at Washington's Wormley Hotel. In return for a Republican pledge that Hayes would withdraw the last federal troops from the South, thus permitting the overthrow of the last Republican governments there, the Southerners agreed to abandon the filibuster.

Actually, the story behind the "Compromise of 1877" is somewhat more complex. Hayes was already on record

Compromise of 1877

favoring withdrawal of the troops, so Republicans needed to offer more than that if they hoped for Democratic support.

The real agreement, the one that won over the Southern Democrats, was reached well before the Wormley meeting. As the price of their cooperation, the Southern Democrats (among them some former Whigs) exacted several pledges from the Republicans in addition to withdrawal of the troops: the appointment of at least one Southerner to the Hayes cabinet, control of federal patronage in their areas, generous internal improvements, and federal aid for the Texas and Pacific Railroad. Many powerful Southern Democrats supported industrializing

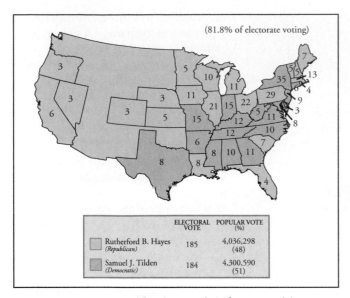

(81.8% of electorate voting)

		ELECTORAL VOTE	POPULAR VOTE (%)
	Rutherford B. Hayes (Republican)	185	4,036,298 (48)
	Samuel J. Tilden (Democratic)	184	4,300,590 (51)

THE ELECTION OF 1876 The election of 1876 was one of the most controversial in American history. As in the elections of 1824, 1888, and 2000, the winner of the popular vote—Samuel J. Tilden—was not the winner of the electoral college, which he lost by one vote. The final decision as to who would be president was not made until the day before the official Inauguration in March. ◆ *How did the Republicans turn this apparent defeat into a victory?*

 For an interactive version of this map go to www.mhhe.com/ brinkley12ch15maps

their region. They believed Republican programs of federal support for business would aid the South more than the states' rights policies of the Democrats.

In his inaugural address, Hayes announced that the South's most pressing need was the restoration of "wise, honest, and peaceful local self-government"—a signal that he planned to withdraw federal troops and let white Democrats take over the state governments. That statement, and Hayes's subsequent actions, supported the widespread charges that he was paying off the South for acquiescing in his election and strengthened those who referred to him as "his Fraudulency." Hayes tried to counter such charges by projecting an image of stern public (and private) rectitude. But the election had already created such bitterness that even Hayes's promise to serve only one term could not mollify his critics.

The president and his party had hoped to build up a "new Republican" organization in the South drawn from Whiggish conservative white groups and committed to some modest acceptance of African-American

Republican Failure in the South

rights. But all such efforts failed. Although many white Southern leaders sympathized with Republican economic policies, popular resentment of Reconstruction was so deep that supporting the party was politically impossible. At the same time, the withdrawal of federal troops signaled that the national government was giving up its attempts to

control Southern politics and to improve the lot of blacks in Southern society.

The Legacies of Reconstruction

Reconstruction made some important contributions to the efforts of former slaves to achieve dignity and equality in American life. And it was not as disastrous an experience for Southern whites as most believed at the time. But Reconstruction was in the end largely a failure. For in those years the United States failed in its first serious effort to resolve its oldest and deepest social problem— the problem of race. What was more, the experience so disappointed, disillusioned, and embittered white Americans that it would be nearly a century before they would try again in any serious way.

Why did this great assault on racial injustice not achieve more? In part, it was because of the weaknesses and errors of the people who directed it. But in greater part, it was because attempts to produce solutions ran up

Ideological Limits

"IS *THIS* A REPUBLICAN FORM OF GOVERNMENT?" The New York artist and cartoonist Thomas Nast marked the end of Reconstruction in 1876 with this biting cartoon in *Harper's Weekly*, expressing his dismay at what he considered the nation's betrayal of the former slaves, who still had not received adequate guarantees of their rights. The caption of the cartoon continued: "Is *this* protecting life, liberty, or property? Is *this* equal protection of the laws?" *(Courtesy The Newberry Library, Chicago)*

against conservative obstacles so deeply embedded in the nation's life that they could not be dislodged. Veneration of the Constitution sharply limited the willingness of national leaders to infringe on the rights of states and individuals. A profound respect for private property and free enterprise prevented any real assault on economic privilege in the South. Above all, perhaps, a pervasive belief among many of even the most liberal whites that African Americans were inherently inferior served as an obstacle to equality. Given the context within which Americans of the 1860s and 1870s were working, what is surprising, perhaps, is not that Reconstruction did so little, but that it did even as much as it did.

Considering the odds confronting them, therefore, African Americans had reason for pride in the gains they were able to make during Reconstruction. And future generations had reason for gratitude for two great charters of freedom—the Fourteenth and Fifteenth Amendments to the Constitution—which, although largely ignored at the time, would one day serve as the basis for a "Second Reconstruction" that would renew the drive to bring freedom and equality to all Americans.

THE NEW SOUTH

The agreement between southern Democrats and northern Republicans that helped settle the disputed election of 1876 was supposed to be the first step toward developing a stable, permanent Republican Party in the South. In that respect, at least, it failed. In the years following the end of Reconstruction, white southerners established the Democratic Party as the only viable political organization for the region's whites. Even so, the South did change in the years after Reconstruction in some of the ways the framers of the Compromise of 1877 had hoped.

The "Redeemers"

By the end of 1877—after the last withdrawal of federal troops—every southern state government had been "redeemed" by white Democrats. Many white southerners rejoiced at the restoration of what they liked to call "home rule." But in reality, political power in the region was soon more restricted than at any time since the Civil War. Once again, the South fell under the control of a powerful, conservative oligarchy, whose members were known variously as the "Redeemers" (to themselves and their supporters) or the "Bourbons" (a term for aristocrats used by some of their critics).

Bourbon Rule

In a few places, this post-Reconstruction ruling class was much the same as the ruling class of the antebellum period. In Alabama, for example, the old planter elite—despite challenges from new merchant and industrial forces—retained much of its former power and continued largely to dominate the state for decades. In most areas, however, the Redeemers constituted a genuinely new ruling class. They were merchants, industrialists, railroad developers, and financiers. Some of them were former planters, some of them northern immigrants who had become absorbed into the region's life, some of them ambitious, upwardly mobile white southerners from the region's lower social tiers. They combined a commitment to "home rule" and social conservatism with a commitment to economic development.

The various Bourbon governments of the New South behaved in many respects quite similarly to one another. Conservatives had complained that the Reconstruction governments fostered widespread corruption, but the Redeemer regimes were, if anything, even more awash in waste and fraud. (In this, they were little different from governments in every region of the country.) At the same time, virtually all the new Democratic regimes lowered taxes, reduced spending, and drastically diminished state services—including many of the most important accomplishments of Reconstruction. In one state after another, for example, state support for public school systems was reduced or eliminated. "Schools are not a necessity," an economy-conscious governor of Virginia commented.

By the late 1870s, significant dissenting groups were challenging the Bourbons: protesting the cuts in services and denouncing the commitment of the Redeemer governments to paying off the prewar and Reconstruction debts in full, at the original (usually high) rates of interest. In Virginia, for example, a vigorous "Readjuster" movement emerged, demanding that the state revise its debt payment procedures so as to make more money available for state services. In 1879, the Readjusters won control of the legislature, and in the next few years they captured the governorship and a U.S. Senate seat. Other states produced similar movements, some of them adding demands as well for greenbacks, debt relief, and other economic reforms. (A few such independent movements included significant numbers of blacks in their ranks, but all consisted primarily of lower-income whites.) By the mid-1880s, however, conservative southerners—largely by exploiting racial prejudice—had effectively destroyed most of the dissenting movements.

The Readjuster Challenge

Industrialization and the "New South"

Many white southern leaders in the post-Reconstruction era hoped to see their region become the home of a vigorous industrial economy. The South had lost the war, many argued, because its economy had been unable to compete with the modernized manufacturing capacity of the North. Now the region must "out-Yankee the Yankees" and build a "New South." Henry Grady, editor of the *Atlanta Constitution,* and other prominent spokesmen for a New South seldom challenged white supremacy, but they did advocate other important changes in southern values.

Henry Grady

The Minstrel Show

The minstrel show was one of the most popular forms of entertainment in America in the second half of the nineteenth century. It was also a testament to the high awareness of race (and the high level of racism) in American society both before and after the Civil War. At the same time, however, African-American performers themselves formed their own minstrel shows and transformed them, at least to a degree, into vehicles for training black entertainers and developing important new forms of music and dance.

Before and during the Civil War, minstrel shows consisted almost entirely of white performers who blackened their faces with cork and presented grotesque stereotypes of the slave culture of the American South. Among the most popular of the stumbling, ridiculously ignorant characters invented for these shows were such figures as "Zip Coon" and "Jim Crow" (whose name later resurfaced as a label for late nineteenth-century segregation laws). A typical minstrel show presented a group of seventeen or more men seated in a semicircle facing the audience. The man in the center ran the show, played the straight man for the jokes of others, and led the music—lively dances and sentimental ballads played on banjos, castanets, and other instruments and sung by soloists or the entire group.

The shows were popular in the South, but they were particularly popular in the North, where black life was less familiar and more exotic and where white audiences (who, whatever their views of slavery, generally held a low opinion of African-Americans) reveled in the demeaning portrayals of slaves. White minstrel performers were so invested in portraying the stupidity and inferiority of blacks that they lashed out savagely at abolitionists and antislavery activists and, during the Civil War, portrayed black soldiers as incompetents and cowards—creating a military stereotype as insulting and inaccurate as the stereotypes they had used to portray slaves.

After the Civil War, white minstrels began to expand their repertoire. Drawing from the famous and successful freak shows of P. T. Barnum and other entertainment entrepreneurs, some began to include Siamese twins, bearded ladies, and even a supposedly 8-foot, 2-inch "Chinese giant" in their shows. They also incorporated sex, both by including women in some

MINSTRELSY AT HIGH TIDE The Primrose & West minstrel troupe—a lavish and expensive entertainment that drew large crowds in the 1800s—was one of many companies to offer this brand of entertainment to eager audiences all over the country. Although minstrelsy began with white musicians performing in black face, the popularity of real African-American minstrels encouraged the impresarios of the troupe to include groups of white and black performers alike. (©Collection of the New-York Historical Society)

Above all, they promoted the virtues of thrift, industry, and progress—qualities that prewar southerners had often denounced in northern society. "We have sown towns and cities in the place of theories," Grady boasted to a New England audience in the 1880s, "and put business above politics. . . . We have fallen in love with work." But even the most fervent advocates of the New South creed were generally unwilling to break entirely with the southern past. That was evident in, among other things, the popular literature of the region. At the same time that white southern writers were extolling the virtues of industrialization in newspaper editorials and speeches, they were painting nostalgic portraits of the Old South in their literature. Few southerners advocated a literal return to the old ways, but most whites eagerly embraced romantic talk of the "Lost Cause." And they responded warmly to the local-color fiction of such writers as Joel Chandler Harris, whose folk tales—the most famous being *Uncle Remus* (1880)—portrayed the slave society of the antebellum years as a harmonious world marked by engaging dialect and close emotional bonds between the races. The writer Thomas Nelson Page similarly extolled the

THE ELECTRIC 3 MINSTRELS For every large troupe such as Primrose & West there were dozens of smaller traveling minstrel bands such as Calley, Haley, and Callan's shown here on the road in the 1880s. In concert, these men performed in exaggerated blackface. Posing for photographs, they tried to exhibit sober, middle-class respectability. *(Brown Brothers)*

shows and, even more popularly, by recruiting female impersonators. One of the most successful minstrel performers of the 1870s was Francis Leon, who delighted crowds with his portrayal of a flamboyant "prima donna."

One reason white minstrels began to move in these new directions was that they were now facing competition from black performers, who could provide more authentic versions of black music, dance, and humor, and usually bring more talent to the task. The Georgia Minstrels, organized in 1865, was one of the first all-black minstrel troupes, and it had great success in attracting white audiences in the Northeast for several years. By the 1870s, touring African-American minstrel groups were numerous. The black minstrels used many of the conventions of the white shows. There were dances, music, comic routines, and sentimental recitations. Some black performers even chalked their faces to make themselves look as dark as the white black-face performers with whom they were competing. Black minstrels sometimes denounced slavery (at least indirectly) and did not often speak demeaningly of the capacities of their race. But they could not entirely escape caricaturing African-American life as they struggled to meet the expectations of their white audiences.

While the black minstrel shows had few openly political aims, they did help develop some important forms of African-American entertainment and transform them into a part of the national culture. Black minstrels introduced new forms of dance, derived from the informal traditions of slavery and black community life: the "buck and wing," the "stop time," and the "Virginia essence," which established the foundations for the tap and jazz dancing of the early twentieth century. They also improvised musically and began experimenting with forms that over time contributed to the growth of ragtime, jazz, and rhythm and blues.

Eventually, black minstrelsy—like its white counterpart—evolved into other forms of theater, including the beginnings of serious black drama. At Ambrose Park in Brooklyn in the 1890s, for example, the celebrated black comedian Sam Lucas (a veteran of the minstrel circuit) starred in the play *Darkest America,* which one black newspaper later described as a "delineation of Negro life, carrying the race through all their historical phases from the plantation, into reconstruction days and finally painting our people as they are today, cultured and accomplished in the social graces, [holding] the mirror faithfully up to nature."

But interest in the minstrel show did not die altogether. In 1927, Hollywood released *The Jazz Singer,* the first feature film with sound. It was about the career of a white minstrel performer, and its star was one of the most popular singers of the twentieth century: Al Jolson, whose career had begun on the black-face minstrel circuit years before.

old Virginia aristocracy. The growing popularity of minstrel shows also reflected the romanticization of the old South (see above). The white leaders of the New South, in short, faced their future with one foot still in the past.

Even so, New South enthusiasts did help southern industry expand dramatically in the years after Reconstruction and become a more important part of the region's economy than ever before. Most visible was the growth in textile manufacturing, which increased ninefold in the last twenty years of the century. In the past, southern planters had usually shipped their cotton out of the region to manufacturers in the North or in Europe. Now textile factories appeared in the South itself—many of them drawn to the region from New England by the abundance of water power, the ready supply of cheap labor, the low taxes, and the accommodating conservative governments. The tobacco-processing industry, similarly, established an important foothold in the region, largely through the work of James B. Duke of North Carolina, whose American Tobacco Company established for a time a virtual monopoly over the processing of raw tobacco into marketable materials. In the lower South, and particularly in Birmingham, Alabama, the iron (and, later, steel) industry grew rapidly. By 1890, the southern iron and steel industry represented nearly a fifth of the nation's total capacity.

Railroad development increased substantially in the

Railroad Development

post-Reconstruction years—at a rate far greater than that of the nation at large. Between 1880 and 1890, trackage in the South more than doubled. And the South took a major step toward integrating its transportation system with that of the rest of the country when, in 1886, it changed the gauge (width) of its trackage to correspond with the standards of the North. Yet southern industry developed within strict limits, and its effects on the region were never even remotely comparable to the effects of industrialization on the North. The southern share of national manufacturing doubled in the last twenty years of the century, to 10 percent of the total. But that percentage was the same the South had claimed in 1860; the region, in other words, had done no more than regain what it had lost during the war and its aftermath. The region's per capita income increased 21 percent in the same period. But at the end of the century, average income in the South was only 40 percent of that in the North; in 1860 it had been more than 60 percent. And even in those areas where development had been most rapid—textiles, iron, railroads—much of the capital had come from the North. In effect, the South was developing a colonial economy.

The growth of industry in the South required the region to recruit a substantial industrial work force for the first time. From the beginning, a high percentage of the factory workers (and an especially high percentage of textile workers) were women. Heavy male casualties in the Civil War had helped create a large population of unmarried women who desperately needed employment. Factories also hired entire families, many of whom were moving into towns from failed farms. Hours were long (often as much as twelve hours a day) and wages were far below the northern equivalent; indeed one of the greatest attractions of the South to industrialists was that employers were able to pay workers there as little as one-half what northern workers received. Life in most mill towns was rigidly controlled by the owners and managers of the factories, who rigorously suppressed attempts at protest or union organization. Company stores sold goods to workers at inflated prices and issued credit at exorbitant rates (much like country stores in agrarian areas), and mill owners ensured that no competitors were able to establish themselves in the community. At the same time, however, the conditions of the mill town helped create a strong sense of community and solidarity among workers (even if they seldom translated such feelings into militancy).

Some industries, textiles for example, offered virtually no opportunities to African-American workers. Others—tobacco, iron, and lumber, among others—did provide some employment for blacks, usually the most menial and lowest-paid positions. Some mill towns, therefore, were places where black and white culture came into close contact. That proximity contributed less to the growth of racial harmony than to the determination of white leaders to take additional measures to protect white supremacy.

At times, industrialization proceeded on the basis of no wage-paying employment at all. Through the "convict-lease" system, southern states leased

gangs of convicted criminals to private interests as a cheap labor supply. The system exposed the convicts to brutal and at times fatal mistreatment. It paid them nothing (the leasing fees went to the states, not the workers). And it denied employment in railroad construction and other projects to the free labor force.

Tenants and Sharecroppers

Despite significant growth in southern industry, the region remained primarily agrarian. The most important economic reality in the post-Reconstruction South, therefore, was the impoverished state of agriculture. The 1870s and 1880s saw an acceleration of the trends that had begun in the immediate postwar years: the imposition of systems of tenantry and debt peonage on much of the region; the reliance on a few cash crops rather than on a diversified agricultural system; and increasing absentee ownership of valuable farmlands (many of them purchased by merchants and industrialists who paid little attention to whether the land was being properly used). During Reconstruction, perhaps a third or more of the farmers in the South were tenants; by 1900 the figure had increased to 70 percent. That was in large part the result of the crop-lien system, the system by which farmers borrowed money against their future crops and often fell deeper and deeper into debt.

Tenantry took several forms. Farmers who owned tools, equipment, and farm animals—or who had the money to buy them—usually paid an annual cash rent for their land. But many farmers (including most black ones) had no money or equipment at all. Landlords would supply them with land, a crude house, a few tools, seed, and sometimes a mule. In return, farmers would promise the landlord a large share of the annual crop—hence the term "sharecropping." After paying their landlords and their local furnishing merchants (who were often the same people), sharecroppers seldom had anything left to sell on their own. The crop-lien system was one of several factors contributing to a particularly harsh social and economic transformation of the southern backcountry, the

Transformation of the Backcountry

piney woods and mountain regions where cotton and slavery had always been rare and where farmers lived ruggedly independent lives. Subsistence agriculture had long been the norm in these areas; but as indebtedness grew, many farmers now had to grow cash crops such as cotton instead of the food crops they had traditionally

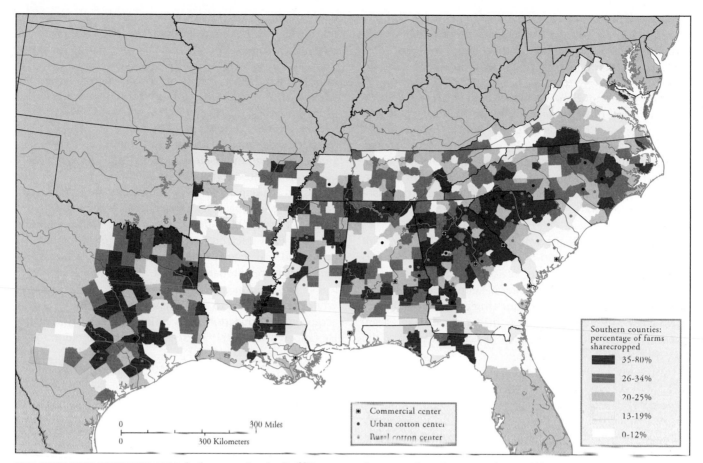

THE CROP-LIEN SYSTEM IN 1880 In the years after the Civil War, more and more southern farmers—white and black—became tenants or sharecroppers on land owned by others. This map shows the percentage of farms that were within the so-called crop-lien system, the system by which people worked their lands for someone else, who had a claim (or "lien") on a part of the farmers' crops. Note the high density of sharecropping and tenant farming in the most fertile areas of the deep South, the same areas where slaveholding had been most dominant before the Civil War. ◆ *How did the crop-lien system contribute to the shift in southern agriculture toward one-crop farming?*

OLC For an interactive version of this map go to www.mhhe.com/brinkley12ch15maps

cultivated in order to make enough money to pay off their loans.

But the transformation of the backcountry was a result of other factors as well. Many backcountry residents had traditionally subsisted by raising livestock, which had roamed freely across the landscape. In the 1870s, as commercial agriculture began to intrude into these regions, many communities began to pass "fence laws," which required farmers to fence in their animals (as opposed to fencing off their crops, as had once been the custom). There were widespread protests against the new laws, and at times violent efforts to resist them. But the existence of the open range (which had once been as much a part of life in the backcountry South as it was in the American West) could not survive the spread of commercial agriculture. Increasingly, therefore, opportunities for families to live largely self-sufficiently were declining. At the same time, opportunities for profiting within the market remained slim. The people of the backcountry would be among the most important constituents for the populist protests of the 1880s and 1890s.

African Americans and the New South

The "New South creed" was not the property of whites alone. Many African Americans were attracted to the vision of progress and self-improvement as well. Some blacks succeeded **Black Middle Class** in elevating themselves into a distinct middle class—economically inferior to the white middle class, but nevertheless significant. These were former slaves (and, as the decades passed, their offspring) who managed to acquire property, establish small businesses, or enter professions. A few blacks accumulated substantial fortunes by establishing banks and insurance companies for their race. One of those was Maggie Lena, a black woman who became the first female bank president in the United States when she founded the St. Luke Penny Savings Bank in Richmond in 1903. Most middle-class blacks experienced more modest gains by becoming doctors, lawyers, nurses, or teachers serving members of their own race.

A cardinal tenet of this rising group of blacks was that education was vital to the future of their race. With the support of northern missionary societies and, to a far lesser extent, a few southern state governments, they expanded the network of black colleges and institutes that had taken root during Reconstruction into an important educational system.

The chief spokesman for this commitment to education, and for a time the major spokesman for his race as a whole, was Booker T. Washington, founder and president of the Tuskegee Institute in Alabama. Born into slavery, Washington had worked his way out of poverty after acquiring an education (at Virginia's famous Hampton Institute). He urged other blacks to follow the same road to self-improvement.

Booker T. Washington

Washington's message was both cautious and hopeful. African Americans should attend school, learn skills, and establish a solid footing in agriculture and the trades. Industrial, not classical, education should be their goal. Blacks should, moreover, refine their speech, improve their dress, and adopt habits of thrift and personal cleanliness; they should, in short, adopt the standards of the white middle class. Only thus, he claimed, could they win the respect of the white population, the prerequisite for any larger social gains. Blacks should forgo agitating for political rights, he said, and concentrate on self-improvement and preparation for equality. In a famous speech in Georgia in 1895, Washington outlined a philosophy of race relations that became widely known as the Atlanta Compromise. "The wisest among my race understand," he said, "that the agitation of questions of social equality is the extremest folly." Rather, blacks should engage in "severe and constant struggle" for economic gains; for, as he explained, "no race that has anything to contribute to the markets of the world is long in any degree ostracized." If blacks were ever to win the rights and privileges of citizenship, they must first show that they were "prepared for the exercise of these privileges." Washington offered a powerful challenge to those whites who wanted to discourage African Americans from acquiring an education or winning any economic gains. He helped awaken the interest of a new generation to the

The Atlanta Compromise

TUSKEGEE INSTITUTE, 1881 From these modest beginnings, Booker T. Washington's Tuskegee Institute in Alabama became the preeminent academy offering technical and industrial training to black men. It deliberately deemphasized the traditional liberal arts curricula of most colleges. Washington considered such training an unnecessary frill and encouraged his students to work on developing practical skills. *(Bettmann/Corbis)*

possibilities for self-advancement through self-improvement. But his message was also an implicit promise that blacks would not challenge the system of segregation that whites were then in the process of erecting.

The Birth of Jim Crow

Few white Southerners had ever accepted the idea of racial equality. That the former slaves acquired any legal and political rights at all after emancipation was in large part the result of federal support. That support all but vanished after 1877. Federal troops withdrew. Congress lost interest. And the Supreme Court effectively stripped the Fourteenth and Fifteenth Amendments of much of their significance. In the so-called civil rights cases of 1883, the Court ruled that the Fourteenth Amendment prohibited state governments from discriminating against people because of race but did not restrict private organizations or individuals from doing so. Thus railroads, hotels, theaters, and the like could legally practice segregation.

Eventually, the Court also validated state legislation that institutionalized the separation of the races. In *Plessy* v *Ferguson* (1896), a case involving a Louisiana law that required separate seating arrangements for the races on railroads, the Court held that separate accommodations

Plessy v. Ferguson

did not deprive blacks of equal rights if the accommodations were equal, a decision that survived for years as part of the legal basis of segregated schools. In *Cumming* v. *County Board of Education* (1899), the Court ruled that laws establishing separate schools for whites were valid even if there were no comparable schools for blacks.

Even before these decisions, white southerners were working to strengthen white supremacy and to separate the races to the greatest extent possible. One illustration of this movement from subordination to segregation was black voting rights. In some states, disfranchisement had begun almost as soon as Reconstruction ended. But in other areas, black voting continued for some time after Reconstruction—largely because conservative whites believed they could control the black electorate and use it to beat back the attempts of poor white farmers to take control of the Democratic Party. In the 1890s, however, franchise restrictions became much more rigid. During those years, some small white farmers began to demand complete black disfranchisement—both because of racial prejudice and because they objected to the black vote being used against them by the Bourbons. At the same time, many members of the conservative elite began to fear that poor whites might unite politically with poor blacks to challenge them. They too began to support further franchise restrictions.

In devising laws to disfranchise black males the southern states had to find ways to evade the Fifteenth Amendment, which prohibited states from denying anyone the right to vote because of race. Two devices emerged before 1900 to accomplish this goal. One was the

Restricting the Franchise

poll tax or some form of property qualification; few blacks were prosperous enough to meet such requirements. Another was the "literacy" or "understanding" test, which required voters to demonstrate an ability to read and to interpret the Constitution. Even those African Americans who could read had trouble passing the difficult test white officials gave them. Such restrictions were often applied unequally. Literacy tests for whites, for example, were sometimes much easier than those for blacks. Even so, the laws affected poor white voters as well as blacks. By the late 1890s, the black vote had decreased by 62 percent, the white vote by 26 percent. One result was that some states passed so-called grandfather laws, permitting men who could not meet the literacy and property qualifications to be enfranchised if their ancestors had voted before Reconstruction began, thus barring the descendants of slaves from the polls while allowing poor whites access to them. In many areas, however, ruling elites were quite content to see poor whites, a potential source of opposition to their power, barred from voting.

The Supreme Court proved as compliant in ruling on the disfranchising laws as it was in dealing with the civil rights cases. The Court eventually voided the grandfather laws, but it validated the literacy test (in the 1898 case of *Williams* v. *Mississippi*) and displayed a general willingness to let the southern states define their own suffrage standards as long as evasions of the Fifteenth Amendment were not too glaring.

Laws restricting the franchise and segregating schools were only part of a network of state statutes—known as the Jim Crow laws—that by the first years of the twentieth century had institutionalized an elaborate system of segregation reaching into almost every area of southern life. Blacks and whites could not ride together in the same railroad cars, sit in the same waiting

White Control Perpetuated

rooms, use the same washrooms, eat in the same restaurants, or sit in the same theaters. Blacks had no access to many public parks, beaches, and picnic areas; they could not be patients in many hospitals. Much of the new legal structure did no more than confirm what had already been widespread social practice in the South since well before the end of Reconstruction. But the Jim Crow laws also stripped blacks of many of the modest social, economic, and political gains they had made in the more fluid atmosphere of the late nineteenth century. They served, too, as a means for whites to retain control of social relations between the races in the newly growing cities and towns of the South, where traditional patterns of deference and subjugation were more difficult to preserve than in the countryside. What had been maintained by custom in the rural South was to be maintained by law in the urban South.

The Origins of Segregation

Not until after World War II, when the emergence of the civil rights movement forced white Americans to confront the issue of racial segregation, did historians pay much attention to the origins of the institution. Most had assumed that the separation of the races had emerged naturally and even inevitably out of the abolition of slavery. It had been a response to the failure of Reconstruction, the weakness and poverty of the African-American community, and the pervasiveness of white racism. It was (as W. J. Cash argued in his classic and controversial 1941 study, *The Mind of the South*) the way things had always been.

The first major challenge to these assumptions, indeed the first serious scholarly effort to explain the origins of segregation, was C. Vann Woodward's *The Strange Career of Jim Crow* published in 1956. Not only was it important in reshaping scholarship. It had a significant political impact as well. As a southern liberal, Woodward was eager to refute assumptions that segregation was part of an unchanging and unchangeable southern tradition. He wanted to convince scholars that the history of the South had been one of sharp discontinuities; and he wanted to convince a larger public that the racial institutions they considered part of a long, unbroken tradition were in fact the product of a particular set of historical circumstances.

In the aftermath of emancipation, and indeed for two decades after Reconstruction, Woodward argued, race relations in the South had remained relatively fluid. Blacks and whites did not often interact as equals, certainly, but black southerners enjoyed a degree of latitude in social and even political affairs that they would subsequently lose. Blacks and whites often rode together in the same railroad cars, ate in the same restaurants, used the same public facilities. African Americans voted in significant numbers. Blacks and whites considered a number of different visions of how the races should live together, and as late as 1890 it was not at all clear which of those visions would prevail. By the end of the nineteenth century, however, a great wave of racist legislation—the Jim Crow laws, which established the basis of segregation—had hardened race relations and destroyed the gentler alternatives that many whites and blacks had considered viable only a few years before. The principal reason, Woodward argued, was the Populist political insurgency of the 1890s, which mobilized blacks and whites alike and which frightened many white southerners into thinking that African Americans might soon be a major political power in the region. Southern conservatives, in particular, used the issue of white supremacy to attack the Populists and to prevent blacks from forming an alliance with them. The result was segregation and the disfranchisement of African Americans (along with many poor whites).

Woodward's argument suggested that laws are important in shaping social behavior—that laws had made segregation and, by implication, other laws could unmake it. Not all historians agreed. A more pessimistic picture of segregation emerged in 1965 from Joel Williamson's study of South Carolina, *After Slavery*. Williamson argued that the laws of the 1890s did not mean very much, that they simply ratified a set of conditions that had been firmly established by the end of Reconstruction. As early as the mid-1870s, Williamson claimed, the races had already begun to live in two separate societies. Blacks had constructed their own churches, schools, businesses, and neighborhoods; whites had begun to exclude blacks from white institutions. The separation was partly a result of pressure and coercion from whites, partly a result of the desire of blacks to develop their own, independent culture. Whatever the reasons, however, segregation was largely in place by the end of the 1870s, continuing in a different form a pattern of racial separation established under slavery. The laws of the 1890s did little more than codify an already established system.

In the same year that Williamson published his argument, Leon Litwack joined the debate, even if somewhat indirectly, with the publication of *North of Slavery*. Litwack revealed the existence of widespread segregation, supported by an early version of Jim Crow laws, in the North before the Civil War. In almost every northern state, he revealed, free blacks experienced a kind of segregation not very different from what freed slaves would experience in the South after the Civil War. A few years later, Ira Berlin argued

More than legal efforts were involved in this process. The 1890s witnessed a dramatic increase in white violence against blacks, which, along with the Jim Crow laws, served to inhibit black agitation for equal rights. The worst such violence—lynching of blacks by white mobs, either because the victims were accused of

Lynchings

crimes or because they had seemed somehow to violate their proper station—reached appalling levels. In the nation as a whole in the 1890s, there was an average of 187 lynchings each year, more than 80 percent of them in the South. The vast majority of victims were black.

The most celebrated lynchings occurred in cities and towns, where large, well-organized mobs—occasionally with the tacit cooperation of local authorities—seized black prisoners from the jails and hanged them in great public rituals. Such public lynchings were often planned well in advance and elaborately organized. They attracted large audiences from surrounding regions. Entire families traveled many miles to witness the spectacles. But such great public lynchings were relatively rare. Much more frequent, and more dangerous to blacks because less visible or predictable, were lynchings performed by small vigilante mobs, often composed of friends or relatives of in *Slaves Without Masters* (1974) that in the antebellum South, too, white people had created a wide range of discriminatory laws aimed at free blacks and ensuring segregation. The postbellum regime of Jim Crow, such works suggested, emerged naturally out of well-established precedents from before the Civil War, in both the North and the South.

Other scholars have challenged all these interpretations by attempting to link the rise of legal segregation to changing social and economic circumstances in the South. Howard Rabinowitz's *Race Relations in the Urban South* (1978) linked the rise of segregation to the new challenge of devising a form of race relations suitable to life in the growing southern cities, into which rural blacks were moving in substantial numbers. The creation of separate public facilities—schools, parks, waiting rooms, etc.—was not so much an effort to drive blacks out of white facilities; they had never had access to those facilities, and few whites had ever been willing to consider granting them access. It was, rather, an attempt to create for a black community that virtually all whites agreed must remain essentially separate a set of facilities where none had previously existed. Without segregation, in other words, urban blacks would have had no schools or parks at all. The alternative to segregation, Rabinowitz suggested, was not integration, but exclusion.

In the early 1980s, a number of scholars began examining segregation anew in light of the rising American interest in South Africa, whose system of apartheid seemed to them to be similar in many ways to the by-then largely

THE NEGRO GALLERY.

(Reproduced from Every Saturday, *Gift of the Louisiana Museum Foundation)*

dismantled Jim Crow system in the South. John Cell's *The Highest Stage of White Supremacy* (1982) used the comparison to construct a revised explanation of how segregation emerged in the American South. Like Rabinowitz, he considered the increasing urbanization of the region the principal factor. But he ascribed different motives to those whites who promoted the rise of Jim Crow. The segregation laws, Cell argued, were a continuation of an unchanging determination by southern whites to retain control over the black population. What had shifted was not their commitment to white supremacy but the things necessary to preserve it.

The emergence of large black communities in urban areas and of a significant black labor force in factories presented a new challenge to white southerners. In the city, blacks and whites were in more direct competition than they had been in the countryside. There was more danger of social mixing. The city therefore required different, and more rigidly institutionalized, systems of control. The Jim Crow laws were a response not just to an enduring commitment to white supremacy, but to a new reality that required white supremacy to move to its "highest stage," where it would have a rigid legal and institutional basis.

the victim (or supposed victim) of a crime. Those involved in lynchings often saw their actions as a legitimate form of law enforcement; and indeed, some victims of lynchings had in fact committed crimes. But lynchings were also a means by which whites controlled the black population through terror and intimidation. Thus, some lynch mobs killed blacks whose only "crime" had been presumptuousness. Others chose as victims outsiders in the community, whose presence threatened to disturb the normal pattern of race relations. Black men who had made any sexual advances toward white women (or who white men thought had done so) were particularly vul-

nerable to lynchings; the fear of black sexuality, and the unspoken fear among many men that white women might be attracted to that sexuality, was always an important part of the belief system that supported segregation. Whatever the reasons or circumstances, the victims of lynch mobs were denied the protection of the laws and the opportunity to prove their innocence.

The rise of lynchings shocked the conscience of many white Americans in a way that other forms of racial injustice did not. Almost from the start there was a substantial anti-lynching movement. In 1892 Ida B. Wells, a committed black journalist, launched what became an

A LYNCH MOB, 1893 A large, almost festive crowd gathers to watch the lynching of a black man accused of the murder of a three-year-old white girl. Lynchings remained frequent in the South until as late as the 1930s, but they reached their peak in the 1890s and the first years of the twentieth century. Lynchings such as this one—published well in advance and attracting whole families who traveled great distances to see them—were relatively infrequent. Most lynchings were the work of smaller groups, operating with less visibility. *(Library of Congress)*

international anti-lynching movement with a series of impassioned articles after the lynching of three of her friends in Memphis, Tennessee, her home. The movement gradually gathered strength in the first years of the twentieth century, attracting substantial support from whites in both the North and South (particularly from white women). Its goal was a federal anti-lynching law, which would allow the national government to do what state and local governments in the South were generally unwilling to do: punish those responsible for lynchings.

But the substantial white opposition to lynchings stood as an exception to the general white support for suppression of African Americans. Indeed, just as in the antebellum period, the shared commitment to white supremacy helped dilute class animosities between poorer whites and the Bourbon oligarchies. Economic issues tended to play a secondary role to race in southern politics, distracting people from the glaring social inequalities that afflicted blacks and whites alike. The commitment to white supremacy, in short, was a burden for poor whites as well as for blacks.

White Unity

CONCLUSION

Reconstruction, long remembered by many white Americans as a vindictive outrage or a tragic failure, was in fact a profoundly important moment in American history. Despite the bitter political battles in Washington and throughout the South, culminating in the unsuccessful effort to impeach President Andrew Johnson, the most important result of the effort to reunite the nation after its long and bloody war was a reshaping of the lives of ordinary people in all regions of the nation.

In the North, Reconstruction solidified the power of the Republican Party and ensured that public policy would support the continued growth of an advanced industrial economy. The rapid growth of the northern economy continued and accelerated, drawing more and more of its residents into an expanding commercial world.

In the South, Reconstruction did more than simply bring slavery to an end. It fundamentally rearranged the relationship between the region's white and black citizens. Only for a while did Reconstruction permit African Americans to participate actively and effectively in southern politics. After a few years of widespread black voting and significant black officeholding, the forces of white supremacy forced most African Americans to the margins of the southern political world, where they would mostly remain until the 1960s.

But in other ways, the lives of southern blacks changed dramatically. Overwhelmingly, they left the plantations. Some sought work in towns and cities. Some left the region altogether. But the great majority began farming on small farms of their own—not as landowners, except in rare cases, but as tenants and sharecroppers on land owned by whites. The result was a form of economic bondage, driven by debt, only scarcely less oppressive than the legal bondage of slavery. But within this system, African Americans managed to carve out a much larger sphere of social and cultural activity than they had ever been able to create under slavery. Black churches organized in great numbers. African-American schools emerged in some communities, and black colleges began to appear in the region. Some former slaves owned businesses and flourished. In southern cities and towns, a fledgling black middle class began to emerge.

The system of tenantry, which emerged in the course of Reconstruction, continued after its end to dominate the southern economy. Strenuous efforts by "New South" advocates to advance industry and commerce in the region produced significant results in a few areas. But the South on the whole remained what it had always been, an overwhelmingly rural society with a sharply defined class structure. It was also a region with a deep commitment among its white citizens to the subordination of African Americans—a commitment solidified in the 1890s and the early twentieth century when white southerners erected an elaborate legal system of segregation (the "Jim Crow" laws). The promise of the great Reconstruction amendments to the Constitution—the Fourteenth and Fifteenth—remained largely unfulfilled in the South as the century drew to its close.

INTERACTIVE LEARNING

The *Primary Source Investigator CD-ROM* offers the following materials related to this chapter:

- Interactive maps. **U.S. Elections** (M7); **Barrow Plantation** (M18); and **African Americans and Crop Lien** (M19).
- Documents, images, and maps related to the Reconstruction era following the Civil War, including examples of black codes passed by southern states and communities early in the aftermath of the Civil War, several firsthand accounts from former slaves, the Fourteenth and Fifteenth Amendments to the U.S. Constitution, and an image of the Tuskegee Institute.

 Online Learning Center (www.mhhe.com/brinkley12)

For quizzes, Internet resources, references to additional books and films, and more, consult this book's Online Learning Center.

FOR FURTHER REFERENCE

Eric Foner, *Reconstruction: America's Unfinished Revolution, 1863–1877* (1988), the most important modern synthesis of Reconstruction scholarship, emphasizes the radicalism of Reconstruction and the role of freed people in the process of political and economic renovation. Thomas Holt, *Black over White: Negro Political Leadership in South Carolina During Reconstruction* (1977) examines Reconstruction in the state where black political power reached its apex. C. Vann Woodward, *Origins of the New South* (1951), is a classic work on the history of the South after Reconstruction after forty years, and argues that a rising middle class defined the economic and political transformation of the New South. Edward Ayers, *The Promise of the New South* (1992) offers a rich portrait of social and cultural life in the New South. Jacqueline Jones, *Labor of Love, Labor of Sorrow* (1985) examines the lives of African-American women after Emancipation. Leon Litwack, *Been in the Storm So Long: The Aftermath of Slavery* (1979) is a major study of the experiences of freed slaves. Steven Hahn, *A Nation Under Our Feet: Black Political Struggles in the Rural South from Slavery to the Great Migration* (2003) is an excellent, wide-ranging history. C. Vann Woodward, *The Strange Career of Jim Crow* (rev. 1974) claims that segregation emerged only gradually across the South after Reconstruction. The "Woodward Thesis" has been challenged by, among others, Joel Williamson, *After Slavery: The Negro in South Carolina During Reconstruction* (1965); John W. Cell, *The Highest Stage of White Supremacy: The Origins of Segregation in South Africa and the American South* (1982); and Howard N. Rabixnowitz, *Race Relations in the Urban South, 1865–1890* (1978).

Appendixes

The United States

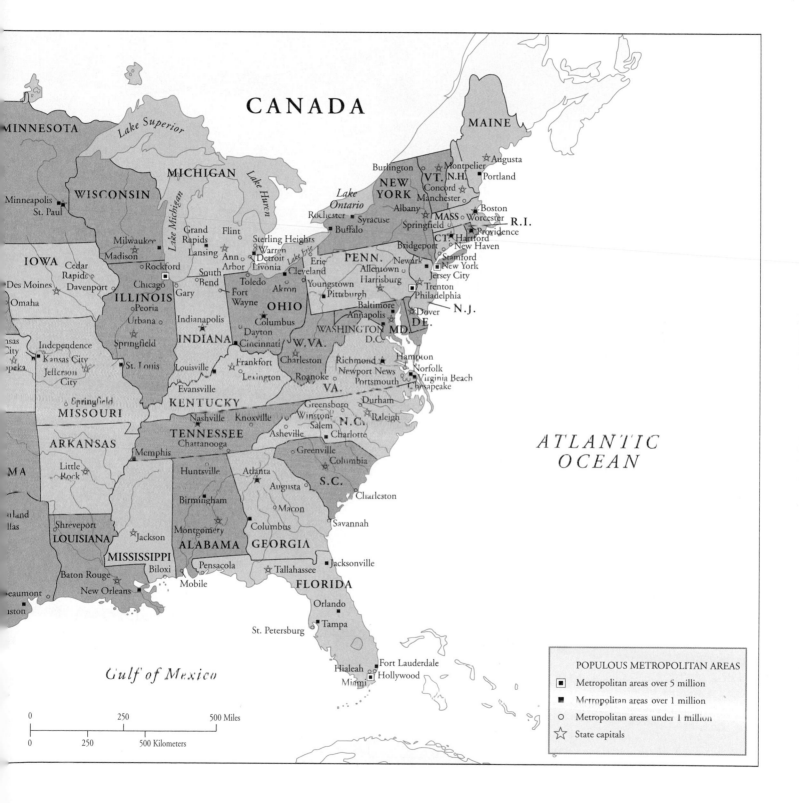

CANADA

MINNESOTA

Lake Superior

MICHIGAN

MAINE

Lake Huron

Lake Michigan

WISCONSIN

Burlington

☆ Montpelier

☆ Augusta

VT. N.H. ■ Portland

NEW YORK

Concord ☆

Minneapolis
St. Paul

Milwaukee

Grand
Rapids

Flint

Sterling Heights

Manchester

Lake Ontario

Albany ■

Rochester

☆

Boston

Warren

Syracuse

Springfield ■ MASS. ■ Worcester

R.I.

IOWA

Madison

Cedar
Rapids

Lansing

Ann
Arbor

Detroit
Livonia

Buffalo ■

☆

Providence ■

CT. ■ Hartford

Rockford

South
Bend

Bridgeport ■

New Haven

Des Moines
Davenport

Chicago

Gary

Toledo

Lake Erie

Erie

Cleveland

PENN.

Newark ■

Stamford

☆

■ New York

ILLINOIS

Peoria

Fort
Wayne

Akron

Youngstown

Allentown ■

Jersey City

Omaha

Urbana

Indianapolis

OHIO

Dayton

Harrisburg ☆

Trenton ☆

N.J.

☆

Columbus

Pittsburgh

Baltimore ■

Philadelphia ■

sas
City

Independence

Springfield

INDIANA

Cincinnati

W.VA.

Annapolis ☆

Dover ■

DE.

peka

Kansas City

☆ Jefferson
City

St. Louis

Louisville

Frankfort ☆

Charleston

WASHINGTON MD.
D.C.

Evansville

Lexington

Roanoke ○

Richmond ☆

Hampton ■

Newport News ■

Norfolk ■

Springfield

MISSOURI

KENTUCKY

VA.

Portsmouth ■

Virginia Beach

Chesapeake

Durham ■

Greensboro ■

Nashville

Knoxville

Winston ○

Raleigh ☆

ARKANSAS

TENNESSEE

Chattanooga

Salem

N.C.

Asheville ○

Charlotte ■

MA

Little
Rock

Memphis ■

Greenville ○

Columbia ☆

ATLANTIC
OCEAN

S.C.

Huntsville

Atlanta ☆

land
llas

Augusta ○

Charleston ■

Birmingham

Macon ○

Shreveport

Montgomery ☆

Columbus

Savannah ■

LOUISIANA

ALABAMA

GEORGIA

eaumont

MISSISSIPPI

Biloxi

Pensacola

Jacksonville ■

Baton Rouge ☆

☆ Tallahassee

ston

New Orleans

Mobile

FLORIDA

Gulf of Mexico

Orlando ■

Tampa ■

St. Petersburg

Hialeah ○

Fort Lauderdale ■

Hollywood

Miami ○

0	250	500 Miles
0	250	500 Kilometers

POPULOUS METROPOLITAN AREAS

■ Metropolitan areas over 5 million

■ Metropolitan areas over 1 million

○ Metropolitan areas under 1 million

☆ State capitals

Topographical Map of the United States

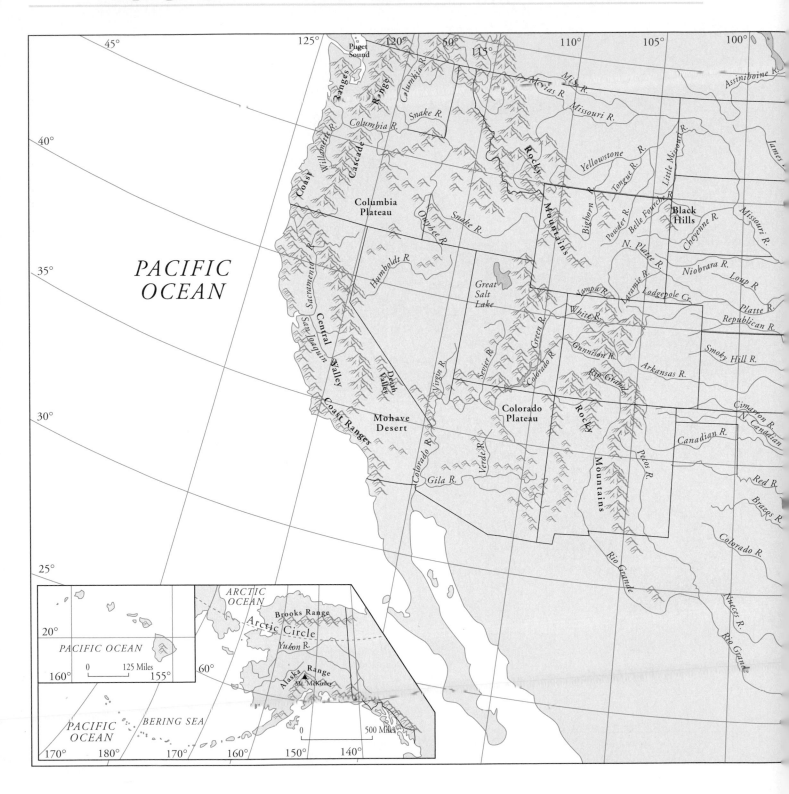

PACIFIC OCEAN

Puget Sound

Coast Ranges

Cascade Range

Columbia R.

Snake R.

Mts. R.

Missouri R.

Assiniboine R.

Willamette R.

Columbia R.

Columbia Plateau

Snake R.

Rocky Mountains

Yellowstone R.

Tongue R.

Little Missouri R.

James R.

Owyhee R.

Snake R.

Bighorn R.

Powder R.

Belle Fourche R.

Black Hills

Cheyenne R.

Missouri R.

Coast

Sacramento R.

Humboldt R.

Great Salt Lake

Yampa R.

White R.

Laramie R.

N. Platte R.

Lodgepole Cr.

Niobrara R.

Loup R.

Central Valley

San Joaquin R.

Death Valley

Virgin R.

Sevier R.

Green R.

Colorado R.

Gunnison R.

Rio Grande

Arkansas R.

Platte R.

Republican R.

Smoky Hill R.

Coast Ranges

Mohave Desert

Colorado R.

Gila R.

Verde R.

Colorado Plateau

Rocky Mountains

Canadian R.

Pecos R.

Cimarron R.

N. Canadian R.

Red R.

Brazos R.

Colorado R.

Rio Grande

Nueces R.

Rio Grande

ARCTIC OCEAN

Brooks Range

Arctic Circle

Yukon R.

PACIFIC OCEAN

125 Miles

Alaska Range

Mt. McKinley

PACIFIC OCEAN

BERING SEA

500 Miles

95° 90° 85° 80° 75° 70° 65°

Lake Superior

St. Croix R.

Mississippi R.

Minnesota R.

Lake Michigan

Lake Huron

Des Moines R.

Cedar R.

Iowa R.

Rock R.

Fox R.

Kankakee R.

Illinois R.

Wabash R.

Lake Erie

Scioto R.

Ohio R.

Allegheny R.

Adirondack Mts.

Lake Ontario

Mohawk R.

Hudson R.

Susquehanna R.

Delaware R.

Connecticut R.

Kennebeck R.

St. Lawrence R.

Potomac R.

Mts.

Central   Plains

Missouri R.

Osage R.

Ozark Plateau

White R.

Arkansas R.

Mississippi R.

Ohio R.

Cumberland R.

Tennessee R.

Allegheny

Kanawha R.

Shenandoah Valley

James R.

Roanoke R.

Chesapeake Bay

Appalachian Mountains

Blue Ridge Mts.

Atlantic   Coastal   Plain

ATLANTIC OCEAN

Mississippi R.

Ouachita R.

Yazoo R.

Tombigbee R.

Red R.

Sabine R.

Pearl R.

Alabama R.

Chattahoochee R.

Savannah R.

Saluda R.

Altamaha R.

Coastal   Plain

Galveston Bay

Gulf of Mexico

0   250   500 Miles

0   250   500 Kilometers

The World

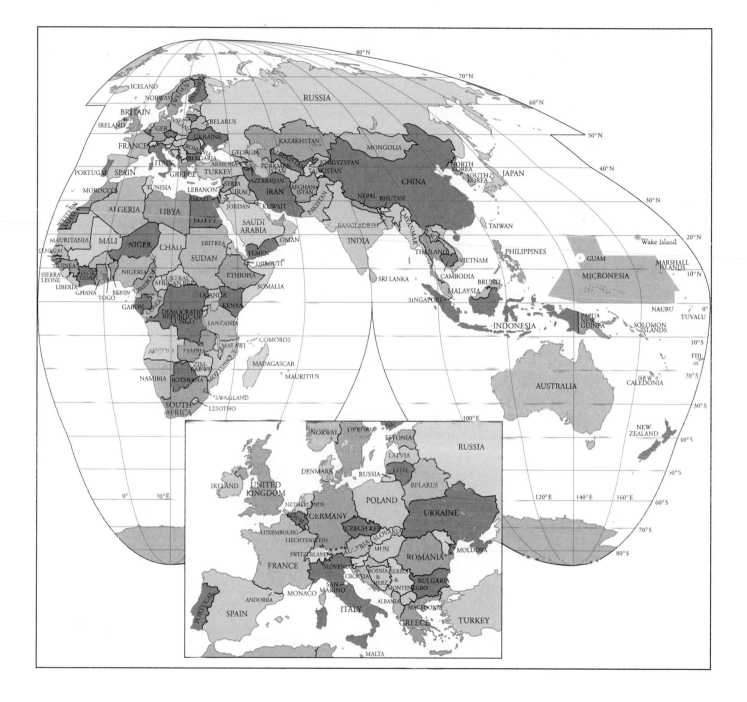

United States Territorial Expansion, 1783–1898

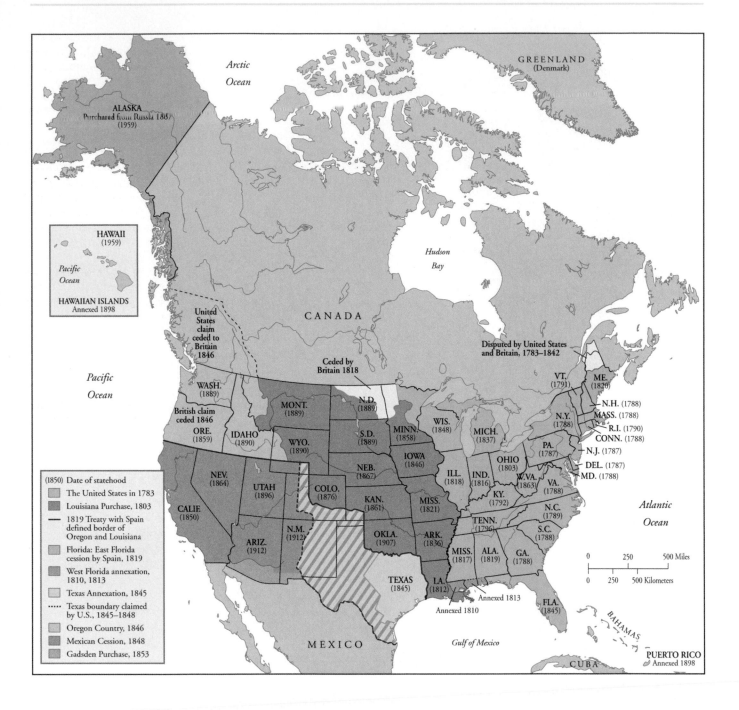

The Declaration of Independence

In Congress, July 4, 1776,

The Unanimous Declaration of the Thirteen United States of America

When, in the course of human events, it becomes necessary for one people to dissolve the political bands which have connected them with another, and to assume, among the powers of the earth, the separate and equal station to which the laws of nature and of nature's God entitle them, a decent respect to the opinions of mankind requires that they should declare the causes which impel them to the separation.

We hold these truths to be self-evident, that all men are created equal; that they are endowed by their Creator with certain unalienable rights; that among these, are life, liberty, and the pursuit of happiness. That, to secure these rights, governments are instituted among men, deriving their just powers from the consent of the governed; that, whenever any form of government becomes destructive of these ends, it is the right of the people to alter or to abolish it, and to institute a new government, laying its foundation on such principles, and organizing its powers in such form, as to them shall seem most likely to effect their safety and happiness. Prudence, indeed, will dictate that governments long established, should not be changed for light and transient causes; and, accordingly, all experience hath shown, that mankind are more disposed to suffer, while evils are sufferable, than to right themselves by abolishing the forms to which they are accustomed. But, when a long train of abuses and usurpations, pursuing invariably the same object, evinces a design to reduce them under absolute despotism, it is their right, it is their duty, to throw off such government and to provide new guards for their future security. Such has been the patient sufferance of these colonies, and such is now the necessity which constrains them to alter their former systems of government. The history of the present King of Great Britain is a history of repeated injuries and usurpations, all having, in direct object, the establishment of an absolute tyranny over these States. To prove this, let facts be submitted to a candid world:

He has refused his assent to laws the most wholesome and necessary for the public good.

He has forbidden his governors to pass laws of immediate and pressing importance, unless suspended in their operation till his assent should be obtained; and, when so suspended, he has utterly neglected to attend to them.

He has refused to pass other laws for the accommodation of large districts of people, unless those people would relinquish the right of representation in the legislature; a right inestimable to them, and formidable to tyrants only.

He has called together legislative bodies at places unusual, uncomfortable, and distant from the depository of their public records, for the sole purpose of fatiguing them into compliance with his measures.

He has dissolved representative houses repeatedly for opposing, with manly firmness, his invasions on the rights of the people.

He has refused, for a long time after such dissolutions, to cause others to be elected; whereby the legislative powers, incapable of annihilation, have returned to the people at large for their exercise; the state remaining, in the meantime, exposed to all the danger of invasion from without, and convulsions within.

He has endeavored to prevent the population of these States; for that purpose, obstructing the laws for naturalization of foreigners, refusing to pass others to encourage their migration hither, and raising the conditions of new appropriations of lands.

He has obstructed the administration of justice, by refusing his assent to laws for establishing judiciary powers.

He has made judges dependent on his will alone, for the tenure of their offices, and the amount and payment of their salaries.

He has erected a multitude of new offices, and sent hither swarms of officers to harass our people, and eat out their substance.

He has kept among us, in time of peace, standing armies, without the consent of our legislatures.

He has affected to render the military independent of, and superior to, the civil power.

He has combined, with others, to subject us to a jurisdiction foreign to our Constitution, and unacknowledged by our laws; giving his assent to their acts of pretended legislation:

For quartering large bodies of armed troops among us:

For protecting them by a mock trial, from punishment, for any murders which they should commit on the inhabitants of these States:

For cutting off our trade with all parts of the world:

For imposing taxes on us without our consent:

For depriving us, in many cases, of the benefit of trial by jury:

For transporting us beyond seas to be tried for pretended offences:

For abolishing the free system of English laws in a neighboring province, establishing therein an arbitrary government, and enlarging its boundaries, so as to render it at once an example and fit instrument for introducing the same absolute rule into these colonies:

For taking away our charters, abolishing our most valuable laws, and altering, fundamentally, the powers of our governments:

For suspending our own legislatures, and declaring themselves invested with power to legislate for use in all cases whatsoever.

He has abdicated government here, by declaring us out of his protection, and waging war against us.

He has plundered our seas, ravaged our coasts, burnt our towns, and destroyed the lives of our people.

He is, at this time, transporting large armies of foreign mercenaries to complete the works of death, desolation, and tyranny, already begun, with circumstances of cruelty and perfidy scarcely paralleled in the most barbarous ages, and totally unworthy the head of a civilized nation.

He has constrained our fellow citizens, taken captive on the high seas, to bear arms against their country, to become the executioners of their friends, and brethren, or to fall themselves by their hands.

He has excited domestic insurrections amongst us, and has endeavored to bring on the inhabitants of our frontiers, the merciless Indian savages, whose known rule of warfare is an undistinguished destruction of all ages, sexes, and conditions.

In every stage of these oppressions, we have petitioned for redress, in the most humble terms; our repeated petitions have been answered only by repeated injury. A prince, whose character is thus marked by every act which may define a tyrant, is unfit to be the ruler of a free people.

Nor have we been wanting in attention to our British brethren. We have warned them, from time to time, of attempts made by their legislature to extend an unwarrantable jurisdiction over us. We have reminded them of the circumstances of our emigration and settlement here. We have appealed to their native justice and magnanimity, and we have conjured them, by the ties of our common kindred, to disavow these usurpations, which would inevitably interrupt our connections and correspondence. They, too, have been deaf to the voice of justice and consanguinity. We must, therefore, acquiesce in the necessity, which denounces our separation, and hold them as we hold the rest of mankind, enemies in war, in peace, friends.

We, therefore, the representatives of the United States of America, in general Congress assembled, appealing to the Supreme Judge of the world for the rectitude of our intentions, do, in the name, and by the authority of the good people of these colonies, solemnly publish and declare, that these united colonies are, and of right ought to be, free and independent states: that they are absolved from all allegiance to the British Crown, and that all political connection between them and the state of Great Britain is, and ought to be, totally dissolved; and that, as free and independent states, they have full power to levy war, conclude peace, contract alliances, establish commerce, and to do all other acts and things which independent states may of right do. And, for the support of this declaration, with a firm reliance on the protection of Divine Providence, we mutually pledge to each other our lives, our fortunes, and our sacred honor.

The foregoing Declaration was, by order of Congress, engrossed, and signed by the following members:

JOHN HANCOCK

New Hampshire
Josiah Bartlett
William Whipple
Matthew Thornton

New York
William Floyd
Philip Livingston
Francis Lewis
Lewis Morris

Delaware
Caesar Rodney
George Read
Thomas McKean

North Carolina
William Hooper
Joseph Hewes
John Penn

Massachusetts Bay
Samuel Adams
John Adams
Robert Treat Paine
Elbridge Gerry

New Jersey
Richard Stockton
John Witherspoon
Francis Hopkinson
John Hart
Abraham Clark

Maryland
Samuel Chase
William Paca
Thomas Stone
Charles Carroll, of
    Carrollton

South Carolina
Edward Rutledge
Thomas Heyward, Jr.
Thomas Lynch, Jr.
Arthur Middleton

Rhode Island
Stephen Hopkins
William Ellery

Connecticut
Robert Sherman
Samuel Huntington
William Williams
Oliver Wolcott

Pennsylvania
Robert Morris
Benjamin Rush
Benjamin Franklin
John Morton
George Clymer
James Smith
George Taylor
James Wilson
George Ross

Virginia
George Wythe
Richard Henry Lee
Thomas Jefferson
Benjamin Harrison
Thomas Nelson, Jr.
Francis Lightfoot Lee
Carter Braxton

Georgia
Button Gwinnett
Lyman Hall
George Walton

Resolved, That copies of the Declaration be sent to the several assemblies, conventions, and committees, or councils of safety, and to the several commanding officers of the continental troops; that it be proclaimed in each of the United States, at the head of the army.

The Constitution of the United States of America[1]

We the People of the United States, in Order to form a more perfect Union, establish Justice, insure domestic Tranquility, provide for the common defence, promote the general Welfare, and secure the Blessings of Liberty to ourselves and our Posterity, do ordain and establish this CONSTITUTION for the United States of America.

Article I

Section 1.

All legislative Powers herein granted shall be vested in a Congress of the United States, which shall consist of a Senate and House of Representatives.

Section 2.

The House of Representatives shall be composed of Members chosen every second Year by the People of the several States, and the Electors in each State shall have the Qualifications requisite for Electors of the most numerous Branch of the State Legislature.

No Person shall be a Representative who shall not have attained to the Age of twenty-five Years, and been seven Years a Citizen of the United States, and who shall not, when elected, be an Inhabitant of that State in which he shall be chosen.

[Representatives and direct Taxes[2] shall be apportioned among the several States which may be included within this Union, according to their respective Numbers, which shall be determined by adding to the whole Number of free Persons, including those bound to Service for a Term of Years, and excluding Indians not taxed, three fifths of all other Persons.][3] The actual Enumeration shall be made within three Years after the first Meeting of the Congress of the United States, and within every subsequent Term of ten Years, in such Manner as they shall by Law direct. The Number of Representatives shall not exceed one for every thirty Thousand, but each State shall have at Least one Representative; and until such enumeration shall be made, the State of New Hampshire shall be entitled to chuse three, Massachusetts eight, Rhode-Island and Providence Plantations one, Connecticut five, New York six, New Jersey four, Pennsylvania eight, Delaware one, Maryland six, Virginia ten, North Carolina five, South Carolina five, and Georgia three.

When vacancies happen in the Representation from any State, the Executive Authority thereof shall issue Writs of Election to fill such Vacancies.

The House of Representatives shall chuse their Speaker and other Officers; and shall have the sole Power of Impeachment.

Section 3.

The Senate of the United States shall be composed of two Senators from each State, chosen by the Legislature thereof, for six Years; and each Senator shall have one Vote.

Immediately after they shall be assembled in Consequence of the first Election, they shall be divided as equally as may be into three Classes. The Seats of the Senators of the first Class shall be vacated at the Expiration of the second Year, of the second Class at the Expiration of the fourth Year, and of the third Class at the Expiration of the sixth Year, so that one-third may be chosen every second Year; and if Vacancies happen by Resignation, or otherwise, during the Recess of the Legislature of any State, the Executive thereof may make temporary Appointments until the next Meeting of the Legislature, which shall then fill such Vacancies.

No Person shall be a Senator who shall not have attained to the Age of thirty Years, and been nine Years a Citizen of the United States, and who shall not, when elected, be an Inhabitant of that State for which he shall be chosen.

The Vice President of the United States shall be President of the Senate, but shall have no vote, unless they be equally divided.

The Senate shall chuse their other Officers, and also a President pro tempore, in the absence of the Vice President, or when he shall exercise the office of President of the United States.

The Senate shall have the sole Power to try all Impeachments. When sitting for that purpose they shall be on Oath or Affirmation. When the President of the United States is tried, the Chief Justice shall preside: And no person shall be convicted without the Concurrence of two thirds of the Members present.

Judgment in Cases of Impeachment shall not extend further than to removal from Office, and disqualification to hold and enjoy any Office of honor, Trust, or Profit under the United States: but the Party convicted shall nevertheless be liable and subject to Indictment, Trial, Judgment, and Punishment, according to Law.

Section 4.

The Times, Places and Manner of holding Elections for Senators and Representatives, shall be prescribed in each State by the Legislature thereof; but the Congress may at any time by Law make or alter such Regulations, except as to the Places of Chusing Senators.

---

[1]This version, which follows the original Constitution in capitalization and spelling, was published by the United States Department of the Interior, Office of Education, in 1935.

[2]Altered by the Sixteenth Amendment.

[3]Negated by the Fourteenth Amendment.

The Congress shall assemble at least once in every Year, and such Meeting shall be on the first Monday in December, unless they shall by Law appoint a different day.

Section 5.

Each House shall be the Judge of the Elections, Returns and Qualifications of its own Members, and a Majority of each shall constitute a Quorum to do Business; but a smaller number may adjourn from day to day, and may be authorized to compel the Attendance of absent Members, in such Manner, and under such Penalties, as each House may provide.

Each House may determine the Rules of its Proceedings, punish its Members for disorderly Behaviour, and, with the Concurrence of two thirds, expel a Member.

Each House shall keep a Journal of its Proceedings, and from time to time publish the same, excepting such Parts as may in their Judgment require Secrecy; and the Yeas and Nays of the Members of either House on any question shall, at the Desire of one fifth of those Present, be entered on the Journal.

Neither House, during the Session of Congress, shall, without the Consent of the other, adjourn for more than three days, nor to any other Place than that in which the two Houses shall be sitting.

Section 6.

The Senators and Representatives shall receive a Compensation for their Services, to be ascertained by Law, and paid out of the Treasury of the United States. They shall in all Cases, except Treason, Felony, and Breach of the Peace, be privileged from Arrest during their Attendance at the Session of their respective Houses, and in going to and returning from the same; and for any Speech or Debate in either House, they shall not be questioned in any other Place.

No Senator or Representative shall, during the Time for which he was elected, be appointed to any civil Office under the Authority of the United States, which shall have been created, or the Emoluments whereof shall have been increased, during such time; and no Person holding any Office under the United States shall be a Member of either House during his continuance in Office.

Section 7.

All Bills for raising Revenue shall originate in the House of Representatives; but the Senate may propose or concur with Amendments as on other bills.

Every Bill which shall have passed the House of Representatives and the Senate, shall, before it become a Law, be presented to the President of the United States; If he approve he shall sign it, but if not he shall return it, with his Objections, to that House in which it shall have originated, who shall enter the Objections at large on their Journal, and proceed to reconsider it. If after such Reconsideration two thirds of that House shall agree to pass the bill, it shall be sent, together with the objections, to the other House, by which it shall likewise be reconsidered, and if approved by two thirds of that House, it shall become a Law. But in all such Cases the Votes of both Houses shall be determined by Yeas and Nays, and the Names of the Persons voting for and against the Bill shall be entered on the Journal of each House respectively. If any Bill shall not be returned by the President within ten Days (Sundays excepted) after it shall have been presented to him, the Same shall be a Law, in like Manner as if he had signed it, unless the Congress by their Adjournment prevent its Return, in which Case it shall not be a Law.

Every Order, Resolution, or Vote to which the Concurrence of the Senate and House of Representatives may be necessary (except on a question of Adjournment) shall be presented to the President of the United States; and before the Same shall take Effect, shall be approved by him, or being disapproved by him, shall be repassed by two thirds of the Senate and House of Representatives, according to the Rules and Limitations prescribed in the Case of a Bill.

Section 8.

The Congress shall have Power To lay and collect Taxes, Duties, Imposts and Excises, to pay the Debts and provide for the common Defence and general Welfare of the United States; but all Duties, Imposts and Excises shall be uniform throughout the United States;

To borrow money on the credit of the United States;

To regulate Commerce with foreign Nations, and among the several States, and with the Indian Tribes;

To establish an uniform rule of Naturalization, and uniform Laws on the subject of Bankruptcies throughout the United States;

To coin Money, regulate the Value thereof, and of foreign Coin, and fix the Standard of Weights and Measures;

To provide for the Punishment of counterfeiting the Securities and current Coin of the United States;

To establish Post Offices and post Roads;

To promote the Progress of Science and useful Arts, by securing for limited Times to Authors and Inventors the exclusive Right to their respective Writings and Discoveries;

To constitute Tribunals inferior to the Supreme Court;

To define and punish Piracies and Felonies committed on the high Seas, and Offenses against the Law of Nations;

To declare War, grant Letters of Marque and Reprisal, and make Rules concerning Captures on Land and Water;

To raise and support Armies, but no Appropriation of Money to that Use shall be for a longer Term than two Years;

To provide and maintain a Navy;

To make Rules for the Government and Regulation of the land and naval forces;

To provide for calling forth the Militia to execute the Laws of the Union, suppress Insurrections and repel Invasions;

To provide for organizing, arming, and disciplining the Militia, and for governing such Part of them as may be employed in the Service of the United States, reserving to the States respectively, the Appointment of the Officers, and the Authority of training the Militia according to the discipline prescribed by Congress;

To exercise exclusive Legislation in all Cases whatsoever, over such District (not exceeding ten Miles square) as may, by Cession of particular States, and the acceptance of Congress, become the Seat of the Government of the United States, and to exercise like Authority over all

Places purchased by the Consent of the Legislature of the State in which the Same shall be, for the Erection of Forts, Magazines, Arsenals, Dockyards, and other needful Buildings;—And

To make all Laws which shall be necessary and proper for carrying into Execution for foregoing Powers, and all other Powers vested by this Constitution in the Government of the United States, or in any Department or Officer thereof.

Section 9.

The Migration or Importation of such Persons as any of the States now existing shall think proper to admit, shall not be prohibited by the Congress prior to the Year one thousand eight hundred and eight, but a tax or duty may be imposed on such Importation, not exceeding ten dollars for each Person.

The privilege of the Writ of Habeas Corpus shall not be suspended, unless when in Cases of Rebellion or Invasion the public Safety may require it.

No bill of Attainder or ex post facto Law shall be passed.

No capitation, or other direct, Tax shall be laid unless in Proportion to the Census or Enumeration herein before directed to be taken.

No Tax or Duty shall be laid on Articles exported from any State.

No Preference shall be given by any Regulation of Commerce or Revenue to the Ports of one State over those of another: nor shall Vessels bound to, or from, one State, be obliged to enter, clear, or pay Duties in another.

No Money shall be drawn from the Treasury, but in Consequence of Appropriations made by Law; and a regular Statement and Account of the Receipts and Expenditures of all public Money shall be published from time to time.

No Title of Nobility shall be granted by the United States: And no Person holding any Office of Profit or Trust under them, shall, without the Consent of the Congress, accept of any present, Emolument, Office, or Title, of any kind whatever, from any King, Prince, or foreign State.

Section 10.

No State shall enter into any Treaty, Alliance, or Confederation; grant Letters of Marque and Reprisal; coin Money; emit Bills of Credit; make any Thing but gold and silver Coin a Tender in Payment of Debts; pass any Bill of Attainder, ex post facto Law, or Law impairing the Obligation of Contracts, or grant any Title of Nobility.

No State shall, without the Consent of the Congress, lay any Imposts or Duties on Imports or Exports, except what may be absolutely necessary for executing its inspection Laws; and the net Produce of all Duties and Imposts, laid by any State on Imports or Exports, shall be for the use of the Treasury of the United States; and all such Laws shall be subject to the Revision and Control of the Congress.

No state shall, without the Consent of Congress, lay any duty of Tonnage, keep Troops, or Ships of War in time of Peace, enter into any Agreement or Compact with another State, or with a foreign Power, or engage in War, unless actually invaded, or in such imminent Danger as will not admit of delay.

Article II

Section 1.

The executive Power shall be vested in a President of the United States of America. He shall hold his Office during the Term of four years, and, together with the Vice President, chosen for the same Term, be elected, as follows:

Each State shall appoint, in such Manner as the Legislature thereof may direct, a Number of Electors, equal to the whole Number of Senators and Representatives to which the State may be entitled in the Congress: but no Senator or Representative, or Person holding an Office of Trust or Profit under the United States, shall be appointed an Elector.

[The Electors shall meet in their respective States, and vote by Ballot for two persons, of whom one at least shall not be an Inhabitant of the same State with themselves. And they shall make a List of all the Persons voted for, and of the Number of Votes for each; which List they shall sign and certify, and transmit sealed to the Seat of the Government of the United States, directed to the President of the Senate. The President of the Senate shall, in the Presence of the Senate and House of Representatives, open all the Certificates, and the Votes shall then be counted. The Person having the greatest Number of Votes shall be the President, if such Number be a Majority of the whole Number of Electors appointed; and if there be more than one who have such Majority, and have an equal Number of Votes, then the House of Representatives shall immediately chuse by Ballot one of them for President; and if no Person have a Majority, then from the five highest on the list the said House shall in like Manner chuse the President. But in chusing the President, the Votes shall be taken by States, the Representation from each State having one Vote; a quorum for this Purpose shall consist of a Member or Members from two-thirds of the States, and a Majority of all the States shall be necessary to a Choice. In every Case, after the Choice of the President, the Person having the greatest Number of Votes of the Electors shall be the Vice President. But if there should remain two or more who have equal votes, the Senate shall chuse from them by Ballot the Vice President.][4]

The Congress may determine the Time of chusing the Electors, and the Day on which they shall give their Votes; which Day shall be the same throughout the United States.

No person except a natural-born Citizen, or a Citizen of the United States, at the time of the Adoption of this Constitution, shall be eligible to the Office of President; neither shall any Person be eligible to that Office who shall not have attained to the Age of thirty-five years, and been fourteen Years a Resident within the United States.

In Case of the Removal of the President from Office, or of his Death, Resignation, or Inability to discharge the Powers and Duties of the said Office, the same shall devolve on the Vice President, and the Congress may by Law provide for the Case of Removal, Death, Resignation, or Inability, both of the President and Vice President, declaring what

---

[4]Revised by the Twelfth Amendment.

Officer shall then act as President, and such Officer shall act accordingly, until the disability be removed, or a President shall be elected.

The President shall, at stated Times, receive for his Services a Compensation, which shall neither be increased nor diminished during the Period for which he shall have been elected, and he shall not receive within that Period any other Emolument from the United States, or any of them.

Before he enter on the execution of his Office, he shall take the following Oath or Affirmation:—"I do solemnly swear (or affirm) that I will faithfully execute the Office of President of the United States, and will, to the best of my Ability, preserve, protect, and defend the Constitution of the United States."

Section 2.
The President shall be Commander in Chief of the Army and Navy of the United States, and of the Militia of the several States, when called into the actual Service of the United States; he may require the Opinion, in writing, of the principal Officer in each of the executive Departments, upon any subject relating to the Duties of their respective Offices, and he shall have Power to Grant Reprieves and Pardons for Offenses against the United States, except in Cases of Impeachment.

He shall have Power, by and with the Advice and Consent of the Senate, to make Treaties, provided two-thirds of the Senators present concur; and he shall nominate, and by and with the Advice and Consent of the Senate, shall appoint Ambassadors, other public Ministers and Consuls, Judges of the supreme Court, and all other Officers of the United States, whose Appointments are not herein otherwise provided for, and which shall be established by Law: but the Congress may by Law vest the Appointment of such inferior Officers, as they think proper, in the President alone, in the Courts of Law, or in the Heads of Departments.

The President shall have Power to fill up all Vacancies that may happen during the Recess of the Senate, by granting Commissions which shall expire at the End of their next Session.

Section 3.
He shall from time to time give to the Congress Information of the State of the Union, and recommend to their Consideration such Measures as he shall judge necessary and expedient; he may, on extraordinary occasions, convene both Houses, or either of them, and in Case of Disagreement between them, with respect to the Time of Adjournment, he may adjourn them to such Time as he shall think proper; he shall receive Ambassadors and other public Ministers; he shall take care that the Laws be faithfully executed, and shall Commission all the Officers of the United States.

Section 4.
The President, Vice President and all civil Officers of the United States, shall be removed from Office on Impeachment for, and Conviction of, Treason, Bribery, or other high Crimes and Misdemeanors.

Article III

Section 1.
The judicial Power of the United States, shall be vested in one supreme Court, and in such inferior Courts as the Congress may from time to time ordain and establish. The Judges, both of the supreme and inferior Courts, shall hold their Offices during good Behaviour, and shall, at stated Times, receive for their Services, a Compensation, which shall not be diminished during their Continuance in Office.

Section 2.
The judicial Power shall extend to all Cases, in Law and Equity, arising under this Constitution, the Laws of the United States, and Treaties made, or which shall be made, under their Authority;—to all Cases affecting ambassadors, other public ministers and consuls;—to all cases of admiralty and maritime Jurisdiction;—to Controversies to which the United States shall be a Party;—to Controversies between two or more States;—between a State and Citizens of another State;[5]—between Citizens of different States—between Citizens of the same State claiming Lands under Grants of different States, and between a State, or the Citizens thereof, and foreign States, Citizens, or Subjects.

In all Cases affecting Ambassadors, other public Ministers and Consuls, and those in which a State shall be Party, the supreme Court shall have original Jurisdiction. In all the other Cases before mentioned, the supreme Court shall have appellate Jurisdiction, both as to Law and Fact, with such Exceptions, and under such Regulations as the Congress shall make.

The trial of all Crimes, except in Cases of Impeachment, shall be by Jury; and such Trial shall be held in the State where the said Crimes shall have been committed; but when not committed within any State, the Trial shall be at such Place or Places as the Congress may by Law have directed.

Section 3.
Treason against the United States, shall consist only in levying War against them, or in adhering to their Enemies, giving them Aid and Comfort. No Person shall be convicted of Treason unless on the Testimony of two Witnesses to the same overt Act, or on Confession in open Court.

The Congress shall have power to declare the Punishment of Treason, but no Attainder of Treason shall work Corruption of Blood, or Forfeiture except during the Life of the Person attained.

Article IV

Section 1.
Full Faith and Credit shall be given in each State to the public Acts, Records, and judicial Proceedings of every State. And the Congress may by general Laws prescribe the Manner in which such Acts, Records and Proceedings shall be proved, and the Effect thereof.

---

[5]Qualified by the Eleventh Amendment.

Section 2.

The Citizens of each State shall be entitled to all Privileges and Immunities of Citizens in the several States.

A Person charged in any State with Treason, Felony, or other Crime, who shall flee from Justice, and be found in another State, shall on demand of the executive Authority of the State from which he fled, be delivered up, to be removed to the State having Jurisdiction of the crime.

No Person held to Service or Labour in one State, under the Laws thereof, escaping into another, shall, in Consequence of any Law or Regulation therein, be discharged from such Service or Labour, but shall be delivered up on Claim of the Party to whom such Service or Labour may be due.

Section 3.

New States may be admitted by the Congress into this Union; but no new State shall be formed or erected within the Jurisdiction of any other State; nor any State be formed by the Junction of two or more States, or parts of States, without the Consent of the Legislatures of the States concerned as well as of the Congress.

The Congress shall have Power to dispose of and make all needful Rules and Regulations respecting the Territory or other Property belonging to the United States; and nothing in this Constitution shall be so construed as to Prejudice any Claims of the United States, or of any particular State.

Section 4.

The United States shall guarantee to every State in this Union a Republican Form of Government, and shall protect each of them against Invasion; and on Application of the Legislature, or of the Executive (when the Legislature cannot be convened) against domestic violence.

Article V

The Congress, whenever two-thirds of both Houses shall deem it necessary, shall propose Amendments to this Constitution, or, on the Application of the Legislatures of two-thirds of the several States, shall call a Convention for proposing Amendments, which, in either Case, shall be valid to all Intents and Purposes, as part of this Constitution, when ratified by the Legislatures of three-fourths of the several States, or by Conventions in three-fourths thereof, as the one or the other Mode of Ratification may be proposed by the Congress; Provided that no Amendment which may be made prior to the Year One thousand eight hundred and eight shall in any Manner affect the first and fourth Clauses in the Ninth Section of the first Article; and that no State, without its Consent, shall be deprived of its equal Suffrage in the Senate.

Article VI

All Depts contracted and Engagements entered into, before the Adoption of this Constitution, shall be as valid against the United States under this Constitution, as under the Confederation.

This Constitution, and the Laws of the United States which shall be made in Pursuance thereof; and all Treaties made, or which shall be made, under the Authority of the United States, shall be the supreme Law of the Land; and the Judges in every State shall be bound thereby, any Thing in the Constitution or Laws of any State to the Contrary notwithstanding.

The Senators and Representatives before mentioned, and the Members of the several State Legislatures, and all executive and judicial Officers, both of the United States and of the several States, shall be bound by Oath or Affirmation to support this Constitution; but no religious Tests shall ever be required as a qualification to any Office or public Trust under the United States.

Article VII

The Ratification of the Conventions of nine States shall be sufficient for the Establishment of this Constitution between the States so ratifying the same.

Done in convention by the Unanimous Consent of the States present the Seventeenth Day of September in the Year of our Lord one thousand seven hundred and Eighty seven, and of the Independence of the United States of America the Twelfth. In Witness whereof We have hereunto subscribed our Names.[6]

George Washington
President and deputy from Virginia

New Hampshire
John Langdon
Nicholas Gilman

Massachusetts
Nathaniel Gorham
Rufus King

Connecticut
William Samuel Johnson
Roger Sherman

New York
Alexander Hamilton

Delaware
George Read
Gunning Bedford, Jr
John Dickinson
Richard Bassett
Jacob Broom

New Jersey
William Livingston
David Brearley
William Paterson
Jonathan Dayton

Pennsylvania
Benjamin Franklin
Thomas Mifflin
Robert Morris
George Clymer
Thomas FitzSimons
Jared Ingersoll
James Wilson
Gouverneur Morris

North Carolina
William Blount
Richard Dobbs Spaight
Hugh Williamson

---

[6]These are the full names of the signers, which in some cases are not the signatures on the document.

Maryland
James McHenry
Daniel of St. Thomas Jenifer
Daniel Carroll

Virginia
John Blair
James Madison, Jr.

South Carolina
John Rutledge
Charles Cotesworth
   Pinckney
Charles Pinckney
Pierce Butler

Georgia
William Few
Abraham Baldwin

Articles in Addition to, and Amendment of, the Constitution of the United States of America, Proposed by Congress, and Ratified by the Legislatures of the Several States, Pursuant to the Fifth Article of the Original Constitution[7]

[Article I]

Congress shall make no law respecting an establishment of religion, or prohibiting the free exercise thereof; or abridging the freedom of speech, or of the press; or the right of the people peaceably to assemble, and to petition the Government for a redress of grievances.

[Article II]

A well regulated Militia, being necessary to the security of a free State, the right of the people to keep and bear Arms shall not be infringed.

[Article III]

No Soldier shall, in time of peace, be quartered in any house, without the consent of the Owner, nor in time of war, but in a manner to be prescribed by law.

[Article IV]

The right of the people to be secure in their persons, houses, papers, and effects, against unreasonable searches and seizures, shall not be violated, and no Warrants shall issue, but upon probable cause, supported by Oath or affirmation, and particularly describing the place to be searched, and the persons or things to be seized.

[Article V]

No person shall be held to answer for a capital or otherwise infamous crime, unless on a presentment or indictment of a Grand Jury, except in cases arising in the land or naval forces, or in the Militia, when in actual service in time of War or public danger; nor shall any person be subject for the same offence to be twice put in jeopardy of life or limb; nor shall be compelled in any criminal case to be a witness against himself, nor be deprived of life, liberty, or property, without due process of law; nor shall private property be taken for public use, without just compensation.

[Article VI]

In all criminal prosecutions, the accused shall enjoy the right to a speedy and public trial, by an impartial jury of the State and district wherein the crime shall have been committed, which district shall have been previously ascertained by law, and to be informed of the nature and cause of the accusation; to be confronted with the witnesses against him; to have compulsory process for obtaining witnesses in his favour, and to have the Assistance of Counsel for his defence.

[Article VII]

In suits at common law, where the value in controversy shall exceed twenty dollars, the right of trial by jury shall be preserved, and no fact tried by a jury, shall be otherwise reexamined in any Court of the United States, than according to the rules of the common law.

[Article VIII]

Excessive bail shall not be required, nor excessive fines imposed, nor cruel and unusual punishments inflicted.

[Article IX]

The enumeration in the Constitution, of certain rights, shall not be construed to deny or disparage others retained by the people.

[Article X]

The powers not delegated to the United States by the Constitution, nor prohibited by it to the States, are reserved to the States respectively, or to the people. [Amendments I–X, in force 1791.]

[Article XI][8]

The Judicial power of the United States shall not be construed to extend to any suit in law or equity, commenced or prosecuted against one of the United States by Citizens of another State, or by Citizens or Subjects of any Foreign State.

[Article XII][9]

The Electors shall meet in their respective States and vote by ballot for President and Vice-President, one of whom, at least, shall not be an inhabitant of the same State with themselves; they shall name in their ballots the person voted for as President, and in distinct ballots the person voted for as Vice-President, and they shall make distinct lists of all

---

[7]This heading appears only in the joint resolution submitting the first ten amendments.

[8]Adopted in 1798.

[9]Adopted in 1804.

persons voted for as President, and of all persons voted for as Vice-President, and of the number of votes for each, which lists they shall sign and certify, and transmit sealed to the seal of the government of the United States, directed to the President of the Senate;—The President of the Senate shall, in the presence of the Senate and House of Representatives, open all the certificates and the votes shall then be counted;—The person having the greatest number of votes for President, shall be the President, if such number be a majority of the whole number of Electors appointed; and if no person have such majority, then from the persons having the highest numbers not exceeding three on the list of those voted for as President, the House of Representatives shall choose immediately, by ballot, the President. But in choosing the President, the votes shall be taken by states, the representation from each state having one vote; a quorum for this purpose shall consist of a member or members from two-thirds of the states, and a majority of all the states shall be necessary to a choice. And if the House of Representatives shall not choose a President whenever the right of choice shall devolve upon them, before the fourth day of March next following, then the Vice-President shall act as President, as in the case of the death or other constitutional disability of the President.— The person having the greatest number of votes as Vice-President, shall be the Vice-President, if such number be a majority of the whole number of Electors appointed, and if no person have a majority, then from the two highest numbers on the list, the Senate shall choose the Vice-President; a quorum for the purpose shall consist of two-thirds of the whole number of Senators, and a majority of the whole number shall be necessary to a choice. But no person constitutionally ineligible to the office of President shall be eligible to that of Vice-President of the United States.

[Article XIII][10]

Section 1.
Neither slavery nor involuntary servitude, except as a punishment for crime whereof the party shall have been duly convicted, shall exist within the United States, or any place subject to their jurisdiction.

Section 2.
Congress shall have power to enforce this article by appropriate legislation.

[Article XIV][11]

Section 1.
All persons born or naturalized in the United States, and subject to the jurisdiction thereof, are citizens of the United States and of the State wherein they reside. No State shall make or enforce any law which shall abridge the privileges or immunities of citizens of the United States; nor shall any State deprive any person of life, liberty, or property, without due process of law; nor deny to any person within its jurisdiction the equal protection of the laws.

Section 2.
Representatives shall be apportioned among the several States according to their respective numbers, counting the whole number of persons in each State, excluding Indians not taxed. But when the right to vote at any election for the choice of electors for President and Vice-President of the United States, Representatives in Congress, the Executive and Judicial officers of a State, or the members of the Legislature thereof, is denied to any of the male inhabitants of such State, being twenty-one years of age, and citizens of the United States, or in any way abridged, except for participation in rebellion, or other crime, the basis of representation therein shall be reduced in the proportion which the number of such male citizens shall bear to the whole number of male citizens twenty-one years of age in such State.

Section 3.
No person shall be a Senator or Representative in Congress, or elector of President and Vice-President, or hold any office, civil or military, under the United States, or under any State, who, having previously taken an oath, as a member of Congress, or as an officer of the United States, or as a member of any State legislature, or as an executive or judicial officer of any State, to support the Constitution of the United States, shall have engaged in insurrection or rebellion against the same, or given aid or comfort to the enemies thereof. But Congress may by a vote of two-thirds of each House, remove such disability.

Section 4.
The validity of the public debt of the United States, authorized by law, including debts incurred for payment of pensions and bounties for services in suppressing insurrection or rebellion, shall not be questioned. But neither the United States nor any State shall assume or pay any debts or obligation incurred in aid of insurrection or rebellion against the United States, or any claim for the loss or emancipation of any slave; but all such debts, obligations, and claims shall be held illegal and void.

Section 5.
The Congress shall have the power to enforce, by appropriate legislation, the provisions of this article.

[Article XV][12]

Section 1.
The right of citizens of the United States to vote shall not be denied or abridged by the United States or by any State on account of race, color, or previous condition of servitude—

Section 2.
The Congress shall have power to enforce this article by appropriate legislation.

---

[10]Adopted in 1865.

[11]Adopted in 1868.

[12]Adopted in 1870.

[Article XVI][13]

The Congress shall have power to lay and collect taxes on incomes, from whatever source derived, without apportionment among the several States, and without regard to any census or enumeration.

[Article XVII][14]

The Senate of the United States shall be composed of two Senators from each State, elected by the people thereof, for six years; and each Senator shall have one vote. The electors in each State shall have the qualifications requisite for electors of the most numerous branch of the State legislatures.

When vacancies happen in the representation of any State in the Senate, the executive authority of such State shall issue writs of election to fill such vacancies: *Provided,* That the legislature of any State may empower the executive thereof to make temporary appointments until the people fill the vacancies by election as the legislature may direct.

This amendment shall not be so constructed as to affect the election or term of any Senator chosen before it becomes valid as part of the Constitution.

[Article XVIII][15]

Section 1.
After one year from the ratification of this article the manufacture, sale, or transportation of intoxicating liquors within, the importation thereof into, or the exportation thereof from the United States and all territory subject to the jurisdiction thereof for beverage purposes is hereby prohibited.

Section 2.
The Congress and the several States shall have concurrent power to enforce this article by appropriate legislation.

Section 3.
This article shall be inoperative unless it shall have been ratified as an amendment to the Constitution by the legislatures of the several States, as provided in the Constitution, within seven years from the date of the submission hereof to the States by the Congress.

[Article XIX][16]

The right of citizens of the United States to vote shall not be denied or abridged by the United States or by any State on account of sex.

Congress shall have power to enforce this article by appropriate legislation.

[13]Adopted in 1913.

[14]Adopted in 1913.

[15]Adopted in 1918.

[16]Adopted in 1920.

[Article XX][17]

Section 1.
The terms of the President and Vice-President shall end at noon on the 20th day of January, and the terms of Senators and Representatives at noon on the 3d day of January, of the years in which such terms would have ended if this article had not been ratified; and the terms of their successors shall then begin.

Section 2.
The Congress shall assemble at least once in every year, and such meeting shall begin at noon on the 3d day of January, unless they shall by law appoint a different day.

Section 3.
If, at the time fixed for the beginning of the term of the President, the President elect shall have died, the Vice-President elect shall become President. If a President shall not have been chosen before the time fixed for the beginning of his term or if the President elect shall have failed to qualify, then the Vice-President elect shall act as President until a President shall have qualified; and the Congress may by law provide for the case wherein neither a President elect nor a Vice-President elect shall have qualified, declaring who shall then act as President, or the manner in which one who is to act shall be selected, and such person shall act accordingly until a President or Vice-President shall have qualified.

Section 4.
The Congress may by law provide for the case of the death of any of the persons from whom the House of Representatives may choose a President whenever the right of choice shall have developed upon them, and for the case of the death of any of the persons from whom the Senate may choose a Vice-President whenever the right of choice shall have developed upon them.

Section 5.
Sections 1 and 2 shall take effect on the 15th day of October following the ratification of this article.

Section 6.
This article shall be inoperative unless it shall have been ratified as an amendment to the Constitution by the legislatures of three-fourths of the several States within seven years from the date of its submission.

[Article XXI][18]

Section 1.
The eighteenth article of amendment to the Constitution of the United States is hereby repealed.

[17]Adopted in 1933.

[18]Adopted in 1933.

Section 2.

The transportation or importation into any State, Territory, or possession of the United States for delivery or use therein of intoxicating liquors, in violation of the laws thereof, is hereby prohibited.

Section 3.

This article shall be inoperative unless it shall have been ratified as an amendment to the Constitution by conventions in the several States, as provided in the Constitution, within seven years from the date of the submission hereof to the States by the Congress.

[Article XXII][19]

No person shall be elected to the office of the President more than twice, and no person who has held the office of President, or acted as President, for more than two years of a term to which some other person was elected President shall be elected to the office of the President more than once.

But this Article shall not apply to any person holding the office of President when this Article was proposed by the Congress, and shall not prevent any person who may be holding the office of President, or acting as President, during the term within which this Article becomes operative from holding the office of President or acting as President during the remainder of such term.

This article shall be inoperative unless it shall have been ratified as an amendment to the Constitution by the legislatures of three-fourths of the several states within seven years from the date of its submission to the states by the Congress.

[Article XXIII][20]

Section 1.

The District constituting the seat of Government of the United States shall appoint in such manner as the Congress may direct:

A number of electors of President and Vice-President equal to the whole number of Senators and Representatives in Congress to which the District would be entitled if it were a State, but in no event more than the least populous State; they shall be in addition to those appointed by the States, but they shall be considered, for the purposes of the election of President and Vice-President, to be electors appointed by a State; and they shall meet in the District and perform such duties as provided by the twelfth article of amendment.

[19]Adopted in 1961.

[20]Adopted in 1961.

Section 2.

The Congress shall have power to enforce this article by appropriate legislation.

[Article XXIV][21]

Section 1.

The right of citizens of the United States to vote in any primary or other election for President or Vice President, for electors for President or Vice President, or for Senator or Representative in Congress, shall not be denied or abridged by the United States or any state by reason of failure to pay any poll tax or other tax.

Section 2.

The Congress shall have the power to enforce this article by appropriate legislation.

[Article XXV][22]

Section 1.

In case of the removal of the President from office or of his death or resignation, the Vice President shall become President.

Section 2.

Whenever there is a vacancy in the office of the Vice President, the President shall nominate a Vice President who shall take office upon confirmation by a majority vote of both Houses of Congress.

Section 3.

Whenever the President transmits to the President Pro Tempore of the Senate and the Speaker of the House of Representatives his written declaration that he is unable to discharge the powers and duties of his office, and until he transmits to them a written declaration to the contrary, such powers and duties shall be discharged by the Vice President as Acting President.

Section 4.

Whenever the Vice President and a majority of either the principal officers of the executive departments or of such other body as Congress may by law provide, transmit to the President Pro Tempore of the Senate and the Speaker of the House of Representatives their written declaration that the President is unable to discharge the powers and duties of his office, the Vice President shall immediately assume the powers and duties of the office as Acting President.

Thereafter, when the President transmits to the President Pro Tempore of the Senate and the Speaker of the House of Representatives his written declaration that no inability exists, he shall resume the powers and duties of

[21]Adopted in 1964.

[22]Adopted in 1967.

his office unless the Vice President and a majority of either the principal officers of the executive departments or of such other body as Congress may by law provide, transmit within four days to the President Pro Tempore of the Senate and the Speaker of the House of Representatives their written declaration that the President is unable to discharge the powers and duties of his office. Thereupon Congress shall decide the issue, assembling within forty-eight hours for that purpose if not in session. If the Congress, within twenty-one days after receipt of the latter written declaration, or, if Congress is not in session, within twenty-one days after Congress is required to assemble, determines by two-thirds vote of both Houses that the President is unable to discharge the powers and duties of his office, the Vice President shall continue to discharge the same as Acting President; otherwise, the President shall resume the powers and duties of his office.

[Article XXVI][23]

Section 1.
The right of citizens of the United States, who are eighteen years of age or older, to vote shall not be denied or abridged by the United States or by any State on account of age.

Section 2.
The Congress shall have power to enforce this article by appropriate legislation.

[Article XXVII][24]

No law varying the compensation for the services of Senators and Representatives shall take effect until an election of Representatives shall have intervened.

---

[23]Adopted in 1971.

[24]Adopted in 1992.

Presidential Elections

Year	Candidates	Parties	Popular Vote	Percentage of Popular Vote	Electoral Vote	Percentage of Voter Participation
1789	GEORGE WASHINGTON (Va.)*				69	
	John Adams				34	
	Others				35	
1792	GEORGE WASHINGTON (Va.)				132	
	John Adams				77	
	George Clinton				50	
	Others				5	
1796	JOHN ADAMS (Mass.)	Federalist			71	
	Thomas Jefferson	Democratic Republican			68	
	Thomas Pinckney	Federalist			59	
	Aaron Burr	Dem.-Rep.			30	
	Others				48	
1800	THOMAS JEFFERSON (Va.)	Dem.-Rep.			73	
	Aaron Burr	Dem.-Rep.			73	
	John Adams	Federalist			65	
	C. C. Pinckney	Federalist			64	
	John Jay	Federalist			1	
1804	THOMAS JEFFERSON (Va.)	Dem.-Rep.			162	
	C. C. Pinckney	Federalist			14	
1808	JAMES MADISON (Va.)	Dem.-Rep.			122	
	C. C. Pinckney	Federalist			47	
	George Clinton	Dem.-Rep.			6	
1812	JAMES MADISON (Va.)	Dem.-Rep.			128	
	De Witt Clinton	Federalist			89	
1816	JAMES MONROE (Va.)	Dem.-Rep.			183	
	Rufus King	Federalist			34	
1820	JAMES MONROE (Va.)	Dem.-Rep.			231	
	John Quincy Adams	Dem.-Rep.			1	
1824	JOHN Q. ADAMS (Mass.)	Dem.-Rep.	108,740	30.5	84	26.9
	Andrew Jackson	Dem.-Rep.	153,544	43.1	99	
	William H. Crawford	Dem.-Rep.	46,618	13.1	41	
	Henry Clay	Dem.-Rep.	47,136	13.2	37	
1828	ANDREW JACKSON (Tenn.)	Democratic	647,286	56.0	178	57.6
	John Quincy Adams	National Republican	508,064	44.0	83	
1832	ANDREW JACKSON (Tenn.)	Democratic	687,502	55.0	219	55.4
	Henry Clay	National Republican	530,189	42.4	49	
	John Floyd	Independent			11	
	William Wirt	Anti-Mason	33,108	2.6	7	
1836	MARTIN VAN BUREN (N.Y.)	Democratic	765,483	50.9	170	57.8
	W. H. Harrison	Whig			73	
	Hugh L. White	Whig	739,795	49.1	26	
	Daniel Webster	Whig			14	
	W. P. Magnum	Independent			11	
1840	WILLIAM H. HARRISON (Ohio)	Whig	1,274,624	53.1	234	80.2
	Martin Van Buren	Democratic	1,127,781	46.9	60	
	J. G. Birney	Liberty	7,069		—	
1844	JAMES K. POLK (Tenn.)	Democratic	1,338,464	49.6	170	78.9
	Henry Clay	Whig	1,300,097	48.1	105	
	J. G. Birney	Liberty	62,300	2.3	—	

*State of residence at time of election.

Year	Candidates	Parties	Popular Vote	Percentage of Popular Vote	Electoral Vote	Percentage of Voter Participation
1848	**ZACHARY TAYLOR (La.)**	Whig	1,360,967	47.4	163	72.7
	Lewis Cass	Democratic	1,222,342	42.5	127	
	Martin Van Buren	Free-Soil	291,263	10.1	—	
1852	**FRANKLIN PIERCE (N.H.)**	Democratic	1,601,117	50.9	254	69.6
	Winfield Scott	Whig	1,385,453	44.1	42	
	John P. Hale	Free-Soil	155,825	5.0	—	
1856	**JAMES BUCHANAN (Pa.)**	Democratic	1,832,955	45.3	741	78.9
	John C. Frémont	Republican	1,339,932	33.1	114	
	Millard Fillmore	American	871,731	21.6	8	
1860	**ABRAHAM LINCOLN (Ill.)**	Republican	1,865,593	39.8	180	81.2
	Stephen A. Douglas	Democratic	1,382,713	29.5	12	
	John C. Breckinridge	Democratic	848,356	18.1	72	
	John Bell	Union	592,906	12.6	39	
1864	**ABRAHAM LINCOLN (Ill.)**	Republican	2,213,655	55.0	212	73.8
	George B. McClellan	Democratic	1,805,237	45.0	21	
1868	**ULYSSES S. GRANT (Ill.)**	Republican	3,012,833	52.7	214	78.1
	Horatio Seymour	Democratic	2,703,249	47.3	80	
1872	**ULYSSES S. GRANT (Ill.)**	Republican	3,597,132	55.6	286	71.3
	Horace Greeley	Democratic; Liberal Republican	2,834,125	43.9	66	
1876	**RUTHERFORD B. HAYES (Ohio)**	Republican	4,036,298	48.0	185	81.8
	Samuel J. Tilden	Democratic	4,300,590	51.0	184	
1880	**JAMES A. GARFIELD (Ohio)**	Republican	4,454,416	48.5	214	79.4
	Winfield S. Hancock	Democratic	4,444,952	48.1	155	
1884	**GROVER CLEVELAND (N.Y.)**	Democratic	4,874,986	48.5	219	77.5
	James G. Blaine	Republican	4,851,981	48.2	182	
1888	**BENJAMIN HARRISON (Ind.)**	Republican	5,439,853	47.9	233	79.3
	Grover Cleveland	Democratic	5,540,309	48.6	168	
1892	**GROVER CLEVELAND (N.Y.)**	Democratic	5,556,918	46.1	277	74.7
	Benjamin Harrison	Republican	5,176,108	43.0	145	
	James B. Weaver	People's	1,041,028	8.5	22	
1896	**WILLIAM McKINLEY (Ohio)**	Republican	7,104,779	51.1	271	79.3
	William J. Bryan	Democratic-People's	6,502,925	47.7	176	
1900	**WILLIAM McKINLEY (Ohio)**	Republican	7,207,923	51.7	292	73.2
	William J. Bryan	Dem.-Populist	6,358,133	45.5	155	
1904	**THEODORE ROOSEVELT (N.Y.)**	Republican	7,623,486	57.9	336	65.2
	Alton B. Parker	Democratic	5,077,911	37.6	140	
	Eugene V. Debs	Socialist	402,283	3.0	—	
1908	**WILLIAM H. TAFT (Ohio)**	Republican	7,678,098	51.6	321	65.4
	William J. Bryan	Democratic	6,409,104	43.1	162	
	Eugene V. Debs	Socialist	420,793	2.8	—	
1912	**WOODROW WILSON (N.J.)**	Democratic	6,293,454	41.9	435	58.8
	Theodore Roosevelt	Progressive	4,119,538	27.4	88	
	William H. Taft	Republican	3,484,980	23.2	8	
	Eugene V. Debs	Socialist	900,672	6.0	—	
1916	**WOODROW WILSON (N.J.)**	Democratic	9,129,606	49.4	277	61.6
	Charles E. Hughes	Republican	8,538,221	46.2	254	
	A. L. Benson	Socialist	585,113	3.2	—	
1920	**WARREN G. HARDING (Ohio)**	Republican	16,152,200	60.4	404	49.2
	James M. Cox	Democratic	9,147,353	34.2	127	
	Eugene V. Debs	Socialist	919,799	3.4	—	
1924	**CALVIN COOLIDGE (Mass.)**	Republican	15,725,016	54.0	382	48.9
	John W. Davis	Democratic	8,386,503	28.8	136	
	Robert M. LaFollette	Progressive	4,822,856	16.6	13	
1928	**HERBERT HOOVER (Calif.)**	Republican	21,391,381	58.2	444	56.9
	Alfred E. Smith	Democratic	15,016,443	40.9	87	
	Norman Thomas	Socialist	267,835	0.7	—	

Year	Candidates	Parties	Popular Vote	Percentage of Popular Vote	Electoral Vote	Percentage of Voter Participation
1932	**FRANKLIN D. ROOSEVELT (N.Y.)**	Democratic	22,821,857	57.4	472	56.9
	Herbert Hoover	Republican	15,761,841	39.7	59	
	Norman Thomas	Socialist	881,951	2.2	—	
1936	**FRANKLIN D. ROOSEVELT (N.Y.)**	Democratic	27,751,597	60.8	523	61.0
	Alfred M. Landon	Republican	16,679,583	36.5	8	
	William Lemke	Union	882,479	1.9	—	
1940	**FRANKLIN D. ROOSEVELT (N.Y.)**	Democratic	27,244,160	54.8	449	62.5
	Wendell L. Willkie	Republican	22,305,198	44.8	82	
1944	**FRANKLIN D. ROOSEVELT (N.Y.)**	Democratic	25,602,504	53.5	432	55.9
	Thomas E. Dewey	Republican	22,006,285	46.0	99	
1948	**HARRY S. TRUMAN (Mo.)**	Democratic	24,105,695	49.5	304	53.0
	Thomas E. Dewey	Republican	21,969,170	45.1	189	
	J. Strom Thurmond	State-Rights Democratic	1,169,021	2.4	38	
	Henry A. Wallace	Progressive	1,156,103	2.4	—	
1952	**DWIGHT D. EISENHOWER (N.Y.)**	Republican	33,936,252	55.1	442	63.3
	Adlai E. Stevenson	Democratic	27,314,992	44.4	89	
1956	**DWIGHT D. EISENHOWER (N.Y.)**	Republican	35,575,420	57.6	457	60.6
	Adlai E. Stevenson	Democratic	26,033,066	42.1	73	
	Other	—	—		1	
1960	**JOHN F. KENNEDY (Mass.)**	Democratic	34,227,096	49.9	303	62.8
	Richard M. Nixon	Republican	34,108,546	49.6	219	
	Other	—	—		15	
1964	**LYNDON B. JOHNSON (Tex.)**	Democratic	43,126,506	61.1	486	61.7
	Barry M. Goldwater	Republican	27,176,799	38.5	52	
1968	**RICHARD M. NIXON (N.Y.)**	Republican	31,770,237	43.4	301	60.6
	Hubert H. Humphrey	Democratic	31,270,533	42.7	191	
	George Wallace	American Indep.	9,906,141	13.5	46	
1972	**RICHARD M. NIXON (N.Y.)**	Republican	47,169,911	60.7	520	55.2
	George S. McGovern	Democratic	29,170,383	37.5	17	
	Other	—	—		1	
1976	**JIMMY CARTER (Ga.)**	Democratic	40,828,587	50.0	297	53.5
	Gerald R. Ford	Republican	39,147,613	47.9	241	
	Other	—	1,575,459	2.1	—	
1980	**RONALD REAGAN (Calif.)**	Republican	43,901,812	50.7	489	52.6
	Jimmy Carter	Democratic	35,483,820	41.0	49	
	John B. Anderson	Independent	5,719,722	6.6	—	
	Ed Clark	Libertarian	921,188	1.1	—	
1984	**RONALD REAGAN (Calif.)**	Republican	54,455,075	59.0	525	53.3
	Walter Mondale	Democratic	37,577,185	41.0	13	
1988	**GEORGE BUSH (Texas)**	Republican	47,946,422	54.0	426	50.2
	Michael S. Dukakis	Democratic	41,016,429	46.0	112	
1992	**WILLIAM J. CLINTON (Ark.)**	Democratic	44,908,233	43.3	370	55.2
	George Bush	Republican	39,102,282	37.7	168	
	Ross Perot	Independent	19,721,433	19.0	—	
1996	**WILLIAM J. CLINTON (Ark.)**	Democratic	47,401,185	49.3	379	
	Robert Dole	Republican	39,197,469	40.7	159	49.0
	Ross Perot	Reform	8,085,294	8.4	—	
2000	**GEORGE W. BUSH (Texas)**	Republican	50,459,211	47.89	271	51.0
	Albert Gore, Jr.	Democratic	51,003,894	48.41	266	
	Ralph Nader	Green	2,834,410	2.69	—	
2004	**GEORGE W. BUSH (Texas)**	Republican	62,028,285	50.73	286	
	John Kerry	Democratic	59,028,109	48.27	251	60.0
	Ralph Nader	Independent	463,647	0.38	0	

Note: All data from www.fec.gov (federal election commission) www.fec.gov/pubrec/fe2004/2004presgen.shtml

Vice Presidents and Cabinet Members

The Washington Administration (1789–1797)

Vice President	John Adams	1789–1797
Secretary of State	Thomas Jefferson	1789–1793
	Edmund Randolph	1794–1795
	Timothy Pickering	1795–1797
Secretary of Treasury	Alexander Hamilton	1789–1795
	Oliver Wolcott	1795–1797
Secretary of War	Henry Knox	1789–1794
	Timothy Pickering	1795–1796
	James McHenry	1796–1797
Attorney General	Edmund Randolph	1789–1793
	William Bradford	1794–1795
	Charles Lee	1795–1797
Postmaster General	Samuel Osgood	1789–1791
	Timothy Pickering	1791–1794
	Joseph Habersham	1795–1797

The John Adams Administration (1797–1801)

Vice President	Thomas Jefferson	1797–1801
Secretary of State	Timothy Pickering	1797–1800
	John Marshall	1800–1801
Secretary of Treasury	Oliver Wolcott	1797–1800
	Samuel Dexter	1800–1801
Secretary of War	James McHenry	1797–1800
	Samuel Dexter	1800–1801
Attorney General	Charles Lee	1797–1801
Postmaster General	Joseph Habersham	1797–1801
Secretary of Navy	Benjamin Stoddert	1798–1801

The Jefferson Administration (1801–1809)

Vice President	Aaron Burr	1801–1805
	George Clinton	1805–1809
Secretary of State	James Madison	1801–1809
Secretary of Treasury	Samuel Dexter	1801
	Albert Gallatin	1801–1809
Secretary of War	Henry Dearborn	1801–1809
Attorney General	Levi Lincoln	1801–1805
	Robert Smith	1805
	John Breckinridge	1805–1806
	Caesar Rodney	1807–1809
Postmaster General	Joseph Habersham	1801
	Gideon Granger	1801–1809
Secretary of Navy	Robert Smith	1801–1809

The Madison Administration (1809–1817)

Vice President	George Clinton	1809–1813
	Elbridge Gerry	1813–1817
Secretary of State	Robert Smith	1809–1811
	James Monroe	1811–1817
Secretary of Treasury	Albert Gallatin	1809–1813
	George Campbell	1814
	Alexander Dallas	1814–1816
	William Crawford	1816–1817
Secretary of War	William Eustis	1809–1812
	John Armstrong	1813–1814
	James Monroe	1814–1815
	William Crawford	1815–1817
Attorney General	Caesar Rodney	1809–1811
	William Pinkney	1811–1814
	Richard Rush	1814–1817
Postmaster General	Gideon Granger	1809–1814
	Return Meigs	1814–1817
Secretary of Navy	Paul Hamilton	1809–1813
	William Jones	1813–1814
	Benjamin Crowninshield	1814–1817

The Monroe Administration (1817–1825)

Vice President	Daniel Tompkins	1817–1825
Secretary of State	John Quincy Adams	1817–1825
Secretary of Treasury	William Crawford	1817–1825
Secretary of War	George Graham	1817
	John C. Calhoun	1817–1825
Attorney General	Richard Rush	1817
	William Wirt	1817–1825
Postmaster General	Return Meigs	1817–1823
	John McLean	1823–1825

Secretary of Navy	Benjamin Crowninshield	1817–1818
	Smith Thompson	1818–1823
	Samuel Southard	1823–1825

The John Quincy Adams Administration (1825–1829)

Vice President	John C. Calhoun	1825–1829
Secretary of State	Henry Clay	1825–1829
Secretary of Treasury	Richard Rush	1825–1829
Secretary of War	James Barbour	1825–1828
	Peter Porter	1828–1829
Attorney General	William Wirt	1825–1829
Postmaster General	John McLean	1825–1829
Secretary of Navy	Samuel Southard	1825–1829

The Jackson Administration (1829–1837)

Vice President	John C. Calhoun	1829–1833
	Martin Van Buren	1833–1837
Secretary of State	Martin Van Buren	1829–1831
	Edward Livingston	1831–1833
	Louis McLane	1833–1834
	John Forsyth	1834–1837
Secretary of Treasury	Samuel Ingham	1829–1831
	Louis McLane	1831–1833
	William Duane	1833
	Roger B. Taney	1833–1834
	Levi Woodbury	1834–1837
Secretary of War	John H. Eaton	1829–1831
	Lewis Cass	1831–1837
	Benjamin Butler	1837
Attorney General	John M. Berrien	1829–1831
	Roger B. Taney	1831–1833
	Benjamin Butler	1833–1837
Postmaster General	William Barry	1829–1835
	Amos Kendall	1835–1837
Secretary of Navy	John Branch	1829–1831
	Levi Woodbury	1831–1834
	Mahlon Dickerson	1834–1837

The Van Buren Administration (1837–1841)

Vice President	Richard M. Johnson	1837–1841
Secretary of State	John Forsyth	1837–1841
Secretary of Treasury	Levi Woodbury	1837–1841

Secretary of War	Joel Poinsett	1837–1841
Attorney General	Benjamin Butler	1837–1838
	Felix Grundy	1838–1840
	Henry D. Gilpin	1840–1841
Postmaster General	Amos Kendall	1837–1840
	John M. Niles	1840–1841
Secretary of Navy	Mahlon Dickerson	1837–1838
	James Paulding	1838–1841

The William Harrison Administration (1841)

Vice President	John Tyler	1841
Secretary of State	Daniel Webster	1841
Secretary of Treasury	Thomas Ewing	1841
Secretary of War	John Bell	1841
Attorney General	John J. Crittenden	1841
Postmaster General	Francis Granger	1841
Secretary of Navy	George Badger	1841

The Tyler Administration (1841–1845)

Vice President	None	
Secretary of State	Daniel Webster	1841–1843
	Hugh S. Legaré	1843
	Abel P. Upshur	1843–1844
	John C. Calhoun	1844–1845
Secretary of Treasury	Thomas Ewing	1841
	Walter Forward	1841–1843
	John C. Spencer	1843–1844
	George Bibb	1844–1845
Secretary of War	John Bell	1841
	John C. Spencer	1841–1843
	James M. Porter	1843–1844
	William Wilkins	1844–1845
Attorney General	John J. Crittenden	1841
	Hugh S. Legaré	1841–1843
	John Nelson	1843–1845
Postmaster General	Francis Granger	1841
	Charles Wickliffe	1841
Secretary of Navy	George Badger	1841
	Abel P. Upshur	1841
	David Henshaw	1843–1844
	Thomas Gilmer	1844
	John Y. Mason	1844–1845

The Polk Administration (1845-1849)

Vice President	George M. Dallas	1845-1849
Secretary of State	James Buchanan	1845-1849
Secretary of Treasury	Robert J. Walker	1845-1849
Secretary of War	William L. Marcy	1845-1849
Attorney General	John Y. Mason	1845-1846
	Nathan Clifford	1846-1848
	Isaac Toucey	1848-1849
Postmaster General	Cave Johnson	1845-1849
Secretary of Navy	George Bancrocft	1845-1846
	John Y. Mason	1846-1849

The Taylor Administration (1849-1850)

Vice President	Millard Fillmore	1849-1850
Secretary of State	John M. Clayton	1849-1850
Secretary of Treasury	William Meredith	1849-1850
Secretary of War	George Crawford	1849-1850
Attorney General	Reverdy Johnson	1849-1850
Postmaster General	Jacob Collamer	1849-1850
Secretary of Navy	William Preston	1849-1850
Secretary of Interior	Thomas Ewing	1849-1850

The Fillmore Administration (1850-1853)

Vice President	None	
Secretary of State	Daniel Webster	1850-1852
	Edward Everett	1852-1853
Secretary of Treasury	Thomas Corwin	1850-1853
Secretary of War	Charles Conrad	1850-1853
Attorney General	John J. Crittenden	1850-1853
Postmaster General	Nathan Hall	1850-1852
	Sam D. Hubbard	1852-1853
Secretary of Navy	William A. Graham	1850-1852
	John P. Kennedy	1852-1853
Secretary of Interior	Thomas McKennan	1850
	Alexander Stuart	1850-1853

The Pierce Administration (1853-1857)

Vice President	William R. King	1853-1857
Secretary of State	William L. Marcy	1853-1857
Secretary of Treasury	James Guthrie	1853-1857
Secretary of War	Jefferson Davis	1853-1857
Attorney General	Caleb Cushing	1853-1857
Postmaster General	James Campbell	1853-1857
Secretary of Navy	James C. Dobbin	1853-1857
Secretary of Interior	Robert McClelland	1853-1857

The Buchanan Administration (1857-1861)

Vice President	John C. Breckinridge	1857-1861
Secretary of State	Lewis Cass	1857-1860
	Jeremiah S. Black	1860-1861
Secretary of Treasury	Howell Cobb	1857-1860
	Philip Thomas	1860-1861
	John A. Dix	1861
Secretary of War	John B. Floyd	1857-1861
	Joseph Holt	1861
Attorney General	Jeremiah S. Black	1857-1860
	Edwin M. Stanton	1860-1861
Postmaster General	Aaron V. Brown	1857-1859
	Joseph Holt	1859-1861
	Horatio King	1861
Secretary of Navy	Isaac Toucey	1857-1861
Secretary of Interior	Jacob Thompson	1857-1861

The Lincoln Administration (1861-1865)

Vice President	Hannibal Hamlin	1861-1865
	Andrew Johnson	1865
Secretary of State	William H. Seward	1861-1865
Secretary of Treasury	Salmon P. Chase	1861-1864
	William P. Fessenden	1864-1865
	Hugh McCulloch	1865
Secretary of War	Simon Cameron	1861-1862
	Edwin M. Stanton	1862-1865
Attorney General	Edward Bates	1861-1864
	James Speed	1864-1865

Postmaster General	Horatio King	1861
	Montgomery Blair	1861–1864
	William Dennison	1864–1865
Secretary of Navy	Gideon Welles	1861–1865
Secretary of Interior	Caleb B.Smith	1861–1863
	John P. Usher	1863–1865

The Andrew Johnson Administration (1865–1869)

Vice President	None	
Secretary of State	William H. Seward	1865–1869
Secretary of Treasury	Hugh McCulloch	1865–1869
Secretary of War	Edwin M. Stanton	1865–1867
	Ulysses S. Grant	1867–1868
	Lorenzo Thomas	1868
	John M. Schofield	1868–1869
Attorney General	James Speed	1865–1866
	Henry Stanbery	1866–1868
	William M. Evarts	1868–1869
Postmaster General	William Dennison	1865–1866
	Alexander Randall	1866–1869
Secretary of Navy	Gideon Welles	1865–1869
Secretary of Interior	John P. Usher	1865
	James Harlan	1865–1866
	Orville H. Browning	1866–1869

The Grant Administration (1869–1877)

Vice President	Schuyler Colfax	1869–1873
	Henry Wilson	1873–1877
Secretary of State	Elihu B. Washburne	1869
	Hamilton Fish	1869–1877
Secretary of Treasury	George S. Boutwell	1869–1873
	William Richardson	1873–1874
	Benjamin Bristow	1874–1876
	Lot M. Morrill	1876–1877
Secretary of War	John A. Rawlins	1869
	William T. Sherman	1869
	William W. Belknap	1869–1876
	Alphonso Taft	1876
	James D. Cameron	1876–1877
Attorney General	Ebenezer Hoar	1869–1870
	Amos T. Ackerman	1870–1871
	G. H. Williams	1871–1875
	Edwards Pierrepont	1875–1876
	Alphonso Taft	1876–1877

Postmaster General	John A. J. Creswell	1869–1874
	James W. Marshall	1874
	Marshall Jewell	1874–1876
	James N. Tyner	1876–1877
Secretary of Navy	Adolph E. Borie	1869
	George M. Robeson	1869–1877
Secretary of Interior	Jacob D. Cox	1869–1870
	Columbus Delano	1870–1875
	Zachariah Candler	1875–1877

The Hayes Administration (1877–1881)

Vice President	William A. Wheeler	1877–1881
Secretary of State	William M. Evarts	1877–1881
Secretary of Treasury	John Sherman	1877–1881
Secretary of War	George W. McCrary	1877–1879
	Alex Ramsey	1879–1881
Attorney General	Charles Devens	1877–1881
Postmaster General	David M. Key	1877–1880
	Horace Maynard	1880–1881
Secretary of Navy	Richard W. Thompson	1877–1880
	Nathan Goff, Jr.	1881
Secretary of Interior	Carl Schurz	1877–1881

The Garfield Administration (1881)

Vice President	Chester A. Arthur	1881
Secretary of State	James G. Blaine	1881
Secretary of Treasury	William Windom	1881
Secretary of War	Robert T. Lincoln	1881
Attorney General	Wayne MacVeagh	1881
Postmaster General	Thomas L. James	1881
Secretary of Navy	William H. Hunt	1881
Secretary of Interior	Samuel J. Kirkwood	1881

The Arthur Administration (1881–1885)

Vice President	None	
Secretary of State	F. T. Frelinghuysen	1881–1885
Secretary of Treasury	Charles J. Folger	1881–1884
	Walter Q. Gresham	1884
	Hugh McCulloch	1884–1885

Secretary of War	Robert T. Lincoln	1881-1885
Attorney General	Benjamin H. Brewster	1881-1885
Postmaster General	Timothy O. Howe	1881-1883
	Walter Q. Gresham	1883-1884
	Frank Hatton	1884-1885
Secretary of Navy	William H. Hunt	1881-1882
	William E. Chandler	1882-1885
Secretary of Interior	Samuel J. Kirkwood	1881-1882
	Henry M. Teller	1882-1885

The Cleveland Administration (1885-1889)

Vice President	Thomas A. Hendricks	1885-1889
Secretary of State	Thomas F. Bayard	1885-1889
Secretary of Treasury	Daniel Manning	1885-1887
	Charles S. Fairchild	1887-1889
Secretary of War	William C. Endicott	1885-1889
Attorney General	Augustus H. Garland	1885-1889
Postmaster General	William F. Vilas	1885-1888
	Don M. Dickinson	1888-1889
Secretary of Navy	William C. Whitney	1885-1889
Secretary of Interior	Lucius Q.C. Lamar	1885-1888
	William F. Vilas	1888-1889
Secretary of Agriculture	Norman J. Colman	1889

The Benjamin Harrison Administration (1889-1893)

Vice President	Levi P. Morton	1889-1893
Secretary of State	James G. Blaine	1889-1892
	John W. Foster	1892-1893
Secretary of Treasury	William Windom	1889-1891
	Charles Foster	1891-1893
Secretary of War	Redfield Proctor	1889-1891
	Stephen B. Elkins	1891-1893
Attorney General	William H. H. Miller	1889-1891
Postmaster General	John Wanamaker	1889-1893
Secretary of Navy	Benjamin F. Tracy	1889-1893
Secretary of Interior	John W. Noble	1889-1893
Secretary of Agriculture	Jeremiah M. Rusk	1889-1893

The Cleveland Administration (1893-1897)

Vice President	Adlai E. Stevenson	1893-1897
Secretary of State	Walter Q. Gresham	1893-1895
	Richard Olney	1895-1897
Secretary of Treasury	John G. Carlisle	1893-1897
Secretary of War	Daniel S. Lamont	1893-1897
Attorney General	Richard Olney	1893-1895
	James Harmon	1895-1897
Postmaster General	Wilson S. Bissell	1893-1895
	William L. Wilson	1895-1897
Secretary of Navy	Hilary A. Herbert	1893-1897
Secretary of Interior	Hoke Smith	1893-1896
	David R. Francis	1896-1897
Secretary of Agriculture	Julius S. Morton	1893-1897

The McKinley Administration (1897-1901)

Vice President	Garret A. Hobart	1897-1901
	Theodore Roosevelt	1901
Secretary of State	John Sherman	1897-1898
	William R. Day	1898
	John Hay	1898-1901
Secretary of Treasury	Lyman J. Gage	1897-1901
Secretary of War	Russell A. Alger	1897-1899
	Elihu Root	1899-1901
Attorney General	Joseph McKenna	1897-1898
	John W. Griggs	1898-1901
	Philander C. Knox	1901
Postmaster General	James A. Gary	1897-1898
	Charles E. Smith	1898-1901
Secretary of Navy	John D. Long	1897-1901
Secretary of Interior	Cornelius N. Bliss	1897-1899
	Ethan A. Hitchcock	1899-1901
Secretary of Agriculture	James Wilson	1897-1901

The Theodore Roosevelt Administration (1901-1909)

Vice President	Charles Fairbanks	1905-1909
Secretary of State	John Hay	1901-1905
	Elihu Root	1905-1909
	Robert Bacon	1909

Secretary of Treasury	Lyman J. Gage	1901–1902
	Leslie M. Shaw	1902–1907
	George B. Cortelyou	1907–1909
Secretary of War	Elihu Root	1901–1904
	William H. Taft	1904–1908
	Luke E. Wright	1908–1909
Attorney General	Philander C. Knox	1901–1904
	William H. Moody	1904–1906
	Charles J. Bonaparte	1906–1909
Postmaster General	Charles E. Smith	1901–1902
	Henry C. Payne	1902–1904
	Robert J. Wynne	1904–1905
	George B. Cortelyou	1905–1907
	George von L. Meyer	1907–1909
Secretary of Navy	John D. Long	1901–1902
	William H. Moody	1902–1904
	Paul Morton	1904–1905
	Charles J. Bonaparte	1905–1906
	Victor H. Metcalf	1906–1908
	Truman H. Newberry	1908–1909
Secretary of Interior	Ethan A. Hitchcock	1901–1907
	James R. Garfield	1907–1909
Secretary of Agriculture	James Wilson	1901–1909
Secretary of Labor and Commerce	George B. Cortelyou	1903–1904
	Victor H. Metcalf	1904–1906
	Oscar S. Straus	1906–1909
	Charles Nagel	1909

The Taft Administration (1909–1913)

Vice President	James S. Sherman	1909–1913
Secretary of State	Philander C. Knox	1909–1913
Secretary of Treasury	Franklin MacVeagh	1909–1913
Secretary of War	Jacob M. Dickinson	1909–1911
	Henry L. Stimson	1911–1913
Attorney General	George W. Wickersham	1909–1913
Postmaster General	Frank H. Hitchcock	1909–1913
Secretary of Navy	George von L. Meyer	1909–1913
Secretary of Interior	Richard A. Ballinger	1909–1911
	Walter L. Fisher	1911–1913
Secretary of Agriculture	James Wilson	1909–1913
Secretary of Labor and Commerce	Charles Nagel	1909–1913

The Wilson Administration (1913–1921)

Vice President	Thomas R. Marshall	1913–1921
Secretary of State	William J. Bryan	1913–1915
	Robert Lansing	1915–1920
	Bainbridge Colby	1920–1921
Secretary of Treasury	William G. McAdoo	1913–1918
	Carter Glass	1918–1920
	David F. Houston	1920–1921
Secretary of War	Lindley M. Garrison	1913–1916
	Newton D. Baker	1916–1921
Attorney General	James C. McReynolds	1913–1914
	Thomas W. Gregory	1914–1919
	A. Mitchell Palmer	1919–1921
Postmaster General	Albert S. Burleson	1913–1921
Secretary of Navy	Josephus Daniels	1913–1921
Secretary of Interior	Franklin K. Lane	1913–1920
	John B. Payne	1920–1921
Secretary of Agriculture	David F. Houston	1913–1920
	Edwin T. Meredith	1920–1921
Secretary of Commerce	William C. Redfield	1913–1919
	Joshua W. Alexander	1919–1921
Secretary of Labor	William B. Wilson	1913–1921

The Harding Administration (1921–1923)

Vice President	Calvin Coolidge	1921–1923
Secretary of State	Charles E. Hughes	1921–1923
Secretary of Treasury	Andrew Mellon	1921–1923
Secretary of War	John W. Weeks	1921–1923
Attorney General	Harry M. Daugherty	1921–1923
Postmaster General	Will H. Hays	1921–1922
	Hubert Work	1922–1923
	Harry S. New	1923
Secretary of Navy	Edwin Denby	1921–1923
Secretary of Interior	Albert B. Fall	1921–1923
	Hubert Work	1923
Secretary of Agriculture	Henry C. Wallace	1921–1923
Secretary of Commerce	Herbert C. Hoover	1921–1923
Secretary of Labor	James J. Davis	1921–1923

The Coolidge Administration (1923-1929)

Vice President	Charles G. Dawes	1925-1929
Secretary of State	Charles E. Hughes	1923-1925
	Frank B. Kellogg	1925-1929
Secretary of Treasury	Andrew Mellon	1923-1929
Secretary of War	John W. Weeks	1923-1925
	Dwight F. Davis	1925-1929
Attorney General	Harry M. Daugherty	1923-1924
	Harlan F. Stone	1924-1925
	John G. Sargent	1925-1929
Postmaster General	Harry S. New	1923-1929
Secretary of Navy	Edwin Derby	1923-1924
	Curtis D. Wilbur	1924-1929
Secretary of Interior	Hubert Work	1923-1928
	Roy O. West	1928-1929
Secretary of Agriculture	Henry C. Wallace	1923-1924
	Howard M. Gore	1924-1925
	William M. Jardine	1925-1929
Secretary of Commerce	Herbert C. Hoover	1923-1928
	William F. Whiting	1928-1929
Secretary of Labor	James J. Davis	1923-1929

The Hoover Administration (1929-1933)

Vice President	Charles Curtis	1929-1933
Secretary of State	Henry L. Stimson	1929-1933
Secretary of Treasury	Andrew Mellon	1929-1932
	Ogden L. Mills	1932-1933
Secretary of War	James W. Good	1929
	Patrick J. Hurley	1929-1933
Attorney General	William D. Mitchell	1929-1933
Postmaster General	Walter F. Brown	1929-1933
Secretary of Navy	Charles F. Adams	1929-1933
Secretary of Interior	Ray L. Wilbur	1929-1933
Secretary of Agriculture	Arthur M. Hyde	1929-1933
Secretary of Commerce	Robert P. Lamont	1929-1932
	Roy D. Chapin	1932-1933
Secretary of Labor	James J. Davis	1929-1930
	William N. Doak	1930-1933

The Franklin D. Roosevelt Administration (1933-1945)

Vice President	John Nance Garner	1933-1941
	Henry A. Wallace	1941-1945
	Harry S. Truman	1945
Secretary of State	Cordell Hull	1933-1944
	Edward R. Stettinius, Jr.	1944-1945
Secretary of Treasury	William H. Woodin	1933-1934
	Henry Morgenthau, Jr.	1934-1945
Secretary of War	George H. Dern	1933-1936
	Henry A. Woodring	1936-1940
	Henry L. Stimson	1940-1945
Attorney General	Homer S. Cummings	1933-1939
	Frank Murphy	1939-1940
	Robert H. Jackson	1940-1941
	Francis Biddle	1941-1945
Postmaster General	James A. Farley	1933-1940
	Frank C. Walker	1940-1945
Secretary of Navy	Claude A. Swanson	1933-1940
	Charles Edison	1940
	Frank Knox	1940-1944
	James V. Forrestal	1944-1945
Secretary of Interior	Harold L. Ickes	1933-1945
Secretary of Agriculture	Henry A. Wallace	1933-1940
	Claude R. Wickard	1940-1945
Secretary of Commerce	Daniel C. Roper	1933-1939
	Harry L. Hopkins	1939-1940
	Jesse Jones	1940-1945
	Henry A. Wallace	1945
Secretary of Labor	Frances Perkins	1933-1945

The Truman Administration (1945-1953)

Vice President	Alben W. Barkley	1949-1953
Secretary of State	Edward R. Stettinius, Jr.	1945
	James F. Byrnes	1945-1947
	George C. Marshall	1947-1949
	Dean G. Acheson	1949-1953
Secretary of Treasury	Fred M. Vinson	1945-1946
	John W. Snyder	1946-1953
Secretary of War	Robert P. Patterson	1945-1947
	Kenneth C. Royall	1947
Attorney General	Tom C. Clark	1945-1949
	J. Howard McGrath	1949-1952
	James P. McGranery	1952-1953

Postmaster General	Frank C. Walker	1945
	Robert E. Hannegan	1945–1947
	Jesse M. Donaldson	1947–1953
Secretary of Navy	James V. Forrestal	1945–1947
Secretary of Interior	Harold L. Ickes	1945–1946
	Julius A. Krug	1946–1949
	Oscar L. Chapman	1949–1953
Secretary of Agriculture	Clinton P. Anderson	1945–1948
	Charles F. Brannan	1948–1953
Secretary of Commerce	Henry A. Wallace	1945–1946
	W. Averell Harriman	1946–1948
	Charles W. Sawyer	1948–1953
Secretary of Labor	Lewis B. Schwellenbach	1945–1948
	Maurice J. Tobin	1948–1953
Secretary of Defense	James V. Forrestal	1947–1949
	Louis A. Johnson	1949–1950
	George C. Marshall	1950–1951
	Robert A. Lovett	1951–1953

The Eisenhower Administration (1953–1961)

Vice President	Richard M. Nixon	1953–1961
Secretary of State	John Foster Dulles	1953–1959
	Christian A. Herter	1959–1961
Secretary of Treasury	George M. Humphrey	1953–1957
	Robert B. Anderson	1957–1961
Attorney General	Herbert Brownell, Jr.	1953–1958
	William P. Rogers	1958–1961
Postmaster General	Arthur E. Summerfield	1953–1961
Secretary of Interior	Douglas McKay	1953–1956
	Fred A. Seaton	1956–1961
Secretary of Agriculture	Ezra T. Benson	1953–1961
Secretary of Commerce	Sinclair Weeks	1953–1958
	Lewis L. Strauss	1958–1959
	Frederick H. Mueller	1959–1961
Secretary of Labor	Martin P. Durkin	1953
	James P. Mitchell	1953–1961
Secretary of Defense	Charles E. Wilson	1953–1957
	Neil H. McElroy	1957–1959
	Thomas S. Gates Jr.	1959–1961
Secretary of Health, Education, and Welfare	Oveta Culp Hobby	1953–1955
	Marion B. Folsom	1955–1958
	Arthur S. Flemming	1958–1961

The Kennedy Administration (1961–1963)

Vice President	Lyndon B. Johnson	1961–1963
Secretary of State	Dean Rusk	1961–1963
Secretary of Treasury	C. Douglas Dillon	1961–1963
Attorney General	Robert F. Kennedy	1961–1963
Postmaster General	J. Edward Day	1961–1963
	John A. Gronouski	1963
Secretary of Interior	Stewart L. Udall	1961–1963
Secretary of Agriculture	Orville L. Freeman	1961–1963
Secretary of Commerce	Luther H. Hodges	1961–1963
Secretary of Labor	Arthur J. Goldberg	1961–1962
	W. Willard Wirtz	1962–1963
Secretary of Defense	Robert S. McNamara	1961–1963
Secretary of Health, Education, and Welfare	Abraham A. Ribicoff	1961–1962
	Anthony J. Celebrezze	1962–1963

The Lyndon Johnson Administration (1963–1969)

Vice President	Hubert H. Humphrey	1965–1969
Secretary of State	Dean Rusk	1963–1969
Secretary of Treasury	C. Douglas Dillon	1963–1965
	Henry H. Fowler	1965–1969
Attorney General	Robert F. Kennedy	1963–1964
	Nicholas Katzenbach	1965–1966
	Ramsey Clark	1967–1969
Postmaster General	John A. Gronouski	1963–1965
	Lawrence F. O'Brien	1965–1968
	Marvin Watson	1968–1969
Secretary of Interior	Stewart L. Udall	1963–1969
Secretary of Agriculture	Orville L. Freeman	1963–1969
Secretary of Commerce	Luther H. Hodges	1963–1964
	John T. Connor	1964–1967
	Alexander B. Trowbridge	1967–1968
	Cyrus R. Smith	1968–1969
Secretary of Labor	W. Willard Wirtz	1963–1969
Secretary of Defense	Robert F. McNamara	1963–1968
	Clark Clifford	1968–1969

Secretary of Health, Education, and Welfare	Anthony J. Celebrezze	1963–1965
	John W. Gardner	1965–1968
	Wilbur J. Cohen	1968–1969
Secretary of Housing and Urban Development	Robert C. Weaver	1966–1969
	Robert C. Wood	1969
Secretary of Transportation	Alan S. Boyd	1967–1969

The Nixon Administration (1969–1974)

Vice President	Spiro T. Agnew	1969–1973
	Gerald R. Ford	1973–1974
Secretary of State	William P. Rogers	1969–1973
	Henry S. Kissinger	1973–1974
Secretary of Treasury	David M. Kennedy	1969–1970
	John B. Connally	1971–1972
	George P. Shultz	1972–1974
	William E. Simon	1974
Attorney General	John N. Mitchell	1969–1972
	Richard G. Kleindienst	1972–1973
	Elliot L. Richardson	1973
	William B. Saxbe	1973–1974
Postmaster General	Winton M. Blount	1969–1971
Secretary of Interior	Walter J. Hickel	1969–1970
	Rogers Morton	1971–1974
Secretary of Agriculture	Clifford M. Hardin	1969–1971
	Earl L. Butz	1971–1974
Secretary of Commerce	Maurice H. Stans	1969–1972
	Peter G. Peterson	1972–1973
	Frederick B. Dent	1973–1974
Secretary of Labor	George P. Shultz	1969–1970
	James D. Hodgson	1970–1973
	Peter J. Brennan	1973–1974
Secretary of Defense	Melvin R. Laird	1969–1973
	Elliot L. Richardson	1973
	James R. Schlesinger	1973–1974
Secretary of Health, Education, and Welfare	Robert H. Finch	1969–1970
	Elliot L. Richardson	1970–1973
	Caspar W. Weinberger	1973–1974
Secretary of Housing and Urban Development	George Romney	1969–1973
	James T. Lynn	1973–1974
Secretary of Transportation	John A. Volpe	1969–1973
	Claude S. Brinegar	1973–1974

The Ford Administration (1974–1977)

Vice President	Nelson A. Rockefeller	1974–1977
Secretary of State	Henry A. Kissinger	1974–1977
Secretary of Treasury	William E. Simon	1974–1977
Attorney General	William Saxbe	1974–1975
	Edward Levi	1975–1977
Secretary of Interior	Rogers Morton	1974–1975
	Stanley K. Hathaway	1975
	Thomas Kleppe	1975–1977
Secretary of Agriculture	Earl L. Butz	1974–1976
	John A. Knebel	1976–1977
Secretary of Commerce	Frederick B. Dent	1974–1975
	Rogers Morton	1975–1976
	Elliot L. Richardson	1976–1977
Secretary of Labor	Peter J. Brennan	1974–1975
	John T. Dunlop	1975–1976
	W. J. Usery	1976–1977
Secretary of Defense	James R. Schlesinger	1974–1975
	Donald Rumsfeld	1975–1977
Secretary of Health, Education, and Welfare	Caspar Weinberger	1974–1975
	Forrest D. Mathews	1975–1977
Secretary of Housing and Urban Development	James T. Lynn	1974–1975
	Carla A. Hills	1975–1977
Secretary of Transportation	Claude Brinegar	1974–1975
	William T. Coleman	1975–1977

The Carter Administration (1977–1981)

Vice President	Walter F. Mondale	1977–1981
Secretary of State	Cyrus R. Vance	1977–1980
	Edmund Muskie	1980–1981
Secretary of Treasury	W. Michael Blumenthal	1977–1979
	G. William Miller	1979–1981
Attorney General	Griffin Bell	1977–1979
	Benjamin R. Civiletti	1979–1981
Secretary of Interior	Cecil D. Andrus	1977–1981
Secretary of Agriculture	Robert Bergland	1977–1981
Secretary of Commerce	Juanita M. Kreps	1977–1979
	Philip M. Klutznick	1979–1981
Secretary of Labor	F. Ray Marshall	1977–1981

Secretary of Defense	Harold Brown	1977–1981
Secretary of Health, Education and Welfare	Joseph A. Califano Patricia R. Harris	1977–1979 1979
Secretary of Health and Human Services	Patricia R. Harris	1979–1981
Secretary of Education	Shirley M. Hufstedler	1979–1981
Secretary of Housing and Urban Development	Patricia R. Harris Moon Landrieu	1977–1979 1979–1981
Secretary of Transportation	Brock Adams Neil E. Goldschmidt	1977–1979 1979–1981
Secretary of Energy	James R. Schlesinger Charles W. Duncan	1977–1979 1979–1981

The Reagan Administration (1981–1989)

Vice President	George Bush	1981–1989
Secretary of State	Alexander M. Haig George P. Shultz	1981–1982 1982–1989
Secretary of Treasury	Donald Regan James A. Baker III Nicholas F. Brady	1981–1985 1985–1988 1988–1989
Attorney General	William F. Smith Edwin A. Meese III Richard Thornburgh	1981–1985 1985–1988 1988–1989
Secretary of Interior	James Watt William P. Clark, Jr. Donald P. Hodel	1981–1983 1983–1985 1985–1989
Secretary of Agriculture	John Block Richard E. Lyng	1981–1986 1986–1989
Secretary of Commerce	Malcolm Baldrige C. William Verity, Jr.	1981–1987 1987–1989
Secretary of Labor	Raymond Donovan William Brock Ann D. McLaughlin	1981–1985 1985–1987 1987–1989
Secretary of Defense	Caspar Weinberger Frank C. Carlucci	1981–1987 1987–1989
Secretary of Health and Human Services	Richard Schweiker Margaret Heckler Otis R. Bowen	1981–1983 1983–1985 1985–1989
Secretary of Education	Terrel H. Bell William J. Bennett Laura F. Cavazos	1981–1985 1985–1988 1988–1989

Secretary of Housing and Urban Development	Samuel Pierce	1981–1989
Secretary of Transportation	Drew Lewis Elizabeth Dole James H. Burnley	1981–1983 1983–1987 1987–1989
Secretary of Energy	James Edwards Donald P. Hodel John S. Herrington	1981–1982 1982–1985 1984–1989

The George H. W. Bush Administration (1989–1993)

Vice President	J. Danforth Quayle	1989–1993
Secretary of State	James A. Baker III Lawrence S. Eagleburger	1989–1992 1992–1993
Secretary of Treasury	Nicholas F. Brady	1989–1993
Attorney General	Richard Thornburgh William P. Barr	1989–1991 1991–1993
Secretary of Interior	Manuel Lujan	1989–1993
Secretary of Agriculture	Clayton K. Yeutter Edward Madigan	1989–1991 1991–1993
Secretary of Commerce	Robert A. Mosbacher Barbara H. Franklin	1989–1992 1992–1993
Secretary of Labor	Elizabeth Dole Lynn M. Martin	1989–1991 1991–1993
Secretary of Defense	Richard B. Cheney	1989–1993
Secretary of Health and Human Services	Louis W. Sullivan	1989–1993
Secretary of Education	Laura F. Cavazos Lamar Alexander	1989–1991 1991–1993
Secretary of Housing and Urban Development	Jack F. Kemp	1989–1993
Secretary of Transportation	Samuel K. Skinner Andrew H. Card	1989–1992 1992–1993
Secretary of Energy	James D. Watkins	1989–1993
Secretary of Veterans Affairs	Edward J. Derwinski	1989–1993

The Clinton Administration (1993–2001)

Vice President	Albert Gore, Jr.	1993–2001
Secretary of State	Warren M. Christopher Madeleine Albright	1993–1997 1997–2001

Secretary of Treasury	Lloyd Bentsen	1993–1995
	Robert E. Rubin	1995–1999
	Lawrence H. Summers	1999–2001
Attorney General	Janet Reno	1993–2001
Secretary of Interior	Bruce Babbitt	1993–2001
Secretary of Agriculture	Mike Espy	1993–1995
	Daniel R. Glickman	1995–2001
Secretary of Commerce	Ronald H. Brown	1993–1996
	Mickey Kantor	1996–1997
	William M. Daley	1997–2000
	Norman Minetta	2001
Secretary of Labor	Robert B. Reich	1993–1997
	Alexis M. Herman	1997–2001
Secretary of Defense	Les Aspin	1993–1994
	William Perry	1994–1996
	William S. Cohen	1996–2001
Secretary of Health and Human Services	Donna E. Shalala	1993–2001
Secretary of Education	Richard W. Riley	1993–2001
Secretary of Housing and Urban Development	Henry G. Cisneros	1993–1997
	Andrew Cuomo	1997–2001
Secretary of Transportation	Federico Pena	1993–1997
	Rodney E. Slater	1997–2001
Secretary of Energy	Hazel O'Leary	1993–1997
	Federico Pena	1997–1998
	Bill Richardson	1998–2001
Secretary of Veteran Affairs	Jesse Brown	1993–1998
	Togo D. West, Jr.	1998–2000
	Hershel Gober (Acting)	2000–2001

The George W. Bush Administration (2001–09)

Vice President	Richard B. Cheney	2001–
Secretary of State	Colin Powell	2001–2005
	Condoleezza Rice	2005–
Secretary of Treasury	Paul O'Neill	2001–2002
	Kenneth W. Dam (Acting)	2002–2003
	John Snow	2003–
Attorney General	John Ashcroft	2001–2005
	Alberto Gonzales	2005–
Secretary of Interior	Gale Norton	2001–
Secretary of Agriculture	Anne M. Venemen	2001–2005
	Mike Johanns	2005–
Secretary of Commerce	Don Evans	2001–2005
	Carlos Gutierrez	2005–
Secretary of Labor	Elaine Chao	2001–
Secretary of Defense	Donald Rumsfeld	2001–
Secretary of Health and Human Services	Tommy G. Thompson	2001–2005
	Michael O. Leavitt	2005–
Secretary of Education	Roderick Paige	2001–2005
	Margaret Spellings	2005–
Secretary of Housing and Urban Development	Melquiades R. Martinez	2001–2003
	Alphonso Jackson	2003–2005
Secretary of Transportation	Norman Mineta	2001
Secretary of Energy	Spencer Abraham	2001–2005
	Samuel W. Bodman	2005–
Secretary of Veteran Affairs	Anthony Principi	2001–2005
	Jim Nicholson	2005–
Secretary of Homeland Security	Tom Ridge	2003–2005
	Michael Chertoff	2005–

Population of the United States, 1790–2000

Year	Population	Percent Increase	Population per Square Mile	Percent Urban/ Rural	Percent White/ Nonwhite	Median Age
1790	3,929,214		4.5	5.1/94.9	80.7/19.3	NA
1800	5,308,483	35.1	6.1	6.1/93.9	81.1/18.9	NA
1810	7,239,881	36.4	4.3	7.3/92.7	81.0/19.0	NA
1820	9,638,453	33.1	5.5	7.2/92.8	81.6/18.4	16.7
1830	12,866,020	33.5	7.4	8.8/91.2	81.9/18.1	17.2
1840	17,069,453	32.7	9.8	10.8/89.2	83.2/16.8	17.8
1850	23,191,876	35.9	7.9	15.3/84.7	84.3/15.7	18.9
1860	31,443,321	35.6	10.6	19.8/80.2	85.6/14.4	19.4
1870	39,818,449	26.6	13.4	25.7/74.3	86.2/13.8	20.2
1880	50,155,783	26.0	16.9	28.2/71.8	86.5/13.5	20.9
1890	62,947,714	25.5	21.2	35.1/64.9	87.5/12.5	22.0
1900	75,994,575	20.7	25.6	39.6/60.4	87.9/12.1	22.9
1910	91,972,266	21.0	31.0	45.6/54.4	88.9/11.1	24.1
1920	105,710,620	14.9	35.6	51.2/48.8	89.7/10.3	25.3
1930	122,775,046	16.1	41.2	56.1/43.9	89.8/10.2	26.4
1940	131,669,275	7.2	44.2	56.5/43.5	89.8/10.2	29.0
1950	150,697,361	14.5	50.7	64.0/36.0	89.5/10.5	30.2
1960	179,323,175	18.5	50.6	69.9/30.1	88.6/11.4	29.5
1970	203,302,031	13.4	57.4	73.5/26.5	87.6/12.4	28.0
1980	226,545,805	11.4	64.0	73.7/26.3	86.0/14.0	30.0
1990	248,718,000	9.8	70.3	77.5/22.5	83.8/16.2	32.9
2000	281,421,906	13.0	79.6	79.0/21.0	83.0/17.0	35.3

Employment, 1870–2000

Year	Number of Workers (in millions)	Male/Female Employment Ratio	Percentage of Workers in Unions
1870	12.5	85/15	—
1880	17.4	85/15	—
1890	23.3	83/17	—
1900	29.1	82/18	3
1910	38.2	79/21	6
1920	41.6	79/21	12
1930	48.8	78/22	7
1940	53.0	76/24	27
1950	59.6	72/28	25
1960	69.9	68/32	26
1970	82.1	63/37	25
1980	108.5	58/42	23
1985	108.9	57/43	19
1990	118.8	55/45	16
2000	134.3	53/47	13.5

Production, Trade, and Federal Spending/Debt, 1790–2000

Year	Gross National Product (GNP) (in billions $)	Balance of Trade (in billions $)	Federal Budget (in billions $)	Federal Surplus/Deficit (in billions $)	Federal Debt (in billions $)
1790	—	−3	.004	+0.00015	.076
1800	—	−20	.011	+0.0006	.083
1810	—	−18	.008	+0.0012	.053
1820	—	−4	.018	−0.0004	.091
1830	—	+3	.015	+0.100	.049
1840	—	+25	.024	−0.005	.004
1850	—	−26	.040	+0.004	.064
1860	—	−38	.063	−0.01	.065
1870	7.4	−11	.310	+0.10	2.4
1880	11.2	+92	.268	+0.07	2.1
1890	13.1	+87	.318	+0.09	1.2
1900	18.7	+569	.521	+0.05	1.2
1910	35.3	+273	.694	−0.02	1.1
1920	91.5	+2,880	6.357	+0.3	24.3
1930	90.7	+513	3.320	+0.7	16.3
1940	100.0	−3,403	9.6	−2.7	43.0
1950	286.5	+1,691	43.1	−2.2	257.4
1960	506.5	+4,556	92.2	+0.3	286.3
1970	992.7	+2,511	196.6	+2.8	371.0
1980	2,631.7	+24,088	579.6	−59.5	914.3
1985	4,087.7	−148,480	946.3	212.3	1,827.5
1990	5,764.9	−101,012	1,251.8	−220.5	4,064.6
2000	9,860.8	−369.7	1,789.6	+237.0	5,674.2

Index

Note: Some page numbers are in italics and are followed by letters; these refer to illustrations (*i*), maps (*m*), or tables (*t*).

Abolitionism, 330-336
Academy and College of Philadelphia, 93
ACS, 330
Act Concerning Religion, 38
Adams, Abigail, 146, 147
Adams, Charles Francis, Jr., 387
Adams, John, 122, 128, 129, 138, 142-143, 168, 175, 176, 177, 178, 215
Adams, John Quincy, 212, 223, 228-230, 336
Adams, Samuel, 116, 121, 128, 155
Adams-Onis Treaty, 223
African Americans, disenfranchising laws, 427; Jeffersonian era, 186-187; Jim Crow laws, 427, 428-429; lynchings, 428-430; minstrel shows, 285, 423; poverty (1820-1850), 280
African slave trade, 20-23
Africans bound for America, 74*i*
After Slavery (Williamson), 428
Age of Jackson, The (Schlesinger), 236
Age of Reason, The (Paine), 128*i*, 185
Age of revolutions, 142-143
Agassiz, Louis, 360
Agrarians (Ashworth), 237
Agricultural revolution, 8
Agricultural technology, 37-38
Agriculture (1813-1852), 274-275, 288-290
Alabama, 387
Alabama claims, 416
Albany Plan, 103
Albany Regency, 236
Alcott, Bronson, 327
Alexander, Francis, 1/1*i*
Alexander, Thomas B., 418
Algonquin tribes, 7
Alien Act, 176-177
Alien menace, 264
Almanacs, 94-95
Alton anti-abolitionist riot, 358*i*
Amana Community, 321
America (1700), 66*m*
America (1800), 193*m*
America before Columbus, 4-9
American Antislavery Society, 331
American Colonization Society (ACS), 330
American Dictionary of the English Language, An (Webster), 184
American imports and exports (1790-1820), 217*t*
American Museum, 288
American Negro Slavery (Phillips), 306
American Party, 265
American Political Tradition (Hofstadter), 236
American Revolution Considered as a Social Movement, The (Jameson), 130
"American Scholar, The" (Emerson), 318
American Slavery, American Freedom (Morgan), 73
American Slavery as It Is: Testimony of a Thousand Witnesses (Weld/Grimké), 336

American Society for the Promotion of Temperance, 324
American Society of Pewterers, 148*i*
American Spelling Book (Webster), 184
American Star, 158*i*
American System, 228, 250
American Tobacco Company, 423
America's economic revolution (1813-1852), 258-291; agriculture, 274-275, 288-290; artisans, 277-278; birth rate, 283; business, 271-272; canal age, 265-268; child labor, 275, 278; corporation, 271, 274; Erie Canal, 267; factories, 272-273; factory towns, 273; family structure, 282-283; geographical mobility, 281; immigrant work force, 277, 278; immigration, 260*t*, 261-263, 264*i*, 264*t*; journalism, 271; Know-Nothings, 265, 266*i*; labor force, 274-277; leisure activities, 285-288; Lowell System, 276-277; merchant capitalism, 274; middle-class life, 281-282; Native American Party, 264; nativism, 263-265; northeastern agriculture, 288; Old Northwest, 288-290; population, 260-261, 262*m*, 263*m*; railroads, 268-270; rural life, 290; social mobility, 280-281; steamboats, 266; technology, 273; telegraph, 270-271; unions, 277, 278; wealth inequality, 279-280; women, 242*i*, 275, 276-277, 283-285
Amherst, Jeffrey, 106
Amistad case, 336
Anderson, Robert, 360
Andros, Sir Edmund, 61
Anglicans, 144
Anglo-French conflicts, 104-107
Anne, Queen, 105
Antebellum culture and reform, 314-317; asylum movement, 327-328; community living, 319-320; crusade against slavery, 330-336; education, 326-327; health fads, 324-325; Indian reservation, 328; literature, 316-318, 334-335; medical science, 326; Mormons, 321-322; nature, 319; Oneida community, 320-321; painting, 316; phrenology, 325-326; revivalism, 323; Shakers, 321; temperance crusade, 323-324; transcendentalists, 318-319; Utopian community, 319-320; women, 329-330
Anthony, Susan B., 329, 379
Anti-abolitionism, 332-334
Anti-Catholicism, 91
Anti-federalists, The (Main), 165
Anti-Leislerians, 61
Anti-lynching movement, 429-430
Anti-Masons, 249
Anti-Nebraska Democrats, 356
Anti-Nebraska Whigs, 356
Antietam, 393
Antifederalists, 167
Antinomianism, 45

Appomattox Courthouse, 398
Aptheker, Herbert, 306
Arawaks, 53
Aristocrats (Ashworth), 237
Arizona, 56
Ark, 38
Arnold, Benedict, 135, 137, 140
Aroostook War, 254
Ashburton, Lord, 254, 255
Ashley, William, 221
Associated Press, 271
Astor, John Jacob, 220, 343
Astor Place riot, 286, 287*i*
Asylum movement, 327-328
Atlanta (after the burning), 383*i*
Atlanta Compromise, 426
Atlantic World, 22
Attucks, Crispus, 100*i*, 116
Austin, Stephen F., 341, 342
Austin, Texas (1840), 342*i*
Automatic reaper, 289
Aztecs, 4, 5, 12

Bacon, Nathaniel, 39-40
Bacon's Rebellion, 39-40
Bagley, Sarah, 277
Bailyn, Bernard, 131
Balboa, Vasco de, 12
Baldwin, Joseph G., 318
Baltimore, Lord, 38, 61
Baltimore Sun, 255
Bancroft, George, 130
Bank note, 169*i*, 272
Bank of the United States, 170, 216, 246-247
Bank war, 246-247, 248*i*
Banneker, Benjamin, 94
Baptists, 91
Barbados, 49, 53, 54*i*
Barbary Company, 24
Barbary pirates, 198
Barlow, Joel, 184-185
Barnard, Henry, 326
Barnum, P. T., 288, 422
Barron, James, 205
Barrow plantation, 412*m*
Barton, Clara, 379
Baseball, 285, 384-385
Bastille Day, 142*i*
Battle of Brandywine Creek, 137
Battle of Bunker Hill, 134, 136*i*
Battle of Chancellorsville, 393
Battle of Chattanooga, 395
Battle of Chickamauga, 394
Battle of Fair Oaks, 391
Battle of Horseshoe Bend, 209
Battle of Murfreesboro, 390
Battle of Nashville, 396
Battle of New Orleans, 211
Battle of Plattsburgh, 211
Battle of San Jacinto, 342
Battle of Shiloh, 390

Battle of Spotsylvania Court House, 395
Battle of the Seven Days, 391
Battle of the Wilderness, 395
Battle of Tippecanoe, 207–208
Battle of Trafalgar, 204
Battle of Wilson's Creek, 389
Bayonet rule, 418, 419
Beale, Howard K., 418
Bear Flag Revolution, 348
Beard, Charles A., 164, 372
Beard, Mary, 372
Beaumarchais, Caron de, 139
Beauregard, P. G. T., 370, 389, 390
Becker, Carl, 130
Becknell, William, 220
Beecher, Catharine, 329, 330
Been in the Storm So Long (Litwack), 419
Beer's Almanac, 95
Belknap, William W., 415
Bell, John, 363
Benevolent empire, 327
Benin, 20
Benjamin, Judah P., 387
Bennett, James Gordon, 254
Berkeley, Sir John, 51
Berkeley, Sir William, 39
Berlin, Ira, 428
Bernard, S., 241*i*
Biddle, Nicholas, 246, 247
Bierstadt, Albert, 316
Bill of Rights, 168
Bingham, George Caleb, 232*i*
Birney, James G., 336
Birth of a Nation, The, 418
Bismarck, Otto von, 381
Black abolitionists, 331–332
Black academies, 411
Black Belt of Central Alabama, 220
Black Codes, 406
Black Death, 9
Black Family in Slavery and Freedom, The
 (Gutman), 306
Black Hawk, 242, 242*i*
Black Hawk War, 242–243
Black Majority (Wood), 73
Black minstrels, 423
Black Reconstruction (Du Bois), 418
Blackwell, Antoinette Brown, 329
Blackwell, Elizabeth, 329
Blair, Francis P., 239
Blassingame, John, 306
Bleeding, 69
"Bleeding Kansas," 356–357, 358*i*, 361–362
Blithedale Romance, The (Hawthorne), 319
Blood Mary (Queen of England), 26
Bloomer, Amelia, 330
Bloomer costume, 330
Blue-backed speller, 184
Board of Trade and Plantations, 102
Bolivar, Simón, 143, 229
Bombardment of Fort McHenry, 211*i*
Bonaparte, Napoleon, 143, 176, 200
Booth, Edwin, 287
Booth, John Wilkes, 287, 405
Booth, Junius Bratus, Jr., 287*i*
Booth, William Junius, 287
Boston, 42, 61

Boston Massacre, 100*i*, 116–117
Boston Tea Party, 119
Bourbons, 421
Braddock, Edward, 105
Bradford, William, 40, 41
Brady, Matthew, 239*i*, 287*i*, 378
Bragg, Braxton, 385, 390, 394–395
Brant, Joseph, 138
Brant, Mary, 110, 138
Breckinridge, John C., 363
Briggs, Isaac, 95
Bright, John, 387
Bristol, 25*i*
Bristow, Benjamin H., 415
British empire, 52–53, 59–62
Broadside against "nobility," 161
Broadway in 1836, 262*i*
Brook Farm, 319
Brooks, Preston, 300, 357
Brown, Charles Brockden, 185
Brown, John, 336, 357, 362
Brown, Joseph, 382
Brown, Moses, 188
Brown, Robert E., 130, 165
Bruce, Blanche K., 410
Bruff, Joseph Goldsborough, 222*i*
Buchanan, James, 359–362, 368, 373
Bucktails, 236
Buell, Don Carlos, 390
Bull Run, 389, 393
Bullocke, James, 194
Burgoyne, John, 136–138
Burke, Edmund, 122
Burned-over district, 323
Burning of Washington, 180*i*
Burnside, Ambrose E., 393
Burr, Aaron, 178, 202–204
Burr conspiracy, 202–204
Butler, Andrew P., 357

Cabinet (1789), 168
Cabot, John, 23
Cahokia, 5
Cahokia Indian mounds, 6*i*
Calhoun, John C., 209, 219, 223, 239–241,
 250, 253, 343, 353, 359
California, 56, 346–347
California gold rush, 351–353
Calloway, Colin, 131
Calvert, Cecilius, 38, 38*i*
Calvert, Charles, 38
Calvert, George, 38
Calvert, Leonard, 38
Calvin, John, 25, 26*i*
Calvinism, 25
Cammeyer, William, 385
Camp followers, 146, 147*i*
Canal age, 265–268
Candles, 80
Cane Ridge, 92
Caribbean islands, 53–55
Caribbean (17th century), 55*m*
Caribs, 53
Carnegie, Andrew, 389
Carolinas, 48–50
Caroline affair, 253
Carpetbaggers, 410

Carroll, Charles, 84, 144
Carroll, John, 144
Carteret, Sir George, 51
Cartwright, Alexander, 384
Cartwright, Peter, 92
Caruthers, William Alexander, 318
Cash, W. J., 428
Cass, Lewis, 351
Cast-iron plow, 289
Cast-iron stove, 281
Catholic Irish, 77
Catholic missions, 15
Catlin, George, 8
Caucus system, 228
Cavalier image, 298
Cavaliers, 48
Cavelier, René Robert, 104
Cavour, Camillo di, 381
Cell, John, 429
Central Park, 280*i*
Chadwick, Henry, 384
Champlain, Samuel de, 28
Chandler, Winthrop, 64*i*
Chants Democratic (Wilentz), 237
Charles I, 42, 48
Charles II, 48, 50, 52, 60, 61
Charles River Bridge v. *Warren Bridge,* 248
Charles Town, 48, 49
Charleston (1831), 241*i*
Charlestown, South Carolina, 49*m*
Charter of Liberties, 52
Chartered companies, 24
Chase, Samuel, 199
Chatham, Lord, 115, 122
Cherokee Nation v. *Georgia,* 243
Cherokee resistance/removal, 243
Chesapeake, 34–40, 69–70, 78
Chesapeake-Leopard incident, 205
Chicago (1858), 272*i*
Chickasaw, 244
Child labor, 275, 278
Choctawa, 244
Cholera, 324
Christensen, Carl, 322*i*
Church, Frederic, 316
Church of England, 26, 90
Ciboney, 53
Circus, 285, 288
Civil Rights Act of 1866, 406
Civil Rights Act of 1875, 411
Civil rights cases of 1883, 427
Civil War, 366–399; Antietam, 393;
 Appomattox Courthouse, 398; Atlanta,
 383*i*, 396; baseball, 384–385; black
 soldiers, 377; casualties, 398; commanders,
 384–386; Confiscation Acts, 376;
 Crittenden Compromise, 368; draft riots,
 375; Emancipation Proclamation, 376;
 Europe, 387–388; food draft, 382; Fort
 Sumter, 368–370; Gettysburg, 394, 395*i*;
 historian disagreements, 372; irrepressible
 conflict argument, 372–373; King Cotton
 diplomacy, 387; last stage of war
 (1864–1865), 395–398; maps, 369*m*,
 391*m*, 392*m*, 394*m*, 395*m*, 396*m*, 397*m*;
 March to the Sea, 396–398; mobilization of
 the North, 371–379; mobilization of the

South, 379-383; National Bank Acts, 374; nursing/medicine, 378-379; opening clashes (1861), 389-390; Peninsular campaign, 390; railroads, 371*i*, 389; repressible conflict argument, 373; sea power, 386-387; Shiloh, 390; Southern advantages, 371; Southern resources, 370*i*; states' rights, 382; technology of battle, 388-389; telegraph, 389; Thirteenth Amendment, 377; Trent Affair, 387; Union advantages, 370; Union resources, 370*i*; Vicksbury, 394; Virginia front, 390-393, 396*m*; war begins, 370; western theater, 388, 390, 391*i*; women, 378-379, 383

Clark, George Rogers, 139
Clark, William, 202
Class divisions, 7
Clay, Henry, 209, 212, 223, 225, 228, 229, 241, 246, 250, 252, 341, 346, 353
Clay eaters, 303
Clermont, 192, 218*i*
Clinton, De Witt, 236, 266
Clinton, Sir Henry, 139, 141
Coal, 273
Cobden, Richard, 387
Coercive Acts, 120-121
Coffin handbill, 230
Cohens v. *Virginia,* 226
Cole, Thomas, 316
Colfax, Schuyler, 415
College of New Jersey, 93
Colonial almanacs, 94-95
Colonial America, 32-98; agricultural technology, 37-38; almanacs, 94-95; Bacon's Rebellion, 39-40; California, 56; Caribbean islands, 53-55; Chesapeake, 34-40, 69-70, 78; cities, 88-89; colleges, 93; commerce, 81-82; consumerism, 82-83; economy, 78-81; education, 93; Enlightenment, 92-93; Georgia, 57; German immigrants, 76; Glorious Revolution, 61-62; Goode's Rebellion, 61-62; Great Awakening, 91-92; Huguenots, 75; immigration, 75-77; industrial servitude, 66-67, 68*i*; Jamestown, 34-35; law, 96-97; life expectancy, 68, 70; Maryland, 38-39; Massachusetts, 42; medicine, 68-69; merchant class, 82; middle grounds, 58-59; Navigation Acts, 60; New England, 40-42, 61, 68, 70-71; New Jersey, 51; New York, 50-51; North/South Carolina, 48-50; northern economy, 78-80; Pennsylvania Dutch, 76; plantation, 83-86; Plymouth Plantation, 40; politics, 97; Puritan community, 71, 86-87; Quaker colonies, 51-52; religion, 90-92; restoration colonies, 48-52; science, 93-96; self-sufficiency, 81, sex ratio, 68, 70; slavery, 71-75; southeast borderlands, 56-57; southern borderlands, 55-56; southern economy, 78; Spain's northern colonies, 55-56; Stono Rebellion, 86; stratified southern society, 84-85; tobacco, 35, 78; triangular trade, 81*m*, 82; Virginia, 34-35, 39; witchcraft, 87-88, 89
Colonial charters, 30

Colonial cities, 88-89
Colonial commerce, 81-82
Colonial currency, 43*i*
Colonial governments, 97
Colored conventions, 410
Colt, Samuel, 388
Columbia University, 93
Columbiad, The (Barlow), 185
Columbian Centinel, 223
Columbus, Christopher, 11-12
Coming of the Civil War, The (Craven), 373
Command of the Army Act, 408
Committee of the Conduct of the War, 385
Committees of correspondence, 121
Common Sense, 128*i*, 129
Commonwealth v. *Hunt,* 278
Community living, 319-320
Compromise of 1850, 353-355
Compromise of 1877, 417-419, 428-429
Comte, Auguste, 6
Concept of Jacksonian Democracy, The (Benson), 237
Conciliatory Propositions, 122
Concord, Battle of, 122-124
Confederate flag, 368*i*
Confiscation Acts, 376
Congo, 20
Congregational Church, 42
Congregationalism, 90
Connecticut Valley, 43
Conquistadores, 12-14, 18
Constitution of 1787, 163
Consumerism, 82-83
Continental Association, 122
Continental impost, 155
Continental System, 204
Contract theory, 129
Convict-lease system, 424
Coode, John, 61
Cooper, Anthony Ashley, 48, 49
Cooper, James Fenimore, 316
Cooper, Peter, 269*i*
Copley, John Singleton, 150*i*
Copperheads, 375
Cornwallis, Lord, 126*i*, 140-142
Coronado, Francisco, 14
Corporation, 271, 274
Corrupt bargain, 228-229
Cortés, Hernando, 12-13
Cotton, 220, 294-295, 296*m*
Cotton, John, 42, 45
Cotton, slavery, and Old South, 292-313; cavalier image, 298; colonial dependency, 298; cotton, 294-295, 296*m*; cult of honor, 300; education, 302; hill people, 302; manufacturing, 295; plain folk, 301-303; planter class, 298-301; slavery, 303-312; transportation system, 295, 297; women, 301
Cotton gin, 188-189
Cotton Kingdom, 295
Counterblaste to Tobacco, 35
Country Whigs, 117
Countryman, Edward, 131
Coureurs de bois, 28
Courts; Indian tribes, 226-227; Jeffersonian era, 198-200; Marshall, John, 225-227; Taney, Roger B., 247-248

Cowpens, 141
Crackers, 303
Crandall, Prudence, 332
Craven, Avery, 373
Crawford, William H., 228
Creation of the American Republic, The (Wood), 165
Credit, 272, 413
Crédit Mobilier, 415
Creeks, 244
Creole affair, 254
Creoles, 143
"Crime Against Kansas, The" (Sumner), 357
Crisis, The, 128*i*
Critical Period of American History, The (Fiske), 164
Crittenden, John J., 368
Crittenden Compromise, 368
Crockett, Davy, 342
Cromwell, Oliver, 39, 60
Crop-lien system, 412-413, 425*i*
Crosby, Alfred, 9
Crucible (Miller), 89
C.S.S. Tennessee, 397*i*
Cuffe, Paul, 330
Culture, 7
Cumming v. *County Board of Education,* 427
Currency Act of 1764, 111
Currier, Nathaniel, 324*i*
Cushing, Caleb, 255
Cylindrical press, 271*i*

da Gama, Vasco, 11
Dale, Sir Thomas, 35, 37
Dame school primer, 94*i*
Dame schools, 93, 94*i*
Dana, Charles A., 255
Dare, Virginia, 29
Darkest America, 423
Dartmouth College v. *Woodward,* 226
Daughters of Liberty, 119
Davies, Thomas, 141*i*
Davis, Jefferson, 243, 354, 356, 379, 385, 398, 402, 411
Dawes, William, 123
Day, Benjamin, 254
De Bow, James B. D., 297
De Bow's Review, 297-298
de Grasse, François Joseph Paul, 141
De La Warr, Lord, 35
de Soto, Hernando, 13, 15*i*
de Varennes, Pierre Gaultier, 104
de Verger, Jean Baptiste, 133*i*
Death of Lincoln, 405
DeBry, Theodore, 30*i*
Declaration of Sentiments, 329
Declaratory Act, 114
Deere, John, 289
Deerslayer, The (Cooper), 316
Degas, Edgar, 294*i*
Degler, Carl, 72
Democracy in America (Tocqueville), 233
Democrats, 237, 249
Demographic catastrophic, 18
Denevan, William M., 9
Deskilling, 277

Devil in the Shape of a Woman, The
    (Karlsen), 89
Dew, Thomas R., 359
Dias, Bartholomeu, 11
Dickinson, John, 128
Discovery, 34
Disfranchising laws, 427
Distribution act, 250
District of Columbia, 194–198
Disunion, 364
Dix, Dorothea, 327, 329, 378
Djenne, 20*i*
Dobyns, Henry, 9
Doctrine of personal regeneration, 323
Doctrine of predestination, 25
Doctrine of the Inner Light, 52
Doeg Indians, 39–40
Dominion of New England, 61
Donald, David Herbert, 418
Dorr, Thomas L., 235
Dorr Rebellion, 235
Doubleday, Abner, 384
Doughty, Thomas, 316
Douglas, Stephen A., 270, 354, 356, 362, 363
Douglass, Frederick, 311, 331*i*, 332, 332*i*, 333,
    360, 361
Dove, 38
Draft riots, 375
Dragging Canoe, 145
Drake, Sir Francis, 29
Dred Scott decision, 360–361
Drunkard's progress, 324*i*
Du Bois, W. E. B., 418
Duke, James B., 423
Dunning, William A., 418
Dupont, Sophie, 325*i*
Durand, Asher, 316
Dutch, 28–29, 50
Dutch Reformed, 91
Dutch West India Company, 50
Dwight, Timothy, 92

Earl of Shaftesbury, 48
Early North America, 4*m*
East India Company, 24, 118
Eaton, John H., 239
Eclipse-Henry match race, 195
Economic interests, 7
*Economic Interpretation of the Constitution
    of the United States, An* (Beard), 164
Edict of Nantes, 75
Education; antebellum period, 326–327;
    benevolent empire, 327; colonial America,
    93; Jeffersonian era, 182–183; Old South,
    302; reconstruction period, 411; women
    (1820–1850), 283–284
Edwards, Jonathan, 96
1807 war crisis, 206–207
Elections. *See* Presidential elections
Electric 3 Minstrels, 423*i*
Electricity, 96*i*
Eliot, John, 46
Elizabeth I, 26, 27*i*, 29
Elkins, Stanley, 306
Emancipation Proclamation, 376
Embargo, 205
Emerson, Ralph Waldo, 318, 370

Emmanuel, Victor, 380*i*
Empire in transition, 100–125; Albany Plan,
    103; Anglo-French conflicts, 104–107;
    Boston Massacre, 100*i*, 116–117; Boston
    Tea Party, 119; Coercive Acts, 120–121;
    Conciliatory Propositions, 122; Concord,
    Battle of, 122–124; Currency Act of 1764,
    111; Declaratory Act, 114; English
    constitution, 117–118; First Continental
    Congress, 121–122; French and Indian
    War, 103–107; internal and external taxes,
    115; Iroquois Confederacy, 104–107;
    Lexington, Battle of, 122–124; Mutiny Act
    of 1764, 110; Paxton Boys, 112;
    Proclamation of 1763, 108*m*, 110;
    Regulator movement, 112; Seven Years'
    War, 103–107; Stamp Act crisis, 113–114;
    Stamp Act of 1765, 111; Tea Act of 1773,
    118–119; Townshend duties, 115; virtual
    vs. actual representation, 118
Enclosure movement, 24
Encomiendas, 17
Enforcement Acts (Ku Klux Klan Acts), 416
Engerman, Stanley, 306
English canal age, 191
English Caribbean, 53
English Civil War, 48
English constitution, 117–118
English indentures, 68
English Reformation, 25–26
English Restoration, 33, 60
Enlightenment, 22, 92–93, 333
Entertaining Satan (Demos), 89
Equality, 149
Era of Reconstruction, The (Stampp), 419
Erie Canal, 267
Eriksson, Leif, 9
Ernst, Joseph, 131
Espy, James Pollard, 361*i*
Essex Junto, 203
Europe and West Africa (15th century),
    21*m*
Europe looks west, 9–23
European exploration and conquest
    (1492–1583), 13*m*
European Reformation, 24–25, 26*i*
Evangelical Protestantism, 323
Evans, Oliver, 188, 191
Ex parte Marryman, 376
Ex parte Milligan, 376, 409
Expanding settlement (1810–1850), 340*m*
*Experiments and Observations on
    Electricity,* 96*i*

Facing East from Indian Country (Richter), 58
Factor system, 219
Factory Girls Associations, 277
Factory system, 190
Factory towns, 275
Farewell address (Washington), 175
Farmer's Almanac, 94
Farragut, David G., 390, 397*i*
*Fathers and Children: Andrew Jackson and
    the Subjugation of the American Indian*
    (Rogin), 237
Federalist Papers, 166*i*, 167
Federalists, 166–170, 174

Fell, Margaret, 51
Female Labor Reform Association, 277
Female protective unions, 277, 278
Ferdinand of Aragon, 11
Fifteenth Amendment, 408
Fifty-four forty or fight!, 346, 347*i*
Fillmore, Millard, 354, 355, 359
Finney, Charles Grandison, 323
Fire-eater, 368
First Battle of Bull Run, 389
First Battle of Manassas, 389
First Continental Congress, 121–122
First English settlements, 29–30
First party system, 171
Fish, Hamilton, 414, 416
Fiske, John, 164
Fitch, John, 191
Fitzhugh, George, 301
Fletcher v. *Peck,* 225
Flintlock rifle, 47
Floating hell, 204
Florida, 57
Florida, 387
Fogel, Robert, 306
Foner, Eric, 372, 419
Food draft, 382
Force act, 205, 241
Forrest, Edwin, 286
Fort Donelson, 390
Fort Henry, 390
Fort McHenry, 211*i*
Fort Snelling, 219*i*
Fort Sumter, 368–370
Forty-niners, 351
Founding Fathers, 162
Four humors, 69
Fourier, Charles, 320
Fourteenth Amendment, 406
Fourth of July Picnic at Weymouth Landing
    (1845), 214*i*
Fowler, Orson and Lorenzo, 325
Fox, George, 51, 52
Fox-Genovese, Elizabeth, 306
Franco-Prussian War, 381
Franklin, Benjamin, 93, 94–95, 96*i*, 102, 103,
    109, 115, 129, 135, 139, 142–143, 147,
    162, 185
Franklin, John Hope, 419
Frederick the Great, 105
Fredrickson, George, 72
Free blacks, 307–308
Free Soil, Free Labor, Free Men (Foner), 372
Free-soil/free-labor ideology, 357–359
Free-Soil Party, 351, 355
Free-soilism, 336
Freedman's Bank, 411
Freedman's Bureau school, 404*i*, 411
Freethinkers, 188
Frémont, John C., 348, 359
French, 27–28, 47, 58
French and Indian War, 57, 103–107
French Jesuit missionaries, 28
French Revolution, 142*i*, 143, 172, 173
Frey, Silvia, 131
Friendless women, 328
Frobisher, Martin, 2*i*
Fugitive Slave Act, 355

Fugitive slave law convention, 331
"Fugitive's Song," 332*i*
Fuller, Margaret, 255, 320
Fulton, Robert, 192, 218, 218*i*
Fundamental Constitution for Carolina, 48, 49
Fundamental Orders of Connecticut, 43
Funding the debt, 169
Fur trade, 220–221

Gadsden, James, 356
Gadsden Purchase, 356
Gage, Thomas, 122, 123, 134
Galen, 69
Gallatin, Albert, 198, 212, 217
Galloway, Joseph, 121
Gang system, 304
Garibaldi, 380*i*
Garrison, William Lloyd, 330–336, 360
Gaspée, 118
Gates, Horatio, 137, 138, 141
Gates, Sir Thomas, 35
Genet, Edmond, 173
Genius of Universal Emancipation, 330
Genovese, Eugene, 306, 373
Geography Made Easy (Morse), 184
George I, 102
George II, 57, 102
George III, 107, 109, 110*i*, 119
Georgia, 57
Georgia Minstrels, 423
Georgia plantation, 299*m*
German immigrants, 76
German indentures, 68*i*
Gerry, Elbridge, 176
Gettysburg, 394, 395*i*
Ghana, 20
Gheeraerts, Marcus, 27*i*
Gibbons v. Ogden, 226
Gienapp, William, 373
Gilbert, Sir Humphrey, 27, 29
Girls' evening school (1840), 314*i*
Gladstone, William, 159
Gleason, William, 64*i*
Glorious Revolution, 61–62
Godey's Lady's Book, 284
Gold rush, 351–353
Gone With the Wind, 418
Goode's Rebellion, 61–62
Goodyear, Charles, 273
Goodspeed, 34
Gorges, Ferdinando, 45
Grady, Henry, 421–422
Graham, Sylvester, 325
Graham cracker, 325
Grandfather laws, 427
Grant, Ulysses S., 384, 386*i*, 390, 394–396,
  409*i*, 414–415, 417
Grant scandals, 415
Grantism, 414
Granville, Charles Bécard de, 5*i*
Gray, Robert, 343
Great Awakening, 22, 91–92
Great Compromise, 163
Great Swamp of Rhode Island, 47
Great Triumvirate, 250
Greeley, Horace, 414, 417
Greenbackers, 415

Greenbacks, 374
Greene, Nathanael, 141
Grenville, George, 109, 113
Grenville, Sir Richard, 27, 29
Grimké, Angelina, 329, 336
Grimké, Sarah, 329
Griswold, Roger, 177
Growth of New England (1620–1750), 44*m*
Growth of the Chesapeake (1607–1750), 35*m*
Guess, George, 227*i*
Guinea, 20
Guinea Company, 24
Gullah, 85
Gutman, Herbert, 306

Hakluyt, Richard, 24, 33
Hale, John P., 355
Hale, Sarah, 284
Halleck, Henry W., 384
Hamilton, Alexander, 155, 161, 165, 166*i*, 167,
  168, 169, 170, 172, 173, 174, 175, 198, 203
Hamilton, Andrew, 96
Hamilton-Burr duel, 203
Hammond, Bray, 236
Handlin, Oscar and Mary, 72
Hard-money faction, 246
Harpers Ferry Raid, 362, 363*i*
Harper's Magazine, 298
Harris, Joel Chandler, 422
Harrison, William Henry, 206–207, 209, 240*i*,
  250, 252, 343
Harrison Land Law, 206
Hartford Convention, 211, 212*i*
Hartford Wits, 185
Harvard, 93
Harvard, John, 93
Hasenclever, Peter, 79
Hathaway, Rufus, 80*i*
Hauling the Whole Week's Picking (Brown),
  304*i*
Hawley, Nathan, 284*i*
Hawthorne, Nathaniel, 319–320, 334
Hayes, Lemuel, 145
Hayes, Rutherford B., 417–420
Hayne, Robert Y., 240, 241
Head of a Negro (Copley), 150*i*
Headright system, 36, 39
Health fads, 324–325
Henry, Andrew, 221
Henry, Patrick, 113–114, 122
Henry the Navigator, Prince, 11
Henry VIII, 25–26
Herkimer, Nicholas, 137
Herrera, 12*i*
Herskovits, Melville J., 306
Hervieu, August, 301*i*
Hickory Paint, Kansas, 358*i*
Hicks, Edward, 283*i*
Highest Stage of White Supremacy, The (Cell),
  429
Hill, Isaac, 239
Hill people, 302
Hillsborough, Lord, 116
Historical interpretation, 7
History of the Revolution (Warren), 185
*History of the Rise and Fall of the Slave
  Power* (Wilson), 372

*History of the United States from the
  Compromise of 1850* (Rhodes), 372
Hoe, Richard, 271
Hoerder, Dirk, 131
Hofstadter, Richard, 236
Holbrook, Josiah, 360
Holmes, Oliver Wendell, 319, 326, 360
Holt, Michael, 373
Holy Roman Empire, 9
Homer, Winslow, 366*i*, 413*i*
Homespun, 149
Homestead Act of 1862, 374
"Honor," 300
Hood, John B., 396
Hooker, Joseph, 393, 394
Hooker, Thomas, 43
Hooper, Johnson J., 318
Hopeton Plantation, 299*m*
Horse racing, 194–195
House of Burgesses, 36, 113, 114
House of Seven Gables, The (Hawthorne), 320
House slaves, 307
Houston, Sam, 342
Howard, Oliver O., 404
Howe, Elias, 273
Howe, William, 135–138
Howells, William Dean, 255
Huckleberry Finn, 286
Huckleberry Finn, 287
Hudson, Henry, 28
Hudson River School, 316
Huguenots, 75
Hume, David, 166
Humoralism, 69
Hutchinson, Anne, 45, 45*i*
Hutchinson, Thomas, 114
Huxley, Thomas Henry, 6
Hydrotherapy, 325

Ideas, 7
*Ideological Origins of the American
  Revolution, The* (Bailyn), 131
Immigrants/immigration, America's economic
  revolution, 260*t*, 261–263, 264*i*, 264*t*;
  colonial America, 75–77, 77*m*; German
  immigrants, 76
Impressment, 106, 204–205
In the Devil's Snare (Norton), 89
Incas, 4, 5
Independence Day, 132*i*
Independent treasury, 251–252
Indian agricultural techniques, 37
Indian hunters, 352
Indian ring, 415
Indian slavery, 352
Indians of New France, 5*i*
Indigo, 78
Industrial revolution, 189–192, 190–191, 259
Industrial servitude, 66–67, 68*i*
Innocent VIII, Pope, 15
Interchangeable parts, 273
Internal and external taxes, 115
Into the American Woods (Merrell), 58
Ireland, 27
Ironclad Oath, 405
Ironclad warship, 386
Iroquois Confederacy, 7, 59, 104–107, 138

Iroquois women, 10*i*
Irrepressible conflict argument, 372-373
Irving, Washington, 185, 316
Isaac, Rhys, 131
Isabella of Castile, 11

Jackson, Andrew, 194, 209, 211, 223, 228-230,
    233-249, 328, 343
Jackson, Stonewall, 402
Jackson, Thomas J. ("Stonewall"), 390-391
Jacksonian America, 232-257; American
    System, 250; Anti-Masons, 249; Aroostook
    War, 254; bank war, 246-247, 248*i*; Black
    Hawk War, 242-243; broadening the
    franchise, 234-235; *Caroline* affair, 253;
    Creole affair, 254; distribution act, 250;
    Dorr Rebellion, 235; election of 1832,
    247*m*; election of 1836, 250; historian
    disagreements, 236-237; independent
    treasury, 251-252; log cabin campaign,
    252; nullification crisis, 241-242;
    nullification doctrine, 239; Panic of 1837,
    251; removal/expulsion of Indians,
    242-246; Seminole War, 245; spoils system,
    238; Taney court, 247-248; trade with
    China, 255-256; Treaty of Wang Hya, 255;
    two-party system, 237; Webster-Ashburton
    Treaty, 254-255; Webster-Hayne debate,
    240-241; Whig Party, 249-255
Jacksonian America (Pessen), 237
Jacksonian Persuasion, The (Meyer), 236
Jacobin period, 143
James, duke of York, 50, 51
James, Henry, 255
James I, 26, 29-30, 35, 37, 42
James II, 51, 61
Jamestown, 29, 34-35
Jarvis, John Wesley, 242*i*
Jay, John, 142-143, 166*i*, 167, 174
Jay Cooke and Company, 415
Jay's Treaty, 174
Jazz Singer, The, 423
Jefferson, Thomas, 129, 150, 151, 161, 168,
    170, 171, 172, 174, 175, 177, 178, 185,
    193-202, 205, 215
Jeffersonian era, 180-213; Barbary pirates,
    198; Burr conspiracy, 202-204;
    Chesapeake-Leopard incident, 205; cities,
    192-193; courts, 198-200; cultural
    aspirations, 184-185; District of Columbia,
    194-198; education, 182-183; 1807 war
    crisis, 206-207; embargo, 205; Hamilton-
    Burr duel, 203; Hartford Convention, 211,
    212*i*; Indian problem, 206-208; industrial
    revolution, 188-192; Jeffersonian vision,
    181; Louisiana purchase, 201-202;
    medicine, 183-184; Napoleon, 200;
    Napoleonic wars, 204; native Americans,
    183, 187, 206-208; Non-Intercourse Act,
    205; religious skepticism, 185; revolt of
    New England, 211; science, 183-184;
    Second Great Awakening, 185-188;
    shipping, 191; technology, 188-190;
    transportation innovations, 190-192;
    turnpike era, 191; War of 1812, 209-212;
    women, 182, 186
Jenner, Edward, 326

Jensen, Merrill, 164
Jeremiads, 91
Jeremiah, Thomas, 145
Jews, 91
John Brown's raid, 362, 363*i*
Johnson, Andrew, 405-406, 409, 411,
    419, 430
Johnson, Joseph E., 391
Johnson, Sir William, 110, 138
Johnson v. *McIntosh,* 226
Johnston, Albert Sidney, 390
Johnston, Joseph E., 395-398
Joint Committee on Reconstruction, 406
Joint occupation, 343
Joliet, Louis, 104
Jolson, Al, 423
Jones, Jacqueline, 419
Jordan, Winthrop D., 72
Judiciary Act of 1789, 168, 198
Judiciary Act of 1801, 178, 198

Kansas ("Bleeding Kansas"), 356-357, 358*i*,
    361-362
Kansas-Nebraska controversy, 356
Kearny, Stephen W., 348, 350*i*
Keckley, Elizabeth, 307
Kemble, Fanny, 330
Kemmelmeyer, Frederick, 158*i*
Kendall, Amos, 234, 239
Kennan, George F., 360
Kennedy, John Pendleton, 318
Kennesaw Mountain, 396
Kent, James, 235
Keppler, Joseph, 415*i*
Kerber, Linda, 131
Key, Francis Scott, 209, 211
King, Samuel, 235
King Caucus, 228
King Cotton diplomacy, 387
King George's War, 105
King Philip's War, 46-47, 59
King's College, 93
King's Mountain, 141
Kitchen Cabinet, 239
Kleppner, Paul, 373
Knights of the White Camellia, 416
Know-Nothings, 265, 266*i*
Knox, Henry, 168
Kroeber, Alfred, 8
Ku Klux Klan, 416-417
Ku Klux Klan Acts, 416-417

La Salle, Sieur de, 104
La Verendrye, Sieur de, 104
Labor of Love, Labor of Sorrow (Jones), 419
Labor unions, factories (1830-1850), 278;
    female millworkers (1830s), 277; female
    protective unions, 277, 278
Lafayette, Marquis de, 133, 141, 215
Lake, Handsome, 187-188
Lamar, Mirabeau, 342*i*
Land-grant institutions, 374
Land survey (Ordinance of 1785), 154*i*
Lane, Fitzhugh, 258*i*
Last of the Mohicans, The (Cooper), 316
Latin American revolution, 227-228
"Leatherstocking Tales" (Cooper), 316

Leaves of Grass (Whitman), 317
Lecompton constitution, 361-362
Lecture, 288
Lee, "Mother" Ann, 321
Lee, Richard Henry, 128
Lee, Robert E., 362, 385, 386*i*, 391-394,
    396-398, 402
Leisler, Jacob, 61
Leislerians, 61
Lemisch, Jesse, 131
Lena, Maggie, 425
L'Enfant, Pierre, 194, 196*m*
Leon, Francis, 423*i*
Levant Company, 24
Lewis, Meriwether, 202
Lewis and Clark Expedition, 201*i*, 202
Lexington, Battle of, 122-124
Liberator, 330-331
Liberty and Power (Watson), 237
Liberty Party, 336
Life of Washington (Weems), 185
Lincoln, Abraham, 243, 290, 335*i*, 360,
    362-364, 368, 370, 372, 375, 384, 385,
    402, 404, 405, 405*i*
Lincoln, Mary Todd, 307
Lincoln-Douglas debates, 362
Lincoln's 10% plan, 405
Literacy rate, 93
Literacy tests, 427
Literature, 316-318, 334-335
Little Turtle, 154, 155*i*
Litwack, Leon, 419, 428
Livingston, Robert R., 192, 200, 201, 218*i*
Locke, John, 22, 48, 117, 177
Locofocos, 249
Locomotive – horse-drawn carriage race, 269*i*
Log cabin campaign, 252
London Company, 34
Lone Star Flag, 341*i*
Long, Stephen H., 221-222
Long lots, 297*i*
Long-staple (Sea Island) cotton, 294
Longstreet, Augustus B., 318
Lord Dunmore's War, 146
"Lost Cause," 402, 403*i*
Lost Colony, 29
Louis XIV, 56
Louis XVI, 138
Louisiana, 56
Louisiana Constitutional Convention (1868),
    410*i*
Louisiana purchase, 201-202
L'Ouverture, Toussaint, 143, 200
Lovejoy, Elijah, 334, 358
Lowell, Francis Cabot, 216
Lowell, Massachusetts (1832), 258*i*, 275*m*
Lowell lectures, 360
Lowell mills, 258*i*
Lowell Offering, 276
Lowell System, 276-277
Lowery, George, 227*i*
Loyalists, 129
Lucas, Eliza, 78
Lucas, Sam, 423
Lundy, Benjamin, 330
Luther, Martin, 24
Lyceum, 360-361

Lynchings, 428–430
Lyon, Mary, 284
Lyon, Matthew, 177
Lyon-Griswold affair (brawl in Congress),
    177, 177*i*

Machine tools, 273
Macready, William, 286
Madison, Dolley, 208*i*
Madison, James, 155, 161, 162, 163, 165, 166,
    166*i*, 167, 168, 170, 171, 205, 208*i*, 209,
    218, 219, 222
Magellan, Ferdinand, 12
Main, Jackson Turner, 165
Maine, 45
Making of New World Slavery (Blackburn), 73
Malaria, 68
Mali, 20
Manifest Destiny, 340–341
Mann, Horace, 326, 327
Marbury v. *Madison,* 198
March to the Sea, 396–398
Marcy, William L., 238
Maria Theresa, 105
Marion, Francis, 140
Marquette, Jacques, 104
Marshall, John, 176, 199, 200, 225–227, 351
Marx, Karl, 255
Maryland, 38–39, 62
Mason, George, 129
Mason, James M., 387
Mason, John, 45, 46
Massachusetts, 42
Massachusetts Bay Company, 42
Match race, 195
Matchlock rifle, 47
Mather, Cotton, 95
Matrilineal societies, 21, 23
Mayas, 4, 5
Mayflower, 40
Mayflower Compact, 41
Mazzini, Giuseppe, 381
McClellan, George B., 376, 384, 389, 390–393
McCormick, Cyrus H., 289, 344*i*
McCormick, Richard L., 237
McCormick reaper, 289
McCormick Reaper Company, 344*i*
McCulloch v. *Maryland,* 226
McDowell, Irvin, 389, 390, 391
McIntosh, William, 229
McLeod, Alexander, 253, 254
McNeill, William, 9
Meade, George C., 394, 395
Medicine, antebellum period, 324–325, 326;
    Civil War, 378–379; colonial America,
    68–69; Jeffersonian era, 183–184
Meiji Japan, 381
Meiji reforms, 190
Melville, Herman, 317
Memphis race riot (1866), 407*i*
Mennonites, 76
Mercantilism, 24, 59
Merchant capitalism, 274
Merchant capitalists, 24
Merchant class, 82
Merrell, James, 58
Merrett, Susan, 214*i*

Merrimac, 386
Mestizos, 19
Metacomet, 46, 47
Metal works, 79
Methodism, 186
Methodist camp meeting (1837), 187*i*
Mexican War, 347–350
Mexico City, 55
Meyer, Marvin, 236
Meynell, Francis, 74*i*
Middle Ages, 9
Middle Ground, The (White), 58
Middle grounds, 58–59
Middle passage, 72, 74*i*, 82
Middlesex Company Woolen Mills (Lane),
    258*i*
Midnight appointments, 178
Midwives, 69
Militia diplomats, 138
Miller, Alfred Jacob, 238*i*
Miller, Peter, 89
Mind of the South, The (Cash), 428
Minstrel show, 285, 422–423
Minutemen, 122
Missouri Compromise, 224*m*, 225
Mobile Bay (1864), 397*i*
Moby Dick (Melville), 317
Molasses, 54*i*
Monitor, 387
Monroe, James, 174, 201, 205, 222–223, 228
Monroe Doctrine, 228
Monroe's goodwill tour, 222*i*, 223
Montcalm, Marquis de, 107
Montesquieu, Baron de, 165
Montezuma, 12
Montgomery, Richard, 135
Monument to the Lost Cause, 403*i*
Mooney, James, 8
Moore's Creek Bridge, 134
Moran, Thomas, 316
Moravian boys school (1800), 182*i*
Moravians, 76, 182*i*
More, Thomas, 23
Morgan, Edmund S., 130
Morgan, William, 249
Mormons, 321–322
Morrill Land Grant Act, 374
Morris, Robert, 155, 164
Morse, Jedidiah, 184
Morse, Samuel F. B., 270
Morton, William, 326
Mott, Lucretia, 329
Mount Holyoke, 284
Mount Vernon, 160*i*, 174*i*
Mulberry Plantation (1770), 72*i*, 85*i*
Murphy, Isaac, 195
Murray, James, 185
Murray, Judith Sargent, 146, 185
Muscovy Company, 24
Muskogean, 7
Mutiny Act of 1764, 110
Myth of self-sufficiency, 81

Name of War, The (Lepore), 59
Napoleonic wars, 204
Narragansetts, 47

Narrative of the Life of Frederick Douglass
    (Douglass), 332
Nash, Gary, 131
Nast, Thomas, 374, 420*i*
National Bank Acts, 374
National Greenback Party, 415
National Republicans, 230
National Trades' Union, 278
Native American Association, 264
Native American Party, 264
Native Americans, agricultural technologies,
    37; American Revolution, 138, 145–146,
    153–154; antebellum period, 327, 328;
    Battle of Fallen Timbers, 154; Black Hawk
    War, 242–243; education, 327; Five
    Civilized Tribes, 243; Indian hunters, 352;
    Jacksonian America, 242–246; Jeffersonian
    era, 183, 187, 206–208; King Philip's War,
    46–47; labor source, as, 20; Marshall court,
    226–227; middle grounds, 58–59; middle
    passage, 72, 74*i*; Pequot War, 46; post-
    revolutionary period, 172–173; Powhatan
    Indian, 37; praying Indians, 45; pre-colonial
    America, 5, 7–9, 20; Prophet
    (Tenskwatawa), 207; Second Great
    Awakening, 187; Seminole War, 223, 245;
    slavery, 352; Tecumseh, 207–208; Trail of
    Tears, 243–244; Woodland Indians, 5
Nativism, 263–265
Nature, 319
"Nature" (Emerson), 318
Nauvoo, Illinois, 321
Navigation Acts, 60
Negro rule, 410, 419
Neolin, 187
Nevins, Allan, 372
New Amsterdam, 28–29, 28*i*, 50
New England, 40, 48, 61, 68, 70, 71
New Hampshire, 45
New Harmony, 320
New Haven, 44
New Jersey, 51
New Left, 131
New Light dissenters, 186
New Light revivalists, 92, 323
New Market, 194
New Mexico, 55
New Nation, The (Jensen), 164
New Netherland, 29, 50
New Orleans, 192
New Orleans (1803), 203*i*
New York, 50–51, 62
New York City draft riot (1863), 375*i*
New York Herald, 254, 271
New York *Sun,* 254
New York Times, The, 255, 271
New York Tribune, 255, 271
Newburgh Conspiracy, 160
Nicholson, Francis, 61
Nicolls, Richard, 50
Niña, 11
Non-Intercourse Act, 205
North, Lord, 116, 119, 122, 142
North, Simeon, 273
North America (1763), 111*m*
North of Slavery (Litwack), 428
North/South Carolina, 48–50

North Star, 332
Northern Confederacy, 203
Norton, Mary Beth, 131
Nothing but Freedom (Foner), 419
Noyes, John Humphrey, 320
Nullification crisis, 241–242
Nullification doctrine, 239

Oakland House and Race Course
    (Brammer/Van Smith), 194
Oberlin, 283
Oglethorpe, James, 57
Old Light traditionalists, 92
Old Northwest, 220, 280–290
Old plantation, 292*i*, 311*i*
Olmsted, Frederick Law, 303
Oñate, Don Juan de, 17
O'Neale, Peggy, 239
Oneida community, 320–321
Oneida "Perfectionists," 320
Onondaga, 138
Openchancanough, 37
Ordeal of the Longhouse, The (Richter), 58
Ordeal of the Union, The (Nevins), 372
Ordinances of Discovery, 14
Oregon, 343, 346, 347*i*
Oregon Trail, 344
Original Meanings (Rakove), 165
Origins of the Republican Party, The
    (Gineapp), 373
"Origins of the Southern Labor System"
    (Handlin/Handlin), 72
Oriskany, 138, 145
Osceola, 244, 245
Ostend Manifesto, 355
O'Sullivan, John L., 340
Otis, James, 114
Owen, Robert, 320
Owenite experiments, 320

Page, Thomas Nelson, 422
Paine, Thomas, 128*i*, 129, 133, 185
Painting, 316
Pakenham, Sir Edward, 211
Palatinate, 75
Palatinate Germans, 75–76
Pale of settlement, 27
Palmerston, Lord, 253
Panic of 1819, 224
Panic of 1837, 251, 278
Paper money, 43*i*
Paragon, 218*i*
Park Theater, 286*i*
Pastoral America (1848), 283*i*
Paterson, William, 162
Patriarchal Puritan family, 71
Patriarchy, 70
Patroons, 29, 50
Paupers, 280
Pawtucket bridge and falls, 189*i*
Paxton Boys, 112
Peace Democrats, 375
Peace of Paris, 107
Peaceable coercion, 205
Peale, Rambrandt, 197*i*
Peculiar Institution, The (1956) (Stampp), 306
Peggy Eaton affair, 239–240

Peninsular campaign, 390
Penn, William, 52
Pennsylvania, 52
Pennsylvania asylum, 328*i*
Pennsylvania Dutch, 76, 76*i*
Pennsylvania hospital, 184*i*
Penny press, 254–255
Pequot Indians, 46
Pequot village destroyed, 47*i*
Pequot War, 46, 47*i*
Percy, Lord, 124*i*
Perkins School for the Blind, 327
Perry, Oliver Hazard, 209
Personal liberty laws, 356
Pet banks, 247, 250
Philadelphia, 52
Philadelphia Public Ledger, 254–255
Philip II, 29
Phillips, Ulrich B., 306
Phillips, Wendell, 360
Philomath Almanac, 94
Phrenology, 325–326
Phyfe, Duncan, 279*i*
Pickens, Andrew, 140
Pickering, John, 199
Pickering, Thomas, 175
Pickett's Charge, 394, 395*i*
Pidgin, 310
Pierce, Franklin, 355, 356
Pike, Albert, 297
Pike, Zebulon, 201*i*, 202
Pilgrims, 41–42
Pinchback, P. B. S., 410
Pinckney, Charles Cotesworth, 175, 196
Pinckney, Thomas, 174, 175
Pinckney Treaty of 1795, 200
Pinckney's Treaty, 174
Pine-Savage, Edgar, 132*i*
Pinta, 11
Pitcairn, John, 122, 123
Pitcher, Molly, 146
Pitt, William, 106, 109, 115, 122
Pizarro, Francisco, 13, 14*i*
Plague, 41
Plain folk, 301–303
Plantation, 83–86
Plantation model, 27
Plantation slavery, 85–86
Plantation system, 220
Plantations in Louisiana (1858), 297*i*
Platte River crossing, 222*i*
Plessy v. *Ferguson,* 427
Plymouth Plantation, 40
Plymouth Rock, 41
Pocahontas, 37
Poe, Edgar Allan, 317
"Poem on the Rising Glory of America," 184
Political Crisis of the 1850s, The (Holt), 373
Political Economy of Slavery (Genovese), 373
Polk, James K., 346–351
Pollard, Anne, 43*i*
Poor Richard's Almanack, 94–95, 94*i*
Poor white trash, 303
Pope, John, 393
Population, African population (1775), 84*m*;
    African population of British colonies
    (1620–1780), 76*t*; economic revolution

(1820–1840), 260–261; New England
    (1650), 68; non-Indian population of
    Chesapeake (1607–1700), 37*t*; non-Indian
    population of New England (1620–1700),
    44*t*; non-Indian population of North America
    (1700–1780), 67*t*; persons per square mile
    (1820), 262*m*; persons per square mile
    (1860), 263*m*; pre-Civil War (1620–1860),
    260*t*; pre-colonial America, 8–9
Positivists, 6
Post-revolutionary period, 158–179; Alien Act,
    176–177; Anglo-American relations, 173;
    Antifederalists, 167; Bank of the United
    States, 170; Bill of Rights, 168; Cabinet
    (1789), 168; Constitution of 1787, 163;
    election of 1796, 175; election of 1800,
    177–178; Federalist Papers, 166*i*, 167;
    Federalists, 166–170, 174; Founding
    Fathers, 162; French-American relations,
    175–176; funding/assumption of debts,
    169; Great Compromise, 163; Jay's Treaty,
    174; Judiciary Act of 1789, 168; Judiciary
    Act of 1801, 178; Lyon-Griswold affair
    (brawl in Congress), 177, 177*i*; native
    Americans, 172–173; Pinckney's Treaty,
    174; Report on Manufactures (1791), 169;
    Republican Party, 171; Sedition Act,
    176–177; Virginia Plan, 162; Washington's
    farewell address, 175; Whiskey Rebellion,
    172, 173*i*; XYZ affair, 176
Potato famine, 263
Pottawatomie Massacre, 357
Powhatan Indians, 37
Praying Indians, 45, 46
Pre-colonial America, 2–31; African slave
    trade, 20–23; America before Columbus,
    4–9; arrival of English, 23–30; Atlantic
    World, 22; Aztecs, 4, 5; Columbus, 11–12;
    conquistadores, 12–14; Dutch, 28–29;
    Europe looks west, 9–23; first English
    settlements, 29–30; French, 27–28; Incas,
    4, 5; Mayas, 4, 5; Roanoke, 29; Spanish
    America, 14–20
Precision grinding machine, 273
Predestination, 25
Prelude to Civil War, 338–365; Alton anti-
    abolitionist riot, 358*i*; Bear Flag
    Revolution, 348; "Bleeding Kansas,"
    356–357, 358*i*, 361–362; California,
    346–347; California gold rush, 351–353;
    Compromise of 1850, 353–355; disunion,
    364; *Dred Scott* decision, 360–361;
    election of 1860, 363–364; free-soil/free-
    labor ideology, 357–359; Gadsden
    Purchase, 356; Harpers Ferry Raid, 362,
    363*i*; Kansas-Nebraska controversy, 356;
    Lecompton constitution, 361–362; Lincoln-
    Douglas debates, 362; lyceum, 360–361;
    Manifest Destiny, 340–341; Mexican War,
    347–350; Oregon, 343, 346, 347*i*; Ostend
    Manifesto, 355; Pottawatomie Massacre,
    357; pro-slavery defense, 359; railroads,
    356; sectional debate, 351–355; slave
    power conspiracy, 358–359; Texas,
    341–343, 346; westward migration,
    343–346; Wilmot Proviso, 351; Young
    America, 355

Presbyterian Lowlanders, 77
Presbyterianism, 90
Presidential elections (1824–1860), 234t; election of 1796, 175; election of 1800, 177–178; election of 1804, 196; election of 1824, 228–229; election of 1828, 229–230; election of 1832, 247m; election of 1836, 250; election of 1844, 346; election of 1848, 351; election of 1856, 359; election of 1860, 363–364; election of 1864, 376; election of 1876, 417–420
Presidential Reconstruction, 406
Presidios, 15, 56
Prigg v. *Pennsylvania,* 336
Primogeniture, 86
Primrose & West minstrel troupe, 422i
Princeton, 93
Privy Council, 102
Pro-Slavery Argument, 359
Pro-slavery defense, 359
Problem of Slavery in the Age of Revolution, The (Davis), 73
Proclamation of 1763, 108m, 110
Prophetstown, 207
Prosser, Gabriel, 187, 309
Prosser Rebellion, 309
Protection papers, 205i
Protestant Reformation, 24–25
Protestant revivalism, 323
Protestants, 91
Publius, 167
Pueblo revolt of 1680, 17
Pueblos, 17
Puerperal fever, 326
Pukes, 69
Punishment in New England, 97t
Puritan community, 71, 86–87
Puritan democracy, 86
Puritan discontent, 26
Puritan separatists, 26, 40
Puritans, 26
Put-In-Bay, 209

Quaker colonies, 51–52
Quaker meeting, 51i
Quakers, 144, 329
Quantrill, William C., 388
Quartering Act, 115
Quasi war with France, 175–176
Quebec, 28
Queen Anne's War, 57

Rabinowitz, Howard, 429
Race Relations in the Urban South (Rabinowitz), 429
Race riots, 407
Radical Reconstruction, 406–412
Radicalism of the American Revolution, The (Wood), 131
Railroad, America's economic revolution, 268–270; Civil War, 371i, 389; expansion/growth (1850–1860), 270m; Reconstruction, 424; slavery, 356
Rakove, Jack, 165
Raleigh, Sir Walter, 27, 29, 30
Randall, James G., 373
Randolph, Edmund Jennings, 162, 168, 170, 174

Randolph, John, 307
Rapp, George, 320i
Rappites, 320i
"Raven, The" (Poe), 317
Raymond, Henry, 255
Readjusters, 421
Reason, 318
Reconstruction After the Civil War (Franklin), 419
Reconstruction: America's Unfinished Revolution (Foner), 419
Reconstruction, Political and Economic (Dunning), 418
Reconstruction and the New South, 400–431; African-American family, 413–414; *Alabama* claims, 416; Atlanta Compromise, 426; black academies, 411; Black Codes, 406; black middle class, 425–427; black minstrels, 423; Bourbon governments, 421; carpetbaggers, 410; civil rights cases of 1883, 427; colored conventions, 410; Compromise of 1877, 417–419, 428–429; convict-lease system, 424; crop-lien system, 412–413, 425i; death of Lincoln, 405; education, 411; election of 1876, 417–420; Fifteenth Amendment, 408; Fourteenth Amendment, 406; Grant, Ulysses S., 414–415; Grant scandals, 415; greenbackers, 415; historian disagreements, 418–419, 428–429; industrialization, 421–424; Johnson, Andrew, 405–406, 409; Johnson's impeachment, 409; Ku Klux Klan, 416–417; Ku Klux Klan Acts, 416–417; land ownership, 411; Lincoln's plan, 404–405; "Lost Cause," 402, 403i; lynchings, 428–430; map, 408m; Negro rule, 410; presidential Reconstruction, 406; race riots, 407; radical Reconstruction, 406–412; railroads, 424; Readjusters, 421; Reconstruction bills, 407; Redeemers, 421; redemption, 416; scalawags, 409–410; Seward's Folly, 416; sharecropping, 411–412, 424; Social Darwinism, 417; Tenure of Office Act, 408, 409; transformation of backcountry, 424–425; Wade-Davis Bill, 405; white supremacy, 430
Reconstruction bills, 407
Red, White, and Black (Nash), 58
Red Jacket, 245i
Red Shirts, 416
Redeemed, 416
Redeemers, 421
Redemption, 408m, 416
Reed, Charles Wellington, 398i
Regency, Albany, 240i
Regulator movement, 112
Religion, American Revolution, 144, 150; anti-Catholicism, 91; Atlantic World, 22; colonial America, 90–92; Congregational Church, 42; deism, 185; English Reformation, 25–26; Great Awakening, 91–92; Jeffersonian era, 185–188; jeremiada, 91; New Lights, 92; Old Lights, 92; Protestant Reformation, 24; revivalism

(antebellum period), 323; Second Great Awakening, 185–188; slave, 310–312; Spanish America, 15; unitarianism, 185; universalism, 185
Religious toleration, 90
Remini, Robert V., 237
Removal Act, 243
Report on Manufactures (1791), 169
Repressible conflict argument, 373
Republican Party, birth of, 356
Republican Party (1790s), 171
"Resistance to Civil Government" (Thoreau), 319
Restoration colonies, 48–52
Revels, Hiram, 410
Revere, Paul, 100i, 116, 123
Revolt of New England, 211
Revolution of 1800, 178
Rhineland, 75
Rhode Island, 44
Rhodes, James Ford, 372
Rice, 78
Richmond (1865), 402i
Richter, Daniel, 58–59
Rights of Man, The (Paine), 128i
Ripley, George, 319
Rise and Fall of the White Republic, The (Saxton), 237
Rise of American Civilization, The (Beard/Beard), 372
Roanoke, 29, 30i
Rochambeau, Count Jean Baptiste de, 141
Rockingham, Marquis of, 114
Rocky Mountain Fur Company, 221
Rolfe, John, 36, 37
Roll, Jordan, Roll (Genovese), 306
Roman Catholic Church, 9
Romanticism, 315
Roosevelt, Nicholas J., 192
Rosecrans, William, 394
Roundheads, 48
Rousseau, Jean Jacques, 142
Royal African Company, 73
Royal Society of London, 95
Rush, Benjamin, 147, 183
Rush-Bagot agreement, 212

Sacramento (1850s), 348i
Salem Possessed (Boyer/Nissenbaum), 89
Salem witch trials, 87–88, 89
Salt-contaminated water, 68
Salt Lake City, 321
Sambo, 309
Samoset, 41
San Jacinto, 342
San Jacinto, 387
Sand hillers, 303
Santa Anna, Antonio Lopez de, 342
Santa Fe, 17, 56, 348, 350i
Santa Fe Trail, 344
Santa María, 11
Saugus Ironworks, 79
Savannah (1734), 60i
Scalawags, 409–410
Scalp bounties, 107
Scarlett Letter, The (Hawthorne), 320
Scene of "The Road," A (Tattersall), 192i

Schlesinger, Arthur M., Jr., 130, 236
Schuyler, Philip, 137
Science, colonial America, 93–96; Jeffersonian era, 183–184
Scientific societies, 95
Scots-Irish, 76
Scott, Sir Walter, 316
Scott, Thomas, 389
Scott, Walter, 300
Scott, Winfield, 243, 348*i*, 355, 384
Scottish Highlanders, 76
Scrooby, 40
Sea dogs, 29
Searle, John, 286*i*
Seasoning, 68
Second Bank of the United States, 216
Second Battle of Bull Run, 393
Second Battle of Manassas, 393
Second Great Awakening, 185–188
Second Reconstruction, 419
"Second Reply to Hayne," 240
Secoton, 10*i*
Sectional debate, 351–355
Sedition Act, 176–177
Seignuries, 28
"Self-Reliance" (Emerson), 318
Self-sufficiency, 81
Seminole Dance, 223*i*
Seminole War, 223, 245
Seminoles, 244
Semmelweis, Ignaz, 326
Seneca Falls, 329
Sentimental novels, 285, 334–335
Separatists (Puritan), 26, 40
Septicemia, 326
Sequoyah, 227*i*
Servants for sale, 66–67, 68*i*
Seven Pines, 391
Seven Years' War, 57, 103–107
Seward, William H., 326, 353, 372, 405, 416
Seward's Folly, 416
Sewing machine, 273
Sex ratio, 19, 68, 70
Seymour, Horatio, 414
Shaftesbury, Lord, 48, 49
Shakers, 321
Shakespeare in America (1820–1850), 286–287
Shanty Irish, 277
Sharecropping, 411–412, 424
Shattuck, Job, 155*i*
Shays, Daniel, 155
Shelbourne, Lord, 142
Shenandoah, 387
Sherman, William Tecumseh, 383*i*, 385, 396–398
Shiloh, 390
Shoe factories, 272
Short-staple cotton, 294
Siege of Louisbourg (1758), 106*i*
Silbey, Joel, 373
Silliman, Benjamin, 360
Simms, William Gilmore, 318
Singer, Isaac, 273
Slater, Samuel, 188
Slater's Mill, 189*i*
Slave codes, 74–75, 303

Slave culture, 85–86
Slave marriages, 312
Slave music, 310, 311
Slave power conspiracy, 358–359
Slave quarters, 304
Slave religion, 310–312
Slave resistance, 308–310
Slave spirituals, 310
Slave trade, 308
Slavery, abolitionism, 330–336; Africa (pre-colonial America), 20–23; American Revolution, 144–145, 150–151; *Amistad* case, 336; black abolitionists, 331–332; Caribbean settlements, 53–54, Compromise of 1850, 354*m*; cotton, 295, 296*m*; culture, 85–86; Dutch West India Company, 50; economic underpinning, 73; English planters, 53; family life, 312; free blacks, 307–308; free-soilism, 336; gang system, 304; Garrison, 330–336; Gullah, 85; historian disagreements, 306; house slaves, 307; kinship networks, 312; marriage, 312; mortality rates, 305; music, 310, 311; Native Americans, 352; Old South, 303–312; origins, 71–75; paternalism, 312; personal liberty laws, 336; pidgin, 310; plantation, 85–86; popular sovereignty, 338*i*, 351; pro-slavery defense, 359; Prosser Rebellion, 309; religion, 310–312; Sambo pattern of personality, 309; sexual abuse, 307; slave codes, 74–75, 303; slave resistance, 308–310; slave trade, 308; Spanish colonists, 20–23; Stono Rebellion, 86; task system, 304; Turner Rebellion, 309; underground railroad, 335, 337; urban slaves, 307; women, 305–307
"Slavery and the Genesis of American Race Prejudice" (Degler), 72
Slavery (Elkins), 306
Slaves Without Masters (Berlin), 429
Slidell, John, 347, 387
Sloan, Hans, 2*i*
Smallpox among the Indians, 19*i*
Smallpox epidemic, 12, 19*i*
Smallpox inoculation, 95
Smith, Jedediah S., 221
Smith, John, 34, 41, 67
Smith, John Rubens, 279*i*
Smith, Joseph, 321, 322, 322*i*
Smith, Sydney, 316
Social Darwinism, 417
Society of Friends, 51
Society of Pewterers, 148*i*
Soft-money faction, 246
Songhay, 20
Sons of Liberty, 121
South Carolina, 49
Southeast borderlands, 56–57
Southern borderlands, 55–56
Southern plantation (before/after Emancipation), 412*m*
Southwestern expansion (1845–1853), 350*m*
Spain's northern colonies, 55–56
Spalding, Albert G., 384
Spanish America, 14–20
Spanish America (18th century), 16*m*

Spanish Armada, 29
Spanish conquistadores, 12–14
Spanish empire, 17–20, 53, 55
Special electoral commission, 417–418
Specie circular, 252, 253
Specie Resumption Act, 415
Spoils system, 238
"Spout Bath at Warm Springs," 325*i*
Spurzheim, Johann Gaspar, 325
Squanto, 41
Squatter sovereignty, 338*i*, 351
St. Augustine, Florida, 16, 56, 57
St. John Plantation, Louisiana, 300*i*
St. Leger, Barry, 137
St. Luke Penny Savings Bank, 425
St. Mary's, 38
Stamp Act crisis, 113–114
Stamp Act of 1765, 111
Stampp, Kenneth, 419
Standish, Miles, 41, 47
Stanley, Amy Dru, 419
Stanton, Edwin M., 408, 409
Stanton, Elizabeth Cady, 329, 379
"Star-Spangled Banner," 211
Stark, John, 138
Starving time, 34–35
States' rights, 382
Statute of Religious Liberty, 150
Steamboats, 218, 266
Steel plows, 289
Stephens, Alexander H., 379, 406
Steuben, Baron von, 133
Stevens, John, 268
Stone, Lucy, 329
Stoneman, George, 407*i*
Stone's River, 390
Stono Rebellion, 86
Storming the Bastille, 142*i*
Story, Joseph, 234
Stowe, Harriet Beecher, 329, 335, 336
Strange Career of Jim Crow, The (Woodward), 428
Stuart, Gilbert, 155*i*
Stuart Restoration, 48
Stuarts, 26
Stuyvesant, Peter, 50
Subject Matter (Chaplin), 59
Sublime, 316
Subtreasury system, 252
Sudbury, Massachusetts (17th century), 87*i*
Sugar, 53, 54*i*
Sumner, Charles, 300, 357, 376, 405, 417
Sumter, Thomas, 140
Supreme Order of the Star-Spangled Banner, 265
Susan Constant, 34
Svinin, Pavel Petrovich, 218*i*
Swann, Thomas, 266*i*

Talleyrand, Prince, 176
Tallmadge, James, Jr., 225
Tallmadge Amendment, 225
Tamerlane and Other Poems (Poe), 317
Tammany Society, 178
Taney, Roger B., 247–248, 361, 376
Tariff of abominations, 229
Task system, 304

Tattersall, George, 192*i*
Taverns (in revolutionary Massachusetts), 120
Taylor, Zachary, 347, 348, 351, 353, 354
Tea Act of 1773, 118–119
Tejanos, 342
Telegraph, 270–271, 389
Temperance crusade, 323–324
Tenochtitlán, 5
Tenskwatawa, 207
Tenure of Office Act, 408, 409
Terra cotta sculpture, 20*i*
Texas, 56, 341–343, 346
Textile industry, 216
Textile mills, 275
"The Times" (1837), 251*i*
Theocracy, 42
Thirteen colonies (1763), 107*m*
Thirteenth Amendment, 333, 377
Thomas, Jesse B., 225
Thomas Amendment, 225
Thoreau, Henry David, 319
Thresher, 289
Tilden, Samuel J., 417, 420*i*
Time on the Cross (Fogel/Engerman), 306
Tobacco, 35, 78
Tobacco plant, 36*i*
Tocqueville, Alexis de, 233, 322*i*, 331
Tories, 129
Town and Country-man's Almanack, 95
Townshend, Charles, 115, 116
Townshend duties, 115
Trade with China, 255–256
Transcendentalists, 318–319
Transcontinental railroad, 356
Transplantations and borderlands, 32–63
Treaty of Ghent, 212
Treaty of Greenville, 154, 206*i*
Treaty of Guadalupe Hidalgo, 348
Treaty of San Ildefonso, 200
Treaty of Utrecht, 105
Treaty of Wang Hya, 255
Treaty of Washington, 416
Trent, 387
Trent Affair, 387
Triangular trade, 25*i*, 81*m*, 82
Trist, Nicholas, 348, 349
Trunk lines, 269
Tryon, William, 112
Tubman, Harriet, 309*i*
Tucker, Beverly, 318
Tudor England, 23
Tudors, 26
Turner, Frederick Jackson, 236, 281
Turner, Nat, 309, 359
Turner Rebellion, 309, 359
Turnpike era, 191, 265
Turret lathe, 273
Tuskegee Institute (1881), 426*i*
Twelfth Amendment, 228
Tyler, John, 252, 253, 343, 346

Uncle Remus (Harris), 422
Uncle Tom's Cabin (Stowe), 335, 359
Underground railroad, 335, 337
Understanding, 318
Understanding test, 427

Unification of Italy, 380*i*
Universal milling machine, 273
University of Pennsylvania, 93
Urban Crucible, The (Nash), 131
Urban slaves, 307
U.S. Sanitary Commission, 378, 379
U.S.S. Richmond, 397*i*
Utopia (More), 23
Utopian community, 319–320

Vallandigham, Clement L., 376
Van Buren, Martin, 236, 239–240, 241, 246, 250–253, 343, 346, 351
Van Deusen, Glyndon, 237
Vance, Zebulon M., 382
Vancouver, George, 343
Varieties of American nationalism (1813–1828), 214–231; Adams-Onis Treaty, 223; corrupt bargain, 228–229; cotton, 220; election of 1824, 228–229; election of 1828, 229–230; factor system, 219; fur trade, 220–221; Latin American revolution, 227–228; Long's expedition, 221–222; Marshall court, 225–227; Missouri Compromise, 224*m*, 225; Monroe Doctrine, 228; Monroe's goodwill tour, 222*i*, 223; Panic of 1819, 224; plantation system, 220; protective tariff, 218; roads, 217; second Bank of the United States, 216; Seminole War, 223; steamboats, 218; tariff of abominations, 229; textile industry, 216; Virginia Dynasty, 222–223; westward expansions, 219–220
Verdict of the People, The (Bingham), 232*i*
Vergennes, Count de, 139, 143
Vespucci, Amerigo, 12
Vicksburg, 394
Victor Emmanuel II, 381
Vietnam War, 7
Virginia, 34–35, 39
Virginia, 386
Virginia Company, 32*i*, 34, 36, 37, 40
Virginia Dynasty, 222–223
Virginia Plan, 162
Virtual *vs.* actual representation, 118
Voltaire, 142
Vulcanizing rubber, 273

Wade, Benjamin F., 376, 385
Wade-Davis Bill, 405
Wagon train, 344–346
Walden (Thoreau), 319
Walker, David, 332
Walker's Appeal . . . to the Colored Citizens, 332
Walpole, Robert, 102
Waltham system, 275
Wampanoags, 46, 47
War, King William, 105
War of 1812, 209–212
War of the Spanish Succession, 57
Warner, Susan, 334, 335
Warren, John, 326
Warren, Mercy Otis, 119, 185
Washington, Booker T., 426
Washington, D. C. (early century), 196*m*

Washington, George, 82, 105, 132, 136, 137, 141, 143, 146, 150, 160, 161, 162, 168, 170, 172, 173, 174, 175, 183
Washington, Martha, 82, 146
Washington City (1821), 197*i*
Washington Temperance Society, 324
Washington's farewell address, 175
Water cure, 325
Water power, 273
Watt, James, 190
Wayne, Anthony, 154
We the People (McDonald), 165
Wealth distribution in colonial cities (1687–1771), 90*t*
Webster, Daniel, 211, 226, 235, 240–241, 246, 250, 253, 254, 353
Webster, Noah, 184
Webster-Ashburton Treaty, 254–255
Webster-Hayne debate, 240–241
Weems, Mason, 185
Weir, Robert, 397*i*
Weld, Theodore Dwight, 336
Wells, Ida B., 429
Wesley, Charles, 92
Wesley, John, 92, 186
West Point, 198, 199*i*
Western trails (1860), 345*m*
Western Union Telegraph Company, 271
Westward migration, 343–346
Wheelwright, John, 45
When Jesus Came, the Corn Mothers Went (Gutierrez), 58
Whig Party, 249–255
Whiggery, 249
Whigs, 237
Whirling Thunder, 242*i*
Whiskey Rebellion, 172, 173*i*
Whiskey ring, 415
White, Hugh Lawson, 250
White, John, 2*i*, 10*i*, 29
White, Richard, 58
White Leagues, 416
White Over Black (Jordan), 72
White supremacy, 430
Whitefield, George, 22, 92, 92*i*
Whitman, Marcus, 343
Whitman, Narcissa, 343
Whitman, Walt, 317, 317*i*
Whitney, Eli, 188, 189, 273
Wide, Wide, World, The (Warner), 334, 335
Wilberforce, William, 333
Wilhelm I, 381
Wilkes, Charles, 387
Wilkie, William, 284*i*
Wilkinson, James, 203
Willard, Emma, 329
William and Mary, 61, 62
William and Mary College, 93
William III, 104
William of Orange, 61
Williams, Roger, 44, 91
Williams v. *Mississippi,* 427
Williamson, Joel, 428
Wilmot, David, 351
Wilmot Proviso, 351
Wilson, Harry, 372
Wilson's Creek, 389

Winchester, Oliver, 388
Winsor, Joshua, 80*i*
Winthrop, John, 42
Witchcraft, 87–88, 89
Within the Plantation Household (Fox-Genovese), 306
Wolfe, James, 106–107
Woman in the Nineteenth Century (Fuller), 320
Women, American Revolution, 146–148; antebellum period, 329–330; Chesapeake, 69–70; Civil War, 378–379, 383; Declaration of Sentiments, 329; economic revolution (1813–1852), 274*i*,

275–277, 283–288; education (1820–1850), 283–284; female millworkers (1850), 274*i*, 276*i*; female protective unions, 277, 278; Hutchinson, Anne, 45; Jeffersonian era, 182, 186; literacy rate, 93; matrilineal societies, 21, 23; midwives, as, 69; New England, 70–71; Old South, 301; sex ratio, 19, 68, 70; slave, 305–307
Wood, Gordon, 131
Wood, T. W., 407*i*
Woodland Indians, 5
Woodward, C. Vann, 418, 428
Wool trade, 24

Worcester v. *Georgia,* 226, 243
Wright, Mother Lucy, 321

XYZ affair, 176

Yale, 93
Yale, Elihu, 93
Young, Brigham, 321
Young America, 355
Young Mill-Wright's and Miller's Guide, The (Evans), 188

Zenger, John Peter, 96